Calibration: Philosophy in Practice

Second Edition

Fluke Corporation
P.O. Box 9090
Everett, WA 98206–9090

First printing, January 1994
Second printing, May 1994

Library of Congress Catalogue Card Number: 93-90764

ISBN 0-9638650-0-5

Printed in the United States of America

Fluke Corporation asserts that the information in this book is complete and accurate to the best of its knowledge, information and belief. Every reasonable effort has been made to confirm the accuracy and reliability of the information and methods described in this book. Fluke Corporation does not, however, warrant that the same results will be obtained in every calibration or test performed and assumes no liability for use of the information herein.

All product names mentioned in this document are trademarks of their respective manufacturers. While Fluke has made a reasonable effort to identify trademarks and trademark owners, we may have missed some, and our failure to identify them is unintentional. Those that we have identified are as follows:

Evanohm is a registered trademark of the Wilbur P. Driver Co. MS-DOS is a registered trademark of Microsoft Corporation. IBM is a registered trademark of International Business Machines. Datron is a registered trademark of Wavetek. Holt is a registered trademark of Holt Instrument Laboratories. ESI is a registered trademark of ElectroScientific Industries, Inc. L&N is a registered trademark of Leeds and Northrup. Hewlett-Packard and HP are registered trademarks of the Hewlett-Packard Corporation. Tektronix is a registered trademark of Tektronix, Inc. The NVLAP logo is a registered trademark of NIST.

Editorial direction: Fluke Corporation. See Contributors list.
Editorial assistance and typesetting: The Write Stuff
Page design and illustrations: The Davis Group

Contents:

Section One: Introduction

Section Two: Universal Elements of Metrology

Section Three: Primary and Secondary Standards

Contents

Section Four: Calibrators and Calibration

Section Five: Statistics

Section Six: Laboratory Management

Section Seven: Practical Considerations for Metrology

Appendices

Figures

Tables

Introduction

Section One

Chapter 1:

About This Book

Unlike other sources of information on metrology, this volume does not deal with just one aspect of the discipline. *Calibration: Philosophy in Practice* is a single volume consisting of seven separate sections, each dealing with a different area of dc and low frequency measurements. The chapters in each section are grouped around a central theme, such as "Laboratory Management" and "Primary and Secondary Standards."

The information within each section is oriented toward the current state-of-the-art of the topics covered, as well as the likely near- and mid-term developments that may influence the subject in the future.

The book emphasizes the "whole-laboratory" approach. No longer is it appropriate for metrologists to view themselves or their profession as restricted to the laboratory; modern realities dictate that laboratories be successfully run, dedicated to quality, integrated with the needs of their customers, and motivated toward improving themselves. This book is designed to help those things happen.

Which Parts of This Book Should You Read?

This book was written with three types of metrology people in mind: people new to the metrology field, experienced metrology technologists and engineers, and laboratory managers.

People New to Metrology

How does metrology fit into the scheme of everyday life? What is the scope of metrology and measurement, and what are some of the things that the person new to metrology needs to think about? What is the nature of "a standard," and what are the reasons for all of the paperwork? What are the more relevant techniques for measuring and comparing laboratory standards?

For those new to metrology in any capacity, Section Two, "Universal Elements of Metrology," and Section Three, "Primary and Secondary Standards," will help answer some of these questions, and, perhaps more importantly, help determine some more questions to ask.

Experienced Metrologists

The increase in affordable desktop computers has been extremely influential on two areas of metrology: automated calibration and statistical analysis. Primary and secondary standards of high accuracy, stability, and versatility have begun to appear on the scene, as well as computer-ready, super-accurate multifunction calibrators. What are some of the changes that this new equipment has brought to the test and procedure design and implementation stages of the metrology process?

The experienced metrologist will particularly appreciate Section Four, "Calibrators and Calibration," Section Five, "Statistics," and Section Seven, "Practical Considerations for Metrology."

Laboratory Managers

Laboratories must not only be productive in the traditional sense of the word, they must be innovative and accepting of change. Further, they are more visible than ever before, as the inroads being made into narrower and narrower corners of time and space are requiring more and more accurate and precise measuring devices and methods. Metrology is the critical path for many areas of science.

To keep up with these new demands, metrology managers must be informed as to how the changing regulations and improvements in equipment and data resources affect them and their laboratories. They must also learn to make sound decisions on new purchases, not only from a cost standpoint but from a measurement standpoint as well. Laboratory managers will find Section Six, "Laboratory Management," especially useful.

What Are the Sections About?

The seven sections and their central topics are as follows:

Section One: *Introduction*

In addition to this chapter, Section One contains "Romance of Metrology," which takes a somewhat poetic look at metrologists and their work. New metrologists may find it interesting; experienced metrologists may identify with some of the thoughts expressed on these pages.

Section Two: *Universal Elements of Metrology*

This section provides a general overview of metrology. It will help you to "fill in the blanks" that many people have when they first enter the discipline. Recommended for anyone who wants to get a good idea of the total picture of metrology.

Section Three: *Primary and Secondary Standards*

The higher levels of the equipment hierarchy are detailed in this section. The discussion also covers the nature of measurement standards for several important electrical quantities, as well as the proper techniques used to transfer measurement quantities.

Experienced metrologists may find new insights into the care of primary and secondary standards here. Beginning metrologists who will be working in standards laboratories will find this section especially useful.

Section Four: *Calibrators and Calibration*

This section details the advanced measurement methods used with today's more versatile multi-function calibrators. It also treats the developing areas of artifact calibration and automation. Nearly everyone will get something useful from this section, whether it be the new metrologist looking for an explanation of a measurement method, or an experienced metrologist or manager wanting to know more about integrating automated methods into their calibration process.

Section Five: *Statistics*

This section is the A-to-Z of metrology statistics. Experienced metrologists more than anyone else will likely turn to this part of the volume. However, beginning metrologists should read "Introduction to Metrology Statistics."

Section Six: *Laboratory Management*

Intended for managers or anyone else who wants to know more about the "other parts" of metrology, this section covers support, facilities, audits, accreditation, and instrument specifications.

Section Seven: *Practical Considerations for Metrology*

This section will serve as a useful reference for any metrologist who is actually designing tests or performing calibrations. Many important and hard-to-find subjects are covered in "Grounding, Shielding and Guarding," "A Rogues' Gallery of Parasitics," and "AC Lore."

Appendices

In the appendices you will find an extensive glossary, index, and a useful section on metrology resources.

We at Fluke are always receptive to comments and criticisms of our work and products, because it helps us to serve you better. If you have any comments on the material in this volume, you may write or call us at:

Fluke Corporation
P.O. Box 9090 Everett, WA 98206, USA
Fluke Europe B.V.
P.O. Box 1186, 5602 BD Eindhoven,
The Netherlands

In the U.S.,	call	(800) 443-5853
	fax	(206) 356-5116
In Europe,	call	(31 40) 644200
	fax	(31 40) 644222
In Canada,	call	(905) 890-7600
	fax	(905) 890-6866
In other countries,	call	(01)(206) 356-5500

Conventions Used in This Book

Notations for numbers follow the United States' convention of using commas and decimal points as separators. For example, the meter is defined as the length of the path traveled by light in a vacuum during a time interval of 1/299,792,458 second; a digital multimeter display may indicate +9.995 volts.

Most of the circuit diagrams presented in this book have been simplified to present concepts most clearly. The actual circuits are described in detail in the manuals for the equipment referenced.

Variables representing the value of a discrete component or the measured value of its parasitics are denoted by upper case letters. Variables representing the unmeasured circuit parasitics are denoted by lower case letters.

Chapter 2:

The Romance of Metrology

"The romance of metrology." What does that phrase make you think of? Here are some thoughts that you may find stimulating.

Metrologists love definitions and can argue about their interpretation for days on end. Here's one to think about. **Romance**\n ... *3: an emotional attraction or aura belonging to an especially heroic era, adventure, or activity.*

Is there a romance of metrology? Of course there is! The grand adventure of measurements began long ago in our own galaxy. We recall Moses who said "...thou shalt have a perfect and just weight, a perfect and just measure shalt thou have: that thy days may be lengthened in the land which the LORD thy God giveth thee." Also in Asia Minor, in Babylon, there was the Code of Hammurabi. We might ask, "Was Hammurabi the first auditor?" If so, what happened to dishonest auditees? Did they lose their hands or their heads for keeping a slightly shady cubit?

Our tradition of honesty in weights and measures must go back to these ancient times and laws. We recognize that other cultures such as the Harappans at Mohenjo-daro on the banks of the Indus river, the Egyptians whose pyramids we see along the Nile, the Chinese, and even the later Mayans had similar views about integrity in weights and measures. But the genealogy of our traditions of metrology does not go directly through these other cultures.

Greek science opened the door to a rational view of nature. Their ancient philosophers conceived of "logos" as the divine wisdom contained in nature. By Aristotle's time, the consideration of this concept had moved away from mysticism—nature's behavior could be relied on to be rational, consistent, and understandable, and did not reflect the whims of the gods.

In the modern continuation of this heroic idea, we metrologists trust the laws of nature to be the same at all times for all observers. We seek to derive our standards of weights and measures from the very structure of nature itself! When we do this, nature cannot give us a "false measure," or so we believe.

What is the structure of nature? How do we define it? These are deep questions that those marvelous Greeks also addressed. The Pythagoreans thought that nature is mathematical in its ultimate expression. Plato advanced the concept that it has an underlying perfection in form, if not representation.

Today we use mathematics of great power and beauty to describe nature. We speak of ideal values that have no error. But alas, as we have peered more deeply into nature, certainty has vanished. The ideal is but a will-o-the-wisp of probability around which we construct distribution densities for uncertainly-measured realities.

"Pardon our dust, but dig we must." The Con Ed slogan typifies the work of metrologists. We just have to dig and dig to make ever better measurements. As we dig, we find that the practical work of the experimentalist goes hand in glove with the idealistic musings of the theoretician.

It is said that the first experimentalist was Archimedes who, according to legend, ran naked through the streets of Syracuse shouting "Eureka! Eureka!" in reaction to his discovery of the physical relationship between buoyancy and volume. But it was by experiment that he confirmed this law and his equally important law of the lever. And so it is today, every measurement we make is an experiment that tests the fineness of correspondence between the actual performance of an apparatus and its principles of operation.

In electrical metrology, there are those who have enjoyed making new discoveries, such as those marvelous "effects" that the 19th-century physicists discovered, which bear names such as Hall, Peltier, Thomson, and Seebeck. Then there are the theoretical underpinnings of electrical metrology, known by their discoverers as Ohm's law, Kirchoff's laws, and Thévenins' theorem. We take these discoveries for granted and treat them mundanely even though they have produced the core technology by which we prosper and prevail.

Then there was the work of Ampere, Volta, and Oersted, which was experimentally unified by that mathematically-innocent, self-educated genius, Faraday. Faraday's missing mathematics were supplied in due time by Maxwell's equations. Physics moved from Newton's deterministic dynamics to the study of the ephemeral electromagnetic field. This step took it directly into relativity and quantum mechanics, and the need for new metrology to support their progeny, atomic energy and electronics—including the broadcasting of man-made radio frequency waves into the electromagnetic field.

The 19th-century electrical discoveries have led us modern metrologists into the bold adventure of devising various sensors and apparatus of exquisite precision and accuracy that exploit one or another of the wondrous effects they discovered!

Thomas Young thought of energy more rigorously than had previously been the case. His studies, combined with those of Carnot, Clausius, Boltzmann, and Kelvin, led to the science of thermodynamics and the need to accurately measure temperature. These measurements have supported the development of efficient prime movers and other heat engines. The engines have taken the place of human power and horse power. Some of them heat and cool our homes, offices, and metrology laboratories. Others have taken us from travelling slowly on the ground and sea to making rapid journeys through the air and into outer space itself.

What a journey metrology has made as it has gone from dynamics to thermodynamics to electrodynamics. Each milestone has led to new metrology. The metrology of dynamics treated mass, length, and time as separate and independent units. Near the end of the era of dynamics, these quantities were represented by artifact standards. In the metric system, the standards were a platinum-iridium cylinder for measuring mass, a platinum bar representing the meter, and an accurate clock whose swinging pendulum moved gears that subdivided the mean solar day into what was thought to be 86,400 exactly equal seconds.

Thermodynamics led to the discovery of the kelvin scale of absolute temperature. And it was found that the mass and length of material objects are affected by their temperature. So, the romance of metrology has included the need to use calibrated thermometers as a prerequisite to calibrating other standards.

Temperature scales are not extensive, as length or mass are. For example, one can obtain a two-meter-long bar by placing two one-meter rulers end to end. However, one cannot get a temperature of two kelvins by bringing together two samples of material, each at a temperature of one kelvin. As the retroactively-stated zeroeth law of thermodynamics shows, the temperature of the two combined samples remains at one kelvin. The metrology of temperature has revolved around the definition and realization of a scale based on Lord Kelvin's fundamental equations which unite the ratios of mechanical work and temperatures.

But wait, there's more. Maxwell's equations led to electrodynamics and the need for other new metrology. The fundamental unit of this new metrology became the ampere, with other associated units such as the volt and the ohm being derived from it. In actuality, the ampere is defined as an electrical current whose associated magnetic force is measured in terms of the meter, kilogram, and second.

In the 20th century, the metrological plot has thickened. The basic unit of time, the second, is now defined in terms of specified quantum electrodynamic energy transitions inherent to the cesium atom. These atomic clocks have caused us to bid goodbye to the pendulum clocks and to the concept of a uniformly rotating earth. The new metrology lets us measure wiggles and jiggles in the earth's rotation. It also allows us to know that the earth's rotation rate is diminishing by transferring some of its angular momentum to the moon and converting the remainder to heat that's generated by the friction of the oceans on the sea floor associated with the diurnal tides.

The meter is no longer defined by an artifact. Now it's the distance that light travels in an exactly defined fraction of a second. Since the speed of light in a vacuum is taken as a constant of nature, the meter is derived from the duration of time. The definitions, realizations, and representations of the meter and the second are now electromagnetic rather than dynamic in nature. Perhaps amazingly, they are successfully used to measure dynamic phenomena even though a unified theory of dynamics and electrodynamics has not been constructed to date.

The constants of nature have also intruded into temperature. Blackbody theory and experimentation link the frequency distribution of the electromagnetic radiation of heat with the temperature of the radiating object. Planck's discovery of the unifying equation led directly to quantum mechanics and to an extension of temperature metrology into the establishment of blackbody techniques whose results correlate with the earlier kelvin scale.

Quantum mechanics, especially quantum electrodynamics, continues to shape advances in electrical metrology. Recently, the direct voltage produced by a superconducting Josephson junction has become the standard for voltage. The voltage is produced by a quantum electrodynamic effect that, up to a few parts in 10^{17}, has been experimentally shown to produce the same voltage in two differentially connected Josephson junctions which are irradiated with a common source of electromagnetic energy. Thus the volt is taken from the constants of nature as a function of the second.

But then there's the Quantum Hall effect. In this effect, the resistance of a superconducting semi-conductor is precisely quantized when current flows as a two-dimensional electron gas perpendicularly to a magnetic field. So the ohm, too, is taken from the constants of nature as a function of the second.

Our inquisitors may be our peers, adversarial auditors, or even ourselves: Is this a good and true measure? How was it made? What trust can be put in it? The questions draw from the laws of man. Metrologists can give replies that are taken from the very laws of nature. Truly the romance of metrology graces our ancient and honorable profession.

Universal Elements
of Metrology

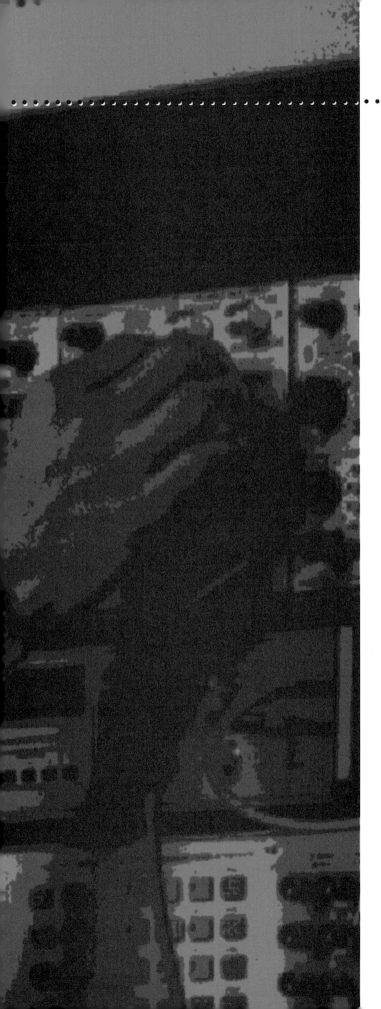

Section Two

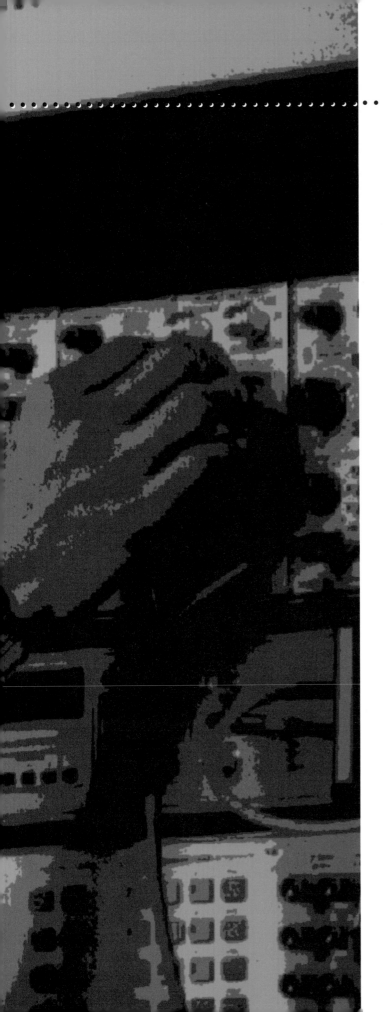

Chapter 3:
Metrology: A Brief Overview

Metrology is so ingrained in everything, most people fail to give it any notice.

Reading this chapter, the reader will get a sense of metrology: its effects, what it involves, where it is done, and where it fits into the general scheme of things. This chapter introduces some terms that will be used throughout the book. These terms need to be understood by anyone concerned with the practical side of metrology—calibration—and the role it plays in the metrology process.

What Is Metrology?

Simply stated, metrology is the science of measurement. Everything that has to do with measurement, be it designing, conducting, or analyzing the results of a test, exists within the metrology realm. These things cover the range from the abstract, comparing statistical methods, for example, to the practical, such as deciding which scale of a ruler to read. It is a broad field; as will be seen, more things can be grouped as metrology-related than might be thought of at first.

What Metrology Means

The effects of the science of measurement can be seen everywhere, allowing people to plan their lives and make commercial exchanges with confidence. For example, most people can assume that the clocks in their homes and the clocks in their work places all display approximately the same time. A pound of hamburger purchased at one grocery store will contain the same quantity of food as the same amount purchased at a store across town. And a screw purchased from Company A will fit into a hole made by a drill purchased from Company B, assuming they are specified to the same size.

Most people also trust that the speedometers in their cars will measure speed the same as the local police's; that 14 karat gold jewelry contains the appropriate amount of gold; and the temperatures indicated by thermostats, ovens, and thermometers are correct. Life would get complicated—and in some cases, more danger-ous—without proper measurements.

What People Need to Know About Metrology

Most people don't need to know anything at all about metrology—as long as things continue to be measured correctly. But people involved in the metrology field will want to know quite a few things, such as who and what regulates metrology; who performs it, and where; what it involves; what calibration is; and what accuracy, uncertainty, and many other terms really mean. This chapter touches briefly on some of the more important topics, and refers to other chapters where specific topics are covered in more detail.

Who or What Controls Metrology?

One of the reasons that things are so consistent when it comes to measurements is that the commercial and legal aspects of metrology are regulated. All governments, whether local, state, or national, have regulations or laws that cover the practice of checking and using weights and measures for commerce and indus-try. In the United States, for example, each state has an organization whose function is to check that all grocery store cash-register scales measure accurately.

In industry, metrology is regulated by contract. Companies that want to do business with national or local governments, for example, usually establish measurement policies that conform to ISO 9000 or MIL-STD 45662A. These standards are discussed in Chapter 28, "Laboratory Quality and ISO 9000"; MIL-STD 45662A is explained in Chapter 30, "Labora-tory Audits." These are documents (not laws) that outline basic metrology requirements. A company found not to conform with a particu-lar metrology rule may not get paid for its ser-vices. Between companies, business contracts can state the metrology requirements. ISO 9000 and MIL-STD 45662A are often the basis for the contractual agreements as well.

Metrology requirements are what dictate the kinds of measurement that are done, how accurate the measurements must be, and how the measurements are documented. Every metrology activity—no matter how simple or complex—has its ruling requirements.

Who Does Metrology?

Metrology affects everyone. As ingrained into everyday life as metrology is, one can hardly escape it. At the center of it all is the metrologist, the one who designs and runs measurement tests.

A metrologist can perform various functions that at first may seem not to have anything to do with measurement. Statistical analysis, database building, and writing automation programs are a few examples. But in today's metrology laboratory, these things have everything to do with metrology. In addition, designing measurement tests, analyzing the results, determining the final accuracy of the device under test, and, perhaps the most important part of metrology, calibration, are all things that a metrologist may do.

Calibration—What Is It?

Calibration is the comparing of a measurement device (an unknown) against an equal or better standard. A standard in a measurement is considered the reference; it is the one in the comparison taken to be the more correct of the two. One calibrates to find out how far the unknown is from the standard.

Where Are Metrology and Calibration Done?

One could say metrology and calibration are done everywhere. But the main work in metrology is done in laboratories, where environmental factors such as temperature, humidity, vibration, and insulation from electronic

interference are tightly monitored and, if possible, controlled. As with most sciences, metrology has a hierarchy; however, in this case, the hierarchy manifests itself to a more visible degree. Metrology has separate laboratories for different levels of metrology and calibration.

There are five main types of metrology laboratories, and each has a different metrology function. Companies may have one or more of these. These are listed below.

Primary Laboratories

This is where the highest level of metrology is done. New research into methods of measuring more accurately or precisely, as well as the calibration of primary and secondary standards are done here.

Secondary Laboratories

In secondary laboratories, calibration of secondary standards and working standards is usually the most important work done. Calibrations of lower accuracy that require specialized techniques may be done here. Mobile calibration units may operate from a centrally-located secondary laboratory.

Research Laboratories

Often the requirements for metrology are different in laboratories that support only research activities. It all depends on the situation. A research laboratory may need the most accurate standards; it may support some of the most abstract projects, such as measuring the current of a single electron.

Calibration Laboratories

Calibration laboratories tend to be oriented toward the production of higher volume calibrations utilizing standards supported by higher echelon laboratories, typically secondary or primary laboratories. A regular calibration laboratory has measurement standards that were calibrated at a secondary metrology laboratory. The emphasis in a calibration laboratory is often on throughput: getting the measurement equipment back to the users as quickly as possible, without sacrificing quality. The larger calibration laboratories may handle tens of thousands of measurement items in a single year.

Mobile Laboratories

Sometimes the logistics of calibration are better served by bringing the calibrator to the test equipment. Examples include military support field calibration, or a mobile laboratory equipped with metrology standards that can be moved to a variety of locations.

What Does the Metrology Process Involve?

Measurement is necessarily a science of comparisons. A voltmeter is calibrated by a multifunction calibrator, or perhaps on an automated test system. The multifunction calibrator has its ranges calibrated with secondary standards that are more accurate than the multifunction calibrator, often at a secondary laboratory. The secondary standards are in turn calibrated against primary standards at a primary laboratory.

The ultimate references for all measurement quantities (length, current, time, and so on) have been agreed upon by international treaties. These references, and the structure of deriving quantities from them, are defined in the International System of Units (SI). This structure is detailed in Chapter 4, "International Metrology."

The basic principles of metrology are simple. Metrology involves measurements and comparisons of a measurement standard to either another measurement standard or to a device of unknown accuracy. It involves the design of tests and methods by which the measurements and comparisons are made, and analysis of the results of the tests.

Standard Units and Measurement Standards

The SI provides a set of standard measurement units by which all measurements are made or referenced. There are seven basic measurement units from which all other measurement units are derived. The seven basic units are:

- meter (length)
- second (time)
- mole (amount of substance)
- candela (light intensity)
- ampere (current)
- kelvin (thermodynamic temperature)
- kilogram (mass)

All of the other measurement units are derived from these seven. The derived units that are described in this book are the:

- volt (electrical potential)
- ohm (electrical resistance)
- farad (capacitance)
- henry (inductance)

Each of these is described in one of the chapters of Section Three, "Primary and Secondary Standards."

Measurement standards, on the other hand, are the devices that represent the SI standard unit in a measurement. For example, a zener reference amplifier is a frequently-used measurement standard that represents the SI volt when calibrating a digital multimeter. A measurement standard is the reference in a measurement.

Traceability

The process of making a measurement is only a part of a calibration. During the measurement, all of the data concerning the test unit's response is recorded, either manually or automatically to disk by a controlling computer. (Often this data is pass/fail rather than actual measured data.) After the measurement is finished, all the information about the measurement standard and the test instrument is placed together with the test data. The information in this test record supports the traceability of the test.

Information should include the calibration and expiration dates of the measurement standard, the test date, and the date the test unit needs calibration again, as well as all the test point data. Many laboratories save even more information in order to conform more closely with the regulating requirements.

Traceability is an unbroken chain of comparisons from the measurement being made to a recognized national, legal standard.

If one were to follow the paper trail up from the calibrated unit through the secondary and primary standards, it would eventually end at the record of an experiment made to establish the quantity in question in terms of one or more of the seven basic measurement units. This is the ultimate in traceability. Usually, though, it is only necessary to show that part of the paper trail is correct. Traceability is detailed in Chapter 6, "Standards and Traceability."

Common Metrology Terms

Working in and around metrology, one will find that there are some terms one needs to know. Following are some of them, defined in plain language. More about these terms can be found in the Glossary.

Accuracy (Measurement Accuracy): A number which indicates the closeness of a measured value to the true value, or the ability of an instrument to make measurements with small uncertainty. Metrologists prefer to use the uncertainty of a measurement (e.g., an uncertainty of ±12 ppm), instead of accuracy (e.g., accurate to 99.9988%).

Calibration: A set of operations, performed in accordance with a definite, documented procedure, that compares the measurements performed by an instrument to those made by a more accurate instrument or standard, for the purpose of detecting and reporting, or

eliminating by adjustment, errors in the instrument tested.

Calibration Label: A label affixed to a measuring instrument to show its calibration status. The label typically indicates the instrument identification, who performed the last calibration and when, and the date of the next scheduled calibration.

Calibration Laboratory (Cal Lab): A work space, provided with test equipment, controlled environment and trained personnel, established for the purpose of maintaining proper operation and accuracy of measuring and test equipment. Cal Labs typically perform many routine calibrations, often on a production-line basis.

Error (Measurement Error): The difference between the measured value and the true value of the object of a measurement. The actual value of an error can never be known exactly, only estimated.

International System of Units (SI): A coherent system of units adopted and used by international agreement.

MSC (Measurement Science Conference): An organization that sponsors and organizes an annual technical conference for metrology and metrology related issues. Also the name of the annual conference.

Measurement: A set of operations performed on a physical object or system according to an established, documented procedure, for the purpose of determining some physical property of the object or system.

Metrology: The field of knowledge concerned with measurement. Metrology includes all aspects of measurements, whatever their level of accuracy and in whatever fields of science or technology they occur.

NCSL (National Conference of Standards Laboratories): An international organization of companies and organizations which have an interest in standards and measurements. NCSL sponsors an annual Workshop and Symposium attended by metrologists and laboratory managers from around the world.

NIST (National Institute of Standards and Technology): The U.S. national standards laboratory, responsible for maintaining the physical standards upon which measurements in the United States are based.

Recall System: A documented process that assures measuring and test equipment is brought into a laboratory for calibration when scheduled.

Specification (Instrument Specification or Spec): A documented presentation of the parameters, including accuracy or uncertainty, describing the capability of an instrument.

Standard (1) (Measurement Standard): An object, artifact, instrument, system, or experiment that stores, embodies, or otherwise provides a physical quantity which serves as the basis for measurements of the quantity.

Standard (2) (Paper Standard or Protocol): A document describing the operations and processes that must be performed in order for a particular end to be achieved. Called by Europeans a "protocol" to avoid confusion with a physical standard. A well known standard is MIL-STD-45662A, which describes the requirements for a calibration system for instrumentation used in producing and testing products sold to the U.S. Military.

Standards Laboratory (Standards Lab): A work space, provided with equipment and standards, a properly controlled environment and trained personnel, established for the purpose of maintaining traceability of standards and measuring equipment used by the organization it supports. Standards laboratories typically perform fewer, more specialized and higher accuracy measurements than Cal Labs.

Test Report (Report of Calibration): A document describing a calibration, including the results, what was done, by whom, under what conditions and using what equipment and procedures.

Tolerance: In metrology, the limits of the range of values (the uncertainty) that apply to a properly functioning measuring instrument.

Traceability: A characteristic of a calibration, analogous to a pedigree. A traceable calibration is achieved when each instrument and standard, in a hierarchy stretching back to the national standard, was itself properly calibrated, and the results properly documented. The documentation provides the information needed to show that all the calibrations in the chain of calibrations were properly performed.

Uncertainty: An estimate of the possible error in a measurement. More precisely, an estimate of the range of values which contains the true value of a measured quantity. Uncertainty is usually reported in terms of the probability that the true value lies within a stated range of values.

Verification: The set of operations that assures that specified requirements have been met, or leads to a decision to perform adjustments, repair, downgrade performance or remove from use.

ppm (parts per million): A convenient way of expressing small fractions and percentages. For example, 12 ppm = 12 ÷ 1,000,000 (fraction), 0.000012 (decimal fraction), and 0.0012% (percentage).

Chapter 4:

International Metrology

This chapter briefly discusses the International System of Units and the role the various laboratories and organizations play in supporting it.

This chapter provides an overview of the global structure of metrology to enable practicing metrologists to gain a better understanding of their positions in the grand scheme of worldwide metrology. It describes the International System of Units, and outlines the features of some other systems of units in use. It touches on the work done in search of standards whose values are based on the constants of nature. Finally, it outlines the three major organizational structures that coordinate the activities of the international metrological community.

The Modern Metric System

The International System of Units (SI) is the foundation of modern metrology. It is sometimes referred to as the "modern metric system" because the names of many of its units are carried forward from the original French metric system. Its abbreviation, SI, is taken from its French name, *Système International d'Unités*. It was established in 1960 by the General Conference of Weights and Measures. The United States and most other nations subscribe to this conference and use the SI for most legal, scientific, and technical purposes.

The SI units are used internationally and are the basis of all modern measurements. In the United States, the national system of measurement is the U.S. Customary System. However, all Customary units, such as the inch, the foot, the yard, and the pound, are defined in terms of the SI base units. For example, an inch is defined as being 2.54 centimeters in length.

The international use of the SI depends on scientific cooperation and legal agreements. Scientific cooperation is focused on improving the definition, realization, representation, and dissemination of the basic units of measurement. Legal agreements ensure that scientific progress can be readily transferred across international borders to provide global support for advances in metrology and commerce.

The SI is a set of definitions. National laboratories conduct experiments to realize (express) the units as defined. Some of these experiments lead to representations of the unit. For example, the volt can be realized via experiments that use the meter, kilogram, and second, but its representation in a Josephson array depends on a strict correlation of the realization with $2e/h$, a ratio of two of the constants of nature.

The System of Units

The SI consists of 28 units (7 base, 2 supplementary, and 19 derivative units).

Base Units

Seven quantities in the SI are the *base units*, the units from which all other measurement parameters are traced. The seven base units are: length, mass, time, electric current, thermodynamic temperature, luminous intensity, and amount of substance. These are all briefly described as follows.

Length
The SI unit of measure for length is the meter (m). It is defined as the length of the path traveled by light in a vacuum during a time interval of $1/299,792,458$ second.

Mass
The SI unit of measure for mass is the kilogram (kg). It is the only unit still defined as a physical artifact, the mass of the artifact cylinder of platinum iridium alloy kept by BIPM at Paris, France.

Time
The SI unit of time is the second (s). It is defined as the duration of $9,192,631,770$ cycles of radiation corresponding to the transition between the two hyperfine levels of the ground state of the cesium-133 atom.

Electric Current
The SI unit of measure for electric current is the ampere (A). It is defined as the electric current producing a force of 2×10^{-7} newtons per meter of length between two long wires, one meter apart in free space. (The newton is briefly defined later.)

Thermodynamic Temperature

The SI unit of measure for thermodynamic temperature is the Kelvin (K). It is defined as $1/273.16$ of the thermodynamic temperature of the triple point of water.

Luminous Intensity

The SI unit of measure for luminous intensity is the candela (cd). It is defined as the luminous intensity in a given direction of a source that emits monochromatic radiation at a frequency of 540×10^{12} hertz, with a radiant intensity in that direction of $1/683$ watts per steradian. (Hertz and steradians are defined later).

Amount of Substance

The SI unit of measure for an amount of substance is the mole (m). It is defined as the amount of substance of a system that contains as many elementary items as there are atoms in 0.012 kilogram of carbon 12.

The SI and Science

The seven SI base units reflect the measurement needs of the major branches of science, charted in Table 4-1. Their construction links the conservation of mass-energy across mechanical, electrical, chemical, and thermodynamic metrology.

Table 4-1. Measurement Needs by Branch and Unit

Branch of Science	m	kg	s	A	K	cd	mol
Classical Mechanics	x	x	x				
Thermodynamics	x	x	x	x	x	x	x
Optics	x	x	x		x	x	
Electrodynamics	x	x	x	x	x	x	x
Chemistry & Metallurgy	x	x	x	x	x		x

Classical Mechanics has been supplanted by Relativity. Quantum Mechanics has unified Optics, Electrodynamics, Chemistry, and Metallurgy. SI not only supports these new needs; it has facilitated their development.

Supplementary Units

There are two supplementary units in the SI system: plane angles and solid angles. These two dimensionless quantities are defined as follows.

Plane Angles

The SI unit of measure for plane angles is the radian (rad). It is defined as a plane angle with vertex at the center of a circle that is subtended by an arc equal in length to the radius.

Solid Angles

The SI unit of measure for solid angles is the steradian (sr). It is defined as the solid angle with vertex at the center of a sphere that is subtended by an area of the spherical circle equal to that of a square with sides equal in length to the radius.

Derived Units

The 19 derived units are obtained by combining the seven SI base units with each other and with other derived or supplementary units. This list has grown with the needs of science; as time goes on, more derived units may be added to the list. Table 4-2 lists the derived units.

Table 4-2. SI Derived Units

Parameter	Unit	Abbrev.	Value
Frequency	hertz	Hz	$1/s$
Force	newton	N	$kg \cdot m/s^2$
Pressure	pascal	Pa	N/m^2
Work or Energy	joule	J	$N \cdot m$
Power	watt	W	J/s
Electric Potential	volt	V	W/A
Electric Resistance	ohm	Ω	V/A
Quantity of Charge	coulomb	C	$A \cdot s$
Electric Capacitance	farad	F	C/V
Conductance	siemens	S	A/V
Magnetic Flux	weber	Wb	$V \cdot s$
Mag. Flux Density	tesla	T	Wb/m^2
Inductance	henry	H	Wb/A
Celsius Temperature	degree	°C	K
Luminous Flux	lumen	lm	$cd \cdot sr$
Illuminance	lux	lx	lm/m^2
Activity	becquerel	Bq	$1/s$
Absorbed Dose	gray	Gy	J/kg
Dose Equivalent	sievert	Sv	$m^2 s^{-2}$

Multiplication Factors

All of the units can be extended over a range of 48 orders of magnitude from their base values. The multiples are all powers of 10, a feature introduced by the original metric system and carried over into SI. Table 4-3 lists the SI standard multiplication factors.

Table 4-3. SI Multiplication Factors

Factor	Name	Symbol
10^{24}	yotta	Y
10^{21}	zeta	Z
10^{18}	exa	E
10^{15}	peta	P
10^{12}	tera	T
10^{9}	giga	G
10^{6}	mega	M
10^{3}	kilo	k
10^{2}	hecto	h
10^{1}	deka	da
10^{-1}	deci	d
10^{-2}	centi	c
10^{-3}	milli	m
10^{-6}	micro	μ
10^{-9}	nano	n
10^{-12}	pico	p
10^{-15}	femto	f
10^{-18}	atto	a
10^{-21}	zepto	z
10^{-24}	yocto	y

Other Systems of Units

Other systems of units are used for different purposes around the world. For example, the centimeter-gram-second (*cgs*) system is used in physics. In this system, the *dyne* is the unit of force. The foot-pound-second (*fps*) system is used in the U.S. (The foot and pound, being units of the U.S. Customary System, are defined in terms of the SI meter and kilogram, however.)

Constants of Nature

It is desirable that the dimensions of the SI units be derived from nature to make intrinsic standards. It is believed, in principle, that this makes them both invariant and locally accessible. Therefore, the determination of the constants of nature is essential to metrology.

The fundamental constants of nature are numbers. Some of these are dimensionless (pure numbers), such as the fine structure constant α. Most are dimensioned, such as Planck's constant h. There are three reasons for using constants of nature. They are:

- The needs of theories. For example, an accurate value for c, the speed of light in a vacuum, is fundamental to the theory of relativity.

- The assigning of values to fundamental particles, such as e, the charge on the electron.

- The assigning of numerical conversion factors. For example, g, the local value of gravitational acceleration which relates mass to force.

In 1983, the value of the speed of light in a vacuum was defined to be exactly 299,792,458 m/s. As a consequence of this definition, the definition of the length of a meter was changed from being a number of wavelengths of krypton-argon radiation to the distance that light travels in 1/299,792,458th of a second.

The numerical values of ratios of the fundamental constants e and h are extremely important to electrical metrology. This is because these ratios are used to define the values provided by the representations of the volt and ohm, through the Josephson and Quantum Hall effects, respectively.

Table 4-4 lists the values of some of the constants of nature that are of interest to electrical metrologists.

National Laboratories

The various national laboratories have participated in defining the SI units and in conducting experiments to establish the values of the constants of nature, in collaboration with physicists and cosmologists. In addition, various national laboratories have conducted experiments to realize the SI units. Finally, all of the national laboratories maintain representations of the units, such as the volt, to which calibrations in their respective countries are legally traceable.

International Metrology Organizations

Three essentially independent international organizations have developed for the standardization of measurements, products, and services. They are the physical standards (treaty) organization, the paper standards (non-treaty) organization, and the supporting technical/professional societies.

It is good to keep in mind that the goal of all these organizations is the effort to ensure that products and services can be confidently traded in the world marketplace. That is, trading partners can know they are receiving and paying a fair price for goods and services; technological products will perform as expected; and applicable laws are being complied with.

Physical Standards Organization

What is here termed the Physical Standards Organization is outlined in Figure 4-1.

This is a treaty organization, in that its origin is in the Treaty of the Meter, to which most technologically advanced countries are signatories. The International Committee for Weights and Measures (CIPM) carries out or oversees the activities required by the treaty. The treaty and CIPM are concerned with establishing, maintaining, and disseminating the particular set of physical parameters that is the international system of units.

Reporting to the CIPM are consultative committees in various disciplines. The Consulting Committee for Electricity (CCE), for example, was involved in proposing, adopting, and implementing the 1990 changes in the volt and ohm. Likewise, the Consulting Committee for Temperature (CCT) proposed and adopted the new ITS-90 temperature scale. Membership in the CCE, CCT, and other committees is made up of scientists and technical experts from the National Standards Laboratories of countries that are parties to the treaty.

Some of CIPM's technical work is carried out by the International Bureau of Weights and Measures (BIPM). This bureau maintains laboratory facilities near Paris, France. BIPM is the custodian of the prototype kilogram, the sole remaining international artifact standard. It also carries out work aimed at achieving agreement among the various physical standards maintained by member countries. Important activities before the adoption of quantum standards for voltage and resistance included arranging and performing periodic intercomparisons of members' voltage and resistance standards.

As shown in Figure 4-1, each nation has set up its own national measurement system consisting of a National Laboratory at the top of the hierarchy and a number of facilities of varying

Table 4-4. *Selected Constants of Nature*

Quantity	Symbol	Value (1σ uncertainty)	Application
Speed of Light in a Vacuum	c	299,792,458 m/s (exactly)	time, frequency, length
Elementary Charge	e	$1.60217733 \cdot 10^{-19}$ C (0.3 ppm)	voltage & current
Josephson Constant	K_{j-90}	483, 597.9 Ghz/V (0.4 ppm)	voltage
Von Klitzing Constant	R_{k-90}	25.812807 kΩ (0.2 ppm)	resistance
Permeability of Vacuum	μ_0	$4\pi \cdot 10^{-7}$ N/A^2 (exactly)	capacitance

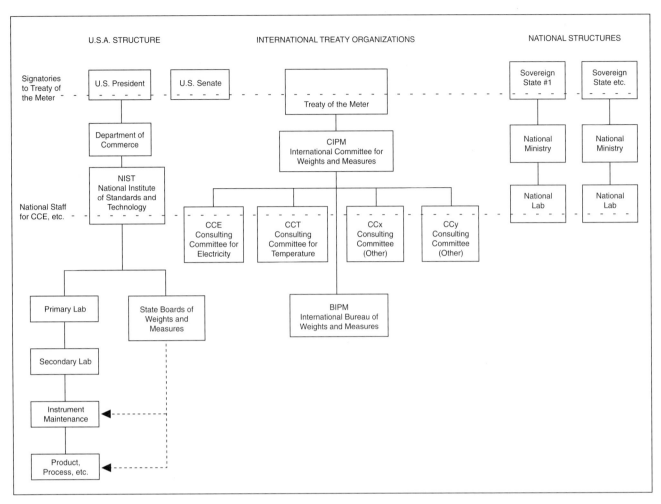

U.S.A. STRUCTURE **INTERNATIONAL TREATY ORGANIZATIONS** **NATIONAL STRUCTURES**

Signatories to Treaty of the Meter

U.S. President

U.S. Senate

Treaty of the Meter

Sovereign State #1

Sovereign State etc.

Department of Commerce

CIPM International Committee for Weights and Measures

National Ministry

National Ministry

National Staff for CCE, etc.

NIST National Institute of Standards and Technology

National Lab

National Lab

CCE Consulting Committee for Electricity

CCT Consulting Committee for Temperature

CCx Consulting Committee (Other)

CCy Consulting Committee (Other)

Primary Lab

State Boards of Weights and Measures

BIPM International Bureau of Weights and Measures

Secondary Lab

Instrument Maintenance

Product, Process, etc.

Figure 4-1. Physical Standards Organization

capability at lower levels in the hierarchy. National laboratories establish, maintain, and disseminate the primary (physical) standards of measurement for the country. Calibration and measurement services are provided by the lower-level laboratories. In general, accuracy and technical expertise diminish, and the number of customers served increases, as one moves downward through the measurement hierarchy.

Many countries have added what may be termed a measurement quality control function to their national laboratories in the form of a laboratory accreditation service. Typically, these services certify a laboratory's ability to make measurements to a certain minimum uncertainty. Then the laboratory can provide measurement service with the authority of the national laboratory, but at a greater uncertainty. Typical of such accreditation bodies are DKD in Germany, NAMAS in Great Britain,

and NKO in The Netherlands. The activities of these European national accreditation bodies are coordinated by the West European Calibration Cooperation (WECC). The U.S. calibration accreditation system is in its infancy, but each state has a Bureau of Weights and Measures which provides a partial system for certain sectors of commercial metrology. See Chapter 29, "Laboratory Accreditation."

Non-Treaty Organization

In addition to the treaty organization for physical standards, there exists a non-treaty ad-hoc organization which has grown to provide what can be termed a quality control function for measurements and testing. This organization is concerned with paper standards (also called protocols or norms) as opposed to physical standards. These standards tell one what to do and how to do it. Some are highly technical, but they are all documents, not artifacts. Figure 4-2 shows some of the important relationships in this informal and largely voluntary organization.

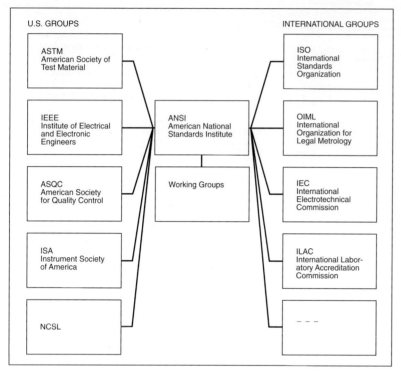

U.S. GROUPS   INTERNATIONAL GROUPS

ASTM
American Society of
Test Material

IEEE
Institute of Electrical
and Electronic
Engineers

ASQC
American Society
for Quality Control

ISA
Instrument Society
of America

NCSL

ANSI
American National
Standards Institute

Working Groups

ISO
International
Standards
Organization

OIML
International
Organization for
Legal Metrology

IEC
International
Electrotechnical
Commission

ILAC
International Labor-
atory Accreditation
Commission

- - -

Figure 4-2. *Informal Non-Treaty Laboratories' Relationship*

The international standardizing bodies with which the electrical metrologist may have to deal are shown in the figure. The International Standards Organization (ISO) has broad standards-writing responsibilities that cut across many disciplines. The International Organization for Legal Metrology (OIML) deals with aspects of metrology affecting law enforcement.

The International Electrotechnical Commission (IEC) writes standards for products and tests in the electrical area. And the International Laboratory Accreditation Commission (ILAC) concerns itself with standardizing the international approach to laboratory accreditation.

ANSI's Role

In the U.S., the national standardizing body is the American National Standards Institute (ANSI). It interfaces with both the technical community within the United States and with the international standards organizations. ANSI's job is to gather the U.S. position on a question, then to communicate that to the international bodies in order to arrive at an international standard that is acceptable to the U.S. Once a standard is accepted internationally, ANSI promotes its use within the U.S.

ANSI has at least two methods of operation. In one, an accepted standards-writing organization will write and gain acceptance for a standard in a fairly narrow area of application, for example, electrical measurements or quality control. ANSI may then expose the standard to the rest of the standards community in order to test its acceptance by the country as a whole. If it is approved, it then becomes an American National Standard, and is recommended for adoption and use throughout the country.

Once a standard is adopted as an American National Standard, ANSI may push for its adoption by one of the international standardizing bodies. Typically, it will not be acceptable in its adopted form, so it will have to be submitted for revision. In this case, ANSI may form a working group to deal with the issues raised. Through a process of negotiations between the parties involved, an effort is made to create a document that will be acceptable to all parties.

In its second method of operation, a standards-writing body in another country will propose that its standard be adopted as an international standard. ANSI then has the responsibility for determining the U.S. position on the standard. It does this through a working group.

As can be seen, this is a process of negotiations aimed at making the standards acceptable to all parties. Figure 4-3 shows the relationships between ANSI and other bodies which have arisen from the establishment of the European Community.

CEN and CENELEC write standards that will be mandatory for all EC countries.

Technical and Professional Societies

There are a number of technical and professional societies that support national and international organizations, and individual metrologists in a variety of ways. These are divided into standards-writing organizations and other organizations.

U.S. Standards-Writing Organizations

For the dc and low frequency metrologist, there are four standards-writing organizations of interest in the U.S. They are: the Institute of Electrical and Electronics Engineers Society for Instrumentation and Measurement (I & M Society of IEEE), the American Society for Quality Control (ASQC), the American Society for Testing Materials (ASTM), and the Instrument Society of America (ISA). Each will be described briefly.

IEEE I & M Society

The Institute of Electrical and Electronics Engineers is a broad-based association of professional electrical and electronics engineers having a wide range of interests and technical abilities. It has a number of member Societies, of which the Society for Instrumentation and Measurement is of major interest to the dc and low frequency metrologist.

The IEEE Society for Instrumentation and Measurement provides two technical conferences: the annual Instrumentation and Measurement Technology Conference (IMTC), and the biannual Conference for Precision Electromagnetic Measurements (CPEM). IMTC tends to focus on new technology related to instrumentation and measurement. CPEM is strongly focused toward standardization and measurement, but tends to be dominated by state-of-the-art measurements in National Laboratories. CPEM must be considered the premier conference for electrical and electronic standardization and measurement. I&M publications, especially the special issues devoted to the conference records, are valuable resources for those who are attempting to be on the cutting edge of electrical measurement technology.

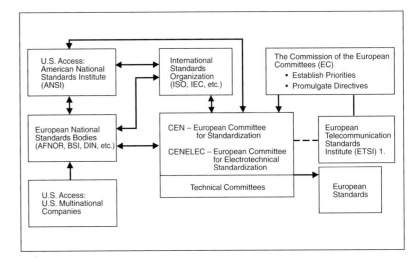

Figure 4-3. *Procedural Standards Organizations*

ASQC

The American Society for Quality Control is not a metrology society, but includes a Metrology division which could become important with proper support from the metrology community. Besides publishing its Journal, ASQC provides training and certification for Quality Engineers and Technicians. Since Quality Assurance functions are the major customer for metrology services in U.S. industry, industrial metrologists can profit by maintaining ties with this organization.

ASTM

The American Society for Testing Materials, as its name suggests, is not directly concerned with metrology either. But, technically speaking, it is one of the strongest standards-writing bodies in the U.S. Its publications can be a useful source of information about measurements.

ISA

Instrument Society of America is strongly focused toward metrology, but the emphasis is on non-electrical measurements. Those who have the opportunity can profit by attending their conferences and reading their publications.

Other U.S. Organizations

Less focused technically, but nonetheless important to metrologists are: the National Conference of Standards Laboratories (NCSL), the Measurement Science Conference (MSC), and the Precision Measurement Association (PMA).

NCSL

The National Conference of Standards Laboratories is international, is more than a conference, and includes many who are not associated with standards laboratories. It publishes a series of Recommended Practices which range from useful to very good, has recently engaged in lobbying Congress on behalf of NIST budgets, and is currently addressing laboratory accreditation.

MSC

The Measurement Science Conference has as its sole reason for existence the staging of the annual Measurement Science Conference. Conferences are well attended, always include strong vendor exhibits, and present a well-balanced technical program that addresses current metrology concerns. In the past, this has been attended mostly by its Southern California members; however, it does draw worldwide participants.

PMA

The Precision Measurement Association publishes a Directory of Metrologists and provides training and information exchange through meetings of local sections.

Key References

NIST, "Guide for the Use of the International System of Units, The Modernized Metric System," NIST *Special Publication 811*

Other references for this chapter are in the Resources Appendix.

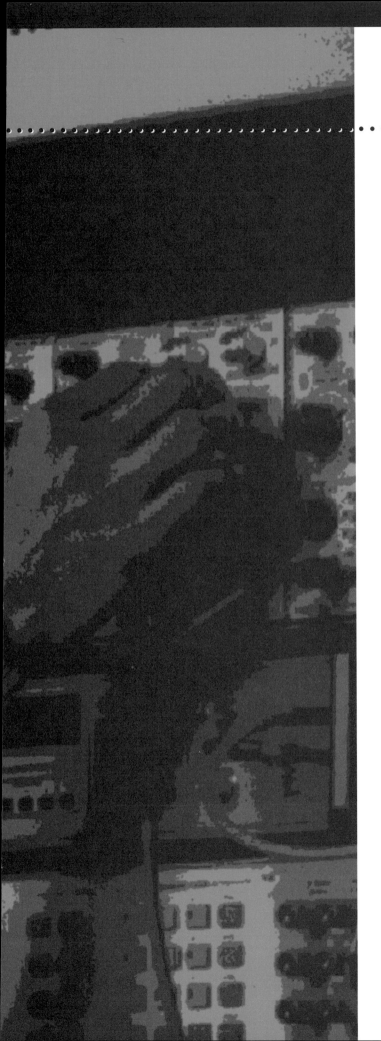

Chapter 5:
Basic DC and Low Frequency Metrology

As the science of measurement, metrology has both a theoretical foundation and a practical expression.

T his chapter provides a new metrologist with background material for this book. Metrology is the science of making measurements, having both theoretical and practical aspects. A measurement is a set of operations whose object is to determine the numerical value of a quantity. The principal quantities, whose measurements are discussed in this book, include voltage, current, resistance, inductance, capacitance, time and frequency. Some general principles for electrical measurements are covered in the following five subtopics:

- Measurement Units
- Measurement Equipment
- Types of Measurements
- Calibration Measurements
- Measurement Uncertainty

Measurement Units

A measurement unit is the basic, or unitary, value of a quantity. One volt, one ohm and one ampere are examples of the basic units of the basic electrical quantities. The International System of Units, abbreviated SI for its French name, Système International d' Unités defines the measurement units used in modern metrology. These units are coherent, uniform and unified. The major legal and scientific aspects of the SI are described in Chapter 4, "International Metrology."

There is a close relationship between mathematics and measurements. All of the quantities measured will have two parts, the name of the unit and its numerical value. For example the quantity 10 volts is ten (10 = numerical value) times as great as 1 volt (volt = name of unit). Moreover, the electrical units can be related to each other by various mathematical operations. For example, the familiar relationship of Ohm's law, $E = I \times R$, shows how the voltage, current and resistance in a dc circuit are strictly related to each other. If the magnitudes of any two of these units are known, the value of the third can be calculated.

Coherent, Uniform and Unified

The SI is a *coherent* system of units for measurements. It consists of seven base units, nineteen derived units and two supplementary units. The base units are considered to be independent of each other. Derived units are combinations of the base units. Multiples and submultiples of the SI units are expressed in a decimal system of systematically defined prefixes. For example, one kilovolt is one thousand volts.

The SI units are *uniform* because, with the exception of the kilogram, its base units are defined by the presumably invariant constants of nature. The units defined in this way can be independently reproduced by an experiment in physics conducted by any competent party.

Finally the SI units are *unified*. Measurements made in dynamics, electrodynamics and thermodynamics can be compared with each other in such a way as to observe the conservation of mass-energy.

Defined, Realized and Represented

The terms "defined," "realized," and "represented" have specific meanings in metrology as discussed next.

An SI *definition* is an exact statement about what a base unit is. A unit is *realized* by a physical object whose observed attributes closely match the definition. For example, the SI unit of time is the second, *defined* as the duration of a number of cycles of radiation emitted by a cesium-133 atom. Anyone who has the time, money, expertise and equipment can make an atomic clock that produces radiation that matches the SI definition of the second. Note that the atomic clock is not the realization of the second; the radiation it produces is the realization.

The SI volt is a key unit in dc and low frequency metrology and is defined as power divided by current. Its definition is realized by experiments that compare electrical power against mechanical power via a force-balance. The results of these experiments are used to assign values to the voltage produced by inexpensive, stable, easily reproduced and maintained devices, such as electrochemical standard cells or electronic zener stabilized voltage standards.

These devices *represent*, rather than *realize*, the SI volt because their principles of operation do not involve a continuous comparison of electrical power with the power produced by realizations of the SI mechanical units.

The best available representation of the SI volt is obtained from a Josephson array. The voltage produced by this device is a function of the frequency of microwaves that irradiate it and the Josephson constant, a universal quantity independent of experimental variables. Experimental realizations of the SI volt have been used to determine and assign the value of this constant.

While the definition is exact, both the realized and represented unit have uncertainties in their magnitudes. At the national level there is a constant effort to reduce the uncertainties by conducting ever more exacting experiments to realize the definition of the unit and by developing improved methods of transferring the realized value to the represented value.

Disseminated and Extended

The values of the national representations of the SI units are transferred, or *disseminated* to representations of the units kept in local laboratories. The devices or artifacts which store or maintain all such representations, national or local, are conventionally called standards. The best local standards are called primary standards. Their values are disseminated to other local standards, usually called working or secondary standards. The values of the secondary or working standards are transferred to devices, usually called calibrators, used to *extend* the value of the SI unit to a wide range of additional values.

All of the electrical units are coherently defined in SI. When properly realized and represented, the use of the SI units assures one that the numerical values obtained for the measurements one makes are compatible with similar measurements made elsewhere.

Measurement Equipment

A new metrologist rarely works with primary laboratory standards. Instead, he or she may use secondary standards but is more likely to use calibrators and related measurement equipment. In order to make the best possible measurements, one should select the best equipment and use it knowledgeably in effective test configurations. The knowledgeable use of measurement equipment requires having an understanding of at least the following:

- Types of measurement equipment
- Their principles of operation
- Imperfections in equipment and test configurations
- Types of measurements that can be made
- Purposes of calibration measurements

Types of Measurement Equipment

Several generic types of calibration equipment are used in dc and low frequency metrology. These include:

- Secondary Standards
- Null Detectors
- Calibrators
- Test Leads

Secondary Standards
Secondary standards typically include devices that disseminate the SI units from the primary local standards, ratiometers and ac-dc transfer standards. Secondary standards are usually used to either calibrate calibrators or enhance the performance of calibrators when extremely accurate measurements are needed, for example when calibrating a laboratory DMM.

Null Detectors
A null detector is a meter that is designed to measure voltage differences. When there is a zero volt difference, the meter's input is at null, hence its name. A typical application is the measurement of the difference in the output of two resistive voltage dividers whose inputs are in parallel across a voltage source. A Wheatstone bridge, discussed in Chapter 9, "DC Ratio," exemplifies this circuit arrangement.

The classical null detector is the galvanometer. A simple galvanometer is an electro-mechanical meter with a pointer that rests at the middle of a deflection scale when there is zero input voltage. This arrangement allows the pointer to indicate both the polarity of the difference in the input voltages and zero when the voltages have equal amplitudes.

In this arrangement, the galvanometer's pointer is deflected by current drawn directly from the output of the two voltage dividers. This fact means that the meter movement should be very sensitive, drawing as little current as possible for an off-null voltage difference. The meter's measurement of the difference of the voltages must not be affected by their amplitude. For example, it must indicate zero volts when both of the voltages at each of its inputs have an amplitude of 1V, 10V or even 100V.

Electronic null detectors are used for the same purposes as galvanometers but they are much more sensitive due to their ability to amplify the voltage difference at their inputs. Fluke model 845AB is an example of a highly sensitive electronic null detector that can accurately measure a null between voltages, each having an amplitude from <1 µV up to 1000V, even at the output of high resistance voltage dividers.

Digital null detectors are available and some laboratory DMMs can also be used for this function. The off-null sensitivity of these instruments is extremely good because they have a high input resistance on their low voltage ranges. In contrast to observing the motion of a meter pointer, it can be very difficult to read these instruments manually because their digital displays are constantly changing.

Calibrators

Calibrators are sometimes called secondary standards, tertiary standards or working standards. They are designed to provide a convenient method of verifying and adjusting the performance of general purpose test equipment such as DMMs and oscilloscopes.

Most modern calibrators are multifunctional. They provide a wide range of values for a number of different SI units. For example, the Fluke 5700A provides dc voltage and current, resis-tance, low frequency and rf ac voltages to 30 MHz as well as low frequency ac current. It is often used to calibrate 5½-digit, bench or systems DMMs.

Modern calibrators can be both manually operated and computer controlled. Their most effective application is the computer controlled calibration of IEEE-488 bus compatible DMMs. In this application, the performance of the DMM is automatically measured, evaluated and even adjusted in much less time, and much more reliably, than when it and the calibrator are manually operated.

Test Leads

Test leads are the wires and cables that are used to connect the measurement equipment and the instrument under test. These leads must be compatible with the measurement that's being made. For example a very low level dc voltage measurement should not be subject to errors caused by the thermo-electric generation of a voltage at the junction of the test lead and an instrument's input connectors. This specific type of error is avoided by using test leads whose connectors are made of the same material as the instrument's connectors and, in addition, generate a low thermal emf when in contact with each other. Other requirements for test leads are discussed in Chapter 32, "Grounding, Shielding and Guarding."

Principles of Operation

Some manually operated measurement equipment has a basic design that dates back to the classical era (19th century) of electrical metrology. Modern equipment uses electronic circuits and microprocessors to improve and increase measurement sensitivity, accuracy and range.

Electrical Measurements

Not all electrical measurement equipment incorporates electronic circuits. Test setups that use this kind of equipment consist simply of resistors, switches and voltage sources. An example of this kind of equipment that continues to be widely used is the Kelvin-Varley voltage divider, a secondary dc ratio standard.

One advantage of this type of equipment is that its principles of operation are usually simple expressions of Ohm's law. Because the measurements are a direct realization of Ohm's law, the results are not subject to errors from the electronic signal processing methods used in modern instruments. On the other hand these measurements are less sophisticated, less sensitive and more difficult to make than is the case when modern instruments are used to make the measurements.

Electronic Measurements

In contrast to the classical electric measurement equipment, modern calibrators and DMMs and other types of measurement equipment make wide use of operational amplifiers and microprocessors and are very compatible with being controlled by computers.

Operational amplifiers were first used to perform the mathematical operations of addition, subtraction, scaling, integration, differentiation and so forth in analog computers. Later, beginning in about 1960, they were incorporated into dc and low frequency measurement equipment to provide amplification and impedance buffering. These applications use two basic circuit configurations, the inverted current feedback amplifier and the voltage follower. These are illustrated in Figure 5-1.

The gain of an inverted current feedback amplifier is determined largely by the values of the feedback resistors, R_{in} and R_f. As the gain of the amplifier without feedback approaches infinity, the gain of the amplifier with negative feedback approaches $-R_f/R_{in}$. The primary function of this circuit is to provide precise gain. This circuit is not an ideal voltage amplifier because R_{in} draws current from the input, which can cause errors. However, its ability to operate on the feedback current allows it to be used for scaling, integration, differentiation and log-antilog operations.

The gain of a voltage follower approaches:

$$1 + \frac{R_f}{R_{in}}$$

as the gain of the amplifier without feedback approaches infinity. The voltage follower is more ideal than the current feedback amplifier

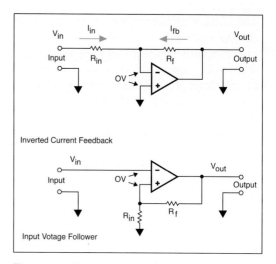

Figure 5-1. *Two Basic Types of Op-Amps*

because of its high input impedance. On the other hand, its use is limited to providing precision gains that are equal to or greater than one. Because of its high input impedance and capability to deliver current to the load, it is often used as a unity-gain impedance buffer between the source and load.

Most modern electronic instruments use microprocessors to increase their measurement capabilities. The microprocessor performs various operations on a digitized signal. In addition to the algebraic operations performed by operational amplifiers, microprocessors easily process the measurement parameters associated with the transcendental and hyperbolic functions as well as the Fourier and other transforms. These powerful capabilities greatly enhance the performance of modern test and measurement instruments at the expense of adding complexity to the signal processing path.

Imperfections in Equipment and Test Configurations

Imperfections in measurement equipment can be described in terms that don't consider the details of the instrument's operation. Instead, the discussion focuses on what the instrument does, not how or why it does it. This method is sometimes called a "black box" analysis because a knowledge of the details of what happens inside an instrument is not needed for the analysis.

Some metrologists find that a black box analysis is not sufficient. They use circuit analysis to know not only what happens, but also how and why it happens. This section will discuss both black box and circuit analysis.

Black Box Analysis
A measurement instrument has some specified sets of behavior. These include the range and accuracy of the nominal values it can measure and the various types of deviations from the nominal value. These considerations will be discussed, using the +10V output of a "black box" calibrator as an example.

A null detector is used to compare the calibrator's freshly adjusted +10V output and the +10V output of a Fluke 732B. The null detector and 732B are assumed to be perfect. At this point the null detector indicates exactly zero volts, so the calibrator's output is exactly +10V. This configuration is maintained for several hours during which slow deflections of up to ±10 μV are observed on the null detector. These deflections are a measure of the calibrator's short term stability.

Next the calibrator is placed in an environmental chamber. As the temperature is changed, its output also changes. After several cycles of temperature changes, the average rate at which the calibrator's output changes is plotted against the temperature change. This measurement determines the calibrator's temperature coefficient per °C.

The calibrator can be turned on and off to see how repeatably it produces its +10V output. An oscilloscope can be placed across its output to observe the peak to peak amplitude of an ac voltage component superimposed on the dc output. This component is commonly called noise. Its rms value can also be measured with a sensitive ac voltmeter.

Other deviations from nominal in the dc voltage function or other functions can be measured. These include linearity deviations over a range of outputs, ac waveform distortion and other imperfections.

The key point is that these imperfections can be measured independently of any knowledge of the calibrator's circuit design. The performance

characteristics of various models of measurement instruments can be readily compared to one another using this method. This method is often used to select test equipment for specific applications.

Circuit and Component Analysis
The principal metrological imperfections of the classical electrical calibration standards are associated with contact resistance and thermal emf's in their manually operated switches. These are generally better than the reed relays and solid state switches used in modern equipment, so when properly used, these instruments can give very good performance. In comparison to electronic calibration standards, the dynamic range of their performance envelope is generally limited due to a lack of sensitivity to small currents and inability to handle input and output load currents.

Operational amplifiers have imperfections in their transfer functions that introduce errors in their mathematical operations. The chief imperfections are caused by voltage offsets and bias currents at their input and gain errors in their output due to imperfections of their associated feedback elements. The former add a constant magnitude of error to the signal that's being measured and the latter introduce a constant proportion of error to the measurement (Figure 5-2).

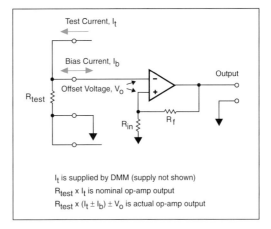

Figure 5-2. Bias Current and Voltage Offset Errors in Op-Amps

Prior to the incorporation of microprocessors in test instruments, the gain, offset and bias current errors of the operational amplifiers were minimized by physically adjusting potentiometers, rheostats and variable capacitors associated with their input and feedback circuitry. In the newest test instruments, the unadjusted analog outputs of the operational amplifiers are digitized and microprocessors digitally operate on the numeric values to compensate for gain, bias current and voltage offset errors.

Test Configurations

A metrologist who uses the classical instruments must be diligent in understanding their principles of operation and their limitations in order to use them effectively. In contrast, metrologists using modern calibration standards with their electronic signal conditioning, processing, analyzing and modification features will find they are very easy to use. However, this ease of use can cause over-confidence about the values they provide or display.

For example, if there are imperfections in the basic interconnections between a calibrator and the standards that are used to calibrate it, its operational amplifiers and microprocessors can be adjusted during the calibration to compensate for errors external to the instrument. The six, seven or eight digits of display will look very authoritative but they can be telling a false story when there are problems in the connections between the measurement standard and the instrument that's being calibrated. So it is wise to behave like a classical metrologist at all times when it comes to establishing the calibration conditions.

Figure 5-3 summarizes the increasing isolation of the metrologist from measurements he or she makes due to the evolution of calibration standards from the classical instruments of the 19th century into today's complex electronic instruments.

In the classical measurement of resistance, a standard resistor, R_{std}, and a test resistor, R_{test}, are connected to the bridge illustrated at the top of Figure 5-3. The bridge dials, symbolized by R_a and $R_{'S'}$ in the figure, are adjusted until the galvanometer indicates zero (null). At this point R_{test} equals R_{std} multiplied by the bridge dial's setting, S. The bridge's operator is fully involved in every step of the measurement procedure.

In the electronically buffered measurement of resistance, the instrument provides a current, I_t, for the test resistor, R_{test}. The voltage drop across R_{test} is processed through the voltage follower to the analog to digital converter (adc). The digitized value is displayed on the instrument's readout.

The instrument's calibration is periodically adjusted via controls inside it. These adjustments set the value of I_t to give a correct reading in the display when a standard resistor of known value is used for R_{test}. During normal operation, offset voltages, V_o, and bias currents, I_b, in the voltage follower and adc can cause errors in the displayed value. Aside from providing a proper test connection at the instrument's input, the operator cannot easily identify or compensate for errors in the electronic circuits.

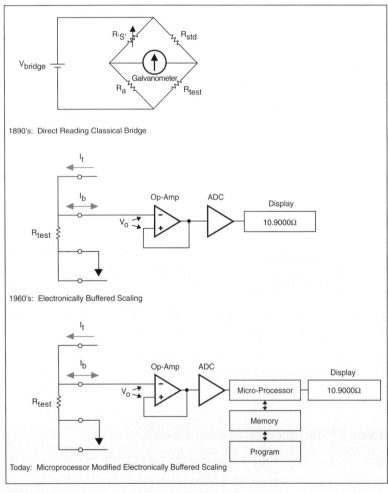

1890's: Direct Reading Classical Bridge

1960's: Electronically Buffered Scaling

Today: Microprocessor Modified Electronically Buffered Scaling

Figure 5-3. Evolution of Calibration Standards

The calibration of the microprocessor modified version of the electronically buffered measurement omits physical adjustments for I_t. Instead the instrument's microprocessor obtains software correction factors to compensate for offsets in its zero reading and to customize the reading for the actual value of I_t. This approach further isolates the metrologist from control of the entire measurement procedure.

Types of Measurements

The measurements discussed here are those that pertain to voltage, current, and impedance (including resistance, reactance and the values of inductors and capacitors). Generally speaking, the measurements made can be categorized as:

- direct measurements
- differential measurements
- transfer measurements
- ratio measurements
- indirect measurements

Direct Measurements

Direct measurements are made by placing an instrument directly into contact with the phenomenon that is to be measured. For example, a Fluke 70 series handheld DMM with its leads placed directly into an electrical power outlet will measure the line voltage directly. In this case, the DMM's LCD readout directly displays the value of the line voltage.

Differential Measurements

Differential measurements are made by using an instrument, such as a galvanometer or null detector, to measure the difference between known and unknown quantities of the same value. Figure 5-4 compares direct and differential measurements. In this case, the Fluke 70 series can measure the difference between the +10V reference and the output of V_{test}. The output of the power supply is the algebraic sum of 10V and the meter reading. This method is more accurate and will provide more resolution

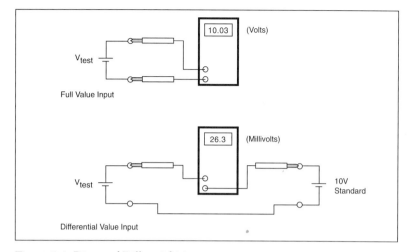

Figure 5-4. *Direct and Differential Measurements*

than would be obtained via direct measurement of the power supply's output with the DMM.

Chapter 22, "Uncertainty Statements," provides an analysis of the uncertainty of these two methods when a Fluke 8840A is used as the DMM.

Transfer Measurements

The differential measurement described above is also a transfer measurement. In essence, the value of the known source of voltage has been transferred to the test source by reducing the voltage difference between the two sources to zero. In this particular case, a like value to like value transfer has been made via a differential measurement.

It's also possible to make transfer measurements where the result of the measurement is not in the same units as the value that's measured. Figure 5-5 provides a simple illustration of this kind of measurement.

In this figure, the voltage drops across the two series-connected resistors are measured. The value of the standard resistor is transferred to the test resistor according to the simple mathematical relationship:

$$V_1 \times R_{std} = V_2 \times R_{test}$$

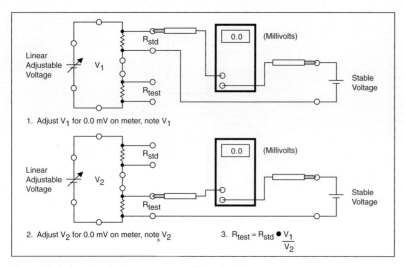

1. Adjust V_1 for 0.0 mV on meter, note V_1

2. Adjust V_2 for 0.0 mV on meter, note V_2   *3. $R_{test} = R_{std} \bullet \dfrac{V_1}{V_2}$*

Figure 5-5. *Transfer Measurements, Differing Units*

Therefore:

$$R_{test} = R_{std} \times \frac{V_1}{V_2}$$

Ratio Measurements

Because the value of R_{std} is transferred to R_{test} via the voltage ratio, this is also a ratio measurement. Ratio measurements are very common in dc and low frequency metrology. Chapters 9, "DC Ratio" and 13, "Immittance and AC Ratio," discuss these measurements.

Indirect Measurements

Indirect measurements find the value of interest from other values. For example dc current is indirectly determined by measuring the voltage drop across a known resistance when the current is flowing in the resistor. The value of the current is computed from Ohm's law.

Another type of indirect method uses a thermal sensor to compare the heat generated in a pure resistor by the alternate application of known dc and test ac voltages to the resistor. If a perfect sensor is used, the dc and ac voltages are equal when the heat generated in the resistor doesn't change as they are alternately applied. This is also a transfer measurement, since the known value of the dc voltage is transferred to the unknown ac voltage.

Calibration Measurements

The preceding types of measurements are often used to calibrate test and measurement instruments. A calibration measurement has a legal connotation that goes beyond determining the numerical value of a quantity. A key requirement is that the calibration measurement is traceable to national standards or other accepted standards. Traceability is discussed in Chapter 6, "Standards and Traceability." The information here summarizes what a calibration measurement is and gives an example of how it's made.

Types of Calibration Measurements

There are three general types of calibration measurement:

- Verify the performance of the test instrument
- Adjust the response of the test instrument
- Obtain correction factors for the test instrument

There is sometimes a tendency to refer to just the second of these as calibration. In fact, all three are defined as calibration by various standards such as MIL-STD-45662A.

Examples of Calibration Measurements

The performance verification of a measurement instrument involves applying a standard value to the instrument and observing how it responds. For example, one might apply +10V to the input of a DMM and observe that its display indicates +9.995V. Depending on the DMM's performance specifications, this reading could indicate that the DMM is performing as specified or that it's out of tolerance.

After its performance has been verified, the DMM's response to the standard values can be adjusted. In older models, these adjustments may involve the physical resetting of potentiometers or capacitors. In newer models, microprocessors calculate correction factors for its response for each of its ranges and functions. The correction factors are stored in memory associated with the microprocessor and are automatically applied to measurements.

Correction factors are sometimes obtained manually during calibration and are written down on a sheet of paper that's kept with the test instrument. For example, an analog pressure gage may have a table of correction factors whose values give a better indication of pressure than the gage's scale.

Reports of Calibration Measurements

The results of calibration measurements performed on a test instrument are recorded and reported. The report can be as simple as a sticker on the instrument's front panel, indicating that it meets its performance specifications.

In other situations a complete report may be required. It will report numerical values of the pre and post adjustment (as found and as left) performance of the instrument and other essential data concerning when and where it was calibrated, the equipment used to calibrate it, the physical environmental conditions, and so forth.

Measurement Uncertainty

In reality, there are no exact measurements. There is always the possibility that errors have occurred that cause the measured and true value to be different. Any such errors raise a degree of uncertainty about how large the difference between the measured and true value is.

Measurement Error

It is a basic assumption of measurement theory that a quantity being measured has a true value, the value that would be obtained by a perfect measurement. However, it's also a premise of measurement theory that there are inevitable imperfections in the measurement process that prevent one from actually measuring the true value. The resolution of this problem has been traditionally handled by invoking the concept of measurement error.

Measurement error is defined as the difference between the result of the measurement and the true value of the quantity measured, after all corrections have been made. Figure 5-6 uses the normal distribution curve to illustrate the situation. It implies that the true value can be anywhere under the curve but it is most likely located at the curve's midpoint.

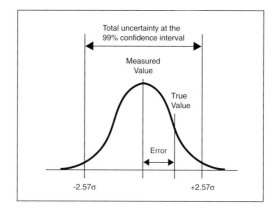

Figure 5-6. *Uncertainty and Error*

A consideration of Figure 5-6 indicates that error is a real physical quantity, but for the most part is both unknown and unknowable. Therefore one is uncertain about the magnitude of the error and hence of the location of the true value in the confidence interval (see below) under the curve.

Error is traditionally viewed as being of two kinds:

Random Error: The result of random, unpredictable differences between measurement results. Often viewed as "random noise" in the measurement process, random error is evaluated by statistical means.

Systematic Error: Differences from the true value which result from imperfections in the measurement system, hence the name.

Some systematic errors are the result of measurable effects (temperature, humidity, pressure, etc.), which can be functionally related to the value of the quantity. Others are simply due to uncorrected offsets in standards. What appears as random error in one instance may be systematic error in another. One example would be temperature effects which appear to influence the measurement in a random fashion in one measurement, but which are analyzed and corrected for in another.

Expressing Uncertainty

The difficulties associated with defining "error" have caused various international metrology organizations to recommend that the concept of measurement uncertainty should be used instead of the concept of measurement error. Chapter 4, "International Metrology," has more information on these organizations.

Uncertainty or measurement uncertainty has traditionally been defined as being a range of values, usually centered on the measured value, which contains the true value with stated probability. This definition doesn't raise the issue of error but emphasizes that the relationship of the observed and true values is uncertain.

"Uncertainty" and "error" are not synonyms. While error is an unknown physical quantity, uncertainty expresses the metrologist's state of mind about the actual value of the measured quantity. The uncertainty statement is intended to provide the customer for the measurement with information which will allow him to compute the risk of using the measurement result.

The ISO *Guide to the Expression of Uncertainty in Measurement* redefines uncertainty as the equivalent of a standard deviation and recommends that uncertainties be placed in two categories, "A" and "B," based on the method by which they are evaluated. Uncertainties evaluated by method "A" are those that are based on a statistical evaluation of a series of measurements. Uncertainties evaluated by method "B" are those that are evaluated by any other method than a statistical evaluation of a series of measurements.

Confidence Interval and Confidence Level

Under the traditional definition of uncertainty, the confidence interval is the range of values which corresponds with the stated uncertainty. "Confidence interval" is a technical term with a precise statistical meaning. It always applies to the mean of several measurements (or equivalent statistical measure) and never to an individual measurement result.

Confidence level is the probability associated with a confidence interval. We would say, "The true value can be expected to lie within ±X units of the measured value with 99% confidence." This means that we have evidence which leads us to believe that if the same measurement were to be performed many times, we would find the true value to be in this interval 99% of the time, which is the same as saying the probability of the true value being in the interval is 99%.

The type "A" method of evaluating uncertainty involves making measurements and using statistical methods to evaluate them. Technically, the type "A" uncertainty is defined as an "uncertainty obtained from a probability density function derived from an observed frequency distribution."

One would normally use this approach to maintain primary standards, for example, when one supports the calibration of a Fluke 732B in a Measurement Assurance Program (MAP). This method is well understood and is extensively used. Section Five, "Statistics," discusses various aspects of this method.

At the time of this writing, there are unresolved issues associated with the type "B" method of evaluating measurement uncertainty. Type "B" uncertainty is defined as "uncertainty obtained from an assumed probability density function based on the degree of belief that an event will occur." The degree of belief is sometimes called "subjective probability" that is said to be "often based on a pool of *comparatively reliable information*." This definition has provoked a good deal of discussion at professional conferences such as the NCSL and MSC (italics added to the quotations above).

In point of fact though, the use of a manufacturer's data sheet could be taken as an example of the type "B" evaluation of uncertainty. This is because the data is accepted as applying to a class of instruments and it is not actually known what the distribution of errors is in a particular instrument. Chapter 20, "Introduction to Metrology Statistics," presents the general principles for getting data from a Fluke 5700A calibrator and using it to construct a type "A" evaluation of its actual performance.

Key References

Taylor, Barry N.; Kuyatt, Chris E., "Guidelines for Evaluating and Expressing the Uncertainty of NIST Measurement Results," NIST *Technical Note 1297*, January, 1993

ISO, *Guide to the Expression of Uncertainty in Measurement*

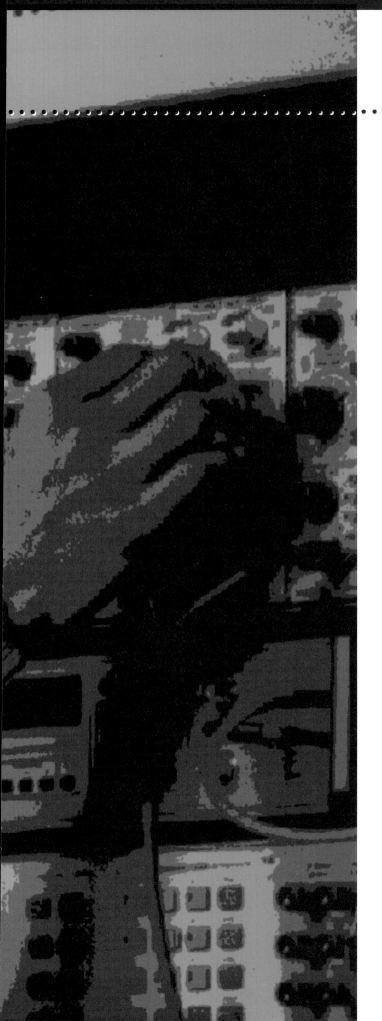

FLUKE®

Chapter 6:
Standards and Traceability

What is a standard? What is traceability? How are they related? In this chapter, you will read about defined standards, and the relationship they have to a system of measurement. You will also read about laboratory practices that produce traceability, as well as services you can use to keep your laboratory traceable to national standards.

Today it is taken for granted that a measurement represents the same quantity everywhere. But it has not always been that way. For example, the cubit was a measure of length that was used by several early civilizations including the Babylonians, Egyptians, Hebrews, and Romans. It eventually came to be recognized as the length of the forearm from the tip of the middle finger to the elbow. But whose forearm? Each group had its own unique definition and standard for the cubit; therefore, the practical length of the cubit varied from place to place. This meant that although reasonable uniformity could be achieved within a region or country, it was guaranteed to differ from one region or country to the next.

Today the likelihood of measurements ending up like the cubit is reduced by the acceptance of international definitions for measurement units as ultimate standards. The process of making sure that our measurements conform to the defined standards, within an acceptable degree of uncertainty, is known as traceability.

These two metrology concepts, defined standards and measurement traceability, are closely interrelated. For a defined standard to be universally accepted, everybody must agree to trace their measurements to it. For us to feel secure that our measurement of a quantity is compatible with that of our neighbors, we must accept the defined standard, and establish traceability to it.

Traceability and the National Measurement System

Traceable calibrations are made within the context of a national measurement system (NMS). Every place in the country that uses instruments to make physical measurements can be considered to be a "measurement station." The software, procedures, protocols, regulations, and so forth, which ensure the functioning of the national measurement system are called the measurement infrastructure (MIS).

The national measurement system ensures that measurements performed in different places in the nation, at the same or different times, will be compatible with one another at levels adequate for each station's purposes. Such measurements are said to be "compatible across space and time" if any two or more stations get the same result within allowed statistical limits when they measure the same or identical items at the same or different times. Note that it is only possible to "measure the same or identical item" if the calibration and testing environments are sufficiently close to being identical.

This definition of measurement compatibility is important in that it emphasizes a measurement's most important characteristic—the degree to which it agrees with other measurements made at different places or different times.

The various national measurement systems of the different countries in the world have a common physical basis by virtue of the International System of Units (SI). A conventional national measurement system includes a national laboratory that serves as a "master station" maintaining the national representations of the SI quantities (the national standards). The national laboratory also provides measurement services that allow other calibration laboratories in the country to relate their standards to the national standards. See Chapter 4, "International Metrology."

In the U.S., the National Institute of Standards and Technology (NIST) is the national laboratory required by law to establish, maintain, and disseminate a consistent and accessible system of standards and measurements. NIST reports to the President of the United States through the Department of Commerce. NIST's standards are, by definition, correct, and all other stations in the country adjust their standards to remove any differences.

While NIST maintains standards (representations) of the SI units, it does not maintain standards or provide measurement services for all of the quantities measured in the country. Some of the quantities used in the national measurement system are established independently by the various calibration laboratories. Measurement assurance programs, described in more detail later in this chapter, may be employed by those laboratories that use these quantities in their calibration activity, to ensure that their work is properly standardized.

Other standardization techniques include the Direct Voltage Measurement Program (DVMP), operated by Fluke; round-robins; Standard Reference Materials, provided by NIST; and Standard Reference Data. Finally, it is possible to achieve standardization through intrinsic standards and measurement systems which may be produced by anyone having the need and resources.

Why Measurements Must Be Traceable

The reasons for traceable measurements extend well beyond the immediate needs of calibration laboratories. Traceable measurements ensure the uniformity of manufactured goods and industrial processes. They support equity in trade as well as compliance to regulatory laws and standards. Traceable measurements are essential to the development of technology.

At this time, it is standard practice for government purchasers to specify that instruments used in testing products which it purchases be traceable. This practice has been picked up and incorporated into other documents, notably those which govern purchases for use in nuclear power generating stations. When traceability is incorporated into a contract, it then becomes a requirement which has legal standing before the courts.

The growing global acceptance of the ISO 9000 quality standards has also led to a general increase in commercial requirements for the traceable calibration of test and measurement equipment. The purpose, with an eye to product safety and fitness for use, is to ensure that the products manufactured in one country will be acceptable in another on the basis of agreed to measurement standards, methods, and practices.

What Is Involved in a Traceable Calibration?

Years ago, in an effort to ensure that measuring equipment was properly calibrated, the U.S. Department of Defense issued MIL-C-45662 as a standard document to govern the calibration of instruments used in qualification of products purchased by the military. MIL-C-45662 has since evolved into the widely used MIL-STD-45662A. One requirement of this and similar standards is that measurements must be traceable to national standards.

In MIL-STD-45662A, traceability is defined as: "The ability to relate individual measurement results to national standards or nationally accepted measurement systems through an unbroken chain of comparisons."

In broader terms, a measurement can be said to be traceable to designated standards within stated uncertainty limits, U, with a coverage factor k, if convincing scientific evidence can be produced which shows that a direct comparison to those standards would produce a result that falls between the stated uncertainty limits with a confidence determined by k. (See Section Five of this book, "Statistics," for discussions of uncertainty limits, coverage factor, and confidence level.)

Both definitions are clearly intended to ensure compatibility of measurements. In both cases, the intent is to ensure the quality of measurements by ensuring that they are properly expressed in terms of standards maintained by NIST, or to accepted measuring systems maintained by others.

Calibration reports are an essential part of traceable calibrations. These provide auditors in the MIL-STD or ISO 9000 environment with evidence of traceability. In addition, metrologists, test engineers, and quality personnel can use the data in calibration reports to improve the accuracy of measurement in a particular facility.

Sections Three and Four describe the key hardware standards and software elements used in a traceable chain of measurements for dc volts, dc resistance, dc current, ac voltage and current, inductance, capacitance, impedance, ac ratio, and time and frequency. Section Five explains how to obtain convincing scientific evidence for the validity of the measurements that are made. Section Six highlights the structure and operation of laboratories that provide traceable calibrations.

Standards

Every unit of measurement has a definition, a realization, and a representation. The definition is the ideal, and it is usually a member of the SI. The realization is achieved by means of an experiment whose result matches the definition as closely as possible. The experiment is most often performed by a national laboratory and is usually time consuming and expensive.

When the realization is obtained, the national laboratory stores its value as a representation of the unit. The national laboratory uses its representation as a master standard to which other representations are compared, as described in this chapter.

The Ideal Standard

Ideally, anyone adopting a defined standard for their measurements of a quantity would expect the following:

1. Everyone considers the definition of the standard as fixed and correct.

2. It is either embodied in an artifact, or can be created on demand through a well-defined scientific experiment.

3. If the standard is embodied in an artifact, there is a controlled means to propagate the embodied value from the master to the standards and measuring devices of all users in their various locations.

4. If the standard is re-created experimentally, the experimental results must be identical at all times and at all places, under all environmental conditions.

5. There is a controlled means to scale the standard value upward and downward.

6. There is no loss of precision or accuracy as a result of the scaling process.

Standards for Your Measurements

All of the measurements you make in your laboratory can usually be traced to a nationally-maintained representation of the unit of measure. The representation of the unit is either embodied in a standard or re-created on demand, by way of an experiment. Not all measurements will trace back to national standards. Depending on the quantity being measured, standards can be any one of the following:

- National standards
- Intrinsic standards
- Ratio type of calibrations
- Consensus standards
- Indirectly-derived quantities

The following sections describe each of these national standards.

National Standards
Every country either maintains a laboratory housing the national standards for each quantity, or makes use of another country's national laboratory. Local laboratories maintain local standards and other standards used to transfer a quantity between a national laboratory and the local laboratory. Transfer standards may be physically transported to the national laboratory for comparison with the national standards.

These national standards usually have years, even decades, of history associated with them. Their stability and uncertainty are therefore proved and accepted. Most calibrations will be traceable to national standards.

Intrinsic Standards
Intrinsic standards of measurement provide a standard quantity considered to be without error (always within a stated uncertainty). For each such standard, there exists a "recipe" or procedure which, if properly followed, will produce a quantity with an uncertainty that does not exceed stated limits. The three intrinsic standards associated with electrical calibration are the Josephson Array for dc voltage, the

Quantum Hall Effect (QHE) standard for resistance, and the cesium standard for time.

In addition, there are a large number of less exotic and expensive candidates for intrinsic standards. These generally rely upon such phenomena as ratios and/or ac-dc transfer. For electrical measurements, examples of such quantities include rf and microwave power, and rf voltage and current.

The interest in such standards originated at least in part from a desire to be less dependent on national laboratories for critical measurement services. If you can duplicate an intrinsic standard locally, you don't need a national laboratory service, at least in theory. However, you must do the work to prove that the standard is as good as it's claimed to be.

Ratio Standards

Ratio standards are used to obtain other values of a unit from a traceable artifact or intrinsic standard. For example, the 10V dc output of a Fluke 732B artifact standard can be extended upward (to higher voltages) and downward (to lower voltages) by using proper ratio techniques. (Ratio standards for dc voltage, ohms, and ac voltage are described in Chapter 9, "DC Ratio.")

There are no national standards for ratio because ratios are unitless and have no physical dimension. Devices that are used to determine exact ratios between like quantities are still laboratory standards, and require periodic checks (if not calibration) to ensure the traceability of the measurements they are used in.

Consensus Standards

A consensus standard can be an artifact or process that is mutually acceptable to a supplier and customer when there is no national or intrinsic standard.

For example, particle contamination is a relatively recent measurement quantity that has no national standards; yet many companies have requirements for levels of purity in laboratories and other clean environments. In such a case, a contractor and supplier might agree to use the performance of two or three calibrated monitoring devices as representative "standards."

Indirect Quantities

Indirectly-derived quantities are inferred by measuring some other quantity. A good example is direct current. Although current is one of the base units in the SI system of units, it is not directly traceable to national standards. The accepted practice today is to standardize current by passing current through a known resistor, measuring the voltage developed across the resistor, and calculating the current by using Ohm's Law.

Traceability

Traceability refers to procedures and records that are used and kept to demonstrate that calibrations made in a local laboratory accurately represent the quantities of interest. The scientific aspects of traceability involve principles of metrology used locally and independently by scientists, engineers, and technicians. The legal aspects of traceability involve a governmentally established and maintained infrastructure within which the measurements are performed. The infrastructure that is in general use today has three major constituents:

- World-wide legal adoption of the International System of Units (SI) as the basic system of units of weights and measure.

- The establishment of national laboratories such as NIST, chartered to maintain representations of the SI units (standards) and to disseminate their values to calibration laboratories.

- Definition, implementation, and use of methods and procedures that allow individual calibration laboratories to compare their local standards with those of the national laboratories.

Establishing And Maintaining Traceability

Traceability includes keeping in-house standards that are compared to one of the previously described standards. More often than not, an unbroken chain of calibrations ends with comparison standards maintained by national authorities such as NIST in the U.S.

Figure 6-1 is a diagram for direct voltage that traces the measurement of a Fluke 8842A back to an intrinsic standard at a national laboratory. Similar diagrams can be made for other units such as resistance, alternating voltage, and so forth.

Within an organization, measurement traceability is maintained by a hierarchy of comparisons up to national standards. A local primary standard is required for this process. Accurate documentation of the process is essential.

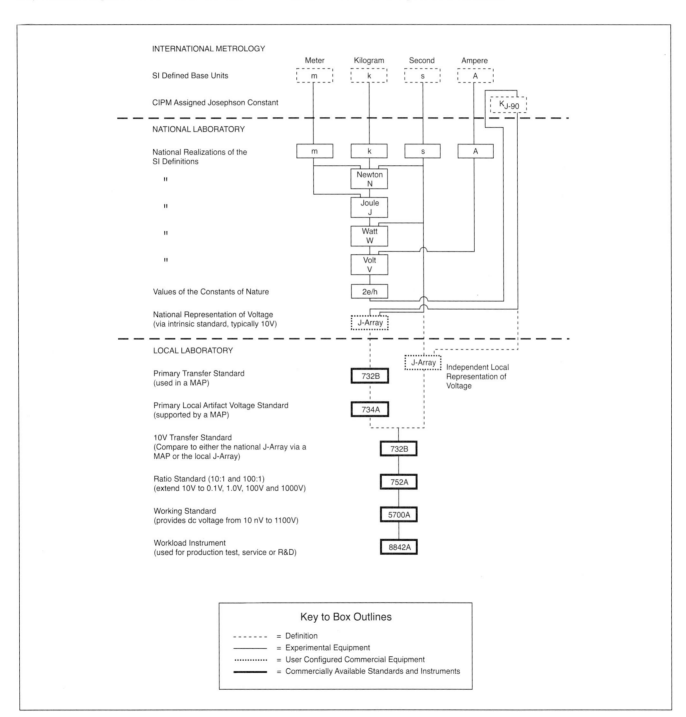

Figure 6-1. *Traceability Diagram for Direct Voltage*

Maintaining a Local Standard

The metrology laboratory must have confidence in the quality of its own internal operations. This normally includes frequent intercomparison of its standards. Although such intercomparisons are not a substitute for periodic calibration by a higher echelon, they create information regarding the stability of the standards. Such checks also reduce the likelihood of a standard unknowingly going beyond its uncertainty limits.

A laboratory may maintain several standards for each unit of measure. Otherwise, it has no way to double-check the standard which it sends to NIST (or other higher-echelon laboratory). Such a double check reduces the possibility of accepting a standard that has been damaged or degraded during the return trip. It also helps to identify the laboratory's systematic errors (offsets) relative to national standards.

A conventional approach to maintaining a local standard is as follows:

1. Acquire at least four nominally identical artifacts, plus a means for comparing them. Three are used to embody the local standard. The fourth is used as a transfer standard.

2. Establish the performance of the transfer standard with respect to the other three (the local standard). Its performance is evaluated in terms of its offset from the local standard, and its drift relative to that standard. The evaluation is accomplished by means of repeated comparisons to the local standard over a period of days, weeks, or months. Statistical models have been developed for these evaluations, the most important of which is linear regression analysis.

3. Have the transfer standard measured by a national laboratory or another qualified supporting facility.

4. When the standard is returned by the supporting facility, determine if the value of the transfer standard, expressed in terms of the local standard, has shifted while it was absent from the facility. If the as-returned

value is within acceptable limits, the process continues to step 5.

5. Compute the value of the local standard in terms of the national standard or other basis for the measurement, using the calibration of the transfer standard and its relationship to the local standard.

This procedure provides a single-point calibration of the local standard. The procedure must be repeated three or more times in order to establish the time stability of the local standard relative to the national standard. Only when that has been done can one assert with confidence that the standard has compatibility across space and time with other standards in the measurement system.

Once the local standard has been established, the laboratory must verify the analysis which assigns an uncertainty to items calibrated against the standard. There are several ways to do this. One of the most convenient is to arrange for the supporting facility to measure an item calibrated by the laboratory, and compare the results. The results should agree within the combined uncertainties that are claimed.

Less Rigorous Methods for Maintaining Traceability

Similar procedures can be carried out at each level in the hierarchy. However, at some level it is no longer cost effective do so. At this point, it is necessary to resort to less rigorous methods of maintaining and stating uncertainty. The most common is pass/fail instrument testing, using the instrument specification. An instrument that passes the test is assumed to meet all of its accuracy specifications for the assigned calibration period. Procedures are commonly established for extending or shortening calibration intervals based upon repeated successes or failures.

Test Uncertainty Ratios (TURs) are frequently used with pass/fail testing. The use of a minimum TUR in lieu of other controls or allowances implies the following: As long as the minimum TUR is met or exceeded, the uncertainties of the standard when assigning an uncertainty to the calibration or measurement can be ignored.

Measurement Services Providing Traceability

There are several ways to keep your quantities fixed in the traceability path. Depending on a laboratory's requirements, a quantity may only need to use one method. Another quantity may need several to ensure direct and industry-wide conformance with the standard units of measure. The services most metrology laboratories need to use are:

- national measurement services
- commercial measurement services
- measurement assurance programs (MAPs)
- reverse MAPs
- the Fluke DVMP

The following sections describe each of these services.

National Measurement Services

The national laboratories of various countries offer a wide variety of calibration services. NIST's offerings include the calibration services for those units of measure which the average metrologist is likely to require. Measurement services are detailed in *Special Publication 250*, available from the Office of Measurement Services, NIST, Gaithersburg, MD. Current prices and announcements of importance to the metrology community appear in the Appendix to SP 250. The Appendix is issued approximately quarterly, and is available from the same office. These publications list phone numbers to call for further information in each of the measurement areas.

NIST places restrictions on the devices that it accepts for calibration. The most important is that they should be compatible with NIST measurement systems. They should have the short-term stability and ruggedness suitable for shipment, storage, and handling. It is advisable

to discuss the requirements with NIST before submitting any new item for calibration.

Commercial Measurement Services

Many manufacturers of test equipment and standards offer calibration services for their products. In addition, a large number of independent laboratories offer calibration and repair services to the public. In general, a commercial calibration service can provide the same services offered by NIST at lower cost, with shorter turnaround time; the tradeoff is usually lower accuracy. There are a few exceptions involving the primary standards laboratories of large companies.

The quality of the service to be obtained from commercial sources ranges from unacceptable to excellent. Many of the large aerospace and defense contractors have established large, well-equipped, and well-staffed primary standards laboratories. Most of these sell services to customers outside the parent company, although long turnaround times can be expected in some cases. Some instrument manufacturers, Fluke, for example, have established primary and secondary calibration laboratories to support the instruments they produce. In some cases, the quality and range of services obtainable from these laboratories rival those of a national metrology laboratory.

Those choosing calibration services should look beyond price. A laboratory's capabilities and operations should be audited before its services are utilized.

The NCSL annual publication *A Directory of Standards Laboratories* lists the services provided by member laboratories. Also listed in a separate section are the name, address, and phone number of a contact person for each facility. It should be kept in mind that NCSL does not check or endorse the services of listed companies, it simply compiles and publishes them.

Measurement Assurance Programs (MAPs)

Traditional calibration services measured a customer's measurement standards in a higher level calibration laboratory. The performance of the standard in the customer's facility was not determined and the customer's ability to make measurements with it was not verified. NBS (now NIST) developed measurement assurance programs (MAPs) to address these shortcomings, and programs are now available for several quantities, including direct voltage (Volt Transfer Program) and resistance (RMAP).

NIST conducts a MAP by first characterizing a transfer standard at NIST, then sending it to a customer's laboratory. The customer makes a prescribed number of measurements using the measurement system, and returns the data and the transfer standard to NIST. After making sufficient measurements to ensure that the transfer standard is operating as expected, NIST evaluates the data and issues a report which not only calibrates the customer's measurement system, but also evaluates the errors and uncertainties associated with the customer's calibration system. Participating in a MAP provides a calibration of the customer's system and standard, at the time the transfer standard was in the facility. More work is required to evaluate the behavior of the system over extended time periods.

Advantages of participating in a MAP include the evaluation of the customer's measuring system and usually a smaller uncertainty than NIST would assign to a simple calibration of a transfer standard. Disadvantages include cost (several times that of a simple calibration), the large investment of time required, and the time span required to complete the calibration. Another factor to consider is the likelihood of failure if the transfer standard proves to be unstable and changes in value while it is absent from NIST.

One variation on the NIST MAP is the regional MAP, or Regional Standards Maintenance Program. In such programs, NIST organizes and oversees a group of laboratories in a region, such as the Los Angeles region or the San Francisco Bay region in California. Member laboratories agree to establish and maintain a regional standard of the quantity of interest. In principle, the regional standard can approach the quality and uncertainty of the standard maintained at NIST. It has the additional advantage of being more readily accessible to the participants. Organizations such as NCSL, PMA (Precision Measurement Association), and MSC (Measurement Science Conference), in addition to NIST, can provide information about these programs.

Reverse MAPs

It was suggested, at an NCSL conference in the early 1980s, that a reverse MAP could provide the same benefits as a regular MAP, without excessively burdening NIST. In this form of MAP, the customer owns the transfer standard, characterizes its performance, then sends it to NIST for calibration. When the standard returns, the customer monitors its performance for sufficient time to ensure that it has not changed in its absence. Then the customer computes the difference between the standard and the NIST standard. As with a regular MAP, a reverse MAP provides a calibration at a particular time; additional work is required to evaluate the behavior of the standard over time.

The FLUKE DVMP

A reverse MAP may be out of reach of a calibration facility which lacks the equipment and expertise needed to properly conduct one. Also, the cost of developing and conducting such a MAP may be prohibitive. Both of these considerations were addressed in the Fluke Direct Voltage Maintenance Program (DVMP), a reverse MAP conducted by Fluke. This program had the added feature that the standards of several customer laboratories were calibrated at the same time as the Fluke standard. This was done by passing the transfer standard through several customer laboratories on its way to NIST. Then, because the standard's performance over time had been properly characterized by Fluke, an accurate value could be assigned to each of the customer standards along with the Fluke standard. In this way, Fluke's expertise and the cost of the program were shared among a large number of laboratories.

Since Fluke acquired its own Josephson Array Voltage Standard, the DVMP has been changed to eliminate sending each transfer standard to NIST.

As with other MAPs, the Fluke DVMP provides a calibration of a customer's standard only at the time that the transfer standard is in the customer's facility. The calibration must be repeated at least three times and statistically analyzed before it is possible to characterize the standard's behavior over time. While other calibration services leave this problem to the customer, the Fluke DVMP provides the customer with predicted values and uncertainties. This program exemplifies the effective use of metrology resources, extending the capabilities of a major laboratory to smaller customer laboratories.

Reports

Reports are primarily generated to provide evidence that the traceability chain is intact, but there are other reasons. For example, reports are generated to document calibration results, manage the calibration workload, obtain data that can be used to improve the calibration activity, and notify equipment users about various matters including a calibration recall. For more information see Chapter 30, "Laboratory Audits."

Proving Traceability

Complete, detailed documentation is necessary to prove that a measurement is traceable. In fact, your contracts may dictate that you supply proof to an inspector or auditor for any or all calibrations on demand.

For some small laboratories, handwritten records are sufficient. Others require more advanced methods of data collection and reporting, such as an integrated database. An electronic database is especially useful if a measurement standard is found to be out-of-tolerance before its interval has expired. A reverse trace, a report of all of the devices calibrated by the out-of-tolerance standard, is nearly

impossible to do with traditional recordkeeping, but is made simple by computerized data collection and storage.

Documenting Calibration Results

Calibration reports are provided for standards that have been calibrated by NIST or another facility. A calibration report states the environmental conditions under which the standard was calibrated, and gives the complete calibration results data along with the estimated uncertainty and its coverage factor. The report is signed and dated by the person who conducted the test.

Certificates of calibration are often provided for calibrators and test equipment such as DMMs. A certificate of calibration states that a traceable calibration was performed on the specific instrument for which the certificate is provided. A certificate may not include results data but will contain other information specific to the tests that were conducted.

Fluke supplies calibration reports at no additional cost for highly accurate standards such as Fluke Models 5700A, 5790A, and 792A.

Calibration stickers are placed on an instrument after it has been calibrated. These stickers typically give the date of the calibration and the due date for the next calibration. They may be color coded to indicate any limitations in how the instrument may be used. Stickers are usually positioned so they will break if someone opens the instrument's covers or makes some other type of calibration adjustment. An intact and current sticker signifies that the instrument is acceptable for service.

Managing the Workload

There is a constant flow of standards, calibrators, and instruments through their specific calibration cycles. This flow must be coordinated to ensure that all of the in-service items in the workload are traceable by virtue of an up-to-date calibration status. Various reports support this need.

For example, one type of report lists all of the instruments in the workload by manufacturer, model, serial number, accounting property number, and calibration interval. Another type of report notifies users when their instrument is due for recalibration. There also can be reports that identify poorly performing instruments which may be removed from the inventory.

There are also management reports showing the status of the calibration activity. These may state the percentage of instruments in-tolerance at the end of the calibration interval. They may give the costs of calibration and state how evenly the workload of instruments flows through the laboratory.

Improving the Calibration Activity

Calibration laboratories can collect an enormous amount of data on the standards, calibrators, and instruments they calibrate. This data can be analyzed to improve the calibration activity. For example, data can be analyzed to help laboratory managers determine the most cost-effective calibration interval for various instruments. In an automated facility, this could yield customized intervals on a per serial number basis. A report containing this kind of data would be used to justify calibration intervals different from the ones recommended by the equipment vendor.

Notifying Users

Various routine notifications need to be provided to users. In the MIL-STD-45662A and other audited environments, there is an important, non-routine requirement to notify users when an item in the calibration chain is "significantly out-of-tolerance." This item could be just the unit under test or, in an extreme case, it could be a calibration standard that has been used to support the calibration of literally thousands of instruments. In either case, a reporting system, such as Fluke's MET/TRACK, must be in place to allow one to report the situation to the users and to take corrective action as needed.

Key References

Huntley, Les, "Is it Time to Adopt Huntoon's Measurement System Paradigm?" ASQC Measurement Quality Conference, 1992

FLUKE®

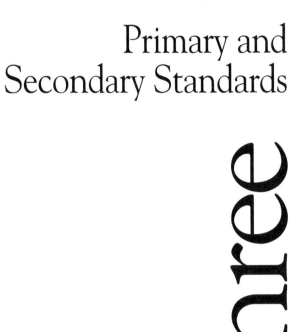

Primary and Secondary Standards

Section Three

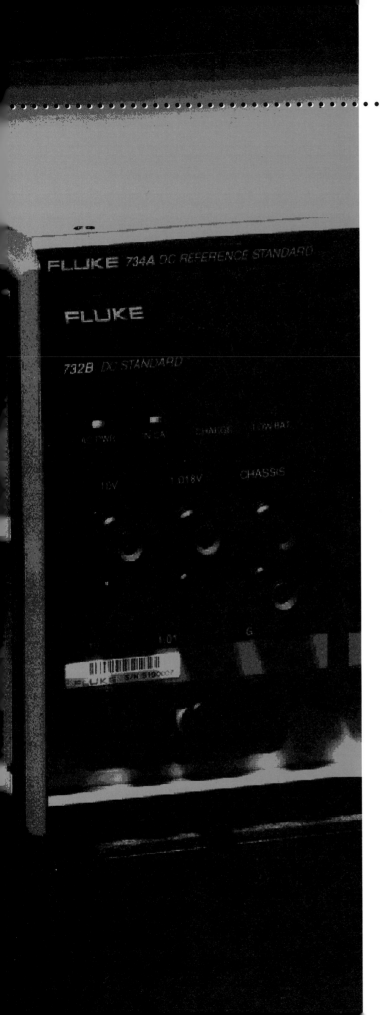

FLUKE®

Chapter 7:

Direct Voltage and Current

Direct voltage and current are key elements in the International System of Units (SI). This chapter discusses the definition, realization, representation and maintenance of the direct volt by voltage standards.

T he chapter presents the SI definition of the volt, via the ampere, in terms of the SI mechanical units. It shows that a Josephson array-based representation of the volt is an intrinsic standard, linked to the SI mechanical units via the constants of nature. The important advantages of using solid state voltage standards for local standards of the volt instead of standard cells are discussed. Direct current is also covered. See Chapter 4, "International Metrology," for a discussion of SI.

The terms "definition," "representation," and "realization" used in this chapter are defined in Chapter 5, "Basic DC and Low Frequency Metrology."

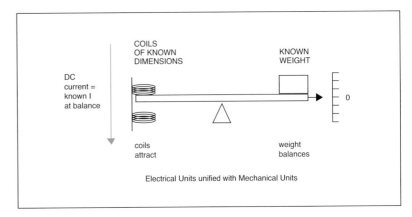

Figure 7-1. *Realization of the Ampere*

SI Definitions of DC Current and Voltage

The ampere is the base unit for electricity in the International System of units. The SI definition of the volt is derived from the ampere and the mechanical unit of the watt.

The Ampere

The SI links the mechanical and electrical units by defining the ampere as "that constant current which, if maintained in two straight parallel conductors of negligible cross section and placed 1 meter apart in a vacuum, would produce between these conductors a force equal to 2×10^{-7} newton per meter of length."

Because the standard ampere is very difficult to realize, the uncertainty of its realization is large, about 15 parts per million (ppm). And it is difficult to maintain for more than a few minutes. Figure 7-1 illustrates the process by which the ampere is realized.

In this simplified drawing, the magnetic fields of the coils on the left side of the balance arm produce an attractive force proportional to the current flowing and the number of turns in each coil. The force is balanced by the weight on the right side of the balance arm. The actual equipment used by NIST in an experiment reported in

the June, 1985, issue of *IEEE Transactions on Instrumentation and Measurement* is more complex.

But what causes the force? According to physics, the force is produced by the electromagnetic field associated with moving electrons. In these terms one ampere is equal to the flow of one coulomb of electrons per second past a given point in an electrical circuit.

Although the ampere is the SI base unit for electricity, it is difficult to realize. For this reason, there is no standard representation of the ampere. Instead it is derived locally from the ratio of the volt and the ohm according to Ohm's law, $I = E/R$. The volt and the ohm are maintained in standards both in a local laboratory and at the national level.

The Volt

The volt is defined in terms of the SI base electrical unit, the ampere, as "the difference of electrical potential between two points of a conducting wire carrying a constant current of 1 ampere, when the power dissipated between these points is equal to 1 watt" (1 watt = 1 joule per second). Based on mechanical units, the volt is:

$$V = W/A$$

$$W = J/s$$

$$J = Nm$$

$$N = kgm/s^2$$

Where:

W = watt (SI derived unit for power)

A = ampere (SI base unit for electricity)

J = joule (SI derived unit for work/energy)

s = second (SI base unit for time)

kg = kilogram (SI base unit for mass)

m = meter (SI base unit for length)

Direct Voltage Representations

Various national laboratories have conducted basic experiments in physics that have supported the realization of the ampere, volt, and ohm as defined. But discoveries in quantum mechanics have led to representations of the volt and ohm by the Josephson and Quantum Hall effects. As shown later, the reproducibility and stability of the representations of these units can and do exceed that of their realizations. The realization of the SI volt is believed to have an uncertainty of 0.4 ppm, one standard deviation relative to its definition.

Solid state voltage standards and saturated standard cells are also used to represent the volt, that is, as local standards of voltage. These provide easier reproducibility and better stability than the more difficultly-obtained realization of the definition of the volt. Accordingly, standards laboratories usually maintain the volt and ohm as primary units, while the ampere and the watt are derived from these.

Josephson-Effect Intrinsic Standard

The Josephson effect is a superconducting physical phenomenon that relates voltage to frequency through the ratio of fundamental constants. A Josephson array, using an integrated circuit containing a number of Josephson junctions, is an intrinsic, independently reproducible standard that is used to represent rather than realize the SI volt. The output of a single Josephson-junction is defined as:

$$V_j = \frac{nf}{K_{j-90}}$$

Where:

V_j = junction voltage

f = frequency in GHz

K_{j-90} = 483,597.9 GHz/V

n = a positive or negative integer

In the equations describing the Josephson effect, the generic Josephson constant is represented by K_j which is equal to twice the ratio of the fundamental constants e and h so that:

$$K_j = \frac{2e}{h}$$

Where:

e = elementary charge

h = Planck's constant

In October, 1988, the International Committee on Weights and Measures (CIPM) recommended that all national laboratories use the same value for the Josephson constant. The recommended value is:

K_{j-90} = 483,597.9 GHz/Volt

Where the K_{j-90} is the recommended value that came into effect on January 1, 1990.

Note that K_{j-90} is the value that has been assigned to the Josephson constant. The assigned value of K_{j-90} is not necessarily equal to the physical constant $K_j = 2e/$h, but it is the value used by international agreement. As discussed in Chapter 4, "International Metrology," the determination of the constants of nature is pursued via fundamental experiments conducted by various national laboratories.

Figure 7-2 is a photograph of the Josephson voltage system used at Fluke to represent the volt.

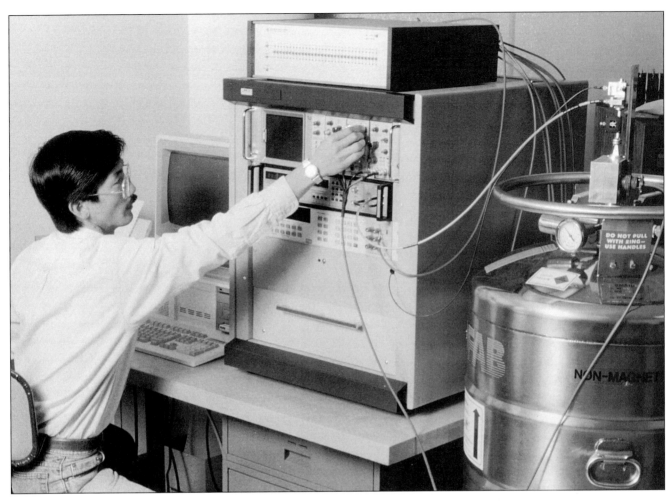

Figure 7-2. *Fluke's Josephson Voltage System*

A Closer Look at the Josephson Junction

Brian Josephson discovered the Josephson effect in 1962. The Josephson effect occurs across two superconductors, separated by a thin oxide insulating barrier (see Figure 7-3).

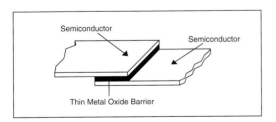

Figure 7-3. *Simplified Structure of Josephson Junction*

A simplified explanation of the Josephson effect, referred to as the ac Josephson effect and oriented toward dc voltage metrology, is as follows. A microwave source irradiates the dc

current biased Josephson junctions in a Josephson array. See Figure 7-4.

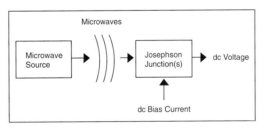

Figure 7-4. *Josephson Device.*

Each junction in the array produces a dc voltage proportional to the frequency of the microwave source.

A series of steps of constant dc voltages appears across the junction due to quantum mechanical tunneling of an ac current through the junction (see Figure 7-5).

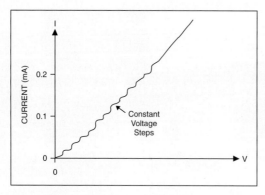

Figure 7-5. *Response of Josephson Junction*

Each step of constant dc voltage is a function of the frequency *f* of the ac current, Planck's constant *h*, elementary charge, *e*, and the number *n* of the step:

$$V = \frac{fnh}{2e}$$

The junction is located in a dewar cooled to below 4.2 Kelvin with liquid helium. It is biased through externally-supplied direct and alternating currents, the ac being at the higher microwave frequencies.

In the early 1970s, many national standards laboratories began to use the ac Josephson effect as the practical standard of dc voltage. In these applications, the previous equation was modified to:

$$V = \frac{fn}{K_j}$$

where K_j is a constant, such that

$$K_j = \frac{2e}{h}$$

(K_j is commonly referred to as the Josephson constant.)

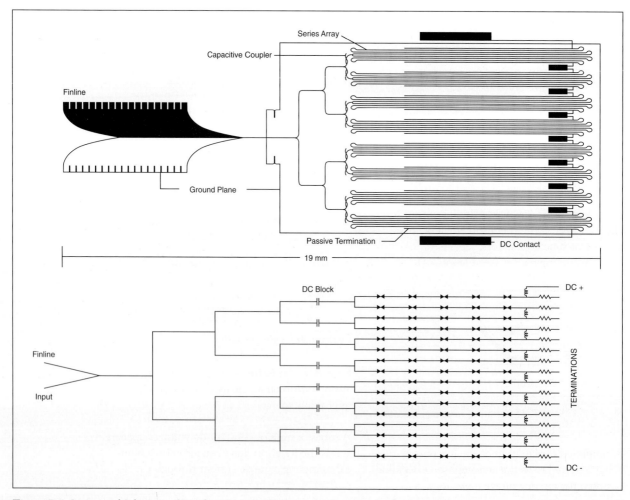

Figure 7-6. *Layout and Schematic of Josephson Junction Array*

Each national laboratory assigned a value to the Josephson constant, K_j, based on the value of dc voltage they used for its representation as maintained in their local standard cell bank. Therefore their Josephson junction-based representations of dc voltage were not identical.

Uniformity in the national Josephson junction-based representations of the dc volt was achieved on January 1, 1990, by the observance of an international agreement on the value to be assigned to the Josephson constant. The assigned value is 483,597.9 GHz/V, symbolized as K_{j-90}.

The early Josephson-junction representations of the volt were difficult to use, primarily because of the low level of voltage, approximately 10 mV, that appeared across a single junction. Attempts to connect the junctions in series to obtain a higher voltage were limited by the need to supply an independent dc bias current for each junction.

The bias current problem is avoided by fabricating junctions with a large capacitance, connecting them in series, and driving them with a microwave ac current whose frequency is well above the junction's plasma frequency. The plasma frequency is a natural resonance set by the junction's inductance and capacitance. This arrangement allows the use of constant voltage steps that cross the zero current axis of the junction when its bias current is near zero.

This technology has been incorporated in an integrated circuit, the 10V Josephson series-array, illustrated in Figure 7-6.

In this array, the dc Josephson voltage is obtained from 18,992 junctions connected in series, insofar as their dc voltage and bias current are concerned.

However, insofar as ac current is concerned, the junctions are organized in 16 parallel groups of 1,187 series-connected junctions. Due to their high capacitance, the 1,187 junctions behave as a microstripline when microwave power launched from a Gunn Diode passes through them to impedance-matching terminations at the far end of each group. Blocking capacitors and inductors are used to keep the dc and ac circuits separated.

This array can produce about 150,000 quantized dc voltages whose values range from −10V to +10V. It is interesting to note that recent experiments have shown that the dc voltage developed by Josephson junctions irradiated by a common source of microwave agrees to within 3 parts in 10^{19} (300 zeta parts).

Who Needs a Josephson Array

While one may derive a lot of satisfaction from owning a state of the art standard like the Josephson Array, they are expensive to acquire and maintain. Before making the investment and commitment of future resources required by the Josephson apparatus, the costs and benefits should be carefully weighed.

Both initial cost and maintenance costs are high. When Fluke acquired its Josephson Array System in early 1992, capital equipment expenses were approximately $85,000, and another $25,000 was expended in engineering time required to get the system operating. Annual operating costs are estimated to be about $10,000, most of which is the cost of liquid helium. Helium costs can be reduced by installing a closed-cycle system which recovers the helium, but the initial cost of a closed-cycle system is considerably higher. An engineer or scientist must be available to deal with the fairly frequent problems with the system, a fact which increases the cost of owning and operating the Array system.

In considering the benefits of owning an Array system, it should be realized that with very few exceptions, these are primarily research tools rather than calibration standards. Very adequate voltage standards can be maintained in a set of four solid state references (described in the next section). Modern statistics-based calibration and maintenance schemes can provide a standard with uncertainty as small as a few tenths ppm, typically 0.1 to 0.3 ppm. The purchase price of such a standard (1993 dollars) is less than $13,000, and annual maintenance costs are less than $3,000.

Fluke's decision to purchase a Josephson Array System was based not on the need for a better voltage standard, but upon the need to verify the linearity of high accuracy digital to analog converters (dac's) used in its calibrators. The uncertainty of Fluke's volt had been maintained for several years at less than 0.35 ppm by frequent transfers to NIST. That uncertainty, now routinely available to anyone, is more than adequate for all but the most demanding calibration requirements. While the Array systems themselves are capable of uncertainties of a few parts per billion, it must be realized that the much greater uncertainties actually achieved are determined primarily by noise and instability in the items calibrated.

Solid-State DC Voltage Standards

Two types of solid-state dc voltage standards are used today. One type uses a reference amplifier with an integrated zener diode. The other uses one or more discrete temperature-compensated zener diodes. Both types overcome most of the limitations of the saturated standard cells described later in this chapter.

Solid state standards are mechanically rugged, are able to sink and source current without damage, and have low temperature coefficients of output. In addition, they can have higher output voltages that minimize the effects of thermal emf's in connecting leads. This makes them easier to use and calibrate.

Reference Amplifier Type
A reference amplifier is an integrated circuit consisting of a zener diode and transistor. Figure 7-7 illustrates a reference amplifier.

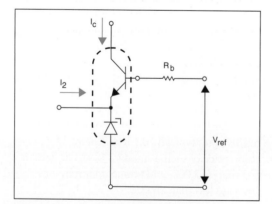

Figure 7-7. *Reference Amplifier Schematic*

The reference voltage, V_{ref}, is the sum of the zener voltage and the voltage across the

base-emitter junction of the transistor. This configuration provides temperature compensation as well as stable operation.

A reference amplifier offers two advantages over the use of a reference zener diode. First, current in the zener, I_2, can be set independently of the transistor's base current. Therefore, the reference amplifier's collector current, I_c, can be adjusted to set up a near-zero temperature coefficient over a narrow temperature range.

Also the reference amplifier's integral transistor can be used as a high-gain first amplifier stage in association with a high-gain, negative feedback amplifier in order to provide a regulated output at a higher reference voltage. The Fluke 732B, Figure 7-8, uses a reference amplifier as depicted in Figure 7-9.

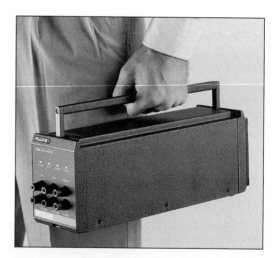

Figure 7-8. *Fluke 732B*

In the schematic, the reference amplifier, U_1, is the reference for the 732B's regulated 10V output. The stability of the 10-volt output is dependent on the stability of the reference amplifier and the ratio stability of the wire-wound resistors R_1 and R_2, which determine the gain, and therefore the output voltage. This circuit provides a low impedance path that delivers significant output current without introducing error in the reference voltage. Because of proper design and attention to detail, the stability of the 732B's feedback-regulated 10V output closely approaches the stability of the reference amplifier voltage.

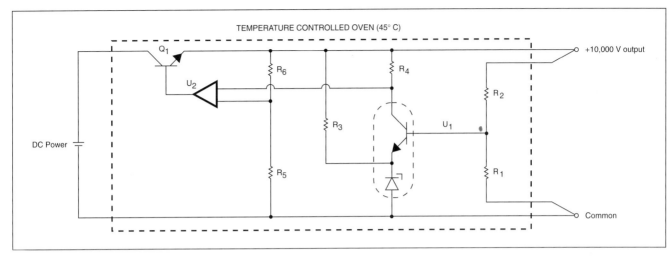

Figure 7-9. Simplified Fluke 732B Schematic

The 732B outputs include reference voltages of 10 and 1.018V (the 1.018V output is not shown). The guaranteed stability of the 10V output is 0.3 ppm/month, and 2.0 ppm/year. Typically, its stability is better than 1.0 ppm of output per year when compared to the predicted value of the 10V output per year. It may be operated from a power line or from internal, rechargeable batteries for more than 72 hours. It is not damaged by a short circuit of the output terminals, and delivers output current of 10 mA with a load regulation change in output voltage that is typically less than 0.1 ppm.

A four module standard, the Fluke 734A, is also available. See Figure 7-10.

Designed with the recommendations of NBS *Technical Note 1239* in mind, the Fluke 734A uses four Fluke 732Bs. Using four 732Bs has the following advantages:

- four independent cells in one enclosure
- 0.3 ppm/month stability
- 2 ppm/year stability
- 72-hour operating battery life
- small size— ¼ rack width per 732B
- light weight—13 pounds per 732B

Each 732B operates independently as required by NBS Technical Note 1239. The performance of one 732B does not affect the performance of the others. It is good practice to maintain a voltage standard as the mean of the output of four to six independent references. The 734A and 732B are, of course, fully compatible with

the Fluke model 732A solid state reference standards. See Figure 7-8.

Four 732Bs are used to maintain a local primary voltage standard because the local volt's assigned value will keep its integrity even if one of the 732Bs fails. Table 7-1 summarizes this.

Table 7-1. Advantages of Multiple References

# of 732Bs in Bank	Possible # of Comparisons	Result of Comparisons
One	None	Can't detect shift
Two	One	Can detect shift, can't identify which 732B shifted
Three	Three	Can detect shift and identify which 732B shifted. Two usable 732Bs left after removing the one that shifted. At risk of losing group average until new 732B stabilizes or another one in the group fails.
Four	Six	Adds redundancy to the local volt. If one 732B fails, it can be replaced with little risk of losing the group average until it stabilizes or if another 732B fails.

Discrete Zener Diode Type

Solid-state physics discoveries in the 1950s included the zener diode, a solid-state voltage regulator. Early zener diodes weren't

Figure 7-10. Fluke 734A

particularly stable and had relatively high noise levels. Today's improved zener diodes can rival saturated cells in stability. However, even when made by the same process in the same batch, some may have widely differing long-term stability characteristics. The difference may not be detectable during short-term testing, but must be determined by selection processes that monitor long-term stability under precisely controlled environmental and electrical operating conditions.

The discrete zener diode does have many desirable characteristics. It is mechanically stable and is unaffected by reasonable levels of shock and vibration. It also is relatively stable following exposure to temperature extremes.

Most diodes do have a temperature coefficient (TC). Individual diodes can be selected for low TC and operated in compensating circuitry which will allow them to approach zero TC over a temperature range of a few degrees (2 or 3°C). Zener diodes intended for reference voltage applications are manufactured to have a positive TC near 2 mV/°C, and are then combined in the same enclosure with a forward-biased silicon diode having a negative TC of about −2 mV/°C. This combination yields a low TC device. Diodes can also be operated in a small, temperature-controlled oven. Zener diodes are used in many digital multimeters and calibrators as the primary dcv reference. Figure 7-11 illustrates a temperature-compensated zener diode with an integrated forward-biased diode.

The typical operating voltage of a zener reference diode is between 6.2V and 6.3V. It is a shunt voltage regulator that is not damaged by a short circuit across its terminals, and it will quickly reestablish its output voltage when the short is removed. If small currents are drawn from it, its reference voltage will change because of *IR* drops across its output impedance, typically about 20Ω.

In applications where the ability to deliver output current at the reference voltage is required, the zener's voltage can be connected to the inverting input of an operational voltage follower. The buffer amplifier's output will supply the needed current. A zener's operating voltage significantly reduces the effect of thermal emf's in connecting leads and switches.

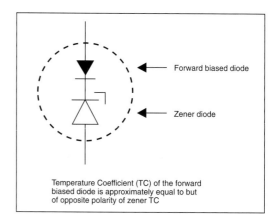
Figure 7-11. Temperature-Compensated Zener Diode

However, 6.2V is not a convenient reference voltage for the laboratory; 10V, or multiples of 10V, are the preferred values. For this reason, most solid-state voltage references used in the laboratory as primary or transfer standards are designed to deliver 10V, or both 10V and 1.018V. To obtain these voltages, the 6.2V zener diode can be used as the reference voltage for a well-regulated, adjustable 10V precision power supply. The amplifier of the power supply provides isolation for the zener reference and the capability for delivering increased output current at the reference voltage as well as current limiting for accidental short circuits.

A disadvantage of the discrete amplifier, in contrast to the reference amplifier, is that it may add significant error terms to those of the reference voltage. Offset drift and noise in the amplifier; drift in the voltage divider; drift in the output adjustment control, all of these add directly to the drift in the zener reference voltage, thus affecting the output voltage at the 10V level. If the standard has 1V and/or 1.018V outputs, they are usually obtained by dividing down the 10V output with one or more resistive voltage dividers. The error in these outputs will then be the sum of errors in the 10V output and any additional error due to drift in the voltage divider and the adjustment potentiometer for the low voltage output.

Maintenance of Solid-State Standards

Solid-state voltage standards are maintained by comparing their outputs as well as by measuring and predicting their stability with time. In the following discussion, the 732B and 732A can be used interchangeably. The unknown reference is compared to a known reference by connecting them in series-opposition and measuring the difference. For references which are within 10 µV of each other, the easiest method is to use a null detector such as the Fluke 845AB or 845AR and a known standard 732B. Figure 7-12 shows the setup.

The technician connects the high side of the 10V output from the 732B under test to the Hi terminal of the 845AB. The high side of the 10V output of the known standard is connected to the Lo terminal of the 845AB. The low side of the 10V output of the known standard and the 732B under test are connected to the Guard terminal of the 845AB with its Guard to Lo strap removed.

Both 845AB inputs are at about 10V relative to measurement common. A voltage difference of a few microvolts between the 732B under test and the known standard is displayed on the 845AB and is the nominal value of the 732B under test ± the uncertainty of the known standard.

The 845AB provides up to 0.1 µV resolution, equivalent to 0.01 ppm when used as a null detector to compare 10V references. A DMM having 0.1 µV resolution should be used when the difference of the voltages being measured is greater than 10 µV.

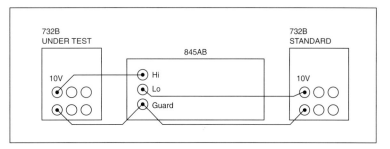

Figure 7-12. *Comparing 732B Outputs*

A solid state reference may exhibit a small permanent change in output when power is removed and re-applied or when its temperature changes. Therefore, for highest accuracy standards, the solid state references should always be maintained under power. This is especially important when solid state references are shipped.

Stability of Output With Time

Statistical techniques are employed to evaluate the stability of the outputs of the individual 732Bs and their group mean with time. These are described in Chapter 21, "Statistical Tools for Metrology."

A linear regression is commonly used to predict the value of the 732Bs output at some future time. See Figure 7-13.

Figure 7-13 shows that the regression line, V_x, for a typical standard is projected through variations in its output that can be conveniently categorized as high or low frequency noise. The low frequency noise can have a period of several days, such as the 10-day event in the figure. Due to the effect of low frequency noise, the linear regression may underestimate the uncertainty of a solid state reference standard's output.

A method that employs a seven period moving average to estimate the uncertainty contributed by both low and high frequency noise was described at the January, 1992, Measurement Science Conference in the paper "A New Approach to Specifying a DC Reference Standard" (reprints available from Fluke). Using this method, the uncertainty of the predicted output obtained via a linear regression is:

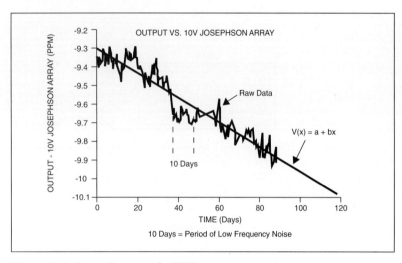

Figure 7-13. *Linear Regression for 732B*

$$U_{tot} = s_1 t_1 \sqrt{\left(\frac{t_2 s_{ra}}{s_1 t_1}\right)^2 + \frac{1}{n} + \frac{\left(x - \bar{x}\right)^2}{\sum\left(x_i - \bar{x}\right)^2}}$$

Where:

U_{tot} = Total uncertainty

s_1 = Standard deviation of the regression

t_1 = Student's t for $n-2$ degrees of freedom

t_2 = Student's t for $(n/7)-2$ degrees of freedom

s_{ra} = Standard deviation of the moving average regression

n = Number of samples

x = Time for which uncertainty is predicted

$\bar{x}$ = Average time of all x sampled

x_i = Value of the ith x (where $i = 1$ to n)

Summary
The solid-state reference standard has many advantages over the typical bank of saturated standard cells. The utility of this device has made it a popular alternative to the standard cell bank in the electrical standards laboratory, and it can be expected to ultimately replace the standard cell bank as the direct voltage reference of choice. The 732-series has become the primary voltage standard in many laboratories around the world for most of the reasons already mentioned. The most telling is the ruggedness of the reference. If the abuse a 732A or B can take is leveled upon a standard cell, the cell may take many months to recover or may be permanently damaged.

Automated systems have been designed and software written to allow maintaining and disseminating a local volt at the 10V level. Many corporations use four or more solid-state references in conjunction with a multichannel scanner, a digital multimeter and a controller to allow intercomparison of the reference standards and transfers of the volt to working standards.

Figure 7-14 is a photo of the Fluke 10V working standard of voltage. Figure 7-15 is its block diagram showing recently added 732Bs used in lieu of the 732As in the photo.

For more information on this type of measurement, see Fluke application bulletin #B0196A, "Technical Information Fractional ppm Traceability Using Your 732A."

Many laboratories began to use the 732A as a transport standard due to its ruggedness in comparison to standard cells. As these laboratories accumulated data on the 732A they put them into banks of four to intercompare like standard cells. They soon found that these banks of 732As would maintain a local primary voltage standard with sub ppm uncertainty. Today many laboratories have multiple 732As or 732Bs that are used to maintain the representation of the volt.

Saturated Standard Cells

Saturated cells are still being used as voltage standards in many calibration laboratories. However, it is now becoming difficult to obtain saturated cells, so new laboratories are likely to use solid-state voltage references as local standards of voltage. These devices are also likely to replace saturated cells in existing laboratories.

Characteristics of Saturated Cells
The saturated cell is illustrated in Figure 7-16.

Figure 7-14. *10V Working Standard of Voltage*

The saturated standard cell, sometimes called the Weston cell, was the accepted artifact standard of voltage for many years. It is also known as the "normal" cell to distinguish it from the unsaturated cell. Cells which are carefully manufactured and carefully used exhibit good voltage uniformity and a long useful life. Their nominal output voltage is 1.0183V at 20°C, although individual cells may differ from nominal by tens of microvolts.

The saturated cell has a large temperature coefficient and must be operated in an environment with a carefully controlled temperature in order to maintain a stable voltage. The equation relating E_t, the emf to temperature, is:

$$E_t - E_{20} = [-40.6(t-20)+0.95(t-20)^2-0.01(t-20)^3] \times 10^{-6}$$

Where:

E_t = emf at a given temperature t

E_{20} = emf at 20°C

The net temperature coefficient at 20°C, −40 ppm/°C, is the algebraic sum of the temperature coefficients of each limb of the cell. These are +0.00031V/°C at the positive terminal and −0.00035V/°C at the negative terminal.

Both limbs of the cell must be kept at the same constant temperature, to ensure a low, stable overall temperature coefficient. A temperature-regulated oil or air bath is used to house the cells. The regulated bath is usually operated at a temperature above room ambient; precise control is easier to maintain by adding heat only, rather than using both cooling and heating.

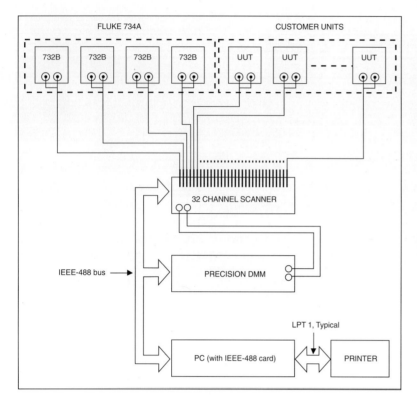

Figure 7-15. *10V Working Standard of Voltage, Block Diagram*

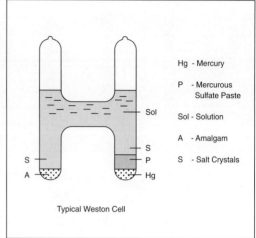

Figure 7-16. *Typical Weston Cell*

Commercial cell enclosures are typically operated at about 30°C.

Saturated cells exhibit substantial change or hysteresis in their output voltage if the temperature of a cell is changed and then returned to normal. A cell's emf is unstable following the change in temperature before it either drifts back to its previous value or arrives at a new stable value. The drift can continue for 60 to 90 days before the cell returns to within 0.5 ppm of its original value.

In addition to the saturated cell's sensitivity to temperature change, any of the following factors may cause a cell bank to drift appreciably for extended periods of time:

- shock or vibration
- tipping
- gas bubble formation at the electrodes
- current flow into or out of the cell

Maintenance of Standard Cells
Since individual standard cells can exhibit unpredictable shifts or drifts in their output voltage, a bank of cells is normally used to represent the volt. The individual cells in a bank

are intercompared to obtain the difference of individual cells from the mean emf of the bank. Banks usually consist of four cells in a temperature regulated enclosure. Up to 12 cells are provided in some enclosures.

A malfunction of temperature control in the common enclosure may go unnoticed and will affect all cells in the enclosure. For this reason, several banks, perhaps three or more, are usually used to confidently maintain an accurate voltage standard. This arrangement also allows a bank to be transported for purposes of maintaining traceability.

Cells in each bank should be intercompared on a regular schedule, with the measurement results plotted on control charts. The comparative measurements are made by connecting two cells together in series-opposition, negative terminals connected together, then measuring the difference with a potentiometer or high resistance microvoltmeter. Test protocols have been developed which make it possible to obtain the desired information with a minimum number of measurements. Such a protocol is outlined in the NBS Technical Note 430, (October 9, 1967).

When using and comparing standard cells, it is extremely important to avoid current flows into or out of the cells. Currents as low as 10^{-15}A, if sustained for several minutes can cause a change in value for which long recovery times are required. This is the reason for connecting the standard cells in series-opposition and using high resistance meters to make the measurement. Small voltage difference and high resistance means low current flow.

Automated test systems can be used to collect the data and perform the statistical analysis of the results. Standard cell scanners are specially designed switching systems with very low thermal emf's. These are commonly IEEE-488 programmable, allowing them to be combined with a programmable DMM, a suitable controller, and a software package to automate the procedure. Such a system interconnects the cells, reads the voltage differences, statistically analyzes the data, and plots the results. Data Proof 160A and 320A Standard Cell Scanners and software make it easy and convenient to automate standard cell comparisons. They are equally effective for automating comparisons of solid state references, such as the Fluke 732B.

Intercomparison of local banks of standard cells does not establish the stability of the bank in comparison to the national standard of voltage. Establishing traceability involves transportation of a group of cells, a transport standard, from a local laboratory to the national standards laboratory.

This process is time consuming because time must be allowed for the cells to stabilize after they're transported. For example, several weeks must elapse at NIST after the cells are received for their outputs to stabilize. Then their outputs can be measured.

Following return of the transport standard to the user laboratory, the cells must again be allowed to stabilize from the effects of transportation. If temperature regulation has not been maintained, a wait of 10 to 12 weeks may be required before the cells can be used to rated accuracy. Only then can they be used for calibration or comparison to other cells maintained in the laboratory. The using laboratory is responsible for discovering and dealing with any change in value that results from return shipment. This is a practical impossibility if only one cell bank, or comparable reference, is maintained, since standard cells in the same bank tend to be influenced similarly.

Summary

The saturated standard cell is far from an ideal voltage standard. It is susceptible to load current or charging current, either of which will cause a voltage shift; a short circuit is even more damaging and can cause irreversible changes in the output voltage of the cell. The high temperature coefficient of the cell makes it necessary to provide elaborate temperature-controlled enclosures. Mechanical shock, vibration, or a change in temperature may cause voltage shifts which may have a slow recovery.

Extending Voltage Values

Whether a Josephson Array, a bank of solid-state reference standards or saturated standard cells are used as the local primary dc voltage standard, it will be necessary to extend the primary value to several working standards at various values. DC voltage ratios and scaling methods are usually used to extend the primary value to other values and standards, for example 10V to 100V. Working standards are usually used to maintain the extended value.

Ratio Techniques

The values of solid state voltage standards are easily disseminated and extended because they can drive voltage dividers without a change in their output. However, be aware that *IR* drops in leads can change the voltage at the divider input. For example, the 10V output of the Fluke 732B can be divided down to 1.0V or 0.1V via the Fluke 752A, or into other values with 1.0 μV resolution via the Fluke 720A Kelvin-Varley divider. See Figures 7-17 and 7-18.

Moreover, the 752A can divide voltages of 1000V and 100V down to 10V. In this case, the 732B's 10V output is bucked against the 752A's output. When this is done, the 732B's output is extended to 100V and 1000V. A similar ratio division can be made with greater uncertainty using the Fluke 720A.

External dividers can also be used to divide voltages down to the level of standard cell

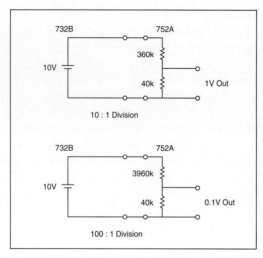

Figure 7-17. *10:1 and 100:1 Division of Fluke 732B Output via 752A*

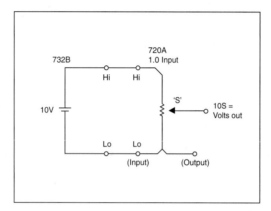

Figure 7-18. *720A Division of 732B Output*

voltages. Care must be taken to prevent damage to the cells, however.

Chapter 9, "DC Ratio," contains comprehensive information concerning the extension and dissemination of dc voltage values.

Working Standards

Solid-state reference standards such as Fluke models 732A and 732B can be used as secondary standards to disseminate fixed levels of dc voltage from the local primary voltage standard to working standards, such as calibrators. The solid-state standard can be easily transported from the primary laboratory to the location of the working standard.

The working standard can be a multi-function calibrator such as the Fluke 5700A and 5100B. Table 7-2, at the end of this chapter, provides a summary of the traceability from primary standards through secondary to the working standards.

DC Current

Although the ampere is the SI unit for electricity, national laboratories do not maintain a national standard of current. Instead, the value of current is derived locally in terms of a traceable voltage drop across a traceable resistor. The current that flows in the resistor is established by Ohm's law as:

$$I = \frac{E}{R}$$

Where:

I = intensity of current in amperes

E = electromotive force in volts

R = resistance in ohms

Hookup Considerations

The cables and connectors used to connect the various standards should have low series resistance, including low contact resistance, and low thermal emf's at their junctions. The insulation resistance of the cables should be very good to reduce leakage currents and other dielectric related errors. Chapter 33, "A Rogues' Gallery of Parasitics" contains more information concerning these and various other sources of error.

DC Lore

Some information is given here as a historical and technical background for this chapter.

Saturated vs. Unsaturated Weston Cells

Unsaturated and saturated Weston cells are virtually identical. The only difference is that the unsaturated cell doesn't contain cadmium sulphate crystals, so the electrolyte is unsaturated at temperatures down to 4°C. Compared to a saturated cell, an unsaturated cell's voltage is about 0.05% higher and is much less stable but has a better temperature coefficient.

Unsaturated standard cells were used as voltage references in several early Fluke differential voltmeters, models 800, 801 and 803. They were also used as references for the chopper stabilized outputs of the early Fluke calibrators, models 301C and 301E.

History of Standard Cells

Early electrical experimenters recognized the need for a reproducible standard of voltage and turned to the development of an artifact. A voltaic cell, with a chemically developed emf, was the most practical approach at the time. The Daniel cell, consisting of copper and zinc electrodes in conjunction with copper sulphate and zinc sulphate electrolytes was tried but was found to be relatively unstable and short lived. Latimer Clark invented a cell in 1872 which was much more stable. This cell consisted of mercury and zinc amalgam, electrodes and a saturated solution of zinc sulphate sealed in a glass enclosure to prevent evaporation of the electrolyte. While the stability and reproducibility was much better than that of the Daniel cell, the Clark cell had a high temperature coefficient.

In 1892, Weston produced the cadmium cell with further improvements in reproducibility and stability. Today, over 100 years later, this cell is still widely used as a primary standard to represent the volt.

NBS Maintenance Of The Volt

NBS placed twelve saturated Weston cadmium cells in service in 1906 to carry an assigned value for the volt until May of 1910. The emf assigned to these cells was based on a comparison with some Clark cells NBS had constructed prior to 1906. The Clark cells emf was defined by a law passed in 1894.

By May of 1910, experiments with silver voltammeters and mercury columns had fixed the values of the International Ampere and International Ohm. The NBS volt, maintained by the Weston Cells, was found to be 852 microvolts lower than the International Volt. Accordingly, NBS changed the value of its Weston cells by this amount on January 1, 1911.

For the next 61 years, the volt was maintained by a bank of saturated standard cells. Some of the individual members of this bank were replaced from time to time when their emf's became unstable with time. The mean value of the bank was revised in 1933, 1937 and 1944 because of these instabilities. Since July 1, 1972, NBS (now NIST) has used the ac Josephson effect to maintain the national representation of the volt.

Comparison Of Voltage Standards

Table 7-2 identifies and briefly describes several dc voltage standards in descending order according to their ranking as primary, secondary or working standards in the traceability chain.

Table 7-2. *DC Voltage Standards*

Type of Standard	Output	Lowest Uncertainty	Relative to	Application/Description/Comment
Josephson Array Intrinsic Standard	−10V to +10V	0.4 ppm (±1σ)	SI definition of one volt	Primary intrinsic standard used in-lab. Maintained in liquid helium
	−10V to +10V	~10^{-19}	other J-arrays	
Fluke 734A Artifact Standard	+10V	0.15 ppm/month	higher echelon standard	Primary 10V standard, MAP traceable, used in-lab or on-site as the mean output of four independent units. Temperature insensitive, 18–28°C
Fluke 732B Artifact Standard	+10V +1.018V	0.3 ppm/month 0.8 ppm/month	higher echelon standard	Secondary standard, in-lab or on-site. Transfers dc voltage of single unit to calibrators such as the Fluke 5700A. Temperature insensitive, 18–28°C
Fluke 5700A Multi-Function Calibrator	0 to ±1100V	5.4 ppm/ 90 days	NIST volt or other national standard	Working standard, in-lab or on-site. Calibrates dc voltage and current ranges of precision and handheld DMMs. Temperature insensitive, 18–28°C
	0 to ±2A	65 ppm/ 90 days		
Fluke 5100B Multi-Function Calibrator	0 to ±1100V	50 ppm/ 6 months	NIST volt or other national standards	Working standard, in-lab or on-site. Calibrates dc voltage and current ranges of handheld DMMs. Temperature insensitive, 18–28°C
	0 to ±2A	0.017%/ 6 months		

Note: A coverage factor, k, of 2.6 (99% certainty) applies to the uncertainty specifications for all Fluke models.

Key References

"Array Josephson Junction," NCSL RISP-1, *Recommended Intrinsic/Derived Standards Practice*, August, 1991

Field, B., "Solid-State Voltage Standard Performance and Design Guidelines," NBS *Technical Note 1239*, September 1987

Eicke, W. G.; Cameron, J. M., "Designs for Surveillance of the Volt Maintained by a Small Group of Saturated Standard Cells," NBS *Technical Note 430*, October, 1967

"Fractional PPM Traceability Using Your 732A," *Fluke Technical Information*, B0196A

Emery, John; Kletke, Ray; Voorheis, Howard; "A New Approach to Specifying a DC Reference Standard," Measurement Science Conference, January, 1992

Other references for this chapter are in the Resources Appendix.

Chapter 8:
DC Resistance

This chapter discusses the definition, realization, representation, and maintenance of the ohm by resistance standards.

The practical unit of electrical resistance is the ohm, named for a German physicist, Georg Simon Ohm, who lived from 1787 to 1854. This chapter describes the historical development of resistance standards, how different designs behave under environmental changes, and what the ohm is. It also describes different style resistors and what they are best suited for. It considers the maintenance and traceability of a local standard of resistance as well as the derivation of other values for local use. This chapter is essential reading for the student of metrology, and valuable for the working professional who wishes to better understand resistance measurements.

SI Definition of DC Resistance (the Ohm)

The SI definition of dc resistance, based on mechanical units, is:

$R = V/A$

Where:

R = resistance in ohms

$V = W/A$

A = SI base unit, the Ampere

W = watt (SI derived unit for power)

The watt is derived from the joule and the newton, which are derived from the meter, kilogram, and second.

Resistance Representations

The Thomas one ohm standard has been traditionally used by national laboratories to maintain their representation of the ohm. Reichsanstalt and Rosa resistors have also been used as standards. However, the Quantum Hall Effect Resistance Standard is replacing them in many laboratories.

Quantum Hall Effect Intrinsic Standard

By international agreement, since January 1, 1990, the preceding definition of the ohm has been related to the Quantum Hall Effect (QHE) by means of the von Klitzing constant. This allows national laboratories to represent the ohm via the QHE. The QHE representation of the ohm has an uncertainty of 0.2 ppm relative to the SI definition.

In October, 1988, the International Committee on Weights and Measures (CIPM) recommended that all national laboratories use the same value for the von Klitzing constant. The recommended value is:

$R_{k-90} = 25,812.807\Omega$

Where the subscript k–90 indicates that the recommended value was to come into effect on January 1, 1990.

In the physical explanation of the QHE, the von Klitzing constant, R_k, is a universal quantity. Furthermore, there are excellent reasons to believe that R_k is a function of the ratio of the fundamental constants h and e, so that:

$R_k = h/e^2$

Where:

e = elementary charge

h = Planck's constant

Although R_{k-90} is the value that has been assigned to the von Klitzing constant, this does not mean that the assignment of R_{k-90} is necessarily equal to the physical constant $R_k = h/e^2$. As discussed in Chapter 4, "International Metrology," various laboratories conduct fundamental experiments to determine the constants of nature.

A Closer Look at the Quantum Hall Effect Intrinsic Standard

In 1980, Klaus von Klitzing discovered the Quantum Hall Effect (QHE), a discovery of such fundamental importance to physics that he was awarded the Nobel prize in physics in 1985. The heart of a QHE device is the Hall bar, a planar MOSFET or heterojunction transistor constructed to constrain a current of electrons within a thin layer.

The planar transistor is operated in a cryogenic environment at a temperature of less than 4.2 kelvin, typically in the range of 1 to 2 kelvin. A magnetic field of several tesla is applied perpendicular to the plane of the sample. The electron current is applied longitudinal to the plane, and the Hall voltage is measured perpendicular to both the flow of current and the magnetic field. See Figure 8-1.

Due to quantized action of the electrons for a given drive current, the Hall voltage is developed in plateaus of constant values, rather than as a continuous ramp, as the strength of the magnetic field is varied. Thus, small instabilities in the intensity of the field have no effect on the amplitude of the Hall voltage. The Hall voltage, V_h, and Hall resistance, R_h, are given as:

$$V_h = R_{k-90}I/i$$

$$R_h = V_h/I = R_{k-90}/i$$

Where:

V_h = Hall voltage

R_{k-90} = assigned value of von Klitzing constant

I = current flowing in MOSFET or heterojunction Hall bar

i = an integer representing the number of the Hall plateau where the value of R_h is measured

R_h = Quantum Hall resistance

Specialized potentiometers and null detectors are used to transfer the value of R_h from the cryogenic interior of a dewar to a standard resistor in the laboratory. The construction and use of these devices is described in the June, 1986, issue of *Metrologia*, the April, 1989, issue of *IEEE Transactions on Instrumentation and Measurement*, and in NIST Technical Note 1263.

In the transfer, the laboratory resistor, R, and the longitudinal plane of the QHE semiconductor are series-connected so that the current I flows through both of them. See Figure 8-2.

In this case, the value of the laboratory resistor, R, is:

$$R = R_h \frac{V_r}{V_h}$$

Where:

R_h and V_h are as given above and V_r is the voltage drop measured across R.

Early adopters of this technology report that there are a number of practical limitations to

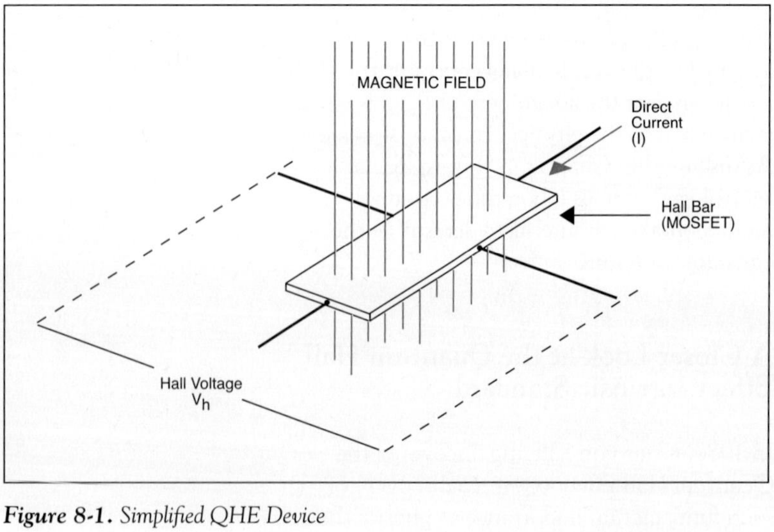

Figure 8-1. Simplified QHE Device

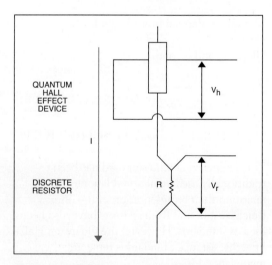

Figure 8-2. Hall Bar to Resistor Connection

this procedure. For practical reasons, the value of the step number i is either 2 or 4. The current flowing through the Hall bar and test resistor, I, is approximately 25 to 37 μA. In order to avoid leakage effects in the overall test system, the discrete resistor should have a value of 6,400 or 12,900Ω. A cryogenic current comparator is sometimes used to compare V_h with V_r. In addition, the value of the discrete test resistor must be transferred using ratio techniques to the 1Ω and 10 kΩ artifact standards in common use.

Thomas One Ohm Standard

The Thomas one ohm standard was developed for maximum stability and has its resistance element enclosed in a hermetically sealed, double-walled metal container. These resistors have a relatively high temperature coefficient of resistance and must be maintained in a temperature-controlled oil bath.

When immersed in an oil bath, the oil is in contact with the walls of the container but not the resistance element. Heat transfer for this construction is not as good as for the Reichsanstalt type, described next, but long-term stability is far superior.

Standards laboratories traditionally use Thomas one ohm standard resistors as their primary resistance standard and compare their higher value standards to the one ohm standards using bridge methods. This is done because the Thomas one ohm resistor is the most stable resistor available. For example, Fluke's Thomas one ohm resistors exhibit a drift of −0.02 ppm per year.

Reichsanstalt Artifact Standard

Low-value standard resistors, from 0.1 to 0.001Ω, which are subjected to high current in the course of their use, are frequently constructed in a design known as the Reichsanstalt. This design has the resistance wire wound on a metal tube which is then enclosed in a perforated container that can be immersed in a constant temperature oil bath. This allows free circulation of the oil over the resistance element, thereby aiding in cooling of the resistor

when it is used in high current test conditions where self heating would produce large resistance changes. The oil bath also serves to minimize the temperature effect on the standard.

Rosa Artifact Standard

Standard resistors with resistance values of 10Ω and higher are often made using the design proposed by Rosa. Rosa design resistors are also known as the NBS type. This construction has the resistance element wound on an insulated metal tube which is then suspended in an oil-filled outer can. A concentric inner tube supports the insulated resistor form and provides a thermometer well for checking resistor ambient temperature. The oil in the can provides heat transfer from the resistance element to the outer wall of the can and increases heat capacity of the resistor, making it less susceptible to resistance changes when subjected to momentary high currents. The resistor is used in an oil bath, which further stabilizes the temperature of the outer can and aids in heat transfer.

ESI SR104

The ESI® SR104, built by Electro Scientific Industries, is a widely-used 10 kΩ standard of resistance. It does not require a stirred oil bath and can be used outside of the laboratory.

The ESI SR104 contains groups of specially aged and temperature-coefficient selected Evanohm® resistors. These are mounted in a hermetically sealed, silicon oil-filled container. The container is enclosed in a thermally lagged outer case. This resistor is specified to have 1 ppm per year stability and a low temperature coefficient of ±0.2 ppm per °C. It features a built-in copper temperature sensor that can be used to measure the resistor's internal temperature and, through a convenient table of correction factors, provides temperature corrections for the resistor's value at the local ambient temperature. Its value can be extended to other resistors using ratio techniques described in Chapter 9, "DC Ratio."

Maintenance of Resistance Standards

Primary and secondary standards laboratories maintain working standards of resistance for use in calibration of current shunts, bridges, voltage dividers, other resistive devices, and resistance measuring instruments. Traceability of the working standards is maintained by periodic comparison to the laboratory primary resistance standards.

Single-valued standard resistors of the types previously described are commercially available in decade-related values ranging from 0.00001Ω to 100 MΩ. The mechanical design of these standards has evolved over many years from the requirements for improved stability, low power coefficient of resistance, and low thermal emf when connected with copper conductors.

Local standards laboratories usually have groups of these resistors, kept in stirred oil baths in order to maintain them at a standard temperature. Their values are intercompared with each other and NIST-traceable transport standards or with a local QHE device. The techniques used for intercomparison are discussed later, in the section "Intercomparing Resistors."

Transport standards usually have values of either 10 kΩ or 1Ω, although other values can be used. The NIST-assigned value for these is transferred to the resistors in the local group. Then the resistors in the local group are used to assign values to working standards, such as Fluke 742As.

One advantage of maintaining the laboratory primary resistance standards at 10 kΩ instead of at 1Ω is that there is less accumulative error when its value is extended to other resistor values. For example, calibration of the 1 MΩ standard starting with a 1Ω primary standard would require six 10:1 ratio measurements and would accumulate some error in each step. Starting with a 10 kΩ primary standard, the calibration could be accomplished with only two 10:1 ratio measurements.

An ideal situation would be to maintain primary laboratory standards at both 1Ω and at 10 kΩ. This would reduce cumulative errors for both high- and low-value laboratory standards. It would also allow one to get a good check on the accuracy and repeatability of the laboratory measurement processes by comparing the difference in calibration of decade resistors between 1Ω and 10 kΩ by ratioing up from the 1Ω standard and down from the 10 kΩ standard.

Intercomparing Resistors

Accurate resistance measurements can be made by comparing the unknown resistance to the known value of a standard resistor. Assuming the measurement equipment is stable and repeatable for the time period involved in the measurement, it is possible to compare two resistors with a high degree of accuracy, low uncertainty. The error decreases as the difference between the two resistors decreases. The limiting factor in this approach will, of course, be the uncertainty in the value of the standard.

2- and 4-Terminal Resistors

One method of measuring a resistance is to pass a known current through the resistance and then measure the resulting voltage drop across it. The results obtained can vary, depending on how the current-carrying and potential-measurement connections are made. Consider the connections at one end of the resistor where the test leads, terminated in spade lugs, are connected to a screw terminal. If the current-carrying lead is on the bottom, closest to the resistance element, the potential-measurement lead will sense not only the potential drop in the resistance element but also the potential drop caused by current flow through the contact resistances of the current-carrying lead. See Figure 8-3.

This contact resistance can vary, depending on how clean the contacts are, the contact surface area, and how well the screw terminal is tightened. Typically, the variation can be several milliohms. If the variation is 2 milliohms (one milliohm at each end) and the standard resistor is 1Ω, the error is 0.2%, unacceptable for an accurate measurement. If the test leads are reversed so that the measurement lead is closest to the resistance element, the error will be considerably reduced, but contact variations will still be excessive for standards laboratory quality measurements.

No matter what measurement technique is used, the resistance of a 2-terminal resistor will be affected by the way the connections are made. For this reason, low-resistance standard resistors and current shunts are constructed with four terminals, two for current connections and two for potential connections. As shown in Figure 8-4, the input current through the resistance is conducted through the current terminals on the left while the voltage drop across the resistance appears across the terminals on the right. The resistance of a 4-terminal resistor is defined as the resistance measured between the potential terminals.

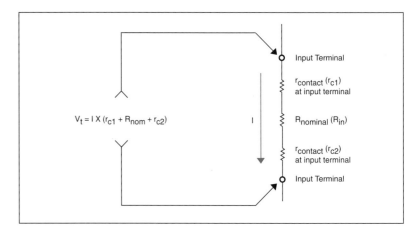

Figure 8-3. *2-Terminal Contact Resistance*

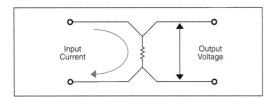

Figure 8-4. *4-Terminal Resistor*

Standards with values of 100 kΩ and above are usually 2-terminal resistors, since 2 mΩ variation in 100 kΩ would be an error of only 0.2 ppm. For more information on contact resistance and thermal emf's, see Chapter 33, "A Rogues' Gallery of Parasitics."

Precise measurements of resistance are usually made with bridge methods. Uncertainties of less than one part per million are readily obtained in the comparison of nominally equal resistances. Where this level of uncertainty is not necessary, other more convenient measurement methods can be used. The following sections discuss some of the more popular methods.

Digital Ohmmeters
Deflection-type measurement instruments have, for the most part, been supplanted by digital instruments which are more accurate and provide other performance advantages. The accuracy of resistance measurements for a high quality digital multimeter is on the order of several ppm for mid-range (1 kΩ to 1 MΩ) readings, and reduces to 100 ppm for high- and low-range readings. Typical accuracy for inexpensive digital meters, such as handheld multimeters, is on the order of 0.5%.

Beyond the advantage of a digital readout, ohmmeter circuits in a digital multimeter are linear with respect to linear changes in the measured resistance. Therefore, they are capable of much improved resolution and accuracy over the deflection-type ohmmeter. A typical 2-terminal resistance connection to a DMM's input is shown in diagram form in Figure 8-5. Chapter 17, "Digital Multimeter Calibration," provides detailed information on the DMM circuitry.

A known constant current from the "source" terminals is connected to the resistance to be measured, R_x, and the voltage drop produced across R_x is measured at the "sense" terminals. Since the current magnitude is known and is constant, the voltage reading can be converted to resistance in ohms.

An important factor which contributes to accuracy when measuring high resistances is the very high input resistance of the voltage measurement circuit, typically greater than 10,000 MΩ. For increased accuracy on the low resistance ranges of the more expensive multimeters, the current source and voltage measurement terminals can be connected to the resistance separately as a 4-terminal ohmmeter connection (Figure 8-6).

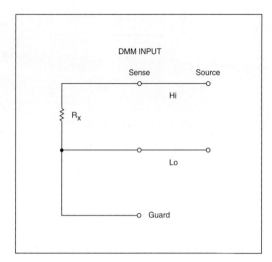

Figure 8-5. *Typical 2-Terminal DMM Resistance Circuit*

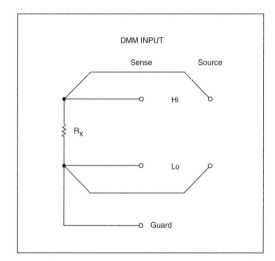

Figure 8-6. *4-Terminal Measurement*

This improves the accuracy over the 2-terminal connection, as shown in Figure 8-5, because the resistance of the connecting leads is not measured as a part of the resistance.

DMM Transfer Measurement
Some modern 7½- and 8½-digit DMMs have a very good resistance measurement capability. While they typically do not have extremely low uncertainty in their resistance readings, their high resolution, excellent linearity and short-term stability make them very useful for comparing nearly equal resistors. See Figure 8-7.

Using this method, the following equation is used to solve for R_{meas}:

$$R_{meas} = R_{std}\left(\frac{Rdg_a}{Rdg_b}\right)$$

Where:

R_{meas} = value of the unknown resistor

R_{std} = value of the standard resistor

Rdg_a = DMM reading of R_{meas}

Rdg_b = DMM reading of R_{std}

This method works best for values greater than 1 kΩ, obtaining transfer uncertainties of about 1 ppm. Thermal emf's may be measured by switching the DMM to the dcv mode. If thermal emf's are present, they can be partially compensated by reversing the leads at the DMM, repeating the measurements, and averaging.

In this configuration, the voltage drop across the resistors is measured by the DMM, and R_{meas} is computed as above except that the DMM readings are in dc volts rather than in ohms.

Extending Resistance Values

Ratio techniques are used to extend resistance values from the 1Ω or 10 kΩ primary standards to other values in working standards. Two ratio techniques that are often used are the potentiometer and the bridge methods. These are summarized here but are described in detail in the section "Resistance Ratio" in Chapter 9, "DC Ratio." Working standards are described in this chapter.

Ratio Techniques

Figure 8-8 illustrates how ratio techniques are used to extend the value of a standard resistor, R_{std}, by connecting it in series with another resistor, R_{meas}, and applying a dc voltage or current to the pair. The two respective voltage drops, V_{std} and V_{meas}, are measured and their ratio is multiplied by R_{std} to find R_{meas} as shown:

$$R_{meas} = R_{std} \left(\frac{V_{meas}}{V_{std}} \right)$$

A constant current source will be used for resistors of 10 kΩ and below. A constant voltage source is used for higher value resistors. (For more information on this method, see *An Automated System for the Comparison of Resistance Standards from 1Ω to Several kΩ*, and *A Wheatstone Bridge for the Computer Age*, available from Fluke.)

The Potentiometer Method
In this method, the voltage applied across the two resistors must be both accurate and stable and the value of the voltage drops across the two resistors must also be accurately measured. These goals can be met with modern voltage sources and DMMs, as discussed in Chapter 9, "DC Ratio."

Bridge Methods
Bridge methods also use the principle of proportional voltage drops but the voltage drops across R_{std} and R_{meas} are compared to the voltage drops across two other series-connected resistors that have a known ratio. In this method, the voltage that is applied does not need to be either very accurate or stable and a null detector is used to differentially measure the voltage drops in the two arms of the bridge. Please refer to Chapter 9, "DC Ratio," for a comprehensive discussion of resistance bridges.

Working Standards

Working standards of resistance are available in a variety of configurations ranging from the single-value, NBS-type standard resistor used as a transfer standard in primary standards laboratories to the programmable, multi-valued resistor set, Fluke 5450A or Fluke 5700A, used for ohmmeter calibration in automated test systems.

Working standard resistors such as the Fluke 742A are designed for use in air at normal laboratory conditions. Unlike the Thomas one ohm, which uses higher TC Manganin wire, they are often constructed with resistance elements made of Evanohm, an alloy which has several desirable properties. In addition to a

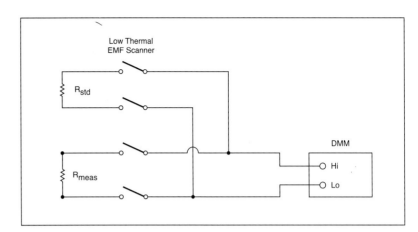

Figure 8-7. *Comparing Resistors of 1 kΩ or Greater Value (DMM in Resistance Mode)*

low, relatively linear temperature coefficient of resistance at room temperature, Evanohm has high resistivity, low thermal emf against copper, and high tensile strength, important when the wire is drawn out to small cross sections for making high value resistors. Because the temperature coefficient curve for Evanohm is roughly linear through the zero temperature coefficient (TC) region, it is possible to process the wire to obtain both +TC and −TC resistors. This makes it possible to select groups of resistors with a net, near zero, TC.

The ESI SR104 and a large number of resistor sets in a variety of different configurations for use in calibration laboratories, such as decade resistor sets and equal value voltage divider sets, are available. Most standards laboratories will maintain a set of resistance standards consisting of one or more resistors of each decade value from 1Ω up to 100 MΩ. Many laboratories

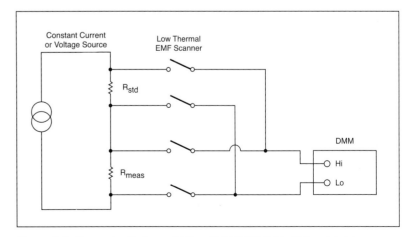

Figure 8-8. *Comparing Resistors of 1Ω to 10 MΩ (DMM in Voltage Mode)*

maintain decade values from 1.9Ω to 19 MΩ to facilitate calibration of their multifunction calibrators. If the laboratory is called on to calibrate high current shunts, it will probably maintain lower-value standards of 1, 10, and 100 mΩ resistance also.

Fluke 742A

The Fluke 742A is a series of standard resistors of decade values covering the 1Ω to 10 MΩ range. 1.9Ω, 19Ω, and 19 MΩ are also available. See Figure 8-9.

Their values can be extended using ratio techniques. See Chapter 9, "DC Ratio," for bridge methods covering a broad range of resistance values.

The 742A resistors are wire wound using nickel/chromium alloy wire which is modified with cobalt and aluminum (MOL3 Wire). The resistors are hermetically sealed in a dry nitrogen environment to improve their stability. Their resistance values are typically derived from multiple resistors in parallel. Their low TC is achieved by using pairs of resistors with the same nominal value but equal and opposite TCs. The pairs, 2 to 10, depending on the resistance value, of resistors are trimmed with wirewound resistors to provide the 742A final value. These standards are designed to be used in a 23 ±5°C air environment. They do not have to be immersed in an oil bath. They give the metrologist the ability to take accurate resistance standards to the production floor.

Fluke DMM Calibration Standards

To calibrate the resistance ranges of high accuracy DMMs, working standards of resistance are included in the Fluke 5700A MultiFunction Calibrator.

Their values are applied to the DMMs' input by a switch matrix internal to the 5700A. Fluke 5450A, shown in Figure 8-10, is a dedicated resistance calibrator that provides a more accurately known switched resistor set than the 5700A.

Some metrologists have used statistical techniques to reduce the uncertainty of the 5450A in order to use it as a programmable secondary standard of resistance. For more information on statistical enhancement of performance, see Section Five, "Statistics."

Hookup Considerations

The cables and test leads used to make resistance measurements should have low thermal emf's and low contact resistance at their junctions. When measuring high values of resistance, cables with very high insulation resistance should be used. Also, high values of resistance and the cables used to connect them should be completely enclosed in a continuous, grounded Faraday shield to avoid "noise pickup."

Chapter 33, "A Rogues' Gallery of Parasitics," discusses contact resistance, thermal emf's, Faraday shields, and other topics that pertain to making precision resistance and voltage measurements.

Resistance Lore

Some information is given here as historical and technical background for this chapter.

History Of Resistance Standards

From Ohm's research with electrical currents came the law known as Ohm's law in 1827, which underlies all modern analog circuit theory and electrical measurements. The value of the ohm was determined by a committee of the British Association in 1863 as the resistance of a certain piece of copper wire, and was called the B.A. ohm. In 1884, in Paris, the International Congress of Electricians adopted the so-called legal ohm as a correction to the B.A. ohm, and defined it as the resistance of a column of mercury one square millimeter in section and 106 centimeters high, at a temperature of 0°C. This definition was later modified to be: "equal to the resistance offered to an unvarying electric current by a column of mercury at 0°C, 14.4521 grams in mass, of a constant cross sectional area, and of the height of 106.3 centimeters."

Early experimenters in electricity found differences in the conductivity of various metals and noted that the resistance was proportional to the length of the conducting path and inversely proportional to the cross-sectional area of the conductor. Resistors used by these experimenters were frequently made of iron wire because it was readily available. As the experiments became more refined, the shortcomings of these resistors, such as large temperature coefficient, became apparent.

When the characteristics of other available metals were examined and found unsuitable, attention turned to various alloys. Edward Weston discovered two alloys in 1884, now known as Constantan and Manganin, which had the desirable characteristics of low temperature coefficient of resistance and high relative resistance. However, Constantan, an alloy of 55% copper and 45% nickel, was found unsuitable for resistors used in instrumentation due to the large thermal emf when connected to copper. Manganin (84% copper, 12% magnesium, 4% nickel), on the other hand, had a very low thermal emf against copper, about 2 microvolts per °C, and this material was widely used—and still is—for instrumentation and standard resistors.

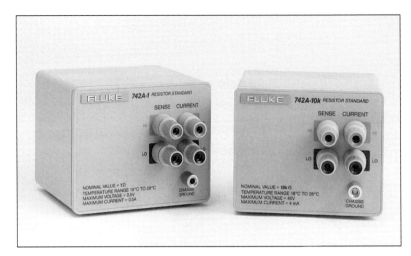

Figure 8-9. *Fluke 742A Working Standard Resistor*

Other alloys have since been developed with further improvements in temperature coefficient characteristics. One of these, Evanohm, is used for most of the precision wirewound resistors found in calibration instruments today. Both Manganin and Evanohm have a zero temperature coefficient point at some temperature in the range of 25°C to 50°C, depending on processing, but the temperature coefficient curve is much flatter for Evanohm. Further improvements in temperature coefficient can be realized by special wire drawing and annealing processes to tailor the characteristics of the wire for specific applications. Evanohm has a resistance of 800Ω per circular mil-foot (CMF). Manganin's value is 280Ω per CMF.

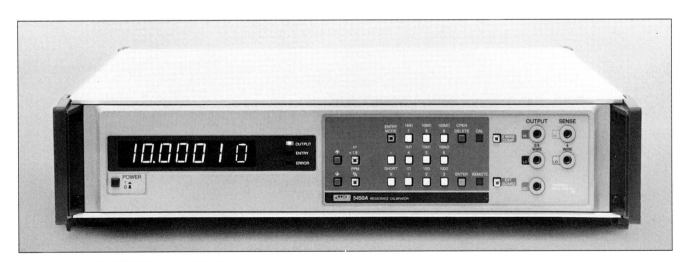

Figure 8-10. *Fluke 5450A Programmable Resistance Set*

NIST Maintenance of the Ohm

Because it is difficult to realize the ohm with accuracy, national standards laboratories such as NIST have historically elected to define the legal national ohm in terms of artifacts. In the United States, from 1901 to 1990, the legal unit of resistance was maintained at the 1Ω level as the mean resistance of a particular group of precision wirewound Manganin resistors, each having a nominal resistance of one ohm. The size of the group has varied from 5 to 17 resistors, but the mean value of the group was assumed to remain constant. Recent absolute-ohm determinations have shown that this is not the case, but it has been remarkably stable. Excluding an adjustment applied in 1948, the change in the ohm as maintained by NIST has been less than 10 ppm.

When the National Bureau of Standards (NBS), now NIST, was established in 1901, the legal unit of resistance for the United States was based on the mercury ohm. At the time, precise measurements of the mercury ohm were being made in Germany at the Physikalisch-Technische Reichsanstalt (PTR), now PTB, and in the UK at the National Physical Laboratory (NPL). Consequently, the original 1Ω resistance standards were a group of Reichsanstalt-type resistors, made in Berlin by the firm of Otto Wolff. Measurements at NBS indicated that these resistors varied as a function of atmospheric humidity, and in 1909 a change was made to that of a sealed resistor developed by Rosa.

From 1909 until 1930, the ohm as maintained by NBS consisted of the mean of a group of 10 Rosa-type resistors. Over the years it was determined that the Rosa-type resistors also drifted. Development work by Thomas resulted in a new resistor design showing improved stability. The major design innovation was to thoroughly anneal the resistance wire before sealing it in dry air between two coaxial brass cylinders. The Thomas-type resistors were more stable immediately following construction than the Rosa-type following aging. Thomas-type resistors were introduced into the primary reference group in 1930, and in 1932 the Rosa-type resistors were withdrawn and replaced by the Thomas-type. Improvements in the original Thomas design were made in 1932

to reduce power coefficient by increasing the cooling surface area and increasing the wire diameter. Until January of 1990, NIST maintained the ohm in a group of five Thomas-type resistors constructed in 1933.

In 1901, when the legal ohm was based on the mercury ohm as defined by public Law #105, the NBS 1Ω standard resistors were compared against standards maintained by PTR and NPL as the closest realization of the mercury ohm. It was not until 1911 that the first NBS determination of the mercury ohm was completed. Absolute resistance experiments at NPL in 1914 and at PTR in 1920 indicated that the absolute ohm was less than the international ohm by about 500 ppm. Further experiments during the period from 1936 to 1939 by NBS, NPL, PTR, LCE (France, now LCIE), and ETL (Japan) substantiated this finding. An international committee recommended the abandonment of the mercury ohm and adoption of the absolute ohm as the basic unit effective January 1, 1940. Because of World War II, the change was delayed until January 1, 1948.

In order to conform to the agreed-upon value of the absolute ohm, the NBS resistance standards were increased by 495 ppm on January 1, 1948. This was the first adjustment to the ohm since the establishment of the Bureau in 1901. In the second adjustment in 1990, both the value and drift rate of the ohm were adjusted to bring them into line with the internationally agreed-upon value.

Early measurements of resistance in terms of the absolute ohm were made by comparing the resistance of the resistors to the impedance of a mutual inductor. The impedance of the inductor could be calculated accurately from physical measurements of the dimensions of the inductor and measurement of the frequency of the applied current. Using this method, NBS was able to determine the absolute value of the ohm to an estimated accuracy of 5 ppm. Another method of deriving the ohm—by comparison to capacitive reactance instead of inductive reactance—resulted from the development of the calculable capacitor in 1956 and the design of transformer comparator bridges. These allow the ratio comparison of very small capacitors with others having values 100,000,000 times larger without detectable increase in the uncertainty of the result.

Since January, 1990, the NIST representation of the ohm has been based on the Quantum Hall Effect, described earlier in this chapter.

Table of Resistance Standards

A number of resistance standards are available to maintain and disseminate the ohm. Table 8-1 briefly describes several dc resistance standards in descending order of their ranking as primary, secondary, or working standards in the traceability chain.

References for this chapter are in the Resources Appendix.

Table 8-1. Resistance Standards

Type of Standard	Output	Lowest Uncertainty	Relative to	Application/Description/Comment
Quantum Hall[1] (QHE) Effect Intrinsic Standard	$\dfrac{h}{ie^2}$	0.2 ppm ($\pm 1\sigma$)	SI definition of the Ohm	Primary intrinsic standard used in-lab. Maintained in liquid helium.
Thomas 1 Ohm Artifact Standard	1Ω	0.05 ppm	higher echelon standard	Primary standard, MAP traceable, at 1Ω level, used in-lab. Maintained in oil bath.
ESI SR104 10 kΩ Artifact Standard	10 kΩ	0.15 ppm	higher echelon standard	Primary standard, MAP traceable at 10 kΩ level used in-lab or on-site. Maintained in air with temperature correction factors supplied.
Fluke 742A[4] Artifact Standard	1Ω to 19 MΩ in 11 discrete values	2.5 ppm 6 months	higher echelon standard	Secondary standard in-lab or on-site. Transfers resistance to calibrators such as the Fluke 5700A. Maintained in air with temperature correction factors supplied.
Fluke 5450A[2,4] Resistance Calibrator	1Ω to 100 MΩ in 17 discrete values	6 ppm 90 days	national standards	Working standard, in-lab or on-site. Calibrates resistance ranges of precision DMMs and calibrators. A user characterized unit can typically have half the specified uncertainty (i.e., 3 ppm, statistically characterized vs. 6 ppm, specified). Temperature insensitive, 18–28 °C.
Fluke 5700A[3,4] Multifunction Calibrator	1Ω to 100 MΩ in 17 discrete values	11 ppm 90 days	national standards	Working standard, in-lab or on-site. Calibrates resistance ranges of precision and handheld DMMs. Temperature insensitive, 18–28°C.
Fluke 5100B[4] Multifunction Calibrator	1 Ω to 10 MΩ in 8 decade values	30 ppm 6 months	national standards	Working standard in-lab or on-site. Calibrates resistance ranges of handheld DMMs. Temperature insensitive, 18–28°C.

1. The output of the QHE standard is 25,812.807Ω when i = 1. (Note: i is a positive integer.)

2. The 5450A resistors are not trimmed to nominal. Their actual vs. characterized values can differ by 50 ppm in the 10 kΩ region and 1000 ppm in the 1Ω region.

3. The 5700A resistors are not trimmed to nominal. Their actual vs. characterized values can differ by 150 ppm in the 10 kΩ region and 500 ppm in the 1Ω region.

4. A coverage factor, k, of 2.6 (99% certainty) applies to the uncertainty specifications for all Fluke models.

Chapter 9:
DC Ratio

This chapter outlines some of the techniques metrologists use for deriving multiples and fractions of the basic DC quantities of voltage and resistance.

T his chapter will present a number of ratio devices and non-ratio scaling techniques in sufficient detail to allow the reader to judge their applicability to specific needs. AC ratios are discussed in Chapter 10, "Principles of AC-DC Metrology."

Electrical metrology as practiced in the 1990s proceeds by careful work to establish the basic unit, such as the ohm, the volt, the farad, etc., then extends the range of application by a scaling experiment. Scaling refers to the establishment of a scale for the quantity, and consists of establishing accurately-known multiples of the basic unit. In electrical metrology, the most common scaling technique is ratioing. Ratio refers to the proportion of one level of a quantity to another level of the same quantity.

Because there are no national ratio standards to calibrate a ratio standard against, the evaluation of a ratio device is an independent experiment. Ratio experiments must be carefully devised and executed in order to account for all significant error sources in the experiment. As an expression of the relationship between one amount of a quantity and another, ratio is dimensionless.

There has been a tendency to believe ratio devices do not require calibration and are exempt from traceability requirements. This is not the case, because the ability to accurately and precisely achieve a given ratio of a quantity requires proper equipment, environment, and technique. Therefore, the prudent metrologist will verify the accuracy of ratios, either by calibrating the ratio device, or by comparing with other facilities devices calibrated using the ratio device.

Non-Ratio Scaling Techniques

The classical example of a non-ratio experiment to establish multiples of a basic quantity is the comparison experiment used for deriving multiples and fractions of the standard kilogram as shown in Figure 9-1.

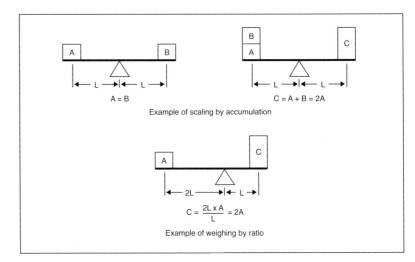

Figure 9-1. *Scaling vs. Ratio*

Series-Connected Cells

An example taken from electrical metrology uses a number of standard cells connected in series to establish a voltage equal to n times the average standard cell voltage. This known voltage is then used to standardize another voltage at the 10V level, using a Kelvin-Varley (K-V) divider (Fluke 720A). See Figure 9-2.

The process is as follows:

1. Preadjust the 10V source to 10V ±0.01%.

2. Set Kelvin-Varley dials to $\dfrac{\Sigma V_{cell}}{10}$

Where:

ΣV_{cell} = Sum of nine certified cell voltages, approximately 9.16V

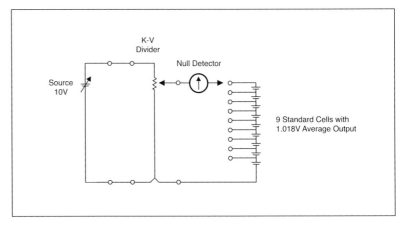

Figure 9-2. *Series-Connect Cells Setup*

3. Connect null detector between the Kelvin-Varley and series-connected cells.

4. Adjust the 10V source for a null on the null detector.

There are several problems with this approach. The K-V divider does not have sufficient resolution, the voltage source used to drive the K-V divider contributes additional noise and drift, and, most importantly, stacking standard cells in series introduces additional leakage paths which make the resultant voltage different from the sum of the cell voltages.

Bruce Field's Method

In June, 1985, Dr. Bruce Field, of NIST, reported another approach to accumulating voltages to establish a known voltage near 10V. He started with 1 kΩ resistors connected in series, with voltage taps available at all 11 resistor connection points. See Figure 9-3.

A stable 10.18V source (a modified Fluke 732A), connected to the input of the resistor string, provided about 1.018V across each resistor.

Each of these voltages was then compared by differential measurements to the voltage of each of four accurately known standard cells. Since the differentially-measured voltages were in the microvolt region, the DMM accuracy did not significantly affect the results.

Upon completion of these tests, Dr. Field had a precisely-known set of voltages ranging from 1.018 to 10.18V in 1.018V steps. These voltages could then be used to calibrate any non-standard voltage in that range, and were used to verify linearity of the DMM. The Field Method was used as the basis of a NIST calibration service which provides 0.3 ppm uncertainty at the 10V level.

Note that when measuring a 10V standard, a DMM is required to measure only about 0.18V, less than 2% of the total voltage. With linearity known, a DMM calibration to within a few ppm does not significantly affect measurement accuracy.

A second decade can be constructed using resistors each having one-tenth the value of those in the main divider. This decade can be calibrated by comparisons to a stable but unknown voltage drop across an individual resistor. In this case, the total voltage across the string is known and the individual voltages are calculated from the difference voltages.

In principle, accumulation techniques could be used for providing multiples and fractions of a standard of resistance. However, the problems are many, and the technique is not often used for high-accuracy measurements. Contact and interconnecting lead resistance are problems for resistors measured as 4-terminal resistors. Leakage resistance on the order of $10^{12}\Omega$ will cause errors at the 1 ppm level for resistors larger than about 1 MΩ.

Standardizing Direct Current

One final example of extending the measurement range by accumulation is the standardization of direct current. Direct current is normally standardized by measuring the voltage drop across a resistor of known high accuracy. This approach works very well if the current to be measured is no larger than the current used in the calibration of the resistor.

However, power and voltage coefficients in the resistor may cause errors at higher currents. The problem can be avoided by connecting several accurately known resistors in parallel, driving the current through them, and then

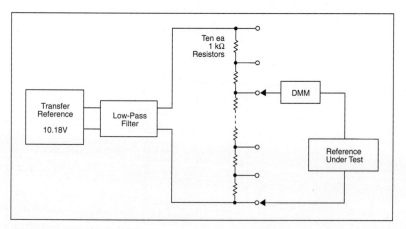

Figure 9-3. Dr. Bruce Field's Divider

measuring the voltage across each resistor as shown in Figure 9-4.

Current division is determined by the values of the individual resistors and the additional contact and connecting resistance which results from their interconnection. The current in each leg of the circuit can be accurately determined by this method, and the sum must equal the total current in the absence of significant leakage resistances. The experiment can be extended to calibrate a single resistor at the higher current level, providing a simpler experiment for future measurements.

Quantum Standards Method

Another non-ratio alternative is the use of quantum standards to provide multiples and fractions of a basic unit. The most striking contemporary example is the Josephson Junction Array voltage standard developed primarily at NIST. This apparatus is capable of generating precisely-known voltages in the range from ±100 μV to ±10V. One application of the apparatus is the accurate calibration of voltage and resistance ratios.

The use of the Josephson Array for calibration of ratios greater than 100:1 is limited by the availability of adequate null detectors. Superconducting Quantum Interference Device (SQUID) detectors might be used in the future to extend the useful range. They operate at a temperature of about 4K, and are virtually free from Johnson and other noise effects which limit ordinary room-temperature detectors.

Voltage Ratio

Four essentially different techniques are currently used for deriving ratios of direct voltage and, by extension, resistance. They are:

■ Hamon resistor
■ Kelvin-Varley divider
■ Ring Reference divider
■ Pulse-Width-Modulated DAC (pwmdac)

Each of these is detailed in the following sections.

The Hamon Resistor

The Hamon resistor relies on a series-parallel equivalence of nominally equal resistances. Figure 9-5 shows the series-parallel equivalence of Hamon-connected resistors.

The principle is demonstrated by using three nearly equal resistors, connected first in series, then in parallel. The average value, R_a, of the three resistors is just:

$$R_a = \frac{R_1 + R_2 + R_3}{3}$$

Define three deltas (δ) thus:

$$\delta_1 = R_1 - R_a$$

$$\delta_2 = R_2 - R_a$$

$$\delta_3 = R_3 - R_a$$

The sum of the three resistors is:

$$R_1 + R_2 + R_3 = 3R_a + \delta_1 + \delta_2 + \delta_3 = 3R_a$$

since the sum of the deviations from average is identically equal to zero. The series resistance is therefore

$$R_s = 3R_a$$

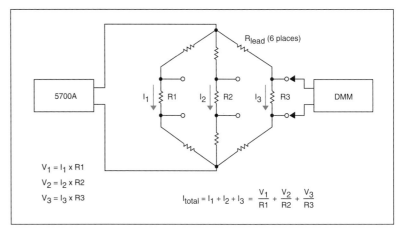

Figure 9-4. *Current Division*

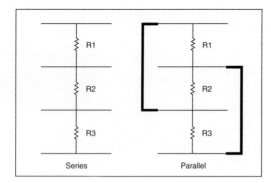

Figure 9-5. *Series-Parallel Equivalence*

Using the normal equations for resistors in parallel, the value of the three connected in parallel, R_p, can be expressed as:

$$R_p = \frac{(R_a + \delta_1)(R_a + \delta_2)(R_a + \delta_3)}{(R_a + \delta_2)(R_a + \delta_3) + (R_a + \delta_1)(R_a + \delta_3) + (R_a + \delta_1)(R_a + \delta_2)}$$

which reduces to

$$R_p = \frac{R_a}{3}$$

since $\delta_1 + \delta_2 + \delta_3 = 0$ and $\delta_1\delta_2$, $\delta_1\delta_3$, $\delta_2\delta_3$, and $\delta_1\delta_2\delta_3$ are insignificant when the δ for each resistor is less than 100 ppm as shown in Table 9-1. The ratio of R_s to R_p equals 9 for three resistors.

Table 9-1. *Significance of Products in ppm Deviation from R_a*

Deviation (δ) of R_1, R_2, or R_3 from R_a	Significance of Deviation vs. Product Given Below	
	$\delta_1\delta_2$ or $\delta_2\delta_3$ or $\delta_3\delta_1$	$\delta_1 \delta_2 \delta_3$
100 ppm	$10(10^{-9})$	$1.0(10^{-12})$
50 ppm	$2.5(10^{-9})$	$0.125(10^{-12})$
10 ppm	$0.1(10^{-9})$	$1.0(10^{-15})$

This approach can be generalized to a large number of resistors. The series-parallel equivalence is accurate to approximately 1 part in 10^8 for resistors matched to 1 part in 10^4, provided proper attention is paid to leakage resistances and connection resistance which tend to make currents divide unevenly.

The useful range of ratios provided by the technique is limited by detector noise and sensitivity at one end and by power and voltage coefficients, and parasite leakage at the other. Recent experiments to determine the SI

value of the volt have used Hamon dividers consisting of about 30 resistors to realize ratios near 1000:1. Ratio errors of less than 1 ppm are claimed for these dividers.

Several manufacturers furnish Hamon resistor devices. These include the ESI SR-1010, which has been used for many years in calibration laboratories around the world, and the more recently introduced Fluke 752A.

ESI SR-1010 Divider

The ESI SR-1010 consists of 12 well-matched resistors connected in series, with each connection point provided with a potential tap.

Shorting bars having very low lead and contact resistances are provided for connecting any number of the resistors in parallel. Current compensators are also provided to ensure proper division of current in the low-valued resistors. SR-1010s are available with individual resistance values ranging from 1 ohm to 100 kΩ, in decade steps. A similar product, the SR-1050, extends the technique into the megohm range.

If the individual resistors are calibrated, the device can act as a 12:n voltage divider, although its use in this way does not capitalize on the advantages of the Hamon technique. Using a properly-chosen number of resistors, the SR-1010 can provide accurate resistance ratios ranging from 4:1 to 144:1. The most common application is for stepping up from a known low value of resistance to a value 100 times as great.

While the SR-1010 is very useful as a ratio device in the Hamon mode, it should not be relied upon as a stable resistor, nor for providing accurate ratios except as a Hamon device. Its wirewound card resistors have fairly high temperature coefficients (on the order of 5 ppm/°C), and are sensitive to changes in barometric pressure. The manufacturer's specifications are conservative; they accurately describe the capabilities of the device.

Fluke 752A Divider

The Fluke 752A is designed to provide very accurate 10:1 and 100:1 ratios. The technique can be considered a modified Hamon approach. Here, three resistors connected in parallel are compared to a fourth resistor, R_4. See Figure 9-6.

R_4 is adjusted to be precisely equal to the resistance of the three in parallel. When connected in series, the three resistors now equal almost nine times the value of R_4, and the series combination of the four provides a very precise 10:1 division.

The 100:1 ratio is formed by connecting three other resistors in parallel, then adjusting one of them until the parallel value is precisely equal to the series combination of the first four. When connected in series with the first four resistors, the combination provides the desired 100:1 ratio.

The 752A is constructed with very careful attention to leakage and contact resistance, and is carefully guarded to eliminate leakage across the divider resistors. It is specified to have uncertainties of less than ±0.2 ppm of output at 10:1 and ±0.5 ppm of output at 100:1, provided it is properly self-calibrated prior to use. It is designed to be used both as a divider and a multiplier for comparing both higher and lower voltages to a 10V standard of voltage. As long as the resistors of nominally-equal values remain within 100 ppm of one another, the 752A can be expected to provide that accuracy indefinitely. Because modern resistor technology cannot eliminate temperature effects at this level of uncertainty, the divider should always be self-calibrated prior to use.

The Kelvin-Varley Divider

While it can be used for generating reasonably accurate fixed ratios (±1 ppm of output at 10:1 in the Fluke 720A), the main application of a Kelvin-Varley divider is to finely subdivide a known input voltage. A Kelvin-Varley divider consists of several strings of resistors interconnected as shown in Figure 9-7.

Although most of these strings consist of more than 10 resistors, they function as decades. Normally the first decade is composed of 11 equal resistors of a value R. To get an over-ranging capability of 10%, as in the Fluke 720A, the first decade is constructed with 12 resistors. At any given setting of the first decade switch, two of these resistors are shunted by the second decade, which is designed to have an input resistance equal to the series value of the two

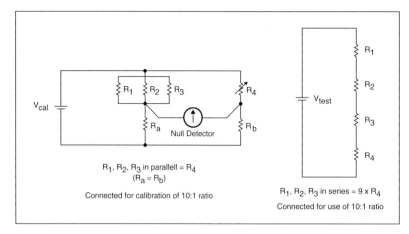

Figure 9-6. *Simplified Fluke 752A Schematic*

resistors being shunted. Due to the combining effect of resistances in parallel, the voltage drop across the two shunted resistors is equal to the voltage across any unshunted first decade resistor. Stated another way, the end-to-end resistance of the decade, as shunted, is equal to the value of 11 resistors, rather than 12.

Two definite advantages are immediately evident: first, the input resistance measured from the input to the common terminal, with the output terminals disconnected or unloaded, is constant. Second, the effect of contact resistance in the switch points is greatly reduced because of the division of current. The second, third, and subsequent decades are also Kelvin-Varley elements. Each decade covers the range of one step of the preceding decade, in steps from one-tenth up to nine-tenths. The last decade consists of 10 equal resistors, and can be set to values of zero through 10. It is only by use of this 11th setting of the last dial that the divider can be set to full scale. This dial's setting is equivalent to a setting of 10, displayed as an X, which is interpreted as 0, carry 1 to the next higher significant decade. For example, a setting of 0.99999X would be interpreted as 1.0 because the carry of 1 from the X is propagated to the first decade setting.

If the basic scheme of the first two decades were to be continued for several subsequent decades, a major problem would be observed. The total resistance of each decade (and therefore of the individual resistors) would have to decrease by a factor of five for each decade. This would soon lead to an impractically-small value of resistance. Therefore the scheme is

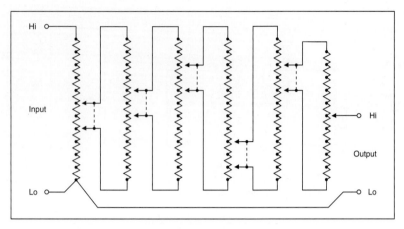

Figure 9-7. *Simplified Kelvin-Varley Divider Schematic*

modified somewhat. Starting with the first decade, the entire decade is shunted by an additional resistor. The value of this resistor is adjusted to make the total shunt resistance seen by the previous decade have the proper value, and to allow the resistors in the string to have some minimum value, such as 1 kΩ. Figure 9-8 is the basic schematic of the Fluke 720A.

Compared with the generic divider previously described, the major difference is that resistors in the first three decades are adjustable.

Linearity Deviation

One of the most important characteristics of a resistive divider such as the Kelvin-Varley, is linearity. This is actually another word for uniformity. If the steps (individual resistors) in a decade of 10 resistors are completely uniform,

then the linearity error is zero. The Fluke 720A has an absolute linearity of ±0.1 ppm of input.

Linearity deviation indicates how far away the output voltage is from the nominal or dialed value, expressed in ppm of the input voltage. This is clear for many applications; however, sometimes the ratio of interest is the ratio between two settings of the K-V. The linearity for this case can be different. Consequently, two linearities are of interest: terminal linearity and absolute linearity. They are defined as follows:

Terminal Linearity defines the division ratio of a divider in terms of the voltages across its input and output terminals. Two types of dividers are considered here: 3-terminal dividers and 4-terminal dividers. See Figure 9-9.

Absolute Linearity defines the linearity of the voltage divider's resistive element independently of the external connections.

To find terminal and absolute linearity in ppm, use the equations in Table 9-2 and multiply the result by 10^6:

Table 9-2. *3-Terminal and 4-Terminal Divider Linearity Equations*

	Terminal Linearity (t)	
	3-Terminal Divider	**4-Terminal Divider**
overall	$\dfrac{V_{'S'}}{V_t} - S$	$S \times \left(\dfrac{V_d}{V_t} - 1 \right)$
at 'S' 1.0	$\dfrac{V_1}{V_t} - 1$	$\left(\dfrac{V_d}{V_t} - 1 \right)$
at 'S' 0.0	$\dfrac{V_0}{V_t}$	0
	Absolute Linearity (a)	
overall	$\dfrac{V_{'S'} - V_0}{V_1 - V_0} - S$	$\dfrac{V_{'S'}}{V_d}$

Where:

a = absolute linearity

t = terminal linearity

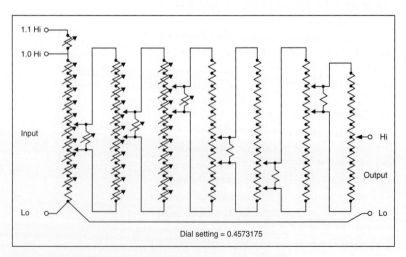

Dial setting = 0.4573175

Figure 9-8. *Parallel Compensation Resistance in Fluke 720A*

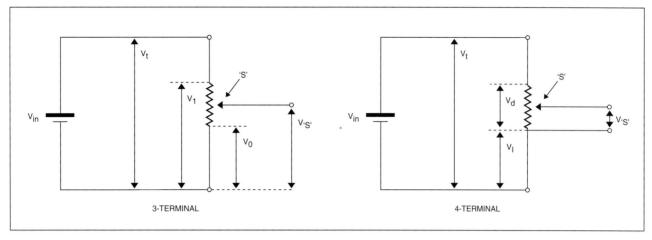

Figure 9-9. *3-Terminal and 4-Terminal Dividers*

S = divider setting

V_t = voltage across input terminals

$V_{'S'}$ = voltage across output terminals at divider setting 'S'

V_1 = $V_{'S'}$ with S = 1.0

V_0 = $V_{'S'}$ with S = 0.0

V_d = voltage across divider element

Lead resistance at its input will reduce a voltage divider's accuracy. The effects of lead resistance are decreased by increasing the values of the resistors that compose the divider's element. However, as the resistance values are increased, the uncertainty of the division ratio is increased by the effects of insulation resistance shunting the resistors. For more information on the effects of insulation resistance, see Chapter 33, "A Rogues' Gallery of Parasitics."

Other Dividers

The Ring Reference Divider
The Ring Reference approach to establishing accurate voltage ratios is based on the fact that the ratio of *n* series-connected voltages will be exactly *n*:1 when averaged over all possible ratios. The principle is illustrated in Figure 9-10, using three references for simplicity of presentation.

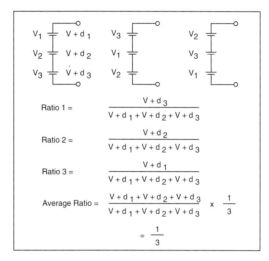

Figure 9-10. *Principle of Ring Reference Divider*

In principle, the technique can be extended to any number of sources, and to *n*:2, *n*:3, etc., ratios. This technique was developed to verify the uncertainty of the 10:1 ratio provided by the Fluke 752A Reference Divider. The implementation used ten Fluke 732As as the voltage sources. A special low-thermal, low-contact resistance measuring setup was constructed to implement the approach.

Conceptually, this approach might be used with resistors in place of the voltage standards. In practice, resistors that have high enough values to be immune to connector resistance errors, are also prone to leakage resistance problems. The very low source resistance of the 732A makes leakage of practical insulators insignificant, and the 732A's well-regulated

10-volt output is essentially immune to connection resistance variations.

The PWMDAC

An alternative to manually-operated direct current comparators consists of instruments that contain Pulse-Width-Modulated Digital-to-Analog Converters (pwmdac). These have accuracy comparable to direct current comparators, while having the additional feature of full automation.

The pwmdac is used to set the output in modern calibrators. It replaces resistive feedback circuits, such as ladder networks or switched-resistor networks previously used in digital-to-analog control circuits. Information on ladder networks and switched-resistor circuits used in calibrators can be found in Chapter 15, "Multi-function Calibrators."

The Fluke 5440B direct voltage calibrator makes use of the pwmdac converter. While a ladder-network, or switched-resistor dac converter can provide digital control, the possible variation in its resistors limits its accuracy.

The pwmdac converter, on the other hand, does not rely on multiple resistors and can therefore be much more accurate. PWMDAC converters consist basically of a low-frequency filter whose input is switched between ground and the reference voltage. The controlled switching action produces a constant-period square wave whose duty cycle depends on the relative time the switch is set to ground or the reference value. The filter smoothes this square wave to a precise, average dc value. Changing the duty cycle from 0% to 100% varies the average voltage appearing at the filter output, from 0 to the value of V_{ref}.

There are several advantages of this type of dac over the switched-resistor type. The device is actually a much simpler circuit with fewer critical components. It also eliminates the need for a large number of precision resistors. Finally, having a repeatable high-precision output depends only on highly reliable digital circuits and the short-term stability of the clock that controls the switching. Figure 9-11 is a schematic diagram of the pwmdac used in the Fluke 5440B calibrator.

DACs of this type are capable of achieving linearity at least as good as the best properly calibrated Kelvin-Varley dividers. And, of course, they have the great advantage of being controlled by computer.

For more detailed information, see the September 8th, 1982, issue of *Electronics* magazine.

Linear ADC in DMM

An 8½-digit DMM with a highly linear analog-to-digital converter (adc) can be used to determine the voltage ratio of a standard cell's unknown emf relative to the known, traceable +10V output of a solid state reference standard. In this method, the negative side of a standard cell is connected to the 10V output, leaving a voltage of a little less than +9V between the cell's high side and the low side of the 10V standard. Two DMM measurements are made and recorded as "V_1" and "V_2" as follows:

$$V_1 = k(V_{std} - V_x)$$

$$V_2 = kV_{std}$$

Where:

k = the scale factor of the DMM

V_{std} = the actual value of the 10V standard

V_x = the actual value of the standard cell

The ratio of the two readings is:

$$\frac{V_1}{V_2} = \frac{k(V_{std} - V_x)}{kV_{std}} = \frac{V_{std} - V_x}{V_{std}}$$

So:

$$V_x = V_{std}\left(1 - \frac{V_1}{V_2}\right)$$

This method can also be used to assign a value to the 10V reference in terms of the known emf of a standard cell. In either case, it relies on the elimination of "floor" errors in the DMM by its autozeroing circuit and on its having extremely good linearity over the +9V to +10V portion of its scale. Chapter 17, "Digital Multimeter Calibration," describes the adc's used in various types of DMMs.

Using Direct Voltage Dividers

This section describes some simple applications of dividers to create integral and incremental multiples and fractions of a known voltage.

Decade Voltage Ratios

One of the simplest applications is illustrated in Figure 9-12. Here a divider of 10:1 ratio is being used to standardize 1V to a known 10V.

Source to divider lead resistance is not significant when the divider is a Fluke 752A. For example, the Fluke 732 can be connected directly to the divider. In this case, input resistances are high enough so that there will be no significant loading of the 732 voltage standard.

Figure 9-13 illustrates another simple measurement—the standardization of a 100V source to a known 10V standard.

The previous paragraphs described 10:1 ratios. 100:1 ratios are also available in the Fluke 752A. A 100:1 ratio is used to divide 1000V down to a known 10V or to divide a known 10V down to 0.1V. The complete set of voltages, 0.1V, 1.0V, 10V, 100V, and 1000V can be used for verifying or adjusting a calibrator's or DMM's ranges.

Two or three 732s can be connected in series to provide the known voltage reference for decade voltage values from 0.2 or 0.3V to 200 or 300V in order to calibrate instruments that use this range structure near full scale. However, the 752A's maximum input is limited to 1000V.

Other Voltage Ratios

The subdivision of 10V using a Kelvin-Varley divider is straightforward. How to use the K-V divider to standardize an odd voltage, such as 752.752V, may not be as obvious. One solution is illustrated in Figure 9-14.

Alternatively, the Fluke 720A can be adjusted for null, and the value of the test voltage read from the 720A dials.

The Fluke 732B does not have external sensing capability. If it were connected directly to the 720A, the voltage at the 720A input would be lower by the voltage drop in the connecting

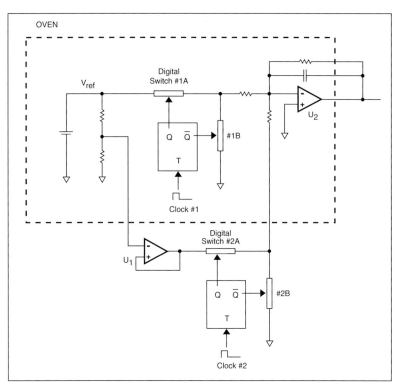

Figure 9-11. PWMDAC in Fluke 5440B

leads. For this reason, it is best to drive the divider with a second source, and standardize that source to the 10 volts provided by the 732B. The 720A and driving source can be replaced with a precision dac which has been standardized at 10V if such is available.

Measurement of small voltages, less than 0.1V, can normally be accomplished using the 720A

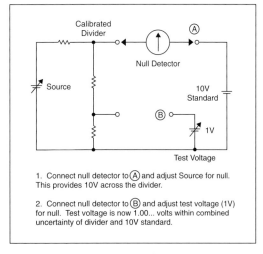

1. Connect null detector to (A) and adjust Source for null. This provides 10V across the divider.

2. Connect null detector to (B) and adjust test voltage (1V) for null. Test voltage is now 1.00... volts within combined uncertainty of divider and 10V standard.

Figure 9-12. Fluke 752A Used as a 10:1 Divider (10V:1V)

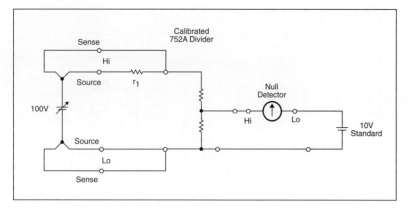

Figure 9-13. *Fluke 752A Used as a 10:1 Divider (100V:10V)*

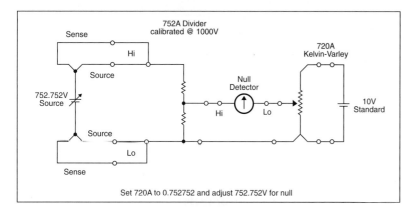

Figure 9-14. *Fluke 720A Used to Standardize 752.752V*

and a 10V or 1V. Noise and thermal emf's in measuring systems are normally the limiting elements in such measurements, not divider accuracy.

Calibrating Direct Voltage Dividers

While many modern dividers are self-calibrating and do not require calibration, there are occasions when it is desirable to compare dividers. Quiet, highly stable voltage sources make it relatively simple to accomplish. See Figure 9-15.

The two sources are set equal by adjusting the variable source for a null on the detector at position A. The detector is then moved to position B and the difference voltage is measured. Optionally, one of the sources can be adjusted to drive the detector to null and the divider difference calculated from the differences in input voltage.

When only a single source is available, or the absolute maximum accuracy of calibration is desired, the bridge comparison circuit of Figure 9-16 should be used.

Here a lead compensator, Fluke 721A, has been added to allow the potentials at both high and low ends of the dividers to be equalized. The 721A is adjusted with the detector at position A, then at position B, and then those adjustments are checked for interaction. When the detector is satisfactorily nulled at both positions, it is moved to position C and the error of the test divider is measured. If one or both of the dividers is adjustable, the detector can be driven to null and the error read from the divider dials.

Dividers are normally calibrated with relatively small voltage inputs. This can lead to problems when using the divider to standardize higher voltages where resistor heating can cause a power coefficient of ratio, and other effects can cause a voltage coefficient. Figure 9-17 illustrates a technique for measuring power coefficient in a divider.

A second general-purpose divider is connected to the source and allowed to stabilize for several hours. The test divider is then connected as shown, and measurements of ratio difference are begun immediately. It is not possible to make such a measurement in zero time, but if several measurements are made at known time intervals, it is easy to extrapolate the curve which represents the divider error back to zero time, where the divider has its low-voltage ratio. From this information, the divider error at high voltage can be computed, and combined with the low voltage error.

While a divider's power coefficient is relatively easy to measure, its voltage coefficient is a different matter. In principle, this can only be done by comparing the divider to one that is known to have no voltage coefficient. At present, the only divider that makes this claim is the Park Divider.

Self-Calibration of the Fluke 720A

The Fluke 720A has three arms of a Wheatstone Bridge built in. Two of the arms are approximately 40 kΩ and the other is approximately 10 kΩ. The object of self-calibration of decades A and B, along with their associated shunt resistors, is to make all resistors appear to be equal in value. All step resistances of decade A and B are substituted into the bridge and adjusted to be equal. Finally, the decade shunts are adjusted so that they, in parallel with the 10 succeeding resistors of the following decade, and two of the preceding resistors of the leading decade, are equal to the standard. A detailed calibration procedure can be found in the Fluke 720A instruction manual.

Independent Calibration of Dividers

The linearity of a divider under test (test divider) can be tested against the absolute division ratio of a user-constructed voltage divider with a known absolute linearity. This divider consists of 10 mutually-compared resistors connected in series.

The following section describes how to make the absolute voltage divider. "Comparing Ten-Tap and K-V Voltage Dividers," described next, shows how to compare a test divider against the absolute divider described here.

How to Make a Ten-Tap Voltage Divider

1. Get ten resistors of nearly the same value in the 10 kΩ to 100 kΩ range. Values should match to about 10 ppm.

2. Get a stable, adjustable voltage source to provide V_{in}. (A Fluke 5700A or 5440B is suitable.)

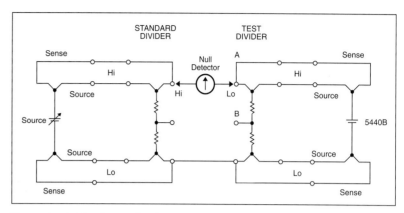

Figure 9-15. *Two Sources Used to Compare Divided Linearities*

3. Get a 10V voltage reference, such as a Fluke 732A or 732B.

4. Get a DMM with 0.1 μV resolution on its lowest ranges, such as Fluke 8842A.

5. Connect these items as shown in Figure 9-18.

6. Identify the resistors as R_1, R_2, . . . R_{10}.

7. Connect the DMM and Fluke 732 to differentially measure the voltage across R_1.

8. Set V_{in} to +100V and adjust it for null ±0.5 μV on the DMM. Record this value as V_1 (V_1 = 10V + DMM reading).

9. Without adjusting V_{in}, differentially measure the voltage across R_2. Record this value as V_2 (V_2 = 10V + DMM reading).

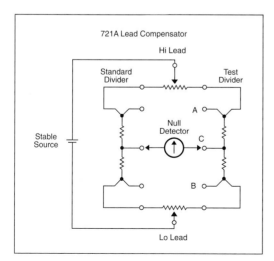

Figure 9-16. *Bridge Comparison of Dividers with 721A Lead Compensator*

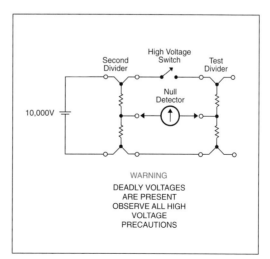

Figure 9-17. *Measuring Power Coefficient in a Divider*

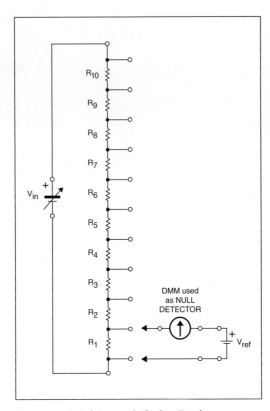

Figure 9-18. *Schematic of Absolute Divider*

10. Continue by differentially measuring the voltage drops across R_3, R_4 ... R_{10}. Record the differences as V_3, V_4, ... V_{10} (add 10V to each DMM reading).

11. Compute the absolute ratios, a_1, a_2, ... a_{10}, as:

$$a_1 = \frac{V_1}{V_1}, a2 = \frac{V_2}{V_1}, ... a10 = \frac{V_{10}}{V_1}$$

12. Add $a_1 + a_2$ ... a_{10} as:

$$\Sigma_a = a_1 + a_2 + ... a_{10}$$

13. Assign an S to each tap of the divider as follows:

$$S_1 = \frac{a_1}{\Sigma_a}, S_2 = \frac{a_1 + a_2}{\Sigma_a} ... S_9 = \frac{a_1 + a_2 + ... a_9}{\Sigma_a}$$

Note that:

$$V_1 = \frac{V_{in}R_1}{R_t}, V_2 = \frac{V_{in}R_2}{R_t}, ... etc.$$

Therefore:

$$a_1 = \frac{R_1}{R_1} = 1, a_2 = \frac{R_2}{R_1}, etc.$$

So:

$$\Sigma_a = \frac{R_1 + R_2 + ... R_{10}}{R_1} = \frac{\Sigma_R}{R_1}$$

$$S_1 = \frac{\frac{R_1}{R_1}}{\frac{\Sigma_R}{R_1}} = \frac{R_1}{\Sigma_R}$$

$$S_2 = \frac{\frac{R_1 + R_2}{R_1}}{\frac{\Sigma_R}{R_1}} = \frac{R_1 + R_2}{\Sigma_R}, ... etc.$$

The settings are absolute, and independent of the values of V_{ref}, V_{in}, and the effects of lead resistances between V_{in} and the divider input.

Notes:

The ratio measurements in this and the following section can be easily accomplished with uncertainties of ±1 ppm of output. However, uncertainties of less than ±0.1 ppm of output are required to check the linearity of a Fluke 720A Kelvin-Varley divider. An uncertainty of ±0.1 ppm of output is difficult to obtain and requires that the following be observed:

■ The experiment should be conducted in a draft-free ambient temperature of 23±1°C.

■ The resistors should have a 24 hour stability of ±0.1 ppm.

■ Thermal emf's in the voltage measurement circuit should be less than 0.5 µV.

■ The contact and lead resistance of the series connected resistors should be less than 1 mΩ and be stable to ±100 µΩ.

Comparing Ten-Tap and K-V Voltage Dividers

This example shows how to compare standard and test dividers, and describes testing the most significant decade of a six-decade Kelvin-Varley (K-V) divider.

1. Get the needed test equipment prior to comparing dividers.

2. Obtain a standard divider. See the preceding discussion, "How to Make a Ten-Tap Voltage Divider."

3. Connect the standard and test dividers as shown in Figure 9-19 (see *Notes* at the end of this procedure).

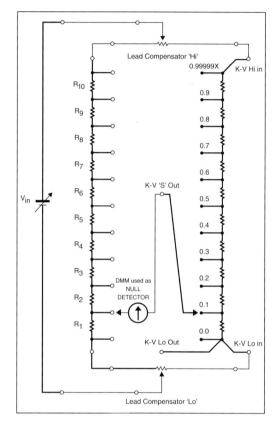

Figure 9-19. *Interconnections for Comparing Voltage Dividers*

4. Set V_{in} to an appropriate level ($\approx 100V$). Observe power and voltage ratings of test and standard dividers.

5. Connect the DMM HI input to the 0.0 tap of the standard divider. Set test divider dials to 0.000000.

6. Adjust LO lead compensator control for null ±0.5 µV.

7. Put null detector HI input on the S_{10} tap of the standard divider. Set test divider dials to 0.99999X.

8. Adjust HI lead compensator control for null ±0.5 µV.

9. Repeat steps 5 through 8 until both nulls are within ±0.5 µV.

10. Record and measure the voltage drop between the high output of V_{in} and tap S_{10}. Measure and record the voltage drop between the low output of V_{in} and tap S_0. Subtract the sum of the voltage drops from V_{in}. Record the results as V.

11. Differentially measure the pairs of outputs of the two dividers in the sequence given in columns 1 and 2 of Table 9-3. Record null detector readings e1, e2, ..., e9 in the third column of the table.

12. Compute and record the true ratios, R_n, for the K-V dial settings in the fourth column as:

$$R_n = S_n - (e_n / V)$$

Where S_n is the standard divider setting.

13. Compute the error, Δ_n in ppm for each setting of the test divider as:

$$\Delta_n = \frac{R_n - D_n}{R_n} \times 10^6$$

Where D_n is the test divider dial setting. Record in the fifth column of Table 9-3.

Notes:

- A calibrated source with an uncertainty of less than 0.01% should be used for V_{in}.

- The lead compensator adjusts voltage drops in divider input leads to make divider voltage drops equal.

- The DMM used to measure the lead compensator voltage drops should have a resolution of 0.1 µV.

- Differential measurements greatly reduce the effect of uncertainty in V_{in}. For example, if V_{in} at 100V nominal is +0.01% high (100.01V), S_1 is 10 ppm low (0.09999), and the output of the test divider is 1 ppm of input high at setting of 0.100000 (.100001), then the computed true ratio will be in error by −0.01 ppm of output (−0.001 ppm of input).

Table 9-3. K-V Voltage Divider Comparison Chart

Set Null Detector Input to:	Set Test Divider Dials to	Record DMM Reading (e_n)	Calculate True Ratio: $R_n = S_n - (e_n/V)$	Calculate error in ppm: $\Delta_n = \dfrac{R_n - D_n}{R_n} \times 10^6$
S1	0.100000	e1=_____		
S2	0.200000	e2=_____		
S3	0.300000	e3=_____		
S4	0.400000	e4=_____		
S5	0.500000	e5=_____		
S6	0.600000	e6=_____		
S7	0.700000	e7=_____		
S8	0.800000	e8=_____		
S9	0.900000	e9=_____		

Resistance Ratio

The Potentiometer Method

In Figure 9-20, an unknown resistance, R_x, is connected in series with a resistance standard, R_{std}, and a current, I, is induced by the voltage source, V.

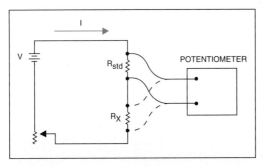

Figure 9-20. *Potentiometer Method*

The voltage drops across the unknown and the standard are measured with a potentiometer or other suitable instrument such as a digital voltmeter which will not draw appreciable current. The value of the unknown resistor can be determined in terms of the known standard as:

$$R_x = R_{std} \left(\frac{S_x}{S_{std}} \right)$$

Where:

R_x = unknown resistor value

R_{std} = standard resistor value

S_x = potentiometer setting for voltage drop across R_x

S_{std} = potentiometer setting for voltage drop across R_{std}

It is essential that the current through the two resistors remain constant during the period of the measurement. Any variation in the current will be reflected as a corresponding error of the same percentage. If variations in the current source do take place and they are random in nature, accuracy could be improved by taking repeated measurements and averaging the results. See Chapter 31, "Instrument Specifications."

Accurate measurements can be made even with changing currents if the changes are linear over this time period, by taking three measurements instead of two in a V_{std}, V_x, and V_{std} sequence. By taking the average of the two V_{std} measurements, the effects can be largely eliminated.

Another source of error is thermal emf's in the measuring circuitry. The effects of these unwanted emf's can be eliminated by reversing the polarity of the source and repeating the measurements. The average of the two measurements is the correct value.

Note that this resistance measurement method is sometimes used with high accuracy digital multimeters where it is relatively easy to make a large number of measurements over a short period of time and calculate an average of the results.

At Fluke, we obtain ±0.25 ppm uncertainty in comparison of 1Ω resistance standards. This is our preferred approach to resistance measurements in the range of 1Ω to 10 kΩ.

Bridge Methods

Because in earlier times it was difficult to maintain a constant current over the period of measurement in the potentiometer method, bridge methods were developed where variations in current do not affect the balance of the bridge.

The Wheatstone and Kelvin double bridge as well as the universal ratio set techniques are presented here. Automated bridges, incorporating their concepts, are now replacing the earlier manually-operated resistance measuring apparatus.

Wheatstone Bridge

The Wheatstone bridge circuit is widely used for the precision determination of resistance. It is useful for measuring resistance over a range from low values to several megohm. This network was first proposed by Christie in 1833 but did not become widely known until 1843 when Sir Charles Wheatstone discovered its usefulness. As shown in Figure 9-21, the circuit consists of four resistors connected in a series-parallel arrangement with a voltage source connected to one pair of opposite corners (*a* and *d*) and a galvanometer connected across the other pair (*b* and *c*).

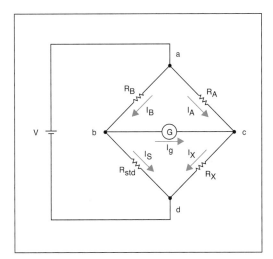

Figure 9-21. Wheatstone Bridge

When the network is used to compare an unknown resistance, R_x, to a standard of resistance, R_{std}, the resistors R_A and/or R_B are adjusted until no potential difference exists between the points *b* and *c*, as evidenced by zero deflection of the galvanometer. For this null condition, the resistor pairs R_A and R_{std}, and R_x and R_B, can be considered to be two parallel voltage dividers with equal division ratio. We can express this equality as:

$$\frac{R_{std}}{R_{std} + R_B} = \frac{R_x}{R_x + R_A}$$

which simplifies to:

$$R_x = R_{std}\left(\frac{R_A}{R_B}\right)$$

In practical instruments, the arms R_A and R_B can be combined in a high-resolution, calibrated voltage divider, such as the Fluke 720A Kelvin-Varley divider, which will provide good null resolution and precise results. Alternatively, R_A and R_B can be selected for a fixed ratio, and the resistance of R_{std} can be the variable. R_{std} would then be a rheostat, a series connection of selectable calibrated resistors with the necessary resolution to achieve a good galvanometer null. Precision commercial bridges are often constructed so that the resistors R_A and R_B are each selectable in decade values over the range of 1Ω to 10 kΩ. This allows the ratio to be set in decade steps anywhere between 0.0001:1 and 10,000:1. Connections to the resistors are arranged to allow any resistor to be placed in either arm.

This is a particular advantage when the bridge is used with equal ratio arms. A measurement of the unknown can be made with one arrangement of the resistance arms R_A and R_B, and then a second measurement can be made with the resistors in R_A and R_B interchanged. As long as the two resistors are reasonably close to the same value, an average of the two readings will eliminate the uncertainty in the ratio arms, leaving only the uncertainty of the variable arm.

There are limitations to the accuracy of the Wheatstone bridge at both the high- and low-resistance ends of the measurement scale. At the high-resistance end, limits are set by the sensitivity of the null measurement galvanometer and by leakage currents in the insulation of the bridge arms and structure. The upper limit of a typical general purpose bridge is about 1 MΩ, but this limit can be extended in a well-designed bridge with special design features.

The lower limit for the Wheatstone bridge is set by the fact that the resistors must be connected in the 4-terminal configuration. For low resistances, the preferred measurement instrument is the Kelvin double bridge.

A recent adaptation of the Wheatstone circuit replaces R_A and R_{std} with two highly stable voltage sources. See Figure 9-22.

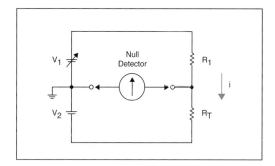

Figure 9-22. *PWMDAC Wheatstone Bridge*

V_1 is a variable voltage obtained from a dc voltage calibrator whose output is controlled by an extremely linear pulse-width-modulated digital-to-analog converter (pwmdac). V_2 is a second voltage source, whose output is fixed during the few minutes that it takes to complete a measurement. R_T is a resistor that must also be stable during the complete cycle. The null detector is a DMM having a 0.1 μV resolution and high input resistance (Fluke 8505A).

The general measurement procedure is as follows:

1. The nominal values of V_1, V_2, and R_T are chosen after selection of the standard resistor, R_{std}, so that the ratios V_1/V_2 and R_{std}/R_T are approximately 1:1 and the voltage drop across them will be in the range of 1 to 10V (depending on the power ratings of the resistors).

2. The standard resistor is connected at R_1.

3. V_1 is adjusted for a null on the DMM. V_1's setting at null is recorded as V_A.

4. The polarity of V_1 and V_2 is reversed, and V_1's setting is adjusted for a null on the DMM. Its setting at null is recorded as V_B. Reversing the voltage compensates for thermal emf in the circuit and any offsets in the DMM.

5. The average of the sum of the absolute values of V_A and V_B ($|V_A| + |V_B|$)/2 is recorded as V_{std}.

6. The test resistor, R_X, is connected at R_1 in place of R_{std}. Steps 2, 3, and 4 are repeated, with the average value recorded as V_X.

The general null equation for the bridge is:

$$\frac{V_1}{V_2} = \frac{R_1}{R_T}$$

Substituting the values of V_{std} and V_X obtained for V_1, and R_{std} and R_X for R_1 in the preceding equation yields the following two relationships:

$$\frac{V_{std}}{V_2} = \frac{R_{std}}{R_T} \quad \text{and} \quad \frac{V_x}{V_2} = \frac{R_x}{R_T}$$

Rearranging and combining these equations yields:

$$\frac{V_x}{V_{std}} = \frac{R_x}{R_{std}}$$

and

$$R_x = R_{std}\left(\frac{V_x}{V_{std}}\right)$$

The value of R_X is therefore determined by the ratio of the two settings of the highly linear pwmdac used in the voltage source. Accordingly, this method provides very accurate measurements.

This automated bridge is used by the Fluke Standards Laboratory to measure resistors from 10 kΩ to 390 MΩ. The uncertainty of comparing two 10 kΩ resistors is typically 0.06 ppm at 95% confidence. For more information on this method, see "A Wheatstone Bridge for the Computer Age," available from Fluke.

Kelvin Double Bridge

In order to understand the Kelvin double bridge, consider the problems of lead resistance and contact resistance when the Wheatstone bridge is used to measure low resistance. As shown in the circuit of Figure 9-23, the unknown resistance, R_X, is to be measured in terms of the standard R_{std}.

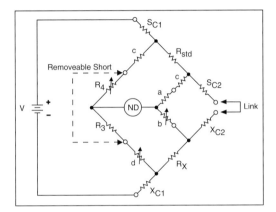

Figure 9-23. Kelvin Double Bridge

The connecting link between R_X and R_{std} has resistance which is significant compared to R_X and R_{std}, when these resistors are of a low value.

Another problem is the contact resistances S_{c1}, S_{c2}, X_{c1}, and X_{c2}. It can be a significant part of the overall resistance if R_X and R_{std} are low-value resistances. Contact resistance is a variable, depending on the cleanliness of contact surfaces and the pressure of the contact. To remove this uncertainty, low-value standard resistors and shunts are usually constructed as 4-terminal resistors, and the resistance is defined as the resistance measured between the potential terminals. To measure and compare this resistance, the Kelvin double bridge accommodates the connection of 4-terminal resistors for R_{std} and R_X.

The circuit for a Kelvin double bridge incorporates a second set of ratio arms, a and b, providing a connection that eliminates the effect of lead resistance in the link. The connections of R_4, R_3, a, and b are made to the potential terminals of the 4-terminal resistors for R_X and R_{std}, eliminating the uncertainty of contact resistances S_{c1}, S_{c2}, X_{c1}, and X_{c2} at the current terminals. C is the contact resistance of the voltage terminals of R_{std}.

The bridge will correctly read the resistance of R_X in terms of R_{std} if $a/b = R_4/R_3$. In a practical bridge, this condition is met by setting $a+c$ equal to R_4+c and b equal to R_3+d. This is done by mechanically coupling the switches which select a and b to those which select R_4 and R_3 so that the inner and outer ratio elements are selected together. If R_4, a, R_3, and b are appreciably higher than R_X and R_{std}, the 4-terminal resistance ratio of R_X to R_{std} can be determined accurately even though the contact and lead resistances associated with R_X and R_{std} are higher than the resistance of R_X and R_{std}. In low impedance bridges where this condition is not met, it will be necessary to balance the lead resistance, and provisions are made for shorting out the ratio arms and adjusting the ratio of the residual lead resistances for a balance as well. With lead resistance ratios equal to the ratio of the inner and outer ratio arms, the bridge will correctly read the ratio of R_X to R_{std}, even though the lead resistances are significant compared to the resistances of the ratio arms.

Current Methods

DC current ratios, based on transformer turns ratios, are sometimes used as an intermediate step to the final resistance ratio. The key technology is a direct current comparator installed in a comparator resistance bridge (CCRB). The use of a transformer's turns ratio at dc may appear to be impossible but the following material shows how it is done.

The Direct Current Comparator

The direct current comparator, illustrated in Figure 9-24, is a current ratio indicator, based on the detection of a balance in the ampere-turns imposed on a pair of magnetic cores.

It consists of two toroidal cores of square-loop magnetic material, a magnetic shield in the form of a hollow toroid which surrounds the cores, and ratio windings over the shield which carry the currents to be compared. An oscillator applies a square-wave alternating voltage to windings on the cores, driving them into saturation twice each cycle. Direct current in the ratio windings causes an even harmonic voltage to be produced which is detected by a demodulator.

The magnetic shield, which is made of high-permeability material, is essential for the operation of the comparator. It shields the cores from external fields and the winding leakage fluxes, so that the need for a special environment and careful ratio winding distribution is practically eliminated, and it suppresses the currents which would be induced by the modulator in the ratio windings.

When the flux in the cores is zero, the ratio of the currents flowing in the ratio windings is equal to the inverse ratio of the turns to a high degree of accuracy, but it is very difficult to maintain this balanced condition manually. The comparator can be made self-balancing by the addition of a slave power supply, controlled by a signal from the demodulator, which supplies the current required to keep the core flux zero. The comparator then acts like a current transformer, which can operate down to zero frequency.

The direct current comparator allows ratio transformer technology, with its very precise and stable ratio, to be used at dc. This technology has been used in resistance bridges (Guildline 9975) and potentiometers (Guildline 9330).

For more information about the direct current comparator, see the MacMartin and Kusters article in the December, 1986, issue of *IEEE Transactions on Instrumentation and Measurement*.

Direct Reading Ratio Set

The calibration of resistive devices can very often be reduced to making nearly a 1:1 comparison of an unknown resistance with a resistance standard of approximately the same value. When the differences are small, it is sufficient to determine the difference with only moderate accuracy in order to accurately calibrate the unknown. For example, if the difference between the unknown and the standard is .01% and the calibration procedure determines the difference with an uncertainty of 1%, the unknown will be calibrated with respect to the standard to an uncertainty of 1 ppm.

The direct reading ratio set is a combination of fixed and variable resistors that can be used in a bridge configuration to compare a resistor to be calibrated to a standard resistor of nearly the same value. The ratio set is calibrated to read small ratio differences between the two resistors.

A typical ratio set can consist of a fixed resistor of 100Ω and a variable resistor set that has a nominal value of 100Ω but is variable between the limits of 99.445Ω and 100.555Ω with a resolution of 0.001Ω. The variable portion of the set is constructed with three switch dials that change the resistance in steps corresponding to variations of 0.1%, 0.01%, and 0.001%, respectively. In use, the ratio set is connected to form two of the arms of a Wheatstone bridge, and the standard resistor and resistor to be calibrated are the other two arms. When balance is achieved, the dials of the ratio set directly read the percent variation, high or low, of the resistor being calibrated with respect to the standard resistor.

Operation of the direct ratio set requires the switching of small increments of resistance, as small as 0.001Ω in the design previously discussed, and this presents a problem if a conventional series combination of switch and resistor is used. Variations in contact resistance of rotary switches are generally in the range of 0.001Ω, the resistance of the element to be switched.

In order to reduce the effect of contact resistance variation, the switched resistors are designed as Waidner-Wolff elements. The Waidner-Wolff element consists of a low-value

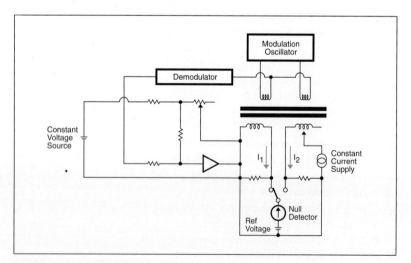

Figure 9-24. Direct Current Comparator

fixed resistor shunted by a switched resistor string of higher value. The switch contact resistance, being in series with the higher value resistance, has very little effect on the overall resistance of the parallel combination. Of course, the resistance of the element cannot approach zero ohms, but this is of no consequence since it is not required in this application.

When the direct ratio set is used to compare a resistor with a standard, the various components of the bridge should be connected, using care to keep the lead resistance and contact resistance low and repeatable. After the initial balance is obtained, by comparing the resistance-under-test to the standard, it is good practice to interchange the positions of the two resistors, take a second balance, and compute the difference as half the difference of the dial readings for the two balances.

Current Comparator Resistance Bridge (CCRB)
The current comparator resistance bridge (CCRB) operates on the current comparison principle. Since the ratios are derived from the turns ratio of transformers, they are highly accurate and highly stable. For example, the Guildline Model 9975 bridge is specified to be within ±0.2 ppm for a 10:1 ratio.

A CCRB is manually controlled, requiring a skilled operator. Making measurements at the sub-ppm level can be tedious and demanding.

It should also be noted that CCRB performance degrades rapidly when calibrating resistors whose values are above 10 kΩ. However, this is the preferred instrument for measuring resistances less than 1Ω.

Hookup Considerations

The same hookup considerations discussed in Chapters 7 and 8, "Direct Voltage and Current" and "DC Resistance," apply to dc ratios. In summary, the key items are low thermal emf's, low series contact and lead resistance, high insulation resistance and good shielding. Chapters 32 and 33, "Grounding, Shielding and Guarding" and "A Rogues' Gallery of Parasitics," also contain further information on these considerations.

Table of Ratio Standards

A number of ratio standards are available to extend and disseminate dc voltages and resistances. The following Table 9-4 briefly describes some ratio standards.

Table 9-4. Ratio Standards

Standard	Ratios	Input Voltage	Lowest Uncertainty	Application/Description/Comment
Fluke 752A	100:1	0 to ±1000V	0.5 ppm of output	Ratio standard used in-lab or on-site. Major application is to establish fixed 10:1 and 100:1 dc voltage ratios.
	10:1	0 to ±100V	0.2 ppm of output	
Fluke 720A	1.1:S 1.0:S	0 to ±1000V	0.1 ppm of input	Ratio standard used in-lab or on-site. Main applications are to establish a wide range of dc voltage and resistance ratios with seven decades of resolution via its setting, 'S'.
PWMDAC in a Fluke 5700A	1.0:S	ref amp internal to 5700A	0.3 ppm of input	Ratio standard embedded in calibrator. Used in-lab or on-site to artifact calibrate the 5700A and to provide seven digits of resolution for its dc and ac voltage and current outputs.
A coverage factor, k, of 2.6 (99% certainty) applies to the uncertainty specifications for all Fluke models.				

Key References

Page, C.H, "Errors in the Series-Parallel Buildup of Four-Terminal Resistors," NBS *Journal of Research*, Vol. 69C, No. 3, July-September, 1965

Morgan, M.L.; Riley, J.C., "Calibration of a Kelvin-Varley Standard Divider," IRE *Transactions on Instrumentation*, September, 1960

Field, B.F., "A Sub-PPM Automated 1-10 Volt DC Measuring System," IEEE *Transactions on Instrumentation and Measurement*, Vol. IM-34, No. 2, June, 1985

Huntley, Les, "A Wheatstone Bridge for the Computer Age," Measurement Science Conference, January, 1992

Voorheis, Howard; Huntley, Les, "Ring Reference Divider for Accuracy Verification of Resistive Dividers," CPEM, 1984

Faulkner, Neil, "An Automated System for the Comparison of Resistance Standards from 1 Ohm to Several kOhms," Measurement Science Conference, January, 1992

Other references for this chapter are in the Resources Appendix.

Chapter 10:

Principles of AC-DC Metrology

The principle of equivalence between ac and dc voltages and currents is the foundation of ac-dc metrology.

This chapter presents the basic theory of ac-dc metrology. It discusses single-element vacuum thermocouple converters and true rms sensors because of their widespread use in ac-dc transfer standards. Chapter 11, "Using AC-DC Transfer Standards," summarizes the practical use of the transfer standards and Chapter 34, "AC Lore," contains related material that covers the measurement of non-sinusoidal ac voltages and currents, including those with dc components. Chapters 12, "Inductance and Capacitance," and 13, "Immittance and AC Ratio," show how ac values are affected by inductance, capacitance, and immitance and can be measured using ac ratio techniques.

Basic Concepts

The output polarity and amplitude of an ideal dc voltage standard is constant at all instants of time during which the desired value is present. In contrast, alternating voltages (and currents) periodically reverse their polarity and their instantaneous amplitude is usually not constant between the polarity reversals. However, each instantaneous ac value has a specific amplitude and polarity.

DC and ac voltages and currents are equivalent when they produce identical average power in a pure resistance. The average power is dissipated as heat, which in turn is usually measured by sensors whose inputs respond directly to temperature and whose outputs provide a dc voltage that is proportional to the heat. This type of sensor is called an electrothermal device.

The main focus of ac-dc metrology concerns using electrothermal devices to measure the average power produced in a pure resistance by an ac voltage in order to assign it a value that is equal to a dc voltage which produces the same power in the same resistor. AC-DC current calibration is usually accomplished by using the electrothermal device to measure the ac and dc voltage drops across a current shunt.

Because electrical power is proportional to the square of the voltage (or current), electrostatic and electrodynamic devices can be used to directly measure the average square of the voltage (or current) and thereby indirectly determine the average power that the voltage or current would produce in a resistor. The relationship of the base-emitter voltage to the collector current in transistors is logarithmic. This relationship is used to determine average power.

Electrostatic and electrodynamic devices are usually not used for precision ac-dc metrology in the zero to 1000V range. The logarithmic methods involve the use of operational amplifiers and other circuits that electronically manipulate the ac and dc voltages and currents in order to obtain their logarithms and anti-logarithms.

The material that follows focuses on using electrothermal devices to measure voltage. It summarizes alternating current measurements and surveys the electrostatic, electrodynamic, and logarithmic methods.

Power Produced by Voltage

When a voltage is applied across a pure resistance, its electromotive force (emf) will cause power to be dissipated in the resistance, at each instant of time, according to the well-known relationship:

$$W = \frac{E^2}{R}$$

Where:

W = power in watts

E = emf in volts

R = resistance in ohms

The instantaneous power produced in an ideal resistor by a dc voltage standard is constant with time. In contrast, the power produced by an ac voltage that is applied to the same ideal resistor will usually be different at each instant of time. A graph of an instantaneous voltage amplitude plotted against time yields a continuous curve called a waveform.

While the waveform for a dc voltage is a flat line, there are an endless variety of ac voltage waveforms. A pure sine wave is the most fundamental type of ac voltage waveform (see Figure 10-1).

AC-DC metrology is primarily concerned with using ac-dc transfer standards to measure the average power produced in a resistor by a pure sine wave and comparing it with the average power produced in the same resistor by a dc voltage.

Sine Wave vs. DC Voltage

A sine wave of voltage consists of a series of instantaneous voltages, V_{ins}. When these voltages are applied across a pure resistance, a series of instantaneous powers, W_{ins}, are produced. Figure 10-2 compares the voltage and power waveforms of a 1V sine wave.

The amplitudes of the instantaneous voltages can be expressed as:

$$V_{ins} = V_{pk}\sin\theta$$

Where:

V_{pk} = peak voltage of the sine wave

$\sin$ = sine of an instantaneous angle, θ

θ = angle in radians in the range of 0 to 2π

The instantaneous power, W_{ins}, for each V_{ins} is:

$$W_{ins} = \frac{V_{pk}^2\sin^2\theta}{R}$$

Where:

R = resistance in ohms

Calculus is used to find the average power, W_{avg}, such that:

$$W_{avg} = \frac{V_{pk}^2}{2R}$$

The constant power, W_{dc}, produced in the resistor by a dc voltage, V_{dc}, is:

$$W_{dc} = \frac{V_{dc}^2}{R}$$

When $W_{avg} = W_{dc}$,

$$\frac{V_{pk}^2}{2R} = \frac{V_{dc}^2}{R}$$

RMS Voltage

Factoring out R and taking the square root of both sides yields:

$$\frac{V_{pk}\sqrt{2}}{2} = V_{dc}$$

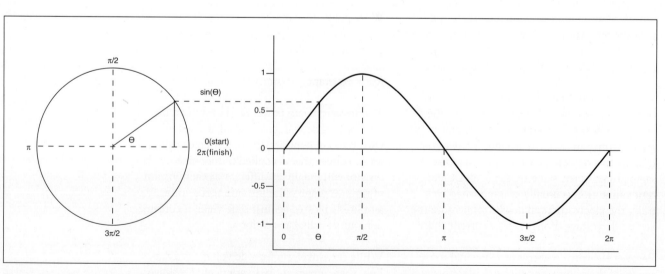

Figure 10-1. *Generation of a Sine Wave*

Due to its derivation, the term on the left is conventionally called the root-mean-square (rms) voltage, V_{rms}.

$$V_{rms} = \frac{V_{pk}\sqrt{2}}{2}$$

The rms voltage, V_{rms}, as defined by this equation has the same power content as the dc voltage, V_{dc}, when $V_{rms} = V_{dc}$.

RSS Voltage

All ac voltages, regardless of their waveform, have an rms value. All waveforms can be constructed from the superposition of a series of sine waves, known as the Fourier series, and a dc component. When this is done, the rms voltage of the composite waveform can be computed as the square root-of-the-sum-of-the-squares (rss) of the values of the ac and dc components. See Chapter 34, "AC Lore," for more information on the Fourier series and the calculation of the rss values of various waveforms.

AC Current

Alternating current is the current that flows in a circuit stimulated by an alternating voltage. Its rms value, I_{rms}, with respect to its peak value, I_{pk}, is related to a dc current, I_{dc}, as follows:

$$I_{rms} = \frac{I_{pk}\sqrt{2}}{2} = I_{dc}$$

Thermal Converters

Joule's law states that a resistor dissipates the power produced in it by a voltage or current as heat. The heat is produced in direct proportion to the power, and the resistor attempts to dissipate it into the ambient surroundings. When heat is generated at a greater rate than it is dissipated, the temperature of the resistor increases until the rate of heat production equals the rate of dissipation. Under this condition, the resistor's temperature is stabilized.

When a dc value is applied to the resistor, there is a lag between the time that the value is applied and the time at which the resistor's

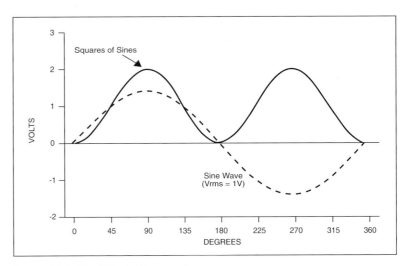

Figure 10-2. *Sine Wave Voltage and Power*

temperature stabilizes. The interval is a function of the thermal time constant of the resistor. A quantitative discussion of the thermal time constant is beyond the scope of this chapter, but can be conceptually understood as being qualitatively similar to the electrical time constants of dc circuits that contain inductance or capacitance in series with a resistance. See Chapter 12, "Inductance and Capacitance," for information on electrical time constants.

When an ac current flows in a resistor, heat is produced in proportion to the instantaneous power in a cycle, going from zero to a peak twice during one cycle of the current. If the cycle time of heat production is much faster than the rate of heat dissipation, the temperature of the resistor will increase until it stabilizes. Under this condition, its temperature will be proportional to the average power in it.

When the temperature of a resistor heated by a direct current is the same as when it is heated by the average power of an alternating current, the rms values of the ac and dc are equal. A two-port device that (1) contains a resistor whose temperature is a function of an ac or dc input, and (2) supplies a dc output proportional to the temperature, is called a *thermal converter*.

AC-DC metrology is organized around thermal converters that have nearly identical outputs to the heat produced in their resistors by the ac and dc voltages or currents at their inputs. A thermal converter is called a thermal voltage converter (TVC) when it is used to measure voltage and a thermal current converter (TCC) when it is used to measure current.

An ideal thermal converter has a true square law response as indicated by the transfer function depicted in Figure 10-3. Note that the output curve is a parabola, a function of the square of the input.

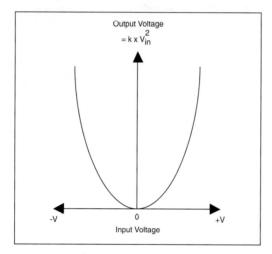

Figure 10-3. *Transfer Function for True RMS Sensing Device*

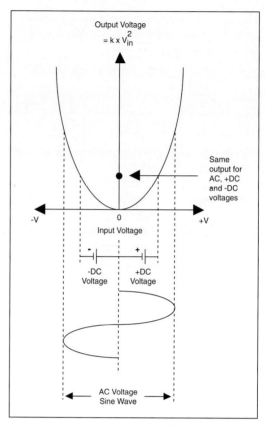

Figure 10-4. *Sensor Output vs. Input*

Square law considerations apply to all thermal converters. Deviations from the true square law response are one factor that can cause a difference in their response to ac and dc signals. Figure 10-4 shows how a true square law device would provide the same dc voltage output for +dc, –dc, and ac voltage inputs.

Any deviation from the true parabolic transfer function on either side of the figure's X axis zero would cause differences in the converter's dc output.

The two most widely-used types of thermal converters are the solid-state true rms sensor and the single-element vacuum thermocouple converter (SEVTC).

The multijunction thermocouple (MJTC) and the log/antilog converter are less widely used in ac-dc transfer devices. The MJTC is a thermal converter, while the log/antilog converter is not. Instead, it uses operational amplifiers and transistors, as described later in the section "Log/Antilog Converters."

Fluke Solid-State True RMS Sensor

A solid-state thermal converter was introduced in the early 1970s. This device used two transistors and a diffused resistor fabricated on a single monolithic chip. To overcome a major drawback of this early solid-state thermal converter, Fluke developed a fabrication process that replaced the diffused resistor with a thin-film resistor and a thermally isolated resistor-transistor assembly on two separate silicon islands. See Figure 10-5.

The islands are supported by the beam leads from the resistor and transistor. This method yields two major benefits: (1) thermal isolation of the islands from each other, and (2) increased thermal resistance of 8000°C/W.

The circuit operates on its input voltage to provide its output voltage as follows (see Figure 10-6):

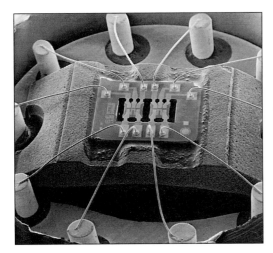

Figure 10-5. *Fluke RMS Sensor*

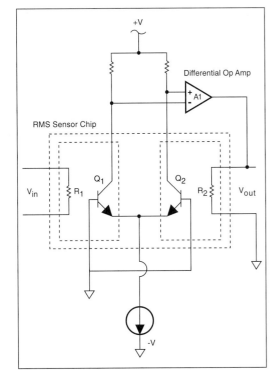

Figure 10-6. *Basic RMS Sensor*

1. $\dfrac{V_{in}^{2}}{R_1}$ heats R_1.

2. Heat in R_1 increases the temperature of Q_1's base, increasing Q_1's collector current.

3. Increased current in Q_1's collector unbalances the inverting (−) input to the amplifier.

4. The amplifier output, V_{out}, heats R_2, causing Q_2's collector current to increase, rebalancing the amplifier's input.

5. In equilibrium, $V_{in} = V_{out}$ (nominally). V_{out} is a dc voltage having the same power content as V_{in}. V_{in} can be an ac, −dc, or +dc voltage.

The relationship between the base-emitter voltage (V_{be}) and the temperature of the transistor's base-emitter junction is given by:

$$V_{be} = \frac{kT_{be}}{q} ln_{(Ic)}$$

Where:

V_{be} = base-emitter voltage

k = Boltzmann's constant

T_{be} = base-emitter temperature (Kelvin)

q = charge on an electron

$ln_{(Ic)}$ = natural logarithm of the collector current, in amperes

It can be seen from this equation that V_{be} varies directly with the temperature, T_{be}, of the base-emitter junction which is proportional to the heat dissipation in R_1 due to the power developed in it by the applied voltage, V_{in}.

In comparison to the single-element vacuum thermocouples that have been used since the 1950s, this converter has a number of advantages. These include the fact that its output voltage at full input is about 2V instead of the 7 mV or so obtained from a vacuum thermal converter. It also has a shorter thermal time constant, superior dc reversal characteristics, and greater ruggedness.

Fluke 5790A and 792A ac-dc transfer standards use this sensor. It is also used in the Fluke 5700A to enable the instrument to intercompare its ac and dc voltage outputs during artifact calibration. The sensor is also used in the Fluke 8506A digital multimeter.

Single-Element Vacuum Thermocouple Converters

The single- (or dual-) element vacuum thermocouple converter (SEVTC) has been used extensively in ac-dc transfer standards, such as the Fluke 540B. It consists of a resistive heater element and a thermocouple. See Figure 10-7.

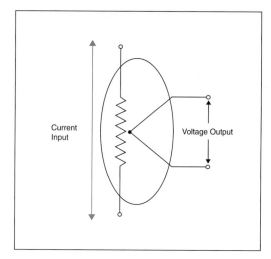

Figure 10-7. *Single-Element Thermal Converter*

Input vs. Output Voltage

Thermocouple action produces an emf proportional to the temperature of the junction of two dissimilar metals. The magnitude of the emf is also dependent on the particular metals used. The rise in junction temperature is proportional to the heat generated in the resistor. Because its output voltage is directly proportional to the heat generated in the resistor, the SEVTC is a thermal converter. Its output voltage varies approximately as the square of the input voltage, and is of an extremely low level, typically 1.75 mV to 7 mV for a 50% to 100% of full-scale span of inputs. The actual output can be expressed as:

$$V_{out} = k \times V_{in}^{n}$$

Where:

V_{out} = output voltage

k = a constant, typically ~ 0.028

V_{in} = input voltage, ≤0.5V

1.6 < n < 1.9 (typical)

Note that n is 2 in a perfect square law device. The values given indicate the empirically determined range of departure from a true square law response in SEVTCs.

In the classical method, used to detect the low-level output of vacuum thermocouples, a sensitive galvanometer is placed between the outputs of the thermal converter and a Lindeck (microvolt) potentiometer. The potentiometer's output is adjusted for a null, plus a few nanovolts, on the galvanometer (see Figure 10-8).

Note that the galvanometer's linearity is not an important consideration, due to the differential measurement that is made. The magnitude of thermal emf's in the galvanometer circuit is not directly important as long as they don't change by more than a few nanovolts during the entire sequence of ac-dc transfers. These usually consist of three pairs of transfers with negligible change in the null indication.

Construction and AC Response

The thermocouple is thermally connected to, but electrically isolated from, the mid-point of the resistive heater. The junction is attached by means of a small insulating glass bead. The thermocouple-heater assembly is supported on the four lead-in wires, two wires from the resistive heater and two wires from the thermocouple, and mounted in an evacuated glass envelope to minimize heat loss and maximize sensitivity.

The ac response of the device is a direct result of how closely the heater resistance, in combination with parasitic reactive elements, approximates a pure resistance over the frequency range of interest. As frequency increases, the capacitance and inductance associated with this resistance tend to have a greater effect on the equivalent impedance. By using compensation networks, it is possible to minimize the impedance change at higher frequencies.

Disadvantages

Vacuum thermocouples do have some intrinsic disadvantages. These include low output voltage, slow response times, and susceptibility to burnout with moderate overvoltage. Long measurement intervals and careful technique are needed to minimize the effects of drift. Low-level null detectors are used with Lindeck potentiometers to measure a thermocouple's low dc output voltage.

Any mechanical asymmetry in the thermocouple mounting results in dc reversal errors, due to the Thomson and Peltier effects discussed in Chapter 34, "AC Lore." Reversal error is the difference in a thermocouple's output voltage with direct current flowing in its resistor in one direction and then in the opposite direction. The effect of reversal error on a measurement is one-half of its magnitude. For example, if the reversal error of a thermocouple were 0.006%, then the error contributed to the measurement (without compensation for reversal error) would be equal to 0.003%. Reversal error may vary as a function of the voltage input.

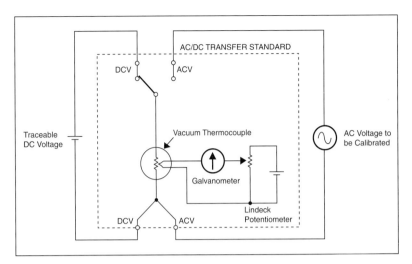

Figure 10-8. *Measuring TVC Output*

Making Transfers

Chapter 11, "Using AC-DC Transfer Standards," describes the electrical standards that are actually used to make ac-dc transfers. It also describes ac-dc transfer procedures and provides information on the calibration of the transfer standards. The following information summarizes the general theory of ac-dc transfer.

Determination of Alternating Voltage

In principle, the amplitude of an ac voltage is determined by sequentially and reiteratively applying it and a known dc voltage to the resistive input of a TVC. The dc voltage is adjusted until the TVC's output voltage is unchanged when the input is switched between the dc and ac voltages. When this condition is met, the traceable value of the known dc voltage at the input is transferred to the ac voltage. See Figure 10-8. In principle, the ac voltage and dc voltage should then be exactly equal.

Reversal Error and AC-DC Difference
The thermal response of practical devices to ac, +dc, and −dc voltages is usually different. The difference in the response to +dc and −dc voltages is the *reversal error* and is determined by sequentially applying a +dc and a larger or smaller −dc voltage that gives the same response as the +dc on the transfer standard. The average

of the absolute values of the forward and reversed dc voltages is used as the nominal dc value. The difference in response to the average dc and the ac is the ac-dc difference and a correction factor, conventionally symbolized by δ, is used to compensate for it. The sign of δ is such that more ac than dc is required for the same output voltage when δ is positive. Consequently, an ac voltage equals the known average dc voltage plus δ. When the average dc voltage value and δ are traceable to a national laboratory, the ac-dc transfer standard measured ac voltage is also traceable. The value of δ for a specific transfer standard is determined and reported by either a national or traceable secondary laboratory.

Determination of Alternating Current

Alternating current is measured by applying a current through a shunt that has a small ac-dc difference. The shunt is placed directly across a TVC's input. The shunt's voltage drop appears across the TVC's input and is measured as a voltage.

Fluke A40 and A40A shunts have a small ac-dc difference and can be used to make transfer measurements with a wide range of sensors or converters. Note that the absolute value of the shunt resistor is not important in a transfer measurement because the dc current provides the reference voltage for the sensor or converter. Resistance values are seldom assigned to ac-dc current shunts. The Fluke Y5020 is an exception.

Methods for determining the magnitude of alternating current are detailed in Chapter 11, "Using AC-DC Transfer Standards."

Frequency Effects

Most thermal converters have a frequency sensitive response. Characteristics change below 10 Hz, from 10 to 40 Hz, from 40 Hz to 20 kHz, and above 20 kHz.

Below 10 Hz
If the ac frequency is very low, relative to the thermal time constant of the converter, the temperature of a thermal converter's resistor tends to follow the instantaneous power in it. Under these conditions the output of a SEVTC will at ever lower frequencies tend to become a sine wave that reproduces the power waveform at twice the frequency of the applied ac voltage. The output of the Fluke rms sensor will also tend to follow the input power. At very low frequencies, this will usually render the transfer standard unusable.

10 Hz to 40 Hz
Between 10 Hz and 40 Hz, most thermal converters continue to partially integrate and partially follow the temperature of their resistor. The transfer standard is usable in this region with increased uncertainty.

40 Hz to 20 kHz
At any frequency above 40 Hz, most thermal converters have a stable output. For frequencies ranging from 40 Hz to 20 kHz, frequency-dependent errors for most thermal transfer standards are negligible. In multi-range instruments, there is some frequency dependence, due to skin effect in the internal wiring and dielectric loss inherent in individual range resistors.

Nevertheless, an ac-dc difference due to thermal rather than circuit considerations occurs at these frequencies. A number of factors cause the ac-dc differences. In solid-state sensor-based standards, the difference can be due to slight departures from a true square law response over the operating range of the rms sensor.

Above 20 kHz
At frequencies above approximately 20 kHz, several factors contribute to frequency-dependent errors. Capacitance, dielectric loss, inductance, and skin effects are the predominant contributors. These kinds of errors are discussed in Chapter 33, "A Rogues' Gallery of Parasitics."

Other AC-DC Devices

A number of other devices can be used to make ac-dc transfers. One of these is the multijunction thermocouple converter (MJTC), a true thermal device. Non-thermal devices include the log/antilog converter as well as electrostatic and electrodynamic instruments.

Multijunction Thermocouple Converters (MJTC)

A multijunction thermocouple converter (MJTC) has a much better transfer function than a SEVTC. It has a single heater whose heat is sensed by many series-connected thermocouples. See Figure 10-9.

The thermocouple outputs are connected in series, providing an output voltage of about 100 mV at full scale. The basic advantage of this approach is an increase in the thermoelement output voltage. Also, multiple thermocouples reduce the dc reversal error by reducing the sensitivity to their placement on the heater and by operating at lower temperatures. In effect, the output voltage of an MJTC represents the average temperature along the length of the heater.

However, the mechanical constraints of constructing a device with large numbers of thermocouple elements limits the output to values less than one volt. Like the SEVTC, it suffers from electrical and mechanical fragility, and is difficult to construct. Careful testing and selection are required to ensure adequate performance.

Uncertainties in the ac-dc difference of less than 1 ppm are claimed for frequencies up to 5 kHz, increasing rapidly at higher frequencies.

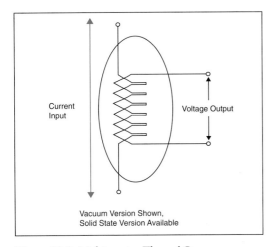

Figure 10-9. *Multijunction Thermal Converter*

The cost and frequency response of these hand-made elements have largely precluded their commercial use. Efforts are under way in several national laboratories to fabricate thin-film multijunction thermal converters using modern microcircuit technology to solve the problems of cost and frequency response.

Log/Antilog Converters

A log/antilog converter's output is equivalent to the true rms of the input voltage even though a temperature measurement is not made. In fact, its operation is based on the same equation that is used for the Fluke rms sensor but it operates on the ac input in the logarithmic domain. It first obtains the logarithm (log) of the instantaneous ac or dc input voltage as $2\log V_{in}$, where V_{in} is the input voltage. It integrates these values to obtain their mean, V_m. Finally, it provides an output that is the antilog of $0.5\log V_m$. Chapter 17, "Digital Multimeter Calibration," gives a more detailed discussion of its operation.

Electrostatic and Electrodynamic Instruments

The direct measurement of an ac emf can be obtained by using devices whose physical operation is based on electrostatic or electrodynamic principles. Accordingly, their indications are a direct measurement of the emf. These devices are normally used for measuring ac voltages of very high amplitude (100 kV to 1 MV). Due to lack of sensitivity, they are not generally used for measurements within the millivolt to 1 kV range. These devices inherently provide a square law response.

Electrostatic methods depend (for their operation) on the force between charged conductors, and are considered by some as the only true rms voltage responders. Instruments using this technique are inherently sensitive to vibration and require relatively high voltages for adequate sensitivity. High currents can be measured by measuring the voltage drop across a shunt.

An interesting example of a combination of electrostatic and electrodynamic techniques is the *ring electrodynamometer* developed by NBS, now NIST. This device suspends a conducting ring in the space between the center and outer conductors of a coaxial line. The period of oscillation of the ring is a function of both the electrical and magnetic fields within the line. The device has an uncertainty of approximately 0.1% at frequencies to 30 MHz.

Electrodynamic instruments depend on the force between current-carrying conductors. They are useful as transfer instruments over a range of frequencies for which the average torque is the same with direct and alternating currents. Such instruments are capable of about 0.1% uncertainty at frequencies up to about 1 kHz.

Key References

Agy, David L., "Alternating Voltage Metrology: Thermocouple to RMS Sensor," Measurement Science Conference, January, 1989

Szepesi, Leslie, L., Jr., "Recent Developments on Solid State Thermal Voltage Converters," Measurement Science Conference, January, 1986

Stott, Harold, L., Jr., "A Multirange Standard for AC/DC Difference Measurements." IEEE *Transactions on Instrumentation and Measurement*, Vol. IM-35, No. 4, December, 1986

Other references for this chapter are in the Resources Appendix.

Chapter 11:

Using AC-DC Transfer Standards

This chapter discusses the key features and operation of several models of both rms sensor-based and vacuum thermocouple-based transfer standards. It also presents information about the calibration of the transfer standard itself.

This chapter summarizes the typical sequence of test events during a thermal transfer, describes proper test lead hookups, and notes error sources to be aware of. The chapter emphasizes the use of the Fluke rms sensor-based 5790A and 792A. It provides some information about the classical vacuum thermocouple-based Fluke 540B and Holt® Model 11. Chapter 34, "AC Lore," contains additional information on classical applications of vacuum thermocouple-based transfer standards.

There are a number of models of ac-dc transfer standards in use today. Table 11-1, at the end of this chapter, compares the major capabilities of four of the models.

The solid-state sensor-based models 5790A and 792A were introduced in the early 1990s. The older, vacuum thermocouple-based 540B (no longer available from Fluke) and Holt Model 11s are widely deployed and have been in use for many years. Their technology was developed in the 1950s from work done at NBS (now NIST).

All of these ac-dc transfer standards are basically designed to make voltage transfers. The solid-state sensor-based units have built-in millivolt ranges, in contrast to the vacuum thermocouple units whose lowest ranges are in the 0.5V to 1.0V region. Current shunts can be used with all of the models for current calibrations. Other accessories are available for the vacuum thermocouple models to extend their areas of application.

Types of AC-DC Transfer Standards

There are two widely-used kinds of thermal transfer standards, those based on the Fluke rms sensor, and those based on vacuum thermocouple technology.

Fluke RMS Sensor-Based Standards

In comparison to vacuum thermocouple-based transfer standards, Fluke rms sensor-based standards are easier to use, have a greater number of self-contained voltage ranges, and allow the completion of transfers at higher voltages in a minute or less on all ranges.

Fluke 5790A

The 5790A, shown in Figure 11-1, is a completely self-contained, microprocessor-controlled, automated ac measurement standard. Its operator push button selects its mode of operation to make ac voltage measurements, ac-dc voltage transfers, and various current measurements. Fluke Models A40 and A40A current shunts can be used with it to make ac-dc current transfers. It can be computer controlled via the IEEE-488 bus or an RS 232 data link.

Figure 11-1. *Fluke 5790A Automated AC Measurement Standard*

In its voltmeter mode, an unknown ac voltage can be applied to either of its two type N input connectors. The 5790A will automatically scale the voltage and compare it to an internally-generated dc reference voltage. This mode of operation is very accurate and requires no operator intervention to accomplish the measurement.

In its voltage transfer mode, the operator connects the ac and dc sources to its inputs. The operator needs only to reverse the polarity of the applied dc when making the transfers. The 5790A automatically computes and uses the average value of the forward and reversed dc during the transfer. NIST-traceable test-reported ac-dc differences, indicated in this chapter by the symbol δ, are stored internally in the 5790A's firmware for use by its micro-processor.

Fluke 792A
Compared to vacuum thermocouple-based devices, the Fluke Model 792A, shown in Figure 11-2, dramatically reduces the time required to make highly accurate, manual ac-dc transfers.

This is especially noteworthy when making transfers at 200V and above. The improvement in performance is obtained by use of the Fluke rms sensor and Fluke thin-film resistors, and by placing the high voltage input resistor in close thermal contact with an efficient heat sink. The designs of the thin-film resistors and the heat sink virtually eliminate errors due to power and voltage coefficients in the divider's resistor, allowing very high accuracy transfers of up to 1000V to be made in a minute or two instead of in half an hour or more as with the older, vacuum thermocouple-based units.

The 792A's settling time and transfer time are short and stable, so one can make a number of measurements before having to recheck the reference. One must supply a 6½-digit DMM to monitor the direct voltage output of the 792A's rms sensor. The output of the 792A is approximately +2V at full-range input on any range, and is linear with the alternating voltage input rather than varying as the square of the ac voltage input.

A DMM that measures ac voltages and currents can be used to pre-measure the ac voltage or current in order to facilitate the selection of the 792A range. The 792A is protected against damage from the inadvertent application of an over-voltage on any range. If the DMM is IEEE-488 bus-compatible, it can be used with a computer to semi-automate the transfers. The computer can automatically add the correction factor for the ac-dc difference to the DMM's reading.

Vacuum Thermocouple-Based Standards

The vacuum thermocouple has been used for many years in high quality ac-dc transfer standards. The long history of vacuum thermocouple-based standards is reflected in the fact that

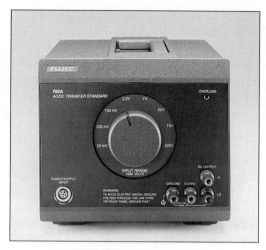

Figure 11-2. *Fluke 792A*

NIST-supplied reports of calibration for the Holt Model 11 show very low uncertainties (to 5 ppm) in its stated ac-dc difference.

However, the application of the vacuum thermocouple can be quite demanding when implementing the conceptually simple technique of making ac-dc transfers, especially when high voltages are being measured. Patience is required because numerous controls are reset time and again until the unit thermally stabilizes. Then the transfer must be quickly and accurately accomplished.

Due to the long thermal time constant of the thermocouple and range resistors, the reference voltage may need to be applied continuously for 30 minutes or longer before the standard reaches thermal stability. Then, due to minute-to-minute temperature instabilities, the ac-dc balance of the inputs must be confirmed by three transfers made in less than a minute.

Fluke 540B Manually-Operated Units
The 540B, depicted in Figure 11-3, is a self-contained transfer standard.

A large number of these standards are used today by skilled technicians. This unit includes separate inputs for voltage, current, and rf voltage measurements. A number of front panel controls are used to facilitate ac-dc transfers. The unit is overload-protected, and includes a low accuracy ac voltmeter used to assist its operator in selecting the proper range.

The 540B's basic range is its 0.5V range. The lowest input it can accurately measure is 0.2 volts, 40% of the 0.5V range. The 40% of range limitation applies to the other ranges, so its voltage range structure has a 0.5, 1.0, 2.5, 5.0 . . . sequence up to 1000V maximum. Its basic frequency range is 5 Hz to 1 MHz. Model A55 thermal voltage converters are used with it to measure voltages with frequencies of up to 50 MHz. Model A40 and A40A shunts are used with it to measure current.

The 540B's built-in meter measures the ac voltage at its input in order to assist the operator in choosing the proper range. This meter is average-responding, not true rms-responding, and it doesn't respond to the dc component of the input. Its reading can be substantially low if it is measuring a non-sinusoidal signal with a large dc component.

Fluke A55 UHF Converters
Fluke A55 converters use a uhf pattern thermocouple. The heater of a uhf pattern thermocouple is basically a straight, short wire that exhibits a constant resistance with small reactance to frequencies as high as 100 MHz. The A55s were designed to be used with the 540B to measure up to 50 volts at up to 50 MHz. They are not compatible with the 5790A or 792A. Each A55 is a stand-alone thermal converter, having a range resistor in series with its thermocouple.

A55s have nominally 200 ohms per volt input impedance. External impedance-matching resistors can be placed across their input to provide an effective impedance of 50Ω at frequencies to a few hundred kilohertz. The shunt capacitance of an A55 causes the effective impedance to go down as frequency is increased and is most noticeable in A55s with the higher voltage ratings.

In practice, an A55 is plugged into a mating receptacle on a 540B. The unknown ac and known dc voltages are manually connected to its input in the proper sequence. The 540B's normal controls are used in the conventional manner to measure the A55's thermocouple output. A55s don't have overload protection.

Holt Model 11 Coaxial Thermal Converters
The Holt model 11 is a system of coaxial ac-dc

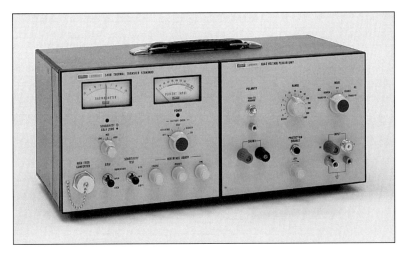

Figure 11-3. Fluke 540B

transfer components. The coaxial components are plugged together to make transfers. The coaxial construction of its components greatly reduces the effects of parasitic capacitance. This system gives excellent results when used by a patient, careful, and skilled technician.

The coaxial component set consists of three thermal voltage converters plus five ranging resistors, for a total of 18 separate voltage ranges. The converters are rated for 1V (2.5 mA), 2V (5 mA), and 4V (10 mA). The five ranging resistors scale the fundamental ranges by ×3, ×10, ×30, ×100, and ×300, up to a maximum input of 1200V. Frequency response is specified from 20 Hz to as high as 30 MHz. The vacuum thermocouple outputs for the thermal voltage converter (TVC) are nominally 7 mV, measured by additional equipment, such as a nano-voltmeter.

A true rms-responding, 3½-digit DMM can be used to preselect the proper range for measuring the approximate amplitude of the voltages or currents to be applied in order to select the proper range on the standard.

AC-DC Voltage Transfers

There are three generic types of transfers:

■ Adjusting an ac voltage or current relative to a known dc voltage or current

- Measuring an ac voltage or current relative to a known dc voltage or current

- Comparing two or more ac voltages or currents

The basic procedure for making ac-dc voltage transfers is to alternately apply a known dc voltage and the ac voltage to be measured to an ac-dc transfer standard's thermal converter through appropriate scaling circuitry. This procedure is outlined in Figure 11-4.

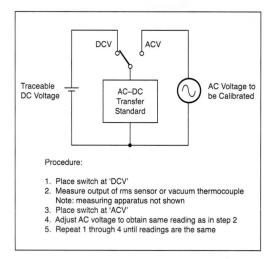

Procedure:

1. Place switch at 'DCV'
2. Measure output of rms sensor or vacuum thermocouple
   Note: measuring apparatus not shown
3. Place switch at 'ACV'
4. Adjust AC voltage to obtain same reading as in step 2
5. Repeat 1 through 4 until readings are the same

Figure 11-4. Simplified AC-DC Transfer

The known dc voltage corrected for reversal error and the ac-dc difference, δ, of the transfer standard, is the true value.

TVCs respond differently to positive and negative dc voltages. This behavior causes what is known as dc reversal error. Reversal error is eliminated during the measurement by taking the average of the forward and reverse supply voltage. The ac-dc difference is given on a test report for the transfer standard as the percent (or ppm) difference of the ac response of the standard with respect to its dc response and is defined as:

$$\delta = \frac{V_{ac} - V_{dc}}{V_{dc}}$$

Where:

δ = ac-dc difference

V_{ac} = rms value of ac voltage

V_{dc} = average of the absolute values of a dc voltage applied in a forward and reverse direction across the transfer standard

δ is reported in either percent (%) or parts per million (ppm). In the equations herein, it is treated as having been converted to a decimal fraction. To convert the reported value of δ to a decimal fraction, divide it by 10,000 when it is given in percentage or 1,000,000 when it's in ppm and drop the units. For example, if δ is reported as −50 ppm, its converted value is −0.00005. If its reported value is +0.01%, its converted value is 0.0001.

NIST-traceable test reports state the ac-dc differences at various voltages and frequencies. Note that the ac-dc differences on a given range and for a given frequency may be different for full-range and down-range inputs. NIST Technical Note 1166, "The Practical Uses of AC-DC Transfer Instruments," provides a comprehensive discussion of ac-dc differences.

The converted value of ac-dc difference, δ, is applied to ac-dc transfers as a correction factor in such a way that:

$$V_{ac} = V_{true} = V_{dc}(1 + \delta)$$

Except for 5790A applications, δ is applied as a correction factor for the dc voltage value by the operator of the transfer standard. The operator reads this value from a test report for the transfer standard and manually offsets the setting of the dc voltage value from nominal by the appropriate amount. The 5790A stores the values of δ for each reported point in its internal memory and automatically uses them when making transfers.

To properly perform the transfer, the plane of reference for the measurement and the effects of the associated connectors and cables must be considered.

Plane of Reference

In any measurement, a plane is defined as its reference position. See Figure 11-5. For very accurate measurements, it is important to define this plane of measurement. Anything that affects the voltage, current, or phase of the

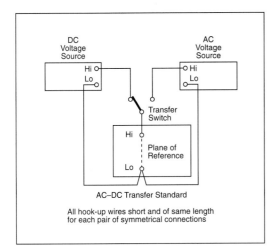

Figure 11-5. Plane of Reference

ac value to be measured must be defined if the measurement is to be duplicated and repeatable. Cables and interconnects can cause errors. Therefore, the cabling and interconnects used in a setup should be carefully planned for accurate and repeatable measurements, as discussed under "Avoiding Transfer Errors" later in this chapter.

For most calibrators, the plane of reference is at its output binding posts. The effects of cabling and interconnects from the binding posts of the calibrator to the input connectors of the ac-dc transfer standard must be taken into account when evaluating the results of the measurement.

Frequency Response

The response of a transfer standard varies with frequency mainly because of the effects of parasitic capacitances. In a lumped parameter model, these can be considered as being in parallel with the resistive element, or from the body of the resistive element to some other circuit conductor such as ground. Figure 11-6 illustrates two parasitic capacitances, C_{Prr} in parallel with the Range Resistor and C_{Pte} in parallel with the Vacuum Thermocouple of a 540B.

Careful design, including the use of frequency compensation techniques for resistive dividers as described in Chapter 13, "Immittance and AC Ratio," minimizes the effects of these parasitic capacitances. But, as the frequency

increases, their effects ultimately prevail and they limit the usefulness of the transfer standard above some upper frequency. Frequency response is the major contributor to the ac-dc difference at higher frequencies.

Making the Transfers

The following sections cover the procedures used to accomplish various categories of transfers with the Fluke 792A. A user-supplied 6½-digit DMM is used with the 792A to measure its 0 to 2 volts dc output.

Vacuum thermocouple-based transfer standards can be used to make these measurements, but their operation is more difficult because of the need to repetitiously adjust low-level potentiometers for a null on a specialized low-level null detector. The instruction manuals for these standards describe how to make the adjustments.

The basic models of these standards are limited to a minimum input of 200 mV although micropots and other external equipment can be used with them to extend their calibration capabilities down to the low millivolt area. In terms of today's technology, the additional equipment is cumbersome to use.

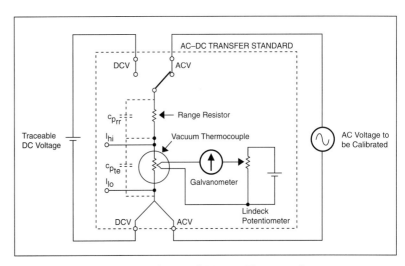

Figure 11-6. Range Resistor in Series with Vacuum Thermocouple

Using the 792A Between Calibration Points

These detailed discussions assume that an ac calibrator and a dc calibrator will be used to apply voltages to the transfer standard.

NIST calibrations of the 792A are obtained at a large number of voltages and frequencies, and strictly speaking, the uncertainty reported by NIST applies only within ± 1% of voltage and ± 1% of frequency. However, as with any instrument which operates over a range of voltages and frequencies, the instrument is calibrated at relatively few voltage-frequency points, and values at other points are obtained by interpolation between calibration points.

In the 792A on the 2.2 volt range and above, frequency response is related to a combination of square-root of frequency and frequency-squared. At lower frequencies, from 100 Hz to about 300 kHz, the dominant effect is skin effect, which increases as square root of frequency. Above about 300 kHz, the frequency-squared effects begin to dominate. These result from the effects of small residual inductances and capacitances in the circuitry.

The frequency response is independent of voltage level at frequencies between about 100 Hz and 300 kHz. At higher frequencies, heating of attenuator resistors can cause small changes in residual reactances, which changes δ. That is to say, ac-dc differences above about 300 kHz can be affected by voltage level. This dependence is proportional to voltage-squared, since it is related to the power dissipated in resistors. In the 792A, these effects are much smaller than the uncertainty of the calibration, and can usually be ignored.

AC-DC differences below about 100 Hz result from the fact that more heat is lost from the heater resistor at maximum power than at minimum power. At frequencies of 100 Hz and above, the time between maximum and minimum power is short enough that the temperature of the heater is essentially constant. At lower frequencies, the temperature tends to track the input signal (at twice frequency) and the temperature peaks are flattened as more heat is lost at voltage maximum than at minimum. This flattening lowers the average

power generated in the sensor, and more ac than dc is required for the same output signal (positive δ).

These low frequency effects are proportional to voltage-squared, being related to the power dissipated in the heater resistor. They are also proportional to $1/f^2$ where f is the frequency in Hz. Acceptably accurate interpolations between frequencies and/or levels can be made using this information.

For lower voltage levels, where amplifiers are used to bring signals to a level compatible with thermal sensors, frequency and level response are determined by amplifier characteristics. In these cases, the general rules for interpolation do not apply. A relatively safe approach is to use linear interpolation between adjacent calibration points, and to increase the uncertainty if the difference between the two points is comparable to the largest assigned uncertainty.

The general rule for assigning uncertainties to values obtained by interpolation between calibration points is to assign the larger of the two uncertainties to the result. The 792A's specified uncertainty varies as frequency-squared below 100 Hz, so uncertainties in this frequency range may be interpolated using the same rule as is used for interpolating between values.

Preparing to Make Transfers

Gather the needed equipment and connect it together with the appropriate cables. Perform the transfers as described.

Adjust the Amplitude of an AC Voltage
To adjust the amplitude of an ac voltage, follow these steps:

1. Select the proper 792A range.

2. Apply a known dc voltage to the 792A's dc input. Note that the known voltage is the nominal voltage multiplied by (1+δ), where δ has been converted to its decimal equivalent as previously described. Reminder: δ may be either positive or negative.

3. Let the DMM's reading stabilize for the time required for the range being used (as specified in the 792A instruction manual) and record the reading.

4. Reverse the dc voltage input.

5. Record the stable DMM reading with the reversed dc voltage input.

6. Compute the average of the absolute values of the two DMM readings.

7. Apply the ac voltage from the ac voltage source to the 792A.

8. Adjust the amplitude of the ac voltage for a DMM reading equal to the average value computed in step 6.

Due to the stability and repeatability of the solid-state rms sensor used in the 792A, it is not necessary to repeat any of the steps. At the end of step 8, the rms value of the adjusted ac voltage equals the value of the average of the forward and reversed dc voltage, including the ac-dc difference, δ.

Measure the Amplitude of an AC Voltage
To measure the amplitude of an ac voltage, follow these steps:

1. The approximate value of the ac voltage must be known to select the proper 792A range. If it isn't known, measure it with any rms-responding, dc-coupled DMM.

2. Set the 792A to the proper range for measuring ac voltage. Turn the power supply "on."

3. Apply the unknown ac voltage to the 792A's input. If the voltage is too high for the range, an alarm will sound. Switch up to higher ranges until the alarm stops on the proper range. The DMM measuring the 792A's output will read between 0.6 and 2 volts.

   Note: The 792A won't be damaged by this procedure. It is protected against overloads for inputs of up to 1000V rms.

4. Let the DMM reading stabilize, and record it.

5. Apply a dc voltage appropriate for the 792A range.

6. Adjust the dc voltage until the DMM reading equals its reading in step 4.

7. Record the DMM reading for step 6.

8. Reverse the dc voltage input, then record the stable DMM reading.

9. Compute the average DMM reading of the forward and reversed dc voltage.

10. Readjust the dc voltage source until the average value of the forward and reversed voltages equals the ac voltage reading taken in step 4.

11. Repeat steps 3 through 10 until the DMM readings of the ac voltage and the average value of the forward and reversed dc voltages are equal.

12. Determine the correct value of the ac voltage by applying the ac-dc correction factor, δ, to the average value of the dc voltage. The ac voltage is the dc voltage times $(1+\delta)$. If δ is positive, the ac voltage is larger than the dc voltage. If δ is negative, it is smaller.

Compare the Amplitude of Two AC Voltages
When measuring approximately equal voltages at several frequencies, time and effort can usually be saved by comparing them to the voltage at some convenient frequency (1 kHz, for example) then measuring that voltage by an ac-dc transfer. With the reference voltage known, the voltage at different frequencies can be calculated. The time saving comes from the fact that only one ac-dc transfer is required.

To compare the amplitudes of approximately equal voltages at different frequencies, follow these steps:

1. Apply the unknown ac voltage to the 792A's input.

2. Record the stabilized DMM reading as V_1.

3. Adjust the frequency to the reference frequency (for example, 1 kHz), and adjust

the amplitude for a DMM reading near V_1. (Or, set the amplitude to provide a known voltage at the reference frequency.)

4. Record the stabilized DMM reading as V_2.

5. The value of V_{unk} in terms of V_{ref} is:

$$V_{unk} = V_{ref}\left[\frac{V_1(1+\delta_{unk})}{V_2(1+\delta_{ref})}\right]$$

where δ_{unk} and δ_{ref} are known ac-dc differences at the frequency of the test voltage and at the frequency of the reference voltage, respectively. Reminder: δ may be either positive or negative.

6. If the value of V_{ref} is not known, make an ac-dc transfer to determine its value, then complete the calculation.

A similar approach can be taken to measure the relative accuracy (flatness) of a voltage source. Starting with a reference level and frequency, adjust the source to provide the desired frequencies, maintaining the level setting constant. Record the reading of the 792A DMM at each frequency. Flatness (in percentage) is computed from:

$$\text{Relative Flatness}\,(\%) = \left[\frac{V_1(1+\delta_{test})}{V_2(1+\delta_{ref})}\right] \times 100$$

where V_1 is the DMM reading at the test frequency and V_2 is the DMM reading at the reference frequency. The ac-dc differences are obtained from the 792A Test Report.

These tests rely on the 792A DMM being linear over the range of voltages which will be encountered. If the linearity of the DMM is in doubt, the Differential Method, discussed below, should be considered.

Notes on Using a DMM with the 792A

The DMM used to monitor the 792A's dc output voltage must be capable of measuring approximately 0.2V to 2V. It should have at least 6½ digits, with 1 µV of resolution, for direct measurement of the voltage. A differen-

tial measurement can be made by using a 4½-digit or 5½-digit DMM in conjunction with an accurate dc voltage source. In this case, the DMM should be able to resolve a dc voltage change of 1 µV on its most sensitive range.

When the direct method is used, the DMM must have extremely good linearity over the range of 792A output voltages that occur during the ac-dc transfers.

For example, suppose you want to measure the ac-dc difference of 0.7V inputs to 5ppm or better. Due to the effects of the test-reported ac-dc differences, δ, of the 792A, ac and dc inputs of identical amplitude may yield 792A outputs whose amplitudes differ by up to 0.02% (140 µV) from each other around the expected 0.7V nominal value.

For best results, make sure that the DMM used as a detector has a linearity of around 1 or 2 ppm of input over the 0.02% span of 792A outputs it measures. In some instances, the small-scale linearity of a DMM may not be specified by its manufacturer. If not, you can experimentally find the linearity of the DMM by comparing its readings to a range of inputs supplied by a very linear dc calibrator, such as Fluke Models 5700A or 5440A/B. Otherwise, you can use the differential method discussed next.

In the differential method, the DMM measures the difference of the 792A's output and the output of an extremely stable, linear dc source (see Figure 11-7).

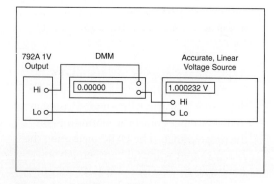

Figure 11-7. *Differential Measurement of 792A Output*

In this configuration, the DMM is used as a differential null detector, and so its linearity is of little significance to the measurement.

However, the linearity of the dc voltage source is important.

Using Shunts for AC-DC Current Transfers

The same generic kinds of ac-dc calibrations are performed for current as for voltage, the only difference being that the external apparatus consists of constant current dc and ac sources instead of voltage sources. The resistance element of the shunts need not be very accurate because the shunt's ac-dc difference at various frequencies is used as a correction factor for the ac current measurement, relative to the accurate dc current source.

Fluke Models A40 and A40A current shunts are accessories for the 540B, 792A, and 5790A. They are used to calibrate ac currents greater than 5 mA. Their full-scale current ratings extend from 10 mA to 20A in a 1, 2, 5 sequence. Their frequency response is typically 0.02% to 20 kHz, 0.03% to 50 kHz, and 0.05% to 100 kHz. Characterization data is available for the shunts; use of the ac-dc difference data from a NIST test report allows a reduction of the uncertainties to as little as 20 ppm for frequencies up to 20 kHz.

A40s are designed to be used directly across the 540B's 90Ω vacuum thermocouple. An external adapter is used with the 5790A and 792A to supply an input resistance of 90Ω on their

0.7V ranges. The adapter draws about 5mA of current at full scale and therefore looks somewhat like a vacuum thermocouple to the shunt.

Using the A40s with the 540B is depicted in Figure 11-8. (Using the A40s with the 792A and 5790A is similar except that the adapter is placed across the voltage terminals, the shunt is connected to the adapter, and the transfer standard is used on its 0.7V range.)

In this configuration the resistance of the shunt in parallel with the 90Ω thermocouple heater resistance establishes a current divider which causes rated current to flow through the heater resistor when full-scale current is flowing in the external shunt. The voltage drop across the parallel-connected current shunt and heater resistor is between 0.2V to 0.5V for currents between 40% and 100% of the shunt's rating.

When using a shunt with the 540B, it is best to calibrate the shunt with the 540B it will be used with because the 540B draws 5 mA of the total current. It is acceptable to use a shunt with a different 540B if you algebraically add the ac-dc differences for the shunt and the transfer standard.

The shunt adapter and the shunt should be calibrated together when the shunt is used with the 5790A or 792A. The shunt and adapter can be used with any 5790A or 792A. This is because the high input impedance (10 MΩ) on the 700 mV ranges of these standards does not

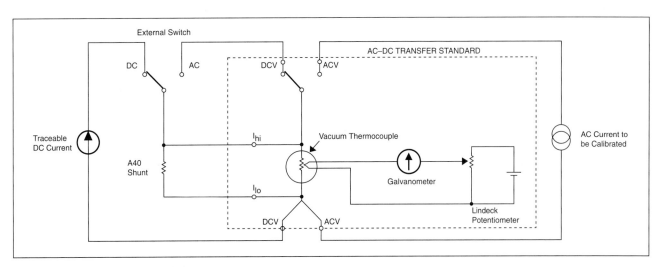

Figure 11-8. Using A40 Shunt with 540B

draw significant amounts of current when connected in parallel with the shunt current.

Avoiding Transfer Errors

Transfer errors can be caused by:

- Improper test configurations
- Poor hookups
- Parasitic reactances
- Signal contamination
- Insufficient settling time

The following information will help avoid errors from these sources. For further information, consult Chapters 33, "A Rogues' Gallery of Parasitics," and 32, "Grounding, Shielding and Guarding."

4-Terminal Connections

During voltage transfers, up to 5 mA of current from the ac and dc sources flows through test leads, switches, connections and the transfer standard. When 2-terminal connections are used, the voltage drops that occur along the signal path will cause the voltage across the plane of reference to be different from the output voltages of the sources. In addition, it is unlikely that the voltage drops in the ac and dc paths will be equal. Four-terminal (4-T) connections are used to make sure that the signals at the plane of reference faithfully reproduce the outputs of the sources. Figure 11-9 illustrates a 4-terminal connection.

In current transfers, common error sources include leakage around one or more sensors, thermal voltages, and inductive coupling between source and sense leads. Unwanted inductive coupling is the dominant error source at high frequency and at high current. This coupling can be minimized by using well-shielded, twisted-pair leads and by making sure source and sense leads are at right angles to one another. This problem can often be detected by moving one set of leads and watching for a change in output.

Connector Considerations

There may be one or more connectors between the transfer standard's signal input and the plane of reference. These can have parasitic effects that degrade the accuracy of transfers. The principal parasitic effects are:

- Unequal contact resistance in the dc and ac paths
- Series inductance and shunt capacitance in the ac path
- Thermal emf's in the dc paths

Connectors can also have peak voltage ratings that limit the maximum amplitude of voltage which can be applied to them.

GR 874-Type Connectors
GR 874-type hermaphroditic connectors were adopted by NBS as the standard for the plane of reference of its calibration reports. These connectors have a great deal of mating surface area and they are compatible with sine wave voltage inputs to 1200V rms. The gold-plated models, whose coaxial contact is soldered to the center conductor of the connecting cable, have insignificant connector-induced errors.

Type N Connectors
After a thorough evaluation of many types of connectors, including the GR 874-type, Fluke selected type N connectors from a specific vendor for use with the 792A and 5790A. The selected connector has extremely low and repeatable contact resistance and is compatible with sine wave voltage inputs to 1000V rms.

UHF Connectors
UHF connectors, as supplied on the 540B's ac voltage input, offer repeatable contact resistances and good high-frequency performances.

5-Way Binding Posts
5-way binding posts using spade lugs provide repeatable contacts, but are prone to thermal voltage generation unless binding posts and lugs are made from the same material. Banana plugs provide less repeatable contact resistance and the nickel-plated type will generate large thermal emf's when plugged into gold-plated or copper jacks. Tellurium copper binding posts and mating banana plugs, used for the 792A, limit thermal voltages to less than 1 µV.

The connections for the Fluke 792A have eliminated much of the problem since its switch is connected to its transfer unit via a type N connector, but the ac and dc sources are connected to the transfer switch via tellurium copper binding posts.

Hookup Considerations

Transfer accuracy is easily degraded by inadequate attention to detail regarding the cables used to interconnect the transfer standard, the ac and dc calibrators, and other devices. The contact resistance of the connectors used on the cables should be low to avoid voltage drop errors similar to the ones previously noted. In addition, the connectors should present a low thermal emf when mated to the connectors used in the various dc paths. Their internal series resistance and their shunt capacitance should be low.

Electromagnetic interference (emi) and radio frequency interference (rfi) can be particularly troublesome with low current thermal elements. The thermocouple in the 540B is encased in a steel shield to minimize stray field pickup. Strong fields can still interfere with the very low level dc output voltages of single-element vacuum thermocouples. Solid-state sensors, used in the 792A, have a much higher output voltage and are much less susceptible to errors from this type of interference. EMI/RFI interference can be detected by changing cable lengths and positions. Short coaxial leads should be used when possible, especially at high test frequencies.

Various guarding, grounding and shielding schemes can also be used. Guarded coaxial cables, with the guard leads tied to the transfer device's guard terminal and to the ac or dc source's guard terminal, may give the best results. Ground loops are eliminated by having just one point where guard and ground are connected. If the transfer device does not have separate guard and ground terminals, then the source's guard should be connected to the transfer device's LO input terminal.

Parasitic Reactances
Parasitic shunt inductance is the most significant cause of frequency related ac-dc differ-

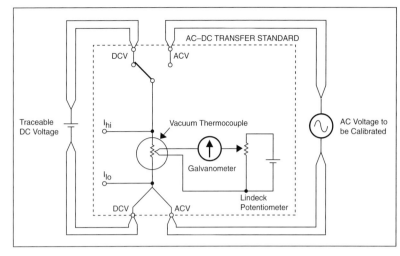

Figure 11-9. 4-Terminal Connection

ences in current measurements. Shunt capacitance in a well designed shunt, such as the A40, has very little effect because of the small resistance of the shunt element. For example, shunting the 10 mA shunt and the 540B thermal element with 10 pF will cause an error of only 5 ppm at 1 MHz.

While inductance is the most significant cause of frequency-related ac-dc difference in current measurements, both inductance and capacitance affect voltage measurements. Capacitance shunting the input and attenuator resistors and lead and component inductance will affect the frequency response of the instrument.

The operator has no control over these parasitics. Proper design and construction are required to control these elements.

Distortion and Noise

Distortion and noise on an ac waveform can affect the accuracy of the measurement of the signal. Distortion of ac signals, usually specified in percent, is defined as the degree to which the signal deviates from a pure waveform. Noise is more loosely defined, generally referring to low frequency and broadband noise, as well as bursts of noise associated with the ac signal. In modern electronic ac sources, some high frequency noise is always present due to the use of digital electronics.

In the strictest sense, all the harmonics and noise associated with a particular signal make up the true rms value of that signal. The bandwidth of the measurement device is what determines the number of harmonics and the amount of noise that are measured as part of the signal. The wider the bandwidth of the measurement system, the more harmonics and noise will contribute to the magnitude of the measured signal.

While a wide bandwidth in the measurement system can permit noise-related errors in sine wave measurements, wide bandwidth is essential for accurate measurement of signals containing significant harmonics, such as square waves. Therefore, the metrologist must be sure he is measuring what he thinks he is.

Transfer Standard Calibration

AC-DC transfer standards are usually calibrated at a national laboratory, or a well-equipped primary laboratory traceable to the national laboratory. The following information considers key elements of these calibrations.

AC-DC Difference

AC-DC differences are usually given in parts-per-million (ppm) or percent. AC-DC difference is a function of the ac performance of the scaling circuits and the associated switching in addition to the basic characteristics of the thermal element used in the transfer standard.

The ac-dc differences, δ, of a transfer standard are determined by comparing its performance with another transfer standard whose ac-dc differences are known. The equipment and techniques required for this calibration are so demanding that only a few laboratories perform the calibration. Calibration services that measure and report δ are available from national laboratories and the manufacturers of the transfer instruments. Even the well-equipped laboratories and the manufacturers of transfer standards who can calibrate δ must ultimately

use a transfer standard whose ac-dc differences have been determined by a national laboratory such as NIST.

NIST test reports of the ac-dc difference for transfer standards are defined as applying at the center of a "TEE" connector, specifically a GR874 TEE. The dot in the center of the TEE connector in Figure 11-10 is the plane of reference.

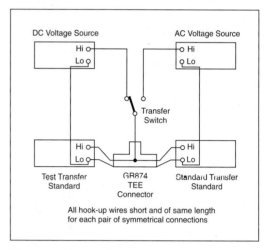

Figure 11-10. *NIST Setup*

In this configuration, the distance from the center of the TEE to each transfer standard must be nearly equal, to minimize the differences in the voltage drops for each path. In addition, the distances should be short, to reduce frequency response errors due to lead inductance and capacitance.

Range Intercomparison by Half-Scale Bootstrapping

A variation of the classical half-scale bootstrapping method of calibration is used by the 5790A to extend the calibration of its 70 mV range down to its 2.2 mV range. The classical technique is used to intercompare the various modules of the Holt Model 11. The 5790A method will be summarized here, and the classical method will be described briefly.

5790A Method

1. The 22 mV output of an ac source is applied to the 70 mV range of the 5790A. The 5790A's reading is noted by its operator.

2. The setting of the ac source is not disturbed and the 5790A is switched to its 22 mV range. The 5790A reading, recorded in step 1, is entered in its firmware from its front panel by its operator. The 5790A automatically compares its internally measured value of the 22 mV input voltage with the entry and obtains a correction factor for the internal measurement that makes its reading equal to the entered reading.

3. This correction factor is used for all inputs on the 22 mV range.

4. The output of the ac source is set to supply 7 mV to the 22 mV range of the 5790A. The 5790A's reading is noted by its operator.

5. Steps 2 and 3 are repeated with the 7 mV input from step 4 being applied to the 5790A's 7 mV range.

6. Step 4 is repeated with 2.2 mV applied on the 5790A's 7 mV range.

7. Steps 2 and 3 are repeated with the 2.2 mV input from step 4 being applied to the 5790A's 2.2 mV range.

Classical Method

In the classical method, a full-scale ac input is calibrated via an ac-dc transfer on the lowest range of the transfer standard. The output of the dc standard is noted. Then the ac value is applied as a half-scale input to the next higher transfer standard range. An ac-dc transfer is made. The output of the dc standard is noted and compared with its previous value. The two dc outputs should be equal.

One limitation in this process is the assumption that the TVC has linear frequency response between half scale and full scale. If the assumption is incorrect, an unknown error has been introduced into the process. Also, half-scale input measurements can be affected by noise as well as by the low sensitivity of the detecting circuitry. At higher frequencies, the changes of impedances associated with changes in the voltage range being used can affect the plane of reference of the measurement.

Key References

Williams, Earl S, "The Practical Uses of AC-DC Transfer Instruments," NBS *Technical Note 1166*, October, 1982

Other references for this chapter are in the Resources Appendix.

Table 11-1. Comparison of Four Major AC-DC Transfer Standards

Parameter	RMS Sensor Based AC/DC Transfer Standards		Vacuum Thermocouple Based AC/DC Transfer Standards	
	Fluke 5790A	Fluke 792A	Fluke 540B	Holt Models 11 and 12
Configuration	self-contained	four modules Transfer Unit Power Pack 1000V Range Resistor Transfer Switch user-supplied DMM	self-contained	Model 11: 3 thermal elements (TEs) 5 range resistors (all 8 plug together) Model 12 Low Voltage micropot / TE Transfer Voltmeter
Typical Transfer Time	4 sec to 1 min	30 sec to 1 min	1 min to 30 min	1 min to 30 min
Transfer Function	linear	linear	square law	square law
Operation	automated	manual, using external DMM on 1V dc range to monitor rms sensors hi level output	manual, using internal galvano-meter to measure –10 mV output of 2 series connected vacuum TCs	manual, using external transfer voltmeter to measure 2.5, 5, and 10 mV outputs of TEs
Input Level Monitor	true rms built-in measurement for both ac and dc voltages	user-supplied DMM	built-in, ac coupled average responding, rms indicating meter	user-supplied DMM
Best Uncertainty	18 ppm	5 ppm (NIST test report) 10 ppm (Fluke test report)	20 ppm (NIST test report)	5 ppm, Model 11 (NIST test report)
Voltage Ranges	2.2 mV to 1 kV (13 ranges)	2.2 mV to 1 kV (9 ranges)	0.5V to 1 kV (11 ranges)	Model 11: 1.0V to 1.2 kV, combining range resistors and TEs Model 12: 2.4 mV to 240 mV (7 ranges)
Self-contained Ranges	all	to 220V (8 ranges)	all	Model 11: 1V only Model 12: All
External Range Resistor	none	1000V	none	Model 11: 5 Model 12: None
Minimum Useful Signal Level	600 µV	2 mV	0.25V	Model 11: 0.25V, 1V range Model 12: 800 µV, 2 mV range
Frequency Range	AC-DC Transfer Mode: 10 Hz – 20 kHz, to 1000V 20 kHz – 50 kHz to 220V Measurement Mode: 10 Hz – 100 kHz, to 1000V 100 kHz – 500 kHz, to 220V 500 kHz – 1MHz, to 70V Wideband Option: 10 Hz – 30 MHz, 0.25 to 7V	10 Hz – 100 kHz: 234 points, 2.2 mV – 1000V 300 kHz: 23 points, 2.2 mV – 200V 500 kHz, 800 kHz, and 1 MHz 57 points, 2.2 mV – 20V	5 Hz – 50 kHz, to 1000V 50 kHz – 100 kHz, to 500V 100 kHz – 500 kHz, to 50V 500 kHz – 1 MHz, to 10V	Model 11: 20 Hz – 100 kHz, to 1200V 100 kHz – 3 MHz, to 400V 3 MHz – 30 MHz, to 40V Model 12: 20 Hz – 100 kHz, to 200 mV
Current	0.25 mA – 20A using A40 & A40A shunts	0.25 mA – 20A using A40 & A40A shunts	0.25 mA – 20A using A40 & A40A shunts	via CS1 shunts across thermocouple
Overload Protection	yes	yes	yes for voltage; no for current	no
Programmable	IEEE–488 and RS–232	no	no	via Holt 6B calibrator

Chapter 12:

Inductance and Capacitance

This chapter discusses the definition, realization, and representation of standard inductors and capacitors. It considers how inductors and capacitors react to voltages and currents in dc and ac circuits both individually and in combination with each other and resistors.

This chapter addresses the theoretical aspects of inductance and capacitance. It describes the principles of construction for standard inductors and capacitors, and identifies the principal parasitics associated with them. The chapter also considers the behavior of inductors and capacitors in dc and ac circuits. In conjunction with Chapter 8, "DC Resistance," and Chapter 9, "DC Ratio," it lays the groundwork for Chapter 13, "Immittance and AC Ratio."

Inductance and capacitance are inherently present in electrical conductors and dielectrics. Artifacts can be constructed that are excellent inductors and nearly perfect capacitors. The value of the inductance or capacitance is a function of the relative geometry and the materials used in their construction. For this reason, standard values of inductance and capacitance are calculated from the physical dimensions of the objects that represent them.

The SI units of inductance and capacitance are, respectively, the henry (H) and the farad (F), and they affect the behavior of both dc and ac circuits. Fundamental realizations of these units at the national level employ artifacts called the "calculable inductor" and "calculable capacitor."

In this chapter, rectangular and polar notation and vectors are used for the mathematical treatment of reactance and impedance. Operator *j* is used as the symbol for the imaginary number *i*, the square root of minus 1. In mathematics, *i* is used to symbolize this root, but in electricity and electronics *j* is substituted in order to avoid confusion with the symbol *i* used for current.

Understanding reactance and impedance is important to fully understanding the calibration of workload equipment such as watt and watt-hour meters, phase meters, complex ratio bridges, LCR meters, capacitance and inductance bridges, resistive voltage dividers, and current shunts. Such knowledge is also important for calibrating standard capacitors, inductors, and impedance bridges.

Inductance

Inductance is the property of an electrical circuit that opposes any change in the magnitude of the current flowing in the circuit. Energy is stored in the magnetic field associated with a current flowing in the circuit. When the current changes, a voltage is induced into the conductor by the magnetic field. The polarity of the induced voltage acts to oppose the change in current, and is therefore called a "counter emf."

There are two types of inductance: self-inductance and mutual inductance. Self-inductance causes the counter emf in the circuit carrying the current. Mutual inductance causes a voltage to appear (be induced) in another circuit. The conductors of the other circuit can be physically isolated but magnetically coupled to the circuit that contains the inducing current. The behavior of inductors such as current chokes results from self-inductance. A transformer's operation results from mutual inductance.

SI Definition of Inductance

The henry (H) is the SI unit of inductance. The henry is derived from the volt (V), second (s), and ampere (A), via the weber (Wb), the SI unit of magnetic flux, and is defined as follows:

$$1H = \frac{1\,Wb}{1A}$$
$$1\,Wb = 1V \times 1s$$

In other words, the self-inductance of an inductor of one henry reacts to a current flowing through it whose amplitude is constantly changing at the rate of one ampere per second by producing a voltage across it whose amplitude is constantly equal to 1V. This is shown in Figure 12-1.

Similarly, a one-henry mutual inductance in a transformer produces a constant 1V output across the secondary when the current flowing in the primary is changing at a constant rate of one ampere per second.

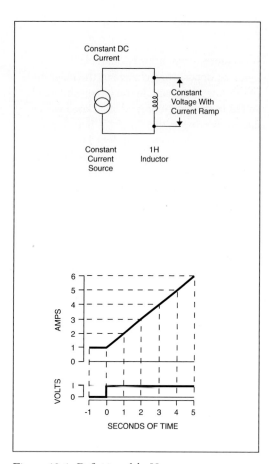

Figure 12-1. *Definition of the Henry*

Standard of Inductance

A calculable standard of inductance can be obtained by constructing a solenoid on an insulating core. A solenoid is a coil whose length is greater than its radius, as shown in Figure 12-2.

The solenoid's wire should be of uniform cross-sectional area and composition, and its turns should be of uniform diameter and spacing. When these constraints are met, the inductance of the solenoid can be calculated from its dimensions as follows:

$$L = \frac{4\pi^2 \times 10^{-7} N^2 r^2}{S}$$

Where:

L = inductance in henries

N = number of turns in the solenoid

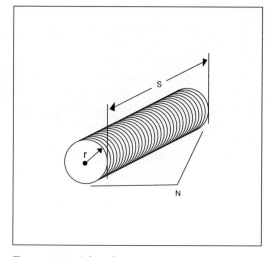

Figure 12-2. *Solenoid*

r = radius of solenoid in meters

S = length of solenoid in meters (very much larger than r)

There are difficulties associated with implementing this procedure. These are primarily due to the effects of mechanical stresses in the wires and the insulating core, and the shielding of the inductor from external electromagnetic fields. Moreover, it is much easier to construct extremely accurate standard capacitors, and use them to assign values to inductors. Consequently, experiments to construct standard realizations of inductance at the national primary level are infrequent.

Traceable Standards of Inductance

A laboratory can have several values of commercially available standard inductors. These are usually four-terminal devices that should be returned to NIST every two years or so for calibration against the NIST working standards for inductance. The best NIST uncertainty for inductance calibrations is ±0.02%. The associated NIST test report demonstrates that their traceability is up to date.

Time Constant of Inductance and Resistance in DC Circuits

When a constant dc voltage, V, is applied across a series-connected inductor, L, and resistor, R, the current, I, increases exponentially from zero to a maximum value equal to the voltage divided by the total series resistance, including the dc resistance of the inductor. This is shown in Figure 12-3.

The expression for the increase in current versus time, t, is:

$$I = \frac{E}{R}\left(1 - e^{-(tR/L)}\right)$$

Where:

e = base of natural logarithms

E = applied emf in volts

R = resistance in ohms

t = time in seconds

L = inductance in henries

The curve in Figure 12-3 illustrates the increase in current. This curve is a universal time constant curve in which the time constant is defined as L/R. When t equals L/R, the current has reached about 63.2% of its final value. In each additional interval of t, the current in the inductor increases by 63.2% of the difference between the current at the beginning of the interval and the current at the end of 15 or more multiples of t (the current is within 0.3 ppm of its final value at $t \times 15$).

The relationship of t, R, and L means that inductors can be used with resistors in precision timing circuits and LR oscillators. However, this is not usually done because less bulky capacitors can be substituted for inductors and used for the same purpose.

Inductive Reactance in AC Circuits

When a pure sine wave of voltage, V, is applied across a pure inductor, a pure cosine wave of current, I, flows in the inductor (see Figure 12-4).

A cosine wave has the same shape as a sine wave but, in the circuit described, lags the voltage that is applied across the inductor by 90°.

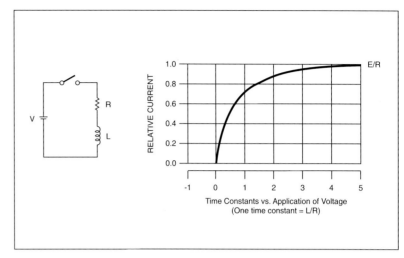

Figure 12-3. *Constant Voltage Across Series Resistance and Inductance*

In other words, the maximum value of current through the inductor occurs when the changing ac voltage across the inductor is passing through zero volts. The cosine wave of current induces a sine wave of counter emf in the inductor. The counter emf is 180° out of phase with the applied emf. It continuously reacts against the changing current to oppose its change.

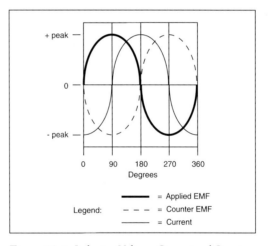

Figure 12-4. *Inductive Voltage, Current and Counter EMF*

The relationship of the voltage and current in an ac circuit is usually represented by vectors. For this reason, vector diagrams rather than sine wave plots will be used here to illustrate phase and amplitude relationships in ac circuits. Figure 12-5 illustrates the vector relationship of the current and voltages shown in Figure 12-4 as sine waves in a pure inductance.

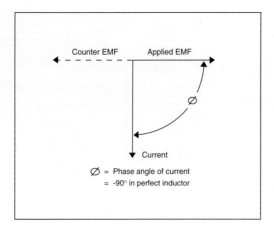

Figure 12-5. *Inductive Voltage and Current Vectors*

The result of the reaction of the counter emf to the applied emf is that the current flowing in the inductor is less than it would otherwise be if limited solely by the inductor's resistance. This characteristic of an inductor is its inductive reactance, X_L, and is equal to:

$$X_L = 2\pi f L$$

Where:

f = frequency of the applied sine wave of voltage in hertz

L = inductance of the inductor in henries

The magnitude of the rms current, I_{rms}, through the inductor is:

$$I_{rms} = \frac{E_{rms}}{X_L}$$

Note that this expression describes the relationships of the amplitudes of the quantities in the same form as the relationship of dc voltage, current, and resistance in Ohm's law. This expression does not define the phase relationship of the voltage and current. Nevertheless, it is important to keep in mind that the current is a cosine wave which lags the voltage by 90° and that the average power consumed by an inductance is zero.

It is impossible to construct a pure inductance. The wire used in constructing an inductor will have some resistance per unit of length. This resistance will act as though it were in series with the inductance. In addition, there will be capacitance across the inductor and between

its turns. Figure 12-6 illustrates parasitics in a practical standard inductor.

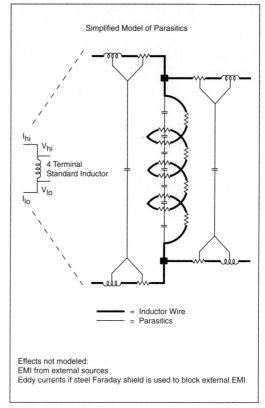

Figure 12-6. *Parasitic Capacitance and Resistance in Inductors*

The ratio, Q, of a coil's inductive reactance to its series resistance provides a figure of merit for the inductor. Q is defined as:

$$Q = \frac{X_L}{R}$$

In metrology, the inductance, L, and the Q of primary, secondary, and working standard inductors are calibrated as described in Chapter 13, "Immittance and AC Ratio." For inductors used in audio frequency applications, these values are obtained at one or more standard frequencies, such as 100, 400, 1000, and 10,000 Hz. The measurements involve an impedance determination where both the amplitude and phase of the voltages and currents are evaluated to obtain the inductor's L and Q.

A complete method for expressing the phase angle and magnitude of the currents and voltages in circuits that contain resistance, inductance, and capacitance is given in Chapter 13, "Immittance and AC Ratio." Connection methods are also provided there under the subheading "Connectors and Hook-Up Considerations."

Capacitance

Capacitance is the property of an electrical circuit that opposes a change in the magnitude of the voltage across the circuit. Capacitance refers to the ability of a conductor to store charge in its conductors and associated dielectric and thus store energy in an electric field.

There are two general categories of capacitors: electrostatic and electrolytic. Electrostatic capacitors are constructed to use vacuum, gas (that is, air or nitrogen), ceramic, or liquid dielectrics. Electrostatic capacitors don't need to have a polarizing dc voltage applied across them. In contrast, electrolytic capacitors feature a metallic oxide film dielectric and require a polarizing dc voltage for their operation. Further discussion in this chapter is limited to electrostatic capacitors.

SI Definition of Capacitance

The farad (F) is the SI unit of capacitance. The farad is derived from the volt (V), second (s), and ampere (A), via the coulomb (C), the SI unit of electric charge, and is defined as follows:

$$1F = \frac{1C}{1V}$$

$$1C = 1A \times 1s$$

In other words, a one-farad capacitor reacts to a constant current of one ampere by continuously increasing the voltage across it at a constant rate of one volt per second (see Figure 12-7).

Realization of the Farad

A realization of the farad is obtained by constructing a calculable capacitor. Figure 12-8 illustrates the principle of operation for the Thompson-Lamphard "cross-capacitor."

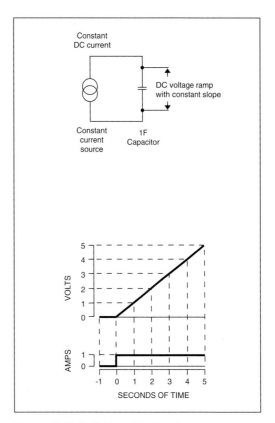

Figure 12-7. *Definition of the Farad*

In this simplified drawing, four rigid rods are placed in a frame so that they are at the vertices of a rectangle when viewed end on. The two diagonally opposite sets of rods each constitute one capacitor. These are C_1, between rods A and B, and C_2, between rods C and D.

When the rods have nearly the same diameter and their lateral and diagonal spacing is nearly the same, the average capacitance, $(C_1 + C_2)/2$, per meter of length of the diagonally opposite pairs of rods is constant to a high degree of accuracy for any set of rods, even when there are small variations in their spacing and cross sectional areas. The constant, average value of the capacitance is given by:

$$\overline{C} = \epsilon_0 L \left[\frac{\ln 2}{\pi} \right] \left[1 + .087 \left(\frac{(C_2 - C_1)}{\overline{C}} \right)^2 \right] + \ldots$$

Where:

$$\overline{C} = \frac{(C_1 + C_2)}{2}$$

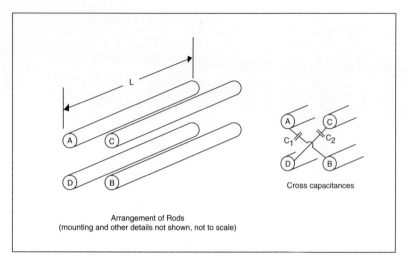

Figure 12-8. *Cross Capacitor*

L = distance between ground rods in meters

$$\epsilon_0 = \frac{1}{\mu_0 c^2}$$

μ_0 = permeability of the vacuum

c = speed of light in a vacuum

0.087 = a constant, *k*, due to deriving this equation from cgs system of units

. . . = symbolizes fourth order and higher terms of the form

$$0.087\left(\frac{(C_1 - C_2)^n}{\overline{C}}\right)$$

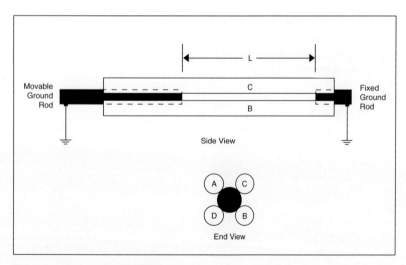

Figure 12-9. *Reducing End Effects with Movable Ground Rod*

The fourth-order and higher-order terms can be disregarded and the capacitance is about 2 pF/m. So, the cross-capacitance of the rods serves as a capacitance standard with a highly accurate capacitance per unit length.

"End effects" distort electrical fields in the areas near the ends of the rods, and invalidate the calculations. For this reason, in one version, one fixed and one movable ground rod are inserted between the pairs of rods, as illustrated in Figure 12-9.

A change in capacitance is obtained by displacing the movable ground rod relative to the fixed rod. The displacement is measured by a laser interferometer. If the ends are separated enough, there is no interaction between end effects, and the change in capacitance can be accurately calculated. In another version, "guard" sections are added at the ends of the active sections to maintain nearly uniform fields throughout this active portion of the capacitor.

In contrast to inductors, capacitors are rather easily shielded from the effects of external electromagnetic fields. Figures 12-8 and 12-9 omit shielding for clarity. The uncertainty of the farad as realized is ±0.015 ppm (1σ) relative to the SI definition.

Traceable Standards of Capacitance

A laboratory can have several values of commercially available standard representations of capacitance. These are usually three-terminal, hermetically sealed capacitors with nitrogen dielectrics, as schematically depicted in Figure 12-10.

In this figure, terminals A and B are the input and output of the standard capacitor, while terminal C is a Faraday shield whose application is discussed under "Immittance Calibration" in Chapter 13, "Immittance and AC Ratio."

These parallel plate capacitors usually have C_{std} values of up to 1000 pF, but larger values are available.

Before the cross capacitor, calculable capacitors were constructed as in Figure 12-11. In these

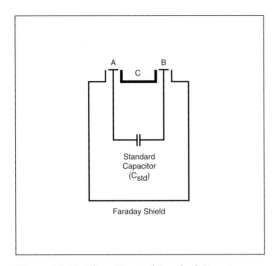

Figure 12-10. *Three-Terminal Standard Capacitor*

capacitors, edge or "fringing" effects make the calculation invalid near the edges.

In order to greatly reduce fringing effects, a guard ring surrounds the active plates (see Figure 12-11). As in the case of the calculable cross-capacitor, their value, C, in picofarads, will be calculated from the area of the plates from:

$$C = 8.8583\left(10^{-4}\right)\frac{Ak}{t}$$

Where:

A = area of active plate shadowing bottom (ground) plate in square millimeters

t = distance between active and ground plate in millimeters

k = a constant, ≈ 1 for air or vacuum dielectric

In these capacitors, the capacitance is uncertain by the small amount of fringing which will occur at the guard ring. The calculable cross capacitor can be known to much better accuracy than a parallel plate capacitor, but the available capacitance is small, about 2 pF.

Five-terminal standard capacitors with air dielectrics are also used. The two additional terminals permit a kelvin (four-terminal) connection to be made. Current is applied to the capacitor via a pair of terminals, and its voltage drop is measured by the other pair. The shield is used as in a three-terminal standard.

Standard capacitors should be returned to NIST every two years or so for calibration against the NIST working standards for capacitance. At the time this is written, NIST uncertainty is ±0.5 ppm for 1000 pF at 1 kHz. The associated NIST test report demonstrates up-to-date traceability. The standards can be compared locally using the ratio techniques discussed in Chapter 13, "Immittance and AC Ratio."

Time Constant of Capacitance and Resistance in DC Circuits

As shown in Figure 12-12, when a constant dc voltage, V, is applied across a series-connected capacitor, C, and resistor, R, the voltage across the capacitor, V_c, increases exponentially from

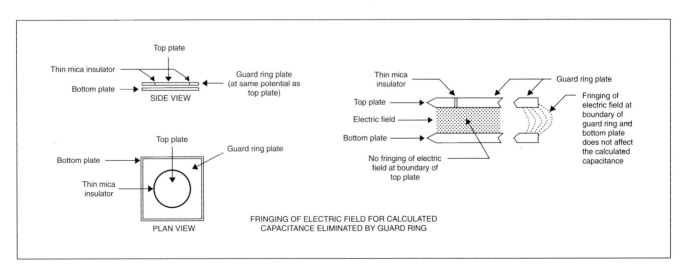

Figure 12-11. *Reduction of Fringing Effects*

zero to a maximum value equal to the applied voltage, V. The expression for the increase in the capacitor's voltage versus time, (t), is:

$$V_c = V\left(1 - e^{-(t/RC)}\right)$$

Where:

e = the base of the natural logarithms

V = applied emf in volts

t = time in seconds

R = resistance in ohms

C = capacitance in farads

The curve in Figure 12-12 illustrates the increase in the capacitor's voltage.

This curve is a universal time constant curve. In this curve, the time constant is defined as RC. For t equal to RC, the voltage across a capacitor whose initial value was zero volts reaches 63.2% of its final value at the end of the initial interval t. In each additional interval of t, the voltage across the capacitor increases by 63.2% of the difference between the voltage at the beginning of the interval and the voltage at the end of 15 or more multiples of t (the voltage is within 0.3 ppm of its final value at t × 15).

The relationship of t, R, and C is used in various electronic circuits, such as timing circuits,

RC oscillators, and operational integrators and differentiators.

Capacitive Reactance in AC Circuits

When a pure sine wave of voltage is applied across a pure capacitor, a pure cosine wave of current flows in the capacitor. The analysis for the relationship between the current and voltage is similar to the one given previously for an inductor except that the current leads the voltage by 90°.

The net effect is to produce a capacitive reactance, X_c, equal to:

$$X_C = \frac{1}{2\pi f C}$$

Where:

f = frequency in Hertz

C = capacitance in farads

The magnitude of the rms current, I_{rms}, that flows back and forth in the conductors connecting the capacitor's plates is:

$$I_{rms} = \frac{E_{rms}}{X_C}$$

Note that as in the case for inductance, the amplitudes of the quantities in this relationship are expressed in the same form as the relationship of dc voltage, current, and resistance in Ohm's law. Also keep in mind that the current is a cosine wave which leads the voltage by 90°.

In contrast to an inductor, constructing a nearly perfect capacitor is relatively easy. Figure 12-13 illustrates both the construction and parasitic qualities of a practical three-terminal capacitor.

The dielectric of the standard capacitor will have a high value of leakage resistance, r_d, around the plates of the capacitor. At a single frequency, r_d behaves as a small value of resistance in series with the capacitor. However, it is better to model this loss as a conductance ($G = 1/r_d$) which does not vary with frequency. The capacitor's connection leads have small

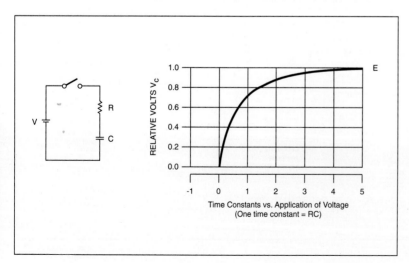

Figure 12-12. RC Time Constant

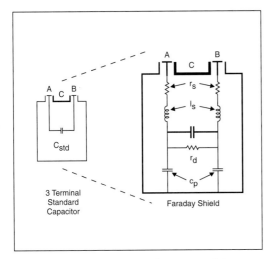

Figure 12-13. *Parasitics of a Three-Terminal Capacitor*

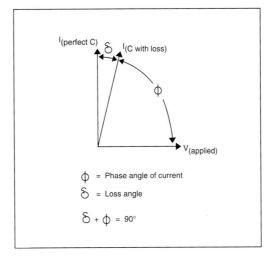

Figure 12-14. *Phase Relationship of Voltage and Current in a Capacitor*

series resistance, r_s, and inductance, l_s. Finally, there is parasitic capacitance, c_p, from the connection leads and the plates of the capacitor to the Faraday shield.

The Faraday shield isolates the electric field of the standard capacitor from the influence of external electric fields. The electric potential on the Faraday shield can be controlled to nullify the effects of the parasitic capacitances. In addition, the leads can be constructed to minimize the effect of lead resistance and inductance over a wide range of test frequencies.

Figure 12-14 illustrates the phase relationships of the voltage and current in a capacitor with losses primarily due to the effects of parasitic resistance.

The effect of losses in a high quality electrostatic capacitor is small, and can be described in three different ways:

1. Power Factor, $PF = \cos \phi = W/IV$

Where:

ϕ = angle by which I leads V when both are sine waves

W = watts

I = rms amperes

V = rms volts

2. Dissipation Factor, $DF = \tan \delta$

Where:

$\delta = 90° - \phi$

3. Quality Factor, $Q = 1/DF = \dfrac{2\pi fC}{G}$

Where:

G = conductance in Siemans (see Chapter 13)

The parasitic resistances in Figure 12-13, when combined at a specific test frequency, yield an equivalent series resistant, R_{esr}.

In this case, PF can be computed as

$$PF = R_{esr} \frac{\sqrt{R_{esr}^2 + X_c^2}}{R_{esr}^2 + X_c^2}$$

Note: R_{esr} varies with frequency.

In metrology, the capacitance, C, and one or more of the loss factors *PF*, *DF*, or *Q* of primary, secondary, and working standard capacitors are calibrated. For capacitors used in audio frequency applications, these values are obtained at one or more standard frequencies, such as 100, 400, 1000, and 10,000 Hz. The measurements involve an admittance determination where both the amplitude and phase of the voltages and currents are evaluated to obtain the capacitor's value, C, and its loss factors (see Chapter 13, "Immittance and AC Ratio").

A complete method for expressing the phase angle and magnitude of the currents and voltages in circuits which contain resistance, inductance, and capacitance is given in Chapter 13, "Immittance and AC Ratio." Connection methods are also provided under the subheading "Connectors and Hook-up Considerations."

High quality electrostatic capacitors are rather easily made. The measurements of their loss factors involve sensitive measurements wherein the capacitor being calibrated must be correctly connected to the calibration apparatus for best results. In fact, determining the Q of high quality capacitors is a difficult challenge which is the subject of continuing investigation. Factors that must be understood and evaluated include the effects of series resistance; shunt resistance; dielectric losses; and the effects of surface films on the plates of the capacitor.

Comparing the Currents in Inductors and Capacitors

Figure 12-15 compares the currents flowing in the series circuits of Figures 12-3 and 12-12.

The current in the inductive circuit is zero when the switch is closed and increases to its maximum thereafter. In contrast, the current in the capacitive circuit is at its maximum when the switch is closed, and decreases to zero thereafter. These two effects are the dc counterparts of the ac current lagging the voltage in inductive circuits and leading the voltage in capacitive circuits: the maximum current lags the maximum voltage across the inductor and leads the maximum voltage across the capacitor in the dc circuits containing series resistances.

These differences reflect the fact that energy is being stored in the magnetic field of the inductor and in the electric field of the capacitor. The time constant is an indicator of the rate at which energy is being stored.

Because a pure sine wave of ac current leads or lags the voltage by 90°, no power is consumed by either a pure inductance or capacitance. Figure 12-16 provides the vector diagrams for the ac inductive and capacitive currents referred to the voltage across the device.

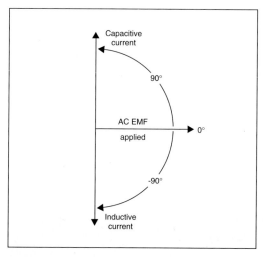

Figure 12-16. *Capacitive and Inductive Current Vectors*

Key References

Free, George; Morrow, Jerome, "Transportable 1000 pF Standard for the NBS Capacitance Measurement Assurance Program," *Precision Measurement and Calibration: Electricity*, NBS Special Publication 705, 1985.

Other references for this chapter are in the Resources Appendix.

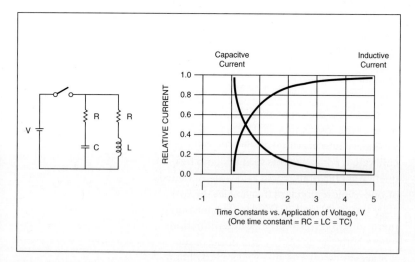

Figure 12-15. *RC, RL Current Comparison*

FLUKE®

Chapter 13:
Immittance and
AC Ratio

*This chapter defines impedance, admittance,
and immittance, and describes equipment used
to measure these parameters.*

Electrical metrology includes the measurement of ac current and ac voltage ratios. AC currents and voltage ratios are functions of the interaction of an ac voltage with the resistance, inductance and capacitance of a circuit or device, such as a ratio transformer. A mathematical understanding of how these parameters affect measurements is essential to the metrologist and involves a consideration of both the amplitude and phase of the circuit elements.

The material in this chapter considers the general relationship of voltage, current, resistance, inductance and capacitance in an ac circuit. Then it describes ac ratio standards whose performance is both based upon and constrained by these relationships.

Impedance, Admittance, and Immittance

An understanding of impedance, admittance and immittance allows one to use Ohm's law for the evaluation of ac standards. These concepts are discussed next.

Impedance

Impedance refers to the combined effects of inductive and capacitive reactance and resistance on the flow of current in a series ac circuit. The symbol for impedance is Z, and its relationship to the rms amplitudes of the sine wave voltage, E_{rms}, and current, I_{rms}, present in the ac circuit is given as:

$$Z = \frac{E_{rms}}{I_{rms}}$$

This expression gives the magnitude of the impedance but does not define the phase relationship of the voltage and current. More informative expressions of impedance are given using either rectangular or polar notation.

Rectangular notation separately states the values of a resistance and reactance connected in series. Polar notation gives the total impedance magnitude and phase angle. The phase angle is the voltage phase angle occurring when the

current is at 0 degrees. The two notations are equivalent, and whichever is most convenient should be used.

Series Connection
When a resistance, R, and reactance, X, are connected in series, the total impedance, Z, is:

Rectangular
$$Z = R \pm jX$$

Polar
$$Z = \sqrt{R^2 + X^2} \; \angle \tan^{-1}(X/R)$$

Where:

R is the series resistance, R_s,

X is the reactance, $j\left(\omega L - \dfrac{1}{\omega C}\right)$ in ohms

$j \;\; = \;\; \sqrt{-1}$

$\omega \;\; = \;\; 2\pi f$ in radians

$f \;\; = \;\;$ frequency in hertz

$L \;\; = \;\;$ inductance in henries

$C \;\; = \;\;$ capacitance in farads

Parallel Connection
When a resistance, R, and reactance, X, are connected in parallel, the total impedance, Z, is:

Rectangular
$$Z = \frac{X^2 R + jXR^2}{X^2 + R^2}$$

Polar
$$Z = XR \frac{\sqrt{X^2 + R^2}}{X^2 + R^2} \; \angle \tan^{-1}(R/X)$$

The reactance is positive for inductance and negative for capacitance.

Figure 13-1 depicts equivalent series and parallel impedances.

Admittance

Admittance, $Y = G + jB$, is a more convenient quantity for expressing the effects of resistance

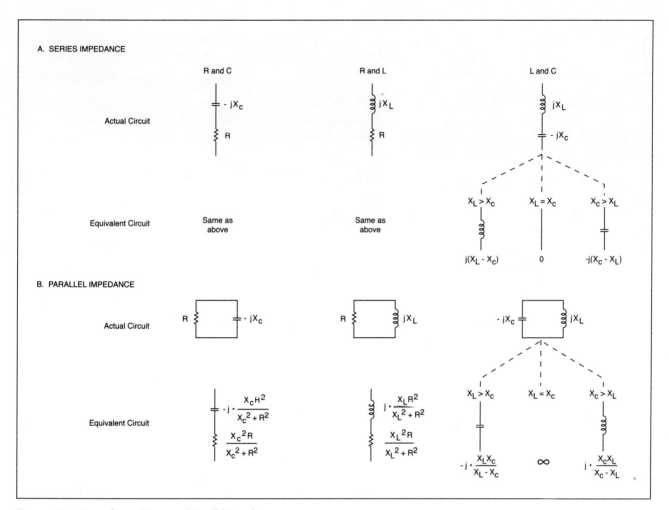

Figure 13-1. *Equivalents of Series and Parallel Impedances*

and reactance when connected in parallel. Here conductance, G, in siemens is:

$$G = \frac{1}{R_p}$$

and susceptance, B, in siemens is:

$$B = j\left(\omega C - \frac{1}{\omega L}\right)$$

Where:

R_p = parallel resistance in ohms.

Simpler algebra results from using admittance to describe parallel circuits and impedance for series circuits. Using the identity $Z \equiv 1/Y$ can simplify the analysis of circuits which contain both series and parallel elements. Current and voltage in parallel-connected circuits are related by $I = EY$.

The relationship between a series impedance, Z, and its parallel equivalent admittance, Y, is:

When: Then:

$Z = R \pm jX$ $Y = G \pm jB$

Where:

$$G = \frac{R}{R^2 + X^2}$$

$$B = \frac{-X}{R^2 + X^2}$$

Immittance

The term "immittance" is a combination of "impedance" and "admittance," and signifies that the quantity should be treated as an impedance or an admittance, whichever is more convenient.

AC Resistance

Unlike dc resistance, which is constant, ac resistance may change with frequency. This change occurs primarily because the magnetic field of alternating current flowing through the resistor tends to force the current to flow in a reduced cross-sectional area near the surface of the resistance element. Because there is less cross-sectional area presented to the current, its resistance per unit of length is greater. Thus, the resistor's resistance is not constant but increases with frequency. This phenomenon is called "skin effect."

Resistors can be designed to reduce skin effect. The effective resistance of a resistor will also change with frequency, because of the associated inductance and capacitance. This is why wirewound resistors cannot be used at high frequencies.

Immittance Calibration

As discussed in Chapter 12, "Inductance and Capacitance," it is much easier to construct and shield a standard capacitor than a standard inductor. Therefore all immittance calibration equipment based on real immittance uses a capacitor as the reactive element.

As symbolized in Figure 13-2, three-terminal capacitors are often calibrated in bridge circuits.

In this figure, the Faraday shields of the test capacitor, C_{test}, and the standard capacitor, C_{std}, are connected to the fixed tap of the tapped inductive divider. Therefore, the parasitic capacitances c_{p2} are across the tapped and fixed portion of the inductive divider. They do load the divider but they don't draw current away from C_{test} and C_{std}. Similarly, the parasitic capacitances c_{p1} shunt the null detector and may reduce sensitivity, but they don't draw current away from C_{test} and C_{std}.

Due to the guarding action of the shields, the ac current that flows in C_{test} is the same as the current that flows in C_{std}. Therefore, in this simple illustration, the value of C_{test} is:

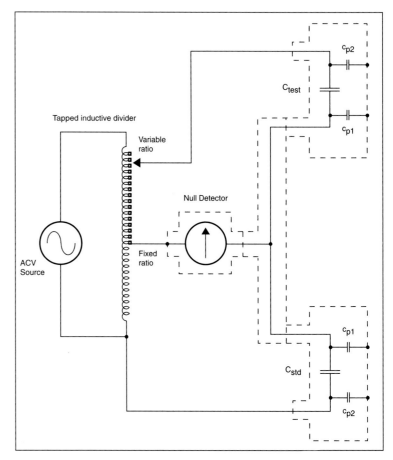

Figure 13-2. *Bridge Calibration of 3-Terminal Capacitor*

$$C_{test} = C_{std} \times \frac{\text{variable ratio}}{\text{fixed ratio}}$$

Figure 13-2 also shows that the Faraday shield is continued around all of the hook-up conductors and the null detector used for this test. Equipment used for immittance calibration often includes elaborate extensions of the Faraday shield throughout the critical circuitry in order to maintain the integrity of the capacitive elements used to obtain immittance via various ratios. For conceptual clarity, guard circuitry which is extensively used in real circuits is omitted from the figures in this chapter to illustrate the concepts of immittance calibration.

Classical Methods

The classical methods of immittance calibration use various bridges and the Q-meter. These are described next. The detector used with the bridges described here will typically be a communications receiver, or other sensitive tunable amplitude detector.

Maxwell Bridge

The Maxwell bridge, shown in Figure 13-3, is used to measure both the inductance, L_x, and series resistance, R_x, of an inductor placed between C and ground (D).

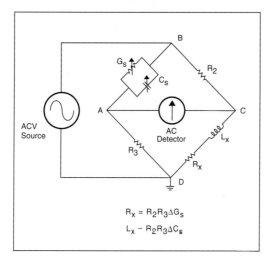

$$R_x = R_2 R_3 \Delta G_s$$
$$L_x = R_2 R_3 \Delta C_s$$

Figure 13-3. *Maxwell Bridge*

The bridge's reactance standard is a calibrated variable capacitor connected between B and A. A high-resistance, calibrated rheostat is used as a conductance standard, and is also connected between B and A. The values of R_2 and R_3 are known.

The current in the left arm (BAD) of the bridge is capacitive and the current in the right arm (BCD) is inductive. The voltage across R_3 is in phase with the current in the left arm and leads the voltage applied by the ac source. The voltage across the inductor under test, symbolized as L_x and R_x, leads the current in arm BCD and, when the bridge is balanced, is equal to and in phase with the voltage across R_3.

A short circuit is initially placed between C and D. C_s and G_s are adjusted for an initial balance and their settings are recorded. Then the test inductor is placed between C and D, and C_s and G_s are readjusted for a new balance. The changes in C_s and G_s are recorded as ΔC_s and ΔG_s, respectively, and are used to calculate L_x and R_x according to the balance equations in the figure.

Parasitic capacitance from C to D limits the bridge to operation at low frequencies or low values of inductance. Resolution and the uncertainty in the impedance of the short set the lower limit of impedance that can be measured.

Schering Bridge

In the configuration illustrated in Figure 13-4, the Schering bridge is used to measure the capacitance, C_x, and conductance, G_x, of a test capacitor placed across R_4 and C_4 (between bridge points C and D).

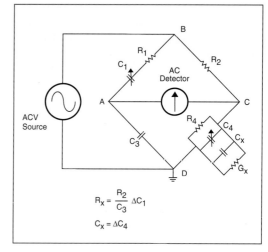

$$R_x = \frac{R_2}{C_3} \Delta C_1$$
$$C_x = \Delta C_4$$

Figure 13-4. *Schering Bridge*

The current in both arms of the bridge is capacitive and, at balance, the voltage across C_3 is equal to and in phase with the voltage across R_4, C_4, C_x, and R_x.

C_1 and C_4 are adjusted for an initial balance before the test capacitor is applied to the bridge. These settings are recorded. The test capacitor is applied and C_1 and C_4 are readjusted. The changes in their settings are recorded as ΔC_1 and ΔC_4, respectively, and are used to calculate C_x and R_x as indicated in the figure. Resolution and the uncertainty in the admittance of the open circuit set the lower limit on admittance which can be measured.

Admittance Ratio Bridge

The operation of this bridge is apparent from the diagram shown in Figure 13-5 because the impedances in the left and right arm are of the same nature from top to bottom.

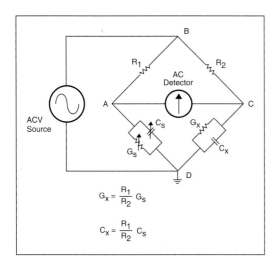

Figure 13-5. *Admittance Ratio Bridge*

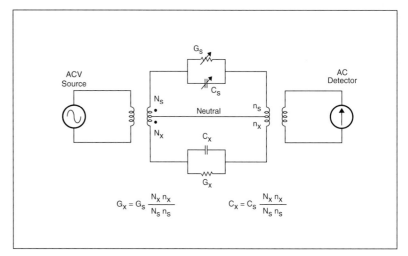

Figure 13-6. *Transformer Ratio Bridge*

C_s and G_s and the ratio of R_1 to R_2 comprise the measurement standards.

Transformer Ratio Bridge
As shown in Figure 13-6, the voltages across the input and output transformer windings are phased to produce zero volts across the ac detector when balance is obtained, via adjustment of C_s and G_s.

C_s and G_s and the ratios of N_x to N_s and n_x to n_s comprise the measurement standards.

Twin-T
Both the left and right arms of this bridge, shown in Figure 13-7, have capacitors at the top and LC tank circuits at the bottom.

Prior to connecting the test admittance, C_5 and C_2 are adjusted for an initial balance and their readings are noted. Then the test admittance of unknown capacitance and conductance, C_x and G_x, is connected and C_5 and C_2 are readjusted. The differences in their readings are used as ΔC_5 and ΔC_2 in the balance equations in the figure.

The twin-T circuit has the unique advantage that both the source and the detector, as well as both adjustable capacitors and the test admittance, all have one terminal tied to ground. This makes it easy to shield, and allows use of ordinary generators and receivers without modification. When properly constructed and adjusted, the twin-T allows resistance

(conductance) to be measured directly in terms of capacitance and frequency, $G = \omega \Delta C$.

The twin-T is not a broadband device, the capacitance balance being a function of frequency-squared.

Q-Meter
The Q-meter's variable capacitor, C, is adjusted to be in series resonance with the test inductor L_x with series resistance R_x (see Figure 13-8).

If L_x and C were perfect, V_1 and V_2 would be zero and infinite, respectively, at resonance. Under these conditions, Q would also be infinite.

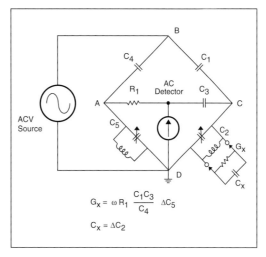

Figure 13-7. *Twin-T*

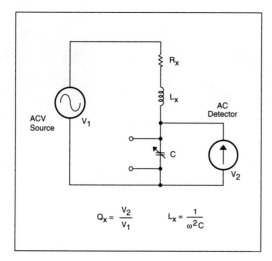

Figure 13-8. *Q-Meter*

However, the test inductor has both inductance, L_x, and series resistance, R_x. The Q-meter measures L_x as an inverse function of the product of the square of the applied frequency, ω^2 and the capacitance standard, C. It measures Q as the ratio of the measured-to-applied voltages.

Electronic Methods

LCR Meter

Figure 13-9 is a simplified diagram of a commercially available digital LCR meter.

This meter can measure L, R_p, C, Q, D, and R_s of inductors, resistors, and capacitors. In Figure 13-9, a capacitor of unknown capacitance, C_x,

and conductance, G_x, is connected to its input terminals. The measurement of these quantities is described herein. The measurement of the other quantities can be inferred from this description.

A sine wave voltage is applied across C_x and G_x, causing an ac current to flow through them into the virtual ground associated with the inverting terminal of the operational amplifier used as the current-to-voltage (I-to-E) converter. The total current flowing into the virtual ground via the test capacitor can be considered to be the sum of a real and capacitive current, as illustrated in Figure 13-10.

The real current flows through the equivalent resistance of G_x, and the capacitive current through C_x.

The feedback current to the inverting terminal from the output of the I-to-E converter is the phase-inverted value of these two currents. The I-to-E converter's output voltage is the product of the two currents and its feedback resistor. Either the voltage output of the I-to-E converter, or the voltage output of the sine wave ac source, is switched to the input of the dual-slope integrator via the phase gate. The phase gate is opened and closed by a clock signal that is either in phase or in quadrature (90° out of phase) with the ac source. The output of the dual-slope integrator is digitized by an analog-to-digital converter (adc) for display on the meter's readout.

To measure C_x, the output of the I-to-E converter is applied to the dual-slope integrator while the quadrature clock signal opens the phase gate. In Figure 13-11, the input to the integrator is indicated by the unshaded portion of the "Quadrature Gate" diagram.

As shown, the current, I_g, flowing in the test capacitor's parallel conductance path, passes through a positive and negative quarter cycle when the gate is open. Its integrated value is therefore zero. However, the dc value of a complete half cycle of the current, I_c, through the capacitor is, in effect, synchronously rectified. Its average value is obtained by integration, and is provided as a dc charge on the integrator's feedback capacitor.

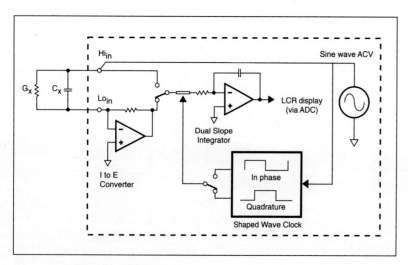

Figure 13-9. *Digital LCR Meter*

When the charge cycle of the integration is completed, the value of the dc voltage on the feedback capacitor of the dual-slope integrator is proportional to $-E\omega C_x T_1$, where E is the ac source voltage and T_1 is the integration period.

After T_1, the input to the dual-slope integrator is obtained from E when the "In-Phase Gate" is open. This causes the integrating capacitor to discharge down to zero volts. The time it takes to discharge is symbolized as T_2.

The complete charge/discharge cycle can be expressed as:

$$-E\omega C_x T_1 = ET_2$$

Therefore:

$$C_x = -\frac{T_1}{\omega T_2}$$

To measure the dissipation factor, D, of the capacitor, the output of the I-to-E converter is applied to the input of the dual-slope integrator while an in-phase clock signal opens the phase gate. In Figure 13-11, the input to the integrator is indicated by the unshaded portion of the "In-Phase Gate" diagram.

As shown, the current, I_c, flowing in the test capacitor passes through a positive and negative quarter cycle when the phase gate is open. Its integrated value is therefore zero. On the other hand, the dc value of a complete half cycle of the current, I_g, through the capacitor's conductance path, G_x, is integrated.

When the charge cycle of the integration is completed, the value of the dc voltage on the feedback capacitor of the dual-slope integrator is proportional to $-EG_x T_3$, where E is the ac source voltage and T_3 is the integration period. At the conclusion of the integration period T_3, the input to the dual-slope integrator is obtained from I_c when the "Quadrature Gate" is open. This causes the integrating capacitor to discharge down to zero volts. The time it takes to discharge is symbolized as T_4. Under these conditions, the charge/discharge cycle can be expressed as:

$$-EG_x T_3 = E\omega C_x T_4$$

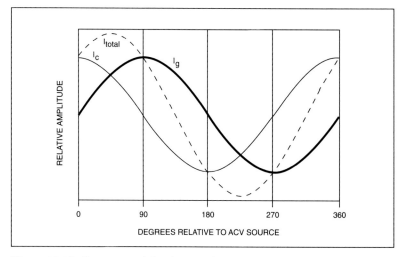

Figure 13-10. *Capacitive and Conductance Currents*

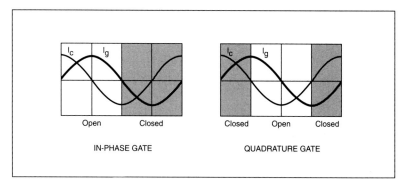

Figure 13-11. *Phase-Gate Selected Integration*

Therefore:

$$D = \frac{G_x}{C_x} = \frac{\omega T_4}{T_3}$$

This is a mathematically correct albeit simplified description of the process by which this meter obtains the values of interest. The meter's actual circuitry is more sophisticated and includes phase inversion and a four-phase gate clock for full-wave synchronous rectification of the signal of interest. It also has circuits to quickly phase-lock the clock signals to the reference voltage and to speed up the integration process.

Wattmeter

A microprocessor-based wattmeter can be employed to measure the loss of high Q capacitors. Figure 13-12 supplies a simplified illustration of the method.

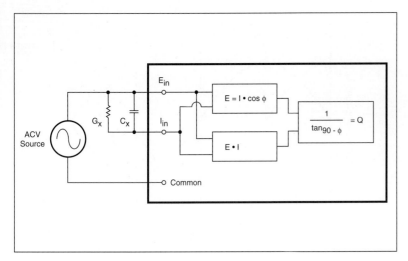

Figure 13-12. *Wattmeter-Measured Q*

A stable, pure sine wave voltage impressed across a parallel conductance and capacitor causes a current to flow into the wattmeter's I_{in} terminal. The ac voltage is also applied to the meter's E_{in} terminal.

The watt's portion of the meter measures the power consumed by the conductance as $EI\cos\phi$. The meter also separately measures E and I (E_{in} and I_{in}) and obtains their product, EI. This product is divided into $EI\cos\phi$ to obtain $\cos\phi$ and then the angle by which I leads E.

Recalling the relationship of Q and DF (dissipation factor) for a capacitor from Chapter 12, "Inductance and Capacitance," Q can be computed as:

$$Q = \frac{1}{\tan(90° - \phi)} = \tan\phi$$

All computations are carried out by the microprocessor in the wattmeter.

AC Ratio

The key requirement for accuracy in ac ratio is that the divider's ratio-determining impedances must be symmetrical. In other words, the equivalent impedance for the numerator and denominator of a complex ratio must be such that:

$$\frac{R_1}{R_2} = \frac{X_1}{X_2}$$

Where:

R and X are the equivalent series resistance and series reactance of the parallel-connected elements of the divider.

In a reactive divider, such as a capacitive divider, the ratio of X_1 to X_2 must be the desired ratio, virtually unaffected by shunting resistors.

These considerations should be borne in mind when reading the following discussion of audio frequency dividers.

Impedance Ratio versus Resistance Ratio

The top portion of Figure 13-13 illustrates a typical dc voltage divider.

The output of this divider is 0.1 × its input. When this divider is used as an ac voltage divider, it is subject to the effects of the parasitic capacitance shunting its resistive elements. This situation is illustrated in the middle portion of Figure 13-13. If the parasitic capacitances, c_p, across each of its resistors have the same value, which is likely if the physical dimensions of the two resistors are nearly the same, the output of the divider can increase from 0.1 times the input to 0.5 times the input as the frequency is increased.

At low frequencies, the capacitive reactance of the parasitic capacitances is high in comparison to the values of the resistors. Under these conditions, the division ratio is primarily set by the resistors. When the frequency of the applied voltage increases, the reactance of C_p becomes small compared to the value of the resistors. Therefore, the division ratio of the divider approaches the division ratio of the capacitive reactances of the two capacitors.

As the divider changes from a resistive divider at low frequencies to a capacitive divider at high frequencies, its impedance changes. The impedance, Z, of the parallel combination of each pair of resistors and parasitic capacitances

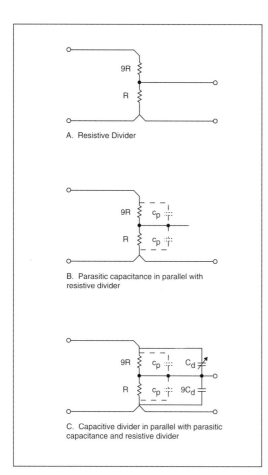

A. Resistive Divider

B. Parasitic capacitance in parallel with resistive divider

C. Capacitive divider in parallel with parasitic capacitance and resistive divider

Figure 13-13. *Typical DC Dividers with Parasitic Capacitance*

in the middle portion of Figure 13-13 can be expressed in rectangular notation as:

$$Z = \frac{X_c^2 R - j X_c R^2}{R^2 + X_c^2}$$

Where:

j = operator j; in electricity, the same as the imaginary number i, the square root of minus 1.

X_c = capacitive reactance of the parasitic capacitance in parallel with a specific resistance element. (Two instances are shown, c_p across $9R$ and c_p across R.)

R = resistance of a specific resistor. (Two instances of generic R are shown in Figure 13-13, with values of $9R$ and R.)

The voltage divider's division ratio can be made less sensitive to frequency by placing discrete capacitors across it whose capacitive reactances have a division ratio equal to the division ratio of the resistors. The lower portion of Figure 13-13 illustrates this method. This approach will cause more current to flow in the divider than in a purely resistive divider, especially at higher frequencies.

This circuit also contains inductance in the resistors, in the capacitor's leads, and in the divider's input and output leads. These inductances will interact with the capacitance and resistance, changing the divider's ratio at high frequencies. For this reason, dividers for use at high frequencies, expected to pass a square wave without distortion, must be constructed as lossy transmission lines. In such dividers, R, L, and C are carefully controlled and are relatively constant across a very large frequency range. (For more information, see "Resistive Dividers," below.)

Similar considerations apply to inductance of the connection wires and the leads of a low resistance high current shunt (Figure 13-14).

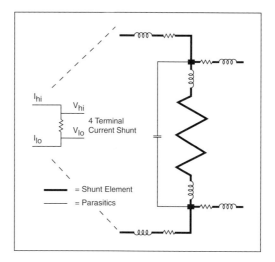

Figure 13-14. *High Current Shunt Parasitics*

In this figure, the impedance Z is:

$$Z = R + j X_L$$

Where:

R = resistance of the shunt element

X_L = inductive reactance of the parasitic equivalent series inductance

The voltage across the shunt leads the current through it as:

$$\theta_{lead} = \tan^{-1}(R/X_L)$$

AC ratio devices can be based on inductive, capacitive, and impedance division ratios. These are considered next.

Audio Frequency Dividers

Resistive Dividers

When designing resistive dividers for use as ac dividers, careful attention must be paid to proper design of the entire divider. Skin effect must be considered, as well as the amount and locations of distributed and discrete inductance and capacitance. Shielding is of great importance, as well.

At audio (roughly 30 Hz to 30 kHz) and higher frequencies, electrical circuits become more complex. Residual impedances begin to affect the operation of even a simple resistive divider. Compared with Figure 13-13, Figure 13-15 more completely illustrates the situation.

Unless care is taken to minimize the effects of inductance and capacitance, the divider can have large frequency-dependent errors.

For the divider shown in Figure 13-15 to have an output that is independent of frequency, the ratios $l_1:l_2$ and $1/c_1:1/c_2$ must be the same as the main ratio, $R_1:R_2$. If current is drawn from the tap, the effect of l_3 must be considered. Current will always be drawn from the tap unless the effect of c_3 is eliminated (by guarding) and the load presents an acceptably high impedance.

This is not to say that resistive dividers should not be used at audio frequencies. Properly designed thin-film resistors, laid down with properly sized shunting capacitors, have been used with good success at 100 kHz and beyond. However, one should always take into consideration the entire circuit, including residual impedances and the effect of the load on the circuit.

Reactive Dividers

At audio and higher frequencies, it becomes practical to consider impedance elements other than resistors for constructing dividers. Dividers constructed of series-connected inductors are not often used, because inductors tend to have relatively low Q and are greatly affected by residual capacitance. Capacitive voltage dividers are practical, however, and have the advantage of being capable of providing high ratios, e.g. 10,000:1.

Figure 13-16 shows one possible configuration.

Such a divider can be constructed from high Q air capacitors that are relatively immune to frequency effects at audio frequencies.

The more important divider at audio frequencies, however, is the transformer-based ratio device. Power frequency applications have long used potential transformers (PT) and current transformers (CT) for providing accurate ratios of voltage and current.

But the most-used divider in this class is the ratio transformer, also known as the Inductive Voltage Divider, shown in Figure 13-17.

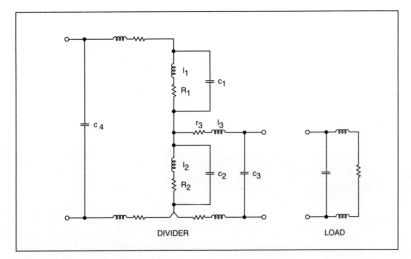

Figure 13-15. Residual Impedances in a Simple 10:1 Divider

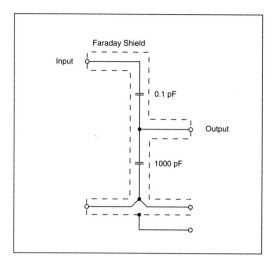

Figure 13-16. *Capacitive Divider for Audio Frequency Ratios*

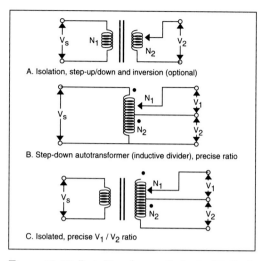

Figure 13-17. *Ratio Transformers (Inductive Dividers)*

These devices are nearly ideal in the frequency range 40 Hz to 1 kHz, and available commercial models are usable to about ±100 ppm to 10 kHz. A recent offering extends the frequency range to 100 kHz, and provides IEEE-488 control. A NIST experimental design provided best accuracy at 100 kHz, and was usable to about ±100 ppm at 1 MHz.

Using Audio Frequency Dividers

Resistive dividers can be used as standards at frequencies where the reactances of the stray elements are either negligible, or their effects can be sufficiently reduced by such techniques as guarding. A diagram of a comparison of two dividers is shown in Figure 13-18, including the

major leakage impedances, generically symbolized as r_p and c_p.

Figure 13-19 shows the application of a third divider and an additional two detectors to provide a guard voltage between the output taps and the cases of the dividers under test.

When the detectors indicate a null, there will be no potential difference between either tap and its case, and the effects of the leakage impedances shown in Figure 13-18 will be eliminated. Either the leakage impedances have no potential across them, or their currents are being supplied by the guard divider.

Inductive voltage dividers, such as ratio transformers, can be calibrated at NIST and used as

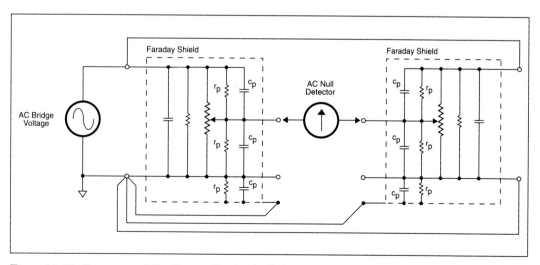

Figure 13-18. *Comparison of Two Resistive Dividers (Including Leakage Impedance)*

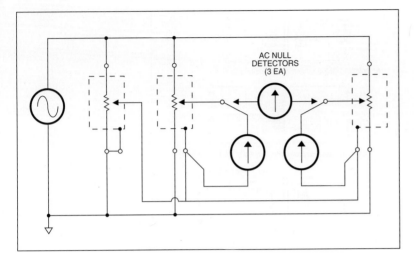

Figure 13-19. *Guarded Audio Frequency Voltage Divider*

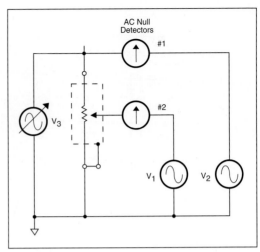

Figure 13-20. *Alternating Voltage Ratio: In-Phase Sources*

standards to calibrate other inductive voltage dividers as well as resistive dividers. Inductive voltage dividers are calibrated at NIST at a frequency of 1 kHz but can be used at other frequencies with degraded accuracy.

Ratio transformers such as the ESI Model DT 72A have a terminal linearity specification of ±0.5 ppm of input at a frequency of 1 kHz and are derated by the square of the frequency to a maximum frequency of 10 kHz. At 10 kHz, the specification for terminal linearity is ±100 ppm. Binary dividers (center-tapped inductive dividers) have not yet been fully exploited. This technique will, no doubt, be significantly expanded in the future.

AC voltage ratios can be established by use of the circuits shown in Figure 13-20 for sources that are in phase. For these techniques to work, the sources must be locked to the same frequency.

In Figure 13-20, V_1, V_2 and V_3 are all in-phase. V_3 is adjusted to equal V_2 via a null on AC Null Detector #1. Then the divider's output is adjusted for a null on AC Null Detector #2. When this null is obtained, $V_1 = SV_2$. 'S' is the divider's setting when both null detectors are at null.

V_3 and AC Null Detector #1 can be omitted when V_2 has a low output impedance or the divider has a high input impedance.

In Figure 13-21, V_1 and V_2 are 180° out of phase and V_2 can directly drive the divider. The divider's setting, S, is adjusted for a null on the AC Null Detector. At null, $V_1 = V_2(1-S)$.

In Figure 13-22, V_3 is in phase with V_2 and is made equal to V_2 by adjusting it for a null on AC Null Detector #1. V_1 is 180° out of phase with V_2 and, when the divider's output is adjusted for a null on AC Null Detector #2, $V_1 = V_2(1-S)$.

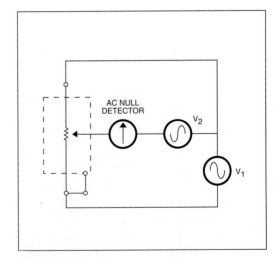

Figure 13-21. *Out of Phase AC Voltage Ratio: High Input Impedance Divider.*

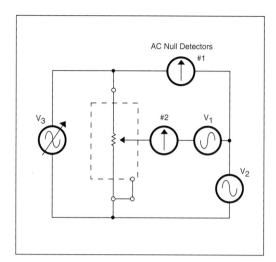

Figure 13-22. *Out of Phase AC Voltage Ratio: Low Input Impedance Divider*

Radio Frequency Ratio

In the radio frequency range, approximately 30 kHz to 300 MHz, electrical circuits are highly susceptible to the effects of residual impedances. The whole circuit must be taken into account, including the connectors and the nonrepeatability of the connection. At these frequencies, skin effect is significant, and resistors, unless properly designed, are not necessarily constant with frequency.

Transmission line effects become significant at radio frequencies, and must be properly accounted for. Typically, matched systems are designed in which source and load impedances are constructed to correspond closely to the characteristic impedance of the transmission lines that connect them. Proper shielding is a necessity.

Banana plugs and other connectors that are taken for granted at lower frequencies are no longer acceptable because they are not shielded, and because they do not present a precisely defined reference plane. The effect of the former problem is that the entire universe becomes part of the circuit, and the effect of the latter is that it is impossible to tell accurately where the standard leaves off and the item tested begins. Precision connectors, such as the GR-900 and the APC-7 connectors, are required for the most accurate work. However, for many applications, especially in matched systems, rf connectors such as type N and TNC are acceptable.

Most ratio devices used at rf can be classified as attenuators, which present a matched impedance to both the source and load when terminated in a Z_0 load. Exceptions to this classification are directional couplers, which extract a portion of the incident signal from the transmission line, and a binary divider developed for use at the lower radio frequencies.

Figure 13-23 shows Pi and T versions of 20 dB resistive attenuators.

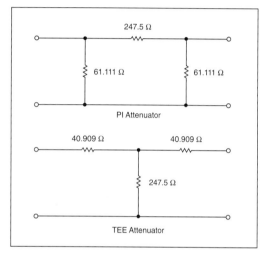

Figure 13-23. *Pi and T 20 dB Attenuators*

Such attenuators of reasonable quality are available in sizes ranging from 3 dB to as high as 40 dB. Skin effect (at rf) and residual impedances are carefully controlled to make the attenuation and input and output impedances essentially independent of frequency over their rated frequency range. These attenuators are constructed in segments of coaxial transmission line, using low reactance disc and rod resistors for the parallel and series elements, respectively.

Attenuators such as these are sometimes used at lower frequencies under the assumption that if they are good up to 2 GHz, they must be good at 10 kHz. Skin effect, which probably is not complete at 10 kHz, and contact resistance, which is not important for 1% measurements, make this a risky assumption for ppm measurements.

The most useful standard of attenuation (ratio) in this frequency range is the Wave Guide Below Cutoff (WGBC) attenuator, shown in Figure 13-24.

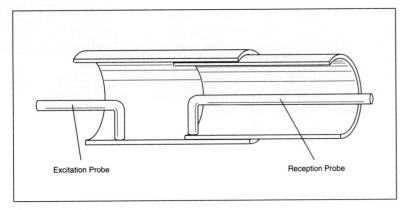

Figure 13-24. *Wave Guide Below Cutoff Attenuator*

A wave launched down a circular waveguide at frequencies below which traveling waves are accommodated will be attenuated at a rate that is dependent only on distance traveled. Guide diameter and material have no effect, but the dielectric constant of the medium in the guide does.

When coupled with a laser interferometer for measuring displacement of receiving probe relative to launching probe, WGBC attenuators are capable of very good accuracy. Excitation and pickup probes are essentially small antennas that must be tuned to present a fixed Z_0 impedance to connecting transmission lines. They are, therefore, fixed frequency devices, with 30 MHz being the usual operating frequency. Extensive apparatus and technique have been developed for measuring ratios of voltage and power at frequencies different from the operating frequency.

The directional coupler is either a three-port or a four-port device. It is designed to extract a portion of either the incident or the reflected wave (three-port) or both (four-port), and to present it to a side port. These devices are widely used in tuning transmission systems, in which the reflected wave is made to vanish, and in measuring mismatch of terminations and other systems. They can, however, be used to generate voltage and power in known ratios to a known standard of voltage or power.

While several varieties of directional coupler exist, the most useful for explaining their operation is the lumped-element directional coupler, shown in Figure 13-25.

Whereas the RF/Microwave Engineer would think of these devices in terms of reflections from mismatched loads, those who deal with voltage, current, and impedance can gain equivalent insight by considering the coupled signals to be the result of coupling between voltage and current in the device.

The output at the side arm is the signal that results from more or less complete cancellation of the divider voltage (proportional to voltage in the main arm) by a voltage that is proportional to the current in the main arm. When the load is matched, the side arm voltage will be zero. When the load is a short, the output will be some maximum value determined by the coupling coefficient. When the load is an open, it will have the same magnitude, but opposite phase. This device is usable into the audio frequency range, but must be calibrated against a standard of some kind.

Connectors and Hook-Up Considerations

Low contact resistance at the connection of the test leads and the terminals of the bridges and meters is essential to the measurement of conductance, series resistance, dissipation factor, power factor, and Q. Even a few milliohms of contact resistance, or hook-up lead resistance, can upset the correct calibration of high Q devices.

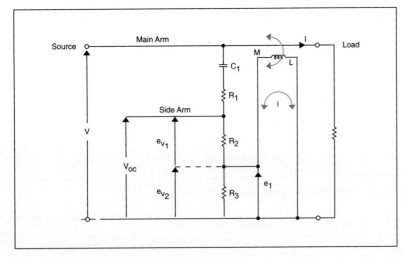

Figure 13-25. *Lumped-Element Directional Coupler*

The Faraday shield of the three-terminal capacitor should be continued as continuously as possible around the device under test, the external standards, the hook-up leads, and the instrumentation. For this reason, coaxial leads and connectors are generally used to complete the circuits.

The inductance of the hook-up leads is also significant. Short, shielded, twisted pair hook-up leads should be used to reject both external magnetic fields and to cancel their self-inductance. The leads should be perpendicular to both the terminals of the device under test and the bridge or meter used to measure its value. See Chapter 32, "Grounding, Shielding and Guarding."

Key References

Jones, R.N.; Anson, W.J., "The Measurement of Lumped Impedance: A Metrology Guide," NBS *Monograph 141*, June, 1974

Hoer, Cletus A.; Smith, Walter L., "A 2:1 Ratio Inductive Voltage Divider With Less Than 0.1 ppm error to 1 MHz," *Journal of Research of the National Bureau of Standards*, Vol. 71C, No. 2, April-June 1967

Judish, R.M.; Jones, R.N., "A Generalized Method for the Calibration of Four-Terminal-Pair Type Digital Impedance Meters," NBSIR 84-3016, August, 1984

Other references for this chapter are in the Resources Appendix.

Chapter 16:

Artifact Calibration

Artifact calibration is a powerful new approach in the design and calibration of measurement and calibration instruments. This chapter covers the technological advances that have enabled the design of artifact calibrated instruments. For calibration to be fully traceable, the instrument must be correctly designed, manufactured, and adjusted. This chapter discusses the traceability issue of artifact calibration in the newer instrumentation.

Artifact calibration is the process of allowing the instrument being calibrated to make ratiometric comparisons to artifact standards. Traditionally such comparisons have been performed external to the instrument, using a wide array of equipment to transfer the value of standards to various ranges and functions of meters and calibrators. With artifact calibration, comparisons are performed using ratio and measurement devices built into the instrument. By including highly stable dc voltage and references, the instrument can use internal software routines to compare its performance to external artifact standards.

Artifact calibration significantly reduces calibration adjustment and maintenance costs. This technique improves user confidence between calibrations. It can also help to implement a program that generates historical data, which may further improve confidence and reduce cost. Using statistical software programs can enhance the user's ability to predict the performance of the instrument.

The benefits include:

■ The effort required to perform a calibration is reduced.
■ Fewer standards are needed to perform a calibration.
■ The possibility of operator error is eliminated.
■ Calibration data is automatically collected.
■ Unstable or faulty operation can easily be detected.

Artifact Calibration Development

Most electronic instruments contain a large number and wide variety of components. The configuration of the circuit and the values of the components determine the characteristics of the instrument. Because the value of any component varies with time, instruments require periodic calibration to ensure continued compliance with specifications.

Until the early 1970s, periodic calibration adjustment generally required the physical adjustment of components within the instrument to bring it into compliance with external standards.

Complex instruments contained dozens of internal, physically-adjustable components such as potentiometers and variable capacitors. The adjustment process might take many hours to accomplish and the process was prone to human error.

In the mid-1970s, instrument designers began using the microprocessor not only to enhance capabilities and operation, but also to simplify the calibration process. For example, the Fluke 8500A DMM was designed to store and use software correction factors to compensate for gain and zero errors on each range of the instrument. This process of storing constants based on comparison to external standards was then used extensively in the calibration of instruments.

By the early 1990s, closed-case calibration had come into use in almost all types of instrumentation. Internal software corrections eliminated the need to remove instrument covers to make physical adjustments. This simplified the calibration process, which is easily automated.

Artifact Calibration Process

Artifact calibration is the process of transferring the assigned value of a standard to more than one parameter. Typically, the term "artifact calibration" is used to describe the process when it is implemented internally in an instrument.

Consider the calibration of a dc voltage source that has several ranges extending from millivolts to one kilovolt. Calibrating such an instrument, whether it uses internally-stored constants or requires manual adjustment, usually requires the following:

■ an external voltage standard such as a zener reference or standard cell
■ a null detector to make comparisons

- a Kelvin-Varley ratio divider (which is usually self-calibrating)
- a decade divider

For calibration, this array of equipment is connected in various configurations to provide the traceable source and measurement parameters.

The artifact calibration process, on the other hand, uses a limited set of standards, such as the Fluke 732B dc reference standard and the Fluke 742A-10K and 742A-1 resistance standards.

The dc voltage source with the capability of artifact calibration would only need to have a 10V dc reference applied. This dc voltage source would have the equivalent of the Kelvin-Varley divider, the null detector, and the decade divider built in. It would then use those built-in devices to transfer the accuracy of the artifact to the many ranges of the instrument.

In essence, an instrument that has artifact calibration capability has taken over the manual metrology functions of establishing ratios and making comparisons. Circuitry, microprocessor control, and software placed inside the instrument perform these same functions.

The incentive for this change has been to reduce the time and equipment costs associated with conventional manual or semi-manual calibration, and to provide more uniform quality by ensuring that the calibration is always performed correctly and consistently.

In the past, highly skilled calibration technicians, working in Type I standards laboratories, used high quality primary standards in conjunction with written procedures to manually calibrate calibrators. Today, with artifact calibration, the 5700A Multifunction Calibrator (MFC) can calibrate itself where it's used. It contains high quality built-in standards, precision switching and microprocessor-controlled firmware calibration procedures to do this. As Figure 16-1 shows, it is as if each and every 5700A includes the skill and experience of Fluke calibration engineers using high quality Fluke standards to perform these calibrations.

Null detectors are built on a chip, ratio systems are reduced to a single circuit board, and thin-film resistor networks replace bulky wirewound resistors. Miniaturization techniques have permitted these revolutionary developments.

The Adjustment Process

Instruments designed for artifact calibration adjust their calibration in the following manner. The instrument:

1. Compares the values of its internal references against external standards and obtains software correction factors for its references.

2. Performs an internal calibration, using its built-in calibration check standards to perform the same ratiometric and ac-dc transfer calibration techniques used by technicians in a calibration laboratory to adjust non-artifact-calibrated devices.

The functions that are calibrated include the ac and dc voltage and current ranges as well as the resistance ranges.

The internal circuits used during artifact calibration include a built-in null detector, dc voltage and resistance references, a pulse-width-modulated digital-to-analog converter (pwmdac) used as a ratiometer, and an ac-dc transfer system.

Examples of Artifact-Calibrated Multifunction Calibrators

5440A

The Fluke 5440A dc voltage calibrator, introduced in 1982, was the first instrument to use artifact calibration. This embodiment of artifact calibration uses an external 10V reference and decade divider as traceable standards. Comparisons are made using an external null detector. Internal references and ranges are calibrated through this process.

Figure 16-1. *Artifact Calibration: The Laboratory in a Box*

5700A

The Fluke 5700A, introduced in 1988, expanded on the capability of the 5440A's artifact calibration techniques. This was done by building in a ratio divider, decade dividers, and null detector, and by including additional calibration circuits to support its added functions of direct and alternating voltage, resistance, and direct and alternating current.

Microprocessor Control
A microprocessor controls all functions and monitors performance, routing signals between modules by way of a switch matrix. As with closed-case calibrated instruments, no physical calibration adjustments are made. Instead, correction constants are stored in non-volatile memory. Numerous internal checks and diagnostic routines ensure that the instrument is always operating at optimum performance.

PWMDAC Ratiometer
A Fluke ultra-linear, pulse-width-modulated digital-to-analog converter (pwmdac) functions as a ratio divider within the calibrator. This divider, like any ratio divider (including a Kelvin-Varley divider), functions on the basis of dimensionless ratio. That is, there are no absolute quantities involved. The repeatable linearity of a pwmdac depends only on a highly reliable digital waveform. To maintain high confidence, this linearity is checked and verified during artifact calibration, by comparing the same two fixed voltages, V_1 and V_2, on different ranges. Figure 16-2 illustrates this comparison.

If the pwmdac is perfectly linear, then:

$$\frac{N_4}{N_3} = \frac{N_2}{N_1}$$

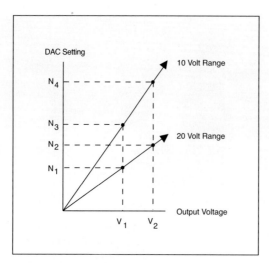

Figure 16-2. *PWMDAC Converter Linearity Verification*

See Chapter 9, "DC Ratio," for more information on the pwmdac.

DC and Resistance References

Two reference amplifiers, similar to those used in the Fluke 732B, maintain the 5700A's dc voltage accuracy and stability. The reference amplifiers are described in Chapter 7, "Direct Voltage and Current." These references are calibrated by comparing them to the external 10V artifact standard. The comparison takes place internally, using the pwmdac and null detector to assign correction values.

Similarly, a 1Ω and 10 kΩ resistor are provided in the 5700A as internal resistance reference standards. The 5700A's microprocessor computes calibration correction factors for these internal standards as it compares them with the external standards via ratio techniques employing the pwmdac and null detector.

The comparisons automatically take place to obtain the updated value for software correction factors for the internal references. The technician must remain in attendance with the instrument for about 15 minutes to connect the artifact calibration standards to its output. Then, the process continues unattended for about another hour.

Null Detector

A built-in 5½-digit DVM provides null detection capability for differential dc voltage measurements. This is essentially the dc por-

tion of the Fluke 8842 DMM. It is used in conjunction with the pwmdac to compare the internal dc voltage and resistance references with the external artifact standards. It is also used to establish voltage and resistance ratios during internal calibration.

DC Voltage Ranges

Decade voltage dividers, such as the Fluke 752A, are used when the dc voltage ranges of an instrument are calibrated via the use of external standards. In effect, these confirm the ratios of the calibrator's internal range resistors. Artifact calibration eliminates the need for decade voltage dividers because it uses its ratiometer to directly measure the ratio of the gain-determining elements. Figure 16-3A illustrates the traditional approach and compares it with the direct measurement of the gain ratio of the dc voltage ranges when artifact calibration is used (Figure 16-3B).

Resistance Ranges

The transfer of resistance references to the 5700A is similar in concept to the transfer of direct voltage described previously. Each resistor is switched in series with the appropriate reference resistor during internal calibration. The dc reference voltage is applied across this series connection and the resistance ratio, and the reference resistor is measured using the pwmdac and null detector. This ratio and the assigned value of the reference resistor are used to obtain the software correction factor for that specific resistor.

Two resistors, having values of 1Ω and 10 kΩ, form the internal resistance references for the calibrator. Their values are assigned using the pwmdac and null detector by comparing them to external resistance artifact standards. The dac and null detector system then establish ratios of various other values within the calibrator, and store their value in non-volatile memory.

AC-DC Voltage Transfers

Two Fluke solid-state thermal rms converters form the alternating voltage measurement reference for the 5700A. One thermal converter makes real time ac-dc comparison measurements to maintain the output voltage at the programmed value. A second is used only during artifact calibration to compare the external dc artifact to the internally generated ac voltages. The traceability of this internal ac-dc reference, used only during artifact calibration, is verified by periodic comparison to an external ac-dc transfer reference. To maintain confidence, an internal software routine directs intercomparison of the two internal converters to ensure that their characteristics track each other.

Artifact Calibration Verification

When an instrument has been artifact calibrated for the first time at the factory, the traceability and integrity of the calibration is confirmed by using external standards to verify the calibration results. Every two years thereafter, external standards should be used to re-verify the continued proper functioning of the internal metrology process.

Traceability of Artifact Calibration

Traceability is defined in MIL-STD-45662A as: "…the ability to relate individual measurement results to national standards or national accepted measurement systems through an unbroken chain of comparisons…"

This requirement must be met with artifact calibration as rigorously as it is with all other calibration methods. This means that no adjustments can be made without comparison to traceable standards, and that all transfer of values must be done using reliable ratiometric techniques.

The block diagram in Figure 16-4 shows the unbroken chain of traceability for the Fluke 5700A.

The 5700A block diagram is clearly analogous to the traditional metrology environment except that in the traditional environment, the ratio transfer and reference devices are external to the instrument.

In the 5700A, the NIST traceable values of the external artifacts are transferred to the internal

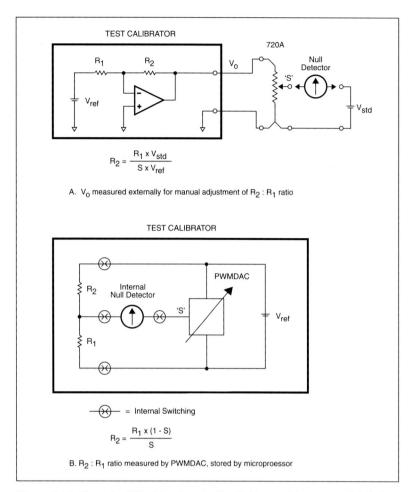

A. V_o measured externally for manual adjustment of $R_2 : R_1$ ratio

$$R_2 = \frac{R_1 \times V_{std}}{S \times V_{ref}}$$

$$R_2 = \frac{R_1 \times (1 - S)}{S}$$

B. $R_2 : R_1$ ratio measured by PWMDAC, stored by microproessor

Figure 16-3. *Example of Traditional vs. Artifact Calibration Measurement Methods*

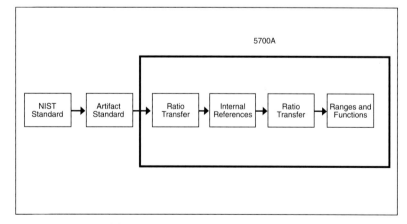

Figure 16-4. *Traceability of Artifact-Calibrated Instrument*

references by the self-calibrating pwmdac. The pwmdac then transfers values from the references to the output parameters. The integrity of the system is enhanced by built-in, self-checking routines.

Design of the MFC

Several important factors are involved in the design and manufacture of an artifact-calibrated instrument to ensure that manufacturing reliably produces instruments that truly and fully meet their specifications. These factors are:

- A design that is correctly analyzed to identify sources of error. The possibility of a design oversight cannot be ignored. Rigorous testing and analysis must be performed during the instrument's development.

- Manufacturing processes which ensure that components and construction meet design criteria. These processes are continually monitored to ensure consistency of production.

- An instrument that has diagnostic routines which verify that its internal calibration system is functioning correctly. These routines establish the same confidence in calibration as is expected with a skilled operator performing manual calibration and using conventional techniques. As is the case with the 5700A, this is achieved by maintaining a set of internal, environmentally controlled references, used as the starting point for periodic internal comparisons.

The Results of Artifact Calibration

If the calibrator is treated as a "black box," the results of an artifact calibration can be determined independently of how the instrument obtained its calibration factors.

After the instrument is artifact calibrated, the values of all of its software correction factors are stored in its memory, ready for use. As with any instrument, its output values may be somewhat displaced from nominal, but they will be well within specified tolerances. A full verification after the initial artifact calibration verifies that the instrument performs to its specifica-

tions. When this has been done, the 5700A calibrator can be used with confidence for two years without further external verifications, provided that artifact calibration has been done periodically.

Data Collection

Production testing of the Fluke 5700A includes over 200 traceable verification points for this artifact-calibrated instrument. Data from each of these verifications is collected and analyzed to ensure that the production process is in control. A selection of data collected is shown in Figure 16-5.

This figure is typical of the data that has been collected from more than 1,500 instruments. This external verification confirms the integrity of the artifact calibration.

The measured results indicated in Figure 16-5 are similar to those that would have been obtained using traditional manual calibration methods. The results are shown to fall in an approximately normal (Gaussian) distribution with the predominant value (mean) centered near nominal, which is the specification center.

Fluke production criteria are set so that each verification point must show a 3σ normal distribution limited to 80% of the instrument's 24-hour specifications. This is equivalent to 3.75σ relative to 100% of the specification.

Periodic Audits

After the initial external verification of artifact calibration, additional external verifications can be performed from time to time to confirm that the artifact calibration process is continuing to perform in a satisfactory manner. Fluke recommends that the performance of the 5700A be verified using external standards every two years. However, Fluke's accumulated experience shows that repeated external verification is not necessary.

Artifact calibration enables the user to collect data and apply the statistical methods outlined in the next section and in Chapters 20, "Introduction to Metrology Statistics," and 21, "Statistical Tools for Metrology." These methods enable the user to verify the performance of the 5700A on an ongoing basis in lieu of repeated external verification.

Calibration Interval and Performance Prediction

The driving force behind artifact calibration has been to reduce the time required to calibrate precision instruments, to reduce the amount of support equipment required, and to obtain consistent control of the calibration process. An additional benefit, one with potentially more impact on the metrology function, is the potential for data generation, collection, and analysis.

To implement artifact calibration in an instrument, that instrument must include sophisticated analog and digital hardware as well as microprocessor-controlled circuits and support software. With internal references and internal comparison capability, the capacity is there to collect data at the time of artifact calibration. Perhaps more significantly, the capability is there to execute these routines between calibrations. This allows the measurement of drift and of performance changes. This data can be analyzed using statistical techniques (see Section Five, "Statistics").

A traditional instrument that is reviewed only during calibration can go out of calibration without the user's knowledge. This lack of awareness can lead to costly and potentially dangerous results, when critical tests rely on the instrument's accuracy.

The ability to run internal calibration checks between external calibrations allows the user to monitor the performance between calibrations. Since the instrument's internal references are well controlled and not sensitive to environmental changes, calibration checks can be performed in the environment in which the

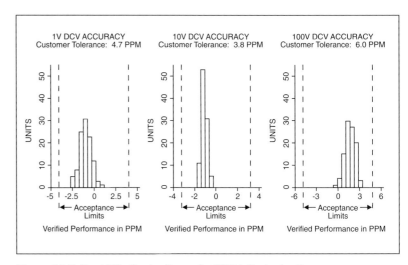

Figure 16-5. *Partial Verification Report for 5700A Production Run*

instrument is to be used. This increases confidence without having to return the instrument to the calibration laboratory. Note that these calibration checks do not adjust the instrument's output, but merely evaluate the instrument's output against internal references. Comparison of the internal reference values to external traceable standards is necessary to make traceable internal adjustments.

Statistical analysis techniques make it possible to analyze the data collected during artifact calibration and internal calibration checks. With a PC and the appropriate software, data can be imported, processed, displayed, and used to assess the performance of the instrument. Figure 16-6 shows the screen from a factory test software package used internally at Fluke which collects and analyzes 5700A internally-generated calibration data.

Figure 16-6 shows data collected using the Calibration Check function of a particular 5700A, where the performance of the 220 mV dc range was measured relative to its internal references.

The display shows:

■ data points collected (dark circles)

■ instrument performance relative to specification (straight regression line and curved predictions band lines)

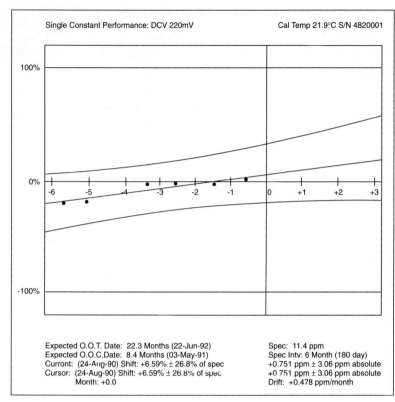

Figure 16-6. *Calibration Analysis Report*

can include various reference components or stimulus values as well as bridges and other instruments. Supporting these complex and lengthy calibrations requires a large and costly array of equipment, processes, and manpower.

Table 16-1 lists some of the major standards that are needed for the manual or closed-case calibration verification and adjustment of a highly accurate conventional calibrator. For further discussion of some of those instruments, see Chapters 17, "Digital Multimeter Calibration," 11, "Using AC-DC Transfer Standards," 7, "Direct Voltage and Current," 8, "DC Resistance," and 9, "DC Ratio." Table 16-2, on the other hand, shows the equipment required for calibration of a 5700A using the artifact calibration method.

Key References

"Artifact Calibration Theory and Application," *Fluke Application Note B0218A*

Goeke, Wayne, "Technical Requirements of Self/Auto Calibration Techniques," 1988 Workshop and Symposium, National Conference of Standards Laboratories, August, 1988

Other references for this chapter are in the Resources Appendix.

- predicted time that instrument performance will exceed the allowed specification, including allowance for confidence limits (OOC, Out of Confidence)

Using the data collected from the instrument, it is possible to detect a potential problem with the instrument. Also, if enough history has been collected on the internal references, it is possible to extend the period between artifact calibrations. This can prevent the effects and cost of an instrument being out of specification during use. Finally, it can reduce future maintenance and calibration costs.

Comparison of Artifact and Traditional Methods

Periodic calibration of a complex multifunction calibrator requires traceable measurement of each of its functions. The calibration equipment or systems used to date have been both manually operated and complex. Such systems

Table 16-1. *Standards Required to Calibrate a Conventional Calibrator*

Standard (Typical Fluke Model)	Used to Calibrate
DC Voltage Reference (732B)	the internal dc voltage reference and the basic dc voltage range, usually the 10V range.
Kelvin-Varley Divider (720A)	linearity of the digits displayed in the readout
Decade Divider (752A)	all other dc voltage ranges
AC-DC Transfer Standard (5790A)	all ac voltage ranges relative to the dc voltage ranges.
DC Voltage Calibrator (5440B)	ac-dc transfer standard dc input
Resistance Standard (742A)	the basic resistance range, usually the 10 kΩ range; and the lowest resistance range, usually the 1Ω range.
Resistance Calibrator (5450A)	all other resistance ranges and the current ranges to 100 mA.
Current Shunts	the 1A and 10A current ranges.

Table 16-2. *Standards Required to Artifact-Calibrate a Fluke 5700A*

Action	How Often	Time	External Standards
Internal calibration check to get data enhancements	Often	< 1 minute to initiate, 1 hour unattended	None
Artifact calibration and internal calibration	Infrequent	15 minutes + 1 hour unattended	Artifact standards
External verification	Very infrequent	4 hours to one or two days, fully attended	Many high performance standards (see Table 16-1)

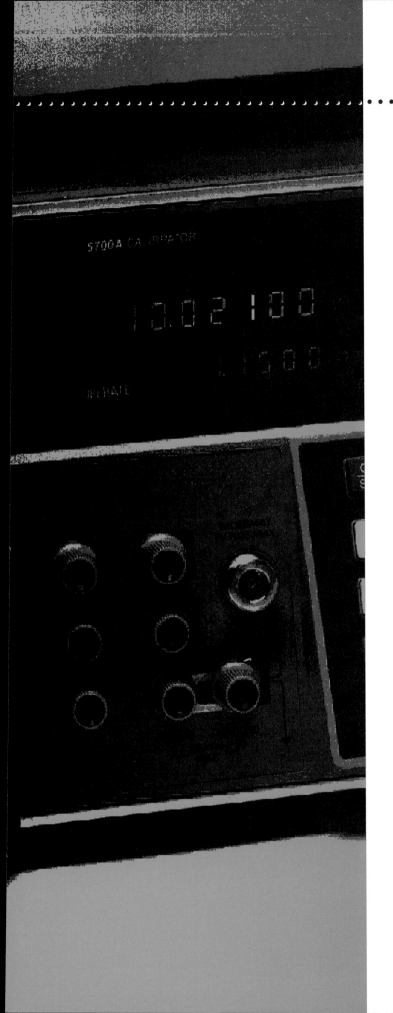

Chapter 17:
Digital Multimeter Calibration

Digital multimeters (DMMs) have evolved from the voltage-only digital voltmeters (DVMs), first introduced in the mid-1950s. Today's digital multimeters have more ranges, more functions, and greater accuracy than ever before, presenting a growing challenge to the metrologist.

This chapter reviews the various types of DMMs that are commonly used in industry, and their characteristics relative to their calibration. Some details of the circuits within DMMs are discussed to present a clearer picture of their calibration needs.

Calibration of DMMs has become less complex with the use of modern multifunction calibrators (MFCs). In the past, a metrologist had to assemble an array of single function calibrators (e.g., dc volts and amps). This led to complicated setups requiring a high degree of skill and a higher probability of making mistakes.

Modern MFCs have greatly eased the DMM calibration process. They are typically controlled through an IEEE-488 bus which makes them ideal for personal computer control with commercially available software such as Fluke's MET/CAL calibration software. These types of modern calibration systems have greatly improved personal productivity and uniformity of calibration, and are less prone to errors and mistakes by calibration personnel.

Types of DMMs

DMMs typically display electrical quantities on their digital displays. However, the method of sensing electrical quantities may alter their response from the calibrated value. This is particularly true when complex ac current and voltage waveforms are measured. Therefore it is important that the metrologist understand the DMM's characteristics in order to conduct a competent calibration.

Of the wide variety of DMMs on the market, three of the most popular will be discussed in the following paragraphs. These are:

- Laboratory DMMs
- Bench/Systems DMMs
- Handheld DMMs

A fourth type of DMM is emerging, the DMM on a card. Due to their relative newness, they are not discussed here but their calibration is similar to the calibration of bench/systems DMMs.

Laboratory DMMs

Laboratory DMMs are usually five-function DMMs that measure dc and ac volts, resistance, and dc and ac current. They typically offer the highest level of accuracy and resolution and may approach the accuracy of the MFC used to calibrate them. They display up to 8½ digits in their readouts and are often automatically calibrated by the closed-loop method using their IEEE-488 bus-compatible systems interface.

These DMMs use similar techniques to measure dc voltage, dc current and resistance. However, they do no necessarily all use the same principles of operation to measure ac voltage and current. Therefore, it is necessary that very pure sine wave quantities be generated by the calibrator since the ac reading displayed assumes and displays a value based on an ideal sine wave.

The modern laboratory DMM makes use of state-of-the-art components such as microprocessor and computer memory chips which allow them to perform complex mathematical computations, including and storing all corrections on all functions and ranges of a DMM, thus eliminating the need for opening the case of the DMM to physically make corrective adjustments.

Bench/Systems DMMs

Bench/Systems DMMs usually measure the same five functions as laboratory DMMs but with less accuracy and resolution, typically 4½ or 5½ digits. They may or may not have an IEEE-488 bus or RS232 interface. If no interface is installed, they are manually calibrated.

In some cases, a manual calibration only involves selecting the range and function and applying the nominal stimulus to which the DMM adjusts itself. Otherwise, the DMM's response is calibrated via adjustment of potentiometers, rheostats, and variable capacitors. These DMMs also use sophisticated components and state-of-the-art circuits and may be as complex as the top end laboratory DMMs.

In many calibration laboratories, the bulk of the workload is composed of bench/systems

DMMs, thus lending them to automated, closed-loop calibration, such as with the Fluke 5700A controlled by a PC running MET/CAL. It is not unusual for a user to purchase an IEEE-488 or RS232 interface option with his DMM to implement automated calibration even though the DMM is used in a manually operated application.

Handheld DMMs

Handheld DMMs are the most commonly used version of the digital multimeter. They are truly multifunctional units that include the five electrical functions plus additional functions such as frequency, continuity, diode test, peak voltage measure and hold, dwell time (in automotive applications), temperature, capacitance, and waveform measurement.

These units typically have a 3½ or 4½ digit display and some also include an analog readout and audible tones for continuity measurements. They tend to be used in a broad variety of applications from very sophisticated electronic circuit testing to automotive maintenance and even some hobbyist use.

These DMMs tend to be small, rugged, and battery operated. At this time, they typically do not have a computer interface to fully automate their calibration. However, with the growing emphasis on quality, and compliance with ISO 9000, future handhelds will likely have some form of interface for calibration to optimize cost-of-ownership and to comply with quality standards.

Calibration of handhelds is not a problem from the standpoint of accuracy. However, due to the increasing number of functions being placed in handhelds, future MFCs will no doubt include more functions to calibrate them.

Anatomy of a DMM

Functional Sections of a DMM

A DMM is really two integrated devices: the measurement section and the control section. See Figure 17-1.

The control section is typically made up of a microprocessor and its support circuitry. The measurement section is made up of the analog conditioning circuits and analog-to-digital converter (adc). The control section requires no calibration adjustment, but is often checked internally during DMM power-up and self tests. The measurement section does require calibration adjustment and verification.

Analog-to-Digital Converter (ADC)

Every input to a DMM is eventually processed by the adc, the heart of any DMM. The purpose of the adc is to digitally represent an analog signal. The adc's used today typically operate over a range of ±200 mV for the less accurate meters; more accurate DMMs have adc's operating over a ±2V, or ±20V range.

There are two major types of adc's in widespread use today: integrating, and successive approximation.

Integrating ADCs
Integrating adc's can operate on dual-slope, multi-slope, or charge-balance schemes. Because of their simple design, and also their ability to deliver high precision, integrating converters appear in every type of DMM from the lowest-cost handheld DMMs, to systems DMMs with precisions of 8½ digits. Integrating adc's are quite effective in rejecting noise, since the analog integrator acts as a low pass filter.

A very basic type of integrating converter is the dual-slope converter. See Figure 17-2.

In a dual-slope converter, the unknown dc input, V_{meas}, is applied via S_1 to an analog integrator for a fixed period of time, and then an internal dc voltage reference, V_{ref}, of opposite polarity is applied to the integrator via S_2 until the output of the integrator reaches zero

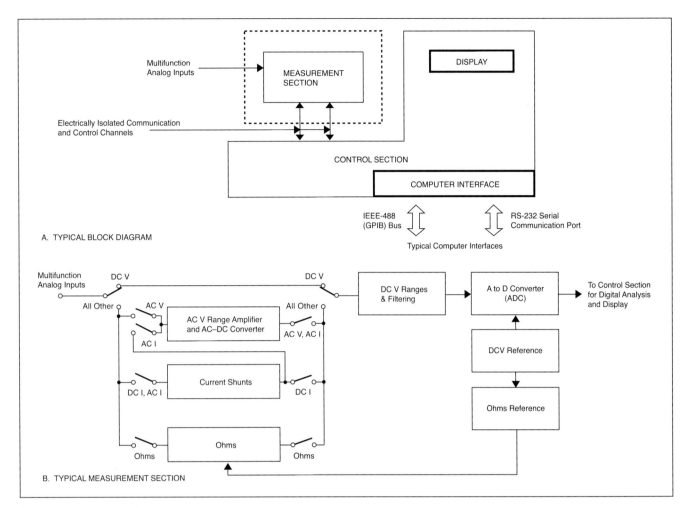

Figure 17-1. *DMM Block Diagram*

again. S_3 is closed to reset the converter between cycles.

The magnitude of the input signal is represented by the time interval required for the de-integration. A fast comparator is used to sense the integrator output. The dual-slope converter, then, is a voltage-to-time converter.

Since crystal oscillators are quite stable, the major source of calibration uncertainty within a dual-slope converter is not the time base, but the dc voltage reference. The uncertainty of the dc voltage reference is directly related to the uncertainty of the adc output. Other uncertainties include the zero or offset stability of the integrator, the dielectric absorption properties of the integrating capacitor, and analog delays in the overall system which result in timing errors.

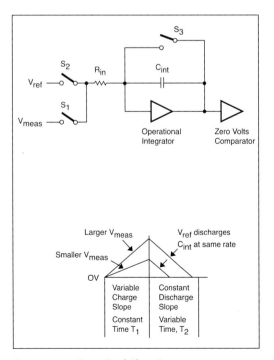

Figure 17-2. *Basic Dual-Slope Converter*

Successive Approximation ADCs and the R^2 Converter

Another common type of adc is the successive approximation adc. The Fluke recirculating remainder (R^2) scheme, a variation on successive approximation, provides the high speed and high precision in many of today's popular DMMs—for example, the Fluke 8506A and 8840A. Combined with external analog and digital filtering, the R^2 converter can have noise rejection characteristics comparable to those of the integrating converter.

The R^2 converter is shown in Figure 17-3.

An unknown dc voltage input, V_{meas}, is compared to the output of the precision digital-to-analog converter (dac). The dac is set to provide an output equal to 10 times the difference between the unknown input and the value of the most significant digit. For example, if the unknown is 9.83 volts, the output of the amplifier would be 8.3 volts.

S_3 is closed so that the dac output, or remainder voltage (8.3 volts in this example), is stored on C_1. After that, S_1 opens to disconnect V_{meas} from the amplifier, and S_2 is closed and the remainder voltage is applied, or recirculated, back to the input. At this point, the cycle repeats. A new remainder (3.0 volts in this example) is generated and stored on the other storage capacitor, C_2. This continues until the signal being measured is digitized to the resolution designed into the converter. Switches S_2, S_3, S_4 and S_5 are operated appropriately in these cycles.

At first glance, it may seem that by measuring one digit at a time, the R^2 converter sacrifices speed for circuit simplicity. In actual practice, the conversion time is a few milliseconds. Furthermore, this basic function has been successfully integrated into an LSI circuit, reducing circuit complexity and execution time.

The sources of calibration uncertainty in R^2 converters are the dac dc voltage reference, the linearity of the dac, and the offset and gain of the amplifier.

Signal Conditioning Circuits

A DMM's dc voltage (dcv) section is used to measure a wide range of input voltages. This section's dc output is scaled to be compatible with the adc input. Additional signal conditioning circuits are used for the other measurement functions.

These circuits consist of amplifiers, attenuators, and filters for each DMM range. Each range scales the input signal to the proper level for the adc. The calibration of each range corrects for zero and gain variations of the amplifier and attenuators. Most DMM filters do not require calibration because filter topologies usually have little effect on uncertainty.

Alternating Voltage Converters (AVCs)

Figure 17-4 is the overall block diagram for typical avc's.

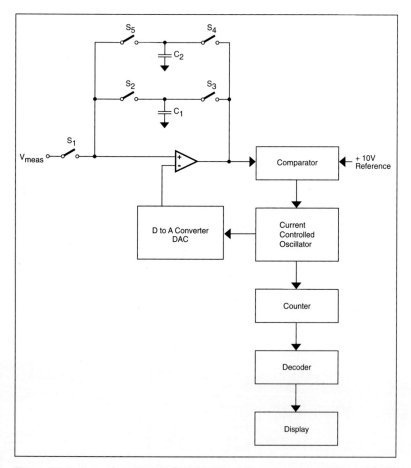

Figure 17-3. Recirculating Remainder (R^2) Converter

The ac voltage range amplifier scales the input ac voltage, ACV_{meas}, to an optimal level for input to the ac-dc converter. The dc voltage output of the ac-dc converter is applied to the adc for digitizing and display.

Average-Responding AC-DC Converters
Average-responding, rms indicating converters process ACV_{meas} via range amplifiers and convert the signal to an equivalent dc voltage level. This is accomplished by a precision operational rectifier. See Figure 17-5.

The resulting dc voltage signal is then digitized by the adc. Usually, the average value is converted to the corresponding rms value by multiplication by a constant. The conversion is made with the assumption that the applied signal is a pure sine wave; otherwise, the conversion factor is not correct and the indication is in error. For a pure sine wave, the conversion formula is:

$$V_{rms} = \frac{\sqrt{2} \times \pi \times V_{avg}}{4} \cong 1.11 \times V_{avg}$$

True RMS Converters
The function of a true rms converter is to accept signals from the input terminals, via range amplifiers, and convert them to a dc voltage value proportional to the rms value of the input. True rms values are mathematically obtained by averaging the squared value of the input, then finding the square root of the average square.

$$V_{rms} = \sqrt{\frac{1}{T} \int_0^T \left[V_{(t)} \right]^2 dt}$$

Where:

T = integration period

t = an instant of time between 0 and T

V = instantaneous voltage at time t

Three major methods are used for true rms ac-dc conversions. They are:

■ Thermal Sensing
■ Log/Antilog Analog Computation

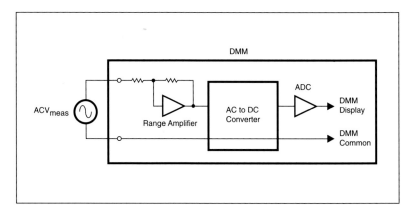

Figure 17-4. *AC Voltage Circuit of a Typical DMM*

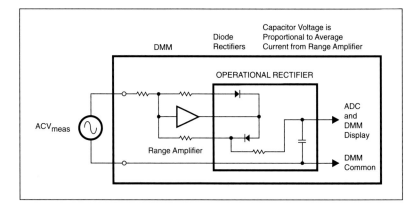

Figure 17-5. *Average-Responding, RMS Indicating Rectifier*

■ Digital Sampling

Thermal Sensing
Figure 17-6 illustrates the version of the thermal sensing technique used in the Fluke 8506A.

In this converter, the output of the range amplifier is applied to a resistor that heats the base of the transistor on the left side of the rms sensor. The transistor's collector current is increased as a result and unbalances the differential amplifier depicted above the two sensor transistors. The differential amplifier supplies a dc current through the resistor on the right side of the sensor. The heat in this resistor increases the collector current in the right transistor and restores the balance of the differential amplifier. The dc voltage drop across the right-hand resistor is proportional to the true rms ac voltage drop across the left hand resistor and is digitized by the DMM's adc for display.

Since this method responds to the power dissipated in the resistors, it responds to the rms

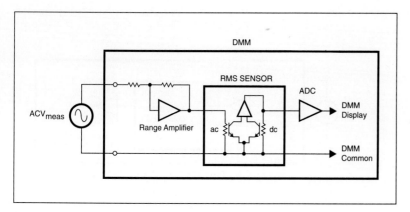

Figure 17-6. *Thermal Sensing Technique*

value of all of the fourier components of the applied waveform, within the bandwidth of the amplifier.

Chapter 10, "Principles of AC-DC Metrology," discusses true rms converters using thermal conversion techniques.

Log/Antilog Analog Computation
Figure 17-7 shows an example of the log/antilog computation (as used in the Fluke 8502A/ 8505A).

The output of the range amplifier is a representation of the input voltage, ACV_{meas}. ACV_{meas} is applied to the input of the absolute value amplifier.

Positive and negative input cycles are converted to a pulsating dc at point 1. (Test points are represented by diamonds in Figure 17-7.) A voltage proportional to the square of the input current is supplied to point 2 by the squaring

amplifier. A current proportional to the voltage at point 2 is supplied to point 3. The output voltage of the integrator, V_o, has a value proportional to the average level of the pulsating dc current supplied to point 3 by Q3.

Since the input current at point 1 is a direct function of the voltage being measured, and the output voltage is a direct function of the average square of the current at point 1, the DMM displays the digitized value of V_o as the true rms value of the input voltage.

Digital Sampling
Figure 17-8 shows an example of the sampling technique (as used in the HP® 3458A).

In this technique, portions of the input waveform are sampled during short intervals of time relative to the period of the waveform. Each sample is quickly digitized by a fast adc. Its value is squared by the DMM's microprocessor and the result stored in the DMM's memory. When a sufficient number of samples have been taken, the DMM's microprocessor takes the square root of the average value of the squares. Mathematically the rms value of samples in the sampling technique is expressed as:

$$V_{rms} = \sqrt{\frac{\sum_{i=1}^{N} V_i^2}{N}}$$

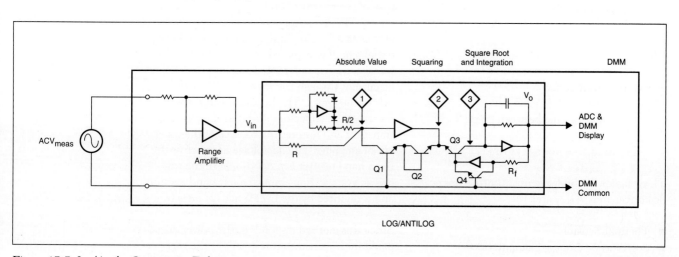

Figure 17-7. *Log/Antilog Computation Technique*

Where:

N = total number of samples

V_i = ith voltage sample

i = sample number such that $1 \leq i \leq N$

This method is extremely accurate and fast for measuring low frequency ac voltages. Its accuracy at higher frequencies is limited by the DMM's sampling rate. In general, the sampling rate of the DMM should be a ×2 or greater integer multiple of the signal frequency.

For more information concerning the relationship between average, rms, and peak values of various waveforms and their fourier components, see Chapter 34, "AC Lore."

Resistance Converters

Two different resistance conversion schemes are commonly employed in today's DMMs: the constant current method and the ratio method.

Constant Current Method of Resistance Conversion

In the constant current method, illustrated in Figure 17-9, constant current sources, from 1mA (for the 200Ω range) to 100nA or less (for the 20 MΩ range), are built into the DMM. This constant current source is applied through R_{meas}, the unknown resistor, and the DMM's voltage amplifier circuits buffer and scale the dc voltage across R_{meas} to the proper level for the adc. Constant current schemes are generally used in the higher end DMMs, such as the Fluke 8840A.

The precision constant current source supplies a current, I, through R_{meas}. The voltage drop, V, across R_{meas} is IR_{meas}. This voltage is scaled by the voltage amplifier in the DMM, and its output is applied to the adc. The control circuits in the DMM calculate and display the resistance, R_{disp}, as:

$$R_{disp} = \frac{V}{I}$$

Ratio Method of Resistance Conversion

The ratio method of resistance conversion,

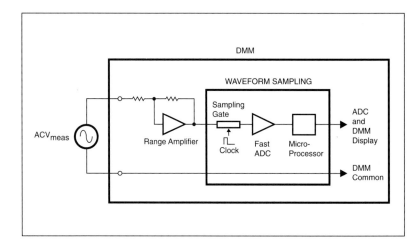

Figure 17-8. Sampling Technique

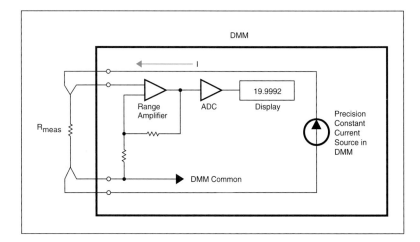

Figure 17-9. 4-Wire Constant Current Resistance Measurement

shown in Figure 17-10, is a method often used with dual-slope (and dual-slope variant) adc's.

Internally, an approximately known current is applied through R_{meas}, the unknown resistor which is series connected to a known reference resistor R_{std}. A simple voltage divider is formed. Now, the unknown resistance value can be determined by solving:

$$R_{meas} = R_{std} \frac{V_{meas}}{V_{std}}$$

Where:

V_{meas} = the voltage across the unknown (R_{meas})

V_{std} = the voltage across the known (R_{std})

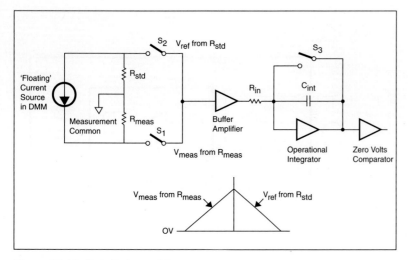

Figure 17-10. *Ratio Resistance Measurement*

This scheme is used with dual-slope converters because a dual-slope converter operates on voltages of opposite polarity taken from R_{meas} and R_{std}. The exact amplitude of the current is not important because the ratio of the resistors is determined by the ratio of the voltage drops. However, the current must be held constant during the two voltage measurements.

Calibration of resistance converters generally consists of zero and gain adjustments. For example, each DMM resistance range is first corrected for zero, then for gain.

The constant current method has primarily gain uncertainties. These are the result of inaccuracies of the precision current source and the gain of the dc voltage sensing amplifier. In the

ratio resistance converters, the gain uncertainty is due to the instability of the reference resistor. Zero uncertainties in resistance converters are due to the voltage offsets of the sensing amplifiers that are part of the dc voltage signal conditioning circuits.

2- and 4-Wire Resistance Converters
Any resistance converter scheme can be set up as a 2- or 4-wire converter. In the 4-wire setup, the sense path—essentially the same circuits as the dc voltage signal conditioning path—is made available on terminals separate from the resistance current source terminals. In this way, the resistance of the connecting leads is eliminated from the measurement. When calibrating DMMs with 4-wire resistance capability, resistance sources should have remote sensing capability, as with the Fluke 5450A Resistance Calibrator and the Fluke 5700A MFC.

Current Converters

The current function of DMMs is usually built with simple current shunts, where either the dc or ac voltage section senses the voltage across the shunt; or by using a feedback scheme, where the unknown current flows to an operational amplifier circuit which generates a proportional output voltage (see Figure 17-11).

General Calibration Requirements

Regardless of the type of DMM, calibration adjustments are performed to reduce instability in the offset, gain, and linearity of the transfer functions of the signal processing circuits. Each of the functional blocks in a DMM's measurement section is subject to these sources of variation in performance.

Theory of Calibration Adjustment

Assume that all of the DMM's signal processing blocks have a transfer function of:

$$y = mx + b$$

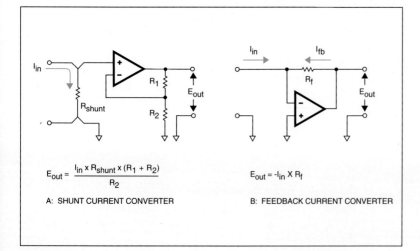

Figure 17-11. *DMM Current Converters*

Where:

y = the output

x = the input

m = the gain

b = the offset from zero

The DMM is designed in such a way that m has an exact nominal value such as 10 and b should be zero. For example, when m is 10 and b is zero, y will equal $10x$.

When m is not equal to its nominal value, all values of y will deviate from nominal by the same percentage. When b is not equal to zero, all values of y will be offset from their correct value by a constant amount. Even though m and b deviate from their nominal values, the slope of y as a function of $mx + b$ should be a straight line. (Departures from a straight line are referred to as nonlinearity.)

A DMM operates under this $y = mx + b$ relationship. It takes an unknown input x (whether in voltage, resistance, or current), and converts it to y (in volts, ohms, or amperes). This is what is displayed by the DMM. Figure 17-12 depicts the variations in gain, offset and linearity for a typical DMM. Traditionally, these deviations are referred to as gain, offset, and linearity errors.

Voltmeter specifications are based primarily on offset, gain, and linearity: the % of reading specification is the gain uncertainty.

Zero uncertainty is due to voltage offsets in the adc amplifiers and comparators; gain uncertainty is tied to inaccuracies of the dc voltage reference and any gain-determining networks of the adc. Linearity uncertainty is due to secondary error sources, such as mismatches in resistive ladders of the dac in R^2 converters, or dielectric absorption errors by storage capacitors, resulting in a drooping response at full scale.

In addition to these sources of uncertainty, some DMMs have spurious voltage spikes, dc bias currents, and pump-out currents present at their input terminals. These can introduce errors in the output of the MFC calibrating the DMM.

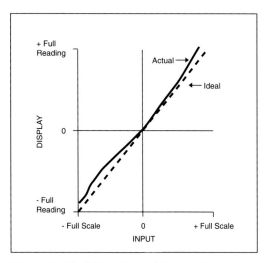

Figure 17-12. *Offset, Gain and Linearity Variations*

Internal References

Every DMM has a dc voltage reference. References range from 1V to 15V. The dc voltage reference is used as the reference for the adc and is the limiting factor for the DMM's best accuracy for all voltage and current measurements. DMMs may or may not require separate calibration of the dc voltage reference. Often, the DMM design is such that an actual measurement (using another DMM) of the dc voltage reference is not required. Instead, a known input voltage is applied to the unit under test (UUT), and an adjustment is made until an accurate representation of the known input voltage appears on the UUT display. Figure 17-13 is an example of a typical high precision direct voltage reference.

Also, in any DMM, there are one or more resistor references that determine the accuracy of the resistance converter. Most DMMs do not require a separate measurement of the reference resistors during calibration. Instead, a standard resistor of known value is applied to the DMM, and the DMM is adjusted for the correct readout. Figure 17-14 illustrates a typical resistance reference.

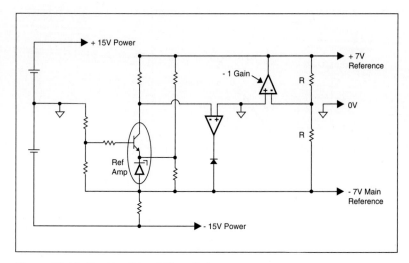

Figure 17-13. *Precision Direct Voltage Reference*

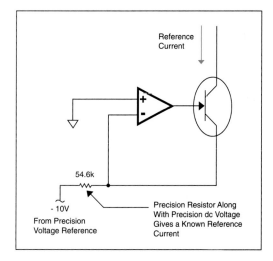

Figure 17-14. *Resistance Reference*

ADC Adjustment Considerations

Since all functions use the adc, it must be calibrated as one of the first steps. Some DMM calibration schemes call out separate adc and reference calibrations; other schemes merely call out dc voltage range calibrations and do not burden the calibration technician with the specific details of the adc calibration. DMMs whose procedures do not call out separate adc adjustments do have internal corrections. The calibration procedure simply calls for an adjustment in the straight-in dc voltage range first. This range, going directly into the adc, has unity gain and thus has no significant error in scale factor. The calibration procedure will

often call for a zero offset adjustment of the dc range, and then the adc is adjusted.

Integrating ADC

The integrating adc has simpler calibration adjustments than successive approximation adc. The major error source of this type of converter is the dc voltage reference; its calibration adjustment can be as simple as applying a known dc voltage of about the same magnitude as the dc voltage reference, and then making an adjustment within the DMM so that the adc's displayed output is the same within an acceptable tolerance, as the applied input.

Some integrating converters have a more complicated calibration adjustment near zero volts. The slew rate of both the integrator and comparator can cause errors near zero volts; these errors are often polarity sensitive. As a result, there may be one or more adjustments near zero volts to correct for this anomaly.

Traditional dual-slope converters often exhibit dielectric absorption in the integrating capacitor. This phenomenon is caused by the capacitor's memory effect which results in a not-as-predicted integrator output voltage over large voltage swings, that is, near full-scale inputs. An uncorrected dual-slope converter will typically droop by 10 to 50 ppm near both positive and negative full scale. To correct for this, the adc is adjusted with a known near-full-scale input applied. For more information on dielectric absorption, see Chapter 33, "A Rogues' Gallery of Parasitics."

R² ADC

The R² converter calibration adjustment procedure generally requires more adjustment points to correct for mismatches in the resistive ladder networks that make up the dac. And certain steps of the calibration may need to be repeated a number of times (iterated) for optimum results. Very specific voltage inputs are required during the calibration, forcing the R² converter to use various combinations of the dac ladder. Iteration allows the matching between the resistors of the ladder to be more accurate. R² calibration is no more demanding than the calibration of a simple dual-slope converter. It is easily accomplished with MFCs such as the Fluke 5700A, which allow quick keyboard entry of any voltage.

DC Voltage Range Calibration

DMMs usually have full-scale ranges of 200V dc, 300V dc, or 1000V dc, typically divided by factors of 10 to determine the lower ranges. Normal calibration practice limits the testing of ranges to just less than full scale. This is because most DMMs are auto ranging, and will go to the next higher range if the input is a certain percentage of full scale. So the calibration voltages for DMMs with full-scale ranges of 200V dc usually follow a 190 mV, 1.9V, 19V, 190V and 1000V dc sequence.

Modern MFCs take advantage of this structure. For example, the lower four of the ranges in the preceding list are very quickly calibrated by the Fluke 5700A by setting up its output on the lowest range and then using its MULTIPLY OUTPUT BY 10 key to step through the next three ranges.

The zero on each range may also need to be adjusted or recorded. This is usually done by applying an external short to the DMM input and taking the appropriate action. After the zero is adjusted or recorded, the full-scale input voltage is applied and the range gain is adjusted.

For example, assume that a DMM's adc operates within the range of ±20V. Its 200 mV dc range scales the input signal × 100 to keep the full-scale adc input to within the proper range, as shown in Figure 17-15. The amplifier used in the 200 mV dc range has a voltage offset error, and the gain provided by the feedback is not exactly 100. This causes a scale-factor error.

The calibration procedure is to apply a short circuit to the input to the amplifier and adjust the DMM reading to exactly 0V dc. This would be followed by an input near full scale, in this case, 190 mV dc. The DMM is then adjusted to display the exact input voltage. In effect, the user is making the gain exactly 100. A DMM calibration may also require an input of opposite polarity, −190 mV. This is to correct either

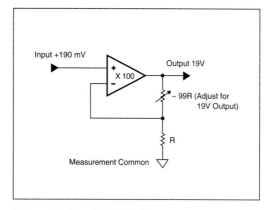

Figure 17-15. *mV Gain Adjustment*

for secondary linearity errors of the range amplifier, or for linearity errors within the adc.

AC-DC Converter Calibration

AC-DC converter calibration is similar for all types of converters. Amplitude adjustments are often made at two or more frequencies on each range. Zero adjustments are not usually made.

Average Responding AC-DC Converters
Calibration adjustment of average responding converters corrects for deviations in the equation $y = mx + b$. However, the b term is solved not for inputs at zero volts, but typically for inputs at $\frac{1}{10}$th or $\frac{1}{100}$th of full scale. This is because precision rectifiers tend not to work well at zero volts input. Near zero volts, they rectify noise that would otherwise ride on the input waveform and average to zero. By moving the b term calibration off of zero, this problem is avoided. For more information, see Chapter 33, "A Rogues' Gallery of Parasitics."

TRMS AC-DC Converters
True rms converters need similar calibration of ranges at full-scale and at near-zero input levels. But true rms circuits have an even greater problem near zero volts than average responding converters. For example, analog log/antilog schemes employ a precision rectifier, resulting in noise rectification problems like those associated with an average responding converter. Also, since the displayed output voltage is:

$$\sqrt{V_{noise}^{2} + V_{sig}^{2}}$$

Where:

V_{noise} = rms value of the noise voltage

V_{sig} = rms value of the signal being measured

Very small input signals cause the noise term to dominate. Consequently, true rms calibrations are accomplished with inputs well above zero volts.

There are additional adjustments to correct for errors in linearity of rms converters. If the DMM has a dc-coupled ac voltage function, there may be zero input adjustments to correct for offset errors of the scaling amplifiers.

The ac voltage converter can have a separate calibration for the true rms converter, but often its calibration is combined into the main ac voltage function calibration. For example, if the true rms module can handle a 2V full-scale waveform, the 2V ac range should be calibrated first; then adjust the true rms module. The other ranges are then adjusted to correct for their gain errors. In some cases, the true rms module needs more than two different inputs to correct for linearity errors. For example, an ac voltage calibration adjustment may call for inputs of 19 mV, 190 mV and 1.9V on the 2V range.

Scaling sections, averaging converters, and true rms converters have resistive and capacitive errors. A major consideration when calibrating ac voltage is frequency response. The general requirement is to use a constant-amplitude cal-

ibrator that covers the entire frequency range of the DMM. The conversion takes some time, and slewing through the pass band is time consuming. Because of this, spot frequency checks are usually made instead.

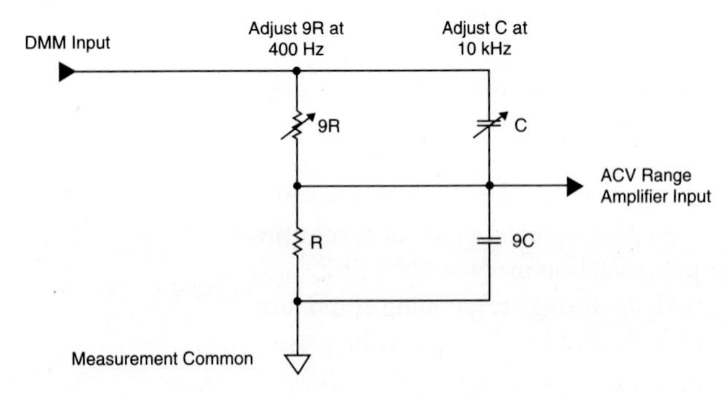

Low frequency calibration is generally performed at 400 Hz to 1 kHz. The high frequency adjustments are done afterwards. The frequencies used for high frequency adjustments are largely determined by the capacitive vs. resistive characteristics of the scaling circuits. When making a high frequency adjustment, one of two actions is performed:

- The actual frequency response of a scaling amplifier or attenuator is physically adjusted. See Figure 17-16.

- The DMM's frequency response at cardinal points is stored in its non-volatile memory. The DMM firmware then displays the correct reading at any frequency by interpolating between frequency points.

The second method requires a DMM with an internal frequency counter to determine input frequency.

Resistance Converter Calibration

Calibration of resistance converters generally consists of zero and gain adjustments. For example, each range of the DMM's resistance function is first corrected for proper zero reading. Then a near-full-scale input is applied to each range, and adjustments are made if necessary.

When calibrating DMMs with 4-wire resistance capability, resistance sources should have remote sensing capability, as with the Fluke 5450A Resistance Calibrator and the Fluke 5700A MFC.

In the 2-wire setup, the sense path and ohms current path are on the same set of terminals. Resistance errors due to the connecting leads can be significant. In general, proper connection of 2-wire resistance calibration for a meter with even 100 mΩ resolution can be a problem. Fluke has addressed this problem in the 5700A, which has its 2-wire ohms compensation feature. The 2-wire ohms compensation

Figure 17-16. Frequency Response Adjustment

feature of the 5700A virtually eliminates the effects of lead resistance in a 2-wire hookup.

Separate 2- and 4-wire resistance calibrations could be specified in calibration procedures. Since the 4-wire sense path is the same as the dc voltage signal conditioning path, all that is required is to correct the gain of the current source for resistance converters with current sources. However, second-order effects cause discrepancies in apparent gain when the dc voltage amplifiers are configured to sense either a dc voltage input directly or the voltage across the unknown resistor. Because of this, many of the higher precision DMMs require calibration for both 2- and 4-wire resistance. For more information on contact resistance, insulation resistance, leakage currents, and bias currents, see Chapter 33, "A Rogues' Gallery of Parasitics."

Current Converters Calibration

Both ac and dc current converters are calibrated by applying a known current and adjusting for the correct reading. Direct current converters correct for zero and gain; alternating current converters correct for down-scale and full-scale response. Typically, there are no high frequency adjustments for alternating current, primarily because current shunts are not inductive enough to cause significant errors relative to the DMM's specifications.

Other DMM Calibrations

There are other characteristics of a DMM that require calibration. The DMM must not only measure dc voltage to a high degree of precision; it must also have a minimal loading effect on the source voltage. One aspect of circuit loading is the bias current error of the DMM's dc voltage amplifiers—how much current does it draw from the circuit under test? Many high-end DMMs, with bias currents in the 10 pA region, require a bias current adjustment of the dc voltage scaling section. These adjustments are made by comparing the DMM reading with a low impedance zero input against a high impedance zero input. The adjustment itself adds or subtracts an actual bias current into the main dc voltage amplifiers.

Simplified DMM Calibrations

Closed-Case Calibration

The calibration of microprocessor controlled, IEEE-488 bus or RS232 communicating DMMs has been simplified by automation. The DMM itself may provide a great deal of the automated capabilities. However, external software, running in a PC, provides even more advanced calibration automation.

DMM manufacturers all realize the benefit of simplifying the calibration task. The HP® 3455A had a removable module containing the direct voltage and resistance references that could be sent to the calibration laboratory separately. However, this also required manual adjustments for complete alternating voltage calibration.

The Fluke 8500A was the first DMM with digitally-stored calibration constants. An optional calibration memory stored various offsets and gain corrections for each range and function in non-volatile memory. This allowed it to be calibrated quickly with the covers on for most functions. The 8500A was not yet a fully digitally-calibrated instrument, because periodically some open-cover high-frequency calibration adjustments were required.

An early DMM to offer full closed-case, digitally-stored calibrations was the Datron® 1061, which extended the concept introduced by the Fluke 8500A to include high frequency adjustments by dac programming of varactor diodes to replace trimmer capacitors. The limitations which older instrument designs had placed on calibration time and requirements for human intervention could now be circumvented.

Since then, the Fluke 8840A has simplified the closed-case calibration process even further: a calibration procedure built into the instrument firmware prompts the user through the exact calibration steps. Average calibration time is approximately 12 minutes in an automated system. Furthermore, the 8840A was one of the first precision DMMs with no potentiometer adjustments at all, eliminating even the so-called one-time-only factory adjustments. This

DMM, from the date of manufacture or after any repair, could be calibrated with all covers on.

Closed-case calibration, along with the advent of IEEE-488 bus controllers and calibration instruments controlled by the IEEE-488 bus, revolutionized the traditional DMM calibration by fully automating it. This automated process is often referred to as closed-loop calibration.

Closed-Loop Calibration

Closed-loop calibration is one of the most significant instrumentation developments in recent years. The loop is the connection between the measurement of an instrument's performance and the actual readjustment of its operating characteristics.

For example, in a manual calibration of an analog voltmeter, the operator first applies a short circuit to the UUT and adjusts the zeroing screw on the face of the meter; then removes the short and applies a known voltage, adjusting a potentiometer for the correct reading at full scale. The loop begins with the technician's interpretation of the reading, goes through the hand that turns the screwdriver, and to the screw being turned. The change in instrument response as the screw is turned is monitored by the technician to complete the loop.

With a programmable source and UUT connected by a suitable digital interface (such as the IEEE-488), the computer can set the source and UUT to the right range and value, then interpret the UUT performance. But if performance is modified by turning a screw on the UUT, either a complex robot arm or a human arm is needed to make the adjustment.

Closed-loop calibration eliminates the need for any kind of arm in the loop. New digital techniques use a microprocessor to store zero and gain corrections into non-volatile memory. These are then applied in real time to modify the displayed reading. Instead of solving the $y = mx + b$ equation by trimming resistor values or dc voltage references, the equation is solved and corrected in software. Electrical parameters of the dc voltage scaling circuits, for instance, are no longer changed; the DMM displays the correct reading y by using its internal micro-

processor to apply calibration constants m and b to the digitized value of input x.

Closed-loop calibration is also possible for those circuits that do require a change in electrical performance. For example, high frequency ac voltage adjustments can consist of dac reprogramming of varactor diodes. Or a dac can be reprogrammed to physically readjust the dc voltage sense amplifier bias current. The programming information is then stored in non-volatile memory.

For a DMM calibrator, the system can send the correct range and function over the IEEE-488 bus, apply the desired stimulus to the analog inputs, take the resultant reading back over the bus, and command a change in the digitally-stored correction. The loop is closed by the system CPU, and the hand on the screwdriver is eliminated. The operator is necessary only to connect leads and initiate the process.

Closed-loop calibration has resulted in faster, more repeatable, higher quality calibrations. Closed-loop calibration has other benefits as well. Customer demand for it has forced DMM manufacturers to actually design a higher quality product. Many DMMs today do not have mechanical potentiometers that wear out. Secondary error sources, such as integrator capacitor dielectric absorption, which are not easily correctable by software, have been eliminated by design.

For more information on closed-case and closed-loop calibration, see Chapter 19, "Automated Calibration."

Artifact Calibration

Another recent development in calibration is artifact calibration and automated internal calibration. This method involves applying a few calibration standards (for example, a 10V dc voltage standard and a 10 kΩ standard), and designing the means inside the DMM to calibrate all of its other ranges and functions using these selected input values. For this purpose, the DMM contains voltage- and resistance-ratio and ac-dc voltage transfer circuitry to determine appropriate range constants for voltage, current, and resistance, and to derive ac voltage range constants from dc voltage ranges. The internal calibration techniques are functionally identical to those ordinarily used in a calibration facility.

In order to take advantage of stability performance that is much better than uncertainty or resolution, it is important that the resolution of the calibration constants be significantly greater than the resolution or uncertainty. Otherwise, recalibration of the instrument will result in noticeable discontinuities in the results, making the instrument unusable for monitoring accurate signal sources with high resolution.

Artifact calibration is treated in detail in Chapter 16, "Artifact Calibration."

Laboratory DMM Calibration

The calibration of laboratory DMMs raises interesting issues because, as their accuracy approaches that of the calibrator, the test uncertainty ratio (TUR) approaches 1:1. In these cases, the metrologist must analyze the uncertainties in his measurements to support using TURs of less than 4:1.

Figure 17-17 is a simplified block diagram of the dc voltage function of a laboratory DMM. Figure 17-18 is a similar block diagram for a precision multifunction calibrator (MFC).

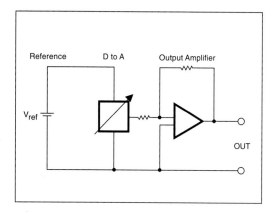

Figure 17-18. MFC *Direct Voltage Function*

As inspection shows, the circuit elements of Figures 17-17 and 17-18 are identical but appear in reverse order. As a matter of fact, it is easier to manufacture the DMM because it uses simple resistive attenuators to reduce high voltage ac voltage inputs to the 10V level at which it processes the attenuated signal.

Because the best calibrators and the best DMMs will have a 1:1 TUR for the dc voltage function, users may wish to use additional test equipment, such as precision voltage dividers and secondary standards of voltage, to enhance the accuracy of the calibrator's direct voltage output (see Figure 17-19).

It is also possible to evaluate the calibration results statistically. For example, if the test limits are set at 1.414 (square root of 2) times the performance specifications for the DMM or calibrator, the distribution of variance in performance for a population of DMMs and calibrators will follow the curve in Figure 17-20.

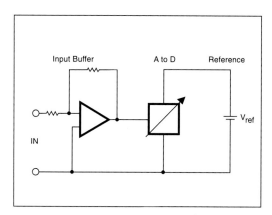

Figure 17-17. DMM *Direct Voltage Function*

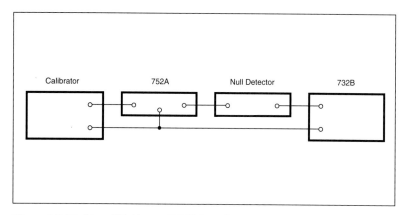

Figure 17-19. *Use of Dividers on DC Voltage Output*

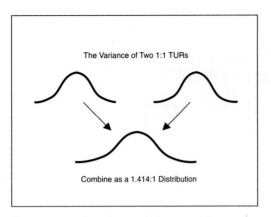

Figure 17-20. *Distribution of Uncertainty for x-Member DMM Population*

A modern calibrator that uses artifact calibration can collect a record of changes in its performance using internal circuits. A personal computer running data analysis software can analyze this record and assign accurate correction factors to the calibrator's output, thereby improving its TUR at each calibration point.

Key References

References for this chapter are in the Resources Appendix.

Table 17-1. *DMM Summary*

Type	Example	Functions	Comment
Laboratory	Fluke 8506A	voltage, current, and resistance	highly accurate, true rms ac voltage sensor
	Hewlett Packard 3458A	voltage, current, and resistance	artifact calibrated, IEEE–488 or manually operated
Bench/ Systems	Fluke 8842A	voltage, current, and resistance	IEEE–488 bus and front-panel controls. Evolved from early bench and systems DMMs of the 1960s and 1970s, such as the Fluke 8300A
Handheld	Fluke 87	voltage, current, resistance, frequency, time, capacitance, diode tests, and more	evolved from early bench DMMs of the 1970s, such as the Fluke 8120A and 8000A

FLUKE®

Chapter 18:

Oscilloscope Calibration

This chapter discusses the process of and considerations for the calibration of oscilloscopes.

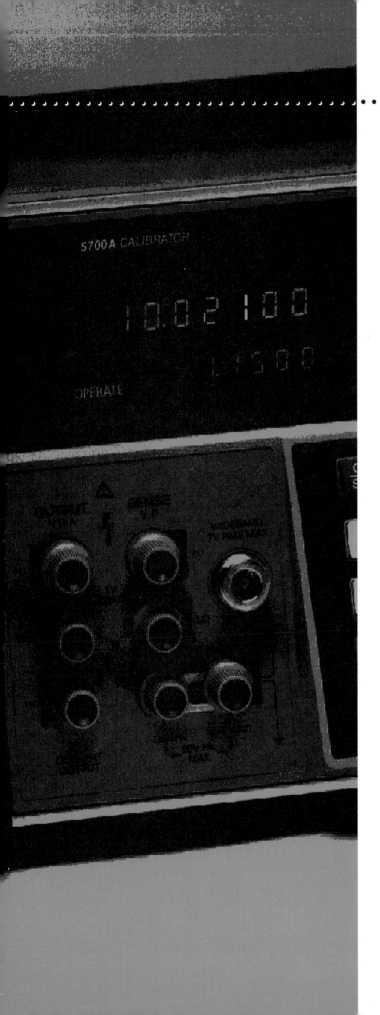

FLUKE®

Single Constant Performance: DCV 220mV   Cal Temp 21.9°C S/N 4820001

Expected O.O.T. Date: 22.3 Months (22-Jun-92)
Expected O.O.C.Date: 8.4 Months (03-May-91)
Current: (24-Aug-90) Shift: +6.59% ± 26.0% of spec
Cursor: (24-Aug-90) Shift: +6.59% ± 26.8% of spec
Month: +0.0

Spec: 11.4 ppm
Spec Intv: 6 Month (180 day)
+0.751 ppm ± 3.06 ppm absolute
+0.751 ppm ± 3.06 ppm absolute
Drift: +0.478 ppm/month

can include various reference components or stimulus values as well as bridges and other instruments. Supporting these complex and lengthy calibrations requires a large and costly array of equipment, processes, and manpower.

Table 16-1 lists some of the major standards that are needed for the manual or closed-case calibration verification and adjustment of a highly accurate conventional calibrator. For further discussion of some of those instruments, see Chapters 17, "Digital Multimeter Calibration," 11, "Using AC-DC Transfer Standards," 7, "Direct Voltage and Current," 8, "DC Resistance," and 9, "DC Ratio." Table 16-2, on the other hand, shows the equipment required for calibration of a 5700A using the artifact calibration method.

"Artifact Calibration Theory and Application," *Fluke Application Note B0218A*

Goeke, Wayne, "Technical Requirements of Self/Auto Calibration Techniques," 1988 Workshop and Symposium, National Conference of Standards Laboratories, August, 1988

Other references for this chapter are in the Resources Appendix.

A. TYPICAL BLOCK DIAGRAM

B. TYPICAL MEASUREMENT SECTION

FLUKE ®

Oscilloscopes are widely used over a broad range of electronic and electri cal measurement applications because of their high versatility. They range in complexity from simple to highly complex and range from general purpose to specifically dedicated in application. The highly sophisticated ones interface into automated, computer-controlled systems and provide very sophisticated functions.

Special purpose oscilloscopes support a wide range of applications or industries that use electronics such as the automotive, medical, machines tool industries, to name a few.

The need to calibrate oscilloscopes appears to be growing because of the focus on quality systems which companies, world-wide, are implementing.

This chapter will focus on the calibration requirements of oscilloscopes in general and will also present information for the metrologist to make informed decisions on the more important aspects of oscilloscope calibration procedure development. It will also cover the more important internal functions of them, to allow one to better understand their characteristics.

Types of Oscilloscopes

Two basic types of oscilloscopes will be covered in this chapter. They are the traditional analog oscilloscope and the relatively newly developed digital storage oscilloscope (DSO). Both types of scopes are sometimes combined into a single instrument which then presents some unique calibration requirements.

Analog Oscilloscopes

Analog scopes are sometimes called real-time scopes because of their inherent ability to sense and display those signals which appear at their input terminals at that instant in time.

In its simplest form the analog scope displays the signals present at its X and Y input terminals. In Figure 18-1 three basic elements of the scope are shown. They are the signal conditioning amplifiers, which present the correct amplitude of the signals, and the cathode ray tube (crt). In this case, if the input signals were repetitive the crt would display Lissajous patterns.

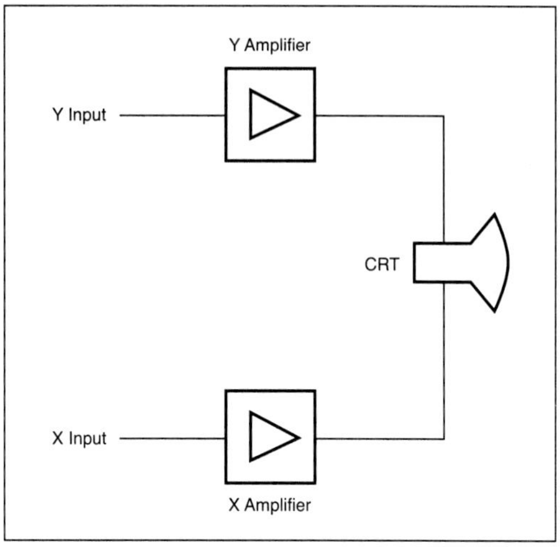

Figure 18-1. *Basic Analog Oscilloscopes*

In most analog scope applications, the display is compared to time or frequency. Therefore, the scope will contain an internal function called a time-base generator. This function generates a sawtooth wave whose repetition time is known. The time-base generator signal is normally applied to the X input of the scope, as shown in Figure 18-2. In order to display a true representation on the crt, it is necessary for the time-base generator to be at precisely the same frequency (or multiple thereof) as the Y input signal. When it is not, the crt may display the Y input signal, as shown in Figure 18-3. Therefore, it is common for scopes to have a scheme which synchronizes the time-base generator to the Y input signal to achieve the desired crt display and thus display a useful image. See Figure 18-5.

Other circuits in a basic analog oscilloscope improve its fundamental usability. Examples include trigger circuits, which allow the user to easily synchronize the time-base generator to the signal to be displayed or to another signal source the user may wish to display. In some oscilloscopes delay lines may be used to help the user get the desired display by delaying the arrival time of the Y input signal to the crt, allowing the synchronizing process to have sufficient time to complete its operation. See Figure 18-4.

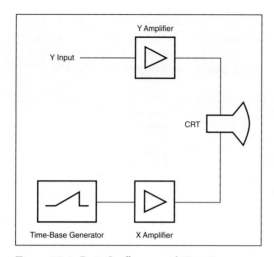

Figure 18-2. *Basic Oscilloscope with Time-Base Generator*

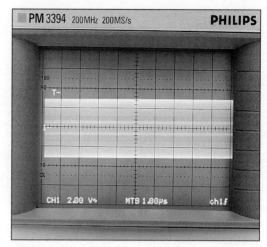

Figure 18-3. *Unsynchronized Time-Base*

As can be seen, the crt face is calibrated in increments of functions selected by the user. In this case, the horizontal divisions are calibrated in time per division (div.) and the vertical in volts per division.

The Basic Analog Oscilloscope

In the basic oscilloscope described, the amplitude and time parameters can be specified as measurement parameters. Amplitudes are measured by comparing the points of interest in a waveform with the graticule lines on the crt, multiplying the number of divisions with the V/div. setting of the instrument controls. Oscilloscopes' displays are limited to measuring differences in instantaneous values of amplitude or

time. Measurements of computed values such as rms voltages are not possible.

In the basic oscilloscope described, calibration of V/div. settings and time/div. settings takes place at the factory, and in subsequent calibrations. Accuracies are expressed as a percentage of reading. Most real-time oscilloscopes offer accuracies in the order of 2 or 3%. Horizontal settings are done similarly but are calibrated in time or hertz/div.

In a performance verification, as part of an oscilloscope calibration, there are other items that need to be verified and possibly adjusted. In the example above, such items include verification and adjustment of the following:

- bandwidth of the vertical channel
- rise time of the vertical channel
- bandwidth of the horizontal channel
- pulse response of the vertical channel
- verification and adjustment of trigger circuits

While the simple instrument described previously has the basic elements of an oscilloscope, most analog oscilloscopes are more complicated.

One example is the number of vertical channels a scope might have. Analog oscilloscopes with the capability to display up to four channels simultaneously are available. Multichannel displays are obtained by employing multiple preamplifiers and attenuators, one set for each channel, and connecting the output of each of these in turn to a fast electronic

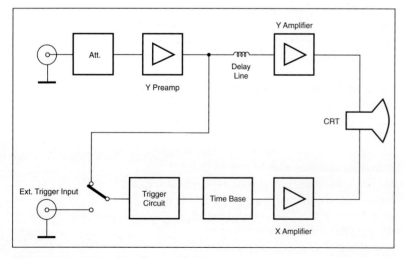

Figure 18-4. *A Typical Oscilloscope Block Diagram*

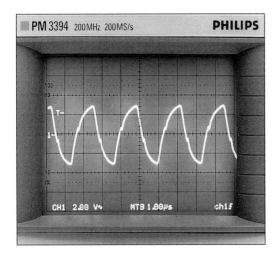

Figure 18-5. *Time-Base Synchronized with Y Input Signal*

switching circuit. The block diagram of such an instrument is shown in Figure 18-6.

Another capability found in a modern oscilloscope is the ability to display a user selectable part of a signal in greater detail. This is obtained by having two time-base generators. One, referred to as the main time-base, generates the display as explained before. Along the sweep of the main time-base, a second time-base generator can be started. The starting point of this second time-base is referred to as the delayed time-base generator, and the length of this second time-base sweep is also user selectable. The purpose of this arrangement is to allow the user to display any portion of the signal in greater detail, in order to make more precise measurements.

Figure 18-7 is a photo of an oscilloscope screen displaying a pulse train on the upper trace. A portion of the pulse train, relative to the main time-base, is intensified. A delayed sweep displaying the intensified part with increased detail is shown in the lower trace. The second time-base also requires calibration.

A fully equipped real-time oscilloscope like the one just described is a fairly complex instrument, as shown in Figure 18-8.

The performance verification of the horizontal circuits includes calibration of the time-base generators, adjusting and verifying triggering circuit sensitivity and symmetry, and calibration

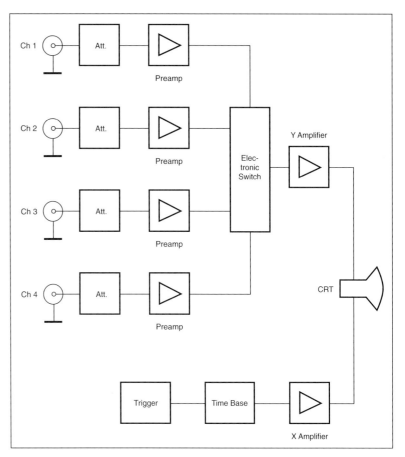

Figure 18-6. *Block Diagram of a Typical 4-Channel Analog Oscilloscope*

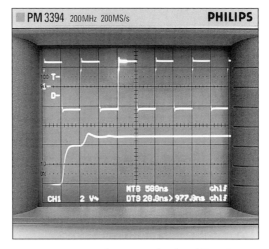

Figure 18-7. *Use of a Main and Delayed Time-Base*

of horizontal amplifiers, similar to the vertical amplifiers.

Digital Storage Oscilloscopes

Digital storage oscilloscopes (DSOs) process and display signals differently than analog oscilloscopes do. The DSO receives its signals, like the analog scope, through the input attenuators and amplifier, but as indicated in Figure 18-9, that is where the similarity ends.

After the signal is processed though the attenuator and amplifier, it is digitized in an analog-to-digital converter (adc), thus converting it to a digital signal at many points (samples) along the waveform, creating a synthesized representation of the analog signal. These digital values are then represented on the crt as dots along the horizontal axes of the display, as shown in Figure 18-10.

The performance parameters of the input are the same as for analog scopes in that bandwidth, rise time, deflection coefficients and calibration, and are expressed in the same values, and verified in the same way.

Once signals are digitized, they are stored in random access memory (RAM) and are made available for processing in a variety of tasks and functions, including display on the crt, the redisplay function, mathematic computations, and data handling, as discussed below.

Redisplay is the process where a stored digitized signal is recalled for display on the crt. In modern DSOs, multiple memories are used to store images and to recall them for comparison to other signals acquired at other times or other test points.

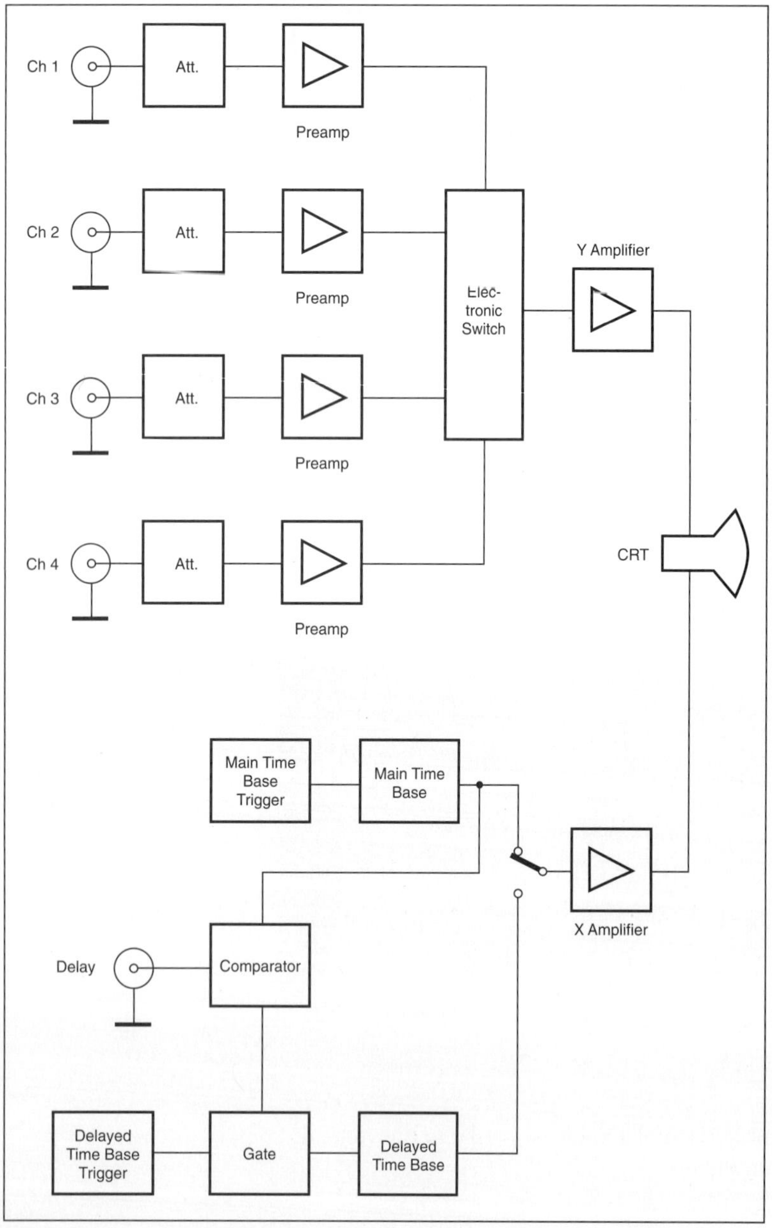

Math Operations

The DSO's microprocessors are also used to perform complex computations on stored data. Computations can be made over a number of functions including rms values of amplitudes and frequencies in the time domain, differentiated values, area under the curve, and displays in the frequency domain. All of these operations are made after the signal is captured and stored. The accuracy of these measurements or the waveform analysis is affected by the calibration of the analog section of the DSO.

Data Handling

DSOs, being primarily digital devices, lend themselves to processing digital information through their interface to printers and computers. This capability also makes the calibration process easier, as is discussed later in this chapter.

Figure 18-8. Fully Equipped Real-Time Oscilloscope

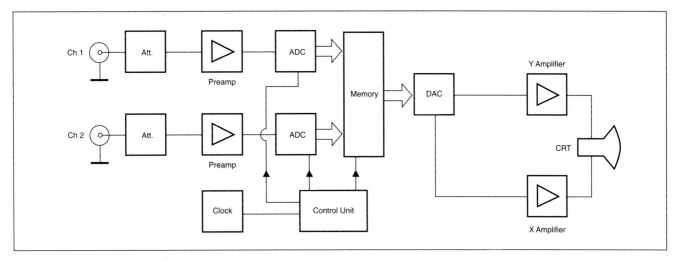

Figure 18-9. *Digital Storage Oscilloscope Block Diagram*

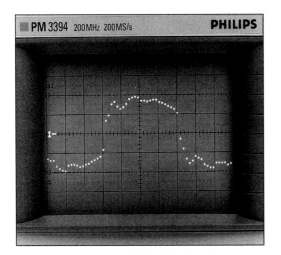

Figure 18-10. *Magnified DSO Waveform Display*

Combination Oscilloscopes

Oscilloscopes with the combined functions of analog oscilloscopes and DSOs are available. They offer the best features of both types of instruments; that is, the ability to faithfully reproduce complex analog waveforms on the analog function and the storage and computational power of the DSO.

The combination oscilloscope is necessarily more complex than either individual type of oscilloscope; however, the same basics apply for calibration and verification.

Oscilloscope Calibration

Important Consideration

The following is a discussion of the basic internal functional elements that the metrologist must deal with when performing oscilloscope calibration or when developing calibration procedures for them. Some of these considerations may or may not apply to specific models of scopes.

Vertical Channels

The amplitude calibration and band pass characteristics are critical to the quality of a measurement display. These amplifiers and associated attenuators are the primary elements affecting the accuracy. However, there are secondary effects on accuracy such as crt trace, focus and resolution.

Well-designed amplifiers remain stable in gain during their calibration interval, as do their frequency response and distortion characteristics, which are more a function of design characteristics than stability with time. While the gain stability of the vertical amplifiers tends to be good, it is noted that the entire vertical system including the attenuator, crt, amplifier delay line, or any other components in the vertical path, is compensated for by adjusting amplifier gain. Vertical channel gain stability in analog scopes is usually about one percent.

That is probably adequate in most cases because the visual resolution is no greater.

Note that the foregoing also applies when horizontal amplifiers are used, as is the case where Lissajous patterns are displayed.

Time Base

The accuracy of the horizontal channel of an analog scope is dependent upon the horizontal amplifier, the time-base generator, and the sawtooth generator that drives the crt's horizontal deflection plates. The accuracy dependencies of the horizontal amplifier are the same as those for the vertical amplifier.

Time-base accuracy of about one percent is normally sufficient. However, the wide range of sweep times, from seconds to nanoseconds per division, causes the calibration to be a time consuming process.

The linearity and accuracy of the horizontal crt drive is also a function of the sawtooth amplitude and linearity. Normally, calibration adjustment of the sawtooth amplitude is adjusted after the horizontal amplifier gain is set. The timing adjustment is made on the RC circuit from which the sawtooth wave is created. The RC circuit time-constant is adjusted to make the final adjustment of the seconds per division calibration.

If a delayed time-base function is contained in the scope, the same calibration considerations are made.

DSO Timing

DSO timing is normally based on a crystal oscillator with stability and accuracy of better than 10 ppm, which is several magnitudes better than an analog scope's time base. Because the crystal oscillator's frequency is inherent and fixed, calibration of its frequency is only verified, not adjusted. The oscillator output is then applied to appropriate frequency dividers to derive sampling speed, time-base rates, and trigger pulses. All of these are checked during the calibration process, but since they are based on the crystal oscillation accuracy, they

are not adjusted. Checking these functions and ranges is done to verify that a catastrophic failure has not occurred. In DSOs, a failure may be caused by component failure or software (firmware) problems.

Performing the Calibration

Oscilloscope calibration, unlike DMM calibration, can be a lengthy process if each range and function is checked. Although the accuracy requirements are much lower than those for DMMs, the technician must make specification judgments based on visual displays on the crt. This is particularly true of analog oscilloscopes where the fidelity of the display is so important. The calibration of DSOs is as exacting, but they lend themselves better to automated calibration because of their interface, typically IEEE-488, and their relatively high degree of accuracy. It is assumed that the appropriate calibration equipment has been assembled and that the technician is familiar with its use. Additional discussion of the calibration equipment is covered further on in this chapter.

The physical steps in the calibration process for analog scopes and DSOs are briefly described.

Analog Scope Calibration

As with any analog instrument, the oscilloscope must have reached thermal equilibrium before calibration can begin. Analog circuits are more susceptible than digital circuits to performance degradation if not stabilized, and this may cause the technician to have to repeat steps in the calibration.

Calibrating the vertical amplifier(s) is usually the first step in the calibrating of the instrument after it is stabilized. It is important that the cable connections are correct and that the proper termination is made. Improperly terminated connectors will lead to gross error in the calibration and may lead to degrading other performance characteristics.

The calibration procedure will specify a sine wave frequency, of relatively low frequency, to do the amplitude calibration. See Figure 18-11.

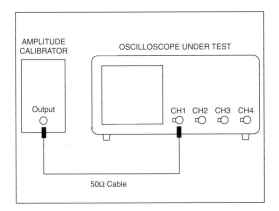

Figure 18-11. *Connection for Amplitude Calibration*

Step two is calibrating and adjusting the square wave response of the vertical amplifiers. Most procedures will call out the application of a high fidelity square wave at some amplitude and frequency to be applied to the vertical channel input terminals. Again, the cabling and proper termination are critical in this step. The verification and/or adjustment is made to display the square wave precisely, as shown in Figure 18-12. The procedure may also call out a low frequency pulse response test.

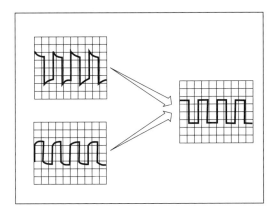

Figure 18-12. *Display of Vertical Channels with Application of a Square Wave*

Finally, the procedure may call out a constant amplitude, wide frequency range generator to perform a frequency response test of the vertical channel. This calibration will call out frequencies up to the amplifiers' 3 dB roll off point.

Because of interaction between the vertical channel characteristics, the calibration procedure may call out repeating some of these steps. Calibration of the horizontal amplifiers is done similarly. However, it is not unusual for the hor-

izontal amplifier to have poorer performance specifications than the vertical amplifiers.

Calibration of the time-base generator is straightforward when using a time-mark generation as the calibrator. The first step is to align the time-mark pulses with the graticule on the display. See Figure 18-13. If the scope has a time-delay generator, the calibration procedure will call out calibrating it the same way after the time-base generator has been calibrated.

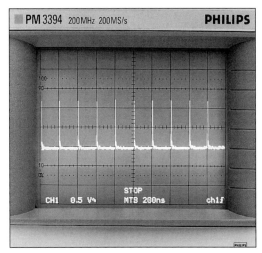

Figure 18-13. *Time-Base Generator Calibrated with a Time-Mark Generator*

The triggering circuits are checked for proper operation as a step in the calibration. Sensitivity and a balance test are made using the calibration equipment to simulate and verify conformance to specifications.

The calibration procedure may require other non-calibration checks to verify performance. Internal power supply voltage may be checked, and tests between interacting circuits are common. An example is the determination of the relative phase angle between vertical and horizontal channels. This test is performed by applying the same sine wave voltage to each channel and noting the phase shift on a Lissajous pattern. The phase angle is determined by comparing ratios of dimensions of the pattern. See Figure 18-14.

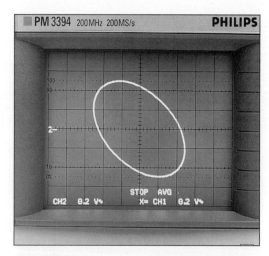

Figure 18-14. *Using Lissajous Pattern to Determine Relative Phase Shift Between Vertical and Horizontal Channels*

Figure 18-15. *Fluke PM3394 DSO*

DSO Oscilloscope Calibration

Calibration of a DSO's analog functions is the same as for analog scopes. The digital portion of the DSO is treated more as a computer, with its microprocessors, RAM, and bus interface,

than a scope. Therefore, the physical calibration of this portion of the DSO may be peculiar to that model, or model series, and will not be discussed further in the chapter because of the diversity in DSOs. Examples of the breadth of oscilloscope types is shown in Figures 18-15 and 18-16: a sophisticated laboratory DSO, Fluke PM3394; and a Fluke ScopeMeter, used for field service installation and maintenance.

Calibration Equipment Considerations

Traditional oscilloscope calibration consisted of gathering the appropriate primary equipment, usually a time-mark, constant amplitude, and pulse generator to make up a work station. These instruments may also appear as modules in a single instrument such as the Tektronix® 4051, which is more convenient to work with.

Whichever instruments are selected, it is important that their specifications and characteristics adequately support the oscilloscope (workload) to be calibrated. Wherever possible, a TUR of 4:1 should be maintained between the calibrator and the scope being calibrated.

Because performing calibrations manually is so time consuming, many calibration procedures are abbreviated, thereby compromising calibration and possibly missing important calibration points. It is therefore even more important that calibration equipment used be able to detect and correct deficiencies in the scope being calibrated. As with DMM calibrations, there has been a trend toward automated calibration. If new oscilloscope calibration equipment is being considered for purchase, one should consider equipment whose setup and data output can be controlled and accessed by a computer's communications bus, even if the initial workload doesn't justify the added cost. Automation costs are coming down.

Automated Oscilloscope Calibration Systems

Modern oscilloscopes are becoming more sophisticated, lending themselves to automated calibration. As is the case of the Fluke PM3394, many of the internal adjustments and checks are done within the instrument itself, and not done externally. This calibration is performed "closed case" and without manual intervention. These features shorten and simplify the external calibration process.

With the wide use of the IEEE-488 bus in modern instruments and the use of popular and low cost personal computers and commercially available software, the automation of oscilloscope calibration has become economical and productive. For example, utilizing the appropriate scope calibration hardware and Fluke's MET/CAL software, provides manual or fully automated calibration.

In the manual mode, MET/CAL steps the technician through each step of the procedure without having to refer to written procedures. The software accepts the calibration data and generates complete documentation, which is acceptable as meeting most quality standards. Manual calibrations take about an hour to complete.

In the fully automated mode, using the same calibration system, the calibration of a modern oscilloscope can be completed in a few minutes. As an example, the Fluke PM 3394 can be fully calibrated with supporting calibration report in under ten minutes. First, the PM 3394 is prompted to execute its internal calibration process, AUTOCAL, which verifies many of the internal settings for time and amplitude against internal references. This takes about four minutes. The PM 3394 is then connected to the MET/CAL system and cardinal points of the scope are calibrated against the scope calibration system. This takes about two minutes.

The result is a complex calibration process, either manual or automatic, being completed fast, repeatably and accurately, and with supporting data which meet quality standards. In addition, with the use of MET/TRACK, other management information such as physical

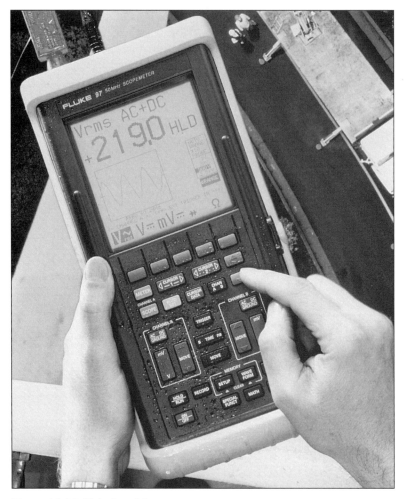

Figure 18-16. *Fluke ScopeMeter*

location and recall interval are conveniently maintained.

Conclusions

Traditionally, oscilloscope calibration has been a relatively complex process requiring skill and a relatively long time when done manually. Detailed written procedures are required to ensure the quality and consistency of the calibration when done by a skilled technician.

In today's modern world, processes, hardware and software are available to greatly improve oscilloscope calibration quality and economy. Fluke's MET/CAL and MET/TRACK software, along with the appropriate hardware under PC control, are examples of modern oscilloscope calibration systems. Present generation oscilloscopes, with closed-case calibration capabilities that interface to the calibration system, further enhance the calibration process.

Key References

"EBR: The Truth About Effective Bits," *Fluke Application Guide B0215B*

"Understanding DSO Bandwidth and Sampling," *Fluke Application Guide B0190D*

"Oscilloscopes: Analog, Digital, or Both?" *Fluke Application Guide B0228A*

"Digital Storage Oscilloscope: Competitive Comparison," *Fluke Application Guide J0341D*

"Measuring Power and Energy with Combi-Scopes,™" *Fluke Application Note B0235A*

Chapter 19:
Automated Calibration

Several functions of the metrology laboratory are excellent candidates for automation. These include the calibration of test equipment, documentation of results, generation of reports, and the maintenance of recall records, thus creating an audit trail for traceability.

All of the actions in the calibration process can be automated to improve the logistics of the calibration process, the quality of calibrations, and accuracy and thoroughness of the related documentation. The degree to which the calibration process is automated depends on each user's workload, quality needs, and audit environment.

Until recently, automation has been implemented only by organizations with significant resources. Improvements in automation technology, such as affordable desktop workstations and powerful application-specific software, have allowed many more companies to automate their calibration processes.

It is important to note that automated calibration does not yet involve software or hardware that thinks for itself. The calibration laboratory manager and technical staff must analyze what they do now, how they would like to improve their work, and where automation would be appropriate and affordable. They should assess their future needs in order to see how automation could be added as time passes.

This chapter should help the laboratory manager and staff successfully define, acquire, install, and integrate an automated calibration system with existing laboratory resources.

The Calibration Process

The successful automation of the calibration process requires an understanding of the actions in the process and their relationship to

Figure 19-1. *PC-Based Calibration Automation*

each other. Some of these actions are more suitable for automation than others. This may lead the laboratory manager to a piecemeal approach that can evolve into islands of automation incompatible with each other.

The calibration process, automated or not, involves many tasks on the part of the calibration laboratory manager, test technicians, and staff. These tasks can be divided into three categories: setup activities, day-to-day operations, and adjustments in workload.

Figure 19-2 illustrates the typical cycle of the overall calibration process.

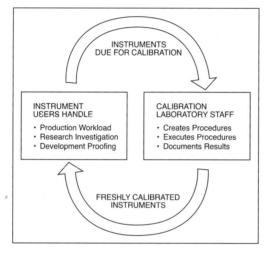

Figure 19-2. *Typical Instrument Calibration Cycle*

There are various activities in each category, as are itemized in the following lists. These lists can serve as guides for calibration laboratory managers who are considering automated calibration in their facilities.

Setup Activities

This category of activities establishes the general calibration protocols and procedures, such as:

■ identifying the instruments to be calibrated

■ establishing calibration intervals

■ setting up an acceptable quality level (AQL) for the instruments

■ documenting the instruments' location and use

■ establishing the kind of calibration procedure to be used to calibrate the various units under test (UUTs)

■ determining whether to calibrate instruments on-site or in the calibration laboratory

■ determining the skill levels required to manage the workload and do the calibrations

■ determining the environment and supporting equipment required

Day-to-Day Operations

Day-to-day operations involve the regular routine of the calibration laboratory. Activities that can be put into the day-to-day category include:

■ bringing instruments to the calibration laboratory or calibrating them on-site

■ locating the appropriate test procedure

■ inspecting and repairing test instruments

■ making as-found or as-left calibration verification (in some environments)

■ making calibration adjustments

■ maintaining measurement standards

■ issuing reports, certificates, stickers, and other pertinent calibration documents to meet the needs of instrument owners and auditors

■ returning completed instruments to service

Adjustments in Workload

From time to time, the calibration laboratory reviews and adjusts its activity. A short list of some of these actions includes:

can be used in conjunction with automated calibration software to carry out a calibration laboratory's mission.

At this time, there are two broad categories of commercially-available metrology software: calibration software, and workload management software.

Calibration software is used to conduct the actual calibrations. This helps to maintain an unbroken chain of measurements traceable to national standards. Workload management software provides the documents and records that serve as the evidence of an operating quality system or of contractual compliance for traceable measurements. This helps to prove that the chain of measurements is indeed unbroken to national standards. For more information, see Chapter 26, "Workload Management."

When an appropriate IEEE-488 bus control card is installed, the computer can be used with Fluke MET/CAL calibration software to control calibrators and UUTs for computer-aided and closed-loop calibrations. MET/CAL software can also be used for operator-prompted calibrations in conjunction with manually-operated calibration equipment.

It is usually not necessary to know how to program in a computer programming language, such as BASIC or C, to use this software. Instead, MET/CAL uses an intermediate applications-oriented language. The basic features of this language are about as easy to learn and use as commercially-available spreadsheet software. These basic features are especially useful for calibrating manually-operated DMMs and for operator-prompted calibration.

There are advanced features of the language whose use is comparable to writing simple macros for use within a spreadsheet or word processor. Typical applications include talking and listening to UUTs on the IEEE-488 bus in closed-loop and closed-case calibration applications.

MET/CAL can call subroutines written in another programming language, such as C, to execute some tasks that could not be accomplished by MET/CAL alone. When the subroutine ends, control returns to MET/CAL. A

typical application for this feature would be the calibration of a Fluke Sigma Series DMM10 in a board-test system. In this application, binary data must be sent to and from the DMM in the board-test system in order to complete its calibration adjustment. A programmer could write a C subroutine that could accomplish this, and the MET/CAL procedure could invoke it for that purpose.

Calibration software should be able to provide traceability information for the calibration standards it controls, as well as generate reports for the units it calibrates. This information should be accessible to workload management software such as Fluke MET/TRACK.

Operator-Prompted Calibration

Operator-prompted calibration can be implemented for completely manual calibrations. In this kind of calibration, both the calibration stimulus and UUT are manually adjusted.

Computer-Aided Calibration

In computer-aided calibration, the computer is used to complete the mundane aspects of documentation and calibration history. The computer may even control the stimulus and UUT devices for a consistent setup each time. The technician still makes the visual measurement and answers questions from the computer as to the accuracy of the UUT.

Closed-Loop Calibration

The ultimate in automation is closed-loop calibration, which allows a technician to connect an instrument to the stimulus device as directed by the computer procedure. The computer then examines the IEEE-488 bus to determine the address of the UUT, and then takes complete control of the calibration. The computer takes as-found test data, analyzes the results, and adjusts the UUT as required. See Figure 19-3.

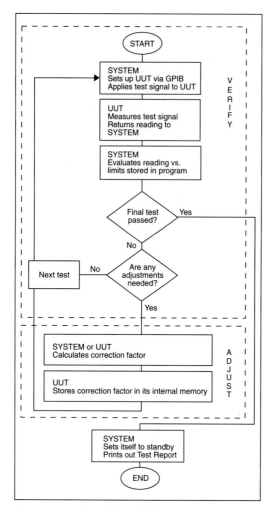

Figure 19-3. *Closed-Loop Calibration*

The majority of these types of calibration involve DMMs, since their readings can easily be transferred to the computer for evaluation. The DMM under test must have the ability to be adjusted without opening the instrument or requiring an action by the operator. The Fluke 8840 series DMMs permit this type of calibration. Because of the increased cost-effectiveness of closed-loop calibrations, the number of UUTs with the capability built in is on the increase.

Calibration Software Requirements

What are the requirements for a good calibration software package? Figure 19-4 depicts the

architecture of a top-quality automated calibration system.

An automated calibration system should:

- provide workload coverage
- be easy to learn and use
- be versatile and execute procedures quickly
- identify out-of-tolerance conditions
- ensure calibration system adequacy
- document traceability
- interface with other metrology software
- offer powerful procedure generation
- ensure operator safety
- provide documented procedures
- be secure from tampering
- be transportable for on-site calibrations

The following sections describe these features in detail.

Workload Coverage
The calibration system supports the majority of the calibration activity carried out by the laboratory. The system can control measurement instruments that support a broad range of applications. The accuracy of these instruments provides adequate TURs. The system is flexible, with the ability to add new instruments as the need arises. Closed-loop capability is available.

Ease of Use
The system is easy to learn and to operate, allowing operators with a wide range of skill levels to use the system. This means that the system operates in an intuitive fashion, with a user-friendly, menu-based interface. The system can display illustrations to help guide the user through new procedures (see Figure 19-5).

Fast, Flexible, and Efficient
There are a variety of operator control modes such as go/no-go, slew, or numeric entry. All mathematical computations are automatic, including calculation of UUT errors and system TURs. The system identifies out-of-tolerance conditions, and records those along with all test data. Out-of-tolerance operator messages should be displayed in real time (see Figure 19-6).

Faster Calibrations
Automation leads to increased workload throughput and, therefore, lowered calibration costs. Table 19-1 compares typical manual and

automated calibration times for hand-held, bench, and systems DMMs.

Table 19-1. Comparison of Calibration Times

Meter Type	Fluke Model	Manual (min.)	Automated (min.)	Time Saved
Hand-held	23	35	20	42%
Bench	45	45	20	48%
Systems	8842A	60	20	66%

The data was compiled using Fluke MET/CAL automated calibration software running on an IBM-compatible 80386 PC. These times do not include additional reductions in time through the automated preparation and delivery of certificates and reports at the end of the procedure.

Flags Out-of-Tolerance Readings

The system identifies marginal, out-of-tolerance, and significantly out-of-tolerance conditions. These conditions are readily identified both on the MET/CAL screen and in the generated reports.

Ensures System Adequacy

TURs are calculated for each calibration test. TURs falling below a user-determined threshold (nominally 4 to 1) are automatically flagged.

Documents Traceability

Calibration results include complete traceability data. Reports are generated automatically at the end of the procedure. The system has provisions for easy modification of the document format as needed, to comply with company policy.

Interfaces with Other Software

The data summary format should be such that it is easy to exchange calibration records between the calibration system, statistical applications packages, and asset management systems as shown in Figure 19-7.

The system provides traceability data on the instruments used during the calibration. This documents the unbroken chain of comparisons leading to NIST or to some other national standard.

Powerful Procedure Generation

The system does not require programming expertise for generating calibration procedures.

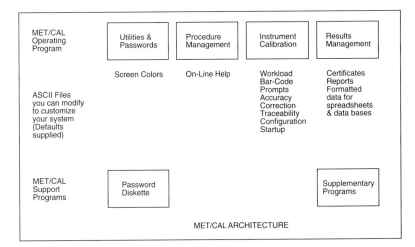

Figure 19-4. Automated System Functional Diagram

Figure 19-5. On-Screen Illustration of Calibration Configuration

Figure 19-6. Out-of-Tolerance Notice Displayed on Screen

Procedures are self-documenting. They resemble familiar manual procedures. Table 19-2 compares equivalent steps of a conventional and MET/CAL automated calibration procedure.

The calibration software allows procedures to be generated easily with error checking, on-line help screens, tolerance calculation, and

TUR checking (see Figure 19-8). The system allows popular text editor software to be used for off-line procedure writing. The system has the ability to display illustrations that show connection points, or show the operator locations of adjustments in the UUT. The system also includes samples of procedures that cover a broad spectrum of instruments. These examples guide the new user through the steps of writing a procedure for an instrument.

Ensures Operator Safety

The system is designed with operator safety in mind and includes an immediate and safe disconnect of all stimulus instruments in case of potentially dangerous conditions.

Provides Documented Procedures

Procedures comply with quality guidelines, helping the laboratory to pass government or commercial audits. The laboratory's operations are documented from procedure generation through text execution to documentation.

Security

The software package has different levels of password protection, to allow the manager to control the overall system. The highest level allows the password holder to change all aspects of the system: system configuration, startup messages, procedures, or document format. Intermediate levels permit tasks such as procedure generation or results management. The lowest levels are restricted to calibrations. Password protection gives the manager control over the system and helps to eliminate unauthorized modifications.

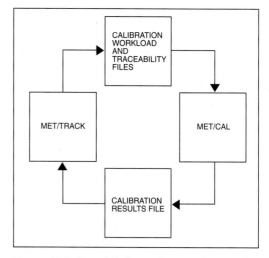

Figure 19-7. *Record Exchanges Between Automated Systems*

Figure 19-8. *MET/CAL TUR Checking*

Goes Where the Workload Is

Often it is necessary to take the calibration system to the workload, for on-site calibrations. The entire calibration system can be rolled out to the test equipment that needs to be calibrated (see Figure 19-9).

Table 19-2. *Conventional versus Automated Calibration Steps*

Conventional	Automated (MET/CAL)
1. Turn on unit under test.	1. DISP Turn on meter
2. Allow 30 minute warm-up.	2. DISP Allow 30 minute warm-up
3. Select meter 10V dc range; then Set calibrator output to 10V dc	3. 5700 10R 10V .005%
4. Adjust 5700A output for a reading of exactly 10V dc on unit under test	
5. Verify that UUT error is not more than 0.005%	

Automation and Company Quality

Automation has made several favorable changes in the calibration process. Instruments are recalled in a timely, efficient manner. Procedures are run, data is accurately reported, and use of human and technical resources is optimized. Documents are prepared to specifications. Equipment is returned to its user quickly. Data to support audits and to make intelligent purchase decisions is readily available. All of this adds up to a calibration laboratory that is a productive contributor to the quality and profitability of the entire company.

For more information on the role of calibration and asset management in a quality assurance system, see Chapter 6, "Standards and Traceability," Chapter 28, "Laboratory Quality and ISO 9000," and Chapter 26, "Workload Management."

Key References

Pirret, Richard, "Software Tools for ISO 9000 Compliance," National 1992 Workshop and Symposium, Conference of Standards Laboratories, August, 1992

"How Metrology Management Software Simplifies MIL-STD-45662A Compliance," *Fluke Application Note B0204A*

Other references for this chapter are in the Resources Appendix.

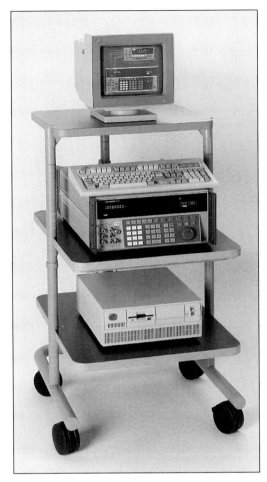

Figure 19-9. *Small, Mobile Automated Calibration System*

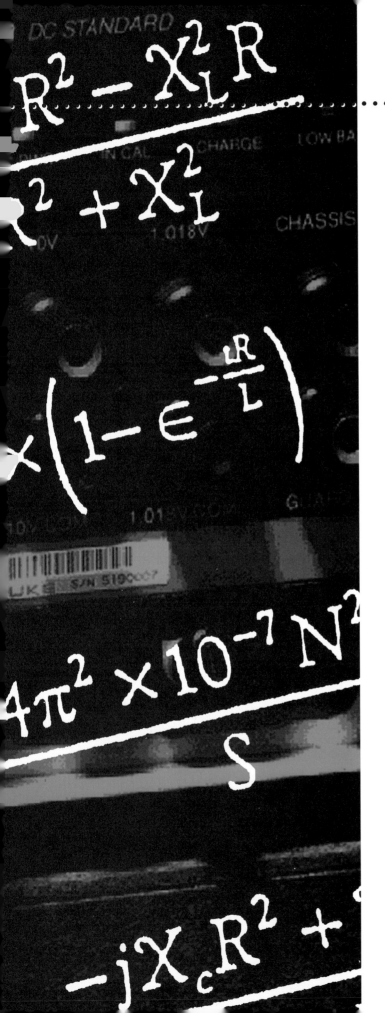

Statistics

Section Five

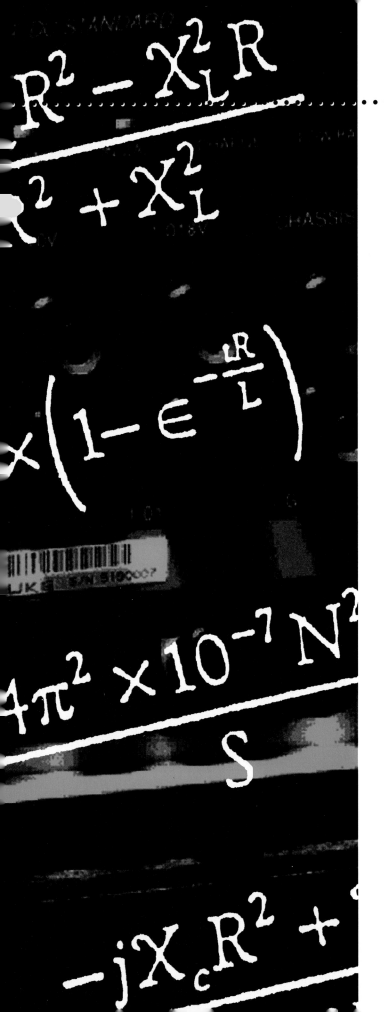

Chapter 20:

Introduction to Metrology Statistics

This chapter discusses the metrologist's use of statistics to predict reliability, accuracies, and calibration intervals of test equipment. Methods in this chapter pertain to all types of measurement instrumentation.

This chapter provides simplified information concerning the relationship of the normal distribution of error to test uncertainty ratios (TURs), prediction of calibration intervals, and enhancing the performance of a calibrator via statistical methods. It also provides a simplified review of the terminology associated with the bell-shaped curve of the Gaussian distribution. Finally, it introduces the use of a linear regression to predict an instrument's performance, using the example of a multifunction calibrator (MFC), and it places prediction limits on the regression. Chapter 21, "Statistical Tools for Metrology," gives a more rigorous discussion of the statistical methods used in metrology.

Populations of Data

The greatest power of metrology is realized when statistics are used to analyze and characterize a population of measurement data. The population of data is a group of like measurements, for example the record of the measured values for a large number of resistance calibrations.

A statistical analysis of a population of data depends on the population's size and distribution. When these factors are known, additional data can be extracted from the data via various statistical methods. The extracted data can then be used to improve all aspects of the metrology operation.

Distributions

The values of the population's data are assumed to be distributed in some way. The distribution is a comparison of the value to some other parameter, such as the frequency of its occurrence. The distribution of values usually occurs in one of a number of well known ways such as normal or Gaussian, skewed, bimodal, Poisson, binomial or rectangular.

For example, an honest coin toss has only two possible outcomes, heads or tails. The distribution of the results of the coin toss consists of two equally likely outcomes. The coin toss is a

simple example of an experiment that leads to the binomial distribution of results. Other examples include the toss of an honest die or the outcome of a process that will produce results that either pass or fail a defined test.

Histograms

A histogram is a bar chart that's commonly used to depict a data distribution. It helps a metrologist visualize the relationships of the key elements of the distribution, its range, mean, median, standard deviation and mode. Plotting a histogram will immediately show such problems as bimodality or other undesirable characteristics in a distribution.

Three histograms are provided in Figures 20-1, 20-2, and 20-3 to illustrate these key elements for three types of distribution, normal, skewed and bi-modal. Each histogram plots the number of occurrences of the integers 1 through 100 from a total population of 4000 integers.

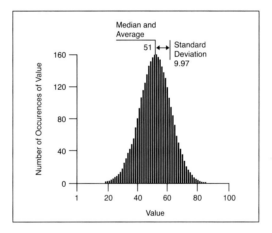

Figure 20-1. *Normal Distribution*

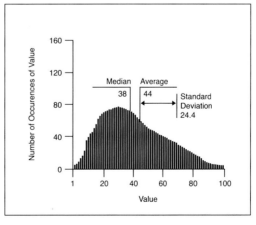

Figure 20-2. *Skewed Distribution*

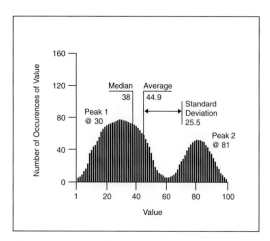

Figure 20-3. *Bimodal Distribution*

Range

The range of a data set is the difference between its largest and smallest value. In each of the three histograms, the range is 100. There are no gaps between the values in these histograms. In actual practice, there may be gaps between most of the data and the highest or lowest values. These extreme values are called "outliers" and their values are often excluded from further statistical analysis when there is good reason to doubt their validity. In this case, the range is the difference between the highest and lowest remaining values.

Mean, Median, Mode and Standard Deviation

The two properties of distributions most useful to a metrologist are the mean (the arithmetic average) and the standard deviation (a measure of the variability of the elements of the distribution). Other properties include the median (point or value below which exactly half the population falls) and the mode (the point or value for which the probability is greatest).

Figure 20-1 is a bar chart of the normal distribution. Due to its extreme importance to metrology, the normal distribution is extensively discussed under the major subheading "Normal Distribution." For comparison to the other histograms, it is noted here that the normal distribution has a single mode, and its average and median values are the same, at the peak. The distribution of the data for this figure has the smallest standard deviation in all of the three figures.

While it may be difficult to amass the data required to prove that a particular population is

normally distributed, there are reasons to believe that the results of most measurement processes are. In those cases where there is a minor deviation from normal distribution, the penalty for assuming normality is small. Metrologists usually assume normality for measurement processes, if the appropriate tests for normality, described in Chapter 21, "Statistical Tools for Metrology," are passed.

In contrast to the histogram for the normal distribution, Figure 20-2 depicts a skewed distribution of the 4000 values. As shown, its average value is greater than its median and its standard deviation is larger than for the normal distribution. Figure 20-3 is a bimodal distribution such that from a value of 1 to its highest peak at a value of 30 the values are distributed as they were in the skewed distribution. Consequently the median is the same but the average value and the standard deviation have increased because of the shifting of several hundred values out of the "trough" near the value of 62 and into the second peak at the value of 81.

One can expect that calibration data will be normally distributed and should perform a statistical test for normality when the assumption of normality is important to the quality of the results. When the distribution of the data is skewed, bimodal or otherwise deviates from normality, the calibration process is probably out of control and needs to be investigated. A histogram provides a quick check for normality in the distribution of data. It is a good idea to plot a histogram even when statistical tests for normality are performed, because it may help in identifying the reasons for non-normal behavior.

Distributions vs. TURs

Manufacturers usually do not specify the individual performance of each instrument they make. Instead, their specifications for a specific model number are based on a calculation of the probability that a large portion of all instruments in the population of that model will be within specifications.

Normal Distribution

It has been empirically determined that the variation in the performance of populations of a wide range of instruments, such as calibrators and DMMs, can be modeled as a function of the area under the standard normal or bell-shaped Gaussian curve, depicted in Figure 20-4. The standard normal curve will be referred to as the normal curve or normal distribution in the material that follows.

The equation for the normal curve is:

$$y_{(\sigma)} = \frac{1}{\sqrt{2\pi}} \times e^{-\frac{\sigma^2}{2}}$$

Where:

$y_{(\sigma)}$ = probability density at σ

e = base of natural logarithms

σ = point on the horizontal scale in standard deviations

The definition of probability density and the derivation of the variance of the normal curve involve a mathematical consideration of an infinite population of values that is beyond the scope of this book. Suffice it to say that the practical counterparts of these concepts are, respectively, probability and sample variance.

The focus of this chapter is on the practical application of the normal curve with respect to the evaluation of the specifications of finite populations of calibrators, DMMs and other instruments. An explanation of the following terminology is essential to this discussion.

- Mean or Average
- Variance
- Sample Variance
- Standard Deviation
- Sample Standard Deviation
- Uncertainty
- Confidence Level
- Confidence Interval
- Student's t

Mean or Average

An average value is simply the arithmetic mean of a series of values. The equation for the average value of a finite data set is:

$$\bar{x} = \frac{1}{N} \sum_{i=1}^{N} x_i$$

Where:

$\bar{x}$ = Mean (average) value of the data

N = Number of items in the data set

x_i = Value of item i in the data set, $i = 1$ to N

In metrology, the series of values can be the results of a number of measurements. When a large number of measurements are made of a presumably invariant parameter, there will be a variation in the measured values. When the distribution of the measured values approximates the shape of the normal curve, the true value of the parameter is most likely equal to the average value. The qualifier in that last sentence is "most likely," and is discussed further under "Uncertainty."

Variance

Variance (σ^2) is the mean square deviation from the average value. The variance of the normal curve equals 1.

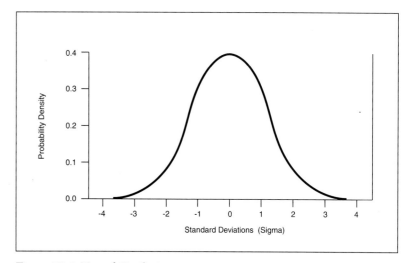

Figure 20-4. Normal Distribution

Sample Variance

The sample variance for a population of data values is an estimate of the true variance for this population. Its equation is:

$$s^2 = \frac{\sum\limits_{i=1}^{N}(x_i - \bar{x})^2}{N-1}$$

Where:

s^2 = Sample variance

N = Number of items in the data set

x_i = Value of item i in the data set, $i = 1$ to N

$\bar{x}$ = Mean (average) value of the data

Standard Deviation

The standard deviation of the normal curve equals 1. The horizontal scale of the normal curve is defined in standard deviations, where one standard deviation is symbolized by the lowercase Greek letter sigma, σ.

Vertical lines projected upward from the horizontal axis at points that are plus and minus 1 σ from the center of the scale intercept the curve at its points of inflection. About 68% of the area under the curve is located between these lines.

Sample Standard Deviation

The sample standard deviation is the square root of the sample variance.

Uncertainty

One cannot be certain that the true value and the average value are identical. The normal curve can be used as a model to calculate the range of values which is likely to contain the true value. This range of values, usually symmetrically centered on the average value, is called the uncertainty. Uncertainty, defined in this way, is equivalent to a confidence interval, which has a confidence level.

Confidence Level

The confidence level is expressed as a percentage. It is the probability that the true value lies in the range represented by the uncertainty. For example, when the points on the horizontal scale are located between -1σ and $+1\sigma$ from the center, about 68% of the area of the curve is between the two points; the confidence level is therefore 68%.

Confidence Interval

The confidence interval is obtained by multiplying the standard deviation by a coverage factor. It is the distance between the two points on the horizontal scale that are used to establish the confidence level. Conventionally, but somewhat confusingly, the phrase "two-sigma confidence" actually refers to the area under the curve from -2σ to $+2\sigma$ on the horizontal scale. This confidence interval implies a confidence level of a little more than 95%.

Student's t

Another very useful distribution is the student's t distribution. It was developed by an Englishman, William Gosset, whose pen name was "Student." This distribution allows the metrologist to draw valid statistical conclusions from small data samples.

Student's t can be considered a special case of the normal distribution, where the population mean and variability are not known but can only be estimated from experimental data. As the number, n, in the sample becomes large, the t distribution approaches the normal distribution. In fact, for $n > 30$ there is little practical difference, and for $n > 100$ the differences can be ignored for all but the most exacting analysis.

Distributions versus Test Uncertainty Ratios (TURs)

Test uncertainty ratio (TUR) is defined as the specified uncertainty of the test instrument divided by the uncertainty of the calibrating instrument. For example, the calibration of a DMM by a MFC is discussed below.

The immediate purpose of calibration is to gain confidence that a UUT is able to make measurements within its specifications. For example, suppose one wants to check a DMM's performance as specified on the 10V range: ±20 ppm of reading, +1.6 ppm of range. The calibration of this DMM can be checked by applying a known 10V from an MFC to its input. If exactly 10V is applied to this DMM, any reading within ±216 µV of 10V will be within specifications.

Calibration laboratories generally don't have access to exact values of stimulus to test DMMs or other equipment. Instead, they must use commercially-available calibrators such as MFCs, which also have uncertainty specifications. For example, data for the Fluke 5700A MFC specifies that the outputs on its 11 volt range are within ±(5 ppm of output ±4 µV) of the true value. When this specification is converted to units, the uncertainty in the MFC's 10V output is ±54 µV or ±5.4 ppm. This is its 99% confidence level (2.6 sigma value). This corresponds to $1\sigma = 5.4/2.6 = 2.08$ ppm.

Computing TURs

If the vendors of the DMM and MFC in this example have based their respective specifications on a normal distribution of uncertainty, and if the confidence interval for the specifications is the same, the TUR between the DMM and MFC is exactly 4:1. According to MIL-STD-45662A and other similar calibration standards, this is an acceptable TUR.

Suppose that the DMM specification is ±15 ppm of input ±20 µV. When 10V is applied to this DMM, readings within ±170 µV of 10V will be within specifications. If you divide the calibrator uncertainty of ±54 µV into this value, you obtain an apparent TUR of 3.148. However, the

DMM specifications have a 2σ confidence interval while the calibrator's specifications have a 2.58σ confidence interval. The difference in the confidence intervals must be taken into consideration to compute the true TUR.

When the specifications for the calibrator and the DMM are based on a normal distribution of uncertainty, the true TUR is computed as:

$$TUR_{true} = TUR_{apparent}\, K_{pcal}\,/\,K_{pDMM}$$

Where:

$TUR_{apparent}$ = ratio of published specifications

K_{pcal} = coverage factor for the calibrator specifications

K_{pDMM} = coverage factor for the DMM specifications

p = probability of instrument meeting its specifications

For the preceding example, the true TUR is:

$$TUR_{true} = 3.148(2.58/2.0) = 4.06$$

A reliable TUR is only obtained when the specifications for the DMM and MFC are correlated according to their respective uncertainty distributions and confidence intervals. You cannot simply divide the smaller number into the bigger number and decide that the TUR is 4:1 when the quotient of the specification ratios is ≥ 4.

Ideal versus Real World Test Results

Ideally, test results should have only two outcomes:

- Good units will be accepted.
- Bad units will be rejected.

Assuming that the population of DMMs is normally distributed, real world test results will add two types of spurious test decisions due to the uncertainty in the specifications for both the instrument being calibrated and the calibrator. These decisions are:

- Good units will be rejected.
- Bad units will be accepted.

The relative rate of occurrence of the four kinds of test decisions will vary according to the TURs and confidence intervals for the DMM and MFC.

The major, and perhaps most surprising result is that the number of in-tolerance DMMs that are falsely rejected always exceeds the number of out-of-tolerance DMMs that are falsely accepted. Figure 20-5 illustrates this situation.

It is assumed that there is a 4:1 TUR and 3σ specifications for the MFC and DMM. The case where the actual output of the MFC is lower than the nominal by the maximum in-specification deviation is illustrated in Figure 20-5.

In terms of the DMM specification, the MFC output is at −0.75σ. Relative to the test limits, the DMMs truly in-tolerance readings extend from −3.75σ to +2.25σ. This is because they are symmetrically distributed around a stimulus that is displaced −0.75σ from nominal.

Therefore, DMM readings between −3.75σ and −3.00σ, relative to nominal, will be falsely out of tolerance. Similarly, readings between +2.25σ and +3σ will be falsely in tolerance. Due to the distribution of probability density for the normal curve, a greater area is under the curve for the falsely out-of-tolerance readings than for the falsely in-tolerance readings.

Inspection of the preceding Figure 20-5 shows that mirror-image results will be obtained when the MFC's output is displaced to 0.75σ. Figure 20-6 summarizes the distribution of false test decisions with 4:1 TURs and 3σ specifications.

Assume that the MFC's actual output is displaced by a very large amount, 50σ from nominal. For practical purposes, all of the DMMs will be rejected even though 99.7% of them are actually in tolerance, with a normal distribution of error.

This discussion has additional practical value. The DMMs or MFCs may have been improperly specified, or abused, or may incorporate unsuspected manufacturing defects. In these cases, the distribution of the test decisions will be different than the specifications would imply. In view of this, it is a good idea to keep a record of the deviations from nominal for each test event of each mode, instead of pass/fail data only. This data can be statistically analyzed to determine the actual (rather than the assumed) confidence level for the DMMs or other instruments of interest.

1:1 TURs

It is becoming more common to find DMMs whose uncertainty specifications are virtually the same as the MFCs. In other words, the TUR approaches 1:1. How can these DMMs be calibrated?

Remember, the distributions and confidence intervals for the respective specifications of the UUT and its calibrator must be strictly correlated before the TUR can be obtained. Now we will consider the case where the strictly correlated specifications of a UUT and its calibrator are about the same.

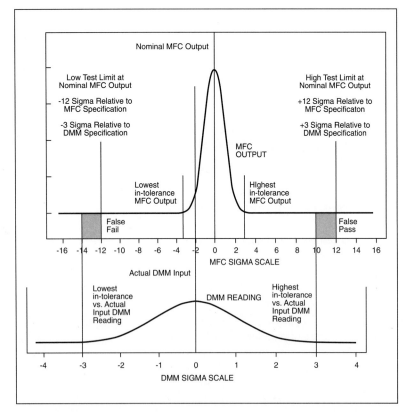

Figure 20-5. *False Test Decisions*

In this case, the nominal TUR is 1:1 and we would reject about 50% of the good DMMs when the MFC output is just within specifications at the $\pm3\sigma$ specification limit (0.15% of all so-specified MFCs will exhibit this condition). To reduce the number of false rejections we must increase the TUR. How can we do this?

One way to increase the TUR is to use high accuracy standards that externally measure the MFC's output. The nominal test parameter is obtained by adjusting the MFC output until the measured value is at nominal. In this scenario, the TUR is the ratio of the uncertainty of the external standards plus the stability of the MFC to the DMM's uncertainty ratio.

However, it is not always necessary to use a full complement of external equipment to enhance an MFC's performance in order to get a better TUR. Statistical methods can be used with a few external standards to characterize the MFC's performance. The uncertainty of the characterized performance, not the specified performance, is what determines the TUR. When this approach is used, some of the principles of statistical process control (SPC) are used to characterize the MFC's performance. For information on SPC, see Chapter 23, "Statistical Process Control."

Improving Performance with Statistics

The rest of this chapter shows how linear regression can be used to predict the performance of a calibrator. Equations for the linear regression and prediction confidence limits are given in Chapter 21, "Statistical Tools for Metrology."

Discussion

A manufacturer proofs the performance of all functions of every MFC during final test prior to shipment. At this time, each MFC output is more accurate than specified because its calibration adjustments have been closely harmonized with the values of the standards used. In

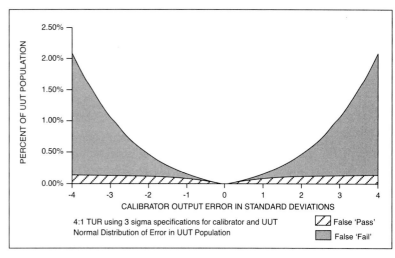

Figure 20-6. *Distribution of False Test Decisions*

general, this is true of artifact, software, and manually adjusted calibrators.

Recall that performance specifications apply to the total population of MFCs during their entire calibration interval and throughout their environmental envelope. For this reason, their performance specifications are not as good as their maximum performance obtained through their initial calibration adjustment at standard reference conditions of temperature and humidity. Experience shows that in the course of time, each output of every MFC is likely to drift from its initially adjusted value. The magnitude and direction of the drift will be unique for each individual output of every MFC, but experience indicates that it is approximately linear with time. This fact allows characterization of the performance of a specific MFC to enhance its performance. The drift history of two hypothetical MFCs is conceptually symbolized in Figure 20-7.

Calibrator A may drift more or less than Calibrator B. However, if one knows what the value of an output was when it was adjusted, and has a record of how much the output has drifted since then, it is possible to algebraically add the relevant data and obtain a prediction of the present output. If the prediction is tested against actual measurements and good correlation is obtained, the predictions can then be trusted to be a true indicator of the actual value of the MFC output.

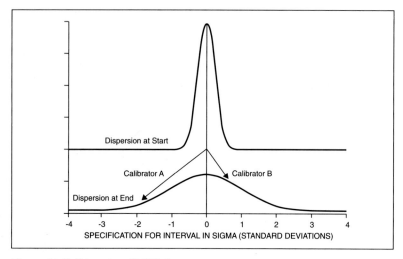

Figure 20-7. *Dispersion of MFC Outputs*

This process is no different than that used for maintaining primary calibration standards. Perhaps a hundred records are kept instead of just a few, but the nature of the records and their applications is the same as for the primary calibration standards.

Detailed Example

To better understand this process, you can conceptually think of any MFC stimulus parameter being generated within the MFC. For example, the +10V output of an MFC can be obtained by the process of dividing the output of a +13V reference amplifier by a pulse-width-modulated digital-to-analog converter (pwmdac), integrating the resultant rectangular wave, and applying the integrated voltage to a buffer amplifier whose output is routed to the MFC binding posts.

Statistical analysis can be used to evaluate this internal MFC process by determining if the MFC stimulus-generating process is in control, is controlled at the right value, and is stable with time.

The Fluke 5700A MFC is able to measure the changes in its outputs relative to internal check standards. It can transmit this data to a personal computer (PC) via an RS-232 or IEEE-488 data bus. A record of these changes can be kept by the PC to evaluate the stability of the 5700A performance against time relative to its internal check standards. The stability of the internal check standards can be separately

obtained by comparing their values with external standards from time to time.

The two sets of data can be automatically combined in a prediction chart using commercially available software, such as a spreadsheet. The PC software can perform linear regressions on the combined data. The linear regression can be used to predict the amount of displacement of the 5700A output from nominal. This has a typical uncertainty two to four times better than the 5700A published specifications.

Under PC control, the predicted displacement in the calibrator output can be used to obtain a correction factor for its programmed output. In this manner, the displacement of the 5700A output from nominal will be small and the consequent TUR will be higher than would be the case if its output were not corrected. The actual output for each function and range can be improved using this method.

In effect, this method amounts to keeping a prediction chart for the calibrator and using it to discipline the displacement of the calibrator outputs. In other words, the statistics of the calibrator's internal metrology process are used to keep its own outputs under tight control.

Data Validation

To test this assumption, the preceding process has been conducted at Fluke with the 5700A. In this experiment, a Fluke 5700A measured the shift in its software calibration constants relative to its internal dc voltage and resistance references once a week. Historical data were kept for each amplitude on each range. Linear regression was then performed on the data. Figure 20-8 is a regression for the 10-volt range of the dcV function.

The dots in Figure 20-8 represent the calibrator's actual output. The straight line is the linear regression, and the curved lines are the prediction limits that bound the slopes of possible regression lines.

In the meantime, the calibrator was periodically returned to the Fluke factory test area and had its performance on each range and function checked against Fluke calibration standards. As with any primary calibration, detailed results of the calibration were recorded.

The calibrator's predicted performance from the linear regressions was correlated with its actual performance as determined by the calibration in the standards laboratory. Figure 20-9 is an XY scatter plot that summarizes the result of the experiment.

Note that measurements of the shift in the calibrator's internal dc voltage and resistance references are critical to obtaining the results in Figure 20-9.

Key References

Youden, W.J., "Experiment and Measurement," *NBS Special Publication 672*, March, 1984

Other references for this chapter are in the Resources Appendix.

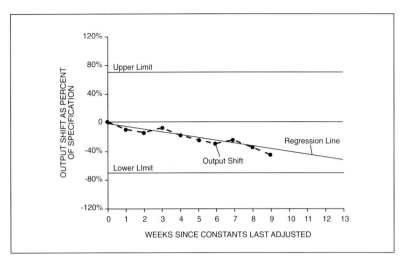

Figure 20-8. *Regression for +10V Range*

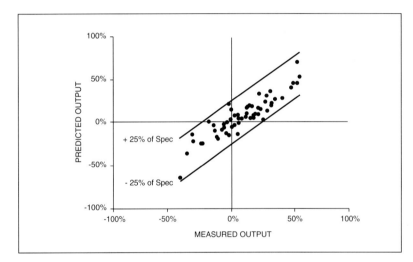

Figure 20-9. *Measured versus Predicted % of Specification Outputs*

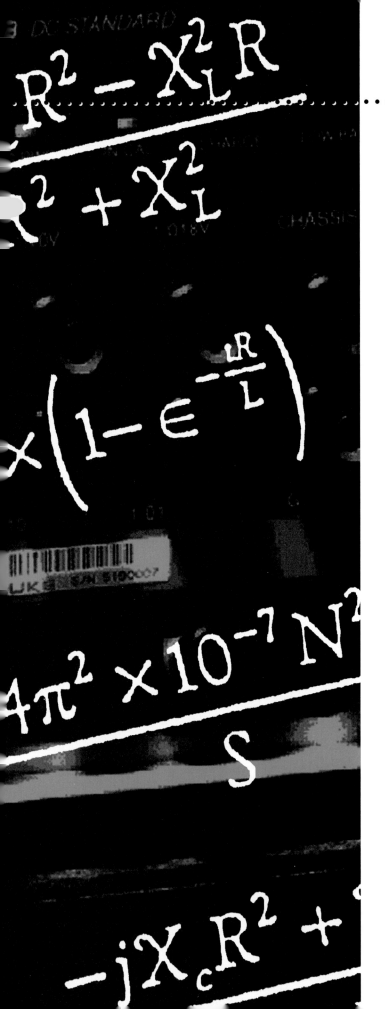

Chapter 21:
Statistical Tools for Metrology

This chapter provides more information on applied statistics for metrology.

The tool known as statistics is to the metrologist what a hammer is to the home craftsman.

This chapter discusses the statistical approach to test data accumulated by a typical metrology laboratory in the areas of:

■ predicting drift rates of standards
■ predicting out of tolerances dates
■ tightening the tolerances of an instrument using statistical techniques
■ statistically showing the reliability of an instrument

Statistics is an essential tool without which the metrologist can do very little. Measurements are made to provide information upon which decisions are based. Decision making almost always involves risk assessment, and risk assessment deals in probabilities. Statistics enables metrologists to assign probabilities in an objective and defensible manner.

Despite their vital role, statistical procedures should not be used in the metrology laboratory unless their benefits outweigh the cost. Typically, statistical analysis becomes cost effective when measurement uncertainties begin to approach the state of the art for the parameter measured.

When to Use Statistics

Measurements made for industrial or commercial purposes can be handled appropriately in almost all of the cases without a detailed statistical analysis. In some cases, instruments having uncertainties much smaller than the required measurement uncertainty are available at relatively low cost. In others, the economic or other penalty for inaccurate measurements is small. When either of these conditions is true, the measurement should be made as easily and economically as possible.

Existing standards, such as MIL-STD-45662A and IEEE-498(1985), encourage the use of arbitrary test uncertainty ratios (TURs) as a means for controlling the penalties associated with inaccurate measurements. In these standards, a

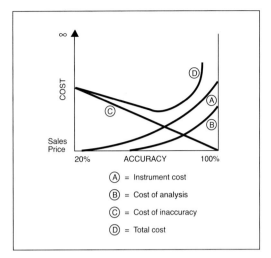

Figure 21-1. Cost versus Uncertainty

TUR of 4:1 is declared to be good enough for the purposes of those invoking the standard.

A TUR of 4:1 means that the specification limits of the parameter tested must be at least four times greater than the uncertainty of the instrument or system used to measure it. For example, one might be asked to measure 120V, ± 1%. A TUR of 4:1 would require that the DMM used for the measurement have an uncertainty specification of ± 0.25% or smaller.

Arbitrary TURs work well where test specifications are wide, and where sufficiently accurate instruments are available at affordable cost. But instrument costs increase rapidly as uncertainties become small. And at least two other costs must be considered in deciding whether it is cost effective to make a detailed uncertainty analysis, the cost of the analysis and the cost which results from making inaccurate measurements.

Figure 21-1 shows how the total cost of this measurement system will be the sum of the three individual costs:

$$C_D = C_A + C_B + C_C$$

Where:

C_D = total cost

C_A = instrument cost

C_B = cost of analysis

C_C = cost of inaccuracy

The point at which arbitrary TURs should be abandoned for detailed uncertainty analysis will be at the uncertainty which produces the lowest total cost.

One should consider making a detailed uncertainty analysis when doing so will be more cost effective than using an arbitrary TUR. Making the graphs upon which to base the decision could involve considerable effort and cost, if this analysis is done accurately. For most cases, a preliminary decision using estimates of the various costs can be made. When it appears that an analysis might be cost effective, the detailed analysis can be made. Such an analysis will always be a statistical analysis.

Statistical Techniques in Metrology

Metrology uses statistics for estimation, prediction, uncertainty analysis, risk assessment, and process control. Statistics serve as the tool by which information is extracted from noisy measurement information. Every measurement process and system is noisy at some level, as is shown by the fact that repeat measurements of the same parameter, on the same device, under the same conditions will differ. In fact, noise is so universally present that the absence of noise in repeated measurements actually tends to reduce a metrologist's confidence in the measurements.

Estimation

The process of assigning values to the results of a set of measurements is called *estimation*. The mean of the set is an estimate of the value of the parameter measured. The standard deviation is an estimate of the noise in the set, and is used in assigning an uncertainty to the result.

Prediction Models

Given a set of measurements taken over time, statistical prediction models, such as linear regression (curve fitting), allow the metrologist

to predict values and uncertainties. Nearly all metrology is an exercise in prediction, whether implicit or explicit. If the present value and uncertainty of a standard are known, then assume that it will have the same value and uncertainty to the next recalibration, or that a statistical analysis is performed to predict its value and uncertainty at some future time.

Risk Assessment

Risk assessment is the process of predicting risk of loss (or gain) to be expected from a particular set of conditions or actions. Given the probability that something will occur, and given the loss (or gain) from its occurrence, an expected value can be assigned to the activity. Risk analysis is a special case of estimation; it estimates the probable gain or loss from a particular activity. It is not normally done by metrologists themselves, but relies on information provided by metrologists.

Statistical Process Control

Statistical process control (SPC), invented in the 1920s, perfected in the 1940s, and forgotten in the United States until the 1980s, is a tool for ensuring the quality of the output of an activity. In the metrology laboratory, SPC is most often used to control the quality of measurements, but has equally important applications in controlling the many non-measurement activities of the laboratory. For a discussion of SPC, see Chapter 23, "Statistical Process Control."

Histogram Analysis

Figure 21-2 shows a histogram, a bar graph representing frequency of occurrence versus parameter value.

A histogram is a useful tool for analyzing distributions. Plotting the histogram will immediately show such problems as bimodality or other non-normal characteristics. Thus it provides a quick check for the normality of the distribution of the data. It is a good idea to plot the histogram even when statistical tests for normality are performed, because it may help

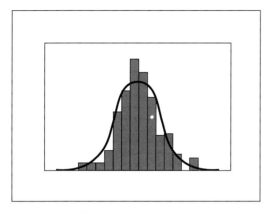

Figure 21-2. *Histogram*

in identifying the reasons for non-normal behavior. One should also perform a statistical test for normality when the assumption of normality is important to the quality of the results.

Statistical Tests

Several statistical tests are useful to the metrologist. These include:

- the t-test for testing whether two means are significantly different

- the chi-square-test for testing whether two samples came from the same process, or for testing whether two processes have the same variability

- the chi-square test for normality (goodness of fit)

- the F-test for fit of a regression to the data

The following sections will briefly describe these tests and then give examples.

t-Tests
The t-test provides an answer to the question, "Is this mean significantly different from another (or standard) mean?" The mean of any finite data set is only an estimate of the true mean of the population. Since there is variation due to noise in the data, it is unlikely that any two means will be the same. How different can they be and still be valid estimators of the same parameter? That question is answered by the t-test and assumes a normal distribution.

Suppose 10 measurements of a 10Ω resistor are made; the mean, m_1, and standard deviation, s_1, are computed. Two weeks later, the same resistor is measured five times on the same system, yielding mean m_2, and standard deviation s_2. The means and standard deviations are different for the two sets of measurements. We want to know whether the resistor has changed value, or the system has developed a problem. In other words, we need an explanation for the differences between the measurement results. If the t-test is failed, that is a good indication that something has changed, either the resistor or the measuring system. Passing the t-test gives less information. It simply means we have no basis for believing anything other than statistical processes are present.

To perform the t-test:

1. First decide what significance level you will test to. A 95% significance level will usually be appropriate. At this level there will be only a 5% chance (1 in 20) that the test will be failed when purely statistical processes are at work. The higher the significance level, the more stringent the test and the greater likelihood that the test will not be failed when other than statistical variations are present.

2. Now calculate t from:

$$t = \frac{\left|m_1 - m_2 - d\right|}{s_0 \left(\frac{1}{n_1} + \frac{1}{n_2}\right)^{\frac{1}{2}}}$$

where d is the difference being tested for (0 in the example), s_0 is the pooled standard deviation, and n_1, n_2 are the number of measurements in each mean (10 and 5 in the example).

3. Then look up student's t for $n_1 + n_2 - 2$ degrees of freedom in a statistics manual. If the computed value of t is greater than student's t, then the test is failed, and it is likely that the two means are really different. In that case, the reason for the difference should be investigated. If the test is not failed, combining the two results will provide a better estimate of the true mean than either one alone.

The pooled standard deviation is computed from:

$$s_0^2 = \frac{(n_1-1)s_1^2 + (n_2-1)s_2^2}{n_1+n_2-2}$$

Continuing the example:

$m_1 = 10.000073,\ s_1 = 3.2(10^{-6}),\ n_1 = 10$

$m_2 = 10.000085,\ s_2 = 2.8(10^{-6}),\ n_2 = 5$

$$s_0^2 = \frac{\left[9(3.2\times10^{-6})^2 + 4(2.8\times10^{-6})^2\right]}{10+5-2} = 9.502\times10^{-12}$$

$s_0 = 3.082\times10^{-6}$

$$t = \frac{1.2\times10^{-5}}{3.082\times10^{-6}\sqrt{\left(\frac{1}{10}+\frac{1}{5}\right)}} = 7.108$$

Student's t at 95% confidence level and 13 degrees of freedom is:

$t_{.05,13} = 2.160$

The test failed because the computed value of 7.108 is greater than the expected value, 2.160. There is reason to believe that there is a real difference in the two measurement results.

Since the standard deviations of two sets of measurements are likely to be different, we might ask if the measuring system has changed between the sets of measurements. This can be determined by performing one of the tests for variances. Remember, the standard deviation is just the square root of the variance. The F test for variances tests whether two data sets were obtained from the same distribution. We will now use the F test to test whether the preceding two sets of resistor measurements were obtained from the same distribution. See the following subsection, "F Test," for more information on F tests.

Assumptions: the measurements are random, independent samples from normal distributions.

1. Compute:

$$F = \frac{s_1^2}{s_2^2}$$

where s_1 is the larger standard deviation so the result is always greater than one.

In the preceding example:

$s_1 = 3.2 \times 10^{-6},\ s_2 = 2.8 \times 10^{-6}$

$$F = \frac{10.24\,(10^{-12})}{7.84\,(10^{-12})} = 1.306$$

2. Using a table of the F distribution, find F for $m = n_1-1$ and $n = n_2-1$ degrees of freedom. In the example, $m = 9$ and $n = 4$.

3. Reject the hypothesis that $s_1 = s_2$ if the computed F exceeds the tabled $F_{\alpha/2,(n-1,n-1)}$. For $\alpha = 0.05$, the tabled value is 6.0, which is greater than 1.306, so the hypothesis is not rejected. There is no evidence to support the idea the two standard deviations are different.

Chi-Square Test (X^2)
The chi-square test for normality is used to test a data set for consistency with the assumption that it was obtained from a normal distribution.

Perform the test by:

1. Grouping the observations in the form of a histogram, and comparing the actual number of results in each group with the expected, or hypothetical, number. The groupings should be such that the theoretical number in each group will be at least five. The groups (bars of the histogram) need not be of the same width, and several of the original or natural groups may be combined to provide at least five in each group.

2. Compute

$$X^2 = \frac{\sum_{i=1}^{r}\left(n_i-e_i\right)^2}{e_i}$$

where r is the number of groups, n_i is the actual number in the rth group, and e_i is the expected (theoretical) number in the ith group. If the calculated value exceeds the tabled value for $F = r-3$ degrees of freedom and significance level α, the distribution should not be considered to be normal.

The histogram shown in Figure 21-2 shows data taken on the 10V output of a Fluke 732A over a period of 180 days. The data are the deviations, in ppm, from a nominal 10V In this case, the evidence indicates that the data are normally distributed.

F Test

An F test can be used for testing the validity of a curve fit (regression) to a series of data. Probably the most common regression relates measurement parameters (values) to time, but many others are used, such as voltage versus temperature, resistance versus pressure, etc.

The F-test compares the pooled standard deviations of subsets of the data to the standard deviation of the whole data set. Here, the data are the residuals, the differences between the measured values and the values computed from the regression line. If the fit is good and the data are normally distributed around the regression line, then the standard deviation of the whole data set will not exceed the pooled standard deviations of the subsets by more than a tabled amount.

This example uses the same 732A data set presented above. Here we have $n = 2$ data points obtained two per day on each of $m = 180$ days.

1. Begin by averaging the m sets of daily points

$$\bar{y}_i = \frac{1}{n_i}\sum_{j=1}^{n_i}(y_{ij})$$

2. Next compute the m variances for the daily point sets

$$s_{1i}^2 = \frac{1}{n_i(n_i-1)}\left[\sum_{j=1}^{n_i}y_{ij}^2 - \left(\sum_{j=1}^{n_i}y_{ij}\right)^2\right]$$

In the example, $n_i = 2$, so the denominator reduces to 2.

3. Now compute the pooled variance, s_1^2

$$s_1^2 = \frac{1}{(N-m)}\sum(n_i-1)s_{1i}^2$$

where N is the total number of points, 360 in this example.

We are testing whether the data set can be represented by a straight line, $y = \alpha + \beta x$, estimated by $y' = a + bx$, obtained by a linear-least squares fit to the data. The constants are estimated by

$$a = \frac{1}{N}\left(\sum n_i\bar{y}_i - b\sum n_i x_i\right)$$

$$b = \frac{N\sum n_i x_i\bar{y}_i - \left(\sum n_i x_i\right)\left(\sum n_i\bar{y}_i\right)}{N\sum n_i x_i^2 - \left(\sum n_i x_i\right)^2}$$

Note that the regression can be easily performed on readily available applications software. Just be sure to perform the regression on the averages, not the raw data set.

4. Now compute the variance for the whole data set:

$$s_2^2 = \frac{1}{m-2}\sum n_i\left(\bar{y}_i - y_i\right)^2$$

where the y_i values are the values computed from the least squares curve fit.

Both s_1 and s_2 are estimates of the standard deviation of points about the regression line. If the fit is good, the two will tend to be of the same magnitude; if otherwise, s_2 will tend to be significantly larger than s_1. We perform the F-test, at 5% significance, by computing

$$F = \frac{s_2^2}{s_1^2}$$

and comparing the result to tabled values of $F_{0.05, (m-2, N-m)}$. The ratio is formed with the larger variance in the numerator so that the fraction is always greater than unity. If the computed value is larger than the tabled value, the hypothesis of linearity must be rejected, and the cause of the rejection investigated.

If the F test is not failed, there is no evidence to support an assertion that the assumed curve (line) does not fit the data, and the fit will be considered good.

A failed F test points to a false assumption somewhere, subject to consideration of the fact that a percentage of good fits will fail the test. Plotting residuals is an essential first step in identifying the cause of the failure. A higher order equation, or equation of another form, such as sine wave, exponential, etc., may fit the data better, or there may be a problem of non-white noise where the Allan analysis will provide a better result. See "Classical versus Non-Classical Statistics," below.

This test is not restricted to testing the fit of a straight line to a data set. It can be extended to testing the fit of any function. Consult a statistics text for details.

Linear Regression (Curve Fitting)

Linear regression is one of the most useful and profitable statistical procedures available to the metrologist. Higher order and other non-linear regressions, as well as multiple regressions, are also often very useful. Only linear regression will be discussed here. See a statistics manual for linearizing procedures and techniques for multiple linear regressions.

Linear regressions establish a relationship between two parameters, one considered the independent and the other the dependent parameter. Probably the most useful regression for the metrologist relates the value of a given parameter to time. From this you are able to compute the parameter's value at times past and to predict its value in the future.

An uncertainty can be assigned to those values, provided the assumptions are met: points normally distributed around the regression line, white noise, and the underlying function really is linear. A regression line which describes a standard's behavior over time provides a better value for the standard than any of the individual measurements or calibrations that may have been made. See Figure 21-3.

The slope of the regression line (also called "Regression Coefficient") is given by

$$b = \frac{n\sum xy - \sum x \sum y}{n\sum x^2 - \left(\sum x\right)^2}$$

and the intercept by

$$a = \frac{\sum y - b\sum x}{n}$$

The variance of points about the line is given by

$$s_{y|x}^2 = \frac{n-1}{n-2}\left(s_y^2 - b^2 s_x^2\right)$$

where s_y and s_x are the standard deviations of the y and x values, respectively.

The standard error of the regression coefficient (slope) is

$$s_b = \frac{s_{y|x}}{s_x \sqrt{n-1}}$$

and a 99% confidence interval for the true slope β is given by

$$\pm t s_b$$

where t is student's t for $\alpha/2 = .005$ and $n-2$ degrees of freedom.

A confidence interval for the intercept is:

$$\pm \frac{t s_{y|x}}{\sqrt{n}}$$

A confidence interval for the true regression line, at any given point x, is given by:

$$ci = \pm t s_{y|x}\left[\frac{1}{n} + \frac{(x-\bar{x})^2}{(n-1)s_x^2}\right]^{\frac{1}{2}}$$

and the uncertainty for any individual value of y, at x, is given by:

$$u = \pm t s_{y|x}\left[1 + \frac{1}{n} + \frac{(x-\bar{x})^2}{(n-1)s_x^2}\right]^{\frac{1}{2}}$$

Both the confidence interval for the line at *x* and the uncertainty of the *y* at *x* assume points normally distributed and data that can really be represented by a straight line. Results at other values of *x* are not independent, so cannot be combined statistically. Confidence intervals and prediction intervals for the whole line are available. Consult a statistics text for details.

It should be kept in mind that a significant risk exists when one projects a line beyond the data on which it is based. But metrologists must take that risk every day because it is impossible to continuously update calibrations so that current values of standards are always known. The common practice of using the last calibration value and uncertainty until the next calibration is a special case of prediction. Here the prediction is that the value will not change during the calibration interval. The prudent metrologist will devise schemes for verifying his assumptions.

An Example: Maintaining and Using a Resistance Standard

The following discussion describes a resistance standard maintained and used by the Fluke Standards Laboratory. The standard consists of three Thomas-pattern one ohm resistors, L&N® 4210. Each of the resistors is sent to NIST for calibration every three years, one resistor per year.

The mean of the values assigned to the three resistors makes up the corporate standard of resistance. A Guildline® 9975 Current Comparator Resistance Bridge is used to ratio up and down from the corporate standard: up to 10 kΩ and down to 1 mΩ. Traceability for 10 kΩ is obtained through participation in the NIST Resistance MAP program, and ratioing to higher valued resistances is accomplished using a modified Wheatstone bridge, described in Chapter 9, "DC Ratio."

NIST calibration data is available for some of the resistors as far back as 1960, and intercomparison data for the three goes back almost that far. Intercomparisons made before 1979 are considered unreliable, because they were made with less accurate equipment before obtaining the Guildline bridge.

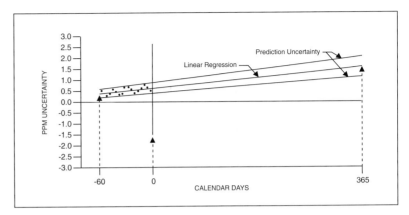

Figure 21-3. *Linear Regression*

First, the difference of each individual resistor from the standard, the mean of the three, is obtained. This is done, ideally, by taking at least three sets of data over a three-day or longer period. Measurements are spread out over several days in order to randomize the effects of small changes in bath temperature and atmospheric pressure. Ideally, the measurements should be made by two or more operators.

The resistors are compared in pairs, with each in turn occupying the position of standard and unknown on the bridge. The results are

$$a_1 = \frac{R_1}{R_2}$$

$$a_2 = \frac{R_2}{R_3}$$

$$a_3 = \frac{R_3}{R_1}$$

where the "*a*"s are the bridge readings (ratios), which should be near unity in each case. We note first that multiplying the three results would yield a value of exactly 1, since each *R* occurs once in both the numerator and the denominator.

That will happen only rarely because of measurement variance (noise), and the difference from unity can be plotted on a control chart as an indication of the noise in the comparison process. Too large a difference points to a problem (bias) that must be corrected before proceeding.

It can be shown that, for resistors which are sufficiently close to the same value,

$$R_1 = R\left(1 + \frac{a_1 - a_3}{3}\right)$$

$$R_2 = R\left(1 + \frac{a_2 - a_1}{3}\right)$$

$$R_3 = R\left(1 + \frac{a_3 - a_2}{3}\right)$$

where R is the mean value of the three resistors. The approximations are good to about 1 in 100 million when the resistors are within 0.01% of the same value. The comparisons are made monthly at Fluke, and the resistors' values are plotted to detect any deviations from expected behavior.

Each set of comparisons provides an estimate of the value of each of the resistors in terms of the mean of the set. A regression over many such comparisons provides an estimate of the resistors' values relative to the Corporate Standard as a function of time. With a sufficient number of comparisons over a sufficient time period, a very accurate determination can be made if the resistors are really drifting in a linear fashion. About 20 measurements over a two- or three-year period give very good confidence in many cases.

Knowing the value of the resistor relative to the standard, we can calibrate the standard by sending any one of the set to NIST for calibration. We send R_1 and receive a value, $R_n \pm U_n$, as the result. From this we can compute the value of the Corporate Standard:

$$R = \frac{R_n}{1 + \left(\dfrac{a_1 - a_3}{3}\right)}$$

Then, using this value for the standard, we can compute the values of the other resistors. The new value for R should be added to the database and a new regression performed. From this, an improved value for R will be obtained. This value will be better than any single NIST calibration of any one resistor might be.

The regression provides the information needed for computing the uncertainty of the difference between our standard and the standard value maintained by NIST. The total uncertainty in the standard has four components:

- the systematic uncertainty in the value assigned by NIST to its standard

- the random uncertainty in the comparison of our standard to NIST's standard

- the uncertainty in the comparison of our transfer standard to the corporate standard

- the uncertainty in the regression used to predict future values of the corporate standard

Except for the first uncertainty, all are random uncertainties. That is, all result from chance variations in measurement processes. In the example case, the systematic error is not reported by NIST, because the ohm is maintained in a bank of resistors which is defined to maintain exactly one ohm without error. We are thus actually computing the error in the Fluke standard relative to the ohm as maintained by NIST.

An acceptably accurate estimate of the uncertainty is simply the square root of the sum of the squares (rss) combination of the individual uncertainties, provided all error sources are approximately normal and all uncertainties are reported at the same confidence level, such as 99%.

Statisticians frown upon the combination of uncertainties in this way, because it is not strictly accurate. However, such a combination will always be conservative regarding the uncertainty, and the error in the estimate is small for moderately large numbers of measurements, 10 or more. All the error distributions must be normal for this approach to be approximately correct.

It is impossible to measure another resistor directly against this standard since it is not directly accessible. Such measurements must be made using one of the individual resistors that make up the standard, which leads to two additional sources of uncertainty: the uncertainty of the individual standard resistor, and the uncertainty of the comparison to the standard.

The uncertainty of the standard resistor will consist of the uncertainty of the composite standard, combined with the uncertainty of the regression which relates the individual resistor to the composite standard. Assuming unbiased comparisons, the uncertainty of the comparison can be obtained by repeat measurements made over a period of several days and the full range of conditions likely to be encountered in the measuring system. Alternatively, if many nominally identical resistors are to be measured, one can be set aside as a check standard and measured periodically. Statistical analysis of the check standard data will yield the information needed to compute the uncertainty of such comparisons, and it is not strictly necessary to make more than one measurement of any one test resistor.

Classical versus Non-Classical Statistics

Scientists at NIST and elsewhere have done much work to apply classical statistical methods to the analysis of measurement uncertainties. However, more recent developments have brought the use of these classical methods into question. Specifically, some scientists now believe that alternative, non-classical statistics developed for use in describing the uncertainties of atomic clocks are more appropriate than classical statistics for describing most measurement uncertainties.

Dr. David Allan of NIST has pointed out that classical statistics assumes white noise, noise that is evenly distributed across the frequency band of the measurements. The frequency band is determined by the measurement system. For example, for dcv measurements, the upper frequency limit might be 10 Hz or less. The lower frequency limit is set by the sampling time of the instrument. For example, a 1-second sample interval effectively sets the lower frequency limit at 1 Hz, because frequencies lower than that will not be detected. When measurements are averaged over many days, the effective lower limit is set by the number of days over which the sample is taken.

Long sampling times are important when flicker noise or random-walk noise is present in the measurement results. In these cases, the classical variance will become very large as sampling time increases. In such cases, the classical variance is not useful for describing measurement uncertainty and other measures. The Allan Variance, or the Modified Allan Variance, should be used instead.

No further discussion about non-classical statistics will be covered here. The metrologist must be aware that classical statistics may not be appropriate for a particular analysis, and should test for white noise in any measurements.

Use the following procedure to test for white noise. The basic requirement is that the classical variance be no larger than a specified multiple of the Allan Variance if noise is white and the assumptions of classical statistics apply.

Testing for White Noise

An estimate of the Allan Variance, $\sigma_y^2(\tau_0)$, for a discrete time series of measurements, y_k ($k = 1$ to N), each taken over a sample time τ_0, can be computed from

$$\sigma_y^2(\tau_0) = \frac{1}{2(N-1)} \sum_{k=1}^{N-1} \left(y_{k+1} - y_k \right)^2$$

The ratio of the classical variance, $\sigma^2(N)$, to the Allan Variance, $\sigma_y^2(\tau_0)$, provides a simple test for white noise.

The classical variance is computed from

$$\sigma^2(N) = \frac{1}{N-1} \sum_{k=1}^{N} \left(y_k - \bar{y} \right)^2$$

If the value $\sigma^2(N) / \sigma_y^2(\tau_0) \leq 1 + 1/\sqrt{N}$, then it is probably safe to assume that the data set is dominated by white noise, and the classical statistical approach can safely be used. A larger ratio is an indication of one or more invalid assumptions.

Failure of the test does not necessarily indicate the presence of non-white noise. What is really tested is the degree of correlation in the data set, which might result from a functional relationship in time. However, failure of the test should be viewed as a warning against applying classical statistics to the data set.

Key References

Ku, Harry H., "Statistical Concepts in Metrology, With a Postscript on Statistical Graphics," *NBS Special Publication 747*, August, 1988

Other references for this chapter are in the Resources Appendix.

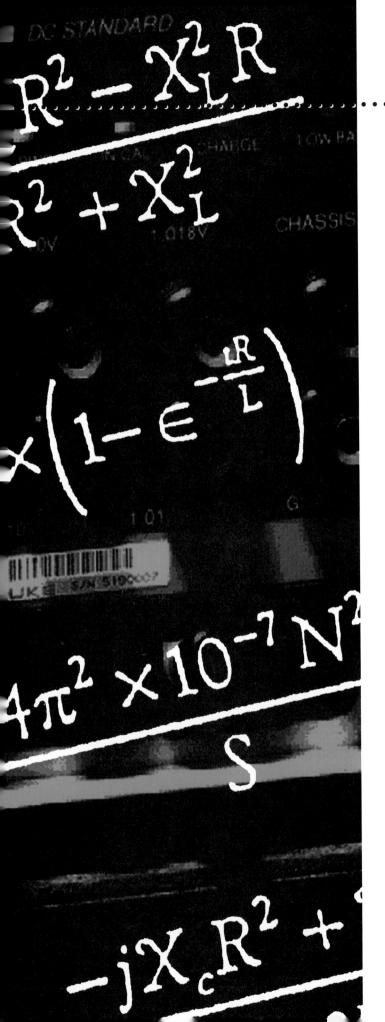

Chapter 22:

Uncertainty Statements

This chapter provides guidance for calculating the total measurement uncertainty in a variety of measurement situations.

This chapter is neither rigorous nor exhaustive, since such discussions require an in-depth discussion of statistics which is not appropriate to many practical measurement situations. The emphasis is on making a safe measurement, rather than on establishing a precisely known uncertainty. This chapter is intended for those who need to know that a measurement is good enough for its intended use.

Documenting Uncertainties

The calculations that go into a measurement and its uncertainty should always be documented, since they, and your competence, may someday be at the center of a dispute and may even be challenged in court. At Fluke, standard operating procedure 34.2 provides documentation for routine measurements. It requires that instruments be maintained to 90-day accuracy specifications, although exceptions must be documented, and that a 4:1 accuracy ratio be maintained between the measurement accuracy required and the accuracy of the measuring instrument. Where a 4:1 accuracy ratio is not maintained, an approved and documented uncertainty analysis must be performed.

When a 4:1 ratio and 90-day specifications are maintained, specific documentation is not needed, since it is assumed that the measurements have been performed correctly. Whenever any of the following accuracy improvement methods in this chapter are used, it is necessary to record what was done. In general, the records should contain sufficient detail to enable another metrologist to duplicate the calculations.

Definitions

The following terms are used frequently in this chapter:

- Error
- Uncertainty
- Confidence Interval
- Confidence Level
- Specified Uncertainty

These are briefly described below. For more complete information on these terms, see Chapter 5, "Basic DC and Low Frequency Metrology" and Chapter 20, "Introduction to Metrology Statistics."

Error

Error is the difference between the result of the measurement and the true value of the quantity measured, after all corrections have been made. Error, which is not the same as uncertainty, has traditionally been viewed as being of two kinds: random error and systematic error. In general, although error always exists, its magnitude cannot be exactly known.

Uncertainty

Uncertainty has traditionally been defined as a range of values, usually centered on the measured value, that contains the true value with stated probability.

A measurement result and its uncertainty traditionally were reported as "Quantity" = "Value" $\pm U$. So the number usually reported and called "uncertainty" was actually half the range defined here. The ISO Guide discussed below redefines uncertainty to be the equivalent of a standard deviation, and thus avoids this problem.

Confidence Interval

When uncertainty is defined as above, the confidence interval is the range of values that corresponds to the stated uncertainty.

Confidence Level

Confidence level is the probability associated with a confidence interval. We would say, "The true value can be expected to lie within $\pm x$ units of the measured value with 99% confidence."

Specified Uncertainty

Specified uncertainty is the range of values, usually centered on the nominal value, that will contain the true measured, or output, value with stated probability for any instrument randomly selected from among all instruments to which the specification applies.

Methods of Combining Uncertainties

Two common methods of combining uncertainties have traditionally been used: linear summing and root-sum-square (rss). Linear summing is simply adding all the uncertainties together and using the sum as the new uncertainty. RSS is the square root of the sum of the squares of each uncertainty. So, where linear summing would give you:

$$U_{TOTAL} = U_1 + U_2 \ldots + U_n$$

RSS yields:

$$U_{TOTAL} = \sqrt{U_1^2 + U_2^2 \ldots + U_n^2}$$

Linear summing of uncertainty components is overly conservative and will result in overstating uncertainties. The International Standards Organization is preparing a document that requires the rss method for combining effective standard deviations, then multiplying by 2 or 3, as appropriate, to obtain a coverage factor, k. This factor is designed to provide a range of values that has a high probability of containing the true value, and, for normal distribution, can be viewed as providing a confidence interval.

At this writing, the rss approach is still controversial among many metrologists who believe that it will underestimate uncertainties, and is not sufficiently rigorous for use in calculating risk factors. The calculation of the risk of nuclear accidents is a good example.

NIST has implemented the recommendations of the ISO Guide, and will report measurement uncertainties with a coverage factor of 2. This provides a confidence level of approximately 95%.

In this chapter, uncertainties are combined by rss. In all cases, it is essential that all the uncertainties have equivalent confidence. That is, all are at 99% confidence, for example. It is not correct to combine uncertainties by rss unless they are known to be based on a normal distribution with the same confidence level. The ISO Guide, however, recommends expressing uncertainty as standard deviations, which are then combined by rss. In that case, it is necessary only to ensure that approximately the same coverage factor is used for all uncertainties.

The rest of this chapter provides four examples of how to use, improve, and combine uncertainties. The examples include:

- simple measurements
- using instruments to better than specified uncertainty
- making indirect measurements using two standards
- scaling using several standards

Several of the examples include detailed descriptions of the measurement procedures used. These are detailed for example purposes. Performing the actual measurements may require other unstated support equipment such as power sources and other laboratory support equipment.

Simple Measurements

This approach applies to the majority of all measurements made. For simple measurements, use the manufacturer's specified uncertainty of the measuring instrument as the total uncertainty of the measurement.

If the instrument is calibrated and maintained as recommended by the manufacturer, and is always found in tolerance on recall, the confidence level of the uncertainty is the manufacturer's stated confidence level. At Fluke, this is 99%. Some manufacturers use other confidence levels, typically 95%.

However, the operation of the recall system determines the confidence level. If the recall system is operated to achieve a different percent in tolerance on recall, such as 85%, then the confidence level maintained is that percentage (85%). Reducing the confidence level is equivalent to increasing the specified uncertainty.

For example, Fluke expects 99% of its instruments to meet all of their accuracy specifications. If a group of Fluke 8840As is recalled every 90 days, and all are always (or 99 times out of 100) found to be in tolerance, their uncertainty can be taken as the 8840A's 90-day specification at 99% confidence.

But if the same 8840As are used in a recall system that achieves 85% of instruments in tolerance on recall, the same uncertainty applies, but only at 85% confidence. The effective uncertainty has been degraded by a factor of 1.8, almost half. Figure 22-1 illustrates this increased uncertainty.

Using an Instrument to Better Than Specification

Occasionally, a measurement must be made with smaller uncertainty (greater accuracy) than can be supported by the instrument specification. There are two approaches to this situation: transferring from a standard, and characterizing the instrument.

Transferring from a Standard

This method, as illustrated in Figure 22-2, can be used either to improve the reading accuracy of a meter, when the standard is a source such as a calibrator; or to improve the output accuracy of a source, when the standard is a DMM.

Valid results will be obtained only if the value of the unknown (test) quantity is near the value of the standard, where linearity error will be negligible.

For measured values near the value of the standard, the value can be found by dividing the measured value of the test quantity, $Rdg_{(x)}$, by the measured value of the standard quantity,

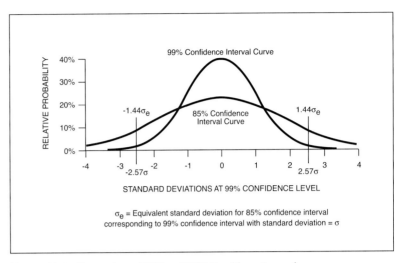

Figure 22-1. *Comparison of 85% and 99% Confidence Intervals*

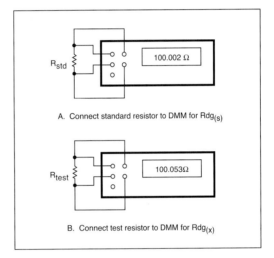

Figure 22-2. *Transferring from a Standard*

$Rdg_{(s)}$, then multiplying by the known value of the standard, R_{std}.

Two uncertainty components are present, the uncertainty of the standard and the transfer uncertainty. The uncertainty of the measurement is the square root of the sum of the squares of the two uncertainties.

An estimate of the transfer uncertainty can be obtained by multiplying the floor specification of the instrument whose accuracy is being enhanced by the square root of 2 (approximately 1.4). The rationale for using the floor specification to obtain transfer uncertainty is that the floor specification reflects the long-term and short-term stability of the zero, as opposed to gain. Thus it includes allowance for instrument noise as well as time stability of the internal circuitry. Therefore, using the floor specification as an indication of the noise in the measurement will tend to overestimate the random uncertainty of the measurement. The value is multiplied by 1.4 because two measurements are required: the standardizing measurement and the measurement of the unknown quantity.

Calculating with the Floor Specification

For this example, assume the following: A Fluke 8840A is specified at ±130 ppm (100 ppm + 3Ω) for the measurement of 100 kΩ on its 200 kΩ range. A 10 ppm, 100 kΩ resistance standard is available. The test current is 10 mA, so the nominal voltage drop is 1V.

When low-thermal emf test leads are used to connect the two resistors to the 8840A, the uncertainty added by the effects of up to a few microvolts of thermal emf can be ignored. This is because 1 μV = 1 ppm of 1V, about 2% of the total uncertainty in the following calculation. For the more sensitive measurements (for example, the ones described in "Scaling a Standard Value"), the uncertainties due to thermal emf must be considered.

When the values of the standard and test resistor have been measured, the value of the test resistor is calculated as:

$$R_x = R_s \frac{Rdg_x}{Rdg_s}$$

Where:

R_x = resistance of unknown

R_s = resistance of standard

Rdg_x = reading of unknown

Rdg_s = reading of standard

The total uncertainty is:

$$U = \sqrt{10^2 + 2 \times 30^2} = 43.6\,ppm$$

Where:

10 = uncertainty of R_s in ppm

2 = total number of measurements

30 = uncertainty of floor specification of 8840A to nominal value of both R_s and R_x in ohms

Because the 8840A resolution is only ±10 ppm, and the standard resistor is known with no better accuracy, we would carry the extra digits in the calculations, then report the uncertainty as 44 ppm.

Calculating with Standard Deviation

The uncertainty obtained in the preceding example might be considered unacceptable for this measurement. A better estimate of the transfer uncertainty can be obtained by taking a fairly large number of measurements (perhaps 10 or more) of both the standard and the test item, then using the averages as the measured values and using the standard deviations to compute the transfer uncertainty. This will lead to the use of statistical tables, in this case the student's t table.

Take 10 measurements each of the standard resistor and the test resistor. Compute the averages, and use them in the equation for computing R_x. Then compute the standard deviations.

Assume that the computed standard deviation is 18 ppm for the standard resistor (s_1), and 21 ppm for the test resistor (s_2). Since the primary noise source for these two measurements is the DMM, the resulting standard deviations should be pooled. This will provide a better estimate of the standard deviation of measurements of 100 kΩ with that particular DMM at that time. So,

$$Pooled\ s = s_p = \sqrt{\frac{s_1^2 + s_2^2}{2}} = \sqrt{\frac{18^2 + 21^2}{2}} = 19.6\,ppm$$

with 18 degrees of freedom.

$$\hat{s} = \frac{s_p}{\sqrt{n}} = \frac{19.6}{3.162} = 6.2\ ppm$$

Where:

$\hat{s}$ is the estimated standard deviation of the mean.

n is the number of measurements of each resistor (10).

Here, degrees of freedom was obtained from the total number of measurements (20) minus the number of parameters (2) calculated from the data (two averages use up two degrees of freedom, leaving 18).

Student's t for 18 degrees of freedom and 99% confidence is 2.878. Obtain the transfer uncertainty (U_t) from:

$$U_t = \sqrt{2}\, t\, \hat{s} = 25.2 \text{ ppm}$$

The total uncertainty is

$$\sqrt{U_R^2 + U_t^2} = 27.1 \text{ ppm}$$

Since the 8840A resolution is only ±10 ppm, and the standard resistor is known with no better accuracy, we would carry the extra digits in the calculations, then report the uncertainty as 27 ppm.

For 10 or more measurements, it is acceptable to use 3 as a 99% multiplier instead of looking up student's t from a table. This approximation will be in error by no more than 16%, which will not significantly affect the usefulness of the uncertainty statement.

For information on standard deviation of the mean, pooled standard deviations, and degrees of freedom, see Chapter 21, "Statistical Tools for Metrology."

Characterizing an Instrument

The rationale for this method is that most instruments are capable of performing much better than specified because measurements of the population of instruments are normally distributed around some value near the nominal value.

This approach is essentially the same as when transferring from a standard, except that the

instrument will not be used immediately after characterization, so an additional allowance must be made for stability. For this reason, the uncertainty will always be larger than for direct transfers from a standard. Also, the option of improving the transfer by multiple measurements is less effective because averaging will not affect the stability terms.

The uncertainty is the square root of the sum of the squares of three uncertainties: the uncertainty of the calibration standard, the transfer uncertainty, and the stability of the characterized instrument. When multiple measurements are made in characterizing the instrument or in using it, the transfer uncertainty is the rss combination of the individual uncertainties.

An allowance for stability can sometimes be inferred from the different specifications for the instrument, such as 30-, 90-, and 360-day specifications. For example, the 8840A 20V dc range is specified at 50 ppm + 3 counts at 90 days and 60 ppm + 3 counts at 1 year. From this we can infer that its drift rate is ≤10 ppm per 9 months, or 13 ppm per year, and that the floor specification holds for the entire year.

Some standards and instruments are specified for stability. For example, the Fluke 732B has a specified stability of ± 2 ppm/year. The stability uncertainty of the 732B is therefore 2 ppm/year.

A safe approach is to assign a reasonable stability uncertainty based on the available information, then check your assumptions by frequently recalling the instrument to verify that its overall uncertainty remains within the assigned limits. This is especially effective where a pool of instruments is maintained to the improved specification. Then the adequacy of the uncertainty assignment can be evaluated relatively quickly.

It is possible to use a standard or instrument to much better than its specified uncertainty if its performance is characterized over time and under different environmental conditions. The approach is to perform many calibrations against superior standards, then use linear regression curve fitting to predict outputs or readings at future times. The uncertainty is computed using the statistics of linear regression.

For more information on characterizing instruments and drift rates, see Chapter 20, "Introduction to Metrology Statistics," and Chapter 21, "Statistical Tools for Metrology."

Indirect Measurements

This method involves measurements in which a quantity is inferred from the measurement of two or more other quantities. A simple example is determining current from measurement of the voltage drop across a known resistor.

Again, the uncertainty is the square root of the sum of the squares of the uncertainties.

Example: determine the direct current output of a Fluke 5700A calibrator at 100 mA.

To complete this example measurement, the following is needed:

■ One calibrated DMM (Fluke 8506A or equivalent)

■ Enough low-thermal emf test leads to make all connections

■ One 10Ω, 4-terminal resistor (Fluke 742A-10 standard resistor or equivalent)

To perform the procedure:

1. Connect equipment as in Figure 22-3.

Note: Power dissipation in the resistor will be 100 mW and there will be a 1V voltage drop across it. Be sure that the resistor used is specified for that level of power. The Fluke 742A-10 standard resistor can be used in this application.

2. Measure the voltage drop across the resistor with a calibrated DMM and record the reading as V.

3. Calculate the current from the known resistance and the measured voltage.

$$I = \frac{V}{R}$$

Assume that the resistor is known to within ±10 ppm (U_1) and the voltage is measured with a Fluke 8506A, which is specified at ±23 ppm (U_2) for 90 days at 1V. The total uncertainty is:

$$U = \sqrt{U_1{}^2 + U_2{}^2} = 25\,ppm$$

The uncertainty of the DMM could be improved by characterization or transferring values from a standard, in which case the total uncertainty would be reduced accordingly.

Scaling a Standard Value

Scaling, or ratioing, is the process of obtaining multiples of a standard value. Fractional values are also considered multiples. In metrology, it is common to derive non-standard values from a standard value, using a ratioing or other scaling experiment. For more information on scaling and ratioing, see Chapters 9, "DC Ratio," and 13, "Immittance and AC Ratio."

This discussion includes three actual measurements. In these procedures, a series of measurements is taken with a certified ratioing device (a Fluke 720A, K-V), and a certified voltage standard (a Fluke 732B) to obtain multiples of the voltage standard.

Testing Linearity

In this procedure, a certified Fluke 732B and a Fluke 720A are to be used to generate calibration voltages for the purpose of testing the

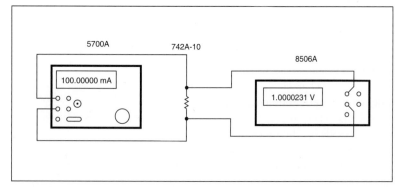

Figure 22-3. *Indirect Current Measurement*

linearity of the dc voltage response of a Fluke 8506A DMM on its 10V range.

For this procedure, the following instruments are needed:

- Fluke 732B Voltage Standard
- Fluke 720A Kelvin-Varley (K-V) divider
- Fluke 8506A DMM
- Enough low-thermal emf test leads to make all connections

To test linearity:

1. Connect equipment as in Figure 22-4.

2. Make and record the DMM reading with K-V divider settings of .1, .2, .3, .4, .5, .6, .7, .8, .9, 1.0, and 1.1.

3. Compute the uncertainty, U, of each reading.

$$U = \frac{0.1}{S} \text{ ppm}$$

In this experiment, the voltage accuracy itself is immaterial (though short-term stability is important). Since this is a linearity measurement, the important specification is the linearity of the K-V divider, which is specified to be ±0.1 ppm of input for settings of 0.1 to 1.1.

For example, the uncertainty at 7V (a K-V setting of 0.7) is 0.14 ppm.

Generating a Known Voltage Using Two Standards

The same equipment used in the previous measurement will be used to generate a known voltage of exactly 4.07254V. The only difference is that the low-thermal emf test leads should be known to produce less than 1 μV of thermal emf.

1. Connect equipment as in Figure 22-4.

2. Make and record the DMM reading with a K-V divider setting of 0.407254.

The uncertainty of this measurement is:

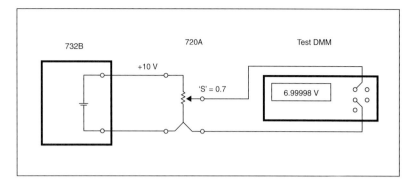

Figure 22-4. Linearity Measurement

$$\sqrt{U_1^{\,2}+U_2^{\,2}+U_3^{\,2}+U_4^{\,2}}$$

Where:

U_1 = the uncertainty of the K-V divider (0.25 ppm)

U_2 = the uncertainty of the 732B (such as 0.93 ppm)

U_3 = the 1 μV uncertainty of thermal emf in the 732B/K-V input circuit (0.1 ppm at 10V)

U_4 = the 1 μV of uncertainty of thermal emf in the DMM/K-V output circuit (0.25 ppm at 4.07254V)

This calculates to 1.0 ppm.

This is not a very realistic measurement for several reasons. The 732B would not ordinarily be connected directly to the 720A since there will be about 100 μA flowing in the connecting leads due to the 720A's 100 kΩ input resistance. Assuming a typical lead resistance of 44 mΩ, the voltage drop in the leads will be 4.4 μV, or 0.44 ppm. Higher resistance leads and the effect of contact resistances can make the error even greater.

This measurement can be improved in two ways:

- Drive the 720A from another source first, such as the Fluke 5440B, and standardize the voltage at the input to the divider by comparing it to the 732B. Then make the measurement. However, this will add another term to the uncertainty—the uncertainty in standardizing the Fluke 5440B. That uncertainty can be evaluated and combined with the total uncertainty.

■ Alternatively, the 732B can be connected directly and the voltage drops in the leads measured. This introduces another source of uncertainty, which is resolved in the next measurement.

Generating a Precise Voltage with Three Standards

A 5700A, a 732B, a 720A, and a 752A are to be used to generate a precise voltage of 333.333 volts.

For this procedure, the following instruments are needed:

■ Fluke 5700A Calibrator
■ Fluke 732B Voltage Standard
■ Fluke 720A Kelvin-Varley divider (or equivalent)
■ Fluke 752A Voltage Divider
■ Fluke 845AB Null Detector
■ Enough low-thermal emf test leads to make all connections. These should be known to produce less than 1 μV of thermal EMF for this application.

The procedure is as follows:

1. Self-calibrate both the 752A and the 720A. For this example, assume the 732B output is known to be 9.999993V ±0.7 ppm at 99% confidence.

2. Connect equipment as in Figure 22-5.

3. Set the 752A to divide by 100.

4. Measure the voltage drop in the leads using a Fluke 845AB. For the purposes of this example, assume the voltage drop to be 3.2 μV ±0.3 μV peak. This makes the voltage at the input to the 720A 9.9999898V (9.999993V − 3.2μV).

5. Connect the 720A Low terminal to the 752A Low terminal.

6. Set the 720A for a reading of 0.3333333 (3.33333/9.9999898).

7. Connect the 845AB between the 752A High and the 720A High. The setup should now be as in Figure 22-6.

8. Adjust the 5700A for null on the 845AB. Assume peak-to-peak noise on the 845AB to be 1.2V at null, and that thermal emf's are known to be less than 1 μV.

We now have 333.333V ± the uncertainty, at the input to the 752A.

The uncertainty, U, is:

$$\sqrt{U_1^2 + U_2^2 + U_3^2 + U_4^2 + U_5^2 + U_6^2} = 1.0 \text{ ppm}$$

Where:

U_1 = the uncertainty of the 732B (0.7 ppm)

U_2 = the uncertainty in the measurement of the lead voltage drop (0.03 ppm)

U_3 = the uncertainty of the 720A at 0.3333333 (0.3 ppm)

U_4 = the 845AB null detector uncertainty (approximately 0.6 μV divided by 3.333333 V = 0.18 ppm)

U_5 = the thermal emf in the null detector circuit (about 0.33 ppm at 3.333333V)

U_6 = the specified uncertainty of the 752A at divide by 1000 (0.5 ppm)

The uncertainty is 0.986 ppm, which would be reported as ±1.0 ppm.

In this example, one half the peak-to-peak noise of the 845AB is used as an estimate of random uncertainty in those measurements, and manufacturer's specifications are used as the uncertainty of the two dividers.

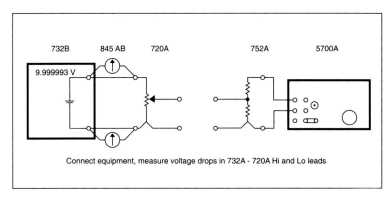

Figure 22-5. *Voltage Measurement—Initial Setup*

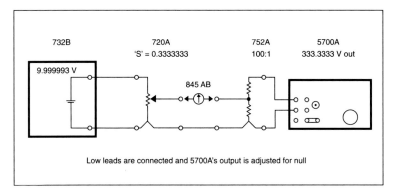

Figure 22-6. *Voltage Measurement—Final Setup*

Key References

Taylor, Barry N.; Kuyatt, Chris E., "Guidelines for Evaluating and Expressing the Uncertainty of NIST Measurement Results," NIST *Technical Note 1297*, January, 1993

ISO, *Guide to the Expression of Uncertainty in Measurement*

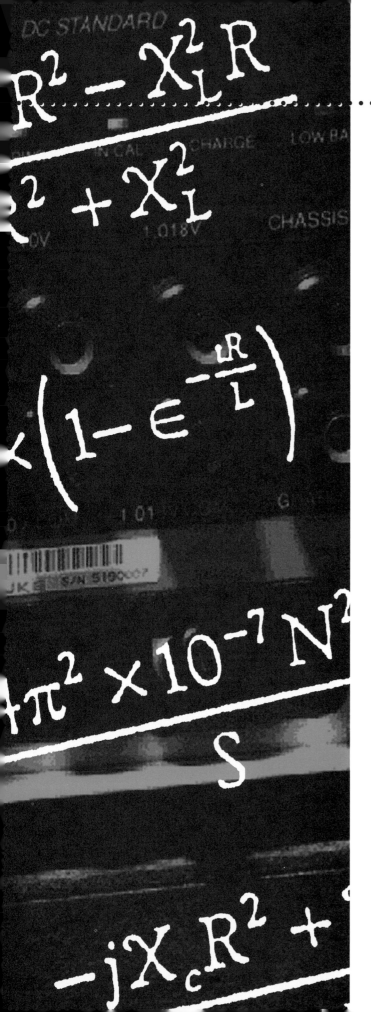

Chapter 23:

Statistical Process Control

This chapter describes the application of Statistical Process Control (SPC) in a metrology laboratory.

T his chapter gives a brief overview of some of the more relevant metrology-related aspects of Statistical Process Control (SPC). It also reports on some of the ways in which the Fluke Standards Laboratory has applied SPC to improving its operations. Perceived benefits of applying SPC in the laboratory include increased profitability resulting from less downtime for internal and external customers, a reduction in the number and magnitude of errors in measurements and in the paperwork associated with measurement, and improved efficiency in the operation.

Adaptation of SPC to metrological processes has had a long but unspectacular history. Churchill Eisenhart, writing at the National Bureau of Standards (NBS), now NIST, in 1962, gave a capsule history of the application of statistics to measurement. He credited Walter A. Shewhart, the creator of SPC, with proposing that measurements can be considered to be the output of a production process amenable to SPC. W. Edwards Deming, in 1950, also clearly understood the improvements that SPC can bring to measurements. Joseph M. Cameron and others at NBS in the 1960s also were discussing measurement as a process.

In spite of this flurry of activity at NBS, there has been little evidence until very recently that the power of SPC is understood by practicing metrologists in industry. ANSI/ASQC M1-1987, American Standard for Calibration Systems, allows one to choose between the "Program Controls Method" and the "Measurement Assurance Method" for maintaining the calibration system and performing calibrations. The former parallels the requirements of MIL-STD-45662A, in which the emphasis is on proper documentation, and the latter implements a version of SPC for controlling the processes that produce measurement results. Perhaps because of the dominant influence of the U.S. military on U.S. industry, there is little evidence that anyone in industry is using the "Measurement Assurance Method" as the basis for controlling a calibration system.

The driving force for any change in the way things are done is, of course, perceived benefit. Generally, in U.S. industry, the perceived benefit is an increase in profitability. Encouraging recent trends affecting profitability include the

movement of metrology and metrologists out of the laboratory and onto the factory floor. Much of this movement is made practical by the renewed emphasis on SPC in the factory, and a recognition that process control involves more than maintaining control charts. By using statistical tools that are familiar to Quality Assurance and Manufacturing personnel in production, the metrologist can establish a common ground for understanding, a common ground largely missing in the past.

Guidelines for Metrology SPC

SPC was designed as a statistical aid to the control of processes. It is not itself a controlling element, but provides evidence of the state of control of the process. SPC can be applied to any repeated operation that has a measurable output, including measurement processes. The simplest application of SPC in the metrology laboratory is in controlling the uncertainty obtained in operating measuring systems.

Controlling Measurement Uncertainties

Figure 23-1 illustrates the three parameters of interest to a metrologist:

- *Error:* the difference between the measured value and the true value

- *Uncertainty:* the range of values that will contain the true value

- *Offset:* the difference between a target (nominal) value and the actual value

Offset is calculated by means of an experiment to determine the absolute value of a parameter, the simplest such experiment being a calibration against a superior standard.

Uncertainty is determined by an uncertainty analysis that takes into consideration the effects of systematic and random errors in all the processes that lead to the assignment of a value

Section 5: Statistics

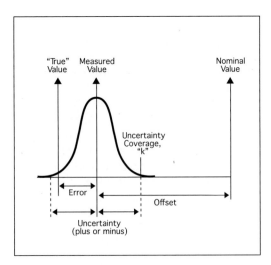

Figure 23-1. *Error, Uncertainty and Offset*

to a measurement result. Both standardization and uncertainty analyses are relatively difficult and costly operations that should not be undertaken more often than necessary. It is most cost effective to perform these analyses once, and then to use process control techniques to provide evidence that the system used is the system analyzed, that is, nothing has changed.

A process can change in two fundamentally different ways: the setpoint can change, or the variability of its processes can change.

A change in setpoint corresponds to a change in the calibration of the system. A change in variability indicates that the uncertainty analysis is no longer valid, since the assumptions upon which it was based have changed. Either change could lead to measurement results outside the range of results expected, based on the uncertainty stated.

Types of Control Charts

SPC monitors setpoint and variability by means of control charts maintained on check standards repeatedly measured on the system. The control charts most often used are the X-bar chart for the measurement means provided by the process, and the R-chart (range) for the variability of repeat measurements. In metrology it is often more appropriate to use the X-bar chart and the S-chart (standard deviation), since the standard deviation, *s*, is just as

easy to compute as the range when data is being processed by computer. When only one measurement is made at a time, it is necessary to use previous data for computing either the range or standard deviation. Typically, the last five measurements are used for this purpose.

Out-of-Control Indicators

Out-of-control indications are evidence that something has changed, and action is required. When the system has a high rate of usage, it is appropriate to measure the check standard only as often as is necessary to maintain confidence in the process. How often is this? The frequency of measurement of the check standard can be approached on the basis of cost-effectiveness. In other words, what is the cost of corrective action if the system is found to be out of control at the next measurement of the check standard? Is this less than the cost of the interim measurements?

If a system is seldom used, it is appropriate to measure the check standard every time the system is operated.

It is not strictly necessary to use a separate, dedicated item as a check standard. When certain items are recalibrated often, it is nearly as effective to maintain control charts on their calibration results. This is especially true when the items are complex instruments and not single value artifacts. The Fluke Standards Laboratory does not maintain a check standard Fluke 5450A Resistance Calibrator, for example. Its working standard 5450A, which contains 17 resistors ranging in value from 1Ω to 100 MΩ, is calibrated monthly, and control charts are maintained for each of the 17 resistors.

Figures 23-2 and 23-3 are examples of a set of control charts that are used to maintain the process by which Fluke 5700A calibrators have their performance verified after they have been artifact-calibrated.

The records of the results of their performance tests are kept in these control charts. The data from the records is inspected to determine whether the process used to verify their performance is in control.

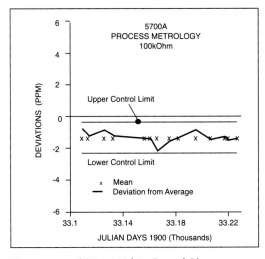

Figure 23-2. *5700A 100 kΩ Control Chart*

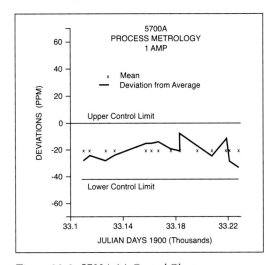

Figure 23-3. *5700A 1A Control Chart*

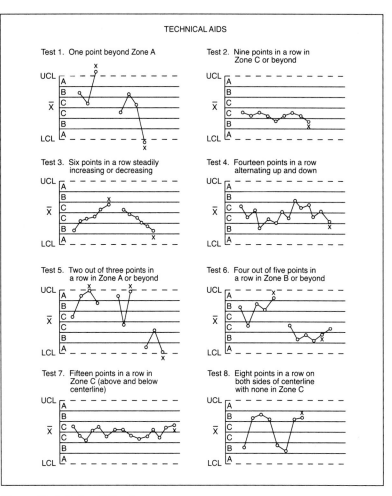

Figure 23-4. *Rules of Thumb*

Figure 23-4 gives some rules of thumb that are used to illustrate a set of rules for interpreting control charts.

In general, any out-of-control indication is a warning that something in the system has changed, and the cause of the change must be identified and corrected if necessary. Keep in mind that the system includes more than the hardware; it includes the operator, the environment, the power lines, and the check standard itself. Changes in offset most often call for calibration of system and/or check standard against a superior standard. Changes in variability are likely to indicate approaching equipment failure, environmental problems, a change in procedures, operator problems, and the like.

Calculating and Working with Drift

A basic assumption of SPC is that the system and the check standard are essentially stable with time. There is no systematic tendency or trend toward different values. Only random variations are present unless the system or check standard has a problem. In many cases in metrology, this assumption is not true. It is not unusual to find a perfectly good standard resistor or voltage standard which exhibits a long-term but highly predictable drift.

It is important to remember that it is not stability that is required, but predictability. Linear regression provides the tools for dealing with these well-behaved yet unstable standards. Linear regression provides us with:

- the drift rate of the standard

- the standard's offset from nominal at some specific time

- the uncertainty of the offset, both at the present time and at times in the future

It takes only a small change in outlook for one to consider the regression line as the center line of a control chart, and the computed uncertainty limits as upper and lower control limits. Of course, the changing value of the standard must be taken into account in order to avoid errors. This can be conveniently done in the software that controls so much of the measuring equipment used in modern metrology laboratories.

SPC Applications

As one example of an SPC-oriented application, the Fluke Corporate Voltage Standard was maintained for several years as the mean of four Fluke 732A DC Reference Standards. The standard drifted at the rate of +0.261 ppm/year for at least six years. Numerous calibrations (72 at the time of this writing) by NIST over that time period established that drift rate with an uncertainty of less than 0.01 ppm/year.

The standard was used daily to calibrate other dc references, a new value being computed each time it was used. This was accomplished by embedding an equation in the software, which computes the measurement results, and the operation is entirely transparent to the operator. Control charts were maintained for the individual references and for the corporate standard as calibrated by NIST.

New applications software just becoming available will make it easy to apply the SPC approach in this manner. For example, a software program for monitoring and displaying trends in the calibration constants of the Fluke 5700A calibrator would combine linear regression and SPC concepts in a user-friendly manner.

One desirable feature in this software is its ability to compute and display the time at which the instrument will become out of confidence. This is the time at which the uncertainty of

the predicted output intersects one of the specification limits. At that point, one can no longer have confidence that the instrument meets its specification, and the instrument should be calibrated, even though there is very small chance that the instrument is actually out of tolerance.

This is one example of the most useful and cost effective applications of SPC to measurement system control. It can be used to give positive information about the need for recalibration. This eliminates the need for periodic recalibrations on a fixed recall schedule, which, in a well-run system, will find that only some 5% or so of instruments actually need calibration. The effect on cost of ownership and downtime is obvious.

It is natural to think of applying SPC and variables control charts to the control of measuring processes, but one should not overlook the many other applications in the metrology laboratory. Examples can be found almost everywhere one may care to look. Attributes control charts of several varieties have many uses in the laboratory, just as in any other situation where repeated operations are performed.

The Fluke Standards Laboratory has applied SPC to monitor and control errors in reports of calibration; turnaround time for the laboratory and for each technician; percent of backlog overdue for shipment; productivity by technician, and many performance factors. The Fluke MET/TRACK laboratory management software package provides easy access to the information needed for such reports.

Attributes versus Variables Charts

There are two types of control charts that metrologists often use. A *variables* control chart is based on numerical data obtained from the measurement of a parameter (which potentially has an infinite number of values). In contrast, an *attributes* chart is used with data obtained by counting yes-no, pass-fail, or other mutually exclusive events. Statistically, the major difference between the two types of charts is that variables charts are based on the normal (Gaussian) distribution and attributes charts are based on the binomial distribution.

The variables chart is the better choice for measurement processes that inherently produce variables data, and that are characterized by relatively small sample sizes. While calibration systems often are formulated around pass-fail criteria suitable for attributes charts, such charts require much larger sample sizes and are much less powerful for indicating problems than are variables charts. On the other hand, pass-fail testing can be much less expensive than variables testing, and for that reason is preferable in many applications. The Fluke Standards Laboratory uses variables testing exclusively in measurements.

For most management and control purposes, variables data is not available, since one is working with such quantities as the number of errors on a report of calibration, the number of instruments found out of tolerance on recall, and the number of on-time deliveries. Often, controlling such parameters will have much more effect on the overall perceived quality (and profitability) of the operation than will controlling measurement processes.

Where to Start

Which should be implemented first, measurement control or management control? The answer should depend on the cost of the implementation weighed against the hidden costs of non-implementation. Unfortunately, calculating such costs is a difficult undertaking.

For example, Fluke Metrology accepted the professional challenge of applying SPC to measurement processes. On the other hand, while few complaints were received about poor or inadequate measurement results or processes, every company does receive complaints about things like cost, late shipments, and long turnaround times. Often the cause of such complaints is beyond the control of the companies involved. Still, resources have been committed to minimize the causes for all complaints coming from Fluke's customers.

The rest of this chapter discusses how SPC was set up and implemented at Fluke, explains some of the problems experienced and how recovery was made from them, and notes the current situation.

Applying SPC at Fluke

The Fluke Standards Laboratory has implemented SPC for those processes and parameters that are most likely to affect the perceived and actual quality of its services. For several years there had been a continuing effort to bring measurement systems under control. More recently, the entire staff was brought into the SPC/TQC process. Significant improvements have been made in the processes targeted for process control. Other observed benefits include notably improved teamwork and a more consistent focus on satisfying customers' needs.

Applications of Attributes Charts

As was stated, SPC was implemented in Fluke's Metrology Laboratories and control charts established for important functions and parameters. Most of the variables control charting had been done by individual metrologists working alone to develop the needed systems. The charts needed for management and control purposes require the input of the entire staff, especially the technicians who are performing the operations. For this reason, the entire laboratory staff was trained in SPC.

In discussions following SPC training, the following SPC objectives were decided on. The first, and the one that drives all the others, was to achieve complete customer satisfaction. In order to do this, operations would need to be monitored to identify and control problems. Secondly, it would need to be ensured that internal customers were properly operating calibrated test equipment, and that the cost of maintaining and using this equipment was optimized. This led to the third objective: monitoring company-owned test equipment to provide information needed to remove the inefficiently operating instruments from the system. Since most of the user complaints concerned turnaround time, the fourth and most urgent objective was to improve throughput for routine calibration services. A goal of five working days for turnaround time for routine calibrations was set.

It was decided that if the Fluke Standards Laboratory staff was to satisfy its customers, it needed to have a clear understanding of who the customers were. Initially, each member of the Metrology staff developed a customer list. Figure 23-5 details the most important customer-supplier relationships.

This was an excellent process because it graphically illustrated the importance of teamwork in the group, and made it very clear who is serving whom. This came as a surprise to some who had originally thought that the technicians existed to satisfy their perceived responsibilities, and who later learned that they existed to support the technicians. It was agreed that, in all cases, the customer wanted services performed as quickly as possible without errors.

Training

The first step in improving the laboratory's throughput was to construct a flow chart that showed the entire calibration process. After the flow chart was completed, problem areas were identified, and it was determined what changes should be made to improve the flow through the laboratory. After the discussions, a new flow chart was prepared, incorporating the suggested changes, as shown in Figure 23-6.

The new flow chart indicated those work areas where control charts were to be used.

Processes in the laboratory that affect throughput are attributes. Attributes reflect qualitative characteristics, such as pass-fail or time overdue. They are plotted on a *U-chart*, a chart that shows the number of nonconformities within a varying sample size. Any instrument that took longer than the targeted five working days was considered an overdue instrument, and therefore a nonconformity.

The control chart for monitoring calibration process time (turnaround time) was based on information obtained from Fluke MET/TRACK Metrology Property Management software. MET/TRACK was decided on because it generates many reports that are valuable for managing the laboratory operation, including:

- number of instruments overdue for recall
- user group and QA Manager to which the overdue instruments belong
- average turnaround time for selected instruments

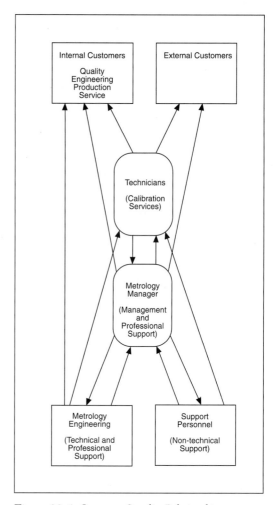

Figure 23-5. *Customer-Supplier Relationships*

- percentage of instruments in tolerance on recall

It also prints out daily schedules for each of the technicians and flags those instruments whose turnaround time has exceeded the targeted five-day turnaround time. The technicians work from these schedules, and the manager uses them to monitor the backlog and turnaround time performance.

Data Collection

After preparing data sheets and blank control charts, the staff began collecting data. The technicians kept track of the number of instruments that were checked in properly as well as the number of errors found on test reports prepared by support personnel. The support personnel kept track of the calibration data sheets prepared by the technicians, making sure that they were legible and that the standards used for

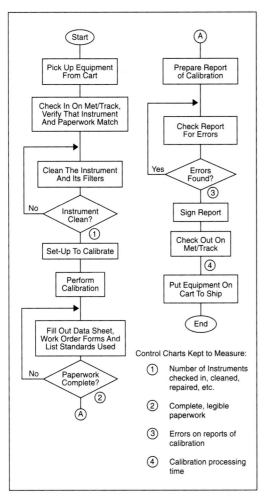

Figure 23-6. *Instrument Flow Through Standards Laboratory*

Control Charts Kept to Measure:

① Number of Instruments checked in, cleaned, repaired, etc.

② Complete, legible paperwork

③ Errors on reports of calibration

④ Calibration processing time

each calibration were listed. The technicians used the daily schedules to chart the percentage of their workload that had exceeded the five working day goal. Each Monday morning the data from the previous week was exchanged by the technicians and support personnel.

Problem Solving

Conflicts between the technicians and the support personnel began almost immediately. The conflicts concerned what were or were not errors or nonconformities. People were taking errors personally instead of as an indication of a process problem that needed correction. Exchanging data once a week did not allow them to correct problems quickly; they could accumulate five days of errors and not know there was a problem until the following Monday.

The problems were solved by reinforcing the idea that SPC was being used to improve processes, not to grade or judge people. To remedy the second problem, the people who were collecting the data provided more information. They would note the error, write a brief description of the problem on the back of the data sheet, and notify the appropriate person as soon as possible. In addition, it was determined that the daily work schedule provided by MET/TRACK must accurately reflect the work that was being performed in the laboratory, as well as what work was complete. That is, there should be no exceptions to the instruments listed on the schedules, and the MET/TRACK database must be kept current.

Control Charts

After data was collected for the first week, the upper and lower control limits and *U-bar* (the average percentage nonconformities) were computed and added to the control charts. If the workload varied by more than 20% for any area in subsequent weeks, new control limits for that area were computed. The *U-bar* was computed and charted weekly regardless of the variations in workload. After the first month, average upper and lower control limits were computed for the whole month, and were plotted on the following month's control chart as a guideline for that month. The goal was to decrease *U-bar* and the control limits each month until an acceptable low level of control was achieved.

Figure 23-7 is a one-month excerpt from the only original chart or graph remaining. It has evolved into a bar graph because the line graph did not present the whole story. For example, 50% overdue might occur when there were only two instruments in backlog.

The control charts for Errors on Data Sheets and Number of Instruments Checked In Properly were discontinued after a few weeks because, by that time, only zeroes were being recorded.

Other useful charts were Percent of Instruments in Tolerance on Recall (Figure 23-8), Average Turnaround Time for Internal Customers (Figure 23-9) and for External Customers (Figure 23-10), and Hours Worked Minus Hours Budgeted (Figure 23-11). The information from

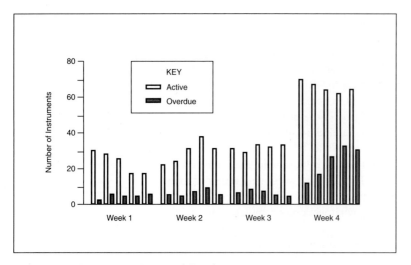

Figure 23-7. *Instruments, Active and Overdue*

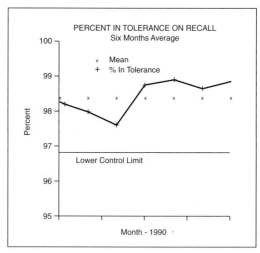

Figure 23-8. *Percent of Instruments In Tolerance on Recall*

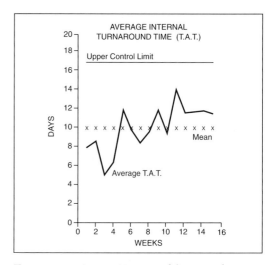

Figure 23-9. *Average Turnaround for Internal Customers*

all but the last chart was obtained from MET/ TRACK (see Chapter 19, "Automated Calibration").

Applications of Variables Charts

Since SPC was instituted in the Standards Laboratory, some of the applications of variables control charts have been fairly routine, while others have been more exotic. Use of X charts was preferred to X-bar charts because, in many cases, only single measurements of a quantity were used. S-charts (standard deviations) are typically used rather than R-charts (range) because most of Fluke's calibration data is processed by computer and it is as easy to compute standard deviation as range. Where one data point for a calibration is available, standard deviations are typically computed for charting from the last five points in a series.

In the world of modern electrical metrology, where sub-ppm uncertainties are becoming commonplace, one seldom has a really stable process or quantity to work with. This necessitates adapting the control chart so that the control line becomes the trend line for the quantity or process involved. Because metrology works with very stable and highly predictable phenomena, only the simplest of trend lines are required (usually linear trends) but sometimes exponential, logarithmic, or square-law are needed.

Resistance Standards

To illustrate the preceding point, consider the problem of calibrating standard resistors. Two resistance standards are maintained, one at 1 ohm and the other at 10 kΩ, each consisting of the mean of three resistors. Until recently, both the 1Ω and 10 kΩ standards were maintained through yearly calibrations by NIST. Maintenance of the 10 kΩ standard is now done by participating in the NIST Resistance Measurement Assistance Program (RMAP).

All of the individual resistors drift with time, and the problem of predicting their values at times different from the date of calibration is unnecessary. These resistors have been drifting linearly for about 20 years, as illustrated in Figure 23-12.

A simple linear regression provides a good means for predicting an individual value. In fact, it has been shown that the regression line provides a more accurate value than any single calibration by NIST.

The regression line is used as the center line of the control charts for these resistors, and standard deviation of points about the regression line establishes upper and lower control limits. S- or R-charts are not maintained in this situation. Figure 23-13 is a control chart for the 10 kΩ standard of Figure 23-12.

Voltage Standard

A more exotic control chart resulted from the maintenance of the voltage standard, maintained at the 10V level in the mean of four Fluke 732A DC Reference Standards. This standard was calibrated approximately monthly through the operation of the Fluke Direct Voltage Maintenance Program (DVMP). The standard, the mean of the four instruments, drifts linearly at the rate of +0.261 ppm/year. These instruments never left the laboratory, and traceability was obtained by means of transfer standards used in the DVMP.

Each transfer standard was calibrated in terms of the Fluke volt prior to being shipped to customers, and was eventually calibrated by NIST and then returned to Fluke. These NIST

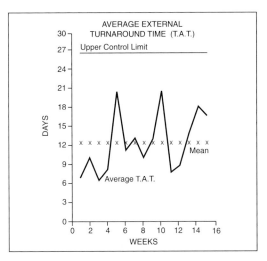

Figure 23-10. Turnaround for External Customers

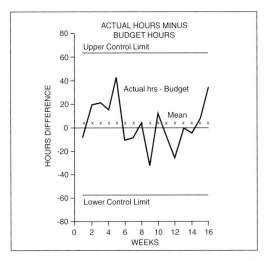

Figure 23-11. Hours Worked Minus Hours Budgeted

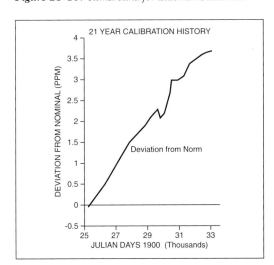

Figure 23-12. Calibration History: 10 kΩ Standard Resistor

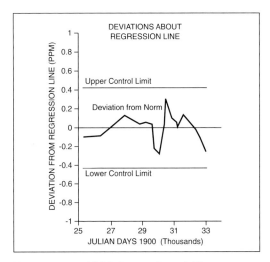

Figure 23-13. 10 kΩ Resistor Control Chart

calibrations provided the data for computing the accuracy with which the Fluke volt was maintained. Equally important, they provided a check on the adequacy of the analysis on which reported uncertainties were based. The difference between the NIST value and the Fluke value for each transfer was plotted on a control chart, the center line of which was the regression line for the standard.

Because uncertainty analysis was tested, control limits in this case were variable, computed for each transfer from the individual uncertainties encountered in the calibrations. Figure 23-14 shows the history of the standard.

It can be seen that too many points fell outside the control limits, indicating that the uncertainty calculations did not include all sources of uncertainty. A standard control chart for the same data is shown in Figure 23-15.

The process appears to be in control, but it is clear that the distribution is not normal; there are far too many points in the 1 to 2 σ range and too few near the extremes and the centerline. As is the case with any process that is in control, any improvements must come from improvements in the process. It is believed that the missing uncertainty was the result of small, long-term, cyclical variations that were not adequately accounted for in the statistical treatment of the data.

5700A Process Metrology

The third, and most exotic, example of a variables chart comes from the system for maintaining traceability for the Fluke factory's Final Test Stations for the Fluke 5700A calibrator. The stations are maintained through process metrology, a recent innovative approach to maintaining traceability of production processes.

The basic idea is to maintain the production test process always in control so that it never makes inaccurate measurements, and to do this in a manner that does not require shutting it down for periodic recalibrations of its instruments. The process is maintained in control by monitoring check standards (two 5700As) which are periodically measured by the Final Test Stations. The process is controlled at the proper setpoints by testing products in the Standards Laboratory. As long as the control

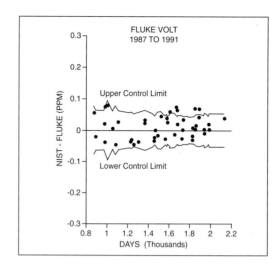

Figure 23-14. *DVMP Uncertainty*

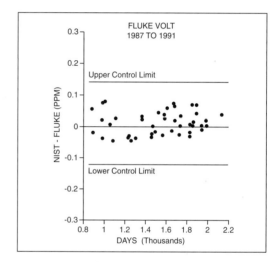

Figure 23-15. *Fluke DVMP/NIST Transfers*

charts for the check standards show control, the process is known to be in control. As long as the differences between the measurements obtained in production and in the Standards Laboratory are in control and at the proper setpoints, the process is judged to be *properly* controlled. Test stations maintained by Process Metrology are certified on the basis of these two kinds of control charts.

Figures 23-16, 23-17, and 23-18 are samples of the control charts obtained from measurements performed on the check standards.

The charts show approximate upper and lower 24-hour specification limits in addition to upper and lower control limits. This is to aid Quality Assurance personnel in quickly spotting parameters that may be in trouble. The data was taken over a nine-month period.

The obvious step at about test 21 in Figure 23-17 resulted from the replacement of the resistance standard in the Final Test Station. The procedure requires testing the check standard immediately upon making any change to instrumentation, and allows for production to continue if the control charts evidence sufficient control.

Figure 23-18 represents a process that is obviously out of control. However, several things should be noted. First, the check standard has remained within 24-hour specifications for a period exceeding nine months. Second, the test station, as shown in Figure 23-3, is in control. An out-of-control condition does not necessarily indicate trouble. It is a flag to alert production personnel to a possible problem. This particular parameter should be controlled around the regression line, not the average, something presently beyond the capability of the software developed for the system.

Histograms

Histograms (Figures 23-19, 23-20, and 23-21) are also generated for each parameter measured, again as an aid to Quality Assurance personnel.

Much information is presented in graphical form. The width of the box represents the factory test specification, usually 80% of 24-hour customer specification. The width of the line above the scale is 24-hour customer specification. The scale is automatically generated by the computer, and its width has no significance.

Figures 23-22, 23-2, and 23-3 are samples of control charts generated from the differences between Final Test and the Standards Laboratory.

These charts are standard variables charts, with upper and lower control limits obtained from standard deviations of points about the control line. The y-scale approximates the upper and lower 24-hour customer specification limits to aid in interpreting the charts.

The 5700A is a complex instrument, for which 166 accuracy-related parameters and 83 secondary-specification parameters are measured.

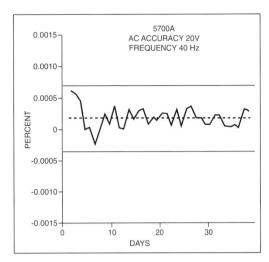

Figure 23-16. *Fluke 5700A Process Metrology: Check Standards at 20V, 40Hz*

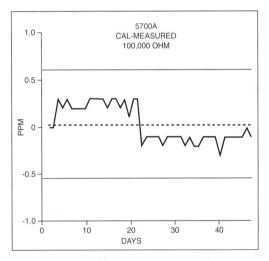

Figure 23-17. *Fluke 5700A Process Metrology: 100 kOhm Check Standard*

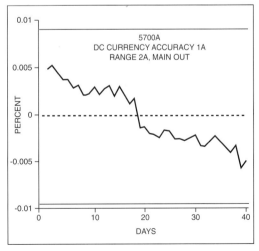

Figure 23-18. *Fluke 5700A Process Metrology: Drift in Check Standard*

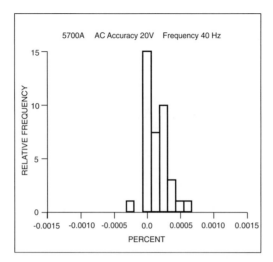

Figure 23-19. *Fluke 5700A Process Metrology: 10V, 40 Hz Check Standard*

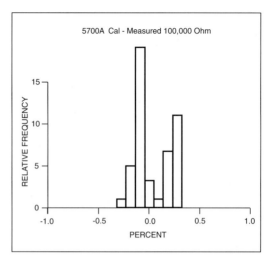

Figure 23-20. *Fluke 5700A Process Metrology: 100 kΩ Check Standard*

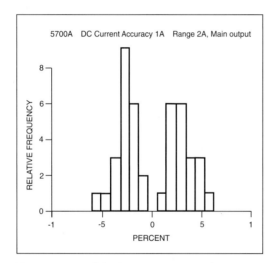

Figure 23-21. *Fluke 5700A Process Metrology: 1A Check Standard*

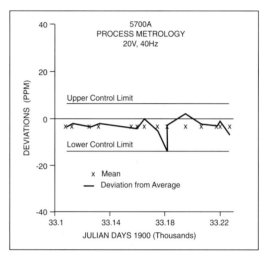

Figure 23-22. *Fluke 5700A Final Test and Standards Laboratory Difference at 20V, 40 Hz*

Control charts are maintained for process control on all 249 points, and for process metrology on the 166 accuracy-related points. Obviously this mass of data must be processed by computer, and developing the computer tools for this complicated procedure was a major undertaking. To eliminate the necessity for examining 249 charts for out-of-control indications, the software incorporated a subset of the Western Electric Rules for interpreting the charts. Quality Assurance personnel have the option of printing all the charts or only those few which fail the selection criteria. This greatly simplifies the problem of dealing with this mass of data.

Costs and Benefits

When Fluke implemented TQC (Total Quality Commitment), resources were routinely allocated to SPC projects. By now, the great benefits of SPC/TQC to production processes have been so often and so well demonstrated that such projects are now required. And there is an ever increasing interest in applying the SPC/TQC concepts to the approximately 80% of the company which is not directly involved in production.

In Fluke's experience, the process that led up to implementing the attributes charts involved the largest number of people and produced the greatest number of obvious benefits. Not the least of the benefits was the improved teamwork that has resulted from a better and more uniform understanding of each person's contribution to the total group objectives. In some ways, the improved teamwork and reduced friction among the staff were the most valuable results of the exercise.

Fluke found SPC to be of great benefit in having information about such parameters as backlog, average turnaround time, instruments out for repair, etc., available to all and reviewed frequently by management. Good people tend to monitor what is perceived to be important, and to correct problems before they become major problems.

Except for routine control charts, the cost of implementing a set of variables control charts can be much greater than the cost for attributes charts. However, this should not discourage anyone from setting up control charts. Substantial benefit was found from setting up even routine charts, largely from the fact that uncertainties became based on objective evidence rather than professional judgment.

Even the substantial costs of setting up the more exotic systems described are easily justified. In the case of the Direct Voltage Maintenance Program (DVMP), the statistical approach allowed Fluke to offer products and calibration services at accuracies that would not have been supportable by more conventional means. In the case of 5700A Process Metrology, the considerable cost is many times recovered in the elimination of downtime and disruption of production that would otherwise result from removing instruments from test stations for routine calibration. In addition, any uncertainty in the quality of the product being shipped has been removed. Rather than trusting that the station is in calibration for the entire calibration period, production now has continuous, objective evidence of process control, and can be highly confident that only in-specification instruments are being shipped.

Another unexpected benefit of 5700A Process Metrology had to do with test ratios in the factory. The factory has always had a tendency to over test. Initially, 5700A testing was performed at 30% to 50% of customer 24-hour specification. A statistical analysis was able to show that over-testing resulted in a very large increase in rework and retest with a very small decrease in non-complying product shipped. In other words, virtually all rejects actually met specifications, and nearly all of those that didn't would be caught by more reasonable test ratios.

Key References

AT&T Technologies, "Statistical Quality Control Handbook," 1956, Indianapolis, IN 46219

Other references for this chapter are in the Resources Appendix.

 FLUKE ®

Laboratory
Management

Section Six

Chapter 24:

Service and Maintenance Policy

This chapter covers aspects of the service philosophy needed by a metrology laboratory to enable its customers to see real value in the calibration service provided. The customer can be either internal or external, but the results have to be the same—customer satisfaction.

There is more to operating a calibration laboratory than simply providing calibration services. Any person managing a metrology laboratory must make a number of policy decisions that involve tradeoffs between cost and quality. This chapter covers a few of the more basic and important decision areas, and suggests appropriate policy and practice.

The Laboratory Mission

The primary function of any calibration laboratory is to maintain traceability and document traceability. The calibration activity itself ensures the accuracy of measurements made in support of the mission of the laboratory's customers. The function of records is to add discipline to the process and ensure that any relevant audits of calibration activity will be successfully passed. This is true whether the laboratory is a department of a larger organization, or deals with outside customers. As with any product or service, there is a required quality level for calibration services. There are also economic limitations which dictate that the services must be provided in a timely manner and within cost constraints.

Calibration Intervals and Adjustment Policy

Two basic and interacting areas of policy and procedure that affect calibration quality are the assignment and adjustment of calibration intervals, and the policy regarding the circumstances under which adjustments are made during the process of calibration. Both of these areas involve technical questions as well as philosophical considerations. While there is little debate regarding the intended results, there is ongoing discussion of the best means of achieving those results.

Calibration Intervals

It is a fact that the assignment of calibration intervals affects both the quality and cost of calibration activity. Since calibration is only a means to an end, it would be desirable to manufacture standards and test equipment that never required calibration, even at the time of manufacture. While this might be possible for some equipment used in quantum experiments, it is not true for the great majority of equipment in use. Calibration at the time of manufacture, as well as periodic recalibration for the assurance of specified accuracy, is a way of life in the industry.

Part of the life-cycle cost of a standard or measurement instrument is the associated cost of periodic calibration. This in turn breaks down to the frequency of calibration as well as to the cost of the individual calibration. Part of the cost of calibration is that of secondary factors involving the loss of use of the standard or instrument during the calibration process. These secondary costs can exceed those of the actual calibration. Thus there are economic advantages in making recalibration both inexpensive and infrequent.

While manufacturers of standards and measurement instruments commonly recommend a recalibration interval, it is the laboratory manager's job to evaluate and, as necessary and desirable, to adjust the interval to meet the laboratory's quality goals and to control costs. A high quality level is more readily ensured by frequent recalibration. Cost reduction is enhanced by reducing the frequency of periodic recalibration. Therefore, it is the manager's job to find the correct point of balance between quality and cost. In this instance, quality is defined as the probability that an instrument will be found to be within tolerance on all ranges and functions when it is returned for routine recalibration.

For example, it may be the laboratory's goal to find 95% of the instrument population fully in tolerance as received by the lab. It is generally assumed that the 100% level is unattainable at any cost. On the other hand, a level below the target value of 95% may be assumed to have unacceptable effects on manufacturing cost, product quality, mission success, or personnel safety, depending on the activities supported by the calibration process.

The methodology for the assignment and adjustment of calibration intervals has been, and still is, the subject of a good deal of study and scientific analysis. The National Conference of Standards Laboratories (NCSL) has both a Recommended Practice RP-1 in this area and a standing committee that studies and encourages communication of theory, practice, and results. In various regulatory and contractual documents, such as MIL-STD-45662A, the assignment and adjustment of calibration intervals is a major area of concern. Anyone who needs to set up an interval adjustment scheme would benefit by obtaining a copy of the NCSL Recommended Practice.

Adjustment Policy

There are two major categories of standards and measurement equipment: those with calibration adjustments, and those without. An example of the latter would be a standard resistor or a saturated standard cell (Weston cell). An example of the former would be any instrument that has one or more potentiometers, variable capacitors, variable inductors, and similar items that affect one or more calibration points. A first generation analog oscilloscope using vacuum tubes as active devices is a prime example of a measurement instrument containing adjustments; the number of adjustable components affecting calibration in such an instrument numbers in the dozens.

While there is no physical way to adjust a Thomas-pattern 1Ω resistor, it might be argued that a reassignment of value would constitute adjustment. However, the "adjust/don't adjust" argument primarily concerns those instruments where physical adjustment is not only possible, but frequently necessary.

One point of view states that, to the extent possible, the calibration process should be carried out so that all adjustments are set during the calibration process. The adjustment is carried out so as to "center up" or "optimize" the actual performance of the instrument. This

applies whether or not any particular checkpoint is found to be out of tolerance.

The opposite point of view states that adjustment should be made only when a checkpoint is found to be out of tolerance, or very close to it. This point of view is frequently modified by allowing (or requiring) adjustment if a checkpoint has used a specified portion of the tolerance "window." For example, assume that the full-scale output voltage on a certain range has a specified maximum of 1.05V and a specified minimum of 0.95V. This is probably specified as a full-scale nominal output of 1.00V, with a tolerance of ±5%. Using the modified philosophy, adjustment would be made if the actual performance deviated from nominal by some lesser amount, such as 3%, rather than the full 5%. On balance, the modified policy (making adjustments only when a specified portion of the tolerance window has been used up) is probably the best approach to adjustment.

In actual practice, many labs do not attempt adjustment unless a point is more than 70% of its specified tolerance. This reduces the chance of having an out-of-tolerance incident, while preserving the advantages of minimal adjustment.

Pros and Cons of the Adjustment Policy

Some arguments favor routine adjustment, and others favor adjustment only when necessary. The validity of each argument depends largely on underlying assumptions as to the nature of the standards or measurement instrumentation being calibrated, as well as the mechanisms leading to out-of-tolerance performance.

One argument opposing routine adjustment is that it tends to obscure information regarding the basic stability of the instrument. Frequent minor adjustments can make it impossible to determine the long-term tendencies of the instrument. Does it have a tendency to drift to a continually higher or lower value? Is the rate of drift uniform and predictable? Does the instrument have a tendency to drift randomly above and below a relatively stable center value? Is there a combination of random drift and single-sided drift with time? What are the relative amplitudes of the two drift actions? What is the time rate of drift for each?

Continual adjustment to compensate for minor drift can obscure the facts needed to make sound decisions on interval adjustment. For example, perhaps an instrument left alone would be found to have a predictable, low rate of drift that would justify a longer calibration interval. Or, leaving it alone for awhile could demonstrate a degree of instability that would lead to the adoption of an even shorter interval.

The actual adjustment takes time and effort. If the average performance is stable, and the random variations are within acceptable limits, then the time spent making minor adjustments may be wasted. Some technicians insist that an instrument is always more useful if it is "right on the money." Others argue that being "on the money" does not change the full specified uncertainty of the instrument.

If an instrument has a stable average value but exhibits random variations that tend to use up most or all of the tolerance range, adjustment at the time of extremes of performance may be counter-productive. Assume, for example, that calibration occurs when the item is randomly near the upper or lower limit of performance. Adjusting the item at that time can be expected to cause the average value to change. Then, when the item drifts to the opposite extreme of performance, it may be "forced" out of tolerance.

In fact, there is no clear calibration strategy for such an item. It probably should be "derated"—assigned a broader tolerance in keeping with its tendency to drift throughout the entire range of specified performance. Unfortunately, this sort of performance is likely to be found when the manufacturer tries to oversell the product's capability.

As stated previously, an instrument adjustment policy that is a compromise between the extreme points of view is probably best for most instruments and most laboratories. However, the laboratory manager must assume responsibility for determining the policy. Note also that this policy can be made for the instrument population as a whole, for individual instruments, or for some in-between category.

The same applies to the adjustment of calibration intervals. Many laboratories adjust calibration intervals for all members of a class consisting of a particular manufacturer-model number combination. Other laboratories adjust intervals for broader classes, such as "3½-digit multimeters" or "low-frequency oscilloscopes." Some laboratories make interval adjustments for the individual item, based on an analysis of individual instrument performance. This method has the advantage of minimum involvement of laboratory engineering or support functions. It is only necessary to establish a periodic check on percent in tolerance at recall of the entire workload to ensure that goals are being met. This is normally done monthly or bi-monthly to track performance to the laboratory's goal for percent in tolerance at recall.

Routine Maintenance

The calibration laboratory manager should also set policy regarding certain aspects of routine maintenance. This could be taken to mean preventive maintenance. However, for a calibration laboratory, routine maintenance is aimed at more than the mere prevention of breakdown between scheduled maintenance activity. Calibration at scheduled intervals does more than keep an instrument "up and running." It provides assurance of measurement accuracy in conformance with specifications. Some types of routine maintenance not only help to prevent breakdown, but also reduce the risk of out-of-tolerance performance.

For example, the loss of cooling efficiency associated with a clogged air filter or an inoperative cooling fan can degrade calibration without actually causing a catastrophic failure (loss of function or gross errors readily detected by the user). Therefore, it is advisable to make maintenance of fans and filters routine whenever an item comes in for calibration, even if maintenance amounts to no more than inspection when all proves well.

Routine maintenance can also pay extra dividends on items that are sent to outside laboratories. This is especially true when the outside laboratory is expensive and has long turn-

Figure 24-1. Fluke Service Engineer and a Calibration System

Fluke 5440B and Fluke 5700A calibrators, use a combination of electronic and relay switching many of the most accurate and precise instruments still depend on manual switches. For example, the Fluke 720A Kelvin-Varley divider contains switches that must have low, repeatable contact resistance in order for the instrument to maintain specified performance. Therefore, this item should be maintained with routine concern for the cleanliness and lubrication of the switches.

Binding posts and broadband rf connectors are susceptible to deterioration, caused by contamination as well as use. Some environments produce contamination and corrosion. The resulting contact resistance, electrochemical voltages, and perhaps other effects can be significant sources of error when working at the state of the art in direct voltage measurement. Intermittent contact resistance and unacceptable levels of voltage standing wave ratio (vswr) can cause problems with high frequency equipment. Careful inspection and maintenance of the associated hardware can reduce long-term calibration and repair cost, as well as provide higher assurance of day-to-day measurement accuracy and precision in the use environment.

Instrument Cleanliness

There are good reasons to routinely clean the exterior surfaces of an instrument when it comes in for calibration or repair. A clean instrument is psychologically more satisfying to the user. The user is also likely to perceive that the service provider is interested in quality and in "going the extra mile" if the appearance of the instrument is better on return than it was when it went in.

As a rule, external surfaces should be cleaned using a soft cloth, a mild detergent, and water. It is important to check the instrument manual to see if there are any special requirements or areas of concern with cleaning due to the item's particular materials and construction methods.

Caution: Care should be taken when spraying cleaner directly on the instrument.

around times. Why be penalized by the time and expense of having routine maintenance performed at such an outside agency? Not only is use of the instrument lost while it is gone, but the whole attempt at calibration could be abortive. Instruments going to NIST and similar laboratories should go there needing only the superior standards and calibration capability they offer. All other repair and maintenance should be taken care of prior to shipping the instrument.

Mechanical Connections

Cables, connectors, and switches are also important in measurement equipment and standards. Wear and tear of wires, switch contacts, and connectors can be a major source of out-of-tolerance conditions. While it is true that many modern instruments, such as the

Take care to avoid getting the cleaning agent inside the instrument or under panel connectors, where it may cause damage or have adverse effects such as leakage resistance to the case. One useful technique is to apply the cleanser to the wiping cloth, rather than directly to the instrument.

Keeping the Customer Informed

The laboratory manager should promptly communicate to the customer anything unusual regarding the condition of the instrument and the required service. This is especially true whenever extra expense or unusual delay is involved. This removes the element of surprise and gives the customer a chance to make responses, or to negotiate the service arrangements. Also, exchanging information may make it easier to service the instrument. Such an exchange may also prevent future problems due to misuse or abuse. It is important, of course, to communicate in a way that is informative and shows concern for the customer. The ability to communicate in an open, non-adversarial way is an important plus for calibration laboratory personnel.

Chapter 25:
The Laboratory Environment

All physical measurements are influenced by the environment. This chapter identifies the major environmental influences affecting calibration measurements.

This chapter discusses the types of physical environment needed for various kinds of calibration laboratories. It also discusses how the strict requirements of the past have been relaxed due to the wider operating temperature band of most modern calibration equipment.

The Need for Environmental Control

The need for controlling the physical environment in which instruments are calibrated and measurements are made becomes evident once one realizes that all physical parameters are influenced to some extent by the environment.

It is the overall goal of calibration and measurement to achieve measurement compatibility. This can be done only when the *same quantity* is being measured. Since the quantity is influenced by the environment, it follows that the environment must be standardized. The environment in a facility must duplicate or compensate for the standard reference conditions that apply to the instruments being calibrated.

The extent to which the environment must be duplicated depends on several factors. These will be discussed in some detail in this chapter. In general, it depends on the degree of compatibility required and the environmental sensitivity of both the measuring system and the item being measured. Because a standards laboratory does a wide variety of the highest accuracy measurements of its organization, it is a general rule that it have the most stringent environmental requirements.

As the lower accuracy, higher volume end of the traceability chain is approached, the environmental requirements are not as strict. Instrument repair facilities, for example, will have much looser environmental requirements than the laboratory that calibrates the repair facility's standards. Fluke has specified levels of environmental control for four general types of measurement facility, ranging from ±0.6°C for a primary laboratory to ±5.0°C for a repair facility doing scopes and handheld meters only.

Relative humidity value also has a similar graduated requirement for the four facility types.

Electrical measurements tend to be much less sensitive to the environment than physical, mechanical, and dimensional measurements. Consequently, the requirements for environmental control of electrical standards and calibration are generally much looser. Usually the parameters that must be considered are:

- temperature
- humidity
- barometric pressure (at times)
- rfi/emi (radio frequency/electromagnetic interference)

Electrical facilities should be kept clean by good housekeeping standards, but the extreme particle count requirements of optical and dimensional laboratories do not apply. In the past, electrical measurements were made with electromechanical-indicating devices where vibration was an issue, but modern electronic instruments have largely negated this requirement.

Some environmental requirements have more to do with worker comfort, health, and safety than instrument susceptibility. Adequate lighting, safe and non-annoying noise levels, good ventilation, and safe and properly grounded electrical supply and equipment are among these requirements.

Construction and design of the calibration or standards laboratory is as important as the selection and operation of the equipment used within it. Equipment eventually becomes obsolete due to technical advances. It also wears out from long-term use. But the laboratory itself may remain in service through generations of equipment. The time and effort put into the design of the laboratory should reflect the value of the facility and its lasting impact on the quality of the work performed in it.

Site Location

It is much easier to obtain tight environmental control when the calibration laboratory location has a modular (room-within-a-room) construction. This provides a buffer that isolates the laboratory from the outside world. The size of the laboratory should be sufficient to allow for future expansion. The cost of expanding an existing laboratory is usually much greater, per square foot, than the initial cost of providing spare room. If modular construction is not possible, location next to an outside wall should be avoided, especially if the wall has a southern exposure. This applies specifically to a laboratory that is located in the northern hemisphere. Since the sun shines on that wall most of the day, the laboratory becomes susceptible to solar heating. Although double-pane windows are acceptable for modular laboratories, and desirable for esthetics and safety, windows of any sort are not advisable when the walls of the laboratory are the building's exterior walls.

Normally, the laboratory should be built on the ground floor, and the floor should be of concrete construction. Where ground vibration is present, it may be necessary to seek out a special low-vibration site for the laboratory. The building chosen for the laboratory site should be of sound and solid construction. Locations above the ground floor or above mezzanines should be avoided because they are susceptible to structural movement and make it difficult to achieve isolation from vibration.

Note: For information on detailed requirements for mechanical calibration facilities, see the description of the NCSL Recommended Practice RP-7 at the end of this chapter.

Laboratory Floor Plan

The actual floor plan for a laboratory will reflect the laboratory's mission and fiscal resources. For example, separate rooms may be used for electrical, temperature, pressure, dimensional, optical and other calibrations. These rooms may be further segregated as to whether primary or working standards are calibrated therein. Some rooms, those used for electrical calibrations of a variety of instruments, may be large and have a number of workbenches. Other rooms may be more modest in size with only one or two workbenches.

A number of calibration laboratories have published information concerning their facilities, including floor plans. Some of this information has been presented at professional conferences, such as the Measurement Science Conference (MSC) or the National Conference of Standards Laboratories (NCSL). Other such information is found in brochures published by these laboratories. Two references to laboratory layout information are given at the end of this chapter.

Construction

The walls of the laboratory must incorporate humidity barriers. These barriers can consist of plastic sheeting inserted into the walls, or of a laminated plastic lining applied to the internal wall surface. The number of doors into the laboratory should be held to a minimum, but must comply with fire and safety regulations. Joints between the doors and frames should be furnished with gaskets that provide an adequate seal. There is some debate as to the benefit of air locks, which were previously considered a necessity. An air lock limits the loss of conditioned air when doors are opened, and also limits the intrusion of dust into the laboratory. Positive air pressure within the laboratory minimizes this problem.

If an air lock is chosen, its dimensions should be sufficient to allow passage of personnel and equipment, such as a cart being pushed through by a technician. This also means that the separation of doors should allow the first door to be closed before the second door is opened; otherwise the lock is ineffective. The separation of the doors should therefore be about nine feet. Some laboratories incorporate door locks that allow only one door to open at a time.

Electrical Power Requirements

Power requirements should be closely calculated when planning electrical outlets for the laboratory. The following list shows typical U.S. power requirements for standards and test equipment, including units under test. It does not include lighting and environmental control requirements. As with other aspects of the laboratory, it is wise to install excessive capacity in new construction to avoid expensive rework later.

- 115/230V ac, 1ϕ, 60 Hz

- 220/440V ac, 3ϕ, 60 Hz ±1 Hz (other voltages for non-U.S. facilities as required)

- 115/230V ac, 1 and 3ϕ, delta, 400 Hz

- 115/208V ac, 3ϕ, wye, 400 Hz ±10 Hz

- 28 Vdc

- provisions for emergency backup power

Most laboratories will require only one outlet each for the 400 Hz and 28V dc sources.

Line Regulation

Today, most laboratory-type measurement instruments have built-in voltage regulators. Therefore their operation is relatively independent of power line voltage variation, as long as it is within the limits of ±10% of the design voltage. With this in mind, it may be acceptable to use the local power company output directly without further line conditioning.

If regulation is needed due to special requirements, equipment outlets should be regulated to maintain voltage within ±2% of average or nominal. The response time of the voltage regulators should not exceed 0.3 second, and total harmonic distortion should not exceed 5% over the full range of loading. Power line noise may also need to be evaluated.

Grounding

A good ground system is required to provide measurement integrity and effective emi shielding. Ground systems maintain a reference potential for instrument safety, protect against static electricity, and limit the system-to-frame voltage to enhance operator safety. Grounding also provides a discharge path for short-duration currents due to lightning, and prevents damage from surges on power lines. Grounding is essential to the protection and operation of electronic process controls and communications. NEC, OSHA, and other electrical standards require a ground system. The resistance within a ground system is composed of the following:

- The resistance of the ground rod and connecting cable.

- The resistance of the contact between the ground rod and the soil directly in contact with the ground rod.

- The resistance of the body of earth surrounding the ground rod.

Generally the resistance of the ground rod, and the contact resistance between the ground rod and soil, will be small compared to the resistance of the body of earth surrounding the ground rod.

For example, assume that the earth surrounding an electrode or ground rod is a series of conductive shells of equal thickness. The current flowing from the ground will flow through the shells. The earth shell closest to the ground rod has the least surface area and, therefore, causes the greatest resistance. The cross sectional area of each shell increases as the distance of the electrode increases. At some point, adding earth shells does not significantly add to the earth resistance surrounding the ground rod. This condition is known as effective resistance area, and it depends mainly on driven depth and diameter of the ground rod. The acceptable ohmic values for a ground bus vary from 2Ω for dc common to 5Ω for ac or power line common.

Measuring Ground Resistance

Ground resistance (or ground rod resistance) is the ohmic resistance between a given grounding electrode and a grounded reference electrode at a remote location. The separating distance eliminates interaction between the electrodes.

Proper grounding is important, but remember that grounding is never absolute. Consider objects in relation to a given ground reference; the lowest possible impedance to the reference should be achieved for all frequencies of concern. Minimize the possibility of circulating ground currents, as well as the coupling of grounding circuits. Inadequate grounding of vans (mobile units) has been experienced in dry, sandy soil, as is found in a desert. Since a convenient water table does not always exist, the solution may be complex and difficult, with uncertain results.

Another example involves grounding problems that were encountered when placing transmitters on Rocky Mountain peaks. Even with a good water table, it is best to use a grid of conductors, or a large metallic sheet, buried in the ground. This is more effective than having a few rods driven into the soil.

Ventilation

Air conditioning systems for a laboratory must provide adequate circulation and ventilation. A well-designed system provides uniform circulation of air, without stratification (layering). It also minimizes temperature gradients in and around the laboratory. Both of these problems occur because heat is generated by the electrical equipment installed in the laboratory and by the body heat of the personnel. A certain stratification of the air is impossible to avoid. Therefore, the laboratory's specifications should be met in the level between 3 and 5 feet from the floor to keep the laboratory equipment from suffering from "hot spots." Air velocity or movement in the working area (3 to 5 feet above the floor) should be 0.71 ±0.28 cubic meters per minute (25 ±10 cubic feet per minute). This includes a minimum acceptable room air

change rate of 0.28 cubic meters (10 cubic feet) per person per hour, or one air change per hour, whichever is more.

Lighting

Use fluorescent lighting in the laboratory area to minimize heating. And use recessed fixtures whenever possible because they lack the ledges and protuberances that catch and hold dust particles. The fixtures should be radio frequency interference-free and equipped with rf line filters.

One standard requires lighting intensity to be 1076 lux (100 foot candles) nominal (shadowless), 860 lux (80 foot candles) minimum, at bench level throughout the laboratory area. However, light level requirements relate mostly to human factors, and the level of this standard is too high for most operations because it causes physical discomfort. Lower levels are acceptable if adequate for the tasks at hand.

Temperature Control

Temperature and humidity control are crucial elements of laboratory design. Since temperature fluctuations also affect humidity, its control is especially important. In many geographical areas, both temperature and humidity require direct control.

Various standards for laboratory temperature apply throughout the industry and around the world. In the mechanical and optical disciplines, the internationally accepted temperature is 20°C. For electronic laboratories, the situation is not clear cut. International comparisons are generally made at 20°C, and many countries have adopted this as their standard. Some countries use 25°C while others, including the United States, have adopted 23°C.

In warmer climates, it is generally advantageous to use a higher operating temperature because the temperature control system requires less capacity for cooling, which results in lower system cost and easier control, and the personnel have a more comfortable working environment. In colder climates, less heating energy is required to maintain a lower temperature. The limiting factor in this case is the comfort of the laboratory staff.

Problems can arise when a laboratory uses a temperature inconsistent with that of the next higher-echelon laboratory. Using a temperature that is different from the country's standard requires that the owner's calibration standards be calibrated at a nonstandard temperature. Or, temperature corrections might have to be developed, increasing the cost and reducing the integrity of the calibration.

The magnitude of deviations from average or nominal temperature is as important as the absolute value of the average. The allowable variation depends on the calibration workload as well as the standards used. This in turn influences the cost of the temperature control system.

Most electronic instruments have some tolerance for temperature change, and many are specified over a range of ±5°C. Still, there are many instruments or standards that require tighter temperature control. State-of-the-art measurement uncertainty combined with temperature-sensitive equipment leads to the most stringent control requirements. A standards laboratory, for example, may require variations of less than ±0.6°C. A less critical laboratory could accept ±1°C. A laboratory calibrating handheld meters with a multifunction calibrator would be quite adequately controlled with ±5°C regulation.

Although tighter control costs more money, most temperature control systems use the same process. First, air is cooled. This air is a mixture of the existing laboratory air combined with a percentage of new air. Cooling the air below its dew point reduces moisture. Then, the air is heated to the desired level, and the correct amount of humidity is added by use of a heated water trough or spray. Finally, the regulated air is vented through the ceiling into the laboratory at various points, where it falls toward the floor. Air turbulence at ceiling level, as well as irregular temperatures across the room surface, can be avoided by using lighting fixtures that

do not obstruct air flow. For this reason, flush-mounted lighting fixtures are recommended.

Another consideration is how much of the laboratory must be closely controlled. Does the critical area extend from the ceiling to the floor? Or is it from 2 feet to 5 feet above the floor? The answer to these questions also has an impact on the environmental control system's cost.

Attempts to cut costs by installing an inexpensive temperature control system will almost certainly prove to be false economy. Higher costs are sure to be incurred due to excessive downtime during out-of-tolerance periods and the inevitable replacement of the system. This cannot be overemphasized.

When selecting a temperature control system, consider what the future use of the laboratory will be. Will more people be added? (Bodies give off heat.) More equipment? Temperature control systems are designed for a certain maximum capacity. If future expansion is anticipated, a larger system should be planned at the outset.

Since temperature-controlled enclosures or oil baths are provided for most standard cells and other sensitive equipment, it can be argued that tight temperature control for the entire laboratory is not required. However, temperature-controlled enclosures operate better in temperature-controlled environments. Ambient temperature fluctuations can affect the temperature of the enclosures. It is important to consider all factors when deciding on the right temperature-control system. For example, thermal time lag in the instrument or system being measured, and in the temperature-control system, can lead to measurement problems, as can those generated between the fixed and varying environment. If an incoming instrument storage area is environmentally controlled, instruments brought into the laboratory will already be acclimated.

The temperature-control system (not including sensors, of course) should be located outside of the laboratory. The noise created by the system can be distracting to laboratory personnel. An outside location also makes the system easier to maintain.

Monitoring Temperature

Monitoring the temperature of the laboratory is important and is usually required. Aside from the inherent value of the information, monitoring is a common contractual or regulatory requirement. When used, temperature monitors should be installed at the correct height for monitoring of the test area. The mounts should be at the equipment or operator level, where they are both effective and easily accessed. Once the temperature control system is installed, its performance must be checked. Two types of tests are normally made, absolute temperature and temperature gradients.

The absolute temperature will be monitored for the duration of the laboratory's life, by connecting a monitor, chart recorder, or some type of digital system to several probes around the laboratory. This data is continually recorded.

Note: It is important that temperature records be maintained for review by laboratory quality auditors.

Temperature gradients are taken by a data logger with numerous probes suspended around the laboratory. Ideally, the measurements are taken with all laboratory equipment turned on and everyone working, as well as with equipment power off and personnel absent. This can be difficult, but it is the only sure way of determining how temperature is being regulated under worst-case conditions. Once satisfactory results are ensured, this system can be removed.

Humidity

Humidity control is very important to a laboratory's operation. Both low and high humidity must be avoided. Static electricity can damage equipment and invalidate measurements at humidities less than 20% rh. Humidities of over 70% rh can cause leakage and erroneous measurements.

As discussed earlier in this chapter, humidity is controlled by the air conditioning system. It is possible to have good humidity control. A generally accepted relative humidity range is

45 ±10% rh. This can vary, depending on the nature of the workload. Multimeters tolerate wider variations than standard resistors. Humidity is also very important if the workload includes high value resistors (1 GΩ and greater).

The resistance of some types of resistors increases during wet seasons. Moisture causes varnishes on the wire to expand; this compresses the resistor wire and causes an increase in resistance. Hermetic sealing eliminates the problem but not all instruments use these more expensive resistors.

Various instruments are available to monitor humidity. One particular type of hygrometer uses several strands of horse hair suspended between two points. When humidity changes, the hairs lengthen or shorten, and a pen attached to the hair records this change on a paper chart. Similar instruments use stretched sheep skin. Electronic instruments such as the hygroscope are now available to measure changes in humidity. These instruments do not depend on organic materials for sensing humidity. They therefore respond much faster, and they have greater sensitivity and stability. One design uses a mirrored surface that is cooled until a vapor forms on it. The presence of vapor is detected opto-electronically; the condensation temperature is combined with a measurement of ambient temperature to display the calculated relative humidity.

Shielding and Filtering RFI

Most laboratories use electronic measurement equipment that is susceptible to interference from radiated electromagnetic energy. As a result, shielding and filtering must be adequate to reduce the average field strength, within the immediate area of the instrumentation, to less than 100 µV/m. For conducted electromagnetic energy on power lines, the measured open-circuit voltage should be no greater than 100 mV.

This simplified statement of maximum tolerable radio frequency interference (rfi) does not take frequency into account. Nor does it address the issue of bandwidth in the measurement of broadband interference. The 100 μV/m limit assumes that the sensitivity of the equipment to wanted information (the signal of interest) must equal or exceed the sensitivity to unwanted signals (interference). It also assumes that the detrimental effects of broad-band interference are no different than those of continuous-wave interference.

A combination of cable, instrument, and room shielding may be required to minimize spurious signals. It is important to assess these details in the planning stage, prior to the construction of the laboratory. Therefore, it is good practice to have an rfi site survey done as part of the planning process. If excessive levels of interference are found, there will be time to design and incorporate the shielding required to reduce interference to tolerable levels.

The most demanding requirements are for measurements on sensitive receivers and similar equipment. This may call for a special enclosure capable of 100 dB of attenuation. Otherwise, adequate shielding can be attained with metal sheets of good conductivity. Single sheets of metallic foil will give 60 dB attenuation if properly installed. In either case, the adequacy of shielding can further depend on the use of well-shielded instruments and cables.

Shielding requirements do not end with cables, instruments, and walls. An effective degree of shielding also depends on the following factors:

- filtering of electrical circuits that lead into an enclosure (such as the laboratory itself)

- proper sealing around pipes and conduits at their entrance into the enclosure

- effective shielding of doors

- shielding of air intakes and exhaust ducts

- shielding of fluorescent fixtures

- PC-generated noise

In combination, these sources of electrical noise and leakage must present a lower level of interference than the residual background level of the shielded enclosure. Otherwise, overall shielding effectiveness will be lost.

There are few references available that set rfi standards in terms of the ambient background level in shielded enclosures (that is, screen rooms). Such a standard would state the permissible level in units of radiated field strength. Instead, the characteristics of shielded enclosures are expressed in terms of their signal attenuation from either inside or outside the enclosure. This factor is often called the "shielding effectiveness" and is expressed in decibels. A typical specification is 100 dB of attenuation from 140 Hz to 10 GHz, or even to 100 GHz. It is reasonable for shielding manufacturers to specify their products in this way. They have no control over field strength "on the other side of the wall," so to speak. Nor can they presume to know the field strength acceptable to the customer.

Military specifications sometimes state maximum radiation limits for an electronic device in terms of radiated field strength. None of these specifications discusses shielded enclosures. One available reference that pertains directly to shielded enclosures is a Russian interference specification, "Norms for Maximum Admissible Industrial Interference," by A. Zharow. In the section pertaining to shielded enclosures, the author states that the radio interference field level in the screen room, from sources outside, shall not exceed 2 μV. This specification covers a frequency range of 150 kHz to 400 MHz.

Low intensity radiated fields are often difficult to measure. Commercial field strength receivers do not accurately measure fields on the order of 1 μV. Most electromagnetic fields within a shielded enclosure are not of sufficient magnitude that a commercial field strength meter can measure them. The chief limiting factor is the internal noise of the field strength meter receiver itself.

As a general rule, special shielding will probably not be required. This is especially true if the laboratory is a secondary rather than a primary laboratory. Exceptions occur when a laboratory is located near a strong source of interference such as a radar or radio station transmitter, or a high power pulsed laser. Again, a site survey, along with a review of the potential changes in industrial use for the area, should enable the potential for future emi problems to be evaluated. Then any necessary shielding measures can be planned.

Industry Guidelines

Other documents exist that serve as industry-wide guidelines for laboratory construction and practices. Two of the most important are the ISA RP52.1, published by the Instrument Society of America, and the NCSL RP-7, published by the National Conference of Standards Laboratories.

ISA RP52.1

Recommended Practice, Recommended Environments for Standards Laboratories, ISA RP52.1, makes specific recommendations for Type I and II standards laboratories. Table 25-1 shows the recommendations.

This document should be required reading for anyone planning to construct a metrology laboratory, not so much for the specifications, but for the detailed explanation of the considerations that led to the specifications. Some of the specifications based on technology as it existed in the early 1970s may be obsolete, but the document is well worth reading for the supporting information.

NCSL RP-7

Recommended Practice—Laboratory Design, *NCSL Information Manual RP-7*, should be read by anyone considering the construction of a laboratory. In addition to the material in the document itself, each chapter contains a broad range of design references that are useful for those who wish to go further into the chapter's subject. The document contains chapters on each of the subjects covered in this chapter, plus additional chapters on subjects relating mainly to design of laboratories for mechanical measurements.

Table 25-1. The ISA RP52.1 Laboratory Practice Guidelines

Acoustical Noise	Type I and II: The maximum level for noise is 45 decibels as measured on a sound level meter using the A or B weighting network.
Dust Particle Count	Type I and II: Less than 7×10^6 particles larger than 1 micrometer per cubic meter. Less than 4×10^7 particles larger than 0.5 micrometers per cubic meter. No particles larger than 50 micrometers.
Electrical and Magnetic Shielding	Type I and II: 100 microvolt/meter maximum radiation field strength. DC ground bus to ground, less than 2Ω. AC ground to ground, less than 5Ω.
Laboratory Air Pressure	Type I and II: Maintain positive pressure of 10 pascals (newtons per square meter), 0.1 millibar, (0.05 inch of water) in the laboratory.
Lighting	Type I and II: 1076 lux (lumens per square meter, approximately 100 foot-candles) at bench level or reading surface.
Relative Humidity	Type I: 35–55% rh around a regulated temperature of 23°C. Type II: 20–55% rh around a regulated temperature of 23°C.
Temperature	Type I: 23 ±1°C. Type II: 23 ±1.5°C.
Vibration	No specific requirements.
Voltage Regulation	Type I and II: Maximum change from average voltage less than 10%, with consideration of holding transients to a minimum. Total rms value of all harmonics should not exceed 5% of the rms value of the fundamental from no load to full load of regulator.

FLUKE.

Chapter 26:
Workload Management

The ability of the laboratory to produce properly documented, traceable calibrations is paramount. But the laboratory also has to provide its services in a timely, convenient, and economical manner.

A calibration laboratory manager has broad and varied responsibilities. He must be a technical specialist, familiar with the principles of metrology. He must be an advocate of the quality that results from the control of measurement accuracy. He must also be an organizer, leader, and business-oriented manager. He is responsible for all aspects of the operation of the laboratory as a service organization.

Getting Down to Basics

The ability to provide timely service depends on many factors, technical, economic and human. It requires the proper set of resources, carefully selected and intelligently managed. In this regard, the laboratory has much in common with a manufacturing organization. Given a set of resources, the workload must be met in a way that is consistent with established objectives. By setting objectives, the manager is able to plan, evaluate, and measure the performance of laboratory operations. While the details vary with the mission and situation of the individual laboratory, the following set of objectives can be considered to be generally applicable to workload management:

- Instruments must be recalled and recalibrated per the established recall schedule.

- The turnaround time for routine calibration must consistently meet established targets. These targets are set and evaluated on the basis of customer need. The customer will view turnaround time as the total time the equipment is away and unavailable for use.

- Other services, such as unscheduled calibration or repair, must have appropriate targets that are consistently met.

- Customers must be routinely informed of unusual delays, such as delay for parts that must be specially ordered. In addition, stocking and ordering procedures must be designed for efficient and economic operation.

- The laboratory must have a strong service orientation, with customer satisfaction an important measure of the quality of operation. Customer convenience is valued. The internal operations aspects of the laboratory, such as the need to subcontract or send items out for calibration, are transparent to the customer. The laboratory takes responsibility for everything that it processes.

An important measure for the individual laboratory is the specific target for turnaround time. Other performance measures take into account such factors as: labor costs; occupancy and other overhead costs set by the parent organization; percent of instruments in tolerance on recall; average days late, etc.

Analyzing the Workload and Laboratory Capacity

In order to understand and deal with the workload, the following information is required:

- Number of items of each type in the inventory. In most cases, this will be by manufacturer-model number combination. In some cases, more generic categories can be used, such as 3½-digit DMM or low-frequency analog oscilloscope, etc.

- Average number of calibrations per year for each category.

- Average calibration time for each category. Consideration must be given to both labor hours and machine hours, as appropriate.

- Similar information regarding unscheduled calibration and/or repair. Since this portion of the workload is by definition not subject to exact prediction, estimates must be made on the basis of the best available information. Accurate historical records are of great value here.

Once the preceding information is available, it would seem a straightforward matter to calculate the number of labor and machine hours necessary to support the workload, as follows:

1. Multiply units by hours by recalls per year for each item (category) for the recall program.

2. Multiply unit submissions by hours for unscheduled service (similar to the preceding step).

3. Add up the numbers for all items (categories) to find the total hours required per year, including both scheduled recall and service on demand.

In fact, there are a number of complications and additional factors that need to be addressed. Most of these involve tradeoffs between capacity, cost, incoming rate of work, and turnaround time. Consider, in particular, the fact that the preceding calculation represents only the total workload for the year, and does not predict the daily, weekly, or monthly rate that will be experienced throughout the year. It is important to consider peak workload as well as the average workload for the year.

Workload, Capacity, and Turnaround Time

In general, fluctuations in the workload will cause fluctuations in turnaround time. Fluctuations in workload are one of the main reasons that turnaround time exceeds the individual processing time for the unit (pipeline time). The laboratory builds up a backlog and increases turnaround time when there is a surge in the incoming rate. The laboratory reduces turnaround time when the incoming rate falls below average. Suppose that a laboratory were to start up operations with no backlog, maintain a constant capacity, and receive work at a constant rate. Then turnaround time should basically equal pipeline time. (Of course, from the customer's viewpoint, pipeline time includes transportation time and all other aspects of pickup and delivery.)

Fluctuations in capacity will affect turnaround time, as will the incoming rate. In the short term, it is the immediate relationship between the two that counts. Capacity seldom goes up without effort, planning, or specific actions

aimed at the increase. Using overtime or extra shifts, hiring additional technicians (temporary or permanent), renting or purchasing equipment, and other factors can increase capacity. Increases in productivity can have the same effect. This could involve improved employee motivation, automation, better scheduling techniques, and so on.

Fluctuations in workload and capacity imply that some amount of turnaround time in excess of pipeline time is unavoidable. To some extent, this can be traded off against cost of operation. Building capacity sufficient for peak levels of demand may ensure minimum turnaround time, but the cost can be excessive. Use of overtime is one way to temporarily meet peak workloads.

Schedule anticipation is a way to prevent or minimize the occurrence of a peak. Items can be recalled ahead of schedule when backlog is low. Many users want to turn in equipment prior to their vacation or a lengthy holiday break. This will cause a peak in workload and increased turnaround time if not anticipated and dealt with. Personnel-related workload capacity is, in part, a function of motivation and morale. It is widely recognized that employee involvement programs, TQC programs or similar activities, can be of great help. A successful program provides positive benefits for the workers and their manager.

There is always the potential for unplanned and unexpected loss of capacity, such as illness, strikes, fires, or other emergencies; or equipment breakdown. These and similar factors can lead to a reduction in capacity, temporary or permanent. For planning purposes, known or expected loss of capacity should be anticipated. This includes items such as scheduled holiday and vacation time, training, equipment maintenance, and so on.

Realistic Assessment of Basic Capacity and Cost Factors

Work Time per Employee

The preceding material focused heavily on fluctuations in workload and capacity. The issue of base workload has already been addressed. Calculation of base capacity is likewise simple for a first-order assessment, but more complicated if an exact determination is to be made.

For example, how many hours does an employee work per year? In a non-leap year, there are 261 work days, if Saturdays and Sundays are excluded. Additional allowance must be made for holidays, vacation, and sick time. Training and group meeting time, scheduled breaks, and the like must be accounted for. Searches for equipment, documents, and materials take time.

Start with 2,080 gross hours per employee, and deduct all known or predictable losses and exclusions. Most managers find that the nominal 2,080 base hours must be multiplied by a factor of 0.8 to 0.9 to get a realistic prediction of time actually on the premises. A similar factor must be used to account for time devoted to activities other than actual calibration and repair work. When all is said and done, 1,600 hours of truly productive time is a likely number, exclusive of overtime.

Labor Rates and Payroll Expense

The cost of an hour of labor is another matter. Both skill level and experience affect base pay, as does a union contract. National and regional labor market situations vary. A high salary at one time and place can be low at another time and place. Promotions, bonuses, merit pay, and other policy matters come into play. The new manager can also be somewhat surprised at the amount of payroll expense that exists, above and beyond base pay. Items include the employee benefit package (health insurance, etc.) as well as employer's contribution to Social Security, and taxes or premiums to cover worker's compensation (accident claims) and unemployment insurance. The amount of expense above base pay can easily be 20 percent or more of base pay.

Laboratory Overhead

The laboratory manager's awareness of, and responsibility for, the expenses associated with operation vary greatly. Entrepreneurs owning their own business are obviously 100 percent involved and responsible. In some government environments, such as a military field installation, the manager may have little knowledge or control over costs. In a typical industrial environment, with a captive lab operation, the manager's role is more like that of the entrepreneur and less like that of the military officer.

Most managers will benefit from a thorough knowledge of costs, cost control, and accounting concepts. They are likely to be accountable for operating within the limits of an expense budget. The manager should be given a role in determining the budget, although upper management is likely to exert limits on the total expenditure, and/or the service charge rates. In some cases, laboratory customers will be given the option of evaluating and using alternative (external) services.

In addition to payroll and related expenses, operational costs include the following:

- costs of materials and supplies

- costs of education, travel, subscriptions, and memberships

- equipment acquisition and ownership expenses, including purchase price for expensed equipment; depreciation expense for capitalized equipment; and calibration, repair, and maintenance

- space or occupancy charges, including leasehold cost or depreciation; repair and maintenance; security, groundskeeping, etc.; insurance and taxes; janitorial, photocopying, and other miscellaneous expenses

- telecommunications, mail, freight, etc.

- indirect salary expense, such as the manager's own salary

The preceding list is not exhaustive. The point is that without prior ownership or management experience, the laboratory supervisor may not be aware of the amount of overhead or burden associated with operations. A captive-laboratory manager may have little if any control over the rates associated with overhead expense. He should also bear in mind the fact that his operation may be overhead for his customers.

Equipment, Facilities, and Procedures

In order for technicians to undertake a calibration or repair as scheduled, they must be free to take on the task. In addition, the necessary equipment and materials must be available, including at least the following:

- a properly approved calibration procedure

- the standards and test equipment called out by the procedure

- instrument controller or test system where called for

- any necessary parts, materials and supplies

- suitable environment (temperature, relative humidity, etc.)

The laboratory must be properly equipped in terms of the types of standards and test equipment available (accuracy, ranges, etc.), and also in terms of the number of such items on hand and their workload capacity. Capacity applies primarily to automatic systems, which have a throughput capacity not necessarily set by operator time or capacity.

Start-up vs. Ongoing Operation

The initial planning and setup of the laboratory must be undertaken with all of the preceding considerations in mind. In essence, the laboratory, as initially designed and installed, comprises a machine that has the capacity to perform a certain number of service operations of a certain nature. Here, nature takes into account factors such as the parameters involved, accuracy, traceability, and environmental control.

Initial capacity of the laboratory should exceed the initial workload. Otherwise, the first growth in workload will create an increased backlog. It is generally less costly to install an increment of capacity than it is to add it later. This is especially true for factors affecting overall size (floor space) and items such as the heating, ventilating, and air conditioning (HVAC) system. It is not necessarily the case for standards and test equipment. However, decisions regarding manual versus automated systems should be made as early as possible.

It is essential that the laboratory have the necessary capacity at the necessary quality level. In most cases, it is also important that the dollar cost of providing capacity and quality represent an efficient and prudent expenditure. However, this adds a dimension to the complexity of laboratory design, installation, and operation. Efficiency results from a multitude of factors, including: equipment, procedures, layout, facilities, personnel selection, and training. An inefficient start-up is likely to be followed by inefficient operation.

Personnel and Staffing Level

The capacity of a laboratory is tied to its staffing level. Classic economic theory suggests that the cost of labor is a variable cost. This implies that workers are readily added to or eliminated from the payroll. This has been and still is true for some operations.

It is difficult if not impossible to change the staffing level to accommodate short-term fluctuations in the workload. Many laboratories are associated with large organizations that attract employees on the basis of long-term employment and relative job security. The supply of qualified and experienced metrology personnel is quite limited. A large percentage come to the laboratory with technical training in mechanical, dimensional, or electrical technology, but without specialized training in metrology. Part-time study and on-the-job training are commonly needed for new laboratory personnel.

It is difficult to rapidly increase the staffing level of a laboratory if a high level of competency is to be maintained. Managers are reluctant to change their staffing level to meet short-term, or even medium-term, fluctuations in workload. It is simply too difficult and too slow a process to rebuild capacity.

Information Systems

Ongoing efficiency and problem solving are greatly aided by having the right information readily available. The laboratory's database or management information system (MIS) must meet this need. It should provide the mechanism for implementing the recall system. In addition, inventory, calibration, repair, and location records are required to support traceability and audit requirements. The inclusion of information related to cost, productivity, etc., eases the management task, and ensures that information for problem solving is readily available. These capabilities were once limited to mainframe systems programmed and controlled by central support organizations. Most laboratories now can meet their needs with a suitable PC (or PC network), running software such as Fluke MET/CAL calibration software and Fluke MET/TRACK property management software. See Figure 26-1.

Test Equipment Management System

While requirements vary from laboratory to laboratory, all high quality asset management systems have certain common elements. A

Figure 26-1. MET/TRACK Asset Management System

good asset management system has the following characteristics:

Meets Contractual Requirements
Many metrology operations exist to ensure compliance with government regulations such as MIL-STD-45662A or international standards such as ISO 9000. There may be market pressures or well-established industrial standards that affect the required management system. In

the case of contracts and regulations, there are specific requirements that must be satisfied, for example, the need to generate reports.

These requirements must be met as the terms of a contract and the cost of doing business. Typical requirements can include forward and reverse traceability, out-of-tolerance reporting, procedure identification, environmental conditions, and so on.

Is Easy to Use

The system should be logical and user friendly. The learning process should be fast and easy. The system should have a limited number of on-screen menus, and use familiar terminology. If the user has a question, simple on-screen help should be available.

Enforces Required Entries

Most databases have certain data fields that must contain data in every record. The system can require that this vital information be entered in the same place, in the same way, every time. For example, if the laboratory is concerned with MIL-STD-45662A or ISO 9000 compliance, the system may require the operator to enter the following information:

- asset or control number
- equipment description, manufacturer, and model number
- information on calibration standards
- ambient environment during calibration
- calibration date
- calibration method used
- calibration technician identification
- procedure used
- out-of-tolerance conditions
- repair data
- program or location where equipment is used and user name

Validates Information for Data Integrity

Validation is a feature that allows only entries which exist in an approved list. This feature ensures uniformity of data, which is necessary for meaningful sorting and reporting.

Examples of validation include:

- Date validation. This feature prevents nonsense dates such as December 32 from being entered as well as calibration dates that are

too old or are in the future. It also prevents a user from entering invalid dates, such as a calibration due date that precedes the last recorded calibration date.

- Traceability validation. When an operator enters traceability information (the standards used), the system verifies that the calibration due dates of the standards have not passed, and that the standards have the proper traceability level. When a standard fails the due date check, the system warns the operator and prevents the standard from being entered.

- Text entry validation. The system should be able to define a set of valid entries for a specific field to maintain consistent usage. For example, the abbreviation "DMM" is always entered the same way, not in other ways such as "D.M.M." or "DVM." The benefit of entering data consistently is most apparent when performing a search of the database. When searching for instruments with the valid description "DMM," all the intended instruments in the system will be found by the search. Figure 26-2 is an example of a Fluke MET/TRACK text entry validation screen.

Computes Due Dates

When supplied with the calibration date, the system then computes the due date based on the recall interval process. Use of an internal calendar also eliminates certain specific dates as due dates. Days to skip might include Saturdays, Sundays, company holidays, or a vacation shutdown period. On those dates, the due date would be rolled back to the last working day prior to the nominal due date.

Accommodates Special Instructions

Special handling or calibration instructions for the technicians can be helpful in meeting special requirements of the organization. Examples include calibration, calibration by vendor, or employee-owned equipment.

Enables Smart Purchase Decisions

Repair and calibration experience for particular models of equipment can be summarized to determine which models provide the lowest cost of ownership.

Figure 26-2. Text Entry Validation Screen

Quick and Easy Searches

In order to view or extract data quickly, search capability is important. The system should be able to make single- or multi-level searches. Multi-level searches allow, for example, the display of all assets made by a particular manufacturer, used at a certain location, on a given program or project. Searches for specific words or segments of fields are handy. You should be able to display the information to the screen or to a printer.

Global Changes

Global change is the ability to manipulate all assets having specified attributes. For example, it might automate the transfer of all assets from test station number S105, located in engineering department number 1010, to the ABC12345 program, in production department number 1500.

Produces an Abundance of Reports

The system supplies meaningful reports to enhance department efficiency. The repertoire of reports includes those devoted to traceability, both to and from national standards. Other commonly required reports include instrument recall notices, out-of-tolerance notifications, overdue equipment reports, laboratory and technician efficiency reports, and equipment status reports.

The system might also print forms for use in the laboratory. In addition, the system should provide a report-writing utility program that allows the manager to generate special reports designed to meet unique requirements.

Network Capable

A Local Area Network (LAN) can give many users simultaneous access to the same database. Having the system on a network can increase productivity, and moves larger organizations to the automated laboratory. The network allows multiple users on the system to share expensive peripherals, such as printers and plotters, in addition to the hard disk containing the database records.

Security

The system should have several levels of access that determine the openness of the system for each user. The ability to view or print sensitive information can then be restricted to certain levels of access. Sensitive information includes data such as labor rates for individual technicians. The ability to change historical records and to make global changes are other examples of restricted access capability. The metrology manager controls who can use the system, and the access level for each user.

Flexibility

Flexibility allows the system to grow and change with the needs of the laboratory. Flexibility covers such things as the ability to change information, and to either suppress or to require information. The system allows the user to customize reports as well as screens, to comply with local needs and customs.

Interfaces with Other Company Systems

Compatibility with other software and hardware systems may be important. The user is able to exchange data with other software or systems, such as spreadsheets, graphics software systems, or even mainframe computers. An example of this is the ability to export calibration results via a network from the asset management system to a mainframe. Likewise, the asset management software should be able to import and export data from a mainframe database or calibration software package.

The foregoing are characteristics of software packages commercially available, such as Fluke MET/TRACK.

Chapter 27:

Selecting New Test Equipment

This chapter considers purchasing test equipment from a manager's point of view. Purchasing test equipment is one of the most important decisions a calibration laboratory manager can make, and it can affect the performance of the laboratory for years to come.

The best long-term purchase is possible only when all of the significant cost/benefit factors are accounted for and carefully considered. The laboratory manager must determine what new capabilities the proposed equipment will provide and what the specifications really mean. Will the new acquisition perform as expected? What are the true costs of acquisition and ownership? What are the risks of purchasing the wrong instrument for the task?

This chapter will help the laboratory manager gather the information to make an informed purchasing decision for equipment to increase the laboratory's capabilities and efficiency.

Buying Considerations

When selecting calibrators and standards, one of the most important considerations will be determining how accurate the new equipment must be. Will the new instrument be used to calibrate meters and other equipment to their manufacturer's specifications or only to the accuracy appropriate for actual use? If calibrating to use, a limited calibration, what accuracy does the application demand? Once the requirements for accuracy, precision, and stability are defined, one must know to what level of uncertainty the calibrations must be performed, and then determine which calibrators and standards are appropriate.

Also, one should base the selection of calibrators on the user's available time, as well as the ability to employ professional metrology techniques in the detection, evaluation, and analysis of the systematic and random errors encountered in the calibration process. A broad spectrum of calibrators and standards exists and they enable the laboratory manager to optimize this trade-off to the best advantage.

When choosing calibration laboratory equipment, one important rule to follow is to select the equipment to adequately satisfy the need.

Another consideration is whether the laboratory can maintain the environment required by the calibrators and standards being considered. Achieving the specified accuracy, precision, and stability is possible only if the environmental characteristics of temperature, relative humidity, and main supply voltage regulation are followed.

Manufacturers clearly define the environmental specifications for their calibrators and standards so that laboratory managers can evaluate the performance of the devices in their environment.

Managers will also want to consider metrology expertise. The lowest levels of calibration uncertainty are achieved in a primary-level laboratory using highly accurate, stable, precision calibrators and standards. The metrology techniques required under these circumstances may be considerably more refined and sophisticated, and demand either extreme expertise or an automated approach to compensate for the lack of that expertise. Most manufacturers recognize the importance of both manual and automated approaches to calibration and offer appropriate solutions to match the need.

The original purchase price is not the most significant cost associated with owning a high accuracy instrument. All too often instrumentation purchases are justified principally on the basis of specifications and initial purchase price. It is true that specifications are critical to evaluating whether a product can perform a required task. However, many factors which are also critical to the overall cost of ownership over the life of the instrument are overlooked when comparisons of similar equipment are based on specifications and purchase price alone.

A laboratory manager must thoughtfully consider many factors any time he is presented with the opportunity of making an equipment purchase or recommendation.

Capabilities

A primary factor, of course, is payback. Will the proposed acquisition sufficiently improve the laboratory's capabilities to justify the cost? Will it handle the workload? Does it provide capabilities that the laboratory currently doesn't possess, or is the new equipment expected to increase efficiency? If the new instrument is only appropriate for handling a few pieces of equipment, perhaps using an outside vendor to perform the necessary calibrations would be a wiser decision. However, there are associated costs both in time and money for using outside laboratories.

The laboratory manager must be able to establish and prioritize the essential criteria to measure the payback of a proposed purchase. Sometimes acquiring a new instrument will significantly improve the laboratory's capabilities. At other times, the improvements will be more subtle but nonetheless meaningful, such as the perception by a laboratory's customers of its expertise and capabilities. Although difficult to quantify, these indirect benefits can be substantial and should be considered.

A key element of calibrator value is ease of use. Usually there are alternative calibrators from several manufacturers which can perform a given task. But some calibrators make the required tasks much easier. For example, the Fluke 5700A multifunction calibrator (MFC) facilitates the task of calibrating DMMs by providing all of the needed functions in one instrument. It is no longer necessary to use several independent calibrators from different parts of the laboratory to complete one DMM calibration. The 5700A can also be taken out of the laboratory environment to calibrate a DMM where it is used. This MFC can do simple range checks with the push of a button, or directly display UUT error with a simple adjustment of the output dial.

The laboratory manager should not only evaluate the drive capabilities of a potential calibrator but should also consider its ease of use characteristics. If the instrument takes a long time to learn to use properly, or intimidates the user, the benefits from the increased capabilities can be lost.

Reliability

When evaluating new equipment, one should make reliability an important consideration. There are reliability factors dealing with confidence in the instrument's performance and in anticipated downtime.

The end user must have confidence that an instrument is working correctly. If a technician or manager believes that a calibrator is not performing to specification, then that calibrator will be thought of as unreliable. The frustration of owning an instrument that is, or appears to be, producing suspect data can be significant. Initially, a user gains confidence by repeatedly verifying an instrument's performance until all doubts have been satisfied. Confidence increases if the instrument incorporates adequate internal self-checks to ensure proper operation. Instrument confidence is acquired over time based on performance, and users will begin to rely on a particular model or manufacturer's reputation.

What about downtime? Periodic performance verification and adjustment takes equipment out of service, and has an associated cost. But there are other factors that contribute to downtime aside from the planned services. It is still true that all electronic equipment will fail eventually. It is the measurement of that "eventually" that has reliability implications, and there are many factors that contribute to an instrument's useful life.

The basic design must be sufficiently robust to tolerate abuse from careless operators. Inadvertently exposing an instrument's output terminals to excessive loads or voltages is a common occurrence. The instrument should have as much protection designed into it as the performance specifications will allow. The last thing a laboratory manager wants to see is a recent investment in a high-performance instrument put out of action by misuse.

Quality manufacturing enhances instrument reliability. At Fluke, statistical quality control is the norm, ensuring that quality is maintained from component test through final assembly and test. In addition, each calibrator built at Fluke is subjected to more than 2g of random vibration to prevent latent imperfections from causing future failures.

When selecting a calibrator, consider the purpose and environment it was intended to serve and has been designed for. For instance, can it withstand the daily rigors of being moved around the laboratory? What about on-site calibration? Are the transportation means protective enough to guard the instrument from unusually rough handling or harsh environments?

Management must also consider how to handle downtime if the new instrument is used in a critical application. Is there other equipment in the laboratory that could be used if the primary instrument becomes unavailable? Should you consider the purchase of a back-up instrument? Does the manufacturer provide fast support for problems that may arise?

A manufacturer's limited support capabilities can make an instrument very expensive to a lab. Acquiring parts can be difficult, particularly if the manufacturer's documentation is insufficiently detailed. It is always safest to select a vendor with complete product support capability. Most major manufacturers are committed to customer support. Fluke has service centers strategically located around the world to repair and calibrate equipment. A domestic module-exchange program is available for most instruments to supply needed replacement modules using priority shipment methods. Fluke also provides maintenance training on most of its popular models.

Favorable instrument reliability can only be obtained with a combination of excellent design, quality manufacturing, fast efficient support, and proper application by the end user and a record of satisfactory performance over time.

Ownership Costs

The cost of maintaining an instrument in calibration needs to be considered because it is an ongoing expense. How often does it need to be calibrated and what type of equipment is required? Is this support equipment available in the laboratory, or should it also be purchased? If not, will the new instrument have to be calibrated outside the laboratory? This leads to the question of what the annual calibration costs will be. If the instrument has to be sent outside the laboratory for calibration, the equipment it supports will have to wait until it returns. A solution to this problem can be to purchase or lease a back-up calibrator. These factors can

add a real expense burden to the laboratory if the time involved in calibration is too long.

Life-Cycle Costs

Many of the ideas discussed thus far in this chapter make statements about the cost, intangible or tangible, of the decision aspects of buying instrumentation. Life-Cycle Cost (LCC) analysis is an approach towards quantifying these considerations that helps laboratory managers put that element in perspective. The theory of Life-Cycle Cost Analysis allows a buyer to make acquisitions that are more economical in the long run. This involves factors that go beyond specifications and purchase price. The LCC approach to instrument selection analyzes the costs associated with ownership over the instrument's projected life span in its application. Life-Cycle Costing computes the total cost of ownership: purchase of the instrument, installing it, maintaining it, special training, maintenance and calibration costs, operating costs, and other factors.

An LCC analysis may result in a decision to purchase the instrument with a higher acquisition cost, but lower lifetime cost. Purchase decisions should be made with the use of LCC concepts in order to correctly evaluate the various cost trade-offs incurred during the life of the instrument.

The cost of an instrument does not end with the purchase price. LCC can be identified and quantified subsequent to purchase. As LCC becomes the standard for instrument purchase justifications, manufacturers will develop new instruments with LCC considerations intrinsic to the design.

To understand the impact of LCC on a particular situation, one should estimate the lifetime costs of the various components making up the total cost of ownership. The leverage of a particular component can vary considerably with the specific application or situation. For example, an instrument or system that meets its performance specification with once-a-year calibration has a substantially lower calibration cost than an instrument that requires calibration every 90 days to meet similar specifications. Typically, an instrument used in a production test system must have the lowest possible downtime.

The first step in determining LCC is to identify the specific elements the buyer must work with. These elements are broken into five cost groups: Acquisition, Training, Operation, Calibration, and Maintenance.

Acquisition Cost (ACQ)

The initial costs associated with instrument purchase are defined as acquisition costs. While the actual purchase price is always considered, there are several other costs associated with acquisition that should not be overlooked. These include: procurement; evaluation; price; setup and installation; freight; and delivery delays. The following equation summarizes the relationship of these elements:

ACQ=PUR+EVAL+PRICE+START+FRE+DEL

Procurement (PUR)
The purchase of instruments includes some overhead costs. Writing the purchase specifications to ensure that the item meets the performance requirements (Request For Quote or RFQ) can be a significant task. The more complex the needs, the more involved the task of writing the RFQ. Direct justification and procurement cost must also be included.

Evaluation (EVAL)
Often a purchase is made using the published performance specifications. At other times a demonstration is acceptable. Specialized systems might require visits to the manufacturer's plant, first article demonstrations, or both. In any event, there are costs associated with evaluating how well the various offerings being considered meet the application needs.

Price (PRICE)
The purchase price is the most obvious factor considered. One can easily identify the money expended, with a purchase order for the instrumentation.

Setup and Installation (START)
These are costs required to bring the instrumentation into the company's system. At the simplest level, an identification label may be the only requirement. On the other hand, software drivers, special facilities (power, space, etc.), integration into the corporate computer system, or environmental alterations may be required. Usually these costs are incurred only once, at the start of operations.

Freight (FRE)
The shipping cost is easy to identify. In most instances, it will not vary greatly from one instrument or supplier to another and is probably not significant.

Delivery Time (DEL)
The delay from the time the purchase order is issued until the purchaser receives the instruments can have cost factors ranging from minor (nuisance factors) to major (program delays).

Training Cost (TRN)

Training is recognized as a necessary part of an instrumentation system's procurement. On-the-job training may seem cheap, or even free, until one considers the cost of problems that can be caused by a lack of proper training. The complexity of the instrumentation has a direct bearing on training requirements. Training cost is even more important when new employees are involved.

The quality and depth of the available training is a relevant consideration. The cost to develop training, when not available from the manufacturer, can be a cost contributing to the LCC. Training costs include: operator training, calibration training, maintenance training, and instructor training. The following equation shows the relationship of these elements:

TRN=OPRTNG+CALTNG+MAINTNG+INSTNG

Operator Training (OPRTNG)
Instrument operator training encompasses everything from front panel operation to software programming, procedures generation, documentation of results, report generation, and applications.

Calibration Training (CALTNG)

The need for calibration training can be assessed from the answers to several questions. Are the calibration procedures required similar to those for existing instruments, or are special procedures necessary? Does training cover special calibration equipment or procedures? Is calibration training available from the manufacturer? As will be shown later, calibration costs affect other elements of the LCC.

Maintenance Training (MAINTNG)

Most instrumentation requires periodic maintenance and repair. If the buyer performs these services, training becomes important. If the equipment is to be sent to an outside firm, the cost of the maintenance service must be considered and is discussed later in this section.

Instructor Training (INSTNG)

In some situations, there is a need to consider the availability of instructor training. This factor applies when the buyer is required to train people from other organizations or locations.

Operation Cost (OPR)

The operational cost may be the most complex component of LCC. Each type of instrumentation has a somewhat different set of elements that comprise cost of operation. This discussion touches only on those elements of operational cost that are most pervasive: float cost, complexity of operation, error forgiveness, automation, documentation cost, specifications, and expandability.

Using these elements, the cost of operation can be expressed as:

$$OPR = FLOAT + COMP + ERR + AUTO + DOC + SPEC + EXPD$$

Float Cost (FLOAT)

When instrumentation is not available for use, as when primary units are in transit for calibration or repair or are otherwise unavailable, a replacement unit is required to maintain operation. These additional units are considered float units. The float cost is directly proportional to the time spent in calibration or repair. The reduction of float cost is one of the major drivers for *in-situ* calibration.

Complexity of Operation (COMP)

The more complex the manually-operated equipment is, the higher the level of operator skill required to use it. Also, more training is likely required for more complex equipment.

Error Forgiveness (ERR)

Sensitivity of an instrument to operator error can have an impact on operational costs. An instrument that is robust and is forgiving of minor errors will cost less. An example of a forgiving instrument is a DMM that will withstand application of high voltage when it is set to measure current.

Automation (AUTO)

Instruments that automatically reduce data and generate reports may reduce the cost of operation significantly. Automation of any previously or normally manual operation will contribute to this critical LCC element.

Documentation Cost (DOC)

Developing procedures that guide the user through its use or calibration is an element of cost. The procedures should meet the documentation standards of the organization, with the goal of reducing or eliminating unnecessary paperwork. The output data must be easily put into a report format that can be readily incorporated into the normal data flow of the group.

The quality of the manufacturer's documentation is an important consideration when estimating the effort required to prepare operating procedures.

Specifications (SPEC)

The extent to which an instrument meets the need or provides the solutions for which it was purchased has a profound effect on operating costs. How well does it do the job? Does it have the right features? The cost of unfulfilled expectations can be many times the investment cost. This element of LCC can be considered a risk factor. It can reduce specification cost (risk) by over-specifying performance. There is a tendency, however, to overlook the fact that this practice increases calibration cost and, in some instances, maintenance costs.

Expandability (EXPD)

If the instrumentation allows for expansion, the future cost of purchasing additional instrumentation may be reduced. The buyer's ability to predict future needs can help to identify those areas where expandability is an asset.

Calibration Cost (CAL)

The life-time calibration costs for an instrument will be significant. These costs can vary as a function of the philosophy and strategy of calibration management, as well as the actual calibration process. Some companies have their own in-house calibration laboratory, while others contract with outside calibration services.

Factors affecting annual calibration cost include: frequency of calibration, calibration time per unit, transportation costs, portability, and the required standards. These factors are shown in the following equation:

$$CAL = CALFRQ * (CALTM + TRANS + PORT + CALSTD)$$

Calibration Frequency (CALFRQ)

The number of times per year that an instrument must be calibrated has a direct impact on calibration cost.

Time to Calibrate (CALTM)

How long does it take to calibrate an instrument? This depends on the instrument's design as well as the laboratory's calibration equipment and procedures. The use of software and closed-loop calibration techniques can reduce calibration time. A large number of internal adjustments, or the calculation and application of constants required for calibration, also increase cost. Can verification be made without adjustment? On-site calibration can save costs associated with downtime and transportation and also reduce float costs. Calibration costs are calculated as the product of calibration time and hourly rate. Hourly rate in turn depends on wages and burden, or overhead, costs.

Transportation Cost (TRANS)

The cost of transportation to and from the calibration laboratory must be included. This is especially important if the laboratory is not local.

Portability (PORT)

The ease with which the equipment can be removed for calibration can have an influence on cost. Is it a bench-top instrument or will it be mounted in a rack? Can one person easily lift it, or does it require more than one person or a cart?

Cal Standards Required (CALSTD)

Are the standards required to calibrate the instrument available in the inventory? It is painful to have to pay for the unexpected need for additional standards. If new standards are required, how available and adequate will they be?

Maintenance Cost (MAINT)

Almost all electronic instrumentation has maintenance costs associated with repair of failures, preventive maintenance, provisioning, and warranty, as shown in the following equation:

$$MAINT = FAIL + RTNMAIN + PROV + WARR$$

Failure Cost (FAIL)

Of the many factors that affect the cost of a failure, the most critical is the number of times it fails. The Mean Time Between Failure (MTBF) is an indication of the expected failure rate. The number of operating hours in a year, divided by the MTBF, gives the expected number of failures during a year. Obviously, the more an instrument fails, the higher the LCC. One high cost of failure is associated with loss of availability, discussed in the preceding discussion of Float Cost.

When a failure occurs, ease and speed of repair are important to minimize costs. Features such as built-in diagnostics, module exchange, readily available spares, and "covers-on repair" influence the Mean Time To Repair (MTTR). The longer it takes to repair a failed instrument, the higher the cost. Other failure costs are associated with special test equipment required, transportation costs to and from the repair facility and overall repair management costs. In turn, these are directly related to the use of in-house versus outside contract services.

Routine Maintenance (RTNMAIN)

The amount of routine maintenance required for today's electronic instrumentation is relatively small. Service contracts are worth investigating when budgeting for routine maintenance.

Provisioning (PROV)

The logistics of spare parts, modules, and float instruments can vary significantly depending on the philosophy used for supporting instrumentation.

Warranty Period (WARR)

Everyone would like to have equipment that never fails. However, when a failure does occur during the warranty period, the actual cost of repair is covered by the manufacturer. But the costs associated with loss of use of the instrument, and with transportation, are normally borne by the user. Hence, those costs are still a part of LCC.

Considerations of Maintenance Costs

The laboratory manager or other purchaser must take into account the source of the product as well as the product itself. This includes the manufacturer's reputation, service capability, and dedication to providing help when needed. All of these can affect the total costs of an instrument. Consider putting the instrument on a manufacturer's service contract, or purchase an extended warranty, so as to minimize downtime and be assured of fixed maintenance costs for a given period of time.

Leverage of Components

There is no one formula that will give the Life-Cycle Cost for every situation because each company's philosophy, resources, and cost basis are unique. However, some elements of LCC are common, one-time costs, while others are repetitive. The important point is to recognize and manage the repetitive cost factors that are multiplied through leverage in your particular situation.

Chapter 28:

Laboratory Quality and ISO 9000

The philosophy that drives modern company management demands a quality-centered operation. This means that metrology laboratories will be more and more involved in the total quality effort of the company.

Because of the link between quality and ISO 9000, laboratories will become more aware of overall company requirements with respect to quality management programs.

This chapter provides an overall view of laboratory quality and the ISO 9000 standard. In "ISO 9000," the first section of this chapter, ISO 9000 is examined as it relates to what metrology laboratories must do to comply with its specifications. The second part of the chapter, "ISO 9000 Registration and Quality," describes the quality program at Fluke, and how it helped to prepare for ISO registration. It is presented as an example of an ISO-9000-oriented quality program in place.

ISO 9000

ISO 9000 is rapidly becoming the internationally-recognized set of standards for a company's quality system. Companies who wish to sell within the $4 trillion European Economic Community or to the U.S. Department of Defense will find ISO 9000 registration an important marketing edge. Obtaining an ISO 9000 registration is a rigorous process involving many areas of the company. Specifically included is the area of test and measurement equipment, as indicated in ISO 9001 paragraph 4.11: "The supplier shall identify, calibrate, and adjust all inspection, measuring, and test equipment . . . at prescribed intervals . . . to nationally recognized standards."

ISO 9000 Defined

ISO 9000 is a set of guidelines for developing a documented quality system. Published by the International Organization for Standardization (ISO) in 1987, it is rapidly becoming the one internationally-recognized standard for quality systems. It consists of five separate documents:

- ISO 9000 provides guidelines for selection and use.

- ISO 9001, 9002, and 9003 provide models for quality assurance intended primarily for use with external suppliers and customers.

- ISO 9004 provides guidelines to quality management and quality-system elements.

ISO 9000 is part of the New Harmonization of Technical Standards, an effort by the European Economic Community to remove trade barriers.

ISO 9000 and the Company

Obtaining ISO 9000 registration will require a significant investment of money and manpower as quality systems are overhauled and carefully documented. It will mean opening company operations to the scrutiny of an audit team from an accredited registrar. But substantial returns accrue to companies willing to make the ISO 9000 investment:

- ISO 9000 can be used to improve product and measurement quality.

- ISO 9000 can be used as a tool to increase overall competitiveness.

- ISO 9000 registration may become the ticket of admission to the European Economic Area—the largest purchasing block in the free world.

- ISO 9000-compliance will be important to companies hoping to do business with the U.S. Department of Defense, which has already announced its intentions to replace MIL-Q-9858A and MIL-I-45208A with ANSI/ASQC Q91, Q92, and Q93. (In the United States, ISO 9000 is known as the ANSI/ASQC Q90 Series.)

A typical ISO 9000 audit will look at all areas of the company, including management, quality systems, purchasing, process control, and training. The audit team will also look at the management of inspection, measuring, and test equipment, which means they will be taking a close look at the metrology operation.

ISO 9000 and the Metrology Laboratory

Quality programs such as ISO 9000 will thrust metrology into the spotlight, as metrology's link to business success becomes clear. The laboratory's workload will increase, as assets that were less rigorously calibrated are forced through the calibration system. The laboratory will undergo tighter scrutiny, as company management, ISO auditors, and other company auditors become intensely interested in the calibration system. In the early stages, there will be more paperwork as the company's quality manual is developed and responds to initial ISO 9000 audits.

The move towards a global economy will force the acceptance around the world of calibration laboratory accreditation. ISO/IEC Guide 25 and the NCSL Calibration Systems Requirement committee are probably today's most reliable sources of information on accreditation. See Chapter 29, "Laboratory Accreditation." ISO 9000 will trigger a shift from MIL-STD-45662A to ISO 9000. The shift will be gradual, as requirements filter down through contracts. The two standards are compared in Table 28-1.

It's All in ISO 9001, Paragraph 4.11

Requirements for calibration are found in several places within the five ISO 9000 documents. The definitive requirements are found in ISO 9001, paragraph 4.11 (or ISO 9002, paragraph 4.10), Inspection, Measuring and Test Equipment, which can be simply paraphrased as follows:

4.11a Select equipment appropriate to the measurements to be made,

4.11b calibrate it at regular intervals to recognized standards,

4.11c using documented procedures, and

4.11d ensure that equipment is capable of necessary accuracy and precision.

4.11e Equipment must indicate its calibration status, and

4.11f calibration records must be kept.

4.11g When equipment is found out of calibration, validity of test results must be assessed.

4.11h Environmental conditions,

4.11i storage, handling, and

4.11j security must be adequate to protect the validity of calibrations.

Table 28-1. *Comparison of MIL-STD-45662A and ISO 9000*

ISSUE	45662A	ISO Guide 25	ISO 9001	ISO 9002	ISO 9003	ISO 9004
Cal System Description	5.1	4.0	4.11a	4.10a	4.6	–
Adequacy of Standards	5.2	8.0	4.11a,d	4.10a,d	4.6	13.2a,e
Environmental Controls	5.3	7.0	4.11h	4.10h	–	13.2a
Calibration Intervals	5.4	8.4	4.11b	4.10b	–	13.2c
Calibration Procedures	5.5	10.0	4.11c	4.10c	–	13.2d
Out-of-Tolerance Conditions	5.6	13.0	4.11g	4.10g	–	13.1, 13.4
Adequacy of Systems	5.7	5.0	4.11a,d	4.10a,d	4.6	13.2d
Calibration Sources	5.8	9.0	4.11b	4.10b	4.6	13.2e
Records	5.9	12, 13	4.11f	4.10f	4.10	13.2d
Calibration Status	5.10	11.0, 8.3	4.11e	4.10e	–	13.2d
Control of Subcontractors	5.11	14.0	4.16	4.15	–	13.3, 13.5
Storage & Handling	5.12	11.0	4.11i	4.10i	–	13.2d
Security	–	–	4.11j	4.10j	–	–
Clarifying Handbooks	MIL-HDBK-52B					

How Software Tools Can Help

For companies seeking ISO 9000 registration, there are five areas where software capabilities can assist in passing the registrar's audit of:

- traceability
- documented procedures
- adequacy of standards
- calibration records
- equipment out of calibration

These are all detailed in the following subsections.

Traceability

ISO 9001 paragraph 4.11b: "The supplier shall identify, calibrate, and adjust all inspection, measuring, and test equipment . . . against certified equipment having a known relationship to nationally recognized standards. . . ."

With the right calibration software package, it is possible to show an auditor complete traceability data back to national standards or other recognized standards. All equipment in the traceability chain can be identified, and the calibration data for each item of equipment can be readily available. An example of an automatically-generated traceability report is shown in Figure 28-1.

Documented Procedures

ISO 9001 paragraph 4.11c: "The supplier shall establish, document, and maintain calibration procedures, including: details of equipment

type, identification number, location, frequency of checks, check method, acceptance criteria, and the action to be taken when results are unsatisfactory."

Calibration systems can satisfy this audit requirement by delivering procedures that are written in plain language, and executed without conversion by the automated system. Such procedures are considered to be self-documenting, and can be written to satisfy all the terms of Paragraph 4.11c. An example of such a procedure is shown in Figure 28-2.

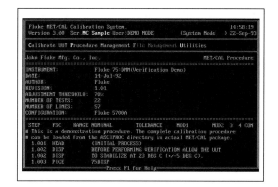

Figure 28-2. *Fluke MET/CAL Procedure Listing*

Adequacy of Standards

ISO 9001 paragraph 4.11d: "The supplier shall ensure that the inspection, measuring, and test equipment is capable of the accuracy and precision necessary."

One measure of adequacy, popularized by MIL-STD-45662A, is a test uncertainty ratio (TUR)

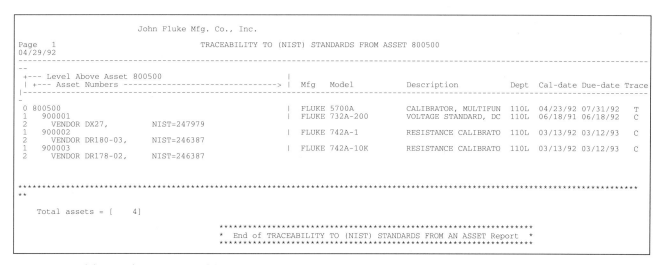

Figure 28-1. *Fluke MET/TRACK Traceability Report*

of 4:1 or better. Calibration software should automatically compute TURs and flag any violations of a predetermined threshold. One example of such a system is shown in Figure 28-3.

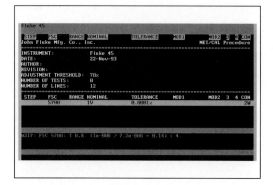

Figure 28-3. *Fluke MET/CAL Software Flags Test Uncertainty Ratios (TURs) Automatically*

Calibration Records

ISO 9001 paragraph 4.11f: "The supplier shall maintain calibration records for inspection, measuring, and test equipment."

In most cases, the auditor will wish to see complete calibration results for selected pieces of equipment. And, in many cases, complete as-found/as-left results will be required. Fortunately, these reports are a simple matter for a good calibration software package. An example of a results report is shown in Figure 28-4.

Figure 28-4. *Fluke MET/CAL Results Report*

Equipment Out of Calibration

ISO 9001 paragraph 4.11g: "The supplier shall assess and document the validity of previous inspection and test results when inspection, measuring, and test equipment is found to be out of calibration."

The difficult part of such an assessment is finding out exactly which other pieces of calibration equipment or final product have been affected by an out-of-tolerance condition. The task is virtually impossible in a paper-based system, and may not be easy with many general-purpose databases. But metrology-targeted software packages are available which support reverse traceability. They can specifically identify all affected calibration equipment during a particular time frame. An example of such a report is shown in Figure 28-5.

Once all equipment has been identified, analysis of the impact of the out-of-tolerance condition can proceed, followed by appropriate corrective action.

ISO 9000 Registration and Quality

The remainder of this chapter is a description of the Fluke quality system including Total Quality Commitment (TQC); Fluke's quality policy; and the corporate Quality Manual and its supporting standard operating procedures. It is presented here as an example of what a company must do if it is seriously considering ISO 9000 registration. This quality system has evolved over a period of time, and was a key ingredient leading to the successful completion of ISO 9001 registration at Fluke.

The Quality System

ISO 9000 is a topic of interest to the Fluke company. It is evident that ISO 9000 registration is necessary to compete in the European community. The connection between ISO 9000 and Fluke's TQC process, patterned after the Malcolm Baldrige National Quality Award (MBNQA), was made several years ago.

No matter what kind of quality system a company has, preparing for an ISO 9000 registration can be a time-consuming task requiring detailed planning, adequate resources, and commitment to get the job done in a timely fashion. Fluke's quality system was developed

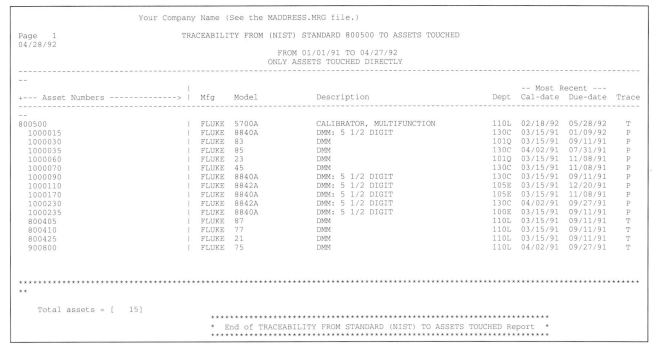

```
                            Your Company Name (See the MADDRESS.MRG file.)

    Page    1                       TRACEABILITY FROM (NIST) STANDARD 800500 TO ASSETS TOUCHED
    04/28/92
                                               FROM 01/01/91 TO 04/27/92
                                               ONLY ASSETS TOUCHED DIRECTLY
    ------------------------------------------------------------------------------------------------------
    --
                                    |                                                      -- Most Recent ---
    +--- Asset Numbers ------------> |  Mfg    Model          Description              Dept  Cal-date  Due-date  Trace
    ------------------------------------------------------------------------------------------------------
    --
    800500                          | FLUKE   5700A          CALIBRATOR, MULTIFUNCTION   110L  02/18/92  05/28/92    T
       1000015                      | FLUKE   8840A          DMM: 5 1/2 DIGIT            130C  03/15/91  01/09/92    P
       1000030                      | FLUKE   83             DMM                         101Q  03/15/91  09/11/91    P
       1000035                      | FLUKE   85             DMM                         130C  04/02/91  07/31/91    P
       1000060                      | FLUKE   23             DMM                         101Q  03/15/91  11/08/91    P
       1000070                      | FLUKE   45             DMM                         130C  03/15/91  11/08/91    P
       1000090                      | FLUKE   8840A          DMM: 5 1/2 DIGIT            130C  03/15/91  09/11/91    P
       1000110                      | FLUKE   8842A          DMM: 5 1/2 DIGIT            105E  03/15/91  12/20/91    P
       1000170                      | FLUKE   8840A          DMM: 5 1/2 DIGIT            105E  03/15/91  11/08/91    P
       1000230                      | FLUKE   8842A          DMM: 5 1/2 DIGIT            130C  04/02/91  09/27/91    P
       1000235                      | FLUKE   8840A          DMM: 5 1/2 DIGIT            100E  03/15/91  09/11/91    P
       800405                       | FLUKE   87             DMM                         110L  03/15/91  09/11/91    T
       800410                       | FLUKE   77             DMM                         110L  03/15/91  09/11/91    T
       800425                       | FLUKE   21             DMM                         110L  03/15/91  09/11/91    T
       900800                       | FLUKE   75             DMM                         110L  04/02/91  09/27/91    T


    **********************************************************************************************************
    **

       Total assets = [   15]
                               ******************************************************************
                               *  End of TRACEABILITY FROM STANDARD (NIST) TO ASSETS TOUCHED Report  *
                               ******************************************************************
```

Figure 28-5. Fluke MET/TRACK Reverse Traceability Report

taking advantage of the implementation of our TQC process and the commitment to ISO 9000 registration.

The quality system is based on Fluke's quality policy:

"Fluke's quality policy is to create and maintain a quality system of continuous improvement of key work processes focused on customer expectations."

This policy was developed by Fluke to give our employees a vision of what quality is to the Fluke company, how Fluke expects employees to incorporate quality into their own processes, how employees are expected to interact with customers, and how progress toward better quality will be measured and enforced.

The quality system consists of the basic elements of ISO 9000 and the MBNQA criteria which together form the TQC process as shown in Figure 28-6.

ISO 9000 focuses on process documentation, process standardization, and the creation of a common language. The MBNQA criteria focus on continuous improvement of processes, the measurement of those processes, and long-term

strategic planning that includes quality as a key element. Both ISO 9000 and the MBNQA criteria will enhance customer satisfaction and define the quality system which the company uses to strive for customer satisfaction.

Focus on Customer Satisfaction

TQC means determining customer expectations; defining, monitoring, and improving processes which support customer expectations; and measuring customer satisfaction in terms of those expectations. If Fluke focuses on customer satisfaction and improves processes based on customer expectations, the Fluke company will be a high quality, low cost producer.

The strategies for creating this customer-oriented TQC environment are realized through a commitment from the top officers and senior managers in the company who provide the following:

- tough goals and the means to measure customer satisfaction

- the means to reward and recognize quality achievement

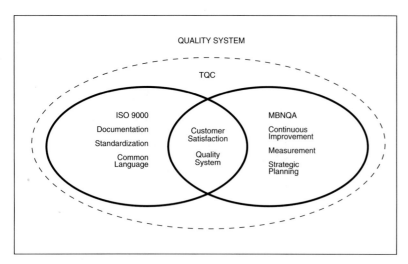

Figure 28-6. *The Total Quality System*

- the environment for partnering and teaming

- an excellent training process to incorporate the cultural change needed in the company to put the focus on customer satisfaction

Individuals work in teams to satisfy customer requirements, and each TQC team or work group needs a process to help it focus on customer satisfaction.

The TQC process flow is shown in Figure 28-7.

First, a team identifies customers and determines customer expectations. Customers can be either internal or external. Teams have to determine how expectations will be measured and how well the product or service which the team provides meets customer expectations.

The next step is to create a flow chart of the process which the team now uses to deliver the product or service to customers. This flow chart will help the team understand exactly how to interact with customers and where the measurement points for process monitoring should be.

Monitoring the results of the work process will point out areas which, if improved, will help to meet customer expectations more efficiently. At this stage, simplification of the process flow occurs, often with huge savings in time and improvements in quality. Improvements are measured in terms of customer satisfaction and are continually monitored for further improve-

ments to ensure that the process remains in control.

All teams use the basic principles, which are:

- Focus on the work process, issue, or behavior—not on the person.

- Maintain the self-confidence and self-esteem of others.

- Maintain strong partnerships with your internal and external customers and suppliers.

- Take initiative to improve work processes and partnerships.

- Lead by example.

These principles help teams focus on process improvement, rather than on each other.

Organization and Structure

Implementing TQC based on MBNQA criteria is not a simple task. A company cultural change is necessary to ensure that the change stays, and has the desired results. A cultural change of this nature requires top-down commitment and focus. The organizational structure shown in Figure 28-8 has the proper top-down commitment and focus for TQC implementation.

The president's staff, consisting of the top officers in the company, serves as the steering committee for TQC implementation. This steering committee is assisted by a Quality System Coordinator, the group and Support Resource Unit (SRU) TQC steering committees, and the TQC strategy committees. These groups consist of the top officers and senior management in the company and provide the support and direction needed to successfully implement TQC. It is no coincidence that the group and SRU steering committees have the remainder of the company's personnel reporting to them.

How does ISO 9000 registration fit into the organizational structure? ISO 9000 registration is the responsibility of the Quality Assurance Joint Council (QAJC). This council is responsible for managing the Fluke quality system and addressing any other corporate issues. Each quality manager of this council reports to a group vice president or senior manager of the company. One of the quality managers acts as the QAJC chairman and, in this capacity, reports to the president of the company. This organization is shown in Figure 28-9.

To begin the ISO 9000 registration process, the ISO 9000 registrar needs to understand the organizational structure of the company, where the company's products and services are manufactured or provided, and how the quality system operates. Fluke's structure is similar to that of many companies. It has several groups which are chartered to manufacture products and several groups which support the manufacture and service of the end product. For ISO 9000 purposes, each organization must understand its processes and how the processes operate and are controlled.

Each organization has many processes. Each process receives inputs from its vendors and generates outputs to its customers. There are also variables which affect the process. Each process owner has to understand how the interface to the next process is controlled and what effect the variables have on the process.

The most important process in any company is the customer interface. Fluke's interface process is shown in Figure 28-10.

The customer interface process is the top-level process in the company. All other processes are built on and support it. ISO 9000 registrars will carefully examine the quality system the customer interface process is built on. Each process that supports this top-level process has to be identified so that the control points can be understood and controlled by each process owner.

Preparing for an ISO Audit

Manufacturing, or operations, is arguably the part of the organization most affected by the ISO 9000 standards and the quality system. A typical operations group organizational structure is shown in Figure 28-11.

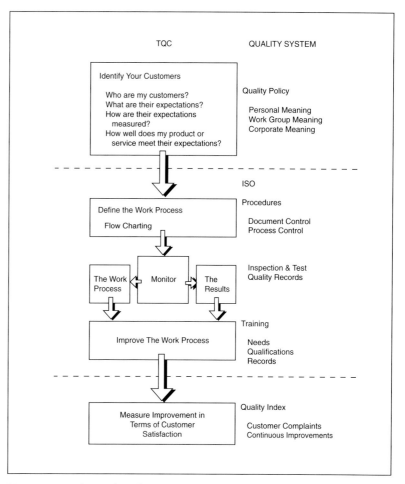

Figure 28-7. *The Total Quality Process*

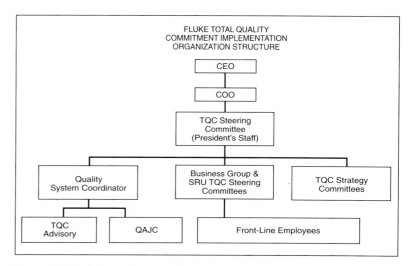

Figure 28-8. *The Top-Down Commitment*

Fluke is a vertically integrated company. In Figure 28-11, the shared processes (A through F) are inputs to the manufacturing process. These inputs provide the needed material and

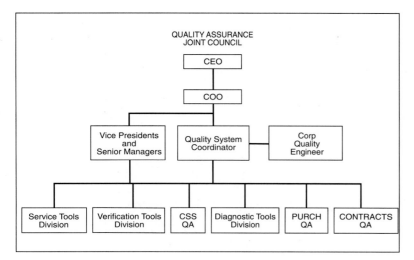

Figure 28-9. The QA Joint Council Structure

support to produce products. Although each product goes through its own assembly flow, there are similar processes that all products go through.

Notice the number of products that are produced through two processes in this particular operations group. Although Figure 28-11 has a good flow, it probably is not enough detail to satisfy ISO 9000 standard controls. This is because the control points and the quality elements are not identified.

Looking at a manufacturing flow in more detail in Figure 28-12, you can see that the links A through D from the shared processes are identified at each point in the process flow.

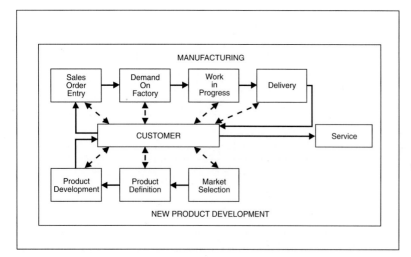

Figure 28-10. The Customer Interface Process

It is the process owner's (typically the supervisor's) task to determine how these links occur and whether the links (inputs and outputs) are in control. If the links are not in control, then the process owner must correct the situation to gain control.

At this point the quality elements pertinent to each step of the process are identified by the process owner. The process owner must review whether the quality element is being used at all, is in need of changing to match the current process, or is being used properly. This is a key step in determining process control.

For example, say the quality element being reviewed is the calibration system for the manufacturing process test equipment. The calibration system procedure calls for a six-month recall cycle, but the "real" procedure being followed is a nine-month recall cycle. The procedure must be changed or enforced to ensure that ISO 9000 registration will be granted.

All employees who need to know about a quality element must have the proper training to enable proper usage of the element. The detail shown in Figure 28-12 may be enough to show and maintain control of a quality system. If the detail is insufficient, the process owner will have to go to the level of detail needed to maintain process control.

Fluke has found that this type of flow diagram is easy to understand. It shows what needs to be done to ensure control, and it shows the deficiencies in the links to inputs, outputs, and quality elements. As such, it provides a means to successful ISO 9000 registration. Any organization can use this method to prepare for a successful ISO 9000 registration.

Support from Top Management

ISO and the MBNQA criteria are part of the TQC process at Fluke. The success of this process and ultimately ISO registration require top management to have a commitment to quality. Top management ensures that all employees are involved in the quality process, and that the quality system operates in a teamwork environment. Finally, top management provides a long-term focus to all actions affect-

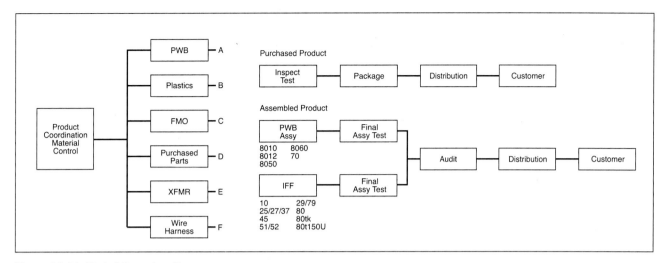

Figure 28-11. *Typical Operations Group*

ing quality and the proper measurements and enforcement necessary.

Quality System and ISO 9000

Fluke's total quality management system, which includes ISO 9000, focuses on customer satisfaction and strives to exceed customer expectations. Fluke has recognized that the only way to accomplish this is by a thorough understanding of all processes, their interactions, and links. ISO 9000 provides the means to implement process thinking into the Fluke company culture in place of the older product orientation. Fluke recognizes that customer perception of quality is an important factor. Fluke has also realized that quality needs to be introduced into the product at the earliest stage of development to be successful. Fluke's vendors are included in its quality plan, and a comprehensive training program for quality is maintained.

Typical Scope of Activities

The typical scope of activities for successful ISO 9000 registration is as follows:

1. Obtain top management commitment.

2. Develop a quality manual patterned after ISO.

3. Begin internal quality auditing.

4. Apply to registrar for assessment scheduling.

5. Identify functional-group process owners.

6. Document processes.

7. Establish and maintain process links.

8. Provide informational training.

9. Conduct on-going internal audits and implement corrective actions.

10. Have registrar perform preliminary audits.

11. Implement improvements based on pre-assessment findings.

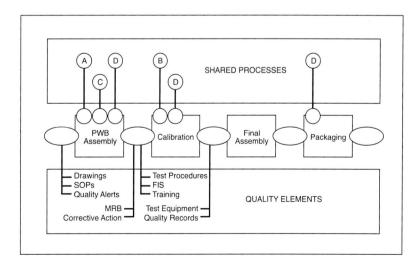

Figure 28-12. *Detail of Manufacturing Process*

12. Obtain registration.

13. Evaluate and measure results expected.

This list of activities can take from one to three years, depending on the level of top management support and the registrar used.

Expected Results

Fluke expects big results from ISO 9000 registration. Taken together with TQC and the MBNQA criteria, Fluke expects to exceed customer expectations and to gain continuous improvement of our processes. This will result in defect prevention because of the employee involvement and empowerment which this type of thinking requires. Although Fluke has traditionally maintained a strong supplier partnership, ISO 9000 requirements solidify that tradition. ISO 9000 delivers the proper quality system guideline to focus the methods and tools, such as TQC, which are used to focus on customer satisfaction. Any company or organization would do well to use ISO 9000 as a means to a well controlled quality system.

Key References

"Metrology, Quality and ISO 9000," Fluke *Application Note B0217C*

Other references for this chapter are in the Resources Appendix.

Chapter 29:

Laboratory Accreditation

This chapter covers the considerations of accreditation for a calibration laboratory— the reasons why a laboratory may need to be accredited, who can do the accreditation and what standard should be used.

When a calibration laboratory becomes accredited it demonstrates that the laboratory meets the standards of quality and technical competency of the accreditation organization. The accreditation is based upon an agreed standard with specified measurement parameters and uncertainties. Accreditation most often involves on-site assessments, proficiency testing and periodic follow-ups.

The term accreditation implies a precisely defined evaluation process that is used in the laboratory approval or registration process. Usually the accreditation is based on a critical evaluation using defined criteria. While these vary from one accrediting body to another, they typically include the following:

- Organization
- Laboratory quality system
- Qualified personnel
- Range of work capabilities and test methods
- Laboratory practices and management system
- Reliable standards and measuring devices
- Laboratory facilities
- Adequate measuring capabilities
- Traceability to national standards
- Calibration records
- Satisfactory completion of audit measurements

Most accrediting bodies make strong statements about what an accreditation is not. It is not a guarantee of laboratory performance, but is an indication of laboratory technical competence. The accreditation must not be construed or represented as an endorsement or certification of any product or material produced by that laboratory. What is accredited is the laboratory's ability to make measurements of specified accuracy. The purpose of accreditation is to provide customers of the laboratory with a high degree of confidence that the laboratory has the technical competency and adequate quality systems to perform calibrations to an agreed standard.

Benefits of Accreditation

A calibration laboratory will find several benefits from being accredited:

- Meet legal requirements
- Reduce the number of separate compliance documents
- Reduce the number of audits
- Measurements accepted through the reciprocity of the accreditation
- Improve measurements quality
- Formal recognition of competency (listed)
- Permission to use "logo" on certificates
- Increase the confidence of customers
- Competitive advantage in the market place—customers may ask for it (especially other accredited laboratories)

Laboratory accreditation is a process that provides customers of measurement services with assurance of the quality of the services provided. High quality measurements consistently fall within the stated uncertainty goals of the laboratory.

Accredited laboratories can display the logo of the accrediting body on their calibration certificates or reports to easily identify them as having met the high standards of the accreditor. For example, a NIST National Voluntary Accreditation Program (NVLAP) accredited laboratory in the U.S. would display the symbol:

Throughout our technological society, many quality issues are measurement issues. While, in the past, most Quality personnel tended to take for granted the accuracy of the measurements upon which they based quality decisions, that is rapidly changing. With the advent of Total Quality Commitment (TQC) programs, Just In Time (JIT) manufacturing, the Malcolm Baldrige Quality Award (USA), and ISO 9000, the importance of adequate measurements has become clear. The fundamental reason for accrediting any laboratory is to provide assurance to its customers that its measurements are correct. In short, customers are demanding high quality in all aspects of business.

Traditionally, in the U.S., the general belief was that demonstrating measurement competence was primarily a matter of displaying adequate documentation to some compliance document. In other parts of the world, especially Europe, it has been recognized for some time that there is a need for documenting the relationship between measurements and national standards, coupled with a demonstration of competence at each step in the process. Accreditation is a means for ensuring that the necessary competence is demonstrated in a uniform and widely understood manner.

Calibration and measurement expenses tend to be highly leveraged. An unsuspecting customer of a substandard laboratory may save on calibration costs, but this savings can be forfeited in the form of lost production time, excessive rework, dissatisfied customers and reduced market share. Accreditation is one means for a calibration laboratory to demonstrate its competence.

Accreditation Process

Laboratory accreditation is provided for a fee, upon successful completion of a preliminary inspection which typically includes measurements of an audit package. In most cases, accreditation is renewed periodically (six months to two years), based on evidence that qualified personnel are maintained on staff plus successful completion of audit measurements (on-site and/or inter-laboratory comparisons).

The accreditation process differs from accreditor to accreditor but the basic steps are:

- Application
- Payment of a fee
- On-site assessment
- Resolution of deficiencies
- Proficiency testing
- Technical evaluation
- Administrative review
- Approval

The on-site assessments are made by auditors from the accreditor who are technical experts in the particular calibration areas for which the laboratory has applied. Their role is more than just assessing (auditing) the capabilities of the laboratory, they can help resolve any identified deficiencies. The on-site visit usually takes one to three days.

As a condition of continued accreditation, the laboratory will need to notify the accreditation body immediately when there are any significant changes in the laboratory (facilities, equipment or people) that could affect calibration performance.

Accreditation Bodies

There are many accrediting bodies around the world. As of this writing, in the U.S. calibration laboratory accreditation can be provided under NVLAP or by the American Association for Laboratory Accreditation (A2LA). Both have important reciprocity agreements with various countries. Picking the right accreditor to meet the needs of the laboratory's customers is important.

NVLAP offers accreditation in eight calibration areas including over 80 parameters. A2LA offers similar areas. They are:

- Dimensional
- DC/Low Frequency
- RF/Microwave
- Optical Radiation
- Mechanical
- Thermodynamic
- Time and Frequency
- Ionizing Radiation

Specialized accreditation bodies in most developed countries accredit laboratories for testing and similar measurements. In the U.S., for example, Underwriter's Laboratories (UL®) accredits laboratories that make safety-related measurements, as does the Canadian Standards Association (CSA) in Canada.

Accreditation Systems Around the World

In some countries, an accredited laboratory is an extension of the national laboratory. That is, a measurement performed by an accredited laboratory has the same authority as if it had been performed by the national laboratory at the uncertainty levels for which the accreditation is granted. In the Western European Calibration Cooperation (WECC), the individual countries accreditation bodies are either part of the national laboratory or have a close affiliation with them.

In other countries, accreditation is a sanction of the laboratory's services by a higher authority. Either the national accreditation agency operates under the authority of the national laboratory or, in some cases, a private non-profit organization operates with the consent of government. In any case, the reciprocity of measurement agreements that the accreditation organization has with other countries will significantly increase the value of the accreditation for dealing in international trade.

Accreditation Standards

The intent of accreditation is to demonstrate compliance of calibration activities with internationally accepted requirements of the ISO 9000 series (ANSI/ASQC Q90 series in U.S.), ISO Guide 25, EN 45000 Series, MIL-STD-45662A and others. An accredited laboratory demonstrates that its operation, measurement capabilities and quality systems are in basic accordance with these standards. Individual requirements differ, but most of the basic requirements are discussed in Chapter 30, "Laboratory Audits."

The NCSL developed a U.S. national standard for calibration laboratories based on ISO Guide 25 and MIL-STD-45662A. NCSL is accredited with ANSI as the standards writing agency for calibration laboratories. Accreditation in the U.S. will be judged against this standard when approved.

Relationship Between Accreditation and ISO 9000

Around the world many companies are becoming ISO 9000 registered while some calibration laboratories are becoming accredited. It is important to recognize the differences between ISO 9000 registration and laboratory accreditation.

First, ISO 9000 registration provides assurance that the company's generic quality systems and procedures meet the standard. This can be true almost independent of the company's business. Calibration laboratory accreditation to a standard such as ISO Guide 25 provides the same assurance in regard to the overall quality systems as well as the competence of the laboratory to make measurements to a specified uncertainty. Accreditation is specific to laboratory environments, quality systems and technical competence.

Many companies that are ISO 9000, 9001 or 9002 registered may want to have their calibration laboratories accredited. The quality management aspects of both standards are complementary but detailed technical laboratory competence specifications are only included in accreditation (ISO Guide 25). In general, laboratories that are accredited will meet the requirements of ISO 9002. However, laboratories that are registered to ISO 9002 may not meet the requirements of accreditation. It is easier to get ISO 9000 registration if the calibration laboratory is accredited because a part of the ISO process is already fulfilled by the accredited laboratory quality system.

Many users of calibration and measurement services will require that their suppliers be accredited to realize the benefits of accreditation. Important decisions that affect product quality, health and safety, the environment, and competitiveness are based on those services.

How Accreditation Fits Into Global Measurements

When a company wants to sell its products in another country, it wants the calibrations made at the point of manufacture to be acceptable and useable to customers in that country. Dr. Joe Simmons, of NIST, in 1993 proposed a possible system of world-wide calibration agreements to meet this need. In his proposal, the world would be grouped into measurement regions (European, North American, Asian Pacific, etc). National laboratories would be encouraged to establish reciprocity (mutual recognition) agreements for measurements between the countries in their region and then extend them down to industrial laboratories through the accreditation system in the region. Interchange of measurements between regions would extend the acceptance of calibration certificates around the world. In Dr. Simmons' proposal (Figure 29-1), inter-comparison measurements would be made not only at the national laboratory level but also at the accredited laboratory level, effectively "closing the loop" on measurement quality.

This process exists in Europe where most national calibration organizations have multilateral agreements of recognition (mutual equivalence) and are participating in the WECC. The WECC is the European regional calibration laboratory accreditation organization that accredits calibration laboratories to EN 45001 and ISO Guide 25. The WECC has four sub-committees that coordinate activities of mutual recognition, technical activities, managing documents and international development. The WECC is an integral part of the metrology infrastructure in Europe.

As more international accreditation systems are implemented and recognized on a global basis, measurements made by an accredited laboratory in one country will be accepted in another country, thereby reducing redundant calibrations and lowering technical and economic trade barriers.

Key References

ISO/IEC, "General terms and their definitions concerning standardization and related activities," *ISO/IEC Guide 2, 1986*

ISO/IEC, "General requirements for the competence of calibration and testing laboratories," *ISO/IEC Guide 25, 1990*

ISO, "Terms and definitions used in connection with reference materials," *ISO Guide 30, 1981*

ISO/ANSI, "Quality management and quality assurance standards," *ISO 9000 Series, 1987, ANSI/ASQC Q90 Series, 1990*

MIL-STD, "Calibration systems requirements," *MIL-STD-45662A, 1988*

NVLAP, *Calibration Laboratories Program Handbook,* NIST, May, 1993

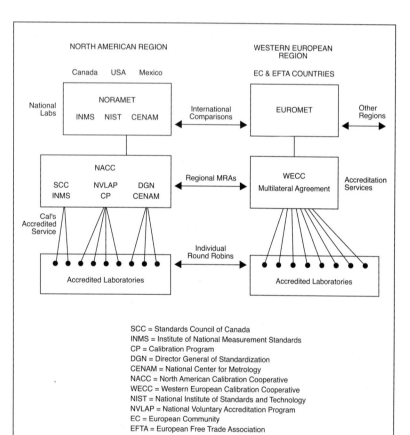

SCC = Standards Council of Canada
INMS = Institute of National Measurement Standards
CP = Calibration Program
DGN = Director General of Standardization
CENAM = National Center for Metrology
NACC = North American Calibration Cooperative
WECC = Western European Calibration Cooperative
NIST = National Institute of Standards and Technology
NVLAP = National Voluntary Accreditation Program
EC = European Community
EFTA = European Free Trade Association

Figure 29-1. *International Reciprocity of Measurements Through Accreditation*

Chapter 30:
Laboratory Audits

This chapter discusses those aspects of a standards or calibration laboratory to be considered when preparing to receive an audit team. It provides general guidelines, illustrated by specific examples, to help the laboratory manager establish techniques to prepare for and pass an audit.

The first part of this chapter discusses the major programs for quality assurance and the auditing effect on companies. The last section presents useful tips for passing audits, using an example of a typical standard.

Companies have many different requirements when addressing an audit. Audits come from various military, end user, and quality assurance programs. Audits all have the same basic requirements—to meet a certain quality standard.

For some organizations, the audit requirements are well defined, as in the aerospace and defense industries or meeting ISO 9000. For others, such as power utilities, there may be engineering policies and procedures for their facilities and thus unique audit requirements. Most modern organizations have test equipment management requirements, and most rely on documents that encompass their requirements in metrology. These documents may include ISO Guide 25, EN 45000, MIL-STD-45662A, ISO 9000 or the proposed new U.S. calibration laboratory standard being developed by NCSL.

Who Requires Audits?

An audit could be required under a customer's contract which involves quality program requirements (ISO Guide 25) and which requires all measuring and test equipment to be controlled according to calibration system requirements (MIL-STD-45662A). An audit could be demanded by an internal quality program. Or, an audit could be performed to meet the requirements of the internationally recognized quality standards of ISO 9001, 9002, or 9003. This is certain to become more common in the future. In 1991, the U.S. Department of Defense (DOD) indicated its intention to replace MIL-Q-9858A and MIL-I-45208A with ANSI/ASQC Q91, Q92, and Q93 (ISO 9001, 9002, and 9003).

Who Performs Audits?

Any company that wants to maintain a standard of quality can audit itself and its suppliers. Often it is simply a good business practice to perform internal and supplier audits. More and more, companies supplying products to ISO registered companies, government or commercial manufacturers are making audits (or accreditation) a requirement. In addition to the internal company audits that are performed to verify conformance to internal quality systems there are numerous private (ISO registrars, contractual, etc.) and government (FDA, NRC, DOD, etc.) auditors that may audit the calibration laboratory.

In most cases, the customer audits the supplier. In the case of subcontractors, the primary contractor has the responsibility for auditing its subcontractors' work. All work by all vendors must meet the same requirements that the primary contractor must meet. So when it comes to test and measuring equipment, quality departments are required to audit the vendors that repair or calibrate their instruments. For an accredited laboratory the audit requirements may be met by accreditation. See Chapter 29, "Laboratory Accreditation."

ISO 9000, an international standard for a company's quality system, is becoming increasingly important for companies selling to customers that are ISO 9000 registered, including the U.S. Department of Defense. While having a broader scope than MIL-STD-45662A, ISO 9000 deals with similar calibration issues. Also see Chapter 28, "Laboratory Quality and ISO 9000," for a more detailed discussion on ISO 9000 and quality systems in general. Table 28-1 shows the relationship of MIL-STD-45662A and various ISO 9000 paragraphs.

Audit Standards

Government auditors, from agencies such as the U.S. Defense Contractor Administration Service (DCASMA), verify that government requirements are being met by contractors. Government representatives normally use Military Handbook 52B (Evaluation of

Contractor's Calibration System) to assess the merit of the contractor's calibration system. While MIL-HDBK-52B is not a standard, an auditor may use it as a guideline. Other quality programs have similar documents. ISO 9000, for example, invokes ISO/IEC Guide 25, which has more detailed calibration laboratory requirements. In the U.S., the Food and Drug Administration (FDA) uses its Good Manufacturing Practices (GMP) and the Nuclear Regulatory Commission (NRC) uses its specific standards.

Resolving Interpretation Questions

One of the problems experienced during audits is that of interpretation between the auditor and the laboratory. Questions arise such as: "Is my interpretation of the Standard the same as the auditor's? Are my requirements the same as any other company? If we differ in interpretation, who is correct? If the auditor and I differ, how do we resolve the issue without major confrontations?"

The same basic principles hold true when being audited by any agency. They will all have a document to check the laboratory measurement quality system for compliance. The document will usually be paraphrased in a handbook that will enable the auditor and the manager to use consistent terminology and definitions during the audit. Some of the requirements stated in a general standard may not be needed for another quality program. Use this chapter to establish techniques to prepare for and pass audits.

Depending on the quality requirement, the fine points could be the basis for negotiation. Though specific requirements will vary from standard to standard, the basics laid out in this chapter are a good starting point.

Care should be taken when using some fairly common terms. For example, calibration versus verification. In this book calibration is defined as including comparison, adjustment (if needed) and verification. Some would say,

"calibration includes all measurement data— verification does not" or "calibration is not made to a specification whereas verification is." Various standards use different definitions that should be considered part of the audit process. Therefore, it is left to the auditor and the laboratory manager to agree on specific definitions and terms covering their specific situation.

Preparing For an Audit

Passing an audit is the result of diligence and attention to detail that reflects an appreciation and understanding of the requirements as well as the ability to implement an effective quality system.

Software tools such as Fluke's MET/CAL and MET/TRACK have been developed to assist in passing an audit. These are detailed in "How Software Tools Can Help" in Chapter 28, "Laboratory Quality and ISO 9000."

First Impressions Count

A clean, uncluttered laboratory, with everything in its place, provides an easy way to get the audit off to a good start. Orderly test-equipment storage areas with proper status identification create a good impression. Complete records that are readily available reflect good management.

The laboratory has to have personnel who are competent, well-trained, confident, and who know the processes for which they are responsible.

Making an auditor wait for the manager to determine the location of an all-important calibration certificate, report, or temperature chart, does not make a good impression.

Preparation Identifies Problems

Self-audits of the laboratory system are the best way to resolve problems before auditors find them. Every quality system should have a mechanism to examine itself on a periodic basis (most standards require it). Not only should the department review itself, but representatives from quality assurance (QA) or corporate headquarters can also offer advice that improves the perspective on the value and validity of the approach to the company's calibration requirements.

Self-Audits

Self-audits of the calibration system tell a story of how the laboratory performs its job. Rehearse the story. Start at its beginning, not in the middle or at the end. Is the story complete? Does it have good continuity? Are there parts that don't seem correct or complete?

Try to anticipate auditors' questions. As the story is told, what questions might be asked along the way? Go over the audit until it can be explained thoroughly.

If problems are found with the system, make a complete examination of how the problem came to be. It may lead to a generic, widespread problem, or a localized problem. Whatever the cause may be, return to the source of the problem and correct it.

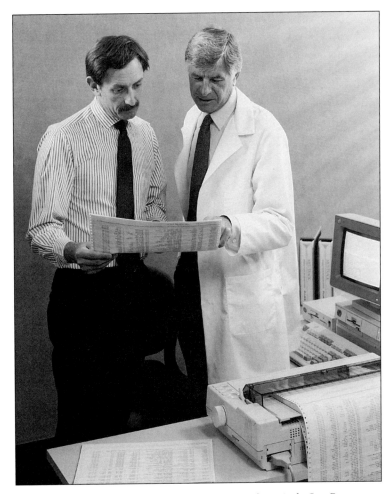

Figure 30-1. *With Preparation and Attention to Detail, an Audit Can Be a Positive Experience*

How Important Are Audits?

Auditors are becoming much better trained in how to perform a meaningful audit. Too frequently, auditors have been looked upon with the same affection shown tax collectors. But they are trying to make sure that the agency they represent (the customer) is getting what it paid for and help improve the quality of the calibrations performed by the laboratory.

Take audits seriously. In recent years, customers are demanding ever increasing levels of quality in the products they buy and that implies high quality in the care and maintenance of the measurement tools used.

Discussion of a Sample Standard

This part of the chapter will discuss and paraphrase the key requirements of the proposed new U.S. standard. Fluke Application Note B0204, *How Metrology Management Software Simplifies MIL-STD-45662A Compliance*, provides information on the automating of record keeping and documentation in the audited environment using Fluke MET/TRACK metrology management software. The information in Application Note B0204 is also valuable for supporting the calibration activity of ISO 9000 registered companies.

This standard applies to measurement and test equipment used anywhere in the company as well as the calibration laboratory's development and implementation of its quality system. It is based on ISO Guide 25 and MIL-STD-45662A.

Organization and Management

An accredited laboratory must first be identifiable as a separate entity and be organized to maintain satisfactory technical performance without undue pressure on its people that might adversely affect the organizational independence, quality or integrity of their work.

All personnel must be aware of the extent and limitations of their responsibilities. There must be a technical manager who has overall responsibility for the technical operations of the laboratory and a quality manager who has responsibility for the quality system and its maintenance. There must be adequate procedures to protect customers' confidential information.

Quality System, Audit and Review

A calibration laboratory must maintain a quality system appropriate to the type, range, and volume of work performed. The quality system must be used by the people in the laboratory and must be maintained current by the quality manager.

Auditors normally will only want to see a small sample of information about the system. Most audits contain very specific information about a few instruments. Frequently this leads to fragmented views of how the system operates. In most cases, it will be quite advantageous to first give the auditor a tour of the laboratory and explain the system so the auditor will have a better overview of the entire operation. Then, as the written procedures are reviewed, there will not be as many secondary questions to address. Generally a tour will help the auditor gain considerable confidence in the calibration system.

The quality manual must contain information or reference documents regarding:

- a quality statement of the objectives and commitments of top management;

- the organization and management structure of the laboratory and the relationships between management, operations, services and the quality system;

- the operational and functional duties and services pertaining to quality;

- job descriptions of key laboratory people;

- reference to the major calibration equipment (and reference measurement standards) used;

- reference to procedures for calibration and maintenance of calibrators used;

- policy for establishing calibration intervals for equipment it controls;

- procedures for control and maintenance of documentation;

- procedures for achieving traceability of measurements;

- policy concerning determination of measurement uncertainty and calibration adequacy;

- arrangements for ensuring that all new work is within the capability of the laboratory before it starts;

- reference to the calibration procedures used;

- procedures for handling calibration items;

- reference to quality assurance practices including inter-laboratory comparisons, proficiency testing and internal quality control schemes;

- procedures for feedback and corrective action whenever measurement discrepancies are detected;

- procedures for dealing with technical complaints;

- procedures for protecting confidentiality and proprietary rights; and

- procedures for audit and review.

The quality system must be systematically and periodically audited by management to ensure the continued effectiveness of the laboratory operations, and any corrective action initiated. Such audits must be recorded together with details of any corrective action taken. Any customer whose work may have been affected by discrepancies or corrective action must be notified in writing.

The overall laboratory quality system must be audited periodically (usually annually) to ensure its continuing suitability and effectiveness. Checks should be made to ensure the quality of results provided to customers using: internal quality control techniques; proficiency testing and inter-laboratory comparisons; duplicate measurements using different methods (parameters); and correlation of results for different characteristics of an item.

Checklist

✔ Complete details for meeting overall standard requirements are documented in the calibration system description.

✔ Planned deviations to any of the detailed requirements are described, with supporting justification, and have been approved.

✔ The calibration system description includes a procedure for obtaining prior approval for deviations from standard practices as requirements arise.

Personnel

The laboratory must have sufficient personnel with the necessary education, training, technical knowledge, and experience to perform their assigned duties. Records on the relevant qualifications, training, and experience of the technical personnel must be maintained and be available to the laboratory.

Checklist

✔ Show organizational chart of laboratory and where each individual fits in.

✔ Show evidence of which people are responsible for which processes.

✔ Records of training sufficient to indicate that each person is adequately trained in areas of responsibility.

✔ Be sure trainer authorizes each individual person's training.

✔ Show records of periodic review of personnel competency.

Facilities and Environment

Anywhere that measurement equipment is used, including the laboratory, facilities, calibration areas, energy sources, lighting, temperature, humidity and ventilation must be sufficient to support proper performance of measurements. Laboratory personnel must monitor, control and record environmental conditions (temperature extremes, dust, moisture, vibration, and emi). Where appropriate, correcting compensations must be applied to measurement results.

Access and use of the laboratory must be controlled in an appropriate manner. Adequate measures must be taken to ensure good housekeeping in the laboratory.

Checklist

✔ Environmental conditions which could affect the accuracy, stability, or calibration of equipment are identified and controlled.

✔ Unusual environmental control requirements are described in the appropriate calibration procedures.

✔ Adequate compensation and/or corrections are applied in instances where the defined environmental conditions are not met.

Equipment and Reference Materials

The laboratory must have access to all equipment (properly maintained) required for the correct performance of the measurements declared in the standard. Instructions for the proper maintenance for those items of equipment must be available.

Any item of equipment which has been subjected to damage, or which gives suspect results, or has been shown by calibration to be defective, must be taken out of service and clearly labeled until it has been repaired and then shown by test or calibration to be performing its function satisfactorily. An investigation must be conducted to assess the effect caused by the defective device and take appropriate action.

Records must be maintained for each major item of calibration equipment. The records must include:

- name of equipment (model & description);

- manufacturer's name and serial number;

- current location;

- dates and results of calibration and date or criteria when calibration expires;

- details of maintenance performed;

- history of any damage, malfunction, modification or repair;

- measured value observed for each parameter found to be out of tolerance during calibration.

Certificates or reports of calibration for measurement standards must be readily accessible and contain the following information: identification of the instrument, identification of the calibration source and report number, date of the calibration, calibration-assigned value(s) with statement of uncertainties, relevant conditions, corrections which must be applied, and a traceability statement.

Measurement equipment must be labeled (calibration sticker) to indicate calibration status. The label must identify specific date calibrated and the specific calibration due date or usage equivalent. Items not calibrated to their full capability or which have other limitations of use, must be labeled or otherwise identified as to the limitations. When it is impractical to apply a label directly to an item, the label may be affixed to the instrument container or some

other suitable means may be used to reflect calibration status.

Measurement Traceability and Calibration

All measuring equipment having an effect on the accuracy or validity of calibrations must be calibrated before being put into service. The laboratory must have a program that ensures the recall or removal from service any standard or measurement equipment which has exceeded its calibration interval, has broken calibration seals, or is suspected to be malfunctioning because of mishandling, misuse, or unusual results or is otherwise judged to be unreliable.

Measurement equipment must be calibrated at periodic intervals established and maintained to assure acceptable reliability, where reliability is defined as the probability that the equipment will remain in tolerance throughout the interval. Intervals must be established for all calibrated equipment unless the equipment is regularly monitored through the use of check standards in a documented measurement assurance process. Check standards must closely represent the item parameters normally tested in the process and the check standard must be verified periodically.

Where intervals are used to ensure reliability, the interval setting system must be systematically applied and must have stated reliability goals and a method of verifying that the goals are being met. Intervals may be based on usage or time since last calibration. All exemptions from periodic calibration must be documented. The recall system may provide for the temporary extension of the calibration due date for limited periods of time under specified conditions that do not unreasonably impair the satisfaction of the customer's requirements.

Calibration intervals are best established based on the performance of individual instruments, with consideration given to their application and calibration history. Two similar instruments can be operated under very different extremes. One may be outside, exposed to the sun, damp air, and dirt, and used two shifts per day, while the other may be in an engineering laboratory and used only occasionally. Some calibration systems are set up to lengthen or reduce calibration intervals by model number or by generic type. Calibration software such as Fluke MET/TRACK can help establish appropriate calibration intervals.

Checklist

✔ Reliability targets (percentage in tolerance) should have been established for all calibration equipment and standards.

✔ Verify that the methodology to initially establish and then adjust the calibration interval to meet the reliability target is acceptable.

✔ All must have assigned calibration intervals that satisfy the reliability target.

✔ Equipment that does not meet the reliability target, even after interval adjustment, must be either restricted in use or removed from use.

✔ Equipment owner must be notified of any out-of-tolerance conditions as soon as possible.

✔ Calibration intervals may be established in terms of calendar time, usage, or a combination of both.

✔ Assure the recall system is effective and prompts release by users.

✔ Overdue notices are issued when recalled items are not submitted in a timely manner.

✔ Instruments overdue for calibration are removed from use or are clearly marked to prevent use.

✔ Temporary extensions of calibration due dates are documented and meet established criteria.

The overall program controlling the calibration of equipment must be designed and operated to ensure that measurements made in the laboratory are traceable to national, international, or intrinsic standards of measurement. The calibration reports must provide the measurement result, as appropriate, associated uncertainty of measurement and compliance with a specification.

A significant number of intrinsic standards, such as the Josephson Array Voltage Standard, have been developed and are now being used by some standards laboratories. These standards are based on well characterized laws of physics, fundamental constants of nature, or invariant properties of materials and make ideal stable, precise, and accurate measurement standards if properly designed, characterized, operated, monitored and maintained. Where intrinsic standards are used, the laboratory should demonstrate by measurement assurance techniques, inter-laboratory comparisons, or other suitable means that its intrinsic standard measurement results are correlated with those of national or international standards.

Where traceability to international, national or intrinsic standards of measurements is not available, the traceability requirement may be satisfied by:

■ Participation in a suitable program of inter-laboratory comparisons or proficiency testing

■ Internationally accepted standards in the field

■ Suitable reference materials

■ Ratio or reciprocity-type measurements

■ Mutual consent standards which are clearly specified and mutually agreed upon by all parties concerned

Calibration Methods

The laboratory must have documented instructions on the use and operation of all relevant calibration equipment and on the handling and preparation of items for calibration. All instructions, standards, manuals, and reference data relevant to the work of the laboratory must be available to people in the laboratory and kept current.

The laboratory must use appropriate methods and procedures for all calibrations and related activities within its responsibility. Calibration procedures must contain the required range and tolerance or uncertainty of each item parameter being calibrated. Methods are usually considered the basic calibration concepts or approaches where procedures are the detailed "step-by-step" descriptions. In addition, the procedures must contain the generic description of the measurement standards and equipment needed with the required parameter, range, uncertainties and specifications for performing the measurement of the calibration and representative types (manufacturer, model, option) that are capable of meeting the generic description for the measurement standards. They must be consistent with the accuracy required, and with any standard specifications relevant to the calibrations concerned.

Checklist

✔ Revisions to procedures and what calibrations were affected can be tracked.

✔ Calibration procedures should be available and used for all calibrations.

✔ The procedures used should describe the required measurement standards to provide an acceptable test uncertainty ratio (TUR) between measurement standards and the instrument being calibrated.

✔ Calibration procedures are kept current by a documented method for making revisions or changes.

The laboratory must ensure that the calibration uncertainties are sufficiently small so that the adequacy of the measurement is not affected. Well defined and documented measurement assurance techniques or uncertainty analysis may be used to verify the adequacy of a measurement process. If such techniques or analyses are not used, then the uncertainty of calibration must not exceed 25% (4:1) of the acceptable tolerance (e.g., manufacturer's specification) for each characteristic of the measuring and test equipment being calibrated.

Checklist

✔ The collective uncertainty of the measurement standards must not exceed 25% of the acceptable tolerance (4:1 TUR, test uncertainty ratio) for any characteristic being calibrated unless documented and justified.

✔ The methodology used for deriving the collective uncertainty of the measurement standards is acceptable.

✔ Traceability requirements are met.

✔ Calibration history is reviewed to ensure that the measurement standards maintain their acceptability in terms of accuracy and reliability.

Where the generic method is not specified, the laboratory should, where practical, select methods that have been internationally established. Where it is necessary to employ non-standard methods, these must be fully documented and subject to agreement with the customer.

All manual calculations and data transfers must be subject to appropriate checks. Where computers are used to derive results, the stability of the system must be such that the accuracy of the results is not affected. This generally implies an ability to detect malfunctions and take appropriate action.

Companies working with the medical industry should be aware of additional standards and requirements. For example, in the U.S., the *Code of Federal Regulations*, 21 CFR, Part 820—Good Manufacturing Practice for Medical Devices: General, Subpart D, Equipment, Section 820.61, *Measurement Equipment*.

This standard describes the calibration requirements for measurement equipment used in the production or service of medical devices or goods. In addition to the requirements of ISO Guide 25, it states that the software used must be validated. To quote the standard, "When computers are used as part of an automated production or quality assurance system, the computer software programs shall be validated by adequate and documented testing. All program changes shall be made by a designated individual(s) through a formal approval procedure." Calibration laboratories regulated by the FDA should be sure that they meet this standard.

Software validation requires there be sufficient control of the documentation, change control and testing processes to ensure that the software actually does what is intended. This can be quite an extensive process, especially for in-house developed software. Software such as Fluke MET/CAL and MET/TRACK are developed according to strict standard procedures that control documentation, changes and testing. Fluke can supply a list of the internal test procedure numbers and applicable standard operating procedure numbers.

Handling of Calibration Items

The laboratory must have a documented system for uniquely identifying the items to be calibrated, to ensure that there is no confusion regarding the identity of the equipment or measurement results.

Upon receipt of the calibration item, any abnormalities in the condition of the equipment must be recorded and agreement must be reached with the customer before proceeding.

Checklist

✔ Equipment and measurement standards should be appropriately protected, handled, and transported to preclude any adverse effects on the capability of the instruments.

✔ Equipment storage areas should provide acceptable environmental conditions.

✔ Instances of improper handling, storage, or transportation are investigated for adverse impacts on affected equipment, and appropriate corrective action is taken.

At all stages of storing, handling, and preparation for calibration, precautions must be taken to prevent damage to the items. A procedure must exist for bonded storage of items where necessary. Tamper-resistant seals must be affixed to operator accessible controls or adjustments that could invalidate the calibration. The requirement to use anti-tamper seals is frequently interpreted differently by auditors. The intent is to prevent operators from tampering with adjustments that could affect calibration.

Checklist

✔ All equipment should be labeled to visually indicate date last calibrated, date calibration due, and any use limitations.

✔ The use and explanation of all calibration status labels are thoroughly described and understood.

✔ Tamper-resistant seals are affixed to operator accessible controls or adjustments.

✔ Instruments for which adjustments seals are broken are removed from use.

Calibration Records

The laboratory must maintain a record system adequate to its particular circumstances and comply with any existing regulations or laws. The records for each calibration must contain sufficient information to permit satisfactory repetition of the calibration. All records and reports must be confidential for the customer.

Individual records should be maintained for all calibrated equipment including the following:

- instrument identification
- current calibration interval
- date of last calibration
- calibration source
- calibration procedure
- results of previous calibrations
- corrective actions taken
- indications of erratic behavior or operational failures
- calibration certificate or report number

Certificates and Reports

When a certificate or report is issued, the results of the calibration, or series of calibrations, carried out by the laboratory must be accurate, clear, unambiguous and objective, in accordance with any instructions in the calibration procedure. The results should normally be reported in a calibration report or certificate and must include all the information necessary for the interpretation of the calibration results and all information required by the method used.

It may not be appropriate to include the measurement data with the calibration certificate or report; for example, the customer wants the laboratory to store the data and give the customer a single page certificate with "meet specifications." Also, not every calibration will require a report or certificate.

Each certificate or report must include at least the following information:

- A title, "Calibration Report" or "Calibration Certificate";

- Name and address of the laboratory;

- Unique report identification (such as serial number);

- Name and address of the customer;

- Description and identification of the item calibrated;

- Characterization and condition of item;

- Date when calibration was performed;

- Identification of the calibration procedure used;

- Reference to sampling procedure, where relevant;

- Any deviations, additions to or exclusions from the calibration procedure, and any other information relevant to a specific calibration;

- Any failures identified;

- When appropriate, measurements, examinations, and derived results, supported by tables, graphs, sketches, and photographs;

- A statement of the estimated uncertainty (where relevant);

- A signature and title of persons accepting technical responsibility for the content of certificate or report, and date of issue;

- A statement to the effect that the results relate only to the items calibrated;

- A statement that the report must not be reproduced except in full without the approval of the laboratory;

- Special limitations of use; and

- Traceability statement.

Particular care and attention must be paid to the arrangement of the certificate or report, especially with regard to the presentation of any calibration results data and ease of assimilation by the reader. The format must be carefully and specifically designed for each type of calibration carried out, but the headings should be standardized as far as possible.

Accredited laboratories can display the logo of the accrediting agency on the calibration certificate or report. For example, in the U.S. a NVLAP accredited laboratory would display the symbol:

NVLAP®

Corrections or additions to a calibration certificate or report after issue must be made only by a further document suitably marked, e.g., "supplement to calibration report serial number... (or as otherwise identified)," and must meet the relevant requirements of the preceding paragraphs.

The laboratory must notify its customers promptly, in writing, of:

- any event such as the identification of defective (out-of-tolerance) calibrator or standard that casts doubt on the validity of results given in any calibration report or certificate. The magnitude of the error created in the calibration results must be quantified;

- any customer's equipment found significantly out of tolerance during the calibration process. Measurement data must be reported so that appropriate action can be taken.

The preceding requirement is more far-reaching than it would at first appear. The real problem has not been how to notify the user of equipment of a significantly out-of-tolerance condition. And the problem has not been how to define what "significant" is. The problem has been to identify everyone who must be contacted when a significantly out-of-tolerance measurement standard is found. This is where metrology management software like Fluke MET/TRACK is useful.

If a reference standard were found to be significantly out of tolerance and it calibrated other, less accurate standards, and those standards calibrated other bench standards, and the bench standards calibrated production test equipment used for acceptance tests, who must be told? What instruments must be recalled and retested? Where were they used? What contracts were affected? What test stations were involved? What interval of time was affected? That is the problem! This is why most users of calibrators with internal check standards (Fluke 5700A) monitor the internal calibration constants between calibrations to increase their confidence that the calibrator is meeting its specifications.

When a measurement standard is found to be significantly out of tolerance, the customer and designated laboratory quality element must be notified of the significantly out-of-tolerance condition. In addition to being notified, they will also be supplied with the measurement data so that appropriate action can be taken.

Significantly out-of-tolerance conditions should be recorded and reported, and appropriate corrective action taken. So now the question becomes, "What is appropriate corrective action?"

The first way to meet the preceding requirement is to provide reverse traceability in the calibration system. This allows the laboratory to see a reverse tree in the calibration system, starting with the highest level of standards and moving down to equipment used with products. It identifies which instruments each measurement standard calibrated. When a significantly out-of-tolerance condition exists, all instruments that may have been affected can be identified and recalled for retest.

Another way to meet the requirement is via an engineering analysis of the instrument's use requirements, the magnitude of the condition, the effect of the out-of-tolerance condition on

the parameter being measured or calibrated, and, ultimately, the effect on the end product of material being delivered to the customer. The best system is a combination of both reverse traceability and an engineering analysis of the effect of the out-of-tolerance condition.

Checklist

✔ Significantly out-of-tolerance conditions are defined.

✔ Significantly out-of-tolerance conditions and supporting data are reported to the respective customer and quality element for evaluation and appropriate action.

✔ Required corrective action resulting from evaluation of significantly out-of-tolerance measurement standards is completed and documented.

Subcontracting of Calibration

When a laboratory subcontracts any part of the calibration, the work must be placed with a laboratory complying with the same required standards. The laboratory must be able to demonstrate that its subcontractor is competent to perform the activities in question and complies with the same criteria of competence as the laboratory with respect to the work being subcontracted. The most conservative method is to choose an accredited subcontractor that is certified (accredited) by a recognized body to the same standard. The laboratory must advise the customer of its intention to subcontract any portion of the calibration to another party.

Checklist

✔ Appropriate requirements should be imposed on suppliers and subcontractors who provide measurements or perform calibrations that can affect the quality of supplies or services presented to the customer.

✔ Suppliers and subcontractors must be audited (if not accredited) to ensure compliance to the specific requirements imposed. Results of the reviews are made available to the customer.

Complaints

The laboratory must have procedures for the resolution of complaints received from customers. A record must be maintained of all complaints received and the corrective actions taken by the laboratory.

Key References

ISO/IEC, "General terms and their definitions concerning standardization and related activities," *ISO/IEC Guide 2*, 1986

ISO/IEC, "General requirements for the competence of calibration and testing laboratories," *ISO/IEC Guide 25*, 1990

ISO, "Terms and definitions used in connection with reference materials," *ISO Guide 30*, 1981

ISO/ANSI, "Quality management and quality assurance standards," *ISO 9000 Series*, 1987, *ANSI/ASQC Q90 Series*, 1990

MIL-STD, "Calibration systems requirements," *MIL-STD-45662A*, 1988

NVLAP, *Calibration Laboratories Program Handbook*, NIST, May, 1993

Federal Register, *Code of Federal Regulations*, 21 CFR, Section 820.61, July, 1978

Other references for this chapter are in the Resources Appendix.

FLUKE®

Chapter 31:

Instrument Specifications

Specifications for precision instruments are often complex and difficult to interpret. Users should consider easily overlooked details in order to properly compare these instruments or apply them to their workload.

The initial selection of prospective equipment is usually based on its written specifications. They provide a means for determining the equipment's suitability for a particular application. Specifications are a written description of the instrument's performance in quantifiable terms and apply to the population of instruments having the same model number. Since specifications are based on the performance statistics of a sufficiently large sample of instruments, they describe group behavior rather than that for a single, specific instrument.

Good specifications have the following characteristics:

■ complete for anticipated applications
■ easy to interpret and use
■ define the effects of environment and loading

Completeness requires that enough information be provided to permit the user to determine the bounds of performance for all anticipated outputs (or inputs), for all possible environmental conditions within the listed bounds, and for all permissible loads. It is not a trivial task even for a simple standard. Designing complete specifications for a complex instrument like a multifunction calibrator is a big challenge.

Ease of use is also important. A large array of specifications, including modifying qualifications and adders, can be confusing and difficult to interpret. Mistakes in interpretations can lead to application errors or faulty calibrations.

The requirement for completeness conflicts somewhat with that for ease of use; one can be traded for the other. The challenge of specification design is to mutually satisfy both requirements.

This is sometimes satisfied by bundling the effects of many error contributions within a window of operation. For example, the listed performance may be valid for six months in a temperature range of 23 ±5°C, for rh up to 80%, for power line voltage of nominal ±10%, and for all loads up to the maximum rated current. This is a great simplification for the user since the error contributions of time, temperature, humidity, power line fluctuations and

loads can be ignored as long as operation is maintained within the listed bounds.

Since specifications are complex for complex instruments, they can be misused and abused both by users and manufacturers. Reputable manufacturers will attempt to describe the performance of the product as accurately and simply as possible without hiding areas of poor performance by omission of relevant specifications.

Much of the following material describes the effects of incomplete specifications, and how specifications can be misinterpreted or abused.

The various specifications fall into three distinct categories; these will be defined later. Each specification must be carefully considered when comparing instruments from different vendors. All of these components combine to describe the performance of a given instrument. Purchasers need to be proficient at adding the contribution of each component to arrive at the actual instrument performance for any given output. This skill will lead to faster and more intelligent purchasing decisions.

Analyzing Specifications

The analysis of specifications as part of the decision making process can be complex. To have a clear picture of the true specifications, laboratory managers, metrologists, and technicians should all be aware of all the components of a specification, and how to extract them from all the footnotes, from the fine print, and from the specification itself.

Advertisements are notorious for their use of footnotes, asterisks, and superscripts. The fine print can turn a data sheet into a reader's nightmare. In general, there are two types of footnotes: those that inform and those that qualify. Always look over all footnotes carefully and determine which have a direct effect on the specification.

Once the main components of the specification are identified, one must interpret and calculate the true specifications. Only after the total specification has been described will the user have a clear understanding of the real instrument specification. This will help to avoid confusing purchasing decisions with extraneous factors. As will be shown, the listed specifications found in advertisements and brochures are often not even half of the total usable specification.

Interpreting Specifications

Consider how a company goes about evaluating electronic instruments for potential purchase. Many companies have complex procedures and tests that an instrument must pass prior to purchase and acceptance. But before that evaluation can begin, one must decide which of the many instruments on the market should be evaluated. The instrument specifications are usually the first step in the process. The specifications must meet the workload requirements if the instrument is to be considered.

Ideally, specifications are a written description of an instrument's performance that objectively quantifies its capabilities. It should be remembered that specifications do not equal the performance, they are performance parameters. They can be conservative or aggressive. Manufacturers are not bound by any convention as to how they present specifications. Some will specify their products conservatively. Such instruments will usually outperform their specifications. Other manufacturers may manipulate the specifications to make an instrument appear more capable than it really is. Impressive specifications touted in advertisements or brochures may be incomplete. They often reflect only a small part of the total usable instrument performance.

The buyer should also be aware that an instrument specification applies to an entire production run of a particular instrument model. Specifications are probabilities for a group, not certainties for an item. For example, the specifications for a Fluke 5700A apply to all the 5700As made. The specification does not describe the actual performance on any individual 5700A. Chapter 20, "Introduction to Metrology Statistics," provides more information on how an instrument gets its specification rating.

Instrument specifications are chosen so that a large percentage of all instruments manufactured will perform as specified. Since the variation in the performance of individual instruments from nominal tends to be normally distributed, a large majority of the units of a specific model should perform well with their specification limits. There are two applications of this information:

- Most individual instruments can be expected to perform much better than specified.

- The performance of an individual instrument should never be taken as representative of the model class as a whole.

Consequently, the instrument purchased will most likely give excellent performance even though there is always a small chance that its performance will be marginal or even out of specification, at some parameter or function.

To compare products from different manufacturers, one will often have to translate, interpret, and interpolate the information so that one can make a logical comparison. Look again at the definition of an ideal specification: "a written description of an instrument's performance that objectively quantifies its capabilities." But what aspects of performance are described? Objective to whom? A manufacturer cannot include every possible specification, so what is included and what isn't?

Confidence

The most critical factor in a calibrator's performance is how small the deviation of its actual output is from its nominal output. Chapter 5, "Basic DC and Low Frequency Metrology," shows that, on the one hand, one will always have a measure of uncertainty as to the magnitude of the deviation. On the other hand, one can have confidence that the deviation is unlikely to be greater than a determined amount. Moreover, confidence can be numerically stated in terms of the confidence level for the specification.

For example, say that vendors X, Y, and Z offer calibrators. Vendor X's specifications state that its calibrator can supply 10V with an uncertainty of 1.55 ppm. Vendor Y's calibrator is specified to provide 10V with 3.03 ppm uncertainty, and vendor Z's specification is 4 ppm uncertainty for the 10V output. None of the data sheets for the calibrators supply a confidence level for the specifications, nor do they state how the uncertainty is distributed.

When questioned, vendors will state that their specifications are based on a normal distribution of uncertainty and have the following confidence levels (or coverage factor, k). Their responses are tabulated in Table 31-1.

Table 31-1. *Specification Comparison*

Vendor	Stated Spec @ 10V	Confidence Level (coverage factor)
X	1.55 ppm	1 Standard Deviation (k = 1)
Y	3.03 ppm	95% (k = 2)
Z	4 ppm	99% (k = 2.58)

As Figure 31-1 shows, the three calibrators can be expected to have identical performance because their confidence intervals apply to different areas under the same curve for the normal distribution of uncertainty.

Fluke uses a 99% confidence level for its specifications for calibrators and standards. As a buyer, one should be alert to the issues surrounding the confidence level for a specification and should ask the vendor to clarify the confidence level when there is doubt as to what it is.

Beware of the Word "Accuracy"

Typically, the number on the cover of a data sheet or brochure will read "Accuracy to *xx* ppm." What it really means is "*xx* ppm uncertainty." This is the result of imprecise language: substituting "accuracy" when "uncertainty" is intended. One also needs to be aware that a specification such as this is often over the shortest time interval, the smallest temperature span, and is sometimes a relative specification.

Components of a Specification

Determining an instrument's true specifications requires that all important specifications be combined. For this discussion, the uncertainty terms comprising calibrator specifications are divided into three groups: baseline, modifiers, and qualifiers.

- Baseline specifications describe the basic performance of the instrument.

- Modifiers change the baseline specifications, usually to allow for the effects of environmental conditions.

- Qualifiers usually define operating limits, operating characteristics, and compliance with industrial or military standards.

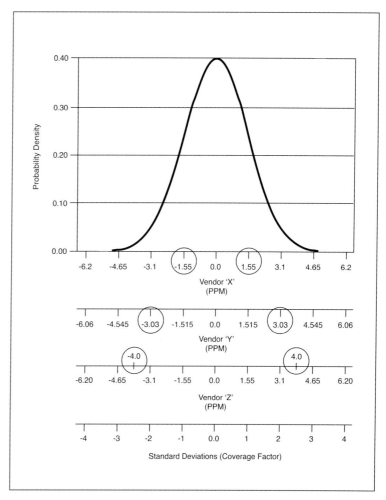

Figure 31-1. *Same Performance, Different Specifications*

The following paragraphs describe each in detail.

Baseline Specifications

Baseline specifications consist of three components. They are listed here along with the name used to represent them in this chapter:

- *output*
- *scale*
- *floor*

The general form for a baseline specification can be expressed as:

$$\pm(output + scale + floor)$$

Where:

output = percent or parts per million (ppm) of the output or setting

scale = percent or ppm of the range, or full-scale value of the range, from which the output is supplied (sometimes given as a fixed value in units or as digits)

floor = a fixed value in units

One or more of these terms will be present in the specification, though not all specifications will include all the terms.

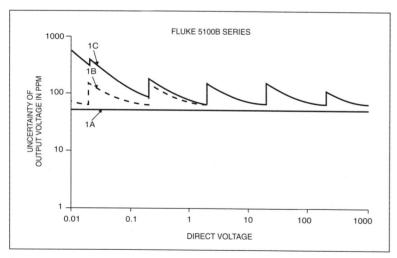

Figure 31-2. Baseline Specifications

The output term of the baseline specification is often quoted casually to describe the instrument's capabilities. But this output uncertainty term alone should not be used to technically evaluate the unit's actual performance. The other two terms can make a significant contribution to the total uncertainty. The following discussion shows how the three terms are combined. Refer to the Fluke 5100B multifunction calibrator specification graph in Figure 31-2.

The Output Term

Line 1A is output—the uncertainty of the basic output signal. This 50 ppm uncertainty term shows up as a horizontal line. It is a constant percentage of output for all settings of the calibrator.

The Scale Term

Line 1B in Figure 31-2 includes scale. The scale term is the uncertainty associated with the output range. Whether specified as a percentage of full scale, or as a percentage of range in units or digits, scale describes the fixed uncertainty for a specific range. This means that although the magnitude of the scale term is the same for all outputs across the range, the effect it has at the low end of the range is greater. At the low end it represents a larger portion of the output than it does at full scale.

Note that Line 1B takes on a sawtooth form. The peaks of the sawtooth are where the next-highest range is selected. This profile is caused by scale being a larger percentage of a fractional scale output. For example, on the 20V range, the 10 ppm uncertainty of the full-scale 20V value is 200 μV. This uncertainty applies to any output on the 20V range whether it is 3.0V or 19.93V.

Two steps are performed here to translate the scale uncertainty term to a specific percentage of any given output value. First, scale was converted to microvolts, using the full-scale output level. This magnitude was then converted to ppm at each specific output value.

The Floor Term

In addition to a calibrator's uncertainty relative to its output and scale, there can be additional uncertainty of a fixed magnitude. This is typically an offset, but can also include noise. This added uncertainty is called the floor, and, for any given range, it is constant across that entire range. For example, often a calibrator specification will include a description such as, "with a floor of 5 µV." This is the floor specification. Because this constant error is a greater percentage of small outputs than of large outputs, it becomes more important as the magnitude of the output decreases.

Line 1C in Figure 31-2 includes floor. This term can vary by range or can be a constant across all ranges. Floor uncertainty is similar to scale and may be combined with the scale term for simplicity. Adding this term to the baseline uncertainty plot shown in Figure 31-2 raises the curve even farther, particularly on the lower end: the constant voltage uncertainty is a large percentage of the total output for smaller voltages. In a more extreme example, a 5 µV floor amounts to an additional 5 ppm uncertainty at 1V, whereas 5 µV is only an additional 0.025 ppm uncertainty at 200V output.

The True Baseline Calculation

Comparing Line 1C with Line 1A shows that the total baseline uncertainty specification is quite different from the basic output uncertainty specification. Yet the total uncertainty specification must be used in determining whether the calibrator will actually fill your needs. This total uncertainty specification must support your application or workload even at the low end of each range.

The comparison of Line 1A to 1C is not as bad as a quick reading of this discussion may first cause you to believe. This is because we are using voltmeters and calibrators as examples. The sawtooth calibration specification in Line 1C is different from 1A, but a voltmeter behaves in the same way and its specifications would reveal much the same pattern so the calibrator could be used to support it at nearly the same Test Uncertainty Ratio (TUR) for all values.

The next questions to be answered are: What do the numbers in the baseline specification include? Under what conditions do these specifications apply? This is where the modifier and qualifier specifications are brought in.

Modifier Specifications

Modifier specifications change the baseline specifications. Most manufacturers include modifiers as part of the baseline specification so that one doesn't need to calculate these, though not all do this. The most important modifiers include instrument stability over time, the time interval for which the specifications are valid, and changes in specifications with changes in temperature (the ambient temperature of the instrument's operating environment rather than its internal temperature). Other secondary specifications include the effect of inductive and capacitive loading, no load versus full load operation, and any changes due to changes in line power.

Modifier specifications are important because the application may require particular aspects of performance to be detailed. Figure 31-3 shows the plot of the secondary specifications for the direct voltage output of a calibrator.

Line 3A is a plot of the basic output uncertainty stated in the manufacturer's data sheet. As previously mentioned, this is the number that is often casually quoted to describe the calibrator's performance. Line 3B is the total baseline uncertainty (*output + scale + floor*) for 24 hours, at an operating temperature of 23 ±2°C at no load. Now the effects of the modifier specifications will be added.

The Time Term

Specifications usually include a specific time period during which the instrument can be

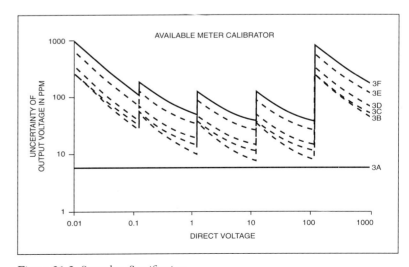

Figure 31-3. *Secondary Specifications*

expected to perform as specified. This is the calibration interval, or the measure of an instrument's ability to remain within its stated specification for a certain length of time.

Limiting this time period or calibration interval is necessary to account for the drift rate inherent in an instrument's analog circuitry. Time periods of 30, 90, 180, and 360 days are common and practical. Any calibrator can be specified to super-high performance levels at the time of calibration. Unfortunately, such levels are good for only the first few minutes following calibration. Any instrument may drift beyond realistic performance levels. If the specifications for an instrument do not state the time interval over which they are valid, a stability factor corresponding to the desired time interval will have to be added.

Some vendors specify the time term as a function of the square root of the years. Recent work at Fluke indicates that the square root of the years method of specifying an instrument may not be appropriate. Fluke experiments indicate that the long term drift of well-aged voltage and resistance standards is nearly linear with time. However there can be short term excursions from a linear regression due to the superposition of low frequency noise on the basic drift. Figure 7-13 in Chapter 7, "Direct Voltage and Current," illustrates this situation. For short periods of time, the accumulated linear drift is small in comparison to the noise excursions, so a short term, e.g. 90 days, uncertainty specification predominantly reflects the uncertainty due to low frequency noise. However, the long term, e.g. 1 year specification, includes the effects of accumulated linear drift.

The calculation of the *time* term due to calibration interval is based on the root/years' square rule. Simplified, it takes the form:

$$rys = y\sqrt{i}$$

Where:

rys = root/year specification

y = 1 year specification

i = desired calibration interval in years

As the equation suggests, an instrument's 1 year specification is published by its vendor. Specifications for other intervals are user computed by multiplying the 1 year specifications by the square root of the number of years for which they are intended to apply. For example, a period of 90 days is about 0.25 years so the square root of 0.25 (0.5) is used to multiply the 1 year specifications to obtain the 90 day specifications.

While the specifications for Fluke calibrators include variation in performance due to the passage of time, other calibrators may not be specified in the same manner. In this case the specification for their stability with time must be added as line 3C in Figure 31-3.

The Temperature Term
Equally important is performance over the specified temperature range. This range is necessary to account for the thermal coefficients in the instrument's analog circuitry. The most common ranges are centered about room temperature, 23 ±5°C. This range reflects realistic operating conditions. It should be remembered that temperature bounds must apply for the whole calibration interval. Thus a temperature range specification of 23±1°C presumes very strict long-term control of the operating environment.

Outside the specified range, a temperature coefficient (TC) is used to describe the degradation of the uncertainty specification. The temperature coefficient is an error value which must be added to an instrument's baseline specification if it is being used outside of its nominal temperature range. Look at the temperature coefficient graph shown in Figure 31-4.

The x-axis is temperature and the y-axis is uncertainty. The dashed portion of Line 4A shows the specified uncertainty for a 23±5°C temperature range common on most Fluke calibrators. Within the span of the dashed line, the uncertainty is within the specifications of 5 ppm. This is in line with a baseline specification of "±5 ppm when used at 23±5°C." This is an absolute range of 18 to 28°C. Beyond this range, the instrument's performance degrades as shown by the solid TC line. TC will usually be given in a specification footnote, and will take the form:

$$TC = x \ \text{ppm}/°C$$

where x is the amount that the performance degrades per change in degree beyond the base range specification. To calculate the uncertainty due to temperatures outside of the given specification, the temperature modifier, t_{mod}, is needed. The formula is:

$$t_{mod} \qquad = \ |TC \times \Delta t|$$

Where:

$\Delta t \qquad$ = operating temperature minus the temperature range limit

$t \qquad$ = the proposed operating temperature

range limit = the range limit that t is beyond

If one wishes to use a calibrator in an ambient temperature outside of its specified range, the effects of TC must be added to the baseline uncertainty specification when calculating the total uncertainty. The t_{mod} term is used to calculate the total specification using the general formula:

$$\text{total spec} = (\text{basic uncertainty at a specific}$$
$$\text{temp. range}) + t_{mod}$$

For example, suppose we have a calibrator whose rated uncertainty is 8 ppm @ 23±2°C. Its TC is 3 ppm/C°. To calculate the uncertainty of the calibrator for operation at 30°C:

$$t = 30$$

$$\text{range limit} = 23+2 = 25$$

$$t_{mod} = 3 \ \text{ppm} \ |30-25| = 3 \ \text{ppm} \ |5| = 15 \ \text{ppm}$$

$$\text{total spec} = 8 \ \text{ppm} + 15 \ \text{ppm} = 23 \ \text{ppm}$$

As can be seen, the specification changes dramatically when the effects of performance due to temperature are considered.

Knowing how to calculate t_{mod} will be necessary when comparing two instruments that are specified for different temperature ranges. For example, Fluke specifies most of its calibrators with a range of 23 ±5°C. However, another

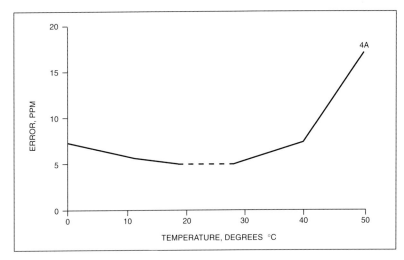

Figure 31-4. *Uncertainty Due to Temperature*

manufacturer may specify a calibrator at 23 ±1°C. To truly compare the two calibrators, one needs to put them in the same terms (23 ±5°C) using the preceding calculation.

The most modern calibrators and instruments are specified to operate in wider temperature ranges. This is because calibration instruments are no longer used only in the closely-controlled laboratory. Calibration on the production floor demands greater temperature flexibility. The preceding equation was used to characterize the degradation in performance that occurs when the calibrator is operated outside the 23 ±2°C temperature range restriction on the data sheet. The result is Line 3D in Figure 31-3.

Power Line and Output Load Terms
In the modifier example, another footnote lists an uncertainty modifier for an assumed line voltage variation of ±10% of rated uncertainty. Adding this results in Line 3E in Figure 31-3. Finally, one last footnote covers an uncertainty modifier for load regulation. This term must be included in the total uncertainty calculation because loading the calibrator is necessary for use. Adding the uncertainty for 0% to 100% load to Line 3E yields Line 3F in Figure 31-3.

The Modified Baseline Specification
Notice how the total uncertainty changes when adding terms of calibration interval, temperature, and line and load regulation. Comparing Line 3A with Line 3F reveals that the actual uncertainty under operating

conditions is 10 to 100 ppm worse than the specified 6 ppm. One must carefully review all of the specifications to assess whether an instrument will really meet the requirements. Again, the instrument must satisfy the application even at the low end of each range where the specification deteriorates.

Qualifier Specifications

The uncertainty terms that can be considered qualifier specifications rarely affect the general specifications or analog performance, but they may be important to the application. These are performance limits and operating characteristics that include emi effects, humidity, and altitude. FCC and military standards such as MIL-T-28800C cover emi emissions and some aspects of emi susceptibility, but there may still be complications. For example, emi from a nearby crt could adversely affect a precision instrument lacking adequate shielding. Compliance with safety standards such as UL, CSA, VDE, and IEC may also be important in your application. These must be kept in mind when comparing instruments.

Relative versus Total Specifications

Uncertainty specifications must also be evaluated as relative or total. Relative uncertainty does not include the additional uncertainty of the reference standards used to calibrate the instrument. For example, when a calibrator's uncertainty is specified as relative to calibration standards, this covers only the uncertainty in the calibrator. This is an incomplete statement regarding the instrument's total uncertainty. Total uncertainty includes all uncertainties in the traceability chain: the relative uncertainty of the unit, plus the uncertainty of the equipment used to calibrate it. This is the true specification of available instrument performance.

A standards laboratory can provide the uncertainties in their calibration standards. These uncertainties must be combined with the specifications relative to calibration standards to determine the performance which is actually achieved. In general, Fluke's practice is to state the more useful total specification, which assumes calibration was in accordance with the instrument operator's manual.

The Units of the Specification

Using different units also adds confusion. Output, scale, and range can be quoted in percentages or parts per million. Scale, range, and floor can also appear as digits or volts. It may be necessary to interpolate between units. The general formulas to convert from % to ppm and back are:

$$ppm = \% \times 10^4$$

$$\% = ppm / 10^4$$

Table 31-2 shows the relationship of some commonly-used ppm and % values.

Table 31-2. The Relationship of PPM to Percent

Percent	PPM
1	10,000
0.1	1,000
0.01	100
0.001	10

As is shown later, a good way to compare specifications for calibrators and DMMs is by converting all of the % and ppm terms to microvolts first. The formulas are:

$$spec_{\mu v} = spec_{ppm} \text{ (output in volts} / 10^{-6})$$

and

$$spec_{\mu v} = spec\% \text{ (output in volts} / 10^{-4})$$

Comparing Specifications: A Detailed Example

Now it's time to compare the specifications for two different models of calibrator. Tables 31-3 and 31-4 depict two typical specification tables found in the literature for modern calibrators.

Table 31-3. Calibrator A

Baseline Specification[1]	± 4 ppm of output ± 2 µV
Uncertainty of Standards	±1 ppm of value
Calibration Interval	90 days
Temperature Range	18°C to 28°C
Line Regulation	n/a
Load Regulation	n/a
Stability	n/a
Range	22V
Full Scale	21.999999V
Confidence Level	99%

[1] Baseline specifications include the uncertainty of standards, temperature coefficient for the temperature range, the effects of line and load regulation as well as stability during the calibration interval.

Table 31-4. Calibrator B

Baseline Specification[1]	± 1 ppm of output ± 0.1 ppm of full scale
Uncertainty of Standards	±1 ppm of output
Calibration Interval	24 hours
Temperature range[2]	23°C ±1°C
Line Regulation	0.1 ppm of output
Load Regulation	0.2 ppm of output
Stability	±(1.5 ppm of output + 0.05 ppm of full scale) for 90 days
Range	10V
Full Scale	19.999999V
Confidence Level	95%

[1] relative to calibration standards
[2] TC = 0.4 ppm/°C

Comparing these two calibrators requires:

- Identifying the specifications that need to be converted
- Converting applicable specifications to microvolts
- Adding the microvolt values
- Adjusting uncertainty for stated confidence interval

Take a look at the process of getting the results.

Identifying the Items to be Converted

List all of the relevant specifications for both calibrators that apply to the situation at hand. Here, it is the comparison of the total uncertainty of both calibrators at an output of 19.99999V. Table 31-5 is a result of the listing. For calibrator A, the baseline specification and the range floor are the only items to be converted to microvolts. All of the other baseline modifiers are included in the baseline specification.

Calibrator B needs several more conversions, because all of its baseline components and modifier specifications are listed individually. Along with the baseline specification and range floor, the standard uncertainty, calibration interval, line regulation, load regulation, and stability must all be converted to the appropriate terms. Calibrator B has a maximum range of 19.99999V. This is effectively 20V, so one would use that for the output value.

Also, although both calibrators have footnotes stating a TC of 0.4 ppm/°C, Calibrator A is exempt from including any temperature modifier because its specifications encompass the widest range. Calibrator B's specification will have to be modified for TC. The pre-conversion Table 31-5 is as follows:

Table 31-5. Pre-conversion Tabulation

Specification	Calibrator A	Calibrator B
Output	4 ppm of 20V	1 ppm of 20V
Floor	2 µV	0.1 ppm of 20V
Standard uncertainty	included	1 ppm of 20V
90-day Stability	included	1.5 ppm of 20V + .05ppm of 20V
TC	included	4° × .4ppm/°C × 20V
Line	included	0.1 ppm of 20V
Load	included	0.2 ppm of 20V
Confidence Level	99%	95%

Converting the Specifications

Convert the baseline specifications for both calibrators to microvolts, then add in the specifications that aren't included in the baseline specifications. This will give the total specified uncertainty for both calibrators at 20V. The results of the conversion and calculation are shown in Table 31-6.

Table 31-6. Microvolt Equivalents and Totals

Specification	Calibrator A	Calibrator B
Output	80 µV	20 µV
Floor	2 µV	2 µV
Standard uncertainty	included	20 µV
90-day Stability	included	30 µV + 1 µV
TC	included	32 µV
Line	included	2 µV
Load	included	0.0 µV
Total	82 µV	107 µV

For the benefit of the doubt, this test assumes a high-impedance DMM load. Even though Calibrator B's load uncertainty is 0.2 ppm of output, its load modifier is 0.0 µV. Low impedance loads could cause this entry to rise to 40 µV at full load current.

Applying the Confidence Interval

In this adjustment, the ratio of the desired to specified confidence interval is used to multiply the total specified uncertainty of each calibrator. This operation yields specifications that have the same confidence level. The ratios of the confidence intervals are used as multipliers because it is assumed that the specifications reflect a normal distribution of uncertainty. In other instances, the t factor is used as a multiplier. For more information on determining the confidence interval, see Chapter 20, "Introduction to Metrology Statistics."

For these purposes, it is enough to know the following:

99% confidence level = 2.58 confidence interval

95% confidence level = 1.96 confidence interval

From this, one can find that the multiplier ratios are 2.58/2.58 = 1.00 for Calibrator A, and 2.58/1.96 = 1.32 for Calibrator B.

Now each total specified uncertainty from the preceding Table 31-6 is multiplied by the multiplier ratios. Using the ratio of desired to specified interval, the specifications for Calibrators A and B are adjusted for the desired (higher) confidence level, 99%. The results are shown in Table 31-7.

Table 31-7. Results of Comparison

Calibrator	A	B
Uncertainty from Table 31-6	82 µV	107 µV
Multiplier Ratio	1.00	1.32
Final Uncertainty	82 µV	141 µV
ppm of output	4.1	7.0

In the original specification, Calibrator B appeared to be four times as accurate as Calibrator A. But with all of the additions and corrections needed to interpret Calibrator B's specifications, it turns out that Calibrator B is about 72% less accurate than Calibrator A. That is, its uncertainty is 72% greater under identical conditions.

Other Considerations

Uncertainty specifications are an important part of determining whether or not a particular calibrator will satisfy the need. There are, however, many other factors that determine which instrument is best suited for an application. Some of these are listed as follows. Refer also to Chapter 27, "Selecting New Test Equipment."

The Workload

Remember that the instrument's specification must match the workload requirements. There is a tendency for manufacturers to engage in a numbers race, with each new instrument having more and more impressive specifications, although often this has little bearing on true workload coverage.

Support Standards

The support standards will typically be three to ten times more accurate than the instruments supported. This is known as the test uncertainty ratio (TUR). Specialized instruments or those that require exotic support equipment on an infrequent basis may best be served by an outside service bureau.

Manufacturer Support

One should also consider the level of manufacturer support. Can the manufacturer provide support as calibration needs grow and vary? Do they have in-house experts who can assist with technical issues? Are training programs available? Are service facilities conveniently located? Do they have an adequate line of support products and accessories?

Reliability

Reliability is another important consideration in how useful an instrument will be. Precision electronic instruments can have a seemingly high failure rate. Any condition that causes the instrument to fall outside of its extremely tight tolerance constitutes a failure. One should ask for a Mean Time To Fail rate (MTTF) to determine when the first failure might occur. Failures upon delivery usually make this interval shorter than the Mean Time Between Failure rate (MTBF). Whichever is quoted, consider whether the number is based on actual field experience or just calculated projections.

Service Philosophy

When an instrument does fail, the manufacturer's approach to service becomes very important. A responsive service organization is essential to getting equipment back in action fast. Issues to consider include service center locations and one's proximity to them, stocking levels for spare parts and subassemblies, avail-

ability of service manuals, and service training for one's own technicians, all of which go into determining how soon equipment can be returned to service.

Reputation

Finally, the manufacturer's reputation should be assessed. Overall, how credible are its claims with respect to performance, reliability, and service? Will the company still be around five years from now? All of these issues define the true cost of owning and using a calibrator.

Key References

"Specifications," *Fluke Technical Data B0174B*

Other references for this chapter are in the Resources Appendix.

49.8mV

876mV

FLUKE®

Practical Considerations
for Metrology

Section Seven

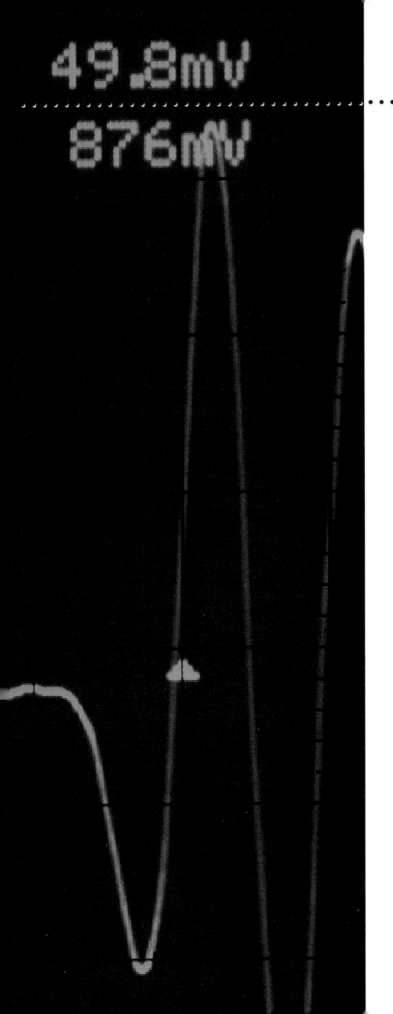

49.8mV

876mV

FLUKE®

Chapter 32:

Grounding, Shielding and Guarding

This chapter discusses the grounding, shielding and guarding of instruments. It focuses on interconnecting cables and how to use them properly to prevent unwanted currents and radiated signals from affecting the accuracy of precision measurements.

T his chapter discusses grounding, shielding, and guarding of interconnected instruments. While these are not measurement techniques, they can have a significant effect on a measurement. By following the basic do's and don'ts in these areas, hard-to-find measurement errors can be avoided. This is particularly true when several instruments and a number of different types of cable are used in precision measurements, as in a test system. There are other possible sources of error in instruments and their interconnections. These include leakage currents, thermal emfs, contact resistance, and transients. They are discussed in Chapter 33, "A Rogues' Gallery of Parasitics."

Measurement set-up schematics and block diagrams show components and circuits in ideal situations for interconnecting instruments and cables. In best-case conditions, connecting wires have no unwanted resistance or reactances; metal-to-metal contacts involve no contact resistance or thermal voltages. Ideally, the laboratory area is free of unwanted signals that can affect the measurement.

In the real world, wires do have unwanted resistance and reactances and there are unwanted signals present which affect the ability to make high quality measurements. Making precision measurements depends on control of these important but sometimes subtle factors.

While the concepts of grounding, shielding, and guarding are not difficult to grasp, the detail of their proper application can be rather complex. Although not all of the material in this chapter may be of interest to the reader with only a casual interest in precision measurement, information included in the subsections titled "Practical Hints" should be of value in common measurement situations. These hints simplify the choice and application of the various wires and cables that are available in the laboratory, and guide one around many of the pitfalls that may be encountered. This chapter will also explain the purpose and application of the various terminals, switches, and connectors labeled guard, shield, ground, and chassis.

Grounding

Ideal vs. Real Ground

An ideal ground has no resistance to current flow. The result is that there is no voltage drop between different points along the ground, regardless of the amount of current flowing. This is illustrated in Figure 32-1 which shows two loops, both of which use a common ground.

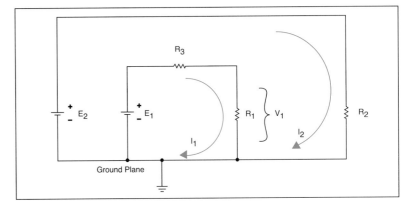

Figure 32-1. *Ideal Ground*

The loop with E_1, R_1, and R_3 is a voltage divider. The output voltage from the divider (V_1) is unaffected by the current in the other loop consisting of E_2 and R_2.

In the ideal case, the divider's output is:

$$V_1 = E_1 \frac{R_1}{R_1 + R_3}$$

In reality, ground has a finite resistance, which results in potential drop along the ground when current is flowing through it. This can cause errors in a measurement system if care is not taken to control the flow of currents. Figure 32-2 illustrates this effect.

The ideal ground is replaced with lumped equivalent resistances, r_1 and r_2. The output of the voltage divider V_1 is now affected by the current in the other loop, I_2.

In the real case, it becomes:

$$V_1 = \left(E_1 - I_2 r_1\right) \frac{R_1}{R_1 + R_3 + r_1}$$

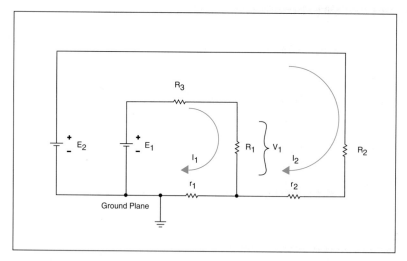

Figure 32-2. *Real Ground*

The addition of the ground resistance r_1 has changed the divider output V_1 in two ways. First, it has added resistance to the divider loop, which changes the division ratio. Secondly, current in r_1 from the second loop I_2 can now affect the value of V_1. The change in division ratio can be handled by ensuring that the value of r_1 remains constant and by changing the value of R_1 or R_3 to compensate for the addition of r_1. The error caused by I_2, which is called a ground loop error, is normally handled by changing the ground connections so that I_2 does not flow through r_1 as shown in Figure 32-3.

Instead of using a common ground for both loops, the ground return is split into two returns, one for each loop.

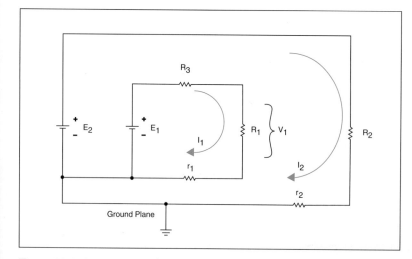

Figure 32-3. *Separate Ground Returns*

Practical Hint

- Use a separate ground return for any loop involving a precision circuit so that only the current from that loop and no other loop flows through it.

Power Line Ground Systems

A typical U.S. power mains connection to an instrument is shown in Figure 32-4.

The High and Neutral wires carry the load current, I_L, to the primary of the power transformer. A safety Ground connection is normally present. It is connected to the case or chassis of the instrument and its purpose is to carry fault current to ground through a low resistance path. Typically, the Neutral connection is grounded at the distribution point and must be isolated from the instrument case so that none of the load current flows through the safety Ground.

Safety-Ground Ground Loop Errors

In a typical laboratory environment, power mains are distributed along a bus connected to the various pieces of equipment. Figure 32-5 shows a power strip which is fed from one end and powers several instruments.

Stray leakage capacitance c_1, c_2, ..., c_n from the High side of the line to the instrument chassis, such as the capacitance in the emi filters or the capacitance in power transformers from the primary winding to the core, causes current to flow through the safety Ground and back to the distribution point. Thus there will be a voltage drop along the Ground line, due to distributed resistance r_g, and the chassis of each piece of equipment will be at a slightly different potential.

This ground current can cause a measurement error when the signal Lo lead is not isolated from ground as shown in Figure 32-6.

The current flowing in the Safety Ground lead splits along two paths. A portion flows through the signal Lo lead, creating a voltage drop that adds to the desired source signal. This drop may be of little consequence if the measuring instrument has good rejection of power line frequencies, as would be the case with a typical dc DMM. However, it may be very significant for an ac DMM.

This problem is often solved by the use of guarding, a technique that will be covered later in this chapter. However, for equipment where the low input or output is grounded, typical of rf equipment, guarding would be ineffective. Here it is important to ensure that all instruments have a common earth return, and that good quality coax cable is used to interconnect them.

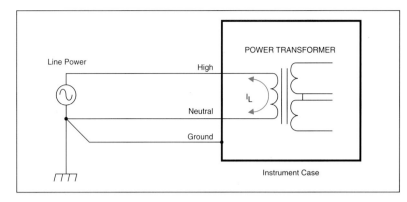

Figure 32-4. *Power Mains*

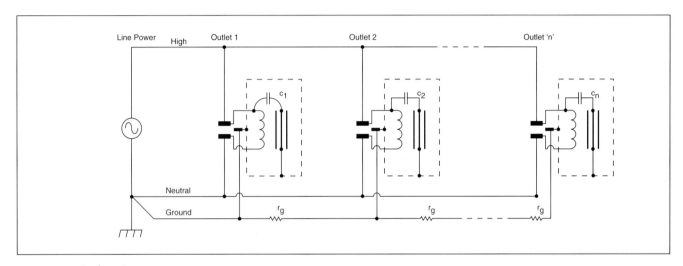

Figure 32-5. *Leakage Capacitance*

Practical Hints

- If possible, plug the power cords of the instruments into the same receptacle. This will minimize the value of r_{ground} and thus the current through r_{Lo} and l_{Lo}.

- If possible, remove the equipment that is putting a lot of current into the Safety Ground and plug it into another branch circuit.

- Keep signal interconnections as short as possible with low resistance cable to reduce resistive and reactive impedances. Coaxial cable is often the best choice, particularly for rf signals.

- Never operate equipment with the connection between chassis ground and power-line ground unconnected. This undesirable situation occurs when using a three-to-two wire

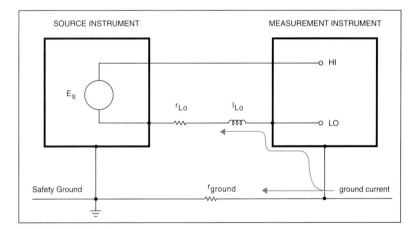

Figure 32-6. *Ground Loop*

adapter (cheater plug). This defeats a prime element of protection against electric shock.

- It is possible for some of the signal current to flow through the safety ground and thus create a ground loop that causes an error in the measurement. Figure 32-7 shows such a situation where the measurement error can be substantial.

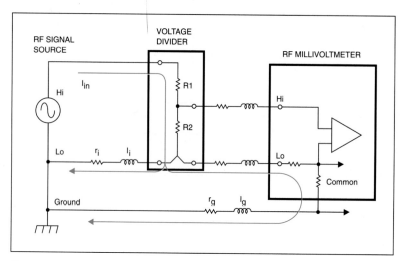

Figure 32-7. *RF Ground Loop*

Here, an rf signal source is connected to the input of a voltage divider with the output going to the input of an rf millivoltmeter. The divider input current, I_{in}, splits at the bottom of the divider and some of it returns to the source through the output cable to the meter Lo lead and the Safety Ground. This current causes a voltage drop in the Lo lead due to the resistance and inductance of the output cable and leads in the meter. This voltage drop adds to the signal from the divider, causing an error in the measurement.

The solution to this problem is to reduce the magnitude and effect of the unwanted ground current by keeping cables short and adding chokes (high impedances) in the unwanted current paths.

■ Decrease the value of r_i and l_i in Figure 32-7 by making the cable from the source to the divider input as short as possible.

■ Place a common-mode choke, T_1, on the output of the divider. See Figure 32-8. The unlabeled components in Figure 32-7 and Figure 32-8 represent other parasitics not discussed here.

The two windings are closely coupled so that their effect on the divider's output current is negligible; but to the ground loop current, it presents a large inductive reactance which substantially reduces the loop current (and thus the error). Such a choke is commonly built by wrapping several inches of the output cable around a ferrite core.

■ Put a common-mode choke in the power cord of the meter. This will work if the ground loop current is mostly through the safety ground and not through some other ground path. Such a choke can be made by wrapping some of the power cord around a ferrite core. Another approach would be to put an inductor in just the safety lead.

Information on designing a ground system for a standards laboratory can be found in Chapter 25, "The Laboratory Environment."

Shielding

Electromagnetic radiation can adversely affect electronic equipment. It can come from many sources, such as power transmission lines, fluorescent lights, electric motors, crt's, communications equipment, cellular phones, high-speed digital logic in computers, transmitters, and many other types of electrical and electronic equipment.

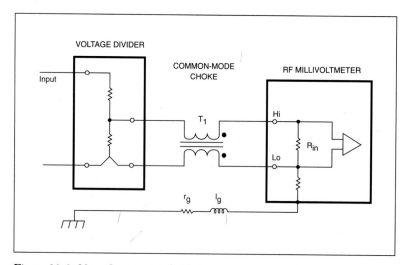

Figure 32-8. *Using Common-Mode Choke*

Electromagnetic Radiation

Electromagnetic radiation is composed of time-varying electric and magnetic fields. These fields will occur in varied relative strengths. Higher voltage, lower current circuits tend to radiate mostly E (electric) fields; lower voltage, higher current circuits will tend to have the H (magnetic) fields dominate in lower voltage, higher current circuits.

Shielding from Electric Fields

Common sources of interfering signals, often called noise, which are predominantly E-field in nature are: fluorescent lights, power lines, crt's, and high-speed digital logic. The simplest model of electric field interference treats the noise generator as a voltage source capacitively coupled into the circuit of interest. Figure 32-9 shows an interfering signal coupled into the input of an ac voltmeter.

The stray capacitance, c_s, causes a current to flow through the input impedance of the meter and the output impedance of the source. This causes an error in the measurement.

In a typical situation involving fluorescent lights, the source voltage is several hundred volts at power line frequency, and the stray capacitance is on the order of picofarads. Depending on the output impedance of the source and the voltage level being measured, the error in the measurement can range from negligible to substantial. It is worst when the source impedance is high and the measurement voltage level is low.

Another common situation involves the presence of digital logic clock signals in close proximity to measurement circuitry. The source of this noise can be a computer, a cable carrying logic signals, or the logic section of another instrument not adequately shielded. Though rather small in amplitude, typically 5 volts peak-to-peak, a clock signal usually consists of a square wave with a rise time of a few nanoseconds, and an operating frequency ranging from 2 MHz to 100 MHz. This can cause large amounts of interference, and therefore errors, due to the high frequency components of the signal.

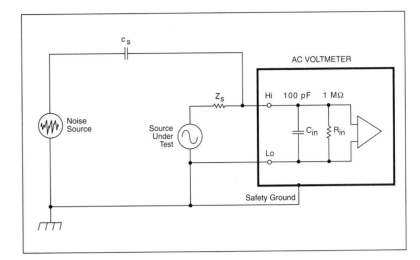

Figure 32-9. *Electric Field Interference*

Reducing the error due to capacitive coupling is best done by a Faraday shield. This shield normally consists of a piece of grounded metal placed between the noise source and the sensitive circuit. Figure 32-10 shows an equivalent circuit using such a shield.

c_{12} is the capacitance from the noise source to the shield; c_{23} is the capacitance from the shield to the sensitive circuit, meter input; and c_{13} is the capacitance through the shield (feed-through capacitance) between the noise source and the sensitive circuit. The value of c_{13} will be several orders of magnitude smaller than the original stray capacitance c_s.

A Faraday shield should completely enclose the circuit with no breaks in it anywhere. Also,

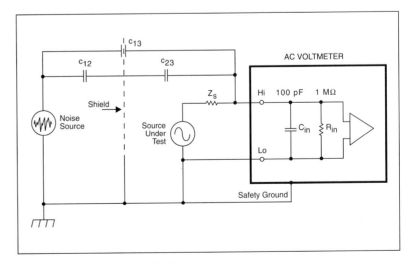

Figure 32-10. *Electric Field Shielding*

because current flows through the shield and back to the source, the shield should be constructed of low resistance material. Otherwise, the current flowing through c_{12} causes a voltage drop along the length of the shield. As a result, current flows through c_{23} into the sensitive circuit at node ①. See Figure 32-11.

Another requirement is that there not be the potential difference $E_{ground2}$ between the shield ground and the circuit ground. If there is, more current will flow through c_{23} into the sensitive circuit. The solution to this problem is to connect the shield to the measurement ground at node ② instead of node ③.

Practical Hint

- Local shielding usually produces the best results. The most complete shielding between a noise source and a sensitive circuit will be achieved if both source and circuit are separately shielded using a tight shield, and each shield is connected to its local ground. See Figure 32-12.

This solution, when generalized, can be applied to both large systems and to instrument design. In the layout of a laboratory, it is common practice to run the power mains wiring through grounded metal conduit, and to use fluorescent fixtures with grounded metal enclosures.

To produce a very quiet electrical environment, fine mesh shielding is used over the opening of such fixtures. In an instrument such as a precision calibrator or DMM, it is common to shield primary power circuits with chassis (power line) ground, to shield digital circuits with the digital supply common, and to use local shielding for sensitive analog circuits.

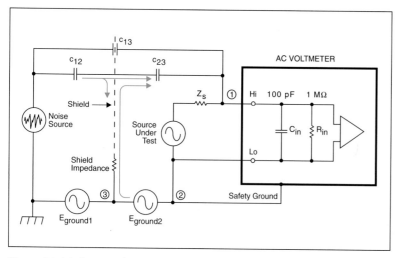

Figure 32-11. *Sources of Error*

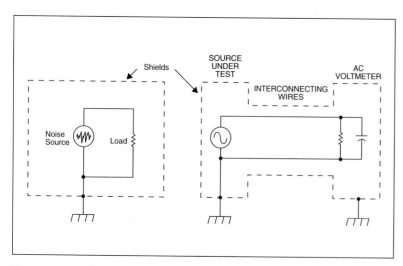

Figure 32-12. *Shielding Sensitive Circuit from Noise*

Magnetic Field Coupling

Some sources of unwanted signals radiate a predominantly magnetic field. Examples of these are motors, power transformers, crt's, and instrument displays. Whenever a sensitive circuit is near a transformer or a circuit with high peak current, there is the possibility of coupling with magnetic fields which can cause a measurement or source error.

For example, a transformer can induce unwanted ac noise into low-level circuitry, whether the circuitry is local or is in a neighboring instrument. Such noise can overload sensitive, narrow-bandwidth dc circuitry. Calibrations performed at power line frequencies may be subject to *beat signals*, where interference from line voltage sources will mix with the signal being measured. Depending on the phase of the two signals, they could effectively double or cancel the signal of interest. Effective use of magnetic shielding, and separation between the error source and the affected circuit, will reduce or eliminate such interference.

A common source of magnetic interference is a transformer with loose coupling between its primary and secondary. In most cases, the interfering signal is induced (picked up) in a loop of circuitry that intercepts a time-varying magnetic field. Figure 32-13 shows magnetic pickup by a loop formed by the wires connecting a source being measured to an ac voltmeter.

The induced current flows through the meter input to cause an error in the measurement. The magnitude of the current is proportional to the magnetic flux density and the loop inductance.

Minimizing Magnetic Pickup

There are two basic approaches to reducing magnetic pickup: reducing the area of the pickup loop, and reducing the magnetic field intensity.

During the design of a precision instrument, it is necessary to consider the enclosed area of low-level, sensitive loops. Careful routing of lands on a printed circuit board can significantly reduce susceptibility to magnetic coupling. Lands that run side by side, or on adjacent sides of the printed circuit board, present a small loop area. Flux density drops off very rapidly with distance from the source, so placing the power transformer and other sources of interference as far as possible from sensitive circuits can substantially reduce pickup. Sometimes the rotation of a transformer will reduce pickup, because pickup is limited to fields that are perpendicular to the loop. Care should be taken when stacking instruments so that the source of magnetic interference in one instrument is not placed close to a sensitive circuit in another instrument. Some types of electronic equipment emit so much magnetic interference that they can't be used near high accuracy meters or sources.

When using test leads, the best method of minimizing magnetic pickup is to twist the leads together. This not only minimizes the area of the loop formed between the leads; it also places the fluxes in direct opposition, and they become mutually canceling. Another way to interconnect instruments is to use coaxial cable (coax). It provides rejection of unwanted

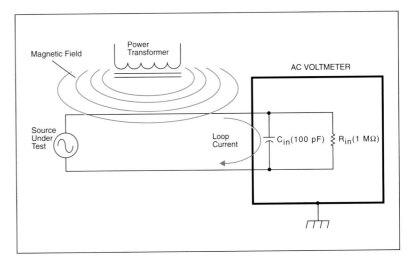

Figure 32-13. *Magnetic Field Pickup*

pickup from both magnetic and electric fields because the center conductor is completely enclosed by the outside shield.

Practical Hints

- Use twisted pairs rather than separate test leads where possible to reduce magnetic pickup and minimize series inductance.

- Use coaxial cables to reduce both magnetic and electrostatic pickup.

  The rejection of interfering fields by coax is related to both the frequency of the interference and the degree of coverage of the outer conductor. Most coax is constructed using a fine-wire braid as the outer conductor. Depending on how tightly this braid is woven, there can be small gaps that reduce its effectiveness at rejecting unwanted radiation or coupling. Coax available on the commercial market varies from 80% to 98% in its coverage. Some coaxial cables use foil shield instead of braid to increase coverage to 100%.

Magnetic Shielding

With properly designed shielding, it is possible to attenuate magnetic interference either at the source or at the point of interference. The primary difference is that the field strength is much higher at the source. Saturation of magnetic materials must be considered. Shielding is achieved with iron as well as iron alloys, and also through the use of high-conductivity materials such as copper or aluminum. Alternating layers of copper and high-nickel magnetic alloy are used for the best shielding.

Iron and its alloys attenuate magnetic interference by concentrating lines of magnetic flux. A common sheet metal steel box, 0.060-inch thick, will have limited effect at power-line frequencies and attenuate magnetic radiation only 3 to 6 dB. By contrast, an 80% nickel alloy, properly annealed and handled with care, can reduce magnetic field strength up to 35 dB.

Practical Hint

- The best material for magnetic shielding is an alloy of nickel and iron known as *Mu-Metal*.

Guarding

From the material covered so far, you can see that one of the biggest measurement problems in interconnecting two or more instruments is keeping extraneous signals out of the interconnecting cables. Ground loops, described previously, are a common cause of such errors.

A related case occurs when the voltage to be measured is elevated (floating) with respect to ground or some other reference point by another voltage, as illustrated in Figure 32-14.

The signal being measured is called the *normal mode* signal. The signal it is floating on is called the *common mode* signal. In fact, the situation shown in Figure 32-6 can be thought of as generating a normal mode signal, floating on a common mode signal, caused by the voltage drop in r_{Lo} due to ground current.

In either case, if the source output Lo and meter input Lo terminals are connected to ground, a current flows through the Lo lead, causing an error in the measurement. Floating the meter Lo above ground will reduce the current flow but not entirely eliminate it, because some current can still flow through the impedance between Lo and ground (z_1). This problem can be solved through the use of guarding.

Instrument Guard

An instrument guard is a Faraday or electric field shield that encloses the analog circuitry of a meter or source and is electrically isolated from the instrument case and ground. In addition to being an electric field shield, it also provides a path to ground for common-mode generated currents so they do not cause an error in the measurement (see Figure 32-15).

The ground loop current now flows through the lead to the guard and then through z_2 to ground instead of through the signal Lo lead.

Figure 32-16 shows an equivalent circuit along with typical values for the various components.

The voltage drop in the guard resistance (r_2) due to current from the 10V common-mode source appears across the Lo lead resistance r_1 and c_1. As a result, a little current does flow through the Lo lead, but its effect is insignificant: the drop is less than 1 nV at 1 kHz. The drop across the guard lead resistance r_2 will also cause some current to flow through c_3 into the meter Hi input. At 60 Hz this is insignificant; at 1 kHz the error would be a few microvolts. Using a guard in this example reduces the errors caused by the common-mode source by a factor of 10,000 (80 db), compared to that seen with a meter without a guard as shown in the preceding Figure 32-14.

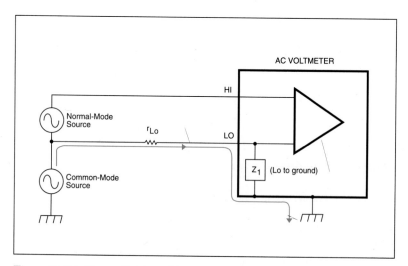

Figure 32-14. *Meter with Elevated Input*

Note that the guard will act as an electric field shield if it is connected to the Lo, either at the meter or at the source, but it will only reduce the error due to ground loop current if it is connected to the Lo at the source.

Practical Hint

- A measurement instrument's guard can be used to reduce common mode errors, as well as provide electric field shielding. It should be connected to Lo at the source terminals.

High-Impedance Measurements

For high-impedance measurements, an instrument guard can be used to reduce the measurement load on a sensitive node to which the Lo lead of a meter is connected. This is done by driving the guard from a low impedance source carrying the same potential as the input Lo. Driving the guard in this manner is known as *active guarding*. Consider the case of using a voltmeter as a null detector to measure the imbalance of a wheatstone bridge, as shown in Figure 32-17.

If an unguarded meter were used, any leakage resistance from the meter Lo to ground would be in parallel with a leg of the bridge, causing a measurement error. If a guarded meter is used and the guard is tied to input Lo (the normal procedure), any leakage resistance from guard to ground would cause an error.

The solution to this problem is to drive the guard with a guard amplifier. This is an amplifier whose gain is unity and whose input is connected to the circuit at the point where the meter Lo connects. Its input impedance is very high, so it doesn't load the circuit; its output connects to the instrument guard. It maintains the guard at the same potential as the Lo; thus no current flows in the Lo lead due to leakage resistance between Lo and guard. Current does flow in the guard lead due to guard-to-ground leakage, but this current is supplied by the amplifier.

An alternative to the guard amplifier is to use a low impedance divider across the bridge source. The output of the divider should be adjusted so that its voltage is equal to that of the bridge

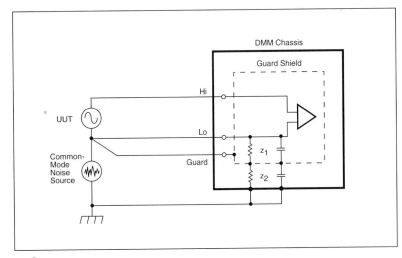

Figure 32-15. *Guarded Meter*

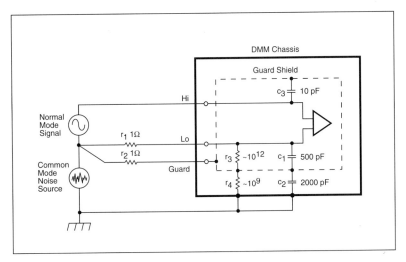

Figure 32-16. *Guarded Meter Parasitics*

centers. This divider output should then be connected to the meter Guard terminal.

Coax Test Leads
In Figure 32-15, input Hi, input Lo, and Guard are shown schematically as separate wires. But the earlier analysis of shielding shows that this would make these inputs susceptible to both electric and magnetic field pickup. A better solution is to use the hook-up of Figure 32-18.

This hook-up uses coaxial cables for both Hi and Lo input leads, with the cable shields connected to Guard. The coax shields provide the required electric field shielding and a connection for the Guard. The hookup also provides adequate rejection of magnetic pickup, when the two pieces of coax are tied together along their length. Coax is constructed with very

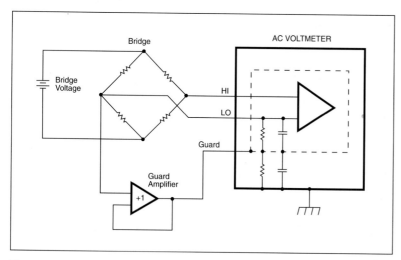

***Figure 32-17.** Using Guard Amplifier*

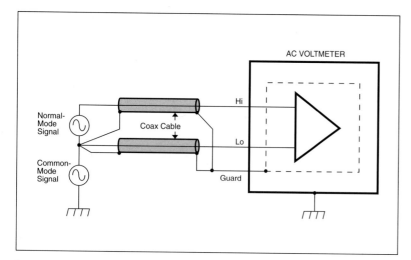

***Figure 32-18.** Using Coax Cable for Interconnections*

good insulating materials and can therefore handle high voltages. There are types that have low per-foot capacitance values (capacitance between the center and outer conductors). Be sure that the coax selected uses a copper inner conductor. Some small-diameter types use copper-covered steel, which results in excessive thermal emf at their connection terminals.

Triax Test Leads

In situations where better magnetic rejection is required, triax can be used instead of parallel coax. Triaxial cable (triax) is like coax but has a second shield over, and insulated from, the first. This is not to be confused with double-shielded coax, which has two shields in contact with each other (two shields providing better coverage than one). In triax, the outer shield is connected to the Guard, the inner shield to

the input Lo, and the center conductor to the input Hi. Triax has all the previously mentioned advantages of coax, but it has the disadvantages of being large in diameter and difficult to terminate the shields to the instruments, so twinax is generally used instead.

Twinax Test Leads

Twinax consists of two insulated wires which are twisted and covered with a braid or foil shield. The input Hi is connected to one wire, the input Lo to the other, and the shield to the Guard, as shown in Figure 32-19.

The twisted wires provide excellent rejection of magnetic pickup and the shield provides electric field shielding and a connection for the Guard. In situations where there is a high intensity rf field present, such as from a nearby broadcast station transmitter or cellular phone, a second shield can be used that is insulated from the first (shown as dotted lines in Figure 32-19). This shield should cover all exposed leads and have a low impedance connection to ground at both ends.

Models of twinax are available that handle high voltage and use excellent insulating materials. Most use copper conductors and a foil shield with a drain wire for easy connection. Connected as shown in Figure 32-19, twinax tends to have higher per-foot capacitance than does coax. Overall, twinax is the best type of cable to use for dc and low frequency ac measurements.

Guarding Current Sources

Under certain conditions, the connection of a precision current source to an external load may require the use of a driven guard to minimize errors. An ideal current source has an infinite output impedance. Regardless of load impedance, the current through the load will be constant. However, capacitance and leakage resistance from Hi to Lo in the interconnecting path can shunt some of the current around the load, resulting in an error in measuring or sourcing the current as shown in Figure 32-20.

The error is in proportion to the load resistance and the square of the frequency, and can reach a significant value both on the 100 μA range of ac calibrators and the highest ohmmeter MΩ or conductance nanoSiemans (nS) ranges. As a result, precision current calibrators provide a current guard, and precision ohmmeters provide an ohms guard.

To understand how such a guard works and is connected, refer to Figure 32-21.

The Current Guard is driven by an amplifier with a gain of unity and whose input is connected to the Hi Out of the current source. Its input impedance is high so that it does not load the current source, and its output connects to a shield around the Hi Out. It maintains the shield at the same potential as the Hi Out so none of the current from the Current Guard is lost due to cable capacitance or leakage resistance. The Current Guard supplies any leakage current due to either capacitance or leakage resistance from the shield to Lo Out.

When a current output is guarded in this fashion, the Lo lead is typically connected with a separate wire. (For minimum magnetic pickup, triaxial cable can be used.) Then the Hi Out is connected to the center lead, the Current Guard to the middle shield, and the Lo Out to the outer shield. This approach is limited by the relatively high shield-to-shield capacitance which loads the Current Guard output; this typically causes increased phase shift at higher frequencies and reduces its effectiveness.

A compromise that has been found to be adequate in all but the noisiest of environments is the use of conventional coax for high and guard connections. A separate insulated return wire is wrapped around the coax. This reduces the susceptibility to magnetic pickup with a smaller capacitive load on the guard amplifier.

Practical Hint

■ Low level, high frequency current measurements are subject to large errors caused by leakage impedances. These errors can be reduced by the use of an active guard (provided by the meter or source) connected to a shield around the Hi lead.

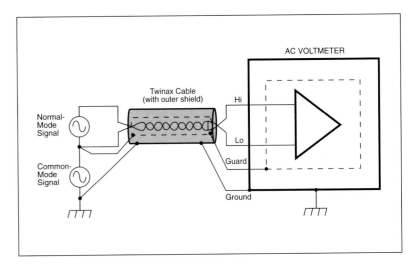

Figure 32-19. *Using Twinax for Interconnections*

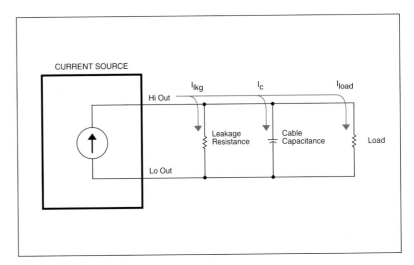

Figure 32-20. *Error in Sourcing Circuit*

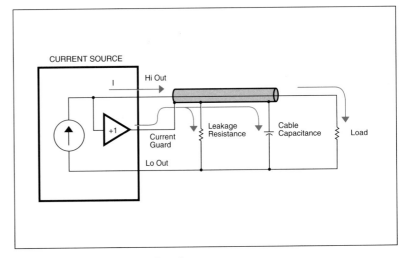

Figure 32-21. *Using Current Guard*

Interconnecting Guarded Instruments

A common operation in the calibration laboratory is the calibration of a DMM with a precision single-function or multifunction calibrator. It is common for both the calibrator and DMM to have a guard. One or both may also have a ground terminal.

The guard will sometimes be labeled V-GUARD, for voltage guard, to differentiate it from the current guard, which may be labeled I-GUARD. Also, the ground is sometimes labeled CHASSIS and may only be available on the rear panel.

Voltage Measurements

Figure 32-22 shows the proper method for interconnecting a calibrator with a DMM. The calibrator's Hi Out, Lo Out, Guard and Ground connect to the DMM's Hi In, Lo In, Guard and Ground, respectively. It is important that the Guard be connected to one of the Lo terminals, usually Lo Out, at the calibrator. Some instruments with guards have a built-in switch that makes this connection; others use a shorting link between the Lo and Guard terminals. Figure 32-2 illustrates the recommended practice of connecting the Lo to Guard at the calibrator but not at the DMM. It is also a good idea to connect the Lo and Guard to Ground. This should be done at only one point (usually at the source). Making this connection will greatly reduce any common mode signal between Lo and Ground, which could cause an error in the measurement.

Beware of confusing the label Grd with ground. Grd means guard. Chassis or Ground mean ground.

Practical Hints

- For dc and low frequency ac, use twinax to connect the source and meter. Hi and Lo are connected with the twisted pairs, and the meter Guard is connected to the shield. The source end of the shield is connected to the Lo Out. If the twinax has a separate outer shield, it should be connected to chassis Ground.

- If you need to minimize capacitance, it may be more appropriate to use two separate pieces of coax. The inner conductors will be used for the signals and the shield will be used to interconnect the meter Guard and Lo Out.

- Sometimes the use of the guard is not required for a measurement, so a simpler interconnection can be made as shown in Figure 32-23.

  Here, the Hi Out and Lo Out are connected to the Hi In and Lo In using coax. At each instrument, the Guard is connected to Lo and the connection to Ground is made only at the calibrator.

- Never leave the Guard-to-Lo connection on an instrument open; always have this connection made somewhere in the system. If the Guard is left floating (unconnected), measurement errors can occur, or the DMM may rise to a hazardous voltage potential.

Resistance Measurements

Methods of interconnecting a guarded resistance calibrator to an ohmmeter depend on whether a two-wire or four-wire connection is being made. Low accuracy meters normally have two input terminals for resistance and no Guard. This type of meter is connected to a calibrator using a two-wire connection. It is not normally required to use the Guard because of the low accuracy involved. The Guard can be connected to the Lo Out at the calibrator and the connection made with coax, like that shown in Figure 32-23. Precision ohmmeters have four input terminals for resistance

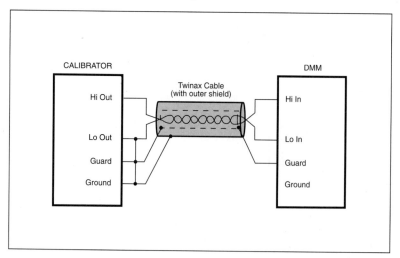

Figure 32-22. Guarded DMM-to-Calibrator Connection

measurement plus a guard. Two of the terminals are connected to an internal current Source and the other two to a voltage measuring circuit. Connecting this type of meter to a calibrator requires a four-wire connection. This can be done, as shown in Figure 32-24, by using two twinax cables, one for the current and one for the voltage.

The Guard is connected to both shields at both ends, but the Lo-to-Guard-to-Ground connection is only made at the calibrator. If the ohm-meter also has an Ohms Guard, it should be connected to a shield around the current Hi lead, as described in the earlier section "Guarding Current Sources."

Practical Hint

■ Four-wire resistance measurements should be made using two twinax cables. One is used for the current source and the other for voltage measurement. Both shields will be connected to the meter's Guard and the source's Guard. The Guard should be grounded at the source.

Frequency Limitations

The application of instrument Guards is subject to some important limitations. Guarding is usually found on dc V and low-frequency ac V instruments for the intended purpose of eliminating measurement errors due to common-mode signals. Most guarding schemes work well at power line frequencies and up through audio frequencies. But above 100 kHz, using the Guard does not always lead to predictable results. The distributed reactance of the Guard shield can introduce errors that would not be present at lower frequencies. For this reason, it may be better not to use the Guard but to use coax instead, as is normally done at rf frequencies. In fact, some instruments disconnect internal Guards above a given frequency, so that the Guard acts more as a grounded shield at the higher frequencies.

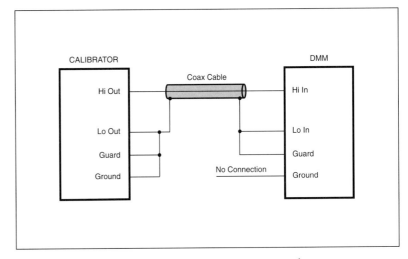

Figure 32-23. *Interconnection When Guarding is Not Required*

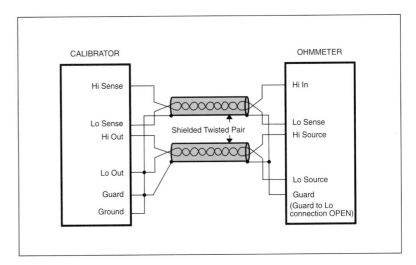

Figure 32-24. *Guarded, Shielded 4-Wire Resistance Interconnection*

Practical Hint

■ In general, guarding is ineffective above 100 kHz. Above 100 kHz, one should adhere to good rf practices, such as using coax. However, for non-50Ω systems, one should be aware of the capacitive loading effects of coaxial cables.

Key References

Morrison, Ralph, *Grounding and Shielding Techniques in Instrumentation*, 2nd Edition, John Wiley and Sons, Inc., 1977

Other references for this chapter are in the Resources Appendix.

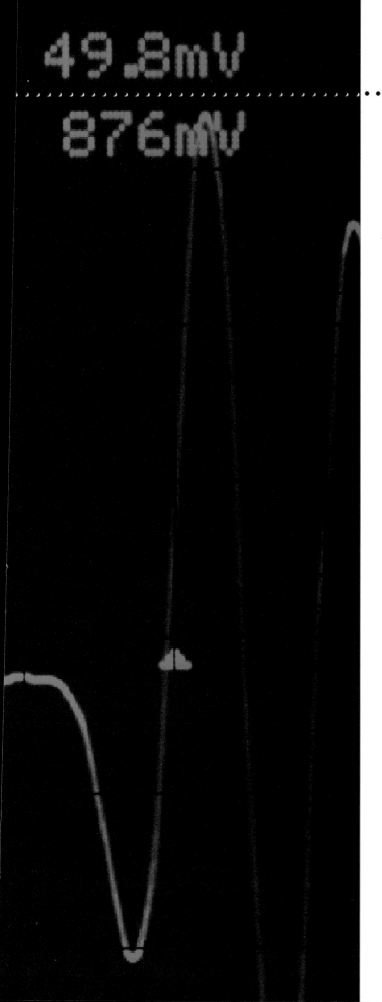

FLUKE®

Chapter 33:
A Rogues' Gallery of Parasitics

This chapter describes parasitic effects that contaminate analog signal processing in precision circuits, and presents some necessary precautions and remedies.

This chapter provides anecdotal examples of the effects of stray voltages, currents, resistances, capacitances, and inductances taken from real-life experiences over the years. It is hoped that they will provoke thoughts about secondary effects on measurements, and will help the reader solve a measurement problem, or structure an experiment more carefully.

Thermal EMFs

Thermal gradients across dissimilar metals, in contact with each other, generate a thermal voltage. This is called the *Seebeck Effect*. Typical points of contact of dissimilar metals include: test lead/calibrator connections, and test lead/UUT connections. See Figure 33-1.

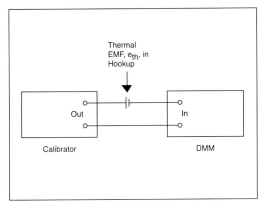

Figure 33-1. *Thermal EMFs*

Thermal emf's are symbolized by e_{th}. Typical magnitudes of thermal emf are from one to a few microvolts per °C. With the connection shown in Figure 33-1, the DMM reading is in error by at least the magnitude of e_{th}, which adds or subtracts from the true measured value.

Gold-flashed spade lugs cinched tightly under gold-flashed or copper 5-way binding posts provide one method of reducing thermal emf's. Pomona 1756-24 is an example of this kind of test lead.

Tellurium copper banana plugs in tellurium copper receptacles also make low-thermal emf connections. Fluke 5440-7002 Low Thermal Cable Set, used in conjunction with the Fluke

5100B, 5130A, 5440B, 5700A, 732A, 732B, 742A, and 792A binding posts, satisfies this requirement.

Nickel-plated banana plugs are likely to cause higher than desired thermal emf's. Their use should be avoided when accuracy in the microvolt region is desired.

Coin silver, tellurium copper, or gold-flashed contacts are adequate for mechanical switches. Typically, these all have thermal emf's of less than a microvolt.

In some differential measurements using bridges, thermal emf's in the null detector circuit can be compensated for by employing low thermal emf reversing switches in the bridge energizing circuit as shown in Figure 33-2.

In Figure 33-2, the dc voltage is obtained from a battery operated source and should be isolated from power line ground.

Two measurements are taken, first with the switch in the forward position and then reversed. In each measurement, the Kelvin-Varley divider is adjusted to obtain a null on the null detector. Let its setting, S, at these two nulls be S_1 and S_2. The average value of S_1 and S_2 is S_A. R_X is computed as:

$$R_x = \frac{R_{std} S_A}{1 - S_A}$$

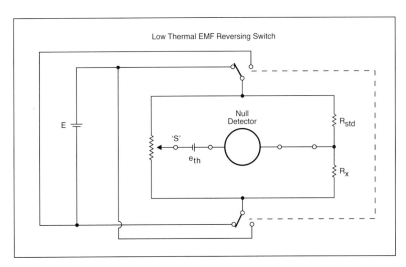

Figure 33-2. *Low EMF Reversing Switch*

Mechanical relays' contacts can conduct the heat generated by the nearby relay coils, causing thermal emfs. Latching relays, with coin silver contacts, have low-thermal emf connections and are recommended for low-level measurements where thermal emf's can have adverse effects on the measurement.

Contact Resistance

Contact resistance, shown in Figure 33-3, as $r_{contact}$ occurs when two conductors come into physical contact.

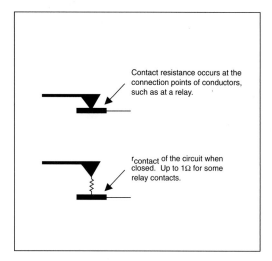

Figure 33-3. *Contact Resistance*

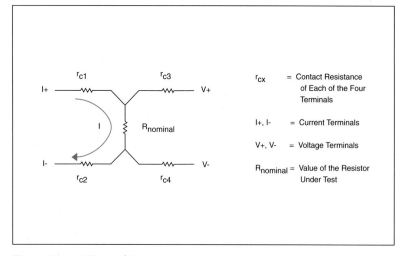

Figure 33-4. *4-Terminal Resistance*

Contact resistance acts as a pure resistance, associated with:

■ test lead/calibrator connection
■ test lead/UUT connection
■ rotary or pushbutton switch contacts
■ relay contacts

The magnitude of contact resistance is typically from a few tenths of a milliohm in a coin silver mechanical switch up to about 1Ω for a mechanical relay. Tightly-cinched spade lug connections also have a few tenths of a milliohm of contact resistance; banana plug connections can range from a few milliohms to a few tenths of an ohm.

Contact resistance acts in series with other resistances in the circuit and can cause errors such as increasing the resistance measured by a 2-terminal ohmmeter. This problem can be greatly reduced by using a 4-terminal connection that separates the voltage and current ports of the resistor. See Figure 33-4.

The current flows through the resistor from $I+$ to $I-$. The current source must be able to provide a compliance voltage, V_c, that is equal to:

$$V_c = I\left(r_{c1} + R_{nom} + r_{c2}\right)$$

The voltage across R_{nom} is proportional to the current through it. This voltage is measured by an instrument with a high input resistance R_{in}. When R_{in} is very high with respect to R_{nom}, r_{c3}, and r_{c4}, the voltage that the instrument responds to, E_{in}, is approximately:

$$V_{in} = I R_{nom} \frac{R_{in}}{r_{c3} + R_{in} + r_{c4}}$$

Two 4-terminal resistors can be connected in series as in Figure 33-5 to create a 4-terminal voltage divider.

In this case, the two voltage drops, V_1 and V_2, are measured separately by a high input resistance device such as a DMM.

It must be noted that contact resistance can be present in the sense (Hi) connection of a calibrator and will cause errors. For example, 2Ω of contact resistance in the sense leads of a dc calibrator with a 1 MΩ sense circuit will cause a

2 ppm error. This problem is alleviated by means of the sense-current cancellation techniques discussed in Chapter 15, "Multifunction Calibrators."

Dielectric films on relay and mechanical switch contacts can cause what is sometimes called *dry* contact resistance. The term dry refers to a contact that has negligible current flowing through it, for example, the potentiometric contacts in the 4-terminal measurements previously mentioned. The wiping action of the mechanical switch is intended to remove this film. Similarly, the contacting action of the relay is also supposed to wipe the film away. The relays used in Fluke calibrators use cross-bar contacts in such a way that the cutting edge of the two bars wipe against each other to remove any dielectric film.

A dry contact with dielectric film can be electrically open even though it is mechanically closed. A typical symptom of dielectric film in dry switch contacts is "floating" DMM readings. The bias current, discussed later, from the DMM is charging its input capacitance. The input capacitance is not shunted by the source resistance of the circuit under test due to the essentially open connection through the dry contact with the dielectric film on it.

In many instances the problem can be corrected by resetting the switch a time or two. If the problem persists, the instrument should be repaired.

Insulation Resistance

Insulation resistance acts like a real resistance between conductors that are supposed to be isolated from each other by the insulation. Insulation resistance acts in parallel with any discrete resistance connected between the conductors. It can also serve as a conduction path for small currents. Figure 33-6 depicts two hookup wires coming from the Hi and Lo sides of a source of emf, V. The insulation around the wires is represented by the shading around each conductor.

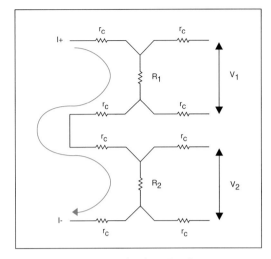

Figure 33-5. *4-Terminal Voltage Divider*

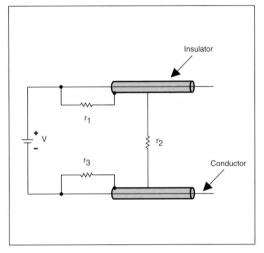

Figure 33-6. *Insulation Resistance*

Insulation resistance between the inner and outer surfaces of the insulation surrounding the wires is symbolized by r_1 and r_3. The insulation resistance between the two wires is symbolized by r_2.

Insulation resistance typically ranges from $10^{10}\,\Omega$ to $10^{13}\,\Omega$, depending on the material used for the insulator. Teflon and diaphthyalate provide the higher value, while various plastics tend toward the lower value.

A DMM often has an input impedance of 10,000 MΩ on its lowest direct voltage ranges. This impedance can be considered the aggregate insulation resistance associated with all of its input components.

If the DMM is placed across the 10:1 output of a Fluke 752A voltage divider, as in Figure 33-7, the loading effects of its insulation resistance, $r_{insulation}$, can add up to 0.4 ppm error above the 0.2 ppm specified uncertainty for the 752A's 10:1 division range. Bias currents can cause similar effects.

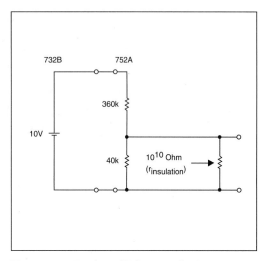

Figure 33-7. *Loading of Voltage Divider Output*

In another instance, up to $10^{12}\Omega$ of insulation resistance connected to the 1000V supply of a differential voltmeter can allow 10^{-9}A of current to flow into the 25 kΩ mid-scale output resistance of its Kelvin-Varley divider. See Figure 33-8. The mid-scale output resistance of the K-V divider is about 25 kΩ, as measured from Common to the K-V's output tap with 'S' = 0.5. It equals half of the divider's 100 kΩ resistance that goes to Common from the tap

in parallel with the other half of the divider's resistance that goes to Common through the 1.01 kΩ resistor.

In the preceding figure, V = 1000V. If S is set to 0.5V on the Kelvin-Varley's 1.0V range, this current multiplied by 25 KΩ will have a 25 mV voltage drop, introducing an error of 50 ppm.

Using insulation materials with high-quality dielectrics provides a way of reducing the loading effects of insulation resistance when attempting to measure voltages from high impedance sources. Teflon-insulated hookup wires have very high insulation resistances and are used for this purpose in many of the Fluke differential voltmeters.

Another technique is to use coaxial cable to guard the key conductors. The guard should be connected to direct voltages taken from low impedance sources (Figure 33-9).

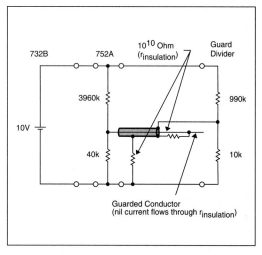

Figure 33-9. *Guarded Insulation Resistance*

The voltage of the sources should be nearly equal, ±1% as a rule of thumb, to the voltage taken from the high impedance source. With equal source voltages, the voltage drop across the insulation resistance is nearly zero, so practically no current flows in it to load the divider.

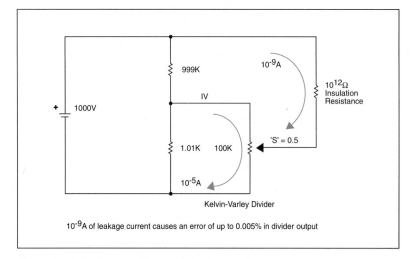

Figure 33-8. *Leakage into Output of Divider*

Surface Leakage

Surface leakage is a current that flows on the outside of an insulator whose surface has been physically contaminated with a conductive substance. The contaminant can be either organic or inorganic in nature. For example, sweaty fingers can put a fine layer of grease and salt on the insulator, shunting it and causing it to carry the leakage current.

Surface leakage is indicated whenever the output of a high resistance voltage divider is erratic or non-linear with the input. A two-stage cleaning process will remove the contaminant. In the first stage an organic cleaner is applied, followed by the application of an inorganic cleaner in the second stage.

Dielectric Absorption

Dielectric absorption is the tendency of certain dielectrics to hold a charge after an electric field has been removed. See Figure 33-10.

In the preceding figure, a virtual capacitor, "Virtual c," is located inside a real capacitor. The insulation resistance of the capacitor's dielectric connects the plates of the virtual and real capacitors. It should be kept in mind that a capacitor can be any two conductors, including hookup wires separated by insulators.

When the capacitor in the sketch is charged, the charge is on its real plates and on the plates of the virtual capacitor within its dielectric. When the real plates are shorted together, they discharge. However, if the short circuit is promptly removed, the virtual capacitor discharges through the insulation resistance of the dielectric back onto the real plates. In other words, the dielectric has absorbed some of the charge when the capacitor was charged and this absorbed charge is leaked back onto the conductors.

In the days of high B+ plate voltages for vacuum tubes, this phenomenon was called the *ham-killer* when oil-filled, paper dielectric power supply capacitors were discharged and the short circuit was prematurely removed.

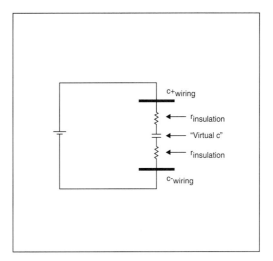

Figure 33-10. *Dielectric Absorption*

This same effect, but with less lethal consequences, can be found in the wiring of a large automatic test system. See Figure 33-11.

In this case, the charge is stored in the dielectric during one test and leaks off during the next. Assume that there is 1 pF of virtual capacitance and that $10^{12}\Omega$ of insulation resistance connects it to the plates of the real capacitors, which are actually the conductors in the wires of the test system.

Further assume that the system has supplied 1000V for about 10 seconds to some load. This is 10 time constants for the virtual capacitor, so at 1000V it is fully charged. Next assume that the system is switched to measure a 10 $M\Omega$ resistor, R_{load}, with a DMM. The DMM is

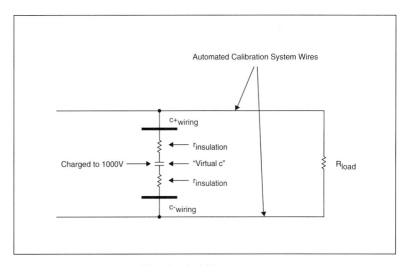

Figure 33-11. *Error Caused by Absorbed Charge*

specified to be able to take an accurate reading within 0.5 seconds after it is connected to the resistor (with filter). 1 μA of test current flows in the resistor.

Under these conditions, the virtual capacitor will have had 0.5 time constants to discharge. The discharge path is through R_{load} under test, and will have a value of 0.6 nA when the DMM measures the resistor. Due to the effect of the discharge current, the reading will be 0.06% high.

The presence of dielectric absorption can be tested by connecting a 6½- or 7½-digit DMM with a 10 MΩ input resistance on its 100V range directly across the circuit of interest. The circuit is then charged by applying a hundred volts or so for a period of ten minutes or more. The charging emf is removed and a short cir-cuit is applied across the DMM's input for up to a minute. Then the short circuit is removed. If the DMM's reading increases abruptly and then more or less slowly decays back to zero, dielec-tric absorption is likely.

Care must be taken to ensure that the DMM is not the source of the problem. For example, the test should be made on the DMM before it is made on the circuit under test. If the DMM reading quickly returns to zero, then it can be used for the test. The short circuit should be applied to the DMM for at least as long as its step-change specification. The readings should not commence after the short is removed until this length of time has elapsed again.

Two remedies to the situation are:

1. Completely discharge the system and then measure all high values of resistance.

2. Let the system settle until the DMM reading is stable. This is an important technique for use with automated calibration stations.

Noise and AC to DC Converters

Different types of ac to dc converters used in DMMs are affected differently by noise. The source of the noise can be inherent in the DMM or riding on the signal. When there is no signal, DMMs respond to this noise differently than when a signal is present.

In an average-responding DMM, noise is recti-fied, and the average rectified value is also mea-sured directly and multiplied by the scaling factor for the DMM. When no input signal is present, the rms value of the rectified noise may at first appear to be a significant amount. See Figure 33-12.

But when a signal is present, an average-responding DMM tends to ignore the noise as the envelope of the applied signal rises above the rectification points for the signal. This means that when a signal is present, the aver-age value of each of the sinusoidal components of the noise will effectively be zero. See Figure 33-13.

A true rms DMM, though, combines the signal and noise as the square root of the sum of the squares (rss) of the rms values of the signal and noise. The effect of noise, then, takes on greater importance, because the noise has a measurable influence on the converted signal, even as the signal to noise ratio increases. For this reason, true rms-responding DMMs will have the in-bandwidth noise measured directly with no signal applied.

An offset reading at zero input is normal for the ac voltage and current function of a properly designed DMM. Fluke does not incorporate ac zero adjustments in its DMMs for this reason.

Parasitic Capacitance

Parasitic capacitance exists between any two conductors. Undesired voltage changes can be coupled from a noise source to sensitive circuits via parasitic capacitance. The noise voltage can be an ac voltage or a change in dc voltage.

Noise from an External Source

In Figure 33-14, a portion of the ac voltage applied to a fluorescent lamp is coupled as a noise signal via parasitic capacitance, c_p, into an unshielded 10 MΩ resistor being measured by a DMM.

The circuit is drawn to show that a circuit is completed through the DMM's line power cord, or any other form of ground. If the distributed capacitance from the fluorescent lamp to the 10 MΩ resistor is 1 pF, its impedance at 60 Hz is about $2.6 \times 10^9 \Omega$. When 115V at 60 Hz is applied to this impedance, the peak-to-peak voltage drop across the 10 MΩ resistor is greater than 0.43V.

In this situation, the DMM digits will fluctuate. The noise can be greatly reduced by placing a Faraday shield around the resistor and the hookup wires connecting it to the DMM (Figure 33-15).

Additional noise attenuation is achieved via the DMM's filter.

Noise from Transformer Windings

Figure 33-16 illustrates a problem that existed in a very early model of a differential voltmeter.

In this meter, the parasitic capacitance between its primary winding and one of the secondary windings of its power transformer caused a circulating alternating current to flow. This caused measurement errors.

The secondary of interest supplies power to the meter's built-in null detector. When the meter's Kelvin-Varley divider was elevated above the internal measurement common, an alternating current flowed through the Kelvin-Varley divider to measurement common. This current caused a voltage drop to appear at the divider's output. This voltage drop was synchronously rectified by a chopper circuit in the meter; the rectified value was algebraically added to the proper direct voltage output of the Kelvin-Varley divider, causing measurement errors.

The solution was to add a variable capacitor between the null detector common and an

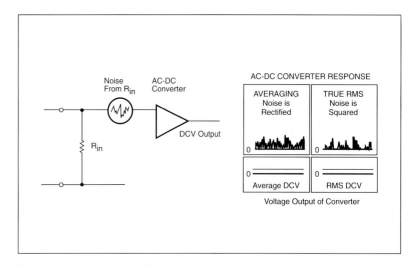

Figure 33-12. *Noise in AC Voltage Converters*

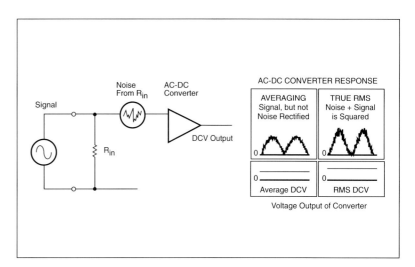

Figure 33-13. *Signals with Noise in AC Voltage Converters*

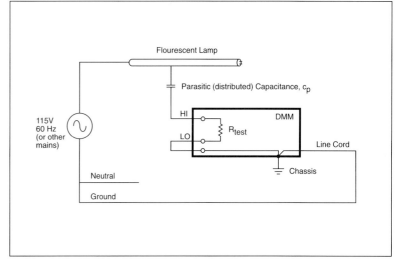

Figure 33-14. *Parasitic Capacitance, External Source*

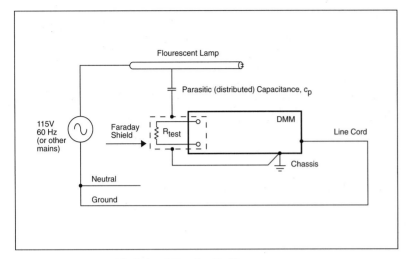

Figure 33-15. *Noise Blocked with Faraday Shield*

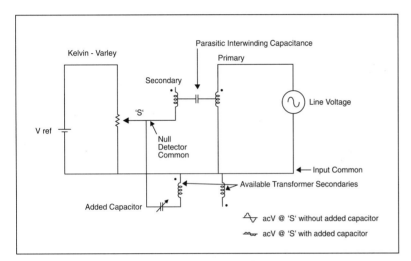

Figure 33-16. *Parasitic Capacitance, Transformer*

oppositely-phased secondary winding. The capacitor was adjusted to provide enough alternating current to cancel the effects of the parasitic capacitance. A slight amount of third-order harmonic was left over, as shown by the waveforms in Figure 33-16.

A variable capacitor with a mica dielectric was chosen for this application because mica has low dielectric absorption qualities and a high dielectric resistance.

Noise from a Change in DCV

In another instance, in another early model of differential voltmeter, the change in the dcv charge on some wires was coupled into its vtvm circuits, symbolized by the Buffer and the Null

Detector, and appeared as a spike on its input terminals. The spike was of relatively low energy but had a high peak voltage that harmed some MOS circuits whose peak voltage rating was 5V. See Figure 33-17.

The solution was to place a Faraday shield around the input resistor and the wires connecting it to other elements of the differential voltmeter. The wires carrying the high voltage were also shielded and certain sensitive sections of the switch decks in the meter were also enclosed in Faraday shields. The end result was the decreasing of the peak value of the transient, as measured on an 85 MHz bandwidth oscilloscope, to less than 5V. For more information, see Chapter 32, "Grounding, Shielding and Guarding."

Parasitic Inductance

John Fluke Sr. founded Fluke with the VAW Meter (volts-amps-watts). This instrument measured true average power, even with highly reactive loads. It had a maximum resolution of 0.1% power factor. The key circuit elements were low effective-inductance current shunts and two varistors whose dc resistance varied with the square of the ac voltage applied. Similar types of devices are known as quarter-square multipliers. Figure 33-18 shows the quarter-square multiplier's block diagram with a capacitive load at its input in series with a current shunt.

The V+A and V−A outputs are applied to two varistors, whose resistance varies as the square of the outputs. The difference of their resistances is indirectly measured to find watts (varistors not shown).

The output of these amplifiers with a purely reactive V input will be equal if the shunt is a pure resistance. The A input to the V+A and V−A amplifiers is developed across R_{shunt} whose voltage drop is negligible with respect to the voltage applied across the series circuit of C_{load} and R_{shunt}. When the shunt is a pure resistance, its *IR* drop leads the voltage by 90° when it is applied to the V+A amplifier. Similarly, it lags the voltage input at the V−A amplifier following its phase inversion at the −1 ampli-fier. Figure 33-19 shows the vector diagrams for these conditions.

The resultant phasors have equal amplitudes. Their squares are identical, so the difference of their squares is zero, as expected for a purely capacitive load.

At high currents, to 30A, the shunt element will inevitably have some inductance. This parasitic inductance appears in series with the shunt's resistance. The voltage drop across the shunt thus contains an inductive component that leads the shunt's *IR* drop by 90°. The phasors, therefore, have unequal amplitudes. See Figure 33-20.

When this component is applied to the input of the V+A amplifier, it leads the V component by 180° and subtracts from its effective magnitude. When it is applied to the input of the V−A amplifier, it is in phase with the V component and adds to its amplitude. Because of this, the outputs of the two amplifiers are no longer equal and the VAW Meter will read in error.

The solution to the problem was to locate small hookup leads on the shunt in such a way that a voltage was induced in them from the current in the shunt. The voltage was equal to, but opposite in phase from the *IX_l* drop across the shunt. See Figure 33-21.

Thus, the A input to the V+A and V−A amplifiers was, for all practical purposes, completely in phase with the shunt's *IR* drop.

The shunt's hookup wires were sealed into their proper position via beeswax. In addition, the varistors were mounted in a small, sealed, can-shaped enclosure with an octal base so that it could be plugged into the regular vacuum tube sockets of the day. This enclosure was called the S (for *squaring*) *can*. The squaring can was filled with castor oil to provide an isothermal environment for the varistors. For those enthusiasts of the by-gone technology: the vacuum tubes that drove the S *can* were a pair of selected 6L6 vacuum tubes.

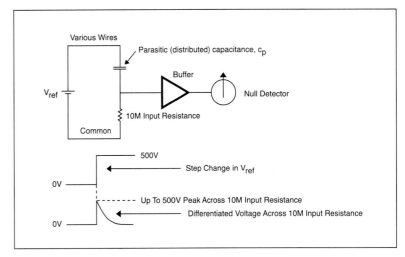

Figure 33-17. *Capacitive Coupling of DC Voltage Change*

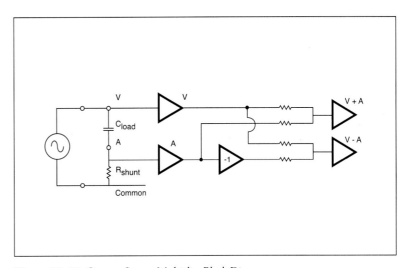

Figure 33-18. *Quarter-Square Multiplier Block Diagram*

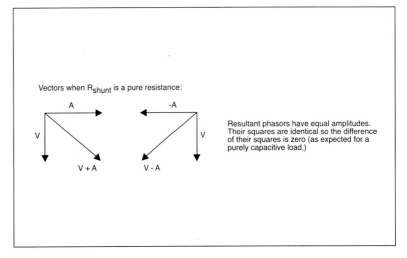

Figure 33-19. *Quarter-Square Vector Diagrams*

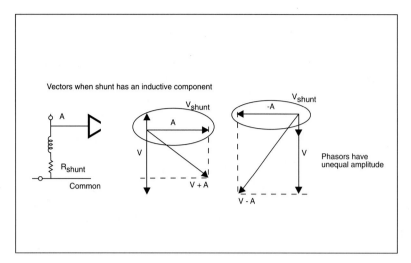

Figure 33-20. *Vectors with Parasitic Inductance Present*

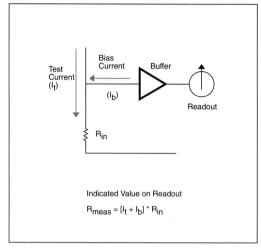

Figure 33-22. *Resistance Measurement Bias Current*

When the DMM measures the voltage drop from a resistive voltage divider, the bias current can also cause measurement errors. See Figure 33-23.

The following equation describes the measurement error which bias current can introduce.

$$V_{meas} = \frac{R_2}{R_1 + R_2}\left(V_x + I_b R_1\right)$$

A bias current can charge a DMM's input capacitance when the DMM is used on its lower dc voltage ranges. On these ranges, the DMM's input resistance is 10,000 MΩ or more. If the DMM's bias current is 10 pA, Ohm's law indicates that the bias current times the input resistance yields a voltage of 0.1V. Accordingly, if the DMM's input is shorted for a time and then the short is removed, its digital display will count up as its input capacitance charges. One time constant for this effect will be on the order of a second or more (the higher the input resistance, the longer the time constant).

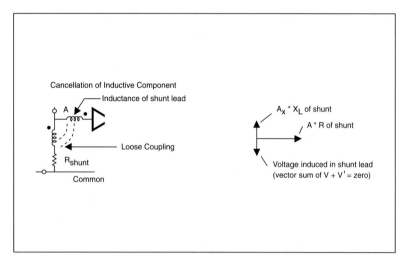

Figure 33-21. *Cancellation of Parasitic Inductance*

Bias Current

Most modern DMMs have small amounts of current flowing from their input terminals. This is the *bias current* and it is developed from the operational amplifiers used in the DMM. Bias current is typically no more than 20 pA. When a DMM is used to measure resistance, the bias current, I_b, from the voltage-measuring circuitry can flow in the test resistor and algebraically add with the test current, I_t. Figure 33-22 shows this effect.

The following equation describes the measurement error which bias current can introduce.

$$R_{meas} = R_{in}(I_t + I_b)$$

A related effect is the analog memory of a DMM reading. For example, if +10V is applied to a DMM on the range with 10,000 MΩ input resistance and then is removed, the DMM's display will slowly count down as its input capacitance discharges through its input resistance. However, the DMM's bias current can cancel out the discharge current, keeping the DMM's reading somewhat constant.

These effects are normal, but can be somewhat disconcerting.

Pumpout Current

Transient noise current (spikes), also known as pumpout current, is often present at the input terminals of some DMMs. This current is usually caused by switching the circuits in the DMM to rearrange its measurement configuration for functions such as auto-zeroing, measurement of resistance by ratio techniques, and reversing polarity to measure negative voltages.

An additional source of pumpout current is capacitively-coupled strobing voltages associated with readouts, notably with plasma display tubes.

As shown in Figure 33-24, the spikes of this pumpout current can get into the sense circuits of DMM calibrators and upset their feedback paths, causing errors in their outputs.

Note that this is a defect of the DMM and that this type of problem can appear to occur in any electronic circuit whose voltages and currents are being measured by a DMM exhibiting this defect. Unfortunately, this defect is usually not noted until the DMM is sent to the calibration laboratory and connected to a multifunction calibrator.

Pumpout current can be detected as indicated in Figure 33-25.

Figure 33-25 shows an oscilloscope making a differential measurement. The signal processing circuits of the oscilloscope could be providing a direct display, or a fourier transform could be applied to the pumpout waveform in order to get the frequency distribution of the fourier components in it.

Almost all DMMs have some pumpout effects. If the peak amplitude of the pumpout waveform is more than a volt or two and the wave is differentiated over a substantial portion of its repetition rate and the repetition rate is 10 or fewer repetitions per second, there is a good chance that the DMM's pumpout current will upset the calibrator.

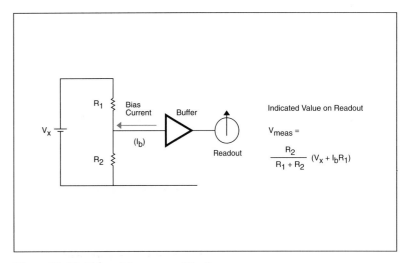

Figure 33-23. *Voltage Measurement Bias Current*

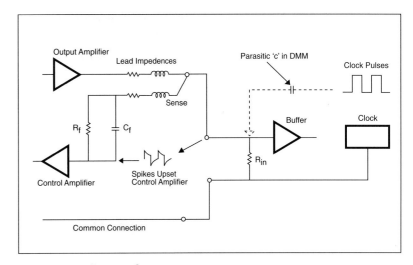

Figure 33-24. *Pumpout Current*

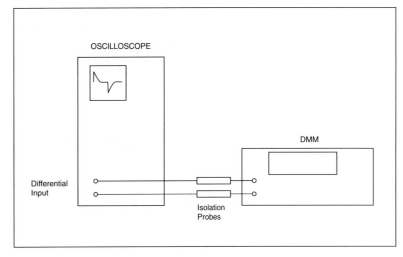

Figure 33-25. *Oscilloscope Detection of Pumpout Current.*

If that problem is experienced, contact the DMM's manufacturer for advice. Note that the DMM that exhibits this kind of problem will most likely disturb the circuits it is intended to test during its normal operation.

Other Rogues

There are other effects that can cause unexpected behavior in sensitive electrical connections:

- The *Hall Effect* causes an emf perpendicular to the current flow in a conductor that is also perpendicular to a magnetic field.

- Distortion of a coaxial cable can cause reflections of the electromagnetic waves it is transporting, causing energy losses and phase errors.

- The *skin effect* occurs when an rf current flows in a conductor. In the skin effect, the current no longer flows through the entire conductor. The conductor resistance will increase with the square root of frequency.

- There can be gross effects, too. For example, triboelectric effects occur when insulators are rubbed against each other. An example of this is the generation of static electricity developed by walking across a nylon rug on a cold, low-humidity day. Static electricity can easily destroy sensitive electronic devices and so it is good to wear a grounding strap when working on circuit cards or components that are sensitive to static electricity.

References for this chapter are in the Resources Appendix.

Chapter 34:
AC Lore

This chapter discusses some additional aspects of classical ac metrology, supplementing material in Chapters 10 and 11, "Principles of AC-DC Metrology" and "Using AC-DC Transfer Standards."

I n addition to discussing ac metrology and standards based on older technology, this chapter also considers ac waveforms. One can use this information to select test equipment and to analyze any differences between the expected and observed performance of standards and instruments. The waveform discussion assumes that the reader is familiar with trigonometry, vectors, and radian measure of angles.

Classical AC-DC Metrology

Chapter 10, "Principles of AC-DC Metrology," introduced the single-element vacuum thermocouple (SEVTC) and its primary attributes for ac-dc metrology. Compared to the Fluke rms sensor, SEVTCs are more prone to error due to Thomson and Peltier heating and are far more difficult to use when making low-level voltage transfers. This section summarizes these aspects of the theory and applications of SEVTCs.

There is an enormous amount of technical literature available containing detailed information on SEVTCs. The Resources section at the end of this book lists numerous key papers that you may wish to consult for detailed information on SEVTCs.

Thomson and Peltier Heating

Thomson heating is a primary source of reversal error and ac-dc differences in SEVTCs. As illustrated in Figure 34-1, Thomson heating is a displacement of the temperature distribution in a SEVTC's heater in the direction of the dc current flow in the heater. In contrast, an ac current does not affect the heater's temperature distribution.

If the thermocouple element of the SEVTC is not placed on the center of the heater, its temperature will be higher when the dc current is flowing in one direction rather than in the other. This temperature difference is the source of the SEVTC's reversal error. Even if the thermocouple element is exactly at the center of

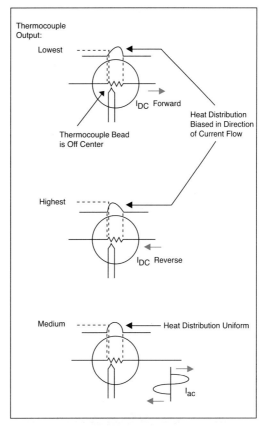

Figure 34-1. *Thomson and Peltier Effects*

the heater, its temperature will be lower when a dc current is flowing than when an ac current is present. This effect is due to the displacement of the heat distribution in the direction of the dc currents, and is a principal cause of ac-dc differences.

Peltier heating also causes second-order reversal errors and ac-dc differences. Peltier heating is caused by a dc current flowing through the junction of dissimilar metals, such as the internal junction of a SEVTC's external connection leads and heater element.

Peltier heat builds up in the input and output junctions of the connection leads and heater when dc is flowing, but is non-existent when ac is absent. Less heat is carried out of the heater element when Peltier heat is present. Thus, the heater is somewhat "hotter" when dc current is flowing, resulting in an ac-dc difference. In addition, the magnitude of the Peltier heating is not exactly the same at each junction, and so it modifies the effects of Thomson heating.

Low-Level Voltage Transfers

Low-level voltage transfers can be made using SEVTCs. In contrast to applications of the Fluke rms sensor-based 792A and 5790A, these transfers require additional equipment, stringent hookup precautions, and greater technical expertise, and have greater uncertainty.

Two methods for making these measurements include the ratio transformer method and the micropot method. The following discussion briefly reviews these methods. Chapter 13, "Immittance and AC Ratio," provides further information on ac ratio.

Ratio Transformer Method

The ratio transformer method of obtaining low ac voltages applies to a frequency range of approximately 10 Hz to 10 kHz. Figure 34-2 illustrates the basic application of the ratio transformer.

An ac-dc transfer at an appropriate level, such as 1V, establishes AC_{v1}, a known ac voltage. This voltage is divided by the ratio transformer (for example, to 0.1V). The ratio transformer's output is applied to an external ac voltmeter. The voltmeter's reading is recorded. Then the ac voltage source is reduced to AC_{v2}, approximately the right level (~0.1V, in the example), and is applied to the meter. Then it is adjusted until the meter's reading matches the recorded reading. This process can be reiterated a number of times.

The ac voltmeter's repeatability and short-term stability are important because it is used as a transfer voltmeter. If the voltmeter lacks sensitivity, low-noise, low-frequency amplifiers can be inserted between the ratio transformer's output and its input to boost the signal level. The amplifier's short-term gain stability is the primary consideration.

Micropot Method

The micropot was developed by NBS (now NIST) in the 1950s. Figure 34-3 illustrates the basic concept of this device.

It consists of a thermocouple in series with a disk-shaped, low-value resistor. The resistor's ac resistance is nearly identical to its dc resistance. A micropot can consist of one thermocouple

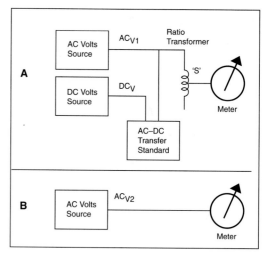

Figure 34-2. *Low-Level, Low-Frequency AC-AC Transfer Connection*

that is plugged into several resistor elements. In contrast, the Holt Model 12 is a single, self-contained unit whose thermocouple is in series with several series-connected resistors.

When a micropot is used to make ac-dc transfers, a stable but adjustable dc voltage is applied across the series-connected SEVTC/resistor. The dc voltage drop across the resistor is measured, for example, by a sensitive DMM. The dc source is adjusted until the voltage drop equals the desired ac voltage. Then the low-level millivolt output of the SEVTC is either measured with a microvoltmeter or balanced against a Lindeck potentiometer.

The dc voltage is reversed in order to find the reversal error of the SEVTC. The mean of the SEVTC's low-level output with forward and reversed dc voltages applied is used as the reference for its output when an ac voltage is placed across the SEVTC/resistor. The amplitude of the ac voltage is adjusted until the SEVTC's output, corrected by its NIST-supplied ac-dc difference factor, δ, matches its mean value with forward and reversed dc applied.

The ac voltage drop across the resistor provides the standard ac voltage, as corrected by any NIST test-reported ac-dc difference for the resistor.

Micropots can also be used with ratio transformers to make ac-ac transfers. This method eliminates the need to measure dc reversal

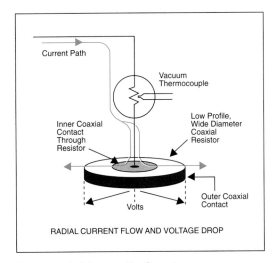

Figure 34-3. *Micropot Configuration*

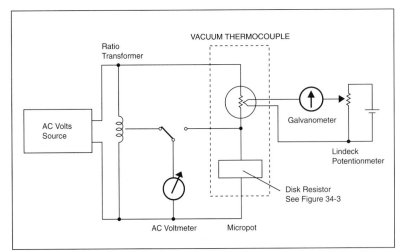

Figure 34-4. *Low-Level, High Frequency AC-AC Transfer Connection*

errors. Figure 34-4 is a simplified illustration of the method.

The ac voltmeter is used to transfer the known output of the rated transformer to the low-frequency ac voltage drop across the micropot's resistor. The Lindeck potentiometer is adjusted to null against the SEVTC's output with the low-frequency ac voltage being applied. Without disturbing the settings of the Lindeck potentiometer, the ratio transformer and voltmeter are removed, the voltage source is switched to the high frequency, and its amplitude is adjusted for a null on the preset Lindeck potentiometer.

Hookup Considerations

The hookups, connectors, and grounding, guarding, and shielding methods used when ratio transformers and micropots provide low-level ac voltages must be carefully considered and implemented. In general, the idea is to keep emi out of the circuits and to keep contact resistances and thermal emfs as low as possible. Of course, the numerous thermal transfers and low-level ac and dc measurements must be carefully made.

Other AC Standards

A number of devices have been developed to measure or supply precision ac voltages and currents. Four of them are briefly surveyed here.

True RMS-Responding Thermopile

An interesting thermal current converter was constructed by NBS, now NIST, several years ago. In order to avoid the effects of residual impedances at high frequencies, the heater was physically separated from the thermopile, i.e., a group of thermocouples. The heat generated in the heater was focused onto the "hot" terminal of the thermopile via an elliptical reflector.

The heater, an extension of the center conductor of a coaxial line, was positioned at one focus of the ellipse; the "hot" terminal of the thermopile at the other focus. The dimensions of the coaxial line and the reflector were designed to make the device non-reflecting up to several GHz. An uncertainty of about 0.1% at 2A was claimed for frequencies up to 10 MHz.

Sampling Voltmeter

A sampling voltmeter reconstructs a measured waveform from precise samples of its instantaneous values. This method is most useful for frequencies lower than 5 kHz and is probably the best approach for measuring voltages at frequencies lower than 5 Hz.

Synthesized Voltage Standard

A similar approach has been used to synthesize ac voltage waveforms. A microprocessor-controlled digital-to-analog converter constructs the waveform from a precision dc voltage reference, as illustrated in Figure 34-5.

This approach provides an ac voltage in a manner that is similar to the output of a solid-state dc voltage reference standard. The approach is said to have uncertainties as low as a few tens of parts-per-million, with the best performance being obtained at the lower frequencies.

AC Standard Cell

A number of years ago, Fluke offered the Model 510A "AC Standard Cell."

This device is no longer manufactured, but quite a few of them are deployed in standards laboratories around the world. The 510A generated a pure and precise 10V sine wave at one of several single frequencies. It was used as though it were an ac standard cell to establish a reference amplitude for the ac-ac transfers and for ratio transformers.

Composite Voltages

This section describes the average-rectified and rms values of several composite voltage waveforms. There are two types of composite voltages, those with sinusoidal waveforms and those with Fourier-series waveforms. This section illustrates their waveforms as they would appear on an oscilloscope, and concludes with a table that summarizes their key characteristics.

For brevity, the composite waveforms are referred to as "voltage waveforms." The values of ac current waveforms are directly analogous to the values of ac voltage waveforms.

Notation for Composite Voltages

The symbol V, with an appropriate subscript, is used herein to denote the average, rms, and peak voltages of composite waveforms. The symbol E, and appropriate subscripts, is used to denote pure sine wave voltages.

Composite Sinusoidal Voltage Waveforms

A pure sine wave is the fundamental component of a composite sinusoidal voltage. Additional components include dc voltages and up to several more sine waves whose frequencies are harmonic multiples of the fundamental wave. Generally speaking, a sinusoidal voltage looks like a sine wave when it is viewed on an oscilloscope.

Sine Wave Plus DC
Figure 34-6 illustrates a sine wave with a dc component.

The rms and average values of a pure sine wave are increased by its dc component. An ac-dc transfer standard will accurately measure these components, as will a true rms-responding DMM operated in its dc-coupled ac voltage mode, if available. Most, if not all, average-responding meters do not respond to the dc component. For example, the "Search" meter on the Fluke 540B does not sense the dc component of any waveform.

The rms value of a waveform with a dc component is equal to the square-root-of-the-sum-of-the-squares (rss) of its components and is denoted herein by V_{rss}, equal to:

$$V_{rss} = \sqrt{E_{dc}^{\,2} + E_{rms}^{\,2}}$$

Where:

E_{dc} = the dc voltage

E_{rms} = the rms value of the sine wave

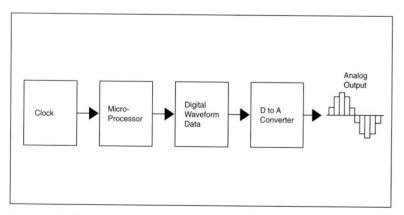

Figure 34-5. Block Diagram of Electronic AC Voltage Synthesis

Harmonically-Distorted Sine Wave

A harmonically-distorted sine wave includes a fundamental sine wave and its harmonics. Figures 34-7 and 34-8 illustrate 2nd and 3rd harmonic distortion, respectively.

AC-DC transfer standards and true rms-responding DMMs accurately measure harmonically-distorted sine waves. Average-responding meters do not; they totally ignore the even harmonics while their response to odd harmonics is a function of the phase relationship of the odd harmonics and the fundamental.

The rss voltage of a waveform with single-harmonic distortion is computed as:

$$V_{rss} = \sqrt{E_{dc}^2 + E_{fund}^2 + E_{harm}^2}$$

Where:

E_{fund} = rms amplitude of the fundamental sine wave

E_{harm} = rms amplitude of the harmonic sine wave in the waveform

If a finite number of harmonics are present in the waveform, the rss voltage is:

$$V_{rss} = \sqrt{E_{dc}^2 + E_{fund}^2 + E_{harm1}^2 + E_{harm2}^2 + ... E_{harmN}^2}$$

Fourier Series of Non-Sinusoidal Voltage Waveforms

A Fourier-series voltage waveform consists of a fundamental frequency and an infinite number of its harmonics. Square waves, triangular waves, and sawtooth waves are examples of voltage waveforms composed of a Fourier series of sine waves. The amplitude and phase relationship of the harmonics is specific to the waveform. Some of these waveforms include a dc component. Their rms amplitude is computed from the Euler number for the squares of the Fourier series.

This section doesn't go into detail concerning the Fourier series or the Euler numbers. More detailed information is given further on in this chapter.

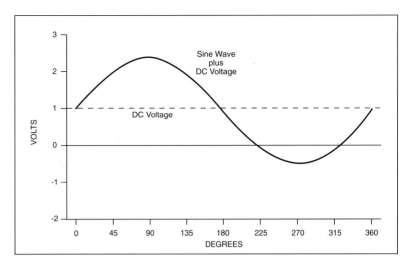

Figure 34-6. *Sine Wave with DC*

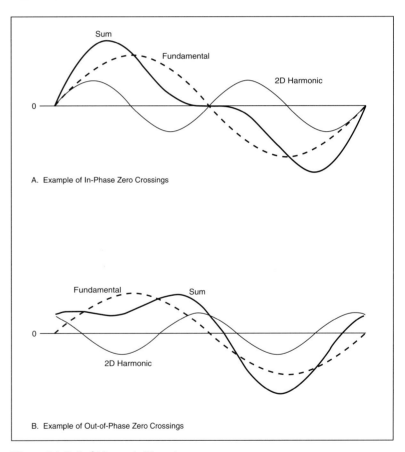

Figure 34-7. *2nd Harmonic Distortion*

Square Waves

A repetitive, symmetrical square wave consists of a simple step change in voltage that alternates between a constant positive and negative value for equal periods of time. The peak, average-rectified, and true rms values of a perfectly symmetrical square wave are identical. These relationships are apparent from Figure 34-9.

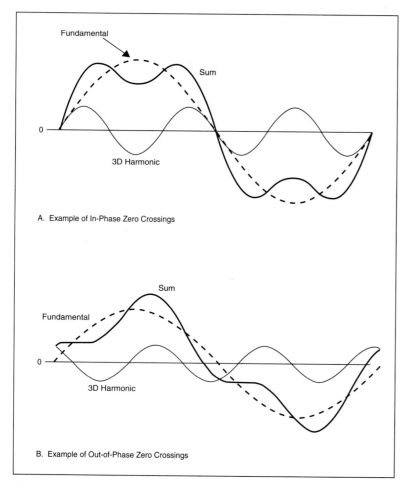

A. Example of In-Phase Zero Crossings

B. Example of Out-of-Phase Zero Crossings

Figure 34-8. *3rd Harmonic Distortion*

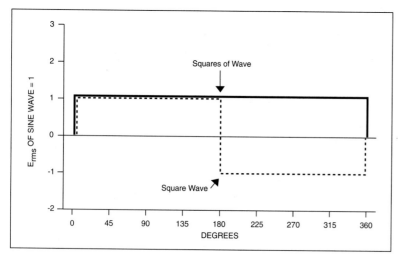

Figure 34-9. *Square Wave and its Squares*

Fourier Components

The Fourier series for a square wave consists of a fundamental sine wave and its odd harmonics. Figure 34-10 illustrates the wave that results from the addition of the instantaneous values of a fundamental and the third, fifth, seventh, and ninth harmonics.

The amplitudes of the harmonics are the amplitude of the fundamental multiplied by the reciprocal of the harmonic number. For example, the amplitude of the fifth harmonic is ⅕th the amplitude of the fundamental. This wave exhibits an approach to being square. Figure 34-11 illustrates the wave that results when the fundamental, third, fifth, and so forth, up to the 501st harmonic, are added.

The ringing near the edges is called *Gibbs phenomenon*. As harmonics are added, these perturbations move closer to the edges of the wave. When there are an infinite number of odd harmonics in the waveform (as required for a perfect square wave), the energy contributed by Gibbs phenomenon is reduced to zero.

Sine Wave for Comparison

Figure 34-12 illustrates a sine wave of voltage and the squares of its sines. This figure is included for reference purposes with respect to the values tabulated in Table 34-1.

Sawtooth and Triangular Waves

The symmetrical sawtooth and triangular waves, illustrated in Figures 34-13 and 34-14, have different Fourier series that sum to the same rms amplitude. The fundamental sine wave provides more of the total energy in a triangular wave than in a sawtooth wave.

Comparing Composite Voltages

Table 34-1 compares the values for composite voltages of both the sinusoidal and Fourier series of non-sinusoidal waveforms. The values of a pure sine wave are included for reference purposes.

Two previously undefined terms, *crest factor* and *form factor*, appear as column headings in Table 34-1. Crest factor is a dimensionless number equal to a waveform's peak voltage divided by its rms voltage. Similarly, a waveform's form factor is the ratio of its peak voltage to its average, rectified voltage.

Analyzing Voltage Waveforms

The key values of any waveform are its peak, instantaneous, average, and rms amplitudes. Various types of instruments are designed to respond to one or another of these values when they are calibrated with a sine wave. Their performance when they are measuring composite voltages can be very misleading. One may need to carefully analyze both the waveform and an instrument's circuit design in order to reconcile differences between its observed and expected performance.

Any repetitive, composite waveform can be constructed as the algebraic sum of a dc level and the instantaneous values of the Fourier series of sine waves. The Fourier series is generally analyzed directly to calculate the average-rectified value of the wave. It is also used in conjunction with the Euler number to calculate the rms value. Euler numbers are described later in this chapter.

Graphs of Waves

A graph of a voltage wave can help you analyze its values. The wave's instantaneous voltages are plotted on the Y axis with respect to time on the X axis. The resultant curve encloses an area with respect to the horizontal axis of the graph. The area under the curve is evaluated via calculus or other methods to find the voltage's average or rms amplitude.

An estimate of the area under the curve can be obtained as follows:

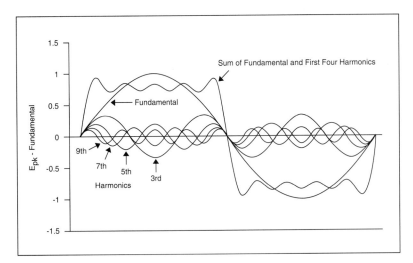

Figure 34-10. *Square Wave with 3rd, 5th, 7th, and 9th Harmonics*

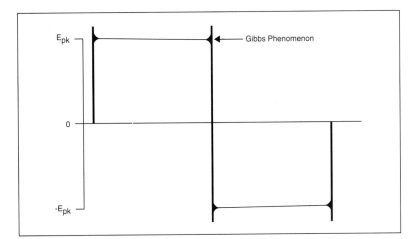

Figure 34-11. *Square Wave with 3rd, 5th,...501st Harmonics*

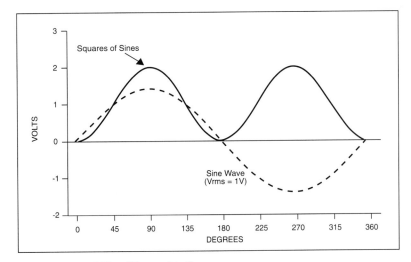

Figure 34-12. *1V Sine Wave and its Squares*

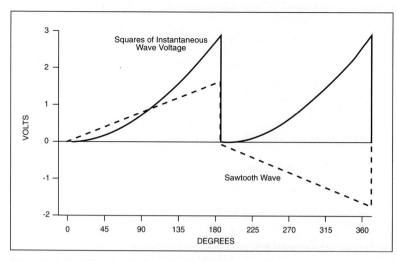

Figure 34-13. *1V Sawtooth Wave and its Squares*

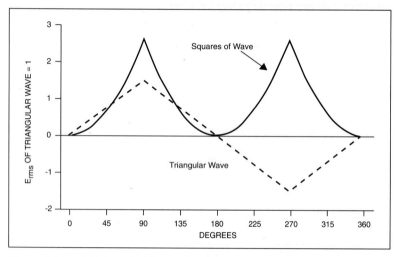

Figure 34-14. *1V Triangular Wave and its Squares*

1. Find the algebraic sum of a large number of its instantaneous voltages that are equally spaced in time.

2. Divide the sum by the number of voltages.

In many instances, a spreadsheet in a personal computer can be used to quickly, easily, and accurately compute the average amplitude of thousands of instantaneous voltages.

Average Voltage

The general method for finding the average voltage of a waveform is:

1. Find the sum of all of the instantaneous areas under its curve between two points of time on the X axis.

2. Divide the sum by the elapsed time between the points.

The two points in time are usually the period of one half cycle for symmetrical waveforms or a whole cycle for non-symmetrical waves.

Since there are an infinite number of instantaneous areas between any two points in time, calculus is used to find the exact area as the integral of the instantaneous areas. A good approximation of the area is found by taking the average of several hundred instantaneous values, separated by equal intervals of time.

RMS Voltage

The general method for finding the rms voltage of any wave is:

1. Square all of the instantaneous values between two points on the X axis.

2. Sum the squares.

3. Divide the sum of the squares by the number of samples.

4. Take the square root of the quotient.

RSS Voltage

The rss method is used to sum the rms values of a composite voltage waveform. When analyzing Fourier-series waveforms, this procedure can be simplified by using the Euler number for the sum of the squares of the series.

Sine Wave Parameters

Understanding the various values associated with a pure sine wave is the foundation for evaluating composite waves via the Fourier series and Euler numbers.

Generation of a Sine Wave

A sine wave is generated by a radius vector whose length equals the peak amplitude, E_{pk}, of the ac voltage being generated and whose origin is the center of a circle (see Figure 34-15).

The vector rotates at a constant rate in a counterclockwise direction around the center of the circle so that its tip traces out the circumference of the circle.

As it rotates, the vector generates an angle with respect to the circle's horizontal diameter. The angle is measured in radians, symbolized by the Greek letter theta, θ. The tip of the vector travels a distance equal to 2π radians on the circumference of the circle in one cycle. Its angular position is sometimes expressed in degrees instead of radians, that is, 360° is equivalent to 2π radians.

Each cycle of a sine wave conventionally begins with a positive-going zero crossing. The phase of two or more sine waves is the difference in time between their positive-going zero crossings, and is conventionally symbolized by the Greek letter phi, ϕ.

The time that it takes for the vector to complete one rotation around the circle is the *period* of the sine wave. The number of periods completed in one second is the *frequency* of the sine wave, given in the SI unit of the Hertz (Hz).

The instantaneous voltage at any point on the curve is $E_{pk}\sin\theta$ and the instantaneous slope of any point on the sine wave is its derivative, $E_{pk}\cos\theta$. The derivative is used by the calculus to determine the area under the curve and to compute inductive and capacitive reactances.

Summary of Amplitude Parameters

A sine wave has quarter-cycle symmetry, as shown in Figure 34-16.

The area under each quarter cycle of the curve is $E_{pk} \times 1$. The corresponding base has a length $\pi/2$ radians. Dividing the base into the area yields the average voltage for each quarter cycle as $2E_{pk}/\pi$. Note that E_{pk} is positive for the first two quarter cycles and negative for the last two. The wave's average and instantaneous amplitudes sum to zero over an entire cycle. However, the average *rectified* value for the two half cycles can always be either positive or negative, depending on the polarity of the diodes in the rectification circuit.

The curve of the squares of the sines also has quarter-cycle symmetry, as illustrated in Figure 34-17.

This curve emphasizes that the power produced in a resistor by a sine wave voltage is always positive. Recall from trigonometry that the sines of angles above 45° are mirror images of the cosines of angles below 45°. Also recall that $\sin^2\theta + \cos^2\theta = 1$. If there are N sines, there are $N/2$ pairs of sums of sines and cosines. Therefore, the root-mean-square voltage, E_{rms}, of a sine wave equals:

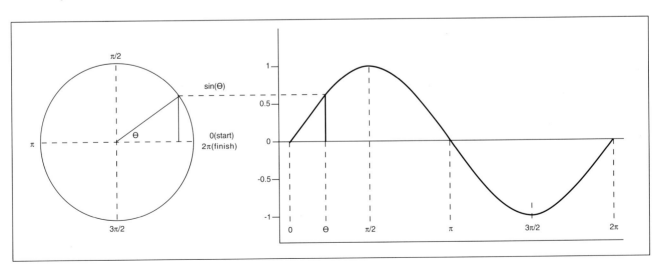

Figure 34-15. *Generation of a Sine Wave*

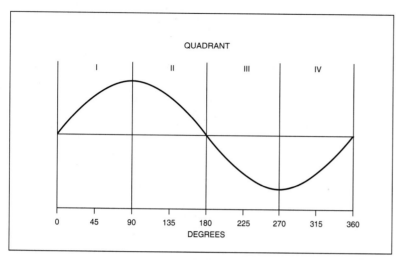

Figure 34-16. *Quarter Cycle Symmetry of Sine Wave*

$$E_{rms} = \frac{|E_{pk}|\sqrt{2}}{2}$$

E_{pk} is the peak value of the sine wave. Its absolute value is used, due to being derived as the positive root of $E_{pk}{}^2$.

Composite RSS Voltages

All composite waveforms consist of a Fourier series of sine waves. They may also have a dc component. Their average rectified value is a function of the areas of the Fourier series, while their rms value is a function of the Euler number for the sum of the squares of the Fourier values:

$$V_{rms} = \sqrt{E_{dc}{}^2 + E_{fund}{}^2 \times (\text{Euler number})}$$

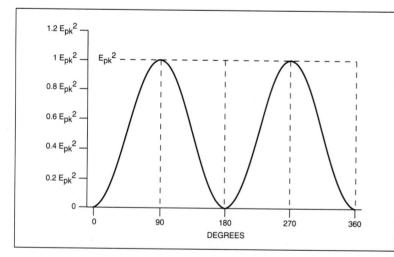

Figure 34-17. *Squares of Sines*

Fourier Series

The 19th-century French engineer Baron Jean-Baptiste Joseph Fourier discovered the fact that any repetitive, composite waveform is composed of an infinite series of sine waves of specific amplitudes, frequencies, and phase relationships. The period of the complex wave equals the period of the lowest frequency or fundamental sine wave in the series. The frequencies of the other sine waves in the series are integral multiples of the fundamental frequency and are called *harmonics*. The phase of the zero crossings of the harmonics is relative to the zero crossing of the fundamental, and the amplitude of the harmonics is a reciprocal of the fundamental's amplitude.

Euler Number

Leonhard Euler was an 18th-century mathematician who discovered how to find the exact sum of an infinite series of the squares of reciprocals of integers (and higher-order, even powers of the reciprocals). The Euler numbers are used to obtain the rms value of the Fourier series. Key Euler numbers are given in Table 34-2.

Measuring Composite AC Voltages

The preceding information indicates that there are many theoretical factors associated with the composition of waveforms. An instrument used to measure sinusoidal or composite ac voltages can have design limitations that cause it to respond improperly to a wave's Fourier series, Euler number, or dc component. The primary areas to evaluate when assessing whether an instrument is suitable for measuring a given waveform are its:

- dc response
- harmonic response
- internal phase shift
- bandwidth
- dynamic amplitude range

Some comments on how these affect the response of DMMs or other meters and ac-dc transfer standards follow.

DC Response

Generally speaking, only true rms-responding DMMs have ac ranges that allow you to measure voltages with a dc component. Average-responding meters do respond correctly to the ac value of a pure sine wave that is superimposed on a dc voltage. If the meter can reject a wave's ac component when it is used in its dc measurement mode, it can accurately measure the dc component via its dc voltage function. The total rms value can be computed as the square-root-of-the-sum-of-the-squares of the two readings.

The presence of a dc component will add Thomson and Peltier heating effects to the ac measurement in SEVTC-based ac-dc transfer standards. If the dc component is small—less than 10% of the total rms value, the effects will be negligible. In order to avoid errors from large dc components, you might consider using a large-value dc-blocking capacitor at the transfer standard's input. The transfer standard will then respond to just the ac component. The dc component can be measured with a DMM and then the total rms value of the quantity can be computed as described in the preceding paragraph.

Harmonic Response

True rms-responding meters and ac-dc transfer standards respond properly to all of the harmonics in a wave that are within their bandwidth. Average-responding meters totally ignore the even harmonics of the fundamental. Their response to odd harmonics is not as well defined. They may completely ignore them, partially add them, or partially subtract them from their overall reading.

These discrepancies are due to the fact that average-responding meters basically add the areas of the harmonic waveforms to the area of the fundamental waveform. The fact that the average value of an unrectified sine wave is zero is the basis for their inability to respond to even harmonics. Their rectifiers act as a gate that passes all of the half cycles of the even harmonics while they are rectifying the fundamental. When odd harmonics are present, their phase relationship to the fundamental determines how much of the area under their waveforms is rectified.

If their zero crossing is in phase with the fundamental, one half cycle of their area will be added to the total value. If their zero crossing is 180° out of phase, a half cycle of their area will be subtracted from the total. If their zero crossing leads or lags the fundamental by 90°, their area will be ignored. Other phase angles cause intermediate discrepancies.

Internal Phase Shift

The internal phase shift of a true rms-responding meter does not degrade its response to waveforms that include harmonics. In contrast, an average-responding meter can incur enormous errors due to its internal phase shift. The same considerations that apply to the average-responding meter's harmonic recognition are responsible.

In summary, form factor errors in average-responding meters arise from phase shifts in the Fourier series of harmonics that comprise the wave, and from bandwidth limitations, discussed next.

Bandwidth

There are an infinite number of harmonics in a Fourier series. Instruments have limited bandwidths and cannot properly integrate the contribution of the energy in all of the harmonics to the total value.

Energy in Harmonics

The use of Euler numbers simplifies the calculation of the rss value of a Fourier series. This number embraces an infinite number of harmonics and implies that an infinite bandwidth is needed to measure the voltage defined by the series.

Practical instruments have limited bandwidths. An approximation of the error in their response to a non-sinusoidal waveform is:

$$Rdg_{err} = \left(\frac{\sqrt{\Sigma}}{\sqrt{\mathrm{Eu}}} \right) \times 100\%$$

Where:

Rdg_{err} = reading error of the instrument

$\sqrt{\Sigma}$ = rss of amplitudes of harmonics in bandwidth

$\sqrt{Eu}$ = square root of Euler number of series

This formula looks benign. However, it shows that if you endeavor to measure a 1 kHz square wave with a DMM that has a 2 MHz bandwidth, the DMM's response will be 0.1068% low, even though the energy in a thousand odd harmonics has been measured.

The remaining 0.1068% of the total energy is in the infinite number of harmonics, excluded by the DMM's bandwidth limitation.

Dynamic Amplitude Range

It is often difficult to measure voltages with a high crest factor because they have a high peak-to-peak value but their rms value is low.

In one practical context, these considerations could lead one to select a DMM's low ac voltage range to provide the best measurement of the low rms value. On the other hand, after further consideration, the user would choose to use a higher ac voltage range to avoid "clipping" the wave's peak values by the DMM's operational amplifiers.

A similar consideration applies when a vacuum thermocouple is used to measure a wave with a high crest factor. As Figure 34-18 shows, the peak-to-peak voltage covers a wide dynamic range of the thermocouple's transfer function.

Deviations from true square law response in the thermocouple will introduce errors into its low dc voltage output. In addition, the peak value of the voltage could be present long enough to burn out the thermocouple's heater if a transfer standard's lower ranges are used to get a measurable reading.

References for this chapter are in the Resources Appendix.

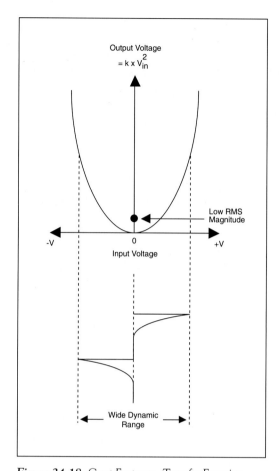

Figure 34-18. *Crest Factor vs. Transfer Function*

Table 34-1. Composite Waveforms

	V_{rss}	V_{avg} Rectified	Fourier Series	Euler Number	E_{rms} of Fundamental	Crest Factor	Form Factor
Square	V_{pk}	V_{pk}	$1 + \frac{1}{3} + \frac{1}{5} + \frac{1}{7} + \frac{1}{9}\cdots$	$\frac{\pi^2}{8}$	$\frac{V_{rss}\sqrt{8}}{\pi}$	$\sqrt{1}$	1
Sine	$\frac{E_{pk}\sqrt{2}}{2}$	$\frac{2E_{pk}}{\pi}$	not applicable (N/A)	N/A	$\frac{E_{pk}\sqrt{2}}{2}$	$\sqrt{2}$	$\frac{\pi}{2}$
Triangle	$\frac{V_{pk}\sqrt{3}}{3}$	$\frac{V_{pk}}{2}$	$1 + \frac{1}{9} + \frac{1}{25} + \frac{1}{49} + \frac{1}{81}\cdots$	$\frac{\pi^4}{96}$	$\frac{4V_{rss}\sqrt{6}}{\pi^2}$	$\sqrt{3}$	2
Sawtooth	$\frac{V_{pk}\sqrt{3}}{3}$	$\frac{V_{pk}}{2}$	$1 - \frac{1}{2} + \frac{1}{3} - \frac{1}{4} + \frac{1}{5}\cdots$	$\frac{\pi^2}{6}$	$\frac{V_{rss}\sqrt{6}}{\pi}$	$\sqrt{3}$	2

Note:
V refers to a value of a composite wave. E refers to a value of a sine wave.

Table 34-2. Key Euler Numbers

Euler number	Sums the reciprocals of	Beginning of Squares of Fourier Series
$\frac{\pi^2}{6}$	squares of all integers	$1 + \frac{1}{4} + \frac{1}{9} + \frac{1}{16} + \frac{1}{25} + \frac{1}{36}\cdots$
$\frac{\pi^2}{24}$	squares of even integers	$\frac{1}{4} + \frac{1}{16} + \frac{1}{36}\cdots$
$\frac{\pi^2}{8}$	squares of odd integers	$1 + \frac{1}{9} + \frac{1}{25}\cdots$
$\frac{\pi^4}{90}$	fourth power of all integers	$1 + \frac{1}{16} + \frac{1}{81} + \frac{1}{256} + \frac{1}{625} + \frac{1}{1296}\cdots$
$\frac{\pi^4}{1440}$	fourth power of even integers	$\frac{1}{16} + \frac{1}{256} + \frac{1}{1296}\cdots$
$\frac{\pi^4}{96}$	fourth power of odd integers	$1 + \frac{1}{81} + \frac{1}{625}\cdots$

FLUKE®

Appendices

Resources

Here are some additional resources. The names and addresses of professional organizations and conferences are listed, along with information about books and periodicals. More chapter references are included here, too.

This appendix contains information that the reader may use as an additional resource to support his or her calibration activity. It is arranged in eight sections as follows:

The Metrologist's Bookshelf
This section lists some books that Fluke believes should be on every metrologist's bookshelf.

National Institute of Standards and Technology (NIST) Information
A list of NIST services with addresses and phone numbers

U.S. Naval Observatory (USNO) Information
A list of USNO services with addresses and phone numbers

Local Services
A place to jot down some additional names, addresses, and phone numbers

Professional Organizations
A list of U.S. organizations

Professional Conferences
A list of conferences

Periodicals
A list of periodicals

Additional Chapter References
An entire section with more references for each chapter

The Metrologist's Bookshelf

National Institute of Standards and Technology Calibration Services Users Guide, NIST *Special Publication 250*, U.S. Superintendent of Documents, U.S. Government Printing Office, Washington DC 20402, Annual Catalog

McCoubrey, A.O., Editor, *Precision Measurement and Calibration: Electricity*, NBS Special Publication 705, 1985

Note: The *Precision Measurement and Calibration* series of reports was begun by NBS in 1961 and updated in 1975. This 1985 volume re-publishes some of the key earlier papers and adds information about new developments between 1972 and 1985.

Military Handbook Evaluation of Contractors' Calibration System, MIL-HDBK-52B, DoD, August, 1989.

International Vocabulary of Basic and General Terms in Metrology, International Standards Organization, P.O. Box 56, CH-1211 Geneva, 20, Switzerland.

National Institute of Standards and Technology (NIST) Information

Calibration and Related Measurement Services (e.g., Electrical Calibration)

Physical Measurement Services Program
Room A112, Building 411
National Institute of Standards and Technology
Gaithersburg, MD 20899
Telephone: (301) 975 2002
FAX: (301) 975 2128

Boulder Services (e.g., Time and Frequency Services)

Measurement Services Clerk
National Institute of Standards and Technology
Boulder, CO 80303
Telephone: (303) 497 3753
FAX: (303) 497 3970

Other Services

National Standard Reference Data System
(see NIST *Special Publication 260*)
Telephone: (301) 975 2208
FAX: (301) 926 0416

Accreditation of Laboratories (NVLAP)
Telephone: (301) 975 4016
FAX: (301) 926 2884

American Association for Laboratory Accreditation (A2LA)
Telephone: (301) 670 1377
FAX: (301) 869 1495

National Center for Standards and Certification Information
(titles and text of standards such as ANSI standards)
Telephone: (301) 975 4040
FAX: (301) 926 1559

Weights and Measures Program
(per NIST *Handbook 44*)
Telephone: (301) 975 4004
FAX: (301) 926 0647

Proficiency Sample Programs
(contact NIST)
Telephone: (301) 975 6704
FAX: (301) 330 1956

U.S. Naval Observatory (USNO) Information

General Information (Recorded Menu)
Telephone: (202) 653 1507

Publications and Products List

**U.S. Naval Observatory
Washington, DC**
Telephone: (202) 653 1507

Local Services

Your National Laboratory

Name: _____

Address: _____

Telephone: _____

Your Calibration Services Laboratory

Name: _____

Address: _____

Telephone: _____

Professional Organizations

American Society for Quality Control, Inc. (ASQC)
310 West Wisconsin Avenue
Milwaukee, WI 53203
Telephone: (414) 272 8575
FAX: (414) 272 1734

National Conference of Standards Laboratories (NCSL)
1800 30th St., Suite 305B
Boulder, CO 80301
Telephone: (303) 440 3339
FAX: (303) 440 3384

Institute of Electrical and Electronic Engineers, Inc. (IEEE)
345 East 47th St.
New York, NY 10017
Telephone: (212) 705 7900
FAX: (908) 981 9667

Instrument Society of America (ISA)
67 Alexander Dr.
Research Triangle Park, NC 27709
Telephone: (919) 549 8411
FAX: (919) 549 8288

Professional Conferences

NCSL: Workshop and Symposium, held annually in various U.S. cities. Regional Meetings, held quarterly in various U. S. cities.

ISA: International Conference and Exhibit, held annually in the fall in various large U.S. cities.

ASQC: Annual Quality Congress, held annually in various large U.S. cities.

MSC: Measurement Science Conference, held annually in January or February in Southern California.

IMTC: IEEE Instrumentation and Measurement Technology Conference, held annually.

CPEM: Conference on Precision Electromagnetic Measurements, held bi-annually in the summer, alternating between U.S. and international cities.

Periodicals

IEEE *Transactions on Instrumentation and Measurement*
Telephone: (212) 705 7900

Metrologia
International Journal of Scientific Metrology (Quarterly)
North America Subscriptions Information
Telephone: (201) 348 4033
All Other Countries
Telephone: (0 30) 82 07 1

ISA Transactions (Quarterly)
Instrument Society of America
Telephone: (919) 549 8411

Additional Chapter References

This section provides additional references for many of the chapters in this book. The references are subdivided into various categories as follows:

Category	Technical Level
NIST Publications	engineering or scientific
Reference Works	engineering or scientific
Technical Articles – A	engineering or scientific
Technical Articles – B	technician
Technical Papers	not categorized, generally engineering
Application Notes	technician
Background Reading	scientifically literate general reader
Supplementary Reading	scientifically literate general reader

Chapter 4: International Metrology

Reference Works

Cohen, E. Richard, "Symbols, Units and Nomenclature," *Encyclopedia of Physics*, Second Edition, BCH Publishers, Inc. New York, NY, 1991

Taylor, B.N., "Constants, Fundamental," *Encyclopedia of Physics*, Second Edition, BCH Publishers, Inc. New York, NY, 1991

70th PTB Symposium, "Fundamental Constants in Physics and Metrology," *Metrologia*, Volume 22, Number 3, 1986

Technical Articles – A

Robinson, Arthur L., "Values of Fundamental Constants Adjusted," *Science*, Volume 235, February 6, 1987

Background Reading

Harrison, Edward R., "The Cosmic Numbers," *The World of Physics, Volume III*, Section X3, page 596, Simon & Schuster, New York, NY, 1987

Barrow, John D., "Constants of Nature," *Theories of Everything*, Chapter 5, page 104, Clarendon Press, Oxford, 1991

Chapter 7: Direct Voltage and Current

NIST Publications

Belecki, Norman B.; Dzluba, Ronald F.; Field, Bruce F.; Taylor, Barry N., "Guidelines for Implementing the New Representations of the Volt and Ohm Effective January 1, 1990," NIST *Technical Note 1263*, June, 1989

Technical Articles – A

Funck, T.; Sienknecht, V., "Determination of the Volt with the Improved PTB Voltage Balance," IEEE *Transactions on Instrumentation and Measurement*, Vol. 40, No. 2, April, 1991

Amato, Ivan, "This SQUID Ain't Sushi," *Science*, Volume 254, December 20, 1991. *This article describes a commercially available SQUID (Superconducting Quantum Interference Device) that can be used as a null detector for a Josephson Array.*

Taylor, B.N., "History of the Present Value of 2e/h Commonly Used for Defining National Units of Voltage and Possible Changes in National Units of Voltage and Resistance," IEEE *Transactions on Instrumentation and Measurement*, Vol. IM-36, No. 2, June, 1987

Olsen, P.T. et al., "The NBS Absolute Ampere Experiment," IEEE *Transactions on Instrumentation and Measurement*, Vol. IM-34, No. 2, June, 1985

Application Notes

Marshall, James, "The Application of Low Noise Switches for Automating Precision Measurements," *Data Proof*, Sunnyvale, CA, 1987

This application note describes a scanner suitable for automating the intercomparison of standard cells or solid-state voltage references.

Chapter 8: DC Resistance

NIST Publications

Belecki, Norman B.; Dzluba, Ronald F.; Field, Bruce F.; Taylor, Barry N., "Guidelines for Implementing the New Representations of the Volt and Ohm Effective January 1, 1990," NIST *Technical Note 1263*, June, 1989

Technical Articles – A

Taylor, B.N., "History of the Present Value of 2e/h Commonly Used for Defining National Units of Voltage and Possible Changes in National Units of Voltage and Resistance, IEEE *Transactions on Instrumentation and Measurement*, Vol. IM-36, No. 2, June, 1987

IEEE *Transactions on Instrumentation and Measurement*, Vol. 38, No. 2, April, 1989, pages 245 ff.

70th PTB Symposium, "Fundamental Constants in Physics and Metrology," *Metrologia*, Volume 22, Number 3, 1986

Background Reading

Halprin, B.J., "The Quantized Hall Effect," *Scientific American*, April, 1986

Chapter 9: DC Ratio

NIST Publications

Park, J.H., "Special Shielded Resistor for High-Voltage DC Measurements," NBS *Journal of Research*, Vol. 66C, January-March, 1962

Technical Articles – A

Burroughs, C.J.; Hamilton, C.A., "Voltage Calibration Systems Using Josephson Junction Arrays," IEEE *Transactions on Instrumentation and Measurement*, Vol. IM-39, No. 6, December, 1990

Delahaye, F.; Reymann, D., "Progress in Resistance Ratio Measurements Using a Cryogenic Current Comparator at LCIE," IEEE *Transactions on Instrumentation and Measurement*, Vol. IM-34, No. 2, June, 1985

Sugiyama, Takashi; Yamaguchi, Keiki, "Pulse-width Modulation DC Potentiometer." IEEE *Transactions on Instrumentation and Measurement*, Vol. IM-19, No. 4, November, 1970

MacMartin, M.P.; Kusters, N.L., "The application of the Direct Current Comparator to a Seven-Decade Potentiometer," IEEE *Transactions on Instrumentation and Measurement*, Vol. IM-17, No. 4, December, 1968

Technical Papers

Faulkner, Neil, "An Automated System for the Comparison of Resistance Standards from 1 Ohm to Several kOhms," Measurement Science Conference, January, 1992

Chapter 10: Principles of AC-DC Metrology

NIST Publications

Hermach, F.L., "An Investigation of the Uncertainties of the NBS Thermal Voltage and Current Converters," *NBSIR* No. 84-2903, April, 1985

Hermach, F.L.; Flach, D.R., "An Investigation of Multijunction Thermal Converters," IEEE *Transactions on Instrumentation and Measurement*, Vol. IM-25, No. 4, December, 1976

Hermach, F.L., "AC-DC Comparators for Audio-Frequency Current and Voltage Measurements of High Accuracy," IEEE *Transactions on Instrumentation and Measurement*, Vol. IM-25, No. 4, December, 1976

Hermach, F.L., "Thermal Converters as AC-DC Transfer Standard for current and Voltage Measurements at Audio Frequencies," *Journal of Research of the National Bureau of Standards*, Vol. 48, No. 2, February, 1952

Technical Articles – A

Inglis, B.D., Franchimon, C.C., "Current Independent AC-DC Transfer Errors in Single-Junction Thermal Converters," IEEE *Transactions on Instrumentation and Measurement*, Vol. IM-34, No. 2, June, 1985

Goyal, Ramesh; Brodie, Benjamin T., "Recent Advances in Precision AC Measurements," IEEE *Transactions on Instrumentation and Measurement*, Vol. IM-33, No. 3, September, 1984

Ott, W.E., "A New Technique of Thermal RMS Measurement, IEEE *Journal of Solid-State Circuits*, Vol. SC-9, No.6, December, 1974

Technical Papers

Widlar, R.J., "An Exact Expression for the Thermal Variation of the Emitter-Base Voltage of a Bi-Polar Transistor," *National Semiconductor Corporation Technical Paper: TP-1*, March, 1967

Inglis, B.D., "Performance Limitations in Thermal AC-DC Transfer Standards," Electrical Measurement Symposium, CISRO-NML, May, 1987

Chapter 11: Using AC-DC Transfer Standards

Technical Papers

Wong, Warren, "Automated Calibration of a Thermal Transfer Standard," Measurement Science Conference, January, 1992

Eccleston, Larry, "Designing an AC Measurement System," Measurement Science Conference, 1991

Matson, Don, "Using a Linear Thermal Transfer Standard for High Precision AV/DV Transfers," CPEM, 1990

Henderson, Bob; Matson, Don, "Design and Evaluation of an AC/DC Transfer Standard," 1990 Workshop and Symposium, National Conference of Standards Laboratories, August, 1990

Application Notes

"Design and Development of the 5790A Automated AC Measurement Standard," *Fluke Application Note B0219A*

Chapter 12: Inductance and Capacitance

NIST Publications

The Rise of the Calculable Capacitor," NBS *Dimensions*, December, 1975 (Note: *Dimensions* is no longer published.)

Technical Papers

Clarke, Kenneth K.; Hess, Donald T., "The Measurement of the Loss in High Q Capacitors," Clarke-Hess Communications Research Corp., New York, NY, 1986

Jones, R.N.; Huntley, Les, "A Precision High Frequency Calibration Facility for Coaxial Capacitance Standards," NBS *Technical Note 386*, March, 1970

Background Reading

Coltman, John W., "The Transformer," *Scientific American*, January, 1988

Trotter, Donald M., Jr., "Capacitors," *Scientific American*, July, 1988

Chapter 13: Immittance and AC Ratio

Technical Articles – A

Hoer, C. A.; Agy, D. L., "Broad-Band Resistive-Divider-Type Directional Coupler," IEEE *Transactions on Instrumentation and Measurement*, Vol. IM-19, No. 4, March, 1982

Allred, C.M.; Manney, C.H., "The Calibration and Use of Directional Couplers Without Standards," IEEE *Transactions on Instrumentation and Measurement*, Vol. IM-25, No. 1, March, 1976

Hall, H.P., "Achieving Fractional-ppm Ratio Precision with Two-Stage Transformers," *EID-Electronic Instrumentation*, February, 1972

Homan, D.N.; Zapf, T.L., "Two Stage, Guarded Inductive Voltage Divider for Use at 100 kHz," ISA *Transactions*, Vol. 9, No. 3, 1970

Russell, D.; Larson, W., "RF Attenuation," *Proceedings of the IEEE*, Vol. 55, No. 6, June, 1967

Huntley, L.E.; Jones, R.N., "Lumped Parameter Impedance Measurements," *Proceedings of the IEEE*, Vol. 55, No. 6, June, 1967

Technical Papers

Clarke, Kenneth K.; Hess, Donald T., "The Measurement of the Loss in High Q Capacitors," Clarke-Hess Communications Research Corp., New York, NY 10011

Chapter 14: Time and Frequency

NIST Publications

Risley, Allan S., "The Physical Basis of Atomic Frequency Standards," NBS *Monograph 140*, May, 1974

Technical Articles – A

Dickey, J.O.; Marcus, S.L.; Steppe, J.A.; Hide, R., "The Earth's Angular Momentum Budget on Subseasonal Time Scales," *Science*, 17 August, 1992

Hide, R.; Dickey, J.O., "Earth's Variable Rotation Rate," *Science*, 9 August, 1991

"Time and Frequency," entire issue of *Proceedings of the IEEE*, Vol.70, No. 7, July, 1991

Ramsey, N.F., "Measurements with Separated Oscillatory Fields and Hydrogen Masers," IEEE *Transactions on Instrumentation and Measurement*, Vol. 40, No. 2, April, 1991

Schuh, Harald, "Earth Rotation Parameters Determined by VLBI Within Project IRIS." IEEE *Transactions on Instrumentation and Measurement*, Vol. 38, No. 2, April, 1989

Dorenwendt, K., "Realization and Dissemination of the Second," *Metrologia*, Volume 22, No. 3, 1986

Wiess, M.; Wiessert, T., "AT2, A New Time Scale Algorithm: AT Plus Frequency Variance," *Metrologia*, Vol. 28, No. 2, 1991

Granveaud, M., "Are the Independent Atomic Time Scales Worthy of Interest?" *Metrologia*, Vol. 26, No. 2, 1989

Ertmer, W.; Penselin, S., "Cooled Atomic Beams for Frequency Standards," *Metrologia*, Vol. 22, No. 3, 1986

Background Reading

Itano, Wayne M.; Ramsey, Norman F., "Accurate Measurement of Time," *Scientific American*, July, 1993

Chu, Steven, "Laser Trapping of Neutral Particles," *Scientific American*, February, 1992

Carter, William E.; Robertson, Douglas S., "Studying the Earth by Very Long Baseline Interferometry," *Scientific American*, November, 1986

Supplementary Reading

Asimov, Isaac, "The Unforgiving Minute," *Out of the Everywhere*, Pinnacle Books, Windsor Publishing Company, New York, 475 Park Avenue South, NY, 10016, 1992. *Asimov's discussion of timekeeping lore from antiquity until now is an easy, fact-filled read.*

Moyer, Gorden, "The Gregorian Calendar," *Scientific American*, May, 1982

Bartley, Ian R.; Harrison, Elizabeth, "Standard and Daylight Saving Time," *Scientific American*, May, 1979

Waugh, Albert E., *Sundials: Their Theory and Construction*, Dover Publications, Inc., 1973. *Waugh's book has a lot to say about local apparent solar time and its relationship to time kept by mechanical clocks.*

Chapter 15: Multifunction Calibrators

Technical Papers

Withrow, Tom, "Semi-Automated Calibration of High Accuracy AC Calibrators," 1990 Workshop and Symposium, National Conference of Standards Laboratories, August, 1990

Eccleston, Larry, "Advancements in Accurate AC Voltage Sources," Measurement Science Conference, January, 1987

Technical Articles – B

Eccleston, L.; Faulkner, N.; Johnston, C.; Prue, W.; Thiemann, M., "Calibrator Brings Record Accuracy, Even to Production and Repair," *Electronics*, September 8, 1982

Application Notes

"Semi-Automated AC Verification of the 5700A Calibrator," *Fluke Application Note B0211A*

"Dialog 5700A," *Fluke Technical Note J0321B*

Chapter 16: Artifact Calibration

Technical Papers

Koeman, Henriecus, "Multifunction, Multi-range Electronic Instrument Performance Prediction," Measurement Science Conference, 1992

Baldock, Paul, "Artifact Calibration," Measurement Science Conference, 1991

Baldock, Paul, "New Design Developments Simplify Calibrator Support," Measurement Science Conference, 1988

Baldock, Paul, "Instrument 'Internal Calibration' Reduces Cost of Ownership and Improves Performance," Measurement Science Conference, 1987

Application Notes

"The Metrology of the 5700A Calibrator," *Fluke Application Note B0175A*

Chapter 17: Digital Multimeter Calibration

Technical Articles – A

Goyal, Ramesh; Brodie, Benjamin T., "Recent Advances in Precision AC Measurements." IEEE *Transactions on Instrumentation and Measurement*, Vol. IM-33, No. 3, September, 1984

Chapel, Roy, "RMS Voltage Measurements— Which Method Works Best," *Electronic Products*, January 15, 1973

Swerlin, Ronald, "Precision AC Measurements Using Digitizing Techniques," Hewlett Packard Company, 815 14th Street S.W., Loveland, CO 80537

Technical Papers

Van Saun, Richard, W., "A New True RMS AC Differential Voltmeter," 1966 National Electronic Conference, Chicago, IL, October 3-4-5

Chapter 19: Automated Calibration

Technical Papers

Mason, Nicholas, "Networking PCs in a Calibration Laboratory," 1990 Workshop and Symposium, National Conference of Standards Laboratories, August, 1990

Withrow, Tom, "Semi-Automated Calibration of High Accuracy AC Calibrators," 1990 Workshop and Symposium, National Conference of Standards Laboratories, August, 1990

Carter, Mark, "Personal Computers Improve Cal Lab Productivity," 1988 Workshop and Symposium, National Conference of Standards Laboratories, August, 1988

Laine, Brian T., "Procedure Driven Software Eases System Control," Midcon, 1985

Bloomer, Jim, "The Future of Instrument Automation and the Impact Upon the Calibration Lab," Measurement Science Conference, January, 1984

Technical Articles – B

Capell, Frank, "New Developments in Automated Calibration Systems," Test and Measurement World, October, 1985

Application Notes

"Metrology, Quality and ISO 9000," *Fluke Application Note B0217C*

Chapter 20: Introduction to Metrology Statistics

Technical Articles – A

Capell, Frank, "From 4:1 to SPC," ISA *Transactions*, Volume 29, No. 4, 1990

Read, S.I., Read, T.R.C., "Statistical Issues in Setting Product Specifications," *Hewlett-Packard Journal*, June, 1988

Eagle, A.R., "A Method for Handling Errors in Testing and Measuring," *Industrial Quality Control*, March, 1954

Technical Papers

Deaver, Dave, "How to Maintain Your Confidence (In a World of Declining Test Uncertainty Ratios)," National Conference of Standards Laboratories, 1993 Workshop and Symposium, July 25-29, 1993

Koeman, Henriecus, "Multifunction, Multirange Electronic Instrument Performance Prediction," Measurement Science Conference, January, 1992

Capell, F., "Performance Proofing a Self-Adjusting Calibrator," 4th Annual ASQC Quality Congress, Milwaukee, WI, May, 1991

Chapter 21: Statistical Tools for Metrology

NIST Publications

Eisenhart, Churchill, "Realistic Evaluation of the Precision and Accuracy of Instrument Calibration Systems," *Journal of Research of the National Bureau of Standards*, Vol. 67C, No. 2, April-June 1963. Reprinted in NBS *Special Publication 300*, Volume 1

Swyt, Dennis A.; Hopp, Theodore H.; Charlton, Thomas, Jr., "Quality Control in Automated Manufacturing," NBS, Center for Manufacturing Engineering

Reference Works

Shewhart, Walter A., "Statistical Method from the Viewpoint of Quality Control," The Graduate School, U.S. Department of Agriculture, Washington, D.C.

Deming, W. Edwards, *Some Theory of Sampling*, John Wiley & Sons, New York, NY, 1950

Technical Articles – A

Schumacher, Rolf B., "Systematic Measurement Uncertainty," *Journal of Quality Technology*, Vol. 13, No, 1, January, 1981

Technical Papers

Huntley, Les; Meyrick, Aaron, "Applying SPC to Calibration Processes in an Industrial Standards Laboratory," Measurement Science Conference, 1991

Haynes, S., "An Automatic Test System for a Multifunction Calibrator," Measurement Science Conference, 1988

Huntley, Les; Murray, Jill Ellen, "An Application of Process Metrology to the Automatic Calibration of Instruments," *Proceedings of the Measurement Science Conference*, January, 1987

Huntley, Les, "The Fluke Direct Voltage Measurement Program," *Proceedings of the Measurement Science Conference*, January, 1984

Application Notes

"Fractional ppm Traceability Using Your 732A," Fluke *Technical Information B0196A*

Chapter 23: Statistical Process Control

NIST Publications

Ku, Harry H., "Notes on the Use of Propagation of Error Formula," NBS *Journal of Research*, Vol. 70C, No. 4, October-December, 1966 (reprinted in NBS *Special Publication 300*, Vol. 1)

Reference Works

Shumway, R.H., *Applied Statistical Time Series Analysis*, Prentice-Hall, Englewood Cliffs, NJ

AT&T Technologies, *Statistical Quality Control Handbook*, 1956, Indianapolis, IN 46219

Technical Articles – A

Huntley, Les, "A Primary Standard of Voltage Maintained in Solid-State References," IEEE *Transactions on Instrumentation and Measurement*, Vol. IM-36, No. 4, December, 1987

Chapter 28: Laboratory Quality and ISO 9000

Technical Papers

Hirning, Jim, "A New Approach to Quality Management," National Conference of Standards Laboratories, 1989 Workshop and Symposium, July, 1989

Korthout, J., "The Impact of New International Quality Standards on Metrology," National Conference of Standards Laboratories, 1991 Workshop and Symposium, Albuquerque, NM, August, 1991

Pirret, Richard, "Software Tools for ISO 9000 Compliance," National 1992 Workshop and Symposium, Conference of Standards Laboratories, August, 1992

Chapter 30: Laboratory Audits

Technical Papers

Berry, G.H., "The Calibration of Software to Audit Survival," National Conference of Standards Laboratories, 1989 Workshop and Symposium, July, 1989

Mason, Nicholas, "Networking PCs in a Calibration Laboratory," National Conference of Standards Laboratories, 1990 Workshop and Symposium, August, 1990

Chapter 31: Instrument Specifications

Technical Papers

Laine, Brian T., "Calibration Synergism: The Embedded Microprocessor and Non-Volatile Memory," Measurement Science Conference, January, 1985

Chapter 32: Grounding, Shielding and Guarding

Reference Works

Ott, H., *Noise Reduction in Electronic Systems*, John Wiley and Sons, Inc., 1976

Reference Data for Radio Engineers, 5th Edition, Howard W. Sams & Co., Inc.

Application Notes

Floating Measurements and Guarding, Hewlett-Packard Company *Application Note 123*, 1970

Chapter 33: A Rogues' Gallery of Parasitics

Technical Papers

Grant, Doug; Wurcer, Scott, "Avoiding Passive-Component Pitfalls," *The Best of Analog Dialogue*, Analog Devices, 1991

Chapel, Roy, "Taming Thermocouple Voltages in Microelectronics," *Proceedings of the 1987 International Symposium on Microelectronics,*

pages 104–112, published by the International Society for Hybrid Microelectronics, P.O. Box 2698, Reston, VA 22090

Chapter 34: AC Lore

Technical Articles – A

Oldham, Niles M.; Hetrick, Paul S.; Zeng, Xiangren, "A Calculable, Transportable, Audio-Frequency AC Reference Standard," IEEE *Transactions on Instrumentation and Measurement*, Vol. 38, No. 2, April, 1989

Widdis, F.C., "The Theory of Peltier- and Thomson-Effect in Thermal AC-DC Transfer Devices," The Institute of Electrical and Electronic Engineers, *Monograph No. 497 M*, January, 1962

Background Reading

Pierce, J.R.; Noll, A.M., "Theories of Communication Fourier to Shannon," Chapter 3 of *Signals*, a *Scientific American* Book, 1990

Dunham, William, "The Extraordinary Sums of Leonhard Euler," Chapter 9 of *Journey Through Genius, The Great Theorems of Mathematics,"* John Wiley & Sons, Inc., 1990

Bracewell, Ronald N., "The Fourier Transform," *Scientific American*, June, 1989

Contributors

This book integrates the ideas and hard work of a number of people, many of whom are acknowledged here. Fluke would like to thank all of those who contributed to this project.

Dave Agy • Bill Allred • Tom Anderson • Mike Arst
Geoff Baker • Paul Baldock • Kelli Barr
Marie Barrett • Arnon Beck • Betty Behrens
Dick Beier • Sharon Bennett • Glen Berry
Anthony Birdsong • Danny Blondia • John Bowman
Ron Brittain • Tom Brockway • Dick Buell
Chace Campbell • Frank Capell • Red Carlson
Mark Carter • Laurie Christian • Warren Collier
Ginger Corley • Rick Crabb • Clark Crain
Wayne Cummings • Don Dalton • Gene Davis
James Davis • Randy Davison • Dave Deaver
Robert Diggins • Frank Doucet • William Driggers
Larry Eccleston • Dan Ellis • William Endow
Doug Erny • Neil Faulkner • Russ Fleming
Dave Flohr • John Flower • Julius Gargyi
Ernest Garner • Val Gersbach • Dick Goodall
Beryl Gorbman • Steve Griffin • Bill Grindele
Warren Hagemeier • Bob Hagger • John Halloran
Bob Hammond • Kazumi Hayakawa • Steve Haynes
John Hines • Jim Hirning • Fred Hubbard
Fred Hume • Les Huntley • Thomas Huttemann
Richard Hyman • Yoshito Ichinomiya • James Ingram
Klaus Jaeger • Tom Johnson • Craig Johnston
Jerry Kaylor • Larry Kimmons • Ray Kletke
Manfred Klonz • Riekus Koeman • Joost Korthout
John Lynch • Vaughn Martin • Joe Martins
David Martson • Nicholas Mason • Dennis McCabe
Kevin McClure • Barbara McGinn • Bob McKelvy
Gary Meyer • Tom Milton • Don Mitchell
Jesse Morse • Tom Moxley • Bob Myers
Hakan Nilsson • Herb O'Neal • Bob Ollweiler
Saburo Oya • Jim Pawluk • Tony Petroske
Rick Pirret • Colin Plastow • Larry Potaro • Walt Prue
Barbara Richardson • Rod Richmond • Harry Rundall
Peter Schneider • Ed Schoenharl • Dick Scott
Doug Severance • Jim Shields • Joe Simmons
Alan Smith • Jack Somppi • Bud Stott • Pat Stuart
Mel Suelzle • Fred Telewski • Sharon Tighe
Hans Toorens • Doug Tracy • Bob Trollinger
Don Tuttle • Richard Van Gilder • Ed Voorhaar
Howard Voorheis • Simon de Vries • Bob Weber
Rick Weller • Bill Wightman • Phil Winfield
Johnnie Winters • Tom Withrow • Warren Wong
Barry Wood • Ken Yoshino

Glossary

The definitions in this glossary are oriented toward their application in dc and low frequency electrical metrology. More detailed and rigorous definitions are supplied in various other works.

This glossary takes note of certain words whose legal and scientific meanings may have subtle shades of difference that may be of great importance in a specific situation. The reader is requested to compare the definitions for these words in the works listed after the definition of the word.

The reference works, arranged by their source of publication, are:

NCSL
  RP3-1988
  RP-2

Military
  MIL-STD-1309C
  MIL-STD-45662A
  MIL-STD-109B
  MIL-STD-721C
  MIL-STD-280A
  DOD-D-4155.1
  NAVAIR 17- FF35MTL-1
  USAF MET HDBK

NIST
  NBS SP 676-1
  NIST Technical Note 1297

INDUSTRY
  ANSI/ASQC STD M1-1987
  ANSI/IEEE STD 100-1977

ISO
  INTL VOC - ISO(84), or VIM
  "International vocabulary of basic and general terms in metrology"

ISO 8402-1986

A2LA: Abbreviation for the American Association of Laboratory Accreditation.

Absolute Uncertainty: (Specifications) The total uncertainty of a specified value, including the uncertainty of its value in comparison to the national standards.

AC Transfer Measurement: The determination of an ac value in comparison to a known dc value by means of an ac-dc transfer standard.

AC-DC Absolute Uncertainty: The complete uncertainty of the ac-dc difference, including the uncertainty of its test-reported difference with the national standards.

AC-DC Difference (δ): The difference in an ac-dc transfer standards response when it is used to compare ac and dc voltages that are known to have the same amplitude.

AC-DC Difference Measurement: The measurement of the unknown ac-dc difference of an ac-dc transfer standard under test in comparison to the known ac-dc difference of a standard ac-dc transfer standard.

AC-DC Relative Uncertainty: An incomplete uncertainty for the ac-dc difference, lacking the uncertainty of its test-reported difference with the national standards.

AC-DC Transfer: The process of comparing an ac voltage to a known dc voltage, thereby transferring the value of the dc voltage to the ac voltage.

AC-DC Transfer Stability: The change in an ac-dc transfer standard's ac-dc difference, δ, over a specified interval of time.

Accuracy: The degree of closeness between a measured value and the true or nominal value (*see* Uncertainty).

Accuracy Ratio: *See* Test Uncertainty Ratio.

Active Ranges, AC-DC Transfer Standard: AC-DC transfer standard ranges that electronically amplify the ac and dc signals at the standard's input prior to applying them to the thermal element.

Adjustment: An operation that is accomplished to initially establish or later restore an instrument's specified performance level. *See* User Adjustment *and* Calibration Adjustment.

Admittance: The electrical inverse, Y, of impedance, Z, equal to 1/Z.

Ampere: The SI base unit of electrical current.

Amplification, Electrical: An increase in the amplitude of an electrical signal.

Amplitude, Electrical: The magnitude of a voltage or current.

Analog Instrument: An instrument whose signal processing circuits do not include digital technology and which often uses meter needle movements to indicate its output or input.

ANSI: Abbreviation for American National Standards Institute.

Artifact Standard: A standard whose value(s) are based on human skill and workmanship.

As-Found, As-Left Calibration: A calibration protocol that records and compares the same calibration data for an instrument both before and after its calibration is adjusted.

Atomic Time: The extremely accurate and uniform measurement of time obtained by counting cycles of an atomic clock.

Attenuation, Electrical: A decrease in the amplitude of an electrical signal.

Audit: Usually a customer's independent inspection of a supplier's records, procedures, facilities and personnel. The audit is conducted to confirm that the supplier's quality system is functioning properly.

Auditor: A person or organization that conducts an audit.

Base Units: Dimensionally independent units in a coherent system of units. All other units are derived from base units. The base units of the SI are the meter, kilogram, second, ampere, kelvin, mole and candela.

Bayesian Probability: A statistical method which uses prior information in the analysis of new measurement data.

Bias Current: An undesired current, typically in the order of a few pA, that flows into or out of an operational amplifer.

BIPM: Abbreviation for International Bureau of Weights and Measures (Fr., Bureau Internationale des poids et mesures).

Burden Voltage: Voltage drop developed across an impedance by the current flowing through it.

Cal Sticker: *See* Calibration Label *or* Calibration Documents.

Calibrated Unit (CU): *See* Unit Under Test.

Calibration: A set of operations, performed in accordance with a definite, documented procedure, that compares the measurements performed by an instrument to those made by a more accurate instrument or standard, for the purpose of detecting and reporting, or eliminating by adjustment, errors in the instrument tested. *Compare* NCSL RP3-1988, MIL-STD-1309C, NBS SP 676-1, INTL VOC - ISO(84), ANSI/ASQC STD M1-1987, MIL-STD-45662A, *and* DOD-D-4155.1.

Calibration Adjustment: The adjustment of an instrument via internal controls or firmware, not accessible during normal operation, in order to initially establish or later restore an instrument's specified performance level.

Calibration Constant: A correction factor that is applied manually or automatically to correct the output or reading of an instrument.

Calibration Cycle (Cal Cycle): The repetitive schedule of removing an instrument from use, calibrating it and returning it to service. The calibration may involve physically moving the instrument from its normal location to the calibration laboratory or it may be done onsite or *in situ*.

Calibration Documents: *See* Calibration Report, Calibration Label, Special Calibration Label, Special Calibration Tag, Limited Calibration Label, No Calibration Required Label, Property Tag, Reject Tag *and* Tamper Seal.

Calibration Due Date: The date that an instrument in the calibration cycle requires calibration. In a properly managed quality system, the instrument cannot be used after this date if the calibration is not accomplished.

Calibration Interval: A specified or designated period of time between calibration adjustments or verifications. During this interval the instrument should remain within specific performance levels, with a specified probability, under normal conditions of handling and use.

Calibration Label: A label affixed to an instrument that shows its calibration status. The label typically indicates the instrument's identification, who performed the last calibration and when, and the date of the next scheduled calibration.

Calibration Laboratory (Cal Lab): A work space, provided with test equipment, controlled environment and trained personnel, established for the purpose of maintaining proper operation and accuracy of measuring and test equipment. Cal Labs typically perform many routine calibrations, often on a production-line basis.

Calibration Procedure, Verification: The documentation or software program that is used to perform or control the measurement processes used to determine, evaluate, and report, but not adjust the performance of an instrument, calibrator or standard in comparison to calibration standards.

Calibration Procedure: The documentation or software program that is used to perform or control the measurement processes used to determine, evaluate, report, or adjust the performance of an instrument, calibrator or standard in comparison to calibration standards.

Calibration Report: A comprehensive record of the calibration of an instrument. The record includes data that describes the performance of the instrument, the environmental conditions under which it was calibrated and the standards used to calibrate it.

Calibration Sticker: *See* Calibration Label *or* Calibration Documents.

Calibration Verification: Checking the functional performance and uncertainty of an instrument or standard without making adjustments to it or changing its calibration constants.

Calibrator: A secondary or tertiary standard that supplies outputs with a known uncertainty for use in checking the accuracy of measurement devices.

Capacitance: The characteristic of an electrical circuit that opposes a change in voltage.

Capacitive Reactance: The opposition to the flow of ac current in an ac circuit due to capacitance.

Cesium Standard: An atomic clock that uses cesium to obtain atomic resonance.

Chassis Ground: The electrical potential of the outer metal chassis of an instrument. This chassis is usually connected to earth ground via the safety ground of the line cord of line power operated instruments.

Check Standard: A stable, well-characterized in-house standard that is remeasured at periodic intervals to determine whether the measurement process is in a state of statistical control.

CIPM: Abbreviation for International Committee for Weights and Measures (Fr., Congress Internationale des poids et mesures).

Coaxial Cable: A transmission line or cable in which a center conductor is surrounded by an insulating medium whose exterior is surrounded by a cylindrical conductor.

Coherent System of Units (of measurement): A system of units composed of a set of base units and coherent derived units.

Coherent Unit (of measurement): A derived unit of measurement which is expressed in terms of base units by a formula in which the proportionality factor is 1.

Common-Mode Noise: An undesired signal that exists between a device's input or output port and earth ground. Common-mode noise has the same potential, relative to ground, on all of the port terminals.

Common-Mode Voltage: A desired voltage signal that exists between a device's input or output port and a common reference point for the port. Common-mode voltage has the same potential, relative to the reference point, on all of the port terminals.

Common: *See* Measurement Common.

Compliance Current: The maximum current that a constant-voltage source can supply.

Compliance Voltage: The maximum voltage that a constant-current source can supply.

Conductance: The inverse of resistance, G, equal to $1/R$.

Conductor: An electrical material that can transport free charge carriers via the application of an emf.

Confidence: In metrology, confidence refers to the degree of assurance one has that a measurement lies within its statistically predicted bounds. These bounds are usually derived from the distribution of probability associated with the normal curve.

Confidence Interval: A range of values under the normal curve for which a specific confidence level applies. The range of values is normally extended symmetrically from the center of the curve, in standard deviations, to a limiting value, typically plus and minus standard deviations.

Confidence Level: The percentage of the area of the normal curve that lies above the confidence interval. A confidence level of 95% is obtained when the range of the confidence is from minus two standard deviations to plus two standard deviations.

Consensus Standard: A standard used by agreement between contracting parties when no national standard is available.

Contact Potential: Voltage (potential) developed across the junction of contacts constructed from two different materials in the absence of current.

Contact Resistance: The resistance at the junction of switch or relay contacts.

Control Chart: A chart devised to monitor one or more processes in order to detect excessive deviation from the desired value (setpoint) of the process.

Correction Factor: A numerical factor used to multiply the result of a measurement in order to compensate for an assumed systematic error.

Correlation: A comparison of independent measurements, calibrations or calibration reports used to establish a common basis for their evaluation.

Coverage Factor: ISO-proposed term, similar to confidence interval.

CPEM: IEEE Conference for Precision Electromagnetic Measurements.

Crest Factor: The ratio of the peak voltage to rms voltage of a waveform (with the dc component removed).

Date: A complete description of the time of an event, including the year, day, hour, minute, and second. It can be given as the day number of a particular year or as the Julian day.

Degradation: A gradual reduction in an instrument's performance that proceeds until the instrument fails to meet its performance specifications.

Derived Units: The units in a coherent system of units that are derived from its base units.

Detector: An instrument or device which indicates the presence of a particular quantity without necessarily providing its value, for example a smoke detector.

Device: As used in this book, a measurement standard, calibrator, instrument or test equipment.

Device Under Calibration (DUC): *See* Unit Under Test.

Device Under Test (DUT): *See* Unit Under Test.

Dielectric: As used in this book, the insulating material between the plates of a capacitor. *See* VIM for a general definition.

Differential Method of Measurement: A method of measurement in which the measurand is compared with a quantity of the same kind, of known value that is usually only slightly different from that of measurand, such that the difference between the two values is measured.

Digital Instrument: An instrument whose signal processing circuits incorporate digital technology and which often uses digital displays to indicate its output or input.

Dimension of a Quantity: An expression which represents a quantity of a system of quantities as the product of powers of the base quantities of the system.

Dimensioned Quantity: A numerical value expressed in units such as 10V.

Dimensionless Quantity: A numerical value that has no units, for example the ratio of two voltages.

Direct Method of Measurement: A method of measurement in which the value of a measurand is obtained directly, rather than by measurement of other quantities functionally related to the measurand.

Distribution: In metrology, the correlation of a set of measured values with their relative frequency of occurrence.

Drift: A slow variation over time in the performance of an instrument. In contrast to Degradation, the instrument may continue to operate within its performance specifications.

Dry Contact Resistance: The resistance at the junction of switch or relay contacts when little or no current is flowing through the contacts.

Earth Ground: Earth ground is a connection through a ground rod to the earth, available in an ac power outlet. The voltage reference point in a circuit is sometimes called ground but is properly referred to as common.

Electrical Reversal Measurement: A measurement wherein the interconnection of a test instrument and standard is reversed in the measurement process in order to cancel out the effects of thermal emf's, lead and contact resistance, etc. The absolute measured value of the test instrument is taken as the mean of the absolute values of its forward and reversed response.

Electrically Neutral: A conductor or system of conductors within which the total electric charge is zero.

Electricity: All phenomena that involve electric charges at rest or in motion.

Electromagnetic Energy: Energy stored in an electromagnetic field.

Electromagnetic Field: A field, described by Maxwell's equations, with electric and magnetic components perpendicular to each other.

Electromagnetic Interference (EMI): The interaction of undesired electromagnetic energy with a desired electrical signal.

Electromagnetic Wave: A wave whose electric and magnetic components and direction of propagation are mutually perpendicular.

Electromagnetism: Phenomena associated with electromagnetic fields.

Electrostatic Field: Electric field whose change with time is negligible.

Electrostatics: Phenomena associated with electrostatic fields and electric charges at rest.

EMI: *See* Electromagnetic Interference.

Environment: The altitude, temperature, humidity, emi and other pertinent conditions that affect the performance of an instrument. *Also see* MIL-STD-721C.

Error: Deviation from the true or nominal value. Different types of error include offset, linearity, random, retrace, reversal, scale, systematic, and transfer error. *Compare* USAF MET HDBK, MIL-STD-1309C, INTL VOC-ISO(84), NCSL RP3-1988 *and* ANSI/IEEE STD 100-1977).

Error Characterization: The development of a table of calibration constants or correction factors for use in correcting the output or reading of an instrument.

Extrapolation: The extension of a data series to a point outside of the data.

F Test: The F test is a statistical test for the fit of a regression to the data sets that were used to determine it.

Faraday Shield: A metal case that completely surrounds the conductors in sensitive circuits in order to protect them from capacitive interaction with a voltage noise source.

Flatness: Variation in the amplitude of a specific ac voltage value as a function of its frequency.

Floor: The part of the uncertainty specification of an instrument that is typically a fixed offset plus noise.

Floor Error: Error that has a constant magnitude relative to all of the signals produced or measured by an instrument.

Form Factor: The ratio of the peak voltage to average voltage of a waveform (with the dc component removed).

Frequency: In this book, frequency refers to the number of cycles of a repetitive ac voltage or current that occurs in one second.

Full Scale: An instrument's maximum reading or output for each of its ranges. This reading or output may have a greater numeric value than the range that measures or provides it. *See* Instrument Range.

Gain Error: Same as scale error. Scale or gain error results when the slope of a device's response curve is not equal to one (1).

Gaussian Distribution: *See* Normal Distribution.

GPTE, General Purpose Test Equipment: *See* Test Equipment.

Ground: *See* Earth Ground.

Ground Loop: Undesirable current that flows when there is more than one chassis ground point in a system of instruments.

Ground Rod: An electrical conductor, driven into the earth and in adequate contact with it, used in an electrical power distribution system to connect and maintain the chassis grounds of electrical devices at a common potential.

Guard: A Faraday shield around sensitive circuitry within an instrument. The guard is often provided with a connection terminal in order to provide a low-impedance path to ground for common-mode noise and ground loop currents, thereby eliminating the errors they would otherwise introduce.

Hall Effect: The Hall effect produces the Hall voltage as a function of the current flowing through the conductor and an externally applied magnetic field. The Hall voltage, the current and the magnetic field are all mutually perpendicular.

Hysteresis: The property of an electrical device or component where its response to an independent variable is a function of both the value of the variable and the previous state of the device. Also called retrace error.

Immittance: A contraction of Impedance and Admittance.

Impedance: The combined opposition of resistance and reactance to an ac current.

In-situ Calibration: An on-site calibration accomplished at the location where the instrument is deployed and used.

Indicating Instrument: An instrument that grossly displays either the presence of a measurand or provides a reading of its approximate value.

Indirect Method of Measurement: A measurement where the value of a measurand is obtained by measurement of other quantities functionally related to the measurand.

Inductance: The characteristic of an electrical circuit that opposes a change in current.

Inductive Reactance: The opposition to the flow of ac current in an ac circuit due to inductance.

Influence Quantity: A quantity which influences the value of the measurand or the indication of the measuring instrument.

Instrument: As used in this book, a calibrator, standard or test equipment.

Instrument Population: The total number of instruments in a particular class. For example, the class could be the number of instruments in the calibration cycle, of a particular model number, or of a particular generic type, such as DMMs.

Instrument Range: Nomenclature used to define an instrument's switch position that is manually selected or computer programmed in order to measure or supply a specified set of input or output values.

Instrument Seal: *See* Calibration Label *and* Tamper Seal.

International System of Units, SI: A coherent system of units adopted and used by international agreement.

Interpolation: The extension of a data series to a point inside of the series for which data has not been collected.

Intrinsic Standard: A standard whose value(s) are inherently derived from the constants of nature or other natural phenomena.

ISO: Abbreviation for International Standards Organization.

Josephson Effect: A quantum effect wherein the dc voltage drop across the junction of two superconducting semiconductors is a highly reproducible function of the frequency of a microwave signal irradiating the junction.

Julian Day (JD): The Julian day number is obtained by counting days with a starting point on noon, January 1, 4713 BC, which was Julian day zero.

Leading Edge: On a narrow pulse like that from a clock, it is the first-occurring change and can be either negative or positive going.

Leap Second: A one-second interval either inserted or deleted in a clock to keep Coordinated Universal Time, UTC, in step with earth time, UT1.

Legal Units: Formerly used in the United States to designate the highest echelon in a system of units.

Life-Cycle Cost: The consideration of all elements contributing to the cost of an instrument throughout its useful life. This includes initial purchase cost, service and maintenance cost, and the cost of support equipment.

Limited Calibration Label: The same as a Special Calibration Label Tag. This term is an older term not in general use today.

Limits: The extremes of a designated range of values that define acceptable performance with respect to a nominal value.

Line Cord: The integral set of electrical conductors, connectors and insulators that is used to provide an instrument with operating power from a line (mains) power outlet.

Linear Regression: A statistical method for fitting a straight line through a set of numerical values, such as measurement results. A linear regression is used to determine the distribution of the numerical values around the line.

Linearity: The relationship between two quantities when a change in the first quantity is directly proportional to a change in the second quantity.

Linearity Error: Linearity error occurs when the response of an instrument deviates from a straight line. The instrument is specified to have a linear response.

Lissajous Patterns: The patterns obtained on a cathode ray tube (CRT) by driving both the horizontal and vertical deflection plates with time varying voltages or currents, usually sine waves. Lissajous patterns are used for frequency calibration and phase measurement.

Load Current: Current flowing in an impedance when a voltage is applied across it.

M&TE, Measuring and Test Equipment: *See* Test Equipment.

MAP (Measurement Assurance Program): A program for a measurement process. A MAP provides information to demonstrate that the total uncertainty of the measurements (data), including both random error and systematic components of error relative to national or other designated standards, is quantified and sufficiently small to meet requirements.

Maxwell's Equations: Equations that completely describe an electromagnetic field.

Mean: The average value of a set of numerical values.

Mean Solar Time: Time based on the mean solar day, which is the average length of all solar days in a solar year. The mean solar second is 1/86,400 of a mean solar day.

Measurand: The quantity that is being measured.

Measurement: A set of operations performed on a physical object or system according to an established, documented procedure, for the purpose of determining some physical property of the object or system.

Measurement Accuracy: The extent to which the measured value of a quantity agrees with the true value of the measurand. *Compare* MIL-STD-1309C, INTL VOC-ISO(84), NCSL RP3-1988, ANSI/IEEE STD 100-1977 *and* ANSI/ASQC STD M1-1987.

Measurement Common: The electrical potential of a circuit element that is used as a reference for other electrical outputs or inputs.

Measurement Correlation: The closeness of the agreement between the results of different measurements of the same measurand, where the individual measurements are carried out under changed conditions such as: method of measurement, observer, measuring instrument, location, conditions of use, time. *Compare* MIL-STD-1309C, NCSL RP3-1988, *and* ANSI/IEEE STD 100-1977.

Measurement Method: A combination of theoretical considerations and practical operations used to perform a measurement.

Measurement Precision: The degree of agreement among independent measurements of a specific measurand under specified conditions. *Compare* VIM, MIL-STD-1309C, INTL VOC-ISO(84), NCSL RP3-1988, ANSI/IEEE STD 100-1977 *and* ANSI/ASQC STD M1-1987.

Measurement Procedure: *See* Measurement Method.

Measurement Reproducibility: The closeness of agreement between the results of measurements of the same measurand at different locations by different personnel using the same measurement method in similar environments.

Measurement Result: The value of a measurand obtained by measurement.

Measurement Standard: An object, artifact, instrument, system or experiment that stores, embodies, or otherwise provides a physical quantity which serves as the basis for measurements of the quantity. Examples include: Artifact, Check, Consensus, Derived, Intrinsic, Primary, Reference, Secondary, Transfer, Transport and Working Standards. *Compare* NCSL RP-3-1988, MIL-STD-45662A, MIL-STD-1309C, INTL VOC-ISO(84), ANSI/ASQC STD M1-1987 *and* VIM.

Measurement System: The complete set of elements required to make measurements. The major items include instruments, standards, procedures and personnel. *Compare* MIL-STD-1309C, INTL VOC-ISO(84), NCSL RP3-1988, ANSI/IEEE STD 100-1977, ANSI/ASQC STD M1-1987 *and* NCSL RP-2.

Measurement Traceability: An unbroken chain of calibration between test equipment and national standards. *See* MIL-STD-45562A.

Measurement Uncertainty: An estimate of the range of values within which the true value of a measurand lies, usually centered on the nominal value. *Compare* MIL-STD-1309C, NBS SP 676-I, INTL VOC-ISO(84), NCSL RP3-1988, ANSI/IEEE STD 100-1977 *and* ANSI/ASQC STD M1-1987.

Metrology: The science of, and the field of knowledge concerned with measurement. *Compare* DOD-D-4155.1, MIL-STD-1309C, INTL VOC-ISO(84), ANSI/IEEE STD 100-1977 *and* VIM.

Metrology Laboratory: An inclusive term for a calibration laboratory or standards laboratory.

Microprocessor Controlled Instrument: A digital instrument that uses a microprocessor to perform mathematical operations in its signal processing or display circuits.

Modified Julian Day: This is equal to the Julian date shifted so its origin occurs at midnight on November 17, 1858; that is, it differs from the Julian day by 2,400,000.5 days exactly.

MSC (Measurement Science Conference): An organization that sponsors and organizes an annual technical conference for metrology and metrology related issues. Also the name of the annual conference.

National Laboratory (National Standards Laboratory): A laboratory that is legally responsible for maintaining the physical standards on which all measurement in the nation is based.

NCSL (National Conference of Standards Laboratories): An international organization of companies and organizations which have an interest in standards and measurements. NCSL sponsors an annual Workshop and Symposium attended by metrologist and laboratory managers from around the world.

NIST (National Institute of Standards and Technology): The U.S. national standards laboratory, legally responsible for maintaining the standards on which all U.S. measurements are based.

NVLAP: Abbreviation for the National Voluntary Laboratory Accreditation Program, available from NIST.

No Calibration Required (NCR) Label: An NCR label is affixed to an instrument to indicate that it does not need to be calibrated.

Noise: A signal containing no useful information that is superimposed on a desired or expected signal.

Nominal Range: The stated value used to test the measurand.

Normal Distribution: A distribution of data around a central point that becomes a bell-shaped curve in the limit.

Normal Mode Noise: An undesired signal at an input or output port.

Null Detector: An instrument that is used to detect the absence (null) of a signal.

Null Measurement: The method of measurement in which the value of the measurand is determined by comparing it via a null detector to a source of like units which have known values. In one implementation of this method, the measurand is compared with an adjustable source whose value is adjusted for a null on the null detector.

Offset: The algebraic difference between the true or nominal value and a measured value.

Offset Error: The reading shown on a meter when an input value of zero is applied is the offset or zero error.

Offset Voltage: An undesired voltage, typically in the order of a few µV or less, that appears at the input of an operational amplifier.

On-Line Calibration: *See* In-Situ Calibration.

On-Site Calibration: A calibration accomplished at the facility where the instrument is used. An on-site calibration is not necessarily an in-situ calibration.

Operational Amplifier: An electronic device that uses analog circuits to perform mathematical operations such as inversion, multiplication, division, addition, subtraction and integrations.

Output Stability, AC-DC Transfer Standard: The change of the rms sensor output over time with a constant input.

Overrange: A value that can be measured or supplied on an instrument's nominal range whose magnitude is larger than the value given for the instrument's range.

Parallax Error: Error caused by apparent shifting of objects when the viewing position is changed.

Parameters: The independent variables in a measurement process such as temperature, humidity, test lead resistance, etc.

Passive Ranges, AC-DC: Transfer standard ranges that apply the ac and dc signals at the input directly, or through range resistors, to the thermal element.

Peltier Effect: Thermoelectric effect in which a current through a junction results in the production or absorption of heat at this junction at a rate proportional to the current and depending upon its direction.

Percent (PCT): A way of expressing decimal fractions that are larger than approximate magnitude 10^{-4}. For example, the decimal fraction 0.00012 equals 0.012%.

Performance Verification (also Performance Test): A test which verifies that an instrument is performing properly.

PME, Precision Measurement Equipment: *See* Test Equipment.

Population: In metrology, the total number of individual values, or members, in a data set composed of measurement results.

Port: The set of terminals on an instrument that supplies or measures a signal. A simple one-port device has a high and low terminal.

Power Line Frequency: The frequency of the ac voltage supplied by a power line. In the United States the power lines are held to a nominal 60 hertz.

PPB (parts per billion): A way of expressing decimal fractions of approximate magnitude 10^{-9}. For example, 12 ppb = 12/1,000,000,000.

PPM (parts per million): A way of expressing decimal fractions of approximate magnitude 10^{-6}. For example, 12 ppm = 12/1,000,000 (fraction).

Precision: The degree of consistency and agreement among independent measurements of a quantity under the same conditions. The coherence or closeness of one result to all of the measurement results.

Predictability: A measure of how accurately the performance of a device can be assumed after a known time following its calibration. If a device is highly stable, it is also predictable.

Predicted Performance: Performance that is expected at some future time, based on a statistical analysis of past and present performance.

Primary Standard: A standard defined and maintained by some authority and used to calibrate secondary standards.

Principle of Measurement: The scientific basis of a method of measurement.

Probability: In metrology, the statistically determined ratio of the likelihood that the measurand will have a specific value relative to all of the values that it could have.

Process Metrology: Tracking the accuracy drift of calibration and other equipment by applying statistical analysis to correction factors obtained during calibration.

Property Tag: A property tag is affixed to an instrument to indicate that it is a capital asset and to be accounted for. This number provides a common control number in lieu of a serial number.

Protocol Standard: A document describing the operations and processes that must be performed in order for a particular end to be achieved. Called by Europeans a "protocol" to avoid confusion with a physical standard. Examples of such standards include MIL-STD-45662A, ANSI/ASQC STD M1-1987, the ISO-9000 Series and ISO GUIDE 25.

Pumpout Current: An undesired current (or voltage) that emerges from the input port of a passive measurement instrument.

Q, Quality Factor of an Inductor: The Q of an inductor is defined as the ratio of its inductive reactance to its resistance.

Quality: The composite total of the characteristics of a product or service that are related to its ability to satisfy a given need. *Compare* DOD-D-4155.1, ISO 8402-1986, NCSL RP-2, MIL-STD-1309C *and* MIL-STD-109B.

Quality Assurance: A planned framework of systematic actions that provide confidence that a product or service will meet its quality requirements.

Quality Audit: A systematic examination of the quality assurance actions.

Quality Control: A system of actions that keeps the quality of goods or services at the level expected by their users.

Quality Plan: A document setting out the specific policies, methods, equipment, procedures, etc., that will be used to support the quality of a product or service.

Quality System: The total framework of organizational structure, responsibilities, procedures, processes and resources that will be used to support the quality of a product or service.

Quantum Hall Effect: The quantization of the Hall voltage in a superconducting semiconductor, such that the voltage appears in constant amplitude plateaus even though there are small instabilities in the current and magnetic fields that establish the Hall voltage. *See* Hall Effect.

Random Error: Error that varies in an unpredictable manner when the same value is measured under identical conditions. *See also* NBS SP 676-1, INTL VOC-ISO(84), NCSL RP3-1988 *and* ANSI/ASQC STD M1-1987.

Range: *See* Instrument Range.

Readability: The relative ease with which the measurement can be distinguished by eyesight.

Recall System (Instrument Recall System): A documented process that ensures that measuring and test equipment is brought into a laboratory for calibration when scheduled.

Reference Amplifier: An integrated solid state voltage regulation device that provides an extremely stable dc voltage output.

Reference Conditions: The environmental and other conditions required for the calibration of a test instrument. A valid comparison of independent calibrations can be made only when the reference conditions are the same, within stated tolerances.

Reference Plane: A plane through the port of an instrument or in a specific connector that defines where a measurement specification applies.

Reference Point: A point within the port of an instrument or in a specific connector that defines where a measurement specification applies.

Reference Standard: The standard that a laboratory uses to maintain its working standards.

Reject Tag: This is a red tag affixed to an instrument, used to indicate that it is being returned in an unserviced and failed state.

Relative Measurement: A measurement where the results are traceable to local standards, rather than to national standards.

Relative Uncertainty: The incomplete uncertainty of a specified value, lacking the uncertainty of its value in comparison to the national standards.

Reliability: The ability of an instrument to perform as specified without premature failure. *See also* ISO 8492-1986 *and* MIL-STD-1309C.

Repeatability: The degree of agreement among independent measurements of a quantity under the same conditions.

Report of Calibration: A document describing a calibration, including the results, what was done, by whom, under what conditions, and using what equipment and procedures.

Reproducibility of Measurements: *See* Measurement Reproducibility.

Resistance: A property of a conductor that determines the amount of current that will flow when a given amount of voltage exists across the conductor. Resistance is measured in ohms.

Resistor: A component designed to have a specific value of resistance.

Resolution (of an indicating device): The smallest change in quantity that can be detected or provided by an instrument.

Retrace Error: *See* Hysteresis.

Reversal Error: Also called turnover error, the difference in output of an ac-dc transfer standard for the same dc input with polarity reversed.

Reverse Recall: The recall of all instruments and standards in the path of reverse traceability.

Reverse Traceability: The unbroken path from the calibration standard to the end user.

RF (Radio Frequency): The frequency range of radio waves; from 150 kHz up to the infrared range.

RMS (Root-Mean-Square): The value assigned to an ac voltage or current that results in the same power dissipation in a resistance as when a dc voltage or current of the same value is applied to the resistance.

RMS Sensor: A device that converts an ac voltage to a traditional dc voltage with great repeatability.

RSS (Root-Sum-Square): The square root of the sum of the squares of a series of rms voltages.

Sample Standard Deviation: The sample standard deviation equals the square root of the sample variance.

Sample Variance: Sample variance, symbolized s^2, is an estimate of the variance of a data set with a finite number of members.

Scale: The total span of the reading range of a measurement device, including overrange capability.

Scale Error: *See* Gain Error.

Seal: *See* Calibration Documents *and* Tamper Seal.

Secondary Standard: A standard maintained by comparison with a primary standard.

Seebeck Effect: Thermoelectric effect in which the contact potential difference increases with temperature.

Self-Calibration Capability: The ability of an instrument to perform a calibration adjustment on itself.

Sensitivity: The degree of response of a measuring device to the change in input quantity.

Settling Time: The time it takes for a device to reach a stable output or indication following the selection or application of the selected parameter. Settling time is often specified as stability to within some percentage of the final value.

Shield: A grounded covering device designed to protect a circuit or component from electromagnetic interference (emi).

SI System of Units: The International System of Units.

Sidereal Time: Time based on observations of stars rather than the sun.

Siemens: The electrical inverse, G, of resistance, R, equal to $1/R$.

Skin Effect: The phenomenon in which the density of an ac current is greater nearer the surface of a conductor than in its interior.

Span: The difference between the two limits of a nominal range of a measuring instrument. *Compare* Instrument Range *and* Full Scale.

SPC: The abbreviation of Statistical Process Control.

Special Calibration Label: A label affixed to an instrument that indicates that the instrument was calibrated but that it does not meet specifications or that one or more functions was defective. A special calibration label is supported by a special calibration tag.

Special Calibration Tag: A tag attached directly to an instrument that is used in conjunction with a special calibration label to identify and define defective performance.

Specification (Instrument): A precisely stated presentation of the parameters, including accuracy or uncertainty, describing the capability of an instrument.

SPETE (Special Purpose Electronic Test Equipment): *See* Test Equipment.

SPTE (Special Purpose Test Equipment): *See* Test Equipment.

Square Law Device: A device whose output is proportional to the square of the applied stimulus.

Stability: The ability of an instrument to have a response or output that is constant with time. *See also* Accuracy, Precision, *and* Resolution.

Standard: *See* Measurement Standard *and* Protocol Standard.

Standard Cell: An electrochemical device used to generate a constant emf.

Standard Deviation: The standard deviation equals the square root of the variance.

Standards Laboratory (Standards Lab): A work space, provided with equipment and standards, a properly controlled environment and trained personnel, established for the purpose of maintaining traceability of standards and measuring equipment used by the organization it supports. Standards laboratories typically perform fewer, more specialized and higher accuracy measurements than Cal Labs.

STE (Special Test Equipment): *See* Test Equipment.

Sticker: *See* Calibration Label.

Student's t Distribution: The Student's t Distribution can be considered to be a special case of the normal distribution for small sets, typically having less than 100 members.

Subjective Probability: Loosely, an evaluation of probability based on experience rather than on the statistical analysis of the data in a set of measurement results.

Superconductor: A material that has zero resistivity below a specified temperature.

Susceptance: The electrical inverse, B, of reactance, X, equal to $1/X$.

System: A collection of instruments, personnel, procedures and other elements that may include computers, peripherals and software that functions as a complete whole, rather than as individual entities. *Compare* MIL-STD-1309C *and* MIL-STD-280A.

System of Units (of measurement): A set of scientific or legal definitions and their inter-relationships used for measurements, for example, the International System of Units (SI).

Systematic Error: Error that varies in a predictable or detectable way. *Compare* NBS SP 676-1, INTL VOC-ISO(84), NCSL RP3-1988 *and* ANSI/ASQC STD M1-1987.

Tamper Seal: A seal of appropriate design and material that is attached to an instrument to clearly indicate tampering. The purpose is to ensure calibration or warranty integrity.

TAMS, Test and Monitoring Systems: *See* Test Equipment.

Temperature Coefficient: A general term used to derate the specifications of an instrument for a change in temperature from the reference conditions.

Temperature Coefficient of AC-DC Difference: The change of an ac-dc transfer standard's ac-dc difference, δ, with a change in temperature.

Terminal: A connector provided on an instrument that is used to connect a cable or test lead to its input or output port.

Tertiary Standard: A standard that is supported by a secondary standard.

Test: As used in this book, a test refers to a procedure or action taken to determine the capabilities, limitations, characteristics, effectiveness, reliability or suitability of an instrument, calibrator, standard or test equipment.

Test Accuracy Ratio: *See* Test Uncertainty Ratio.

Test Equipment: Any equipment that is used to make measurements, or supply stimulus, alone or in conjunction with other equipment. *Compare* MIL-STD-1309C, NAVAIR 17-FF35MTL-1, MIL-STD-45662A, NCSL RP3-1988, ANSI/IEEE STD 100-1977, ANSI/ASQC STD M1-1987 *and* VIM. *Also known as:* GPETE, General Purpose Electronic Test Equipment; GPTE, General Purpose Test Equipment; M&TE, Measuring and Test Equipment; PME, Precision Measuring Equipment; SPETE, Special Purpose Electronic Test Equipment; SPTE, Special Purpose Test Equipment; STE, Special Test Equipment; TAMS, Test and Monitoring Systems; TMDE, Test, Measurement and Diagnostic Equipment. *See also:*

Calibrator, Instrument *and* Measurement Standard.

Test Instrument (TI): *See* Unit Under Test.

Test Procedure: As used in this book, a document that describes step by step the operations required to test an instrument, calibrator, standard or test equipment.

Test Report: *See* Report of Calibration.

Test Uncertainty Ratio (TUR): The test uncertainty ratio (TUR) for a measurand is the specified uncertainty of the instrument under test divided by the specified uncertainty of the calibrator or standard used to test it. The specifications for the instruments must have the same coverage factor.

Thermal EMF: The voltage generated when the junction of two dissimilar metals is heated.

Thermoelectric: The interaction of thermal and electrical phenomena.

Thomson Effect: Thermoelectric effect in which an electric current transports the heat generated in a conductor.

TMDE, Test, Measurement and Diagnostic Equipment: *See* Test Equipment.

Tolerance: In metrology, the limits of the range of values (the uncertainty) that apply to a properly functioning measuring instrument. *Compare* MIL STD 1309C, INTL VOC-ISO(84), NCSL RP3-1988, *and* ANSI/IEEE STD 100-1977.

Traceability: A characteristic of a calibration, analogous to a pedigree. A traceable calibration is achieved when each instrument and standard, in a hierarchy stretching back to the national standard, was itself properly calibrated, and the results properly documented. The documentation provides the information needed to show that all the calibrations in the chain of calibrations were properly performed. *Compare* MIL-STD-1309C, MIL-STD-45662A, ISO 8402-1986, *and* VIM.

Transfer Error: The sum of all new errors induced during the process of comparing one quantity with another.

Transfer Standard: Any standard that is used to compare a measurement process, system or device at one location or level with another

measurement process, system or device at another location or level.

Transport Standard: A transfer standard that is rugged enough to allow shipment by common carrier.

True Value: Also called legal value, the accepted consensus, that is, the correct value of the measurand.

Turnover Error: *See* Reversal Error.

Type A Uncertainty: Uncertainty based on a statistical analysis of the data in a set of measurement values. NIST Special Publication 811 provides further information.

Type B Uncertainty: Uncertainty based on an evaluation that does not include a statistical analysis of the data in a set of measurement values. NIST Special Publication 811 provides further information.

Uncertainty: An estimate of the possible error in a measurement. More precisely, an estimate of the range of values which contains the true value of a measured quantity. Uncertainty is usually reported in terms of the probability that the true value lies within a stated range of values. For the sake of analysis, the lack of knowledge is often considered to be normally distributed around the nominal value of the measurand. *See also* Measurement Uncertainty.

Unit Being Calibrated (UBC): *See* Unit Under Test.

Unit Under Calibration (UUC): *See* Unit Under Test.

Unit Under Test (UUT): A measurement standard, calibrator, instrument, test equipment or any other item that is being tested.

Units: Symbols or names that define quantities.

Universal Time: Universal Time (UT) is a time scale based on the rotation of the earth about its axis.

User Adjustment: The adjustment of an instrument by its user, via controls that are accessible during normal operation, accomplished to obtain the instrument's specified performance. *Compare* Calibration Adjustments.

UUT (Unit Under Test): *See* Unit Under Test.

Value: The expression of a quantity as number of units of measurement.

Variance: Variance, symbolized as σ^2, is the mean square deviation from the average value of a data set with an infinite number of members. *See* Sample Variance.

Volt: The unit of emf in the SI system of units.

Watt: The unit of power in the SI system of units.

Wideband: AC voltage at frequencies up to and including the radio frequency spectrum.

Working Standard: A standard that is used in routine calibration and comparison procedures in the laboratory and is maintained by comparison to reference standards.

Zener Diode: A solid state voltage regulation device that provides a stable dc output voltage.

Index

Contractors
28-4

Control Chart
(*Also see* Attributes Charts *and* Variable Charts)
23-3 to 23-15

Converters
5-8, 9-10, 10-3 to 10-10, 11-5, 15-17, 16-6, 17-4, 17-6, 17-7, 17-13, 33-8

Counter EMF
12-5 to 12-6

Coupler, Lumped-Element Directional
13-16

CPEM (Conference for Precision Electromagnetic Measurements)
4-9

Current
4-3, 5-3, 6-6, 7-3, 7-7, 8-11, 9-5, 9-19, 11-11, 12-7, 12-12, 15-3, 15-4, 22-8
Alternating
(*See* Alternating Current)
Direct (DC)
(*See* DC Current)
Shunts
8-6, 10-9, 11-11, 13-11

Current Comparator Resistance Bridge
9-21, 21-9

Current Converters
17-10, 17-15

Current Guard
32-13

Current Transformer (CT)
13-12

Curve Fitting
21-8 to 21-11

D

Data Collection
6-11, 16-8, 19-6, 23-8

Data Integrity Validation
26-8

DC Current
7-3 to 7-16, 9-4 to 9-20, 10-5, 10-9, 15-8, 15-15, 17-3, 17-10, 17-15

DC Dividers, Typical
13-10 to 13-11

DC Transfer Standards
11-16, 16-10, 16-11

DC Voltage Output, Bi-Polar
15-15

DC Voltage Range Calibration
17-13

DC Voltage Standards
7-8 to 7-12, 7-17 to 7-18

Decade Divider
16-4, 16-6, 16-11

Definition of a Unit
5-3, 5-4

Derived Units
3-5, 4-4

Dielectric Absorption
17-5, 17-11, 17-16, 33-7, 33-10

Difference, AC-DC
(*See* AC-DC Difference)

Differential Measurement
5-9, 9-4, 9-15, 11-10, 33-3, 33-13

Digital LCR Meter
13-8 to 13-9

Digital Multimeter Calibration
8-7, 9-10, 10-11, 15-4, 15-17, 16-10, 17- 3 to 17-17

Digital Ohmmeters
8-7 to 8-8

Digital Sampling
17-7, 17-8 to 17-9, 18-6

Digital Storage Oscilloscope (DSO)
18-3, 18-6 to 18-8, 18-10

Direct Current Comparator
9-19 to 19-20

Direct Measurements
5-9

F

International System of Units (SI)
  4-3 to 4-5, 5-3 to 5-4, 6-3

Intrinsic Standard
  (*Also see* Standards)
  6-5, 7-4, 8-3 to 8-5, 14-3, 30-9

ISA (Instrument Society of America)
  4-9, 25-10

ISA RP52
  25-10 to 25-11

ISO (International Standards Organization)
  4-8, 28-3

ISO 9000
  3-3, 6-4, 17-4, 19-5, 26-7, 28-3 to 28-12, 29-5 to 29-6,
  30-3 to 30-5
  ASQC Q90, 91
  28-3, 30-3
  Registration, Obtaining
  28-3, 28-5 to 28-12, 29-5

ISO Guide 25
  28-4, 29-5, 30-3, 30-6, 30-10

J

Josephson Array Voltage Standard
  6-11, 30-9
  Schematic of
  7-6
  Response of
  7-6
  Simplified Structure of
  7-5

Josephson Junction
  5-4, 6-5, 7-4 to 7-8, 7-18, 9-5, 30-9

Josephson Effect
  7-4

Joule
  4-4, 7-3, 8-3, 10-5

Julian Date, Modified (MJD)
  14-9

K

Kelvin (degree of temperature)
  3-5, 4-4

Kelvin Double Bridge
  9-17 to 9-19

Kelvin-Varley (K-V) Divider
  7-15 to 7-16, 9-7 to 9-9, 9-11, 9-12 to 9-16, 15-4, 22-8
  to 22-11, 24-6, 33-3, 33-6

K_j, K_{j-90}
  (*Also see* Josephson Junction)
  4-6, 7-4 to 7-7

L

Laboratory
  Accreditation of
  (*Also see* Accreditation)
  4-7, 4-10, 28-4, 29-3 to 29-6, 30-3
  Air Pressure in
  25-11
  Audits of
  (*Also see* Audits)
  3-3, 6-11, 29-5, 30-3 to 30-13
  Capacity of
  26-3
  Construction of
  25-10
  Design of
  25-6, 25-10, 26-6
  Floor Plan of
  25-4
  Lighting within
  25-3 to 25-7, 25-11, 30-7
  Managers of
  19-4 to 19-6
  Mission of
  24-3
  Operating Overhead of
  26-5
  Personnel of
  25-7, 30-7
  Practice Guidelines of
  25-11
  Quality of Work in
  3-3, 28-3, 29-5, 30-7

R

W

X

Z